Teaching Science to Every Child

Teaching Science to Every Child

USING CULTURE AS A STARTING POINT

John Settlage and Sherry A. Southerland

Routledge
Taylor & Francis Group
New York   London

National Science Education Standards copyright © 1996 by the National Academy of Sciences, courtesy of the National Academies Press, Washington, D.C. Used by permission.

Routledge
Taylor & Francis Group
270 Madison Avenue
New York, NY 10016

Routledge
Taylor & Francis Group
2 Park Square
Milton Park, Abingdon
Oxon OX14 4RN

© 2007 by Taylor & Francis Group, LLC
Routledge is an imprint of Taylor & Francis Group, an Informa business

Printed in the United States of America on acid-free paper
10 9 8 7 6 5 4 3 2 1

International Standard Book Number-10: 0-415-95637-4 (Softcover) 0-415-95636-6 (Hardcover)
International Standard Book Number-13: 978-0-415-95637-6 (Softcover) 978-0-415-95636-9 (Hardcover)

Library of Congress Cataloging-in-Publication Data

Settlage, John.
    Teaching science to every child : using culture as a starting point / John Settlage and Sherry Southerland.
        p. cm.
        Includes bibliographical references and index.
    ISBN-13: 978-0-415-95636-9 (hb)
    ISBN-13: 978-0-415-95637-6 (pb)
    1. Science--Study and teaching (Elementary) 2. Science--Study and teaching (Middle school) 3. Multicultural education. I. Southerland, Sherry. II. Title.

LB1575.T416 2007
372.3'5--dc22   2006030853

Visit the Taylor & Francis Web site at
http://www.taylorandfrancis.com

and the Routledge Web site at
http://www.routledge.com

#71581728

Contents

Foreword

Gloria Ladson-Billings

One Child's Voice About Science Learning

There are many reasons we can offer to justify putting energy into providing students attending elementary school and middle school with the opportunity to learn science. We have decided to delay listing all the statistical reasons for teaching science to all students, and instead we begin by having you think about the science experiences of a school-aged African American girl who had an interest in science. Gloria is one of countless students who have attended school in the United States. To a certain extent, her story has a happy ending. She is now a nationally recognized professor of education at one of the top universities in the country. Yet her experiences as a science learner are not the kind most of us want to feel we have imposed on children. We feel this is a good starting point as you prepare for a career as someone responsible for teaching science in diverse classrooms.

* * *

I Used to Love Science ... and Then I Went to School: The Challenge of School Science in Urban Schools

As a child growing up in West Philadelphia in the 1950s and 1960s, I have fond memories of my family, community, and school. I was considered a "good" student. I read well, I did my homework, and I was well behaved. However, in my early years I don't remember my elementary school as a place where I experienced much science teaching. Elementary school was a place that focused on the three Rs, and parents and community members seemed to support that focus. No, my science education took place at home. One of my early science memories is of my older brother receiving a chemistry set for Christmas. As we set about trying to perform the experiments provided in the accompanying handbook, we learned quickly that scientists (or at least chemists) sometimes had to improvise. We also learned that there were unintended consequences to scientific experimentation.

For example when we decided to make soap as directed in the chemistry set experiment book, we thought it would be OK to use the previously used cooking grease that my mother kept in a can on the stove top. We didn't know that such impure fat would create a slimy, food-flecked glob that no one in my family would or could use. Another example is when we decided to make the rock candy sugar crystals. Of course, as applied scientists we were less interested in crystal formation than in producing candy. We set out on that experiment during a time when both our parents were gone and our grandfather was left in charge. Again, it did not occur to us that using available resources—in this case, all of the sugar my mother had in the canister—would cause a problem. Our rock candy seemed to form just fine; it was our explanation to our mother upon her return that did not seem to go over well.

Sometime around fifth grade, science became really important in our school. This was the same time that the Russians launched a successful satellite. Suddenly we began receiving science books, and the *Weekly Reader* began to have a very deliberate science message. However, the school's version of science wasn't like the kind of science my brother and I were doing with his chemistry set. There was no mystery, no uncertainty, no unintended consequences, and, most important, no fun. Science—when we had it—was boring. It consisted of reading chapters, memorizing facts, and answering the questions at the end of each chapter. I found it boring, and I was a good reader. I cannot imagine how horrible it was for the struggling readers.

By the time I got to junior high school, I learned that science was a special subject. I knew it was special because we had it in special classrooms. These rooms had big black-covered tabletops with sinks on one end and what I soon learned was a gas outlet for something called a "Bunsen burner." My seventh-grade teacher, Mr. McLean, had a preciseness about him. There was a specific way that the science notebook had to be kept, he said, because scientists work in very precise ways. Already I was starting to get nervous. Mr. McLean insisted that we head our papers in a particular way. He also insisted that we use specific vocabulary—*hypothesis, observations, conclusions*—and that we include precise diagrams and illustrations with our lab work. I liked doing the labs—they reminded me of my chemistry set antics—but I was so nervous about the preciseness of the reporting that I often paid little attention to what I was supposed to be learning. For example I could recite every single part of the microscope, but I don't think I knew what any of those parts really did.

One of the assignments for seventh-grade science was a leaf collection assignment. We were to locate at least ten different kinds of deciduous leaves, mount and label them, and create a booklet. I think the one thing I understood about the assignment was the word *booklet*. The thing that Mr. McLean did not understand about me was that I traveled by trolley and bus to attend that school because my mother thought it would give me a shot at a better education. Most of my classmates lived close to the school, and living close to the school meant that they lived close to Bartram's Garden, the oldest botanical garden in the country. I lived in a neighborhood where the city had removed most of the trees and replanted one species—sycamores. I did not have access to the same variety of leaves that my mostly White classmates did.

My mother, in her attempt to help, talked with a coworker who had a part-time job in a greenhouse. On the eve of the day my leaf booklet was due, my mother came home proudly displaying a set of leaves. They were absolutely beautiful. Unfortunately, they were not deciduous, and neither my mother nor I really knew the difference. I placed my leaves on paper, labeled each one, covered each page with plastic wrap, and made a nice construction paper cover. I failed the project, because while my classmates turned in leaves from maples, oaks, elms, and many other trees native to the Philadelphia environs, I turned in a booklet with leaves from an orange tree, lemon tree, rubber tree, and other trees from a greenhouse. I felt stupid and vowed to try to do science by the book.

In eighth grade, I had a wonderful teacher named Ms. Mowbray. I was excited by the idea that we had a woman as a science teacher. Ms. Mowbray made the science fun. We did lots of experiments and got to ask lots of questions. I did well in her class. However, on one of the last extra-credit assignments, I ran into a problem. We were supposed to construct a "Cartesian diver." Once again I was coming home with an assignment that was beyond my parents' understanding. This time I did understand what Ms. Mowbray wanted. She wanted us to understand "buoyancy" and that an object is buoyant in water because of the amount of water it displaces. She wanted us to know that if the weight of the water that is displaced by an object in water exceeds the weight of the object, then the object will float. I understood that. It helped me understand why people float in large bodies of water. My problem with the project was that it required a glass jar (we did not have plastic bottles), an eyedropper, and a semipermeable membrane. The only component of the project I could get was the semipermeable membrane, which was a balloon. I could not get the glass jar, because glass bottles had a two-cents deposit attached to them. I could not get the eyedropper, because every eyedropper in my house was in use with someone's medicine.

By high school, I had an after-school job and was in a better position to marshal school supplies on my own. I was a good student and earned good grades in science courses, especially chemistry. For a brief moment I considered a career in the sciences. But I have always been puzzled by the way science is seen as the special purview of some students while others are systematically excluded from participation in the sciences.

Examining the Bigger Picture

As an African American student growing up in a working-class household and community, I should be a science education statistic. However, a number of factors converged to ensure that my K-12 schooling experience left me with enough social and cultural capital to enter college and pursue advanced studies. But it is important that we look at what is happening to African American students in science today. In the 2003 Quality Counts report published by *Education Week,* we learned that although many states are doing their best to recruit and retain skilled teachers, few efforts are targeted at finding teachers for students who need them most. Teacher quality is important because the existing research indicates that effective teachers can get an additional year's worth of learning out of students and that the effect of having a string of ineffective teachers is cumulative.

Although we have read about the achievement gap, the digital gap, and the learning gap, we have not addressed the "teacher gap." This gap indicates that students of color in high poverty schools are more likely to have teachers who do not have college majors or minors in the subjects they teach. They are more likely to have teachers who are not certified in the subjects they teach. They are more likely to be inexperienced teachers without the benefit of student teaching before they face a classroom of students.

According to the MetLife 2001 American Teacher Study, "Students overall, and black students in particular, have high expectations for their future. However, teachers and principals in heavily minority schools have lower expectations for their students. Teachers in schools with high proportions of students of color report lower quality teaching and teachers in schools with high proportions of students of color are less satisfied with several school relationships (e.g., with principals, colleagues, students) and less committed to the profession" (p. 10).

The achievement gap we reference emerges in a context that includes a teacher gap (as well as a resource gap). As we look at the National Assessment of Educational Progress data, we know that the largest achievement gaps are in eighth-grade science, in which 40 percent of White students score at or above proficient compared with only 6 percent of African American and 11 percent of Latino students. At each assessed grade level (fourth, eighth, and twelfth), Black and Latino students score significantly lower than their White counterparts (National Center for Education Statistics, 2000).

A number of assumptions are tied to African American students' lack of science proficiency. Some of the usual suspects are that the students lack the motivation, fail to have supportive parents, and do not have prerequisite skills for science learning. Haycock (2001) indicated that when the Education Trust staff queries adults about the racial–ethnic achievement gap, the comments tend to be as follows:

"They're too poor." "Their parents don't care." "They come to school without an adequate breakfast." "They don't have enough books in the home." "Indeed, there aren't enough parents in the home." Their reasons, in other words, are always about the children and their families. Young people, however, have different answers. They talk about teachers who often do not know the subjects they are teaching. They talk about counselors who consistently underestimate their potential and place them in lower-level courses. They talk about principals who dismiss their concerns. And they talk about a curriculum and a set of expectations that feel so miserably low-level that they literally bore the students right out the school door. When we ask, "What about the things that the adults are always talking about—neighborhood violence, single-parent homes, and so on?"—the young people's responses are fascinating. "Sure, those matter," they say. "But what hurts us more is that you teach us less." (Haycock, 2001, p. 3)

In this discussion I want to focus on the idea that the students lack the motivation or aptitude for science. I want to argue that African American students continue to be interested in science but often attend schools where they have little or no opportunity to learn real science. To test student interest in science, I have been interviewing preschool- and kindergarten-age African American students to determine how their interests converge with science. I have purposely not interviewed older students, because the nature of their school science experiences may unduly influence what they believe about science. I have been interviewing four- and five-year-old children at an African American church and five- and six-year-old children who are attending kindergarten. I have been using Brodhagen's (1995) and Beane's (2002) framing questions of "What do you want to know about yourself?" and "What do you want to know about the world?" The following list is a sample of the questions the children posed (I edited out those that were not science questions):

- Why is my shadow long sometimes and short sometimes?
- Why do people have different color skin?
- Why do the leaves fall off the tree in the winter and come back in the summer?
- How can a big airplane stay up in the air?
- Why does stuff come in your eyes when you are sleeping?
- How does the weatherman know what the weather is going to be the day before?
- Why does the moon look different? Sometimes it's a big moon and sometimes it's a little teeny moon.
- How can the moon and sun be out at the same time?

- Why do some of my mother's flowers come back every year and some she has to plant every year?
- Why is it late at my house and early at my grandma's? (I think this is a time-zone question.)
- How does the baby get out of the mommy's stomach?
- Why does your mother say "no jumping" when she bakes a cake?
- How does the thermometer know you're sick?

These questions clearly illustrate that African American students do have an interest in the scientific world. Their questions cut across a variety of science areas—biology, astronomy, chemistry, and physics. Yet we are led to believe that inner-city, urban students of color have little or no interest in science.

How Science Could Be

If the students continue to come to school with interests in science, how can we maintain and invigorate their interests? From my research with teachers who are effective teachers of African American students, I argue that science could be different. Science could incorporate what I have termed "culturally relevant pedagogy." This pedagogy incorporates academic achievement, cultural competence, and sociopolitical consciousness.

Academic achievement is in someway a misnomer for what I mean theoretically. I am not referring merely to student performance on standard measures. Rather I am focusing on student learning as a much broader construct. Thus when it comes to science education, I am referring to what it is important to know. Those of you who have worked with Project 2061 know that science educators have wrestled with this question. Is it necessary to study dinosaurs at every elementary grade level or are there some science concepts and knowledge that students should learn or at least experience at different grade levels?

In the classrooms I studied, teachers demanded that students study and learn to high levels. One teacher taught the students from the graduate curriculum she was studying to obtain her master's degree. In her classroom there were posters of the brain and its various parts. Students use neurological terms and queried their teacher each Thursday morning as to what she studied the day before. In Barb Brodhagen's classroom, her students discussed the earlier questions, such as "What do I want to learn about myself and what do I want to learn about the world?" The students settle on a small set of questions that become the basis for the curriculum. One semester the students decided the question they wanted answered was "Will I live to be 100?" That question provoked study in family and genealogical histories, actuarial charts, environmental effects on life span, and investigation of genetics and genetic diseases (Brodhagen, 1995). What both of these classrooms had in common were knowledgeable and skillful teachers who were unafraid of deviating from prescribed curriculum and challenging students beyond conventional course materials.

The second aspect of culturally relevant pedagogy is cultural competence. This refers to the degree to which student culture is logically and meaningfully incorporated into the curriculum. The typical science attempts at this involve a list of famous African American scientists and inventors. The students rarely see the relevance or connection of these scientists—particularly when they show up only in February—and find their presentation no more meaningful than anything else in the curriculum. Instead, culturally relevant teachers take the time to study the students and their habits and behaviors.

In one classroom of African American students, a teacher asked, "How many people don't like to drink milk?" About one-third of the students raised their hands. She asked, "What is it about milk that you don't like?" Even the way she phrased the question—not "Why don't you like milk?"—invited the students to participate. Her question indicated that there was something about the milk that might be problematic. Some students talked about not liking the taste of the milk. Others talked about not minding the taste but getting sick soon after drinking it. As the students shared their problems with milk, some of the others who were milk drinkers shared stories of siblings and other family members who had trouble drinking milk. The teacher then asked the students what would they think if they learned that in a classroom of White children almost all of the students drank milk. "Wow," exclaimed one boy, "you mean white milk is for White people?" That comment brought a nervous laugh among the students, but the teacher said, "Well, I don't know that white milk is for White people, but it is true that it is difficult for some people of African descent to digest."

This conversation moved the students into a schoolwide survey of milk drinkers. It also gave the teacher an opportunity to teach the students about genetic characteristics, lactose intolerance, and food allergies. The science that most students want to engage in is science that helps them answer their questions. While middle-class students may acquiesce and tolerate the science the school curriculum offers them, many of the students who are struggling to engage with school need a curriculum that engages them.

Cultural competence is important because it helps students understand the strengths and limitations of their culture. In Lee's 1999 study of standards-based science teaching, she learned that although the teachers taught exactly what the curriculum asked of them, students' worldviews are shaped by powerful forces outside of the classroom. In the aftermath of Hurricane Andrew, teachers tried to determine how much of the science learning helped students to understand the weather disaster. Unfortunately, Black and Latino students reported that the hurricane was the result of the wickedness and evil that pervaded the south Florida region. The hurricane was God's way of punishing them. The teachers did not know what to do with this worldview, and students left the school experience with the notion that school and home are strictly separate worlds. The fact that the students experience more success in the world of their home galvanizes their feelings of alienation toward the school.

The third component of culturally relevant pedagogy is sociopolitical consciousness. In my mind, this is the "so what" aspect of schooling. How many times have we heard students ask the question, "Why do we have to learn this?" only to be told, "Because some day you're going to need this." We all know how much we all need the periodic chart of elements in our daily lives. Sociopolitical consciousness helps students understand the way citizens in a democratic society need scientific knowledge to make informed decisions. Maria Torres-Guzmán (1992) studied a group of high school students in an alternative school. The students' major project at the school was investigating a dump site in their neighborhood. The students learned that the site contained toxic materials and ultimately raised questions about the way poor communities of color are vulnerable to environmental racism. The students' passion for this project was fueled by the fact that they understood that what they were doing had a pay-off for the here and now, not the "someday" that teachers often promise.

There is a science out there in which African American students desperately want to participate. This is a science that explains the epidemic of diabetes or AIDS in their community. This is a science that challenges social constructions such as race. This is a science that people can mobilize to fight social injustice and intellectually empower people. This is a science that allows students to do something rather than sit passively while something is done to them.

My focus has been on African American students, but I have begun to see how improving schooling for them is likely to improve schooling for all students. If we begin to strengthen science teaching for those who are most vulnerable in our system, we are likely to strengthen it for everyone. We are no longer in a society that can afford for people to be scientifically illiterate. We are no longer in a society that can afford to weed out students or push them through arbitrary sieves called biology, chemistry, and physics. We are no longer in a society that can afford to send some students to a course called general science that actually would better be called "reading about science." We need all students to leave our schools excited about and engaged in science so that they can have more career and vocational choices open to them and so that they can actively participate in the decision making that democracy requires. We need to turn school into a place where our students can continue to like science. And in case anybody knows Ms. Mowbray, please tell her that I've made my Cartesian diver.

References

Beane, J. A. (2002). Beyond self-interest: A democratic core curriculum. *Educational Leadership, 59*(7), 25–28.

Brodhagen, B. (1995). The situation made us special. In M. Apple & J. Bean (Eds.), *Democratic schools* (pp. 83–100). Alexandria, VA: Association for Supervision and Curriculum Development.

Haycock, K. (2001). Helping all students achieve: Closing the achievement gap. *Educational Leadership, 58*(6), 1–9.

Lee, O. (1999). Science knowledge, world views, and information sources in social and cultural contexts: Making sense after a natural disaster. *American Educational Research Journal, 36*, 187–219.

MetLife. (2001). *The American teacher: Key elements of quality schools.* New York: Author. Available from http://www.metlife.com/Applications/Corporate/WPS/CDA/PageGenerator/0,1674,P2315,00.html?FILTERNAME=@URL\&FILTERVALUE=/WPS/\&IMAGE2.X=0\&IMAGE2.Y=0

National Center for Education Statistics. (2000). *The nation's report card* [Document No. NCES 2002–452]. Washington, DC: U.S. Department of Education.

Torres-Guzmán, M. E. (1992). Stories of hope in the midst of despair: Culturally responsive education for Latino students in an alternative high school in New York City. In M. Saravia-Shore, S. F. Avizu (Eds.), *Language and culture in learning: Teaching Spanish to native speakers of Spanish.* New York: Garland.

Preface

Moving to the Front of the Classroom

At some point in your education program, you will probably have a sudden realization that you are going to be a teacher. Although students enter their educational program with this nebulous goal, at some point they to get a real glimpse of exactly what it means to be a teacher—what responsibilities it entails, what expertise it requires to do well, and the amount of work that seems to lie ahead. Just as with many important life goals, your progress toward becoming a teacher probably has been a mix of your imagination and a considerable amount of hard work. But there is often a moment where each of us realizes that what we have been working toward is about to happen. Before too long, you won't be a student sitting in class being taught by someone else: you are going to be that someone else. The person you have wanted to become—an adult who inspires students, who is enthusiastic about learning, who believes that education opens incredible opportunities, and who serves as a role model for the citizens of tomorrow—believe it or not, that's is where you're headed. This realization is likely to fill you with a combination of excitement and uncertainty.

We recognize this feeling because we've had it ourselves. Even though our names are on the cover of this textbook, most people who know us see us as science teachers. Although our job title says we are education professors, the truth is that we are often in classrooms, working with teachers and working with kids, to help all of us learn science and become better at teaching it. Over the years it has become easier for us to step to the front of a classroom full of students. But it still makes us nervous. Often we don't sleep well the night before we meet a new class. And every now and then, in the midst of a science lesson, we marvel at the fact that we are actually directing a group of students who are learning science. What we want to accomplish with this book is to help you to share in that excitement and enjoy the benefits of helping students become excited about what they are learning and the fact that they are becoming very good at it.

Teaching as a Profession

In discussions about teaching as a career, people often compare our field to the medical profession. There are some similarities: the work involves helping people, individuals who are successful must blend interpersonal skills and intelligent thought, and the preparation for the profession involves a great deal of hands-on training. But there are differences, most notably the discrepancies in pay and prestige. What is often forgotten is that this wasn't the case a hundred years ago (Gregorian, 2004). Medicine and teaching were both highly regarded fields, and only the best and the brightest in a community were seen as suitable for those professions. But times have changed. Now when people in college say they are preparing to become doctors, they receive a response of admiration. When college students say they are preparing to be teachers, the response is something like, "Well, isn't that nice." We suspect that the difference is because one of these fields is cloaked in mystique (and a lab coat) whereas the other seems very familiar to virtually everyone. Unless you've had the unfortunate experience of a major medical problem, it is likely that you've spent a thousand more hours of your life in the presence of teachers than in the presence of physicians. But that shouldn't be a reason to think that teaching is not a profession.

For many teachers the most grueling professional experiences are student teaching and the first year as a full-time classroom teacher. What makes these periods so stressful? There are the physical demands. Teachers are in constant motion as they move about the classroom and the building. The opportunities to take a break and relax are minimal, or nonexistent. There are also the emotional demands. As a teacher you are always "on," and there are often multiple calls for your attention at any given moment. Because you're the authority figure, you must manage students' behavior. The classroom is your responsibility, to manage and to care for the students' safety and well-being while you are teaching what students need to learn.

Clearly, being a teacher is hard work. The stamina that the profession demands is something you can assess by watching teachers at the end of a day of teaching. We point this out to acknowledge that we are very well aware of the challenges required to be a teacher. In the elementary grades a teacher might have to teach up to ten different subjects to the same group of students. At the middle school level, where teachers can sometimes focus on fewer subjects, they are often teaching to multiple groups of students. Here the benefit of having fewer lessons to prepare is balanced by having to become familiar with, understand the needs of, and direct the work of many more students. Although there are variations in schedules and class sizes, for the conscientious professional, teaching will always be demanding.

Our responsibility is to help you to learn to become a successful teacher of science. Given the challenges, you might expect that this book to be a survival guide. However, there are already several books on the market designed for that purpose. Our view is that you, and your students, deserve something better. Both of us teach science methods courses to future elementary and middle school teachers. In addition, we work with teachers in our graduate courses and through the various projects we conduct in schools. We have a pretty clear sense about what teachers require in order to help all of their students to learn science, and the purpose of this book is to help move you in the right direction. As a result we have decided not to create a "science teaching survival manual." Instead we've written a book that will develop your confidence at teaching science in diverse classrooms, provide you with the tools to assist with your instructional decision making, and supply you with concrete strategies for making science accessible to students with a range of ethnic backgrounds, cognitive abilities, and native languages.

Building Science Confidence in Students and Teachers

When we survey the students in our science methods classes, we find that many are unable to recall positive learning experiences from when they were taught science. What memories they do have are often negative, which may explain why they were discouraged about studying science. However, there are always a couple of students who have wonderful stories to tell about their school science experience. These individuals can describe in great detail magnificent field trips they went on. They talk quite passionately about how they were able to pursue questions of their own design without worrying about failing. Often an individual is embarrassed to confess that he or she kept a school science project even though it was completed more than a decade ago. Upon hearing this, this person's classmates express a mixture of surprise and frustration. They are surprised to hear that one of their friends has fond memories of school science when they have little or nothing good to say. They are annoyed that they didn't have a teacher who made them feel as good about science or that they were left not feeling particularly capable in science.

An interesting thing about this scenario is that as their science methods instructors, we cannot predict who is going to share positive stories. You can't look at someone and say, "Oh, she looks like the kind of student who was really good in science." It isn't just the students who wear glasses, are tall or have curly hair, or are males who have positive elementary school science memories. What does this tell us? Outside appearances have nothing to do with students' capabilities to learn science. Based this observation, we have discovered that the factor that seems to make the biggest difference in the quality of the science experience is *the teacher* of those students. We suspect that if we could go back in time and swap the classroom of one of our students who has a great science experience with one of our students who has a negative memory, then the stories they would tell on their first day of their science methods class would be reversed as well.

Now if you are one of those people who had a great science teacher, then you have a model and vision for how this can be accomplished. But for most of the rest of us who weren't as fortunate, we have to develop portraits in our mind of what such classrooms might look and feel like. The goal of your methods course and this book is to help you become the sort of teacher who can make a difference. For those who are sufficiently dedicated and resourceful, it is possible to create a new generation of students who are excited about science, look forward to learning more with every lesson, and realize that they are capable of being successful at it. It is for those future teachers that we have written this methods textbook.

The Importance of Science in the School Curriculum

Historically the centerpiece of education has been language arts and mathematics. What were once the three Rs (i.e., reading, writing, and 'rithmetic) have been replaced by literacy and numeracy. Standardized testing tends to focus on these two areas, starting in elementary school and extending all the way to graduate school. The dominance of these two fields has the potential for pushing all other subjects (social studies, health, the arts, and science) to one side. It's as if all the other subjects are little people in the cafeteria and when the big folks move in (reading and math), they force everyone to adjust to their presence. But if teachers allow that to happen, students will not have as rich of an educational experience as they could. Science is a subject that taps into children's natural curiosity. Science permits students to explore their world and begin to identify patterns and regularities. Science can provide students with the knowledge that helps them learn to be healthy, keep themselves safe, and avoid being ripped off by magical claims about diet pills, get-rich-quick schemes, and other forms of deception. Scientific knowledge can provide students with the skills to make sound decisions. Science can provide students with an amazing amount of power.

Science Enhances Living

One reason that science is so important in a school curriculum is that it helps students to use their knowledge about their world to exert a greater degree of control over their lives. Even though it seems obvious today, humans have not always recognized that germs (bacteria, fungi, and viruses) cause many diseases. It wasn't until the microscope was invented that people knew germs existed. Diseases such as cholera were thought to be caused by bad air and not by unsanitary conditions. In the 1850s physician John Snow discovered that the cholera deaths in London followed a pattern where everyone who became sick was obtaining their drinking water from the same source. When the handle from the pump was removed, forcing residents to obtain their water elsewhere, the cholera epidemic ended. Scientific knowledge saved the day. The knowledge that microorganisms existed and that some cause infections, diseases, and deaths (this is called "germ theory") contributed to improved health practices. This knowledge is useful not only if you are trying to get a drink in London. Consider the fact that in 1918 approximately 40 million people around the world died from the flu. Scientific knowledge led to our understandings of sanitation, vaccinations, and antibiotics. The increase in average heights over the past one hundred and fifty years is evidence of how improved scientific knowledge (prenatal care, nutrition, and sanitation) has had a discernible impact on humans (Cole, 2003). Not only can science help us live better lives, it can help us live. Using this knowledge we see that helping students understand science becomes central to helping humans wisely inhabit the planet.

Professional Opportunities Through Science

Another different but very real reason students need to learn science is that it provides economic prospects and career opportunities. There are many professions in which a knowledge of science is an absolute necessity. By providing students with a science background in elementary school and middle school, you increase the likelihood they will enroll in additional science courses in high school and college.

Not only is scientific knowledge important for many careers but just knowing how to approach problems with a scientific mind is going to prove useful in many jobs. Any career that requires solving problems, gathering data, and using evidence to make informed decisions is going to be much more accessible to those who have had a good background in scientific thinking. An educational experience featuring opportunities for students to learn to *think* scientifically opens doors to jobs and careers.

Given the trajectory of employment in the United States, it is becoming clear that some knowledge of science is an absolute requirement for an adequate quality of life and the hopes of long-term financial security. Science has an economic utility (Postman, 1996) because it can increase students' career possibilities and earning potential. Using this argument, we see how teaching students to learn science is essential in helping them achieve a decent standard of living at the end of their formal education.

Science Within a Democracy

A third justification for making science a regular part of learning is based on the need to prepare students to become good citizens. Admittedly, voting is really not difficult: registered adults show up at the polls on the appointed day, wait their turn in line, and then push a button, punch a card, or throw a lever—it's not all that hard. The trick is knowing how to vote *wisely* so your decision is consistent with your values and informed by facts. Knowing how to sort facts from opinions, knowing how to interpret evidence, and knowing the situation and the ramifications of either of two or more possibilities are all skills that have their basis in scientific thought processes. John Goodlad, who devoted his career to ensuring that democracy is at the core of American education, recently reinforced the important role that schools can play in keeping our democracy strong:

> Schools can help equip us with the skills to search out answers to questions we may have concerning, for example, matters of public policy. Schools can teach us to distinguish between what is and what is not validated, useful information. The difference is important. (Goodlad, Mantle-Bromley, & Goodlad, 2004, p. 39)

Building Knowledge for the Future

A final reason for including science in the curriculum and being committed to the successful teaching of science is that science is part of the passing along of societal norms from one generation to the next. When life was simple and children could learn all they needed to know by watching their parents or apprenticing with other adults, formal schooling was not a necessity. But as the world has become more complicated, careers are becoming increasingly specialized. The knowledge required of mechanics, grocers, florists, and beauticians is so involved that formal instruction is all but required. The romantic notion of parents teaching their children all they need to know as they work side by side is basically a thing of the past. The knowledge accumulated in one generation must be passed to the next to keep modern society functioning. Schools have become the primary mechanism by which knowledge is transmitted from one generation to the next. And science is one of those subject areas in which the knowledge necessarily builds on what is already known.

In summary, there are many purposes to education and science is tightly bound with each of them. Education provides practical knowledge for everyday living, and science knowledge has directly led to improved health. Science is important for our students because it gives them more access to career options. Third, science knowledge creates a more informed citizenry. Finally, science is a subject that is so complex and ever changing that formal instruction is needed to transmit the knowledge across generations. Although some purposes may be more convincing to you than others, we hope you can recognize that it is essential for teachers to teach science, to make every attempt to teach science well, and to strive to teach science to every student in their classroom.

The Philosophy of This Book

As you are probably aware, there is a struggle within teacher education courses between theory and practice. On one hand there is the desire of professors and textbook authors to provide preservice teachers (meaning those in the stage before serving in the capacity of a full-time teacher) with historical perspectives, philosophical analyses, and research findings related to teaching.

Meanwhile future teachers long to know the practical aspects of teaching: what makes a lesson interesting, how students can kept usefully busy, are where to find the best sources of creative activities. We are aware of this tension and appreciate why someone might be seeking a book full of proven hands-on science activities. However, it is our contention that such texts provide only a starting point for the new teacher. Becoming an effective science teacher of all students is about more than activities. What is needed is knowledge and awareness and commitment.

Viewing Teaching as a Profession

Our position is that a course or a book on science methods must be more ambitious than giving you a script you can follow. As we mentioned earlier, we view teaching as a profession. Otherwise teaching science is going to be thought of as a technical skill. When there's a very specific way to do something, such as assembling a piece of furniture that comes in a box, there are certain steps you are supposed to follow. In following these directions, there is no room for creativity. The manufacturer does not expect you to apply any creativity when you are building your desk or bookshelf. When you're doing assembly work, you aren't supposed to do any thinking. Instead you are just the intermediary between taking the pieces as they are delivered and putting them together in the proper way.

What are the problems of a technical approach to teaching? Although components of the furniture have been manufactured and are well known by the people who wrote the directions, the students in your classroom are not as familiar. No two students are the same and no classroom will respond to the same material in the same manner. The scripted approach to teaching science may work for a subset of the students in your classroom, but what about the others? If teachers are to meet the needs of all learners, they must go beyond the technical. They need to assess the situation, make informed decisions, and be capable of judging the effects of those decisions. Teaching real students in real classrooms requires that teachers be professionals, and professionals go far beyond scripts and simplistic approaches.

In this book we assume you have the ambition of becoming a professional teacher and not an educational technician. We believe this is one of the reasons you made the choice to be a teacher, and we are obligated to help you to achieve that goal. In addition, we accept our responsibility to share our experiences and expertise to help you work to create a more scientifically literate generation of students.

Teaching Science With a Sense of Purpose

The act of teaching is so complex it becomes impossible to keep in mind everything you are supposed to be doing. For very practical reasons, it maybe useful to reduce your science teaching "to do" list to something manageable and easy to remember. For that reason we identified three themes for this book, and you will able to detect them throughout every chapter. Just as important, these themes can serve as guidelines for you as a classroom teacher. You can use these themes as you prepare to teach science. You can remind yourself of these themes to help you make decisions in the midst of a science lesson. And you can rely on these themes to help you reflect on your teaching efforts. Our goal is for you to be able to learn enough about these three themes to not only to give your science teaching a sense of purpose during your initial efforts but also to sustain you throughout your teaching career.

Rethinking Science

One theme is the idea of science as a culture. As with each culture, the culture of science consists of participants who understand the norms and traditions of the culture and behave in ways that are consistent with the cultural norms. This view is very different from the view of science as a collection of discoveries and definitions. We are fortunate that the culture of science does not have very tight borders. Science is open to almost anyone who has an interest in learning about it. But as a culture it has certain standards of behavior that are expected of those participating in it.

We will present the details of the culture of science over the next several chapters. For right now we want you to reconsider your ideas of "science" so they expand beyond the stereotypical views. You might even consider science classes to be a form of cultural appreciation, and there are good reasons to think in that way. Using this cultural understanding of science, if you want to help your students learn science, then your task becomes somewhat different from assigning a list of definitions to memorize. Instead you can take on the role of a diplomat who instructs students about the proper ways to behave within a new culture. For those of us who have visited another country or even been the guest in a home that has different traditions, we know how awkward we can feel. Our discomfort becomes much less when someone explains what is going on and the reasons for it. As you reimagine science as a culture, you will recognize that teaching science involves making the rules and traditions plain to those who are unfamiliar with them.

Embracing Diversity

Our second theme addresses student diversity. American schools are supposed to educate every child, and the diversity of students who attend elementary and middle schools is greater now than at any point in our history. Within this book's conceptualization of student diversity, we include three broad categories: ethnicity, home language, and cognitive and physical abilities. Teaching science to a classroom of almost identical students would be relatively simple, but this isn't realistic. Our nation prides itself on the freedoms it provides to its citizens, and one of those freedoms is access to public education to every child. There is no "except for …" in this process. Excluding students from a free and public education because of their skin color, home language, or physical ability is not acceptable in this culture. A quality education for all is only a legal requirement in our society; as authors of this book, we view it as a moral imperative. Given the multiple uses of scientific knowledge and skills (to make personal and societal decisions, to secure employment), this call for a quality education becomes particularly important when we consider science. It is our position that teaching science for all, not just for a select few, is an obligation within American education.

Teachers often feel disadvantaged because they are insufficiently prepared to work with a wide range of students (National Center for Education Statistics, 1998). Part of the reason may be a lack of familiarity with individuals who look, speak, move, or think in different ways. To avoid making this challenge a source of frustration, we will provide you with concrete strategies, conceptual models, and resource materials that will be helpful when teaching in diverse classrooms. A key feature is developing a commitment to teach science so all students can become successful, which requires that teachers move past simply accepting diversity and actually embracing the beauty and benefits of living and learning with a variety of people.

Developing Expertise

Every once in a while we hear a comment indicating a belief that the moment individuals earn their teaching credentials, they are set for a lifetime of teaching. It's an interesting image, kind of like college is a factory where new teachers are assembled and packaged. In actuality becoming an expert teacher is a continual process of refinement and improvement. Maybe this is a secret we shouldn't reveal, but we feel obligated to let you know that the successful completion of student teaching is still only a beginning. If you can accept the fact that you're always going to have opportunities for improving yourself as a teacher, your disappointment will be lessened by those less than perfect teaching days in your future.

For the most part you will have considerable control over the paths you take to become a better teacher. Mentoring programs, summer workshops, and graduate courses can all contribute to what you know about teaching. But you will always be the person who makes the final decision about how your expertise is enacted in a classroom. It would be unkind for us to simply point out that you're going to make mistakes in your teaching, so in this text we will be supplying you with ways to problem solve your teaching. In this way you won't be as frustrated by your errors because you will have ways to think through situations and discover better solutions (Schön, 1990). Being able to examine one's work reflectively and make the appropriate adjustments is a defining characteristic of being a professional.

How This Book Will Be Useful

We believe this book is just one piece in the process of learning how to teach science. We hope it's an important piece, but it's not enough on its own. Our view is that students cannot learn as much about science by reading as they can by doing science with others. In a similar fashion, we cannot foresee how someone might become an effective science teacher by studying a book, no matter how well that book is written. This book will be most useful to you if it not only provides new insights but also causes you to contemplate your role as a teacher of science. As you engage with this text, you should be testing out your ideas and interpretations in conversations with classmates, with your instructor, with veteran teachers, and ultimately through firsthand interactions with children. Learning science is an active process, and the same is true for learning how to teach science. Some might wish that we could provide a simple response to the plea "Just tell me how to teach science!" We do as much of that as we can in these pages. However, you will need to take control of your learning by trying to rethink what is included in science, reimagining who can become successful in science, and accepting the need to continually improve your skills as a teacher of science.

Everything we included in this book is based on activities that have been successful with real kids. A great deal came out of our own work in schools. In areas where we were less certain, we checked in with teachers to be sure we were on target. In addition this book emerged out of our personal experience teaching new teachers over the past several years. What we tried to accomplish is to take the material and approaches we've developed and refined over the many, many times we have taught science methods and put them into a format that extends beyond the courses we personally teach.

One challenge often faced by science methods students is knowing how to think about the course work. For example, in the midst of doing an interesting science activity during the course, you might wonder if you should allow yourself to become caught up in the excitement of learning the science or if your job should be to think about the teaching implications for your future students. We have found it to be useful to conceive of having two different minds that you can switch between during activities.

One of your minds is that of being a science learner. We strongly encourage you to allow that mind to become active during this course. The science learner residing inside each of us is curious, full of wonder, easily excited, and rewarded by the ability to finally understand something that was never fully appreciated. To allow this mind to function is more difficult for some people than for others. For those who have been working hard to become responsible adults, it seems somewhat childish to voice excitement when looking through a magnifier. But you must be open to that possibility.

Only by experiencing firsthand the joys of discovery and the appreciation of understanding something you hadn't previously recognized can you understand the pleasures of doing science. Many students won't have trouble becoming eager about doing science. As their teacher, you must empathize with their enthusiasm, and this is best accomplished if you have experienced that delight yourself. When teachers ask us what they can do to make science fun for their students, we interpret their question to mean they have never personally experienced the fun that is inherent to science. To accomplish this, you will have to allow the science learner mind to come to the surface.

Meanwhile the science teacher mind will also need to become engaged. The science teacher mind is one that tries to recreate science learner enthusiasm so it is channeled toward learning science. The mind of a science teacher accepts the necessity of starting science instruction with direct experiences as a way to encourage curiosity and provoke uncertainty. Student excitement is something that is not just to be tolerated—you should have had those sensations yourself as a science learner. However, as a science teacher you shouldn't be content simply to have your students be enthused. You also accept responsibility for advancing the children's understanding of science as you direct their excitement toward a grander purpose, and the science teacher mind is something we will try to feed throughout this book.

Structure of This Book

This textbook contains the information we use in our science methods courses. One defining part of our teaching philosophy is that the manner in which we teach must be consistent with the ways we expect others to teach. The chapter sequence is intended to reflect that belief. Basically this translates into starting with the most specific and concrete ideas and moving outward toward the more general and abstract material. The information we present in the first few chapters serves as the core. You can think of this beginning as the center of what will become a very large ball of string. With each chapter we gradually build on the information provided in the previous chapters. This doesn't mean we are trying to obscure the initial ideas. Instead we are adding layers of complexity as we progress from one chapter to the next, relying quite deliberately on the ideas resting at the center. When you reach the final chapter, your ball of string won't be finished. However, we will provide you with some clear sources of additional information that will allow you to continue winding more onto the ball as you make the transition to a full-time classroom teacher.

Within the Chapters

We have selected a somewhat informal writing style for readability. The ideas we present and the ways we express them are natural extensions of how we teach. One of the invigorating aspects of teaching is that every individual is able to create his or her own style. Some people are very theatrical; some are very calm. Some are comfortable with a free-flowing atmosphere, whereas others believe learning happens best when there is a considerable structure and regularity. Our motto is that "whatever works for the students" should be the final decision, and by "works" we mean what is successful in helping all students learn science.

In our university courses, we envision each of our students as colleagues. The same holds true for the readers of this text. Because you are becoming one of our science teacher colleagues, we will share our expertise so you can incorporate that information into your personal approach to teaching. We strongly believe we should not provide you with simply a list of recipes for teaching fun science. As a budding professional, you deserve more. We expect you want to become an effective science teacher for every student who enters your classroom. By extension your students require more than to be entertained—they need to learn science.

The activities we included within the chapters are designed for *you* as a future science teacher. If you look at these activities and think they won't work with elementary or middle school students, you would be correct. These activities are to instruct adults about teaching science, which is, after all, the purpose of this book. Nevertheless, we understand the need to view activities for your students, and we will provide those for you when we think you will be able to make sense of them. You should also know that most new teachers require guidance about selecting activities that will be informative, safe, economical, and successful in a classroom. Not every activity book provides all of that. So as you read this text, please be patient, as it will require a little bit of time for us to share with you how to decide which activities to select. For right now, you should understand that the activities we included are designed to help you think about teaching science and are not examples you can photocopy and use with children the next day.

For Reflection & Discussion

Consider these types of questions: "What is the name of … ?" and "What are the parts of … ?" Answering these questions requires pulling information from memory or consulting some reference material. Compare those questions with these: "What could happen if we … ?" and "What do you think we could do … ?" The strategy for answering those questions is much more involved than looking toward some reference materials. It would be helpful to have some background information to assist in forming a response. But there is not a clear right or wrong answer—and one isn't being expected.

This second type of question is characteristic of what you will find sprinkled within the chapters. As the heading indicates, these questions are meant to cause you to reflect as well as prompt you to discuss your ideas with others. The purpose is to encourage you to consider the implications for that chapter's material for your own teaching. There is no answer key. But your responses to these questions will strengthen your thinking about science teaching. Finding ways to compare your responses to others will help to clarify your decisions about teaching.

Connections to Other Information Sources

Learning science is more than having children discover it for themselves. Even though there is some appeal to the idea of allowing students to build their own knowledge about science from the ground up, that isn't very reasonable. First of all, it is impossible for a student to recreate the past two thousand years of scientific thought in the time interval between the first day of kindergarten and high school graduation. Second, science is a social process whereby different people's experiences and interpretations contribute to what becomes accepted as scientifically valid knowledge. Finally, teachers are legitimately expected to guide their students to existing sources of scientific knowledge to assist their students' learning. In other words, learning for oneself often requires making connections to what others have already learned.

In this same way, we provide connections between the information in these chapters and the ideas and experiences of other educators. Sometimes we will subtly point to other people's work by inserting a quick citation within the text. Our sincere wish is that this won't be distracting to you. We have done this not to impress you but to show how the information we supply is built on the work of others. In some places we will describe in greater detail the findings of educational research. Also when it seems appropriate, we will direct you to other sources of information that we simply do not have the space to include. These will range from children's books to science curriculum to Web sites.

One key feature sprinkled throughout the text are the connections to the National Science Education Standards. Because each state develops its own content standards, we do not include those here. Instead, the other portions of NSES are inserted when the text corresponds to a specific standard. Therefore, you will find connections to Teaching, Professional Development, Assessment, and Program Standards.

Point–Counterpoint Feature

We don't want to lead you to believe that all issues related to teaching science for all students have been solved. There are many areas where educators are still uncertain about what is exactly the best way to proceed. In this regard teaching science is similar to science itself: there are many debates about what is known and different people advocate for different approaches. Within the chapters you will find Point–Counterpoint sections in which two different positions about a particular education issue are expressed. Each addresses a topic about which there is genuine dispute. One reason we included the Point–Counterpoint sections is to emphasize the dynamic nature of teaching science. Another reason is to inform you about the stances different groups take toward various educational issues. We consider these to be "awareness building" sections, and they are not designed to demonstrate the superiority of one position over the other. Each represents an issue with which we continue to struggle, and we invite you to consider what your response to each might be.

The Sequence of Chapters

This preface is meant to orient you to the organization of the book and explain the philosophy of the authors. The purpose of the first chapter is to describe two important ideas. The first is to explain why we have chosen to emphasize teaching science to diverse populations. Second, we want to introduce a central premise of the entire text: our focus on teaching the culture of science. At some point in their college careers, most future teachers recognize they will be expected to teach to a wide variety of students. However, they may be uncomfortable because it is not quite clear how to go about doing so. Teaching science by helping students become familiar with a new culture is a useful approach. We will demonstrate why this is so helpful and important.

In chapters 2 and 3 we address the science process skills. Developing these skills is fundamental to learning science. We like to think of science content as being the equivalent to the nouns of a sentence, whereas the science process skills serve as the verbs. Only by thoughtfully combining content and process can we expect students to move toward scientific literacy. Typically science teaching emphasizes content without giving sufficient attention to science process skills. We want to provide balance for that tendency. In addition there are many sources of information available for science content, but not very much is available about science process skills. Finally, learning the science process skills takes a fair amount of time. For all these reasons, we elected to spread the science process skills across two chapters.

In chapters 4 and 5 we begin our discussion of pedagogy, the actual practice of teaching. In chapter 4 we present some history of science teaching to familiarize you with the variety of approaches that have been in vogue. We support each model of teaching with a particular theoretical framework, and we feel it is useful for you to know the reasons why some educators prefer some approaches over others. This leads us to chapter 5, in which we describe the learning cycle—an extremely powerful model for teaching science. There is a particular sequence to the learning cycle approach, and we will provide a great deal of explanation and examples to make this approach very clear for you.

In chapter 6 we focus on using questioning techniques and discussion-leading strategies. As with the learning cycle, these techniques draw on education research, classroom practices, and our personal use in elementary and middle school classrooms. In chapter 7 we add another layer to your knowledge of effective science teaching to all students. Within this chapter you will learn how to modify hands-on activities so they can become more than fun experiences for you and your students. Here we emphasize that there are important distinctions between hands-on science and inquiry science. In this chapter we explain the difference and show how you can create great inquiry lessons from good hands-on activities.

Chapter 8 is in some respects the most challenging. Within this chapter you will encounter the nature of science. This topic attempts to define the philosophical basis of scientific thinking. We included this material because a true understanding of science requires appreciating the particular features of how scientists think. We included it in the middle of the text as we wanted you to first have background experiences that will be useful when approaching this more difficult material. We designed the next few chapters to be practical. Chapter 9 reflects a move from individual lessons to a consideration of entire units of instruction. In chapter 10 we address the idea of integrating science with other subject areas, paying special attention to approaches that support students' entry into the culture of science. In chapter 11 we describe the wide variety of methods that can be used to assess students' science learning, and in chapter 12 we approach the very specific issues of managing a classroom as a safe and productive learning environment.

In the remaining chapters, we take all that has been described to this point and look at the big picture. Within chapter 13 we present the role that technology might play within the teaching of science in elementary and middle school classrooms. In chapter 14 we emphasize the need to connect science learning in the classroom with various communities. Within the idea of community we include the community of science, the community of the students, and your own community as a teacher.

It's Time to Begin

The goal of this book is to help you become the sort of teacher who can make a difference, one who can help students learn *about* science and learn to *do* science. We intend to develop your confidence in teaching science in diverse classrooms, provide you with the tools and mind-set to assist with your instructional decision making, and supply you with concrete strategies for making science accessible to students of every ethnic background, cognitive ability, and native language. It is our position that teachers who strive to be professionals, who understand that they must go beyond the technical, and who are sufficiently dedicated and resourceful can create a new generation of students who are excited about science, look forward to learning more with every lesson, and realize that they are capable of being successful.

References

Cole, T. J. (2003). The secular trend in human physical growth: A biological view. *Economics and Human Biology, 1,* 161–168.

Goodlad, J. L., Mantle-Bromley, C., & Goodlad, S. J. (2004). *Education for everyone: Agenda for education in a democracy.* San Francisco: Jossey-Bass.

Gregorian, V. (2004, November 10). No more silver bullets. *Education Week, 24*(11), 36, 48.

National Center for Education Statistics. (1998). *The condition of eduction.* Washington, DC: U.S. Department of Education.

Postman, N. (1996). *The end of education: Redefining the value of school.* New York: Vintage.

Schon, D. A. (1990). *Reflective practitioner: How professionals think in action.* New York: Basic Books.

Acknowledgments

It would be improper to claim that we wrote this book on our own. There are countless people whose experiences and insights gave shape to what appears within these pages. Knowing that we risk the danger of leaving an important person off this list, we still wish to acknowledge the significant contributors to the ideas that have found their way into print.

First and foremost, we want to acknowledge our families. Sue Stephens has been generous and supportive at every step of the way. Many thanks to her for fielding countless inquiries from friends and families about how the book is going, which came from every direction. At last, she can say, "It's done!" and we're glad to give her that relief. Ben, Will, and Lily Rogers graciously allowed the space and time that was needed to pull some of these ideas together, and we are happy to note that the book is out before Will and Lily enter high school.

Our thoughts for this text have been shaped both by the classroom and research communities and by many people who bridge that divide. We owe a considerable debt to those who first helped us to think about what it is that future teachers need to know about teaching science. Lloyd Barrow, Ron Good, and Jim Wandersee deserve to have their names at the very top of this list. Adam Johnston, Scott Sowell, and Barry Golden were terribly good sports in reading version after version of the nature of science chapter and continually offering useful critiques. Likewise Scott Sowell, Okhee Lee Salmen, Anne Rosebery, and Beth Warren offered profound and insightful comments about chapter 14, "Teachers Negotiating Different Communities." Mike Haudenschild was pivotal in the conceptualization of the technology chapter. More holistic aid came from Leigh Smith, Julie Kittleson, Lee Meadows, Feliica Moore and Mary Burbank, who had long talks about teacher education with each of us and pushed us to complete this seemingly never-ending project. Our deepest thanks go to each of these individuals.

Next, to teacher friends in Cleveland, a heartfelt thanks: Lois Klamar, Matthew Teare, Deanne Urry, Carrie Leutenegger, and Bill Badders were all special informants. In Salt Lake City we were beneficiaries of the collegiality of several key people: Lesley Lewis, Machelle Dahl, Ann Madsen, Kerri Rustad, and Suzie Broughton. In Florida and Georgia teachers in the distance education program read chapter after chapter of this text, offering profound critiques from the viewpoint of practicing teachers. Thanks in particular should go to Karen Rose, Claude Gonzales, and Sheryl Arriola. These teachers from around the country were willing to open their classrooms and their hearts (and maybe those are one and the same) in ways that made us feel welcomed and challenged. The richness of their worlds made ours all the better.

We are deeply indebted to those many researchers, teachers, and teacher researchers who went beyond critique and offered to put their ideas on paper for the Points–Counterpoint features. This text and the discussions it will engender will be so much richer because of their unique and sometimes provocative contributions.

We acknowledge our former college students who convinced us of the need for this book and gave us clues about what such a book should include. Our only regret is that it took us so many years to become smart enough to create the sort of text that they wanted to have in their hands when we first began to work with them.

Finally, we express our deepest gratitude to the children who have participated in countless science activities with us. Their genuineness, their curiosity, and their acceptance of our efforts have helped us the most. Billy Collins wrote a poem called "Schoolsville" in which he noted that if all the students he'd taught were gathered together, there'd be enough to create a small town. If such a gathering were actually possible, we cannot think of a better place where we'd like to reside.

J.S. & S.A.S.

one

Forming Commitments to Science Teaching

Chapter Highlights

- Understand science as a special culture and unique perspective while gaining appreciation for the habits of mind of science (e.g., curiosity, openness, and skepticism).
- Realize the ways in which the mass media and our students' experiences produce powerful images of teachers and teaching.
- Recognize the ways that scientific literacy gives students the intellectual tools to gain control over their lives, attain a wider range of career opportunities, and participate in a more informed citizenry.
- Endorse the idea of "science for all," including girls, all cultures, English language learners, and students with a variety of physical and cognitive abilities.
- Accept the claim that the students are not the cause for the science achievement gaps between students from different demographic groups.
- View the teacher's role as a cultural ambassador who informs students how to participate in the culture of science and how to make use of its materials.

The Culture of Science

Science, as professionals do it, has a culture with its own norms. Any culture can be reduced to stereotypes, and science is no different. The caricature of a scientist is a White man with wild, uncontrollable hair, wearing a lab coat and working in a messy, stinky, and dangerous lab. Famous scientists include Albert Einstein (and he did have the wild hair), Thomas Edison (his lab was full of strange equipment), and the cartoon scientists on television and in movies.

The problem with a stereotype is it uses a fictional person as the representative for the entire culture.

We have no intention of equating racial and ethnic stereotypes with stereotypes of scientists because that would trivialize racism and bigotry. However, there are substantial differences between how science is portrayed in the media compared to how the scientific culture actually operates on a daily basis. What's wrong with that? The stereotyped gender and race of scientists tends to cause students who don't look that way to feel that science is not for them. In other words, if children look to role models based on people with whom they identify, then the stereotype of the White male scientist will not serve as a role model for most students.

Instead of accepting the stereotypes, we will examine science as it really occurs. Along the way we expect you will recognize that science is not something open to only certain types of students. The strategy we'd like for you to consider is this: if we can help children to understand what it means to be a scientist, including the cultural norms of science, then more students will believe they can think like scientists and become more apt to use this way of thinking to understand their lives.

The Worldview of Science

As a culture, science looks at the world through a particular viewpoint. Let's think about the contrasting manner in which a painter and a meteorologist might examine the sky. Even though both could be looking at the same clouds, the ways they think about what they are seeing would be different. The artist might look at the sky and consider how it could be represented using paint: the shades of white, the edges of the clouds, and the gradations of color from straight overhead down to the horizon. In contrast, the scientist looking at the same scene would make sense of the sky in a different way: the shape of the clouds suggests the temperature of the air, the direction of their movement indicates where the low and high pressures are, and the changing color of the clouds gives an idea about the approach of a cold or warm front.

Neither way of looking at the sky is superior. The traditions of the artist and the traditions of the scientist serve different purposes. Instead of trying to argue which way of looking at and thinking about the sky is better, we could recognize that artists and scientists have different worldviews.

A distinguishing feature of the scientific worldview is the principle that there are patterns in the world that we can understand. Through careful examination, scientists feel they will be able to identify the patterns, and they can use this knowledge to make accurate predictions. You might ask, "What's the point of identifying patterns? What's the use in being able to make good predictions?" Scientists are driven to understand the world. Although there are times when scientists want to understand something to solve a problem, at its essence the scientific worldview of being able to understand and explain the universe is the ultimate prize.

> Scientists share certain basic beliefs and attitudes about what they do and how they view their work. These have to do with the nature of the world and what can be learned about it. Scientists presume that the things and events in the universe occur in consistent patterns that are comprehensible through careful, systematic study. Scientists believe that through the use of the intellect, and with the aid of instruments that extend the senses, people can discover patterns in all nature. Science also assumes that the universe is, as its name implies, a vast single system in which the basic rules are everywhere the same. (American Association for the Advancement of Science [AAAS], 1989, pp. 3–4)

The ability to understand the world provides a scientist with power—a power that comes from knowledge. The fulfillment a scientist experiences when he or she is able to understand what had previously been puzzling supplies a feeling of power. Synonyms for *power* include *control, influence, energy, ability,* and *strength.* Does this mean that scientists seek power? Yes, to overcome the discomfort of not knowing something. The need for power that entices some individuals to become leaders is similar to the power that compels others to pursue science. To put this as simply as possible, we quote Francis Bacon, who explained that "knowledge is power." Consequently, the hunger for power within the culture of science becomes the hunger for knowledge.

Habits of Mind

Cultures have their own value systems, and individuals within a culture are judged and shaped by those values. The values you hold influence your actions and your views of others. For example some of us believe working hard is its own reward and that doing a good job should not be based on whether there is some reward waiting for us at the end of the task. People who adhere to this value system look down on those who believe that a person ought to be paid according to how well they did a job. These two value systems are products of contrasting cultures. Another example of a value system is being a vegetarian. This set of beliefs leads to certain behaviors: treating certain foods as acceptable and viewing other foods as objectionable. Sometimes this can create conflicts because people's value systems are in opposition to each other. The point is that what one believes controls how he or she will act. Simultaneously, a person's actions reflect his or her true beliefs.

Because the value system of science influences the way in which individuals think and these ways of thinking are shared traditions, they become the **scientific habits of mind**. These habits are not automatic but have been transmitted from one generation of scientists to the next. People new to science and in the process of becoming members of the culture need to learn to behave in ways consistent with those habits of mind.

Curiosity

The drive to understand something is based on curiosity. Why do some objects sink while others float? Why do plants in one location seem healthy and green while similar plants in another place seem to be weak and yellow? Why is the phase of the moon associated with unusual human behaviors? Questions such as these are a driving force for curious people. Being curious is one of the most important scientific habits of mind.

NSES Teaching Standard B: Teachers encourage and model the skills of scientific inquiry and the curiosity, openness to new ideas and data, and skepticism that characterize science.

Fortunately, most students begin their education with a great deal of curiosity. Every child is curious about objects that move, especially unusual animals (have you ever been at a zoo when a day care group is on a field trip?). The curiosity is there, and it seems appropriate to state that children are predisposed to think like scientists because of their curiosity.

However, it is possible to supress a child's curiosity. If a child is led to believe there are only right or wrong answers and he or she will receive rewards or sanctions based on these answers, then the child's curiosity will be shoved aside. Almost inevitably, and this is one of the many rewards of teaching science, with the right materials and a supportive atmosphere, the curiosity of a child can pop back to the surface and allow the individual to display curiosity as a habit of mind.

Openness to New Ideas

Another habit of mind within the scientific culture is a willingness to consider new ideas. In contrast to the stereotype of the lone scientist working in isolation, science is a social endeavor. Although an individual scientist might make a discovery on his or her own, the discovery has to be considered, discussed, and debated by the scientific community before it is accepted or rejected. As members of the scientific culture, individuals are expected to remain open to the prospect that different explanations for events are possible.

As a culture, science allows for the possibility that the current explanations may not be sufficient. Somebody might gather new data revealing flaws in a current scientific theory or bring a fresh perspective to existing information. There is a long history of old, seemingly factual, scientific ideas being replaced by new and better explanations, and the culture of science accepts the likelihood that better explanations will be developed. That cultural norm translates into the habit of mind that individual scientists must recognize the importance of being open to new ideas.

This can be a source of internal tension. After all scientists are driven by their curiosity to find patterns to explain what is happening. We can imagine the excitement and relief that must accompany the discovery of a pattern someone has long been seeking. Understandably a scientist would feel a sense of accomplishment and ownership of his or her explanation. Indeed there is a tradition in science where the first person to make a discovery (of a new species, of a new star, or of a new theory) has his or her name attached to it. But to then suggest that this person must also be open to new ideas? We can sympathize with scientists' difficulty with this. In a later chapter we will examine a similar tension students experience as they struggle to resolve their personal explanations with those of the scientific community.

Skepticism

The cultural tradition of being skeptical is one of the more unique values of science. When this habit of mind is being stimulated, it is because of such questions as "Are you sure? How can we be sure? What makes me sure?" In certain respects, being open to new ideas and exhibiting skepticism work hand in hand. Even though cynicism is commonly equated with skepticism, the culture of science does not regard skepticism as a negative trait. A cynic is suspicious of people and institutions, suspecting there is always a selfish motivation behind the things others do. In contrast, a skeptic is doubtful about the claims people make and always looks for more evidence to support these claims. A skeptic always needs data to become convinced, whereas there is no amount of data that satisfies a genuine cynic.

The need for data and evidence is a component of the skepticism habit of mind. The more evidence someone uses to support his or her ideas, the more likely other scientists will accept these ideas. Arguments in other fields such as politics or the arts or philosophy don't necessarily rely on data. These fields can rely on persuasiveness, emotion, and beliefs. But in the culture of science, high-quality data are like gold.

Skepticism is also the reason science is often in conflict with other cultures. Skepticism and faith are exact opposites. Skeptics will demand the reasons that support what we know, whereas people with faith are not expected or required to justify their knowledge with data or evidence. Because faith and skepticism place value on conflicting criteria, worldviews based in either of these are going to be in opposition to each other. The way to resolve this dilemma is to think back on the idea of cultural membership: each of us is a member of multiple cultures. Just as you change your role when you go from your home to work, to school, and to worship, individuals can shift their worldviews depending on the situation.

For Reflection and Discussion

How do these scientific habits of mind correspond to the way science is typically represented in schools? What sorts of comments might we expect an instructor to make to students if he or she decided to emphasize the habits of mind throughout the science curriculum?

Images of Teaching

Each of us holds an ideal of who we would like to be as a teacher. Part of this ideal is visual. We imagine how our classroom will appear. We have a notion about what our students will look like. We also have images about what it will be like when we are in the midst of teaching. This imagery comes from multiple sources. Our visions of teaching are informed by stories we've heard that include teachers as characters. Our ideal of a teacher is also built on images of teachers in movies and television shows. We do not deliberately form our views of teachers and teaching while watching these programs, but simply being exposed to these depictions influences our imaginations.

Images of schools are everywhere, and we are not entirely aware of their presence and power. These icons represent teaching and are unique to the context of schools. For example do you remember using lined paper so you could practice writing upper- and lowercase letters? That paper is a distinct school and teacher image. Word-processing programs have fonts with such names as Chalkboard and Schoolbook, and there are countless other school and teaching images: yellow school buses, the alphabet strips on the wall, an apple for the teacher, and recess.

While the objects of teaching, such as a red grading pencil, are much more concrete, the affective dimensions of our ideal of teaching, such as pride in a good grade, are equally powerful. To list the terms associated with these sensations seems to inadequately capture the depth and strength of these ideals. So we provide a short list to illustrate the emotional dimensions of teaching and schools: being part of a classroom community, feeling supported even when you are confused, sensing that the teacher expects great things from you, and feeling the mix of excitement and fear at the start of each new year.

Images Shape Our Thinking

This collection of images and sensations about schools and teaching has led you to this very moment: you have a desire to become a teacher and to help children to learn. Many people feel so irresistibly drawn to the teaching profession that they describe it as a calling. Such individuals claim teaching is not something they chose to do but something that chose them. This shows just how deeply engrained our ideal of teaching can be. Unlike knowing how to maintain control of a classroom or planning an effective lesson, the deep, almost spiritual aspects of teaching are mysterious in their origins—yet their presence is difficult to deny.

Ayers (1995) described those sometimes magical moments when teaching is "transcendent. ... When teaching is done well, it resonates in the deepest parts of your being. It satisfies the soul" (p. 2). In a similar spirit, Palmer (1998) intoned, "Teaching engages my soul as much as any work I know" (p. 9). Yet teaching is not entirely selfless. Guiding others to learn and develop confidence in their capabilities enriches the life of the teacher. Far too many people make career decisions in which they fail to account for the sense of satisfaction that teaching can supply. This is why we are teachers, and we think it's safe to believe that it is a reason why you would like to become one too.

Switching Sides of the Desk

The greatest influences on your view of teaching are the hours you've spent in the presence of teachers. If we think about learning a profession as being an apprenticeship, we can appreciate the suggestion that becoming a teacher is largely an "apprenticeship of observation" (Lortie, 1975). Unlike any other profession, teaching is the one that the largest number of people has experienced for the greatest amount of time. Recognizing that part of our vision of teaching has been shaped by watching teachers on television, can we even begin to appreciate how much greater an influence being a student in classrooms for sixteen years has on us? The problem is that our perspectives as students may not have given us an accurate or complete view of teaching. You will become aware, if you aren't already, that teacher and student views of teaching are very different.

Just as Lortie (1975) reported in the mid-1970s, most beginning teachers find teaching to be much more difficult than expected. As students, few of us appreciated the demands of being a teacher. In fact, a reason teaching is often given such low status by the general public is that the work seems easy (Labaree, 2005). This perception is influenced partly by our passive experience as students and partly by the idea that the knowledge required to teach elementary grades is very basic. This faulty line of thinking suggests that teachers are giving to children the knowledge that all adults possess and that this information is ordinary compared to that needed in professions with greater prestige (Labaree, 2000). Anyone who believes teaching is easy has probably never experienced it firsthand from the teacher's side of the desk.

As teacher educators, we accept our responsibility to help future teachers make the transition from the role of student to the role of teacher. The specific focus of this book is to help with that transition as it applies to elementary and middle school science teaching. Certainly this requires that we provide you with techniques for expanding your teaching strategies. In addition we will point you toward resources you can rely on to help you in the years to come. At least as important are the ideas we will provide you for teaching science, along with descriptions of the instructional decision making that is involved in selecting appropriate teaching strategies. In other words, we will supply you with the "how-tos" and "why-tos" you need to support the science learning of every student.

Discarding Myths About Teachers

A certain amount of idealism is important within teachers, regardless of the number of years they've been in the profession. However it is important to understand that while ideals can become a resource to draw on when you are feeling discouraged, they can also, when unrealistic, compromise your potential in the classroom. As we consider some myths about teaching, you should evaluate which ideals should be discarded in favor of more accurate and powerful visions about teaching.

There are three cultural myths common among new teachers that we suggest need to be replaced (Fenimore-Smith, 2004). Those myths are as follows: (1) everything depends on the teacher, (2) the teacher is the expert, and (3) teachers are self-made. As with many myths, there may be some surface truth present. But these three teaching myths can create problems in the classroom. First, the myth that all things depend on the teacher implies that there is nothing the child, family, or community can contribute. This myth is reinforced by the image of a teacher or professor standing at the front of the classroom and dispensing information to the students. This stereotype of teaching should be replaced by an image of students actively involved in their learning. Students use what they already know, they compare what they hear with others' views, and they build their understandings by putting bits of information into a structure that makes sense to them. The teacher is an important part of the learning, but not everything depends on the teacher.

The second myth of the teacher as expert suggests that teachers are "all knowing" and that their teaching involves transmitting this expertise to students who not only are nonexperts but may know nothing. There are two major flaws that should convince people to discard this myth. First, assuming that the teacher is knowledge wealthy and the students are knowledge poor automatically denies the unique perspectives students bring to the classroom. Second, it is quite impossible for any individual to be an expert in all subjects, even when it comes to teaching kindergarten. For example kindergartners are often curious about nature, and who could expect to have a complete knowledge of all things natural, especially as new discoveries are being made? Teaching at its best is a process of becoming better. Claims of being an expert suggest there is little more for the person to learn.

The last cultural myth to consider is that teachers can become great without any input or assistance from any other source. The biggest flaw with this myth is the suggestion that one person's experience and intuition are sufficient, if not superior, to all others. Admittedly, some people seem to have the interpersonal skills and passion for learning that predisposes them to become better teachers. But the idea that a person can rely exclusively on his or her lived experience as a guide for teaching every kind of learner is shortsighted. How do we resolve the dispute between "teachers are born" versus "teachers are made"? Our preference is to acknowledge that the most effective teachers are a combination of the two. The artistic side of teaching is something that seems innate, whereas the scientific side of teaching comes from studying carefully, consulting with others, and being open to new perspectives. We are comfortable with the idea of teaching as a craft. By this we see artistry being informed by science and science being enhanced by artistry. The key idea is that experience alone is insufficient to create a great teacher—which is why the myth of the self-made teacher is something we should abandon.

Replacing Myths With New Views

Before you experience a sense of loss because we've asked you to discard these myths about teachers, we have some good news. We can provide you with perspectives useful for your quest to become an effective teacher. One very strong recommendation we have for you is to replace a view of the teacher as a performer with the idea of the teacher as an instructional planner and problem solver. For teaching to be effective, it must depend on the interactions among all in attendance.

The most basic instructional problem is helping students to learn something they don't already know. Before you think this is just too obvious, note that it is worth recalling the images of teaching mentioned earlier. The objects of a classroom's culture (projectors, reference books, calculators, pencil sharpeners) and the actions of a classroom (reading silently, taking attendance, writing on the board, lining up at the door) are very rich ideas. But they do not necessarily depict the central purpose of schools, namely, educating children. It is possible to become so caught up in going through the motions that teachers and students may neglect to recognize that the business of schools is about learning.

Teaching for the Purpose of Learning

We propose that teachers should be instructional planners and problem solvers. Within this role the central problem is student learning. To be more specific, and to reinforce the title of this book, we will emphasize the problem of teaching science to all students in elementary and middle schools. Restricting ourselves to science does not mean we will ignore language arts, math, and so on. But science presents unique challenges that make this emphasis justifiable. By excluding high school and college students, we narrow the scope of our work and clarify the range of instructional problems we need to face. This doesn't mean teaching younger students is simpler—it just requires a different combination of talents. In contrast, when we use the phrase "all students," we are not limiting ourselves: *all* means *all*. All students who attend school should have the opportunity to participate in science lessons and activities and to be provided with the support to learn as much science as they are capable. There are really no exceptions.

One substantial barrier to science learning is a teacher's lack of confidence. Perhaps the best model of healthy science confidence a student can witness is the science confidence of his or her teacher. The time to build confidence in your ability to do science and to help students to do so starts right now. Over time, as you broaden your knowledge through readings and activities and by doing some science teaching, you will begin to convince yourself that your science learning self-confidence is reasonable. Sharing your personal history of scientific learning with your students can help you to communicate to them that the difficulty of trying to understand something is sometimes greatest just before a breakthrough.

Developing Science Learning Confidence

When we survey the college students enrolled in our science methods classes, many are unable to recall positive learning experiences from their early science classes. What memories they do have are often negative and may explain why they were discouraged from studying science. However, there are always a couple of students who have wonderful stories to tell about their school science experience. These individuals can describe in great detail the magnificent field trips they went on, and they talk quite passionately about how they were able to pursue questions of their own design without worrying about failing. Occasionally an individual is embarrassed to confess that he or she kept a school science project even though it was completed more than a decade ago. Upon hearing this, other students often express a mixture of surprise and frustration. They feel cheated because they didn't have a teacher who made them feel good about science or who nurtured feelings about being capable in science.

As their instructors, we cannot predict who among our students are going to share positive stories. We can't look at someone and say, "Oh, she looks like the kind of person who was good in science." It isn't just the students who wear glasses or are tall or have curly hair or are men who have positive school science memories. What does this tell us? Outside appearances have nothing to do with one's capability to learn science. We recognize that the factor that makes the biggest difference in the quality of the science experience is the teacher of those students. If we could go back in time and swap the teacher who taught a student who had a great science experience with the teacher of a student who had a negative memory, there is good reason to believe the stories those students would tell on their first day of their science methods class would be reversed as well.

If you are someone who had a great science teacher, you already have a model and vision for how effective science teaching can be accomplished. But those who weren't as fortunate now have to begin developing mental portraits about what a rich science classroom might look and feel like. The goal of this book is to help you develop this portrait so you can become the sort of teacher who can make a difference. For those who are sufficiently dedicated and resourceful, it is possible to create a new generation of students who are all excited about science, look forward to learning more with every lesson, and realize that they are capable of being successful at it. It is for those future teachers that we have written this methods textbook.

NSES Teaching Standard A: Teachers select science content and adapt and design curriculum to meet the interests, knowledge, understandings, abilities, and experiences of students.

A Start on Instructional Problem Solving

We propose three problems related to science teaching that need to be solved. First, we will examine the legitimacy of science within the curriculum. By addressing the question about the role of science within the larger educational system, you will discover that science is essential for elementary and middle school students. After establishing that science has a rightful place in the curriculum, we then look at the problem of defining science, especially in terms of elementary and middle school teaching and learning. Because the phrase is so frequently tossed about in educational circles, we will address the concept of scientific literacy. Our specific interest is clarifying the reasonable expectations for science learning for elementary and middle school students. The third problem is clarifying the implications of the "science for all" movement currently underway in the United States. Interestingly, while many educational programs seem specific to a certain geographic location (e.g., different states or various nations), the "science for all" agenda has worldwide appeal. The secretary general of the United Nations wrote an editorial titled "Science for All Nations" for the journal *Science* in which he proposed an international sharing of science education excellence that will benefit students and citizens in every country on the globe (Annan, 2004). This is all to illustrate that "science for all" is not a short-lived phenomenon but a reform that is likely to be long lasting. You, as a future teacher, and your students will be the beneficiaries of these developments.

Science Within the School Curriculum

Historically the centerpieces of education have been language arts and mathematics. What were once the three Rs (i.e., reading, writing, and 'rithmetic) have been replaced by literacy and numeracy. Standardized testing, starting in the elementary grades and extending all the way into graduate school, focuses on these two areas. The dominance of these two fields has the potential to push all other subjects (social studies, health, the arts, and science) to one side. But if teachers allow that to happen, students will not have a rich educational experience.

One reason science is important in a school curriculum is that it helps students use knowledge to exert greater control over their lives. Even though it seems obvious today, humans have not always recognized that germs (bacteria, fungi, and viruses) are the causes of many diseases. It wasn't until the microscope was invented that people realized germs even existed. Diseases such as cholera were thought to come from "bad air," not unsanitary conditions. In the 1850s physician John Snow famously discovered that the cholera deaths in London were related to an interesting pattern. Everyone who became sick had obtained drinking water from the same source. When the handle from the pump was removed and residents were forced to obtain water elsewhere, the cholera epidemic ended. More generally the knowledge that microorganisms existed and that some could cause infections, diseases, and deaths (this is called the "germ theory") contributed to improved health practices in the mid-nineteenth century. Consider the fact that in 1918, forty million people around the world died from the flu. Scientific knowledge led to our understandings of sanitation, vaccinations, and antibiotics. The increase in humans' average heights over the past one hundred and fifty years is evidence of the way that improved scientific knowledge (prenatal care, nutrition, and sanitation) have had a discernible impact on everyday living (Cole, 2003). Not only can science help us live better lives, it can help us to live. Helping students understand science becomes central for encouraging humans to wisely inhabit the planet.

Economic and career opportunities are other very real reasons students need to learn science. There are many professions in which scientific knowledge is an absolute necessity. By providing students with a science background in elementary and middle schools, you increase the likelihood they will enroll in additional science courses in high school and college. Not only is scientific knowledge important for many careers but just knowing how to approach problems with a scientific mind proves useful in many jobs. Any career that requires the ability to solve problems, gather data, or use evidence to make informed decisions necessitates workers having a good background in scientific thinking. Therefore science has economic utility because it can increase students' career possibilities and earning potential (Postman, 1996). Helping students to learn science increases the odds that they will eventually be able to attain a decent standard of living.

A third justification for including science as a regular part of learning is based on the need to prepare students to become good citizens. Admittedly voting is not very challenging: registered adults show up at the polls on the appointed day, wait their turn in line, and push a button, punch a card, or throw a lever—it's not all that difficult. The trick is knowing how to vote *wisely* so your decision is consistent with your values and informed by facts. Knowing how to sort facts from opinions, knowing how to interpret evidence for oneself, and knowing the situation and the ramifications of choosing between two or more possibilities are all skills that have their basis in scientific thought processes. John Goodlad, who has devoted his career to advocating for democracy to be at the core of American education, has recently reinforced the important role that schools can play in keeping our democracy strong:

> Schools can help equip us with the skills to search out answers to questions we may have concerning, for example, matters of public policy. Schools can teach us to distinguish between what is and what is not validated, useful information. The difference is important. (Goodlad, Mantle-Bromley, & Goodlad, 2004, p. 39)

A final argument for not only including science in the curriculum but being committed to the successful teaching of science involves passing along societal norms from one generation to the next. As the world has become more complicated, careers are becoming increasingly specialized. The knowledge required of mechanics, grocers, florists, and beauticians, for example, is so involved that formal instruction is all but required. Schools have become the primary mechanism by which knowledge is transmitted from one generation to the next, and science is one of those subject areas in which the knowledge necessarily builds on what is already known.

In summary, there are many purposes to education, and science is tightly linked to each. While some purposes may be more convincing to you than others, we hope you can recognize how essential it is for teachers to teach science, to make every attempt to teach science well, and to strive to teach science to every student in their classroom.

Becoming Scientifically Literate

In a traditional sense, being literate has meant knowing how to read and write. This form of literacy roughly describes being competent with the written word. When we mention **scientific literacy,** we mean something more than simply being literate with scientific words. A scientifically literate individual possesses a specialized set of knowledge and skills that allow him or her to participate in science. The AAAS (1989) provided an even more specific definition of scientific literacy in the text *Science for All Americans.* Here are the major components of scientific literacy:

- being familiar with the natural world,
- understanding the key concepts and principles of science,
- employing scientific ways of thinking,
- recognizing that science is a human enterprise, and
- using scientific knowledge and ways of thinking to make informed decisions.

To become scientifically literate, students and teachers must do much more than master the subject matter. Added to a basic understanding of scientific concepts is the need to be able to use this information. There are many adults who believe that learning content must occur before the knowledge can be applied. But when students are pushed to learn material without also having the opportunities to use their knowledge, they generally cannot apply their knowledge to novel situations. Scientific literacy goes beyond having an encyclopedic knowledge of science topics. At least as important is being able to think scientifically and to use the knowledge and thought processes when making decisions about personal and societal issues.

At this point we have considered two challenges or problems associated with the prospects of teaching science. First, we developed a list of justifications for teaching science in elementary and middle schools. If there was any doubt about whether science is a proper subject for students before they enter high school, we expect these doubts have been reduced, if not eliminated. Second, we identified the goals of science teaching and learning for elementary and middle school students. We will continue to develop this idea of "what is science" as we move forward. At least for the short term, we'll be content with the concept of scientific literacy because it includes not only knowledge but also particular ways of thinking. In the next section we will move to the third problem: establishing which students should be expected to become scientifically literate.

In case you are feeling overwhelmed by these challenges, we want to offer you some encouragement. The truth is that the existence of these troubles makes us all the more convinced that we should address the problems head on. We want you to begin your entry into the teaching profession, and specifically science teaching, with your eyes wide open. The problems we are presenting to you are well documented. We are not inventing the problems—we are shining a light so you can notice them. At some point you would have learned about these issues, such as the challenges of teaching science to all students. Our view is that it is more honest to present those issues now so you can think about how you should respond.

The next issue is not one teachers and teacher educators have completely solved. But we know the challenge won't go away if we choose to ignore it. So we have a request for you: would you be willing to work toward the goal of "science for all" even though we aren't yet 100 percent certain how to reach this goal? There are many justifications for taking on this challenge, and they range from the political to the legal to the ethical. We invite you to join us to work toward resolving this challenge. For those who are ready to pitch in, we will supply background information to clarify what we mean by "science for all."

Who Is Included Within "Science for All"?

Why do we teach literature? Why do we teach mathematics? Is it because we expect all students to become best-selling authors or accountants? Probably not. Language arts and mathematics are commonly understood to be essential components of a broader education. They represent a body of knowledge we expect students to master to lead useful, fulfilling lives. We propose that science is no different. The goal of science teaching has moved away from a single-minded pursuit of assembling a new generation of scientists. Instead science teaching now focuses on helping students become scientifically literate, to help them develop a useful and applicable understanding of science, recognizing that some of these students might elect to continue to study science. To teach science only to encourage some students to become scientists is an inappropriate strategy. If science teaching is too closely focused on career preparation and college admissions into scientific fields, far too many students will continue to be turned away from science. Rather than treat science classes as a filter for separating the potential scientists from the nonscientists, we should recognize that knowledge of science represents one important facet of being an educated person. Related to this is the desire for schools to provide every student with equal opportunities to learn science. This claim is being made by more than educators. The largest organization of professional scientists, the AAAS, advocates for this perspective in the book *Science for All Americans:*

> Education has no higher purpose than preparing people to lead personally fulfilling and responsible lives. … The world has changed in such a way that science literacy has become necessary for everyone, not just a privileged few: science education will have to change to make that possible. (AAAS, 1989, pp. xiii–xvi)

Scientists and science educators recognize that scientific knowledge is necessary for everyday life. We recognize that those individuals who have greater skill and stronger understandings will have more control over the choices they make about their lives. As a consequence science instruction should not exclusively, or even primarily, focus on the next generation of scientists. Too often the educational system fails to emphasize knowledge of science as a fundamental necessity for each student. In a school system where every child, regardless of background or ability, receives high-quality science instruction during the elementary and middle school grades, the chances of perpetuating achievement gaps can be reduced. For students who are so inclined or predisposed, high school can be the right time for individuals to begin specializing in science.

Diversity in Many Forms

With the science teaching profession moving past the narrow notion of teaching science for the sole goal of creating future scientists, we can begin to focus on the second component of the earlier quote from the AAAS, the value of teaching science to every student. It is one thing to say "every student"—but what were the AAAS and the related National Research Council thinking in the call for science for all? Who exactly is the "all"? The following definition leaves little room for doubt:

> All students, regardless of age, sex, cultural or ethnic background, disabilities, aspirations, or interest and motivation in science, should have the opportunity to attain high levels of scientific literacy. (National Research Council, 1996, p. 20)

The ambition seems clear: an understanding of science is not a goal we reserve for a certain group of students. Students of all backgrounds, all abilities, and all personality types are to receive the science instruction that will permit them to become scientifically literate. Why is there such an emphasis on the "all" in *Science for All Americans*? Part of the rationale comes from past differential patterns of science achievement among groups of students, part comes from demographic changes in the American population, and part comes from changing educational policy. In the following sections, we will explore some of the categories of students the members of the National Research Council were considering when they authored the *National Science Education Standards* (1996) and explore why these groups have been targeted for scientific literacy.

Gender Diversity

It might be obvious to citizens of a Western industrial nation in the twenty-first century that both girls and boys should receive high-quality science lessons. After all, there is no evidence indicating that success in school science is predetermined by gender. Despite the common stereotype of scientists being men, our society seems to accept the idea that girls can become successful scientists—and we agree. However, this attitude doesn't explain the disparities in science achievement as documented in *The Nation's Report Card* (National Center for Education Statistics, 2003). This report used data from the National Assessment of Educational Progress (NAEP) test, which is administered to students throughout the country every few years. Although the gender gap in science achievement seems to be lessening, differences remain. In 2000, boys had higher average NAEP science scores than did girls at grades four and eight, and between 1996 and 2000, the average score gap favoring boys over girls widened by three points at grade four and by five points at grade eight. Indeed a gap in NAEP science scores for boys and girls remains for students at the highest proficiency level. Echoing such differences, Lynch (2000) reported that only 2.8 percent of girls seriously consider science as a career compared with 10 percent of boys. Although we as a nation aspire to gender equality, boys and girls do not seem to be responding to science education in similar ways.

NSES Teaching Standard E: Teachers display and demand respect for the diverse ideas, skills, and experiences of all students.

Ethnic Diversity

Most students from non-European American cultures do not score as well in science as their more Western, mainstream counterparts. Figure 1.1 shows science NAEP scores for three different grade levels and across five ethnic categories (data for fourth-grade Asian/Pacific Island students were missing from the original report). The graph shows the percentage of students with science scores that placed them in the "below basic" category. In other words, the figure shows the proportion of students who did poorly on this test.

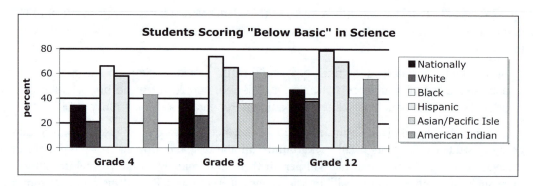

FIGURE 1.1. Students scoring "below basic" in science. From *The Nation's Science Report Card* (National Center for Education Statistics, 2003).

What can we surmise from these data? The percentage of students scoring below basic increases across grade levels. In fourth grade, one-third of students scored below basic, while for twelfth graders this figure reached almost one-half. Compared to the national figures, Whites were consistently more successful in science than their counterparts in other ethnic groups, and that pattern does not seem to be lessening with time. Between 1996 and 2000, no reduction in the gap occurred between the scores of White and African American students or between White and Hispanic students in any of the three grades. This becomes a particularly serious concern when we examine the projected changes in the demographic profile of American schools. In 2000, children of color composed more than 40 percent of America's student population, and estimates indicate that by 2026 this figure will swell to 70 percent (Garcia, 2001). During this time, the greatest growth is expected for Hispanic children. Currently this group represents 16.2 percent of the school-aged population and will increase to 30.5 percent, while Asian Americans, now at 4.2 percent of the student population, will grow to 9 percent. The percentages of African American and American Indian students are expected to stay roughly the same (Hardy, 2000). Clearly, if we are to be successful in helping students across the nation become scientifically literate, then we must address every group of students.

Linguistic Diversity

A defining feature of a cultural group is its language. We would be remiss if we didn't acknowledge how that represents another form of diversity, one different from but related to underlying culture dimensions. English language learners currently make up 5 percent of the American student population (National Center for Educational Statistics, 2003), but this number is increasing at a dramatic rate. One million immigrants move to the United States each year, and 90 percent of them come from non-English speaking countries: in 1998, there were 3.2 million students designated as English language learners, and this figure doubled in less than a decade (Center for Applied Linguistics, 2002).

Many of these students are learning English as a second language even as they attempt to learn subject matter. As suggested by Lee, Fradd, and Sutman (1995), English language learners find science particularly intimidating, as science typically emphasizes vocabulary and abstract thought. Although *The Nation's Report Card* did not report data in terms of student language, a smaller scale research study conducted by Torres and Zeidler (2002) lends empirical support to what many teachers have long suspected: for students learning English, science learning is far more difficult than it is for their English-speaking counterparts. English language learners are placed under a huge burden when placed in an English-speaking science class. One goal of this book is to identify ways in which you, as a teacher, can lessen this burden.

For Reflection and Discussion

What languages might the students in your classroom speak? Visit the Web site for the Office of English Language Acquisition (http://www.ncela.gwu.edu/stats/3_bystate.htm) to investigate the demographics for your state. What are the implications for you as a teacher?

Ability Diversity and Physical Disability

Sharon Lynch (2000), in her analysis of equity in science education, reported that approximately 12 percent of the student population of the United States has some sort of a disabling condition. These conditions include learning disabilities (45 percent of the total number of disabled students), speech and language impairments (20 percent), mental retardation (10 percent), serious emotional impairments (roughly 10 percent), orthopedic impairments (1 percent), hearing impairments (1 percent), and other impairments, including attention deficit disorder (1 percent). With the passage of the Individuals with Disabilities Education Act, many more students with disabilities are being integrated into mainstream classrooms. The national science education reform documents (AAAS, 1989; National Research Council, 1996) urge that science learning be part of the experience of every student, including those who have cognitive disabilities or who are in some way physically challenged.

We propose that those people who endorse the idea that students who have difficulty processing ideas ought not to engage in science are probably taking a too-narrow view of the subject. A deliberate and thorough observation of materials and events is an essential feature of doing science. Manipulating objects to appreciate causes and effects is also considered scientific. When we embrace the complexity of science and realize that mastery of knowledge is not all that is required, we then have access to a new vision of what it means to teach science and who is capable of learning science.

The challenges that people with physical disabilities face can often be regarded as mainly a matter of access, although teacher expectations weigh in heavily here as well. As teachers we should strive to provide every student with access to science, not just for legal reasons but also because of a commitment to the goal of teaching science to all students. Sharon Lynch (2000) brought up a wonderfully insightful point: Albert Einstein, Niels Bohr, and Leonardo da Vinci, all scientific visionaries, had learning disabilities and overcame their disabilities in ways that factored into their eventual success.

Exploring the Reasons Behind Achievement Gaps

It is one thing to claim to teach science to all the children in our classrooms and quite another thing to be successful in doing it. The first step in puzzling this through is to consider possible reasons behind the achievement gaps described previously. Why is it that girls, students of color, students learning English, and students with disabilities tend to lag behind their White, male counterparts in the science classroom? Characteristically answers originate with a focus on the students. Girls are often described as being less interested in science than boys and, for whatever reason (biology or culture), having a lower science aptitude. Simply put, some people suggest that it is harder for girls to think scientifically. This is clearly a controversial remark and continues to be a source of public debate (e.g., Newkirk, 2005).

As we consider the explanations offered for why students fail to do well in science, one common and misleading approach is the suggestion that the student and the student's family are the source of difficulty. If students are not successful in science, it is thought to be because of their deficiencies. Lynch (2000) referred to this as a **deficit mentality,** which is the inaccurate belief that many learners come to school without the prerequisite skills, knowledge, and abilities needed to learn science. According to this deficit mentality, students from certain demographic groups can be expected to make few strides toward the successful learning of science until society can help correct deficiencies.

One of the difficulties of the deficit rationale is that it fails to explain the science success of students from those same groups. In settings where teachers and schools do not subscribe to a deficit mentality, students from a wide range of backgrounds display exceptionally high science achievement. Another perspective for explaining the science achievement gaps shows much promise. Walter Secada (1995) suggested that most attempts to illuminate causes for achievement gaps focus in the wrong direction. His suggestion is that we focus instead on schools and schooling as the causes of these problems. To understand the science achievement of diverse learners, we should consider how we teach them science. For this, we first need to provide a quick lesson about the history of science education.

The traditional curriculum of science, the **culture of science**, is understood to be a uniquely Western and masculine activity, employing mechanistic, causal, reductionist explanations of the natural world (National Science Foundation, 1994). In other words, a Western science view of nature involves an effort to understand something complex and mysterious, such as how a plant grows, by reducing the process to individual parts. Instead of looking at the entire tree, Western science concentrated on the individual cells and ultimately the molecules within the cell. In other words, the Western scientific way of understanding the world attempts to identify cause-and-effect relationships by eliminating all the extraneous factors and aiming for the little pieces that will explain the patterns that are observed.

The traditional way science is taught, and even the way the content is structured, comes to us from over a century of educational inertia (DeBoer, 1991). Historically the students targeted by science teachers and curriculum designers have been White, European American boys. Until recently this was the demographic expected to become the educated elite, the pool from which future scientists would emerge. Unsurprisingly, the curriculum and instruction traditionally employed in teaching science was designed to meet the needs and build on the strengths of this particular group of students. Students not of this group were not targeted by either the teaching or the curriculum—and they not expected to excel in the sciences. There are two sources of concern in the history of science education: expectations and content. We submit that both are areas of particular concern in teaching science for all, because each is an approach that has served to help a few students to learn science but prevented many others from these opportunities.

Geneva Gay (2000), in her book *Culturally Responsive Teaching,* reminded us that teacher expectations substantially influence the quality of teaching provided to students. Although teachers may *believe* that all students can learn, they may not *expect* some students to learn. Thus teachers may challenge and support some students while allowing others to be in classrooms without insisting on engagement in learning. Good and Brophy (1994) labeled this situation a **self-fulfilling prophecy,** a phrase that they claim was first proposed by Merton (1948). If teachers expect students to be high or low achievers, the teachers then act in ways that will cause this expectation to come true. Throughout the past one hundred years of science teaching in this country, teachers and the community expected White boys to succeed in science, and so conditions in the classroom allowed this to happen. Working from a wealth of research literature, Gay described how White boys are asked more difficult questions, given more challenging responsibilities, and provided more acknowledgments of their successes. They are expected to succeed in learning science and so are supported in their learning. Teachers typically do not hold the same science expectations for girls, students of color, or students with disabilities. A vast amount of research describes how these students are asked fewer and lower-level questions, provided less critical feedback, assigned easier tasks, and given less acknowledgment for their success. Less is expected of these students in terms of their science learning, and so fewer opportunities are provided to allow for them to be successful.

Teachers' Potential for Closing the Gap

Teachers can exert powerful influence on students' science achievement through their expectations of students. In addition, we can communicate equitable expectations by monitoring who is asked questions, the difficulty of the challenges, and the praise and feedback we offer to different students.

A second root cause of the science achievement gap is the actual content of science. Given that even the National Science Foundation (1994) recognizes science as a Western, masculine way of thinking, it seems almost inevitable that some students will find scientific thinking much more natural than others. However, just as a teacher ought to hold high expectations for all students, the teacher also has the responsibility for helping students understand scientific ways of thinking. We advocate that this can best be accomplished by reconsidering science as a culture and by making the culture of science an explicit part of science teaching. It is this aspect of science teaching we will address in the next section.

A Clear Sense of Culture

At some point in our lives, each of us begins to identify with a group. For a child this begins with the recognition that he or she is part of a family. This understanding starts with an awareness of parents and siblings and often expands to include the extended family: grandparents, cousins, and so on. As a result, what an individual includes within "me" is more than just himself or herself but also his or her position within the family unit. The center of a person's world shifts from "me" to "we" as he or she sees the environment more broadly. This expansion doesn't stop with the family. Commonly it grows to include friends, neighbors, coworkers, and so on. As a member of each group, the individual learns the standards of the group: what to wear, when to speak, how to behave, and so on. Such is the natural process of becoming a social being. Part of going to school involves learning how to function within a wider variety of groups. Although it may not fit your current conception of the term, we suggest that you consider these groups as each having its own culture.

To explain our use of the term, we are using Sonia Nieto's definition of **culture:**

Culture can be understood as the ever-changing values, traditions, social and political relationships, and worldviews shared by a group of people bound together by a combination of factors that can include a common history, geographic location, language, social class and/or religion. Thus it includes not only tangibles such as foods, holidays, dress, and artistic expression but also less tangible manifestations such as communication style, attitudes, values, and family relationships. (Nieto, 1992, p. 111)

When a culture is isolated from other cultures, the members may not recognize how their own culture is unique. What can happen when people spend much of their life insulated within their own culture is that they believe their cultural traditions are normal. To a certain extent this is accurate. A *norm* is defined as a typical aspect of a group. In testing, the most common score within a group is the norm. Standing when you hear the national anthem broadcast over the school intercom is a cultural norm.

A problem with being confined within a particular culture is that the defining traditions may be left unexamined. As a result people could even claim they do not have any culture. They might believe their ways of thinking and acting are normal and that all other traditions are not. This opinion interferes with the possibility of respecting other people's cultures. Quite naturally people choose to associate with others who share the same traditions. It would be an unusual person who is constantly an outsider from any tradition. But in our current society, we need to not only recognize that each of us is a member of cultures but also come to accept other cultures as legitimate even though they are different.

Unless you teach in a school system completely detached from the outside world, you will need to know how to be effective at teaching many kinds of students. Given that even the most rural schools now have Internet connections, it seems impossible for a school to be entirely disconnected from all other cultures. Thus the notion of culture, both in terms of students and in terms of science, becomes particularly important to consider as one prepares to teach.

Point–Counterpoint

The status of science is a topic of ongoing discussion. Some people hold the view that there is only one kind of science. Others claim that science comes in many different forms and can, and even should, include indigenous people's versions of science. So to the question "How universal is science?" we have the following two perspectives.

Should Science Have Boundaries?

Alejandro Gallard
Science Teacher Educator, Florida State University and Former Middle School and High School Science Teacher

Two of the most powerful processes are observation and communication. Yet for too long we have confined these observations to "scientists" and the "scientific process," which combined together result in unquestionable truth. The notion of truth is rigorously defended by the idea that only "scientists" can do science. The bulk of these truths are found in science journals, in science textbooks, and within phrases such as "independent studies by scientists confirm that… ." Society has a belief that science can come only from a "real scientist"; that is, someone who has the proper academic credentials. To be a "real scientist," these individuals must at least be wearing a white coat and use verbiage such as "objectivity," "empirical evidence," and "data." I wonder how society in general, and scientists in particular, would react to a barely clothed, barefoot man who can communicate only orally because his tribe does not have a written form of communication when he yells, "Run for your life because a man-eating wave is coming!"

Had the villagers of Moken Village on December 26, 2004, waited for a scientist to confirm what they knew, they would have all been killed by the tsunami (Goodnough, 2005). As it turns out, folklore about tide and wave phenomena had been passed on orally from generation to generation. For example Salama Klathalay, chief of the Moken tribe, had been taught by elders to expect a "man-eating wave" whenever the tide receded far and fast. Thus when he observed this phenomenon, he yelled for all to run to high ground. All but one from his village were saved. Another group of Moken in another location noticed that dolphins were very agitated just before the tide receded so severely. Their keen observation allowed for most of that group to survive as well.

How did these villagers know enough to save themselves? Perhaps the answer lies in that they have spent a lifetime collecting informal data and passing on this "native science" to other tribe members through oral stories. Not necessarily the stuff one reads in a science textbook or an objective, rigorous journal of science.

What is the relation between this example and teaching and learning science? Well, what does a science teacher do in a learning situation with the knowledge that John or Mary has about the world around them? To answer this question, one would have to understand that a teacher's beliefs about the nature of science include not only what is science but also who can be a scientist. The complexities of these beliefs form the framework for how teachers react to a student's prior knowledge. I argue that as science teachers, we should not take knowledge that has been built on sometimes years of prior experiences and discard it if that knowledge does not "quack" or "waddle" like the science portrayed in texts. We must, as science teachers, give equal footing to students' extant knowledge about science phenomena by using our own content knowledge to try to understand the implied science phenomena in a man-eating wave. Yes, I do acknowledge that there is legitimate scientific knowledge. However, I am arguing that if a student's observations and ideas about science phenomena and form of communicating this knowledge do not fit the typical patterns of science, then the students' observations and ideas should not be discarded. Instead, what a student knows should be viewed as starting points for more focused science classroom experiences, experiences that serve to enrich rather then deny students' existing knowledge. Placing clear boundaries about what is or what is not science denies students' existing knowledge and so denies the students.

Nature's Laws Are Universal, Not Local

Ron Good
Science Teacher Educator and Former High School Physics Teacher

Nature is ever changing, but nature's laws are not, and discovering nature's laws and building explanatory theories are what natural science is all about. Arguments against the universality of nature's laws are older than science. Religious authorities once argued that the heavens and the Earth are separate spheres and operate according to different laws. Scientists, especially Isaac Newton, showed that nature's physical laws of motion are the same for the heavens and the Earth, uniting the universe into a single system. Religious authorities argued also that humans are separate from other living organisms, but Charles Darwin and modern biologists showed that argument to be wrong as well. Arguments against the universality of nature have a long history in religious doctrine and throughout human societies more generally.

One of the modern arguments against the universality of nature and its laws as discovered by science is known as multicultural/local science. Certain sociologists and other nonscientists argue that because science is done by people, its knowledge base necessarily reflects their personal and cultural biases. The argument goes something like this: science has been dominated by European White men and necessarily reflects their biases, so we should be suspicious of—some say reject—their scientific findings. In their desire to promote multiculturalism, some school systems have included examples of local science into their curriculum. By doing this, they argue, science will be more representative of and fairer to all cultures.

Scientific creationists have used the arguments of local science proponents to inject their own brand of science into the school curriculum. Creation theory or intelligent design, they argue, should be introduced to students as an alternative to evolution theory in the science classroom. After all, both are just theories. Postmodernists argue that scientific knowledge should not be elevated above other ways of knowing because that degrades people whose cultures are not scientific. It seems that nearly everyone wants to elevate their own local knowledge to the category of scientific.

When Albert Einstein called science the most precious thing we have, he was referring to the processes of scientific thought and action that yield universally agreed-on knowledge by people regardless of their local language, beliefs, and customs. And when John Dewey called science the emancipator from local and temporary incidents of experience, he understood that scientific methods are designed to produce knowledge that can be reproduced by all people, regardless of their personal habits and predilections.

Multiculturalism and postmodernism try to preserve local beliefs and customs, whereas science, like nature, is indifferent to them. Science seeks consensus among those who study nature's laws while at the same time requiring that minds remain open to new discoveries that might result in changes to current knowledge. Until a scientific community reaches consensus on an important issue, vigorous heated debates can occur. However, in the end it is nature that settles the debates, for scientific theories must be consistent with nature, and that role of nature as final arbiter is important as it ensures the universality of science.

Science arrived late in human history because it is often counterintuitive and opposed to local knowledge and authority. It is revolutionary in the sense that it can disrupt local customs and beliefs that have been in place for a long time. Its value or preciousness lies in its ability to evaluate local beliefs and to assist in settling disagreements about nature and reality that arise when local customs and intuitions of one society contradict those of another.

Science follows nature and distinguishes itself from other "ways of knowing" by eliminating, as much as is humanly possible, personal bias in its methods. Thus science, like nature, is not Western or Eastern or Northern or Southern. It is just science.

Two Components of Culture

Cultures consist of two components: the objects and the actions. The **objects** of a culture include physical tools and culturally specific knowledge about how to use the tools. The **actions** of a culture are the ways in which participants in the social group think and interact with each other. In the culture of a particular ethnic group, the objects would include their clothing, language, food, and knowledge base, and the actions would include their beliefs, traditions, social structure, and communication styles.

When we travel to a place where the culture is different from our own, we aren't always sure how to fit in. We may not know the language, we may not be wearing the right clothes, and we may not even know how to read the road signs (see Figure 1.2). Each of these belongs within the objects of the culture. We realize that certain actions of the culture are foreign to us when we're not sure about the traditions for forming a line, how to appropriately acknowledge an older person, or which of our behaviors might be viewed as rude and insensitive.

FIGURE 1.2. It is important to know the culture of traffic symbols: This sign from Mexico indicates there should be no parking here.

Such an awareness of cultural differences seems to happen only when we find ourselves in an unusual circumstance. This doesn't mean you must fly to a distant country to experience these sensations. Even though you might not have had the *object* and *actions* terminology to help you sort out your sensations, you have probably experienced these notions when attending a celebration in someone's house of worship, shopping in an ethnic store, or eating a meal in a unique restaurant. The odd and often uncomfortable sensations we encounter when we are quite literally "out of place" highlight other cultures as well as our own.

Often it isn't until we become immersed in another culture that we become aware of the defining features of the culture that is our own. When a person attains this awareness, he or she can recognize that culture is not something exotic, foreign, and remote. Instead that person can recognize culture as something that is a part of each one of us. Those who think about themselves as not having any cultural affiliation or somehow regard their traditions as just normal have not had enough thoughtful exposure to other cultures. When someone from a different culture asks you to explain your holiday traditions and you recognize that your experiences are not necessarily shared by everyone, then you are closer to seeing that you are a member of a culture. It seems necessary to acknowledge a personal cultural identity to become sensitive and effective in working with students from a wide array of cultural backgrounds.

Rather than think about cultures that are exotic, the stuff of public television documentaries, we are going to emphasize two cultures very close to home. We will begin by considering a classroom for its cultural elements, and then we will shift our attention to science as a culture. The purpose of this approach is to prevent our thinking about culture as being something "out there" and that has significance only when we travel to distant societies or talk to people from other countries. The fact is that we are all members of a culture and probably several overlapping cultures. Let's begin a view of culture by considering a setting that is very close to our hearts: a classroom.

Describing a Classroom Using a Cultural Lens

Picture a classroom. Maybe it's the one where you learned from your favorite teacher. Perhaps it's a classroom you recently visited. It doesn't have to be an ideal classroom, but it should be one that is easy for you to visualize. The important thing is to have a vivid sense of a classroom. With that classroom in your mind, consider how you would describe it to different people.

What are the features of the classroom you would describe to someone who is employed by a construction firm? You might think about this classroom in terms of features that would be of primary interest to someone who often views his or her world from the vantage point of ceilings and floors, lights and windows, ventilation and acoustics, and other parts of the physical environment. Your description should give a construction expert a sense about the room at different times of the day and during various seasons. If the classroom has windows, then the quality of light that comes in and the view that one has by looking out will change. If your efforts to describe this classroom to the construction expert are to be effective, you need to anticipate the sorts of things the expert would have an interest in. Given the construction person's professional interests, he or she would probably be curious more about where and how the books are stored within the classroom than about the types of books the children will read.

Now let's describe the classroom for the benefit of an anthropologist. This description is going to be quite different because an anthropologist will likely be interested more in the people in the classroom and the things they do than in the heating and cooling systems. To describe a classroom to the anthropologist, you would emphasize the actions of the people: the manner in which they talk to each other, the ways they organize themselves into groups, the types of objects they use, and the routines in which they participate. This description would need to include the changes taking place in the interactions throughout a school day and from one time of the school year to another. The furniture of the classroom would be important but only to the extent that it informs the anthropologist's understanding of the social aspects of the classroom.

Because you are learning about teaching science to children, you already have a sense of elementary and middle school classrooms. There are all kinds of things special about classrooms that make them very different from other spaces where people work. One obvious difference is the furniture: it's all built in proportion to the children, which can make for a comical situation when adults gather in a classroom. Another characteristic of classrooms are the learning tools: crayons and paper, posters and chalkboards, overhead projectors and pencil sharpeners. Many teachers have these materials organized so they are available at the very moment they are needed and there are enough for every person.

Is there only one correct way to organize the classroom: the furniture, the schedule, the climate, and the books? No, there are hundreds of arrangements that could promote an effective learning environment. We admit that teachers are constrained by the kinds of desks the school provides, the types of educational materials the board of education adopts, and the size of the room. But the teacher has an immense amount of influence over the classroom, especially when we take into account the features of a classroom that we would describe to an anthropologist. In short, the culture of the classroom is one of its most defining aspects.

A dozen teachers, provided with identical materials for use in the exact same space, would be expected to create different classroom cultures. The classroom culture is partially an extension of the teacher: his or her views of the purposes of education, his or her own experiences as a student, and his or her beliefs about the ways to help children learn. The classroom's culture also reflects the students in this room. Just as the teacher brings his or her background into work, so do the children. The ideals of the students, their ways of communicating, their personal aspirations, and the need to define themselves as members of society all contribute to the classroom culture that is formed.

Not only is the classroom culture the by-product of the personalities of those present but it is also an ever-evolving entity. We wouldn't be at all surprised if a classroom changed from the first day of school to two months later. In more subtle ways, the classroom would be perceptibly different at the start of the school day until partway through. The physical arrangement of the students (doing independent writing versus participating in a whole group discussion), the kinds of tools being used (watching a video versus doing an activity), and the general tone of voices (teacher giving directions as the class prepares to leave the room versus children telling each other about their favorite music) are all examples of shifts in the classroom culture.

Altogether, these features and many others define a culture. We should recognize that class-rooms are a type of culture and begin to consider what teachers might do to define and sculpt a classroom so it becomes an environment that supports everyone's learning.

The Boundaries of a Culture

A culture is described by the traditions of a particular group of people. Individuals sharing a culture have a common language. The people have certain standards of clothing, favored foods, and music preferences. There are certain routines distinguishing a group, such as the holidays celebrated, the ideas that are honored, and other features that bind and unify a group of people. The forces leading some individuals to have higher status than others within a culture are yet another social tradition. These sorts of power relationships will also define who is included and who is excluded from a culture. You cannot simply join a new culture because you want to. To become a member of a culture, you must understand the norms of that culture, and your degree of understanding of those norms will determine your acceptance by the culture.

Often when people refer to a cultural group, they are thinking about a nationality and all the stuff of the culture (styles of communicating, ways of dressing, types of food). A person who is born and raised within a city in Taiwan is a member of a culture that is very different from the culture of someone who grew up within a Navajo community. If we would bring together persons from these two cultures, they would not automatically understand each other and for reasons that go beyond language differences. A substantive difference between the two people would be the ways they interact with other people within their culture. Another difference would be their ways of engaging in worship. Individuals from the two cultures might legitimately feel their own ways are normal and that the traditions of the other person are odd.

We might anticipate that a child would be proud of his or her culture. This child would see that the person he or she is becoming is an extension of the cultural traditions of previous gen-erations. Certainly cultures change over time as new words are invented and new tools become incorporated into the culture. But we hope that a child would not believe that other cultures are somehow odd, inferior, or wrong. Instead we expect that people would come to accept other cultures, and the people who are members of those cultures, as different but not in a way that puts cultures into a ranking from best to worst. We feel most comfortable and natural when we function within our own culture, and we expect that others will respect our culture for that very reason.

Membership in Multiple Cultures

Up until this point, we've associated cultures with nationalities. This doesn't mean just geo-graphic boundaries because someone can be a member of a culture even when he or she moves beyond the national borders. We wouldn't expect someone to stop being Kenyan or Russian just because he or she traveled outside of that country. Your being a member of a culture involves much more than simply where you live.

Most of us are members of more than one culture. This statement requires us to recognize that *culture* has a more specific definition than one's nationality. Imagine a group of friends who share certain music preferences, enjoy similar types of food and beverages, have particular words or phrases they use all the time, and share a relatively similar type of clothing. We could describe this circle of friends as a cultural group.

If a culture is defined by a collection of shared and accepted traditions, then we can begin to recognize the incredible variety of cultures that exist. A group of women who meet to play cards and socialize represent a culture. Forest firefighters who work, eat, and live together throughout the fire season are a culture. People who gather online to discuss their lives and dreams are also a culture. In each instance, there are characteristics defining the culture, such as ways of communicating and interacting. Someone who is not a member of a certain culture has a hard time understanding the vocabulary or recognizing the acceptable ways of behaving. He or she would probably feel awkward trying to fit in. But over time, a new person might begin to get the hang of the abbreviations that are used in the chat room or the significance of the bids made in the card game. Over time the person might learn enough of the cultural norms to become accepted into that culture.

Recognizing that a culture is much more specific than just a certain country a person is from, perhaps you can identify the cultures with which you are associated. Anytime you join a group with which you develop new ways of thinking or acting, you become a member of a new culture. These groups might be found at school, church, or work. If you have a job, then you know there are certain words and phrases one needs to know. In addition there are certain ways in which things are done, whether it's how to answer the phone or how to arrange the utensils on the table. You may have different ways of acting when you are in the role of a student. An important part about learning to become a teacher is developing skills at functioning within the culture of teaching.

A Broader View of Culture

A cultural group is defined by its traditions. While in everyday language we might primarily use the word *culture* to refer to a particular ethnic group, we might also use it to talk about cliques. Often a group of children from widely varied family backgrounds will have a common passion for a particular musician or author, and that shared interest will come to define who is in their group and who is not—this could be appropriately identified as a cultural group. Professions also act to define cultural groups. Nurses can be thought of as a cultural group, as can bus drivers, bank tellers, and bartenders. Even though members of these groups may all speak English and live in the same town, there are features of their work lives that distinguish them from other professionals. This includes the accepted attire, the hours that they work, the equipment that they use, and the manner in which they communicate.

> A clique, a club, a gang, the prisoners in a jail, provide educative environments … as truly as a church, a labor union, a business partnership, or a political party. Each of them is a mode of associated or community life, quite as much as is a family, a town, or a state. The activity of each member is directly modified by knowledge of what others are doing. (Dewey, 1916/1944, p. 82)

People learn as a result of being members within a cultural group. If you grew up with others who had a shared set of religious beliefs, then you learned about that religion by being associated with others who were practicing it. In this regard, a culture is more than a group of people with a shared set of traditions—a culture becomes a force that can educate its members. John Dewey took a very broad view of how cultural groups become sites for educating their members.

One view about the purpose of schools is that we want all students to be able to learn to think about their world in many different ways. Although it's an oversimplification, we could think about the school curriculum as a collection of appreciation courses. Students cannot be realistically expected to learn all of the content in science, history, music, economics, math, sports, and so on. But we would like for them to have a taste for all of these. If we wanted to design a curriculum that used subject-area appreciation as a guiding principle, what sorts of learning would occur? Obviously we wouldn't be satisfied with having the students memorize the terms associated with every subject area; there is much more to history than knowing dates. Instead we'd want the students to experience these subjects in ways parallel to the ways the professionals experience them. Our curriculum would require a thoughtful combination of concepts (the "nouns") and skills (the "verbs"). For art this would mean learning some color theory and some painting techniques. For math this would be learning shapes and how to solve problems. Let's consider how this might apply to science.

As we've mentioned, cultural groups are described by their objects (such as the clothing and tools) and their actions (such as their styles of communicating). The objects and actions of a culture should parallel the concepts and skills of an academic field. Art and math might share an interest in shapes, but the way that artists and mathematicians approach their subjects is quite different.

Learning to become a skilled member of a culture requires being able to recognize and use the tools and objects of that culture. To our list of cultural objects, which includes boomerangs, kayaks, and weaving looms, we can add Bunsen burners and thermometers—just to reinforce that the scientific culture has its particular objects. What is maybe less obvious to you, and perhaps entirely unfamiliar to your future students, is an appreciation of the cultural actions of science. This is perhaps why the idea of studying (or teaching) science makes so many people uncomfortable. When you aren't sure about the proper etiquette of a different country, you're naturally concerned about making a major mistake (or, if in France, a *faux pas*). But if someone familiar with the culture educates you about the proper way to think and behave, then your comfort level rapidly rises. This same diplomacy is necessary when teaching science. To help students become comfortable and proficient within the culture of science, you will need to serve as their tour guide. You could imagine science teaching as the task of introducing a group of students to this culture by giving them the terms, skills, and thought processes that will permit them to participate within the culture. In what follows, we will provide information about some actions from the science culture.

Science as a Culture for Students

Perhaps the closest you've been to learning about the actions of science occurred when a teacher encouraged you and your classmates to "think like scientists"—and you were left to imagine how to go about doing such a thing. Our position is that the learning of the actions of the culture of science should not be left to students to figure out for themselves. Instead their teacher must make the traditions clear, acting as if he or she is a cultural emissary for science. Our list of three scientific habits of mind is a fairly straightforward starting point. Curiosity, openness, and skepticism are traits we can define for students and encourage them to use as they do science. Students will more clearly understand a directive such as "As we discuss this activity, I would like for you to practice your skepticism" than one such as "Think like a scientist." Making the subtle features of the culture of science obvious to students removes the guesswork and uncertainty.

Imagine how much easier it would be if, when you were faced with a new setting, the cultural traditions were clear. Having someone who is willing to explain the traditions of a culture to you would not only make you feel more comfortable but also permit you to more smoothly function within the culture. One example of a cross-cultural misunderstanding is physical proximity. On one side, an individual may feel as if his or her personal space is being violated by the closeness, if not actual physical contact, that members of another culture initiate. But on the other side, an individual might perceive a culture as being too remote and cold because others don't engage in warm greetings or even maintain eye contact. Think about your willingness to engage with members of another culture. Having the power of knowledge of another culture provides you with a greater sense of being able to regulate your environment. You feel more competent as you develop increasing skill within this culture—and all because you understand the objects and actions of the culture.

We are suggesting this is the same disposition to undertake when teaching science. When teaching science we can imagine that we are ambassadors representing the culture of science. Rather than expect students to absorb the culture of science by being immersed in it, a science teacher should support students by providing unambiguous information about the objects and actions of science. There is no special formula to do this. A skillful tour guide will look for examples to illustrate the points he or she wants to make. Likewise when teaching science, the teacher should be attentive to opportunities to, for example, highlight the habits of mind that are distinguishing features of the science culture. One might say that the goal of science teaching is to share power with students so they can become confident as they navigate within the culture of science. By being more explicit about the cultural norms of science, the teacher can guide students to know when and how to act in ways appropriate to that culture.

NSES Teaching Standard B: Teachers recognize and respond to student diversity and encourage all students to participate fully in science learning.

As science teachers we recognize science is not a subject that attracts a sufficiently diverse range of individuals. It seems this could be because the dynamic nature of science has not been made explicit to students. To increase students' interest in doing science and their confidence in their personal abilities requires teachers providing them with a better sense of the culture of science. The habits of mind we have introduced are just the starting point. There are additional actions of the science culture, including inquiry and the nature of science, which you will encounter in subsequent chapters. But for right now, we want to introduce the idea of the actions of science and explain how this is fundamental to learning science.

We can create a considerable mess if we compare cultures with the expectation or assumption that one is superior to the other. This applies especially when helping students make the connections between their home cultures and the culture of science. The goal is to create a healthy and respectful balance between the culture of science and the cultures of the students in your classroom (Aikenhead, 2000). Science, for all its marvelous accomplishments, has its limitations. There are questions we might ask that a scientific worldview is unable to answer. If you've heard about multiple intelligences, then you are aware there are many ways of being "smart." You can have musical smarts, interpersonal relationships smarts, athletic smarts, and so on. Scientific smarts cannot be a substitute for these other types of intelligences because thinking in a scientific way is constrained by the need for data.

Taking a Long, Broad Look

Today's classrooms are not homogeneous places. Changing economic conditions, changing demographics, and changing legislation have brought students with a wide variety of ethnic backgrounds, socioeconomic conditions, primary languages, and behavioral and cognitive abilities into the classroom. One thing that is certain is that this variety, this heterogeneity, will only increase during your career as a classroom teacher. Until this point our goal has been to alert you to the complexity of science teaching and also begin providing you with a mental framework for thinking about what you will do when you begin teaching science at the elementary or middle school level.

Our view is that teaching science in ways effective for a diverse student population requires a teacher to reconsider unexamined assumptions. It is important for teachers to continually refine their practices, always aiming to become better but also accepting the inappropriateness of the goal of perfection. There are many groups in the education and scientific community that advocate a "science for all" approach to education. This is connected to the belief that all children are capable of learning science and that the individual teacher has tremendous opportunities, if not the duty, to make this happen. One step toward the realization of this goal is to regard science as a culture. Adopting a perspective of science as a culture implies that we as teachers must become skilled at science. But we must also provide our students with access to the scientific culture. The description of the culture of science, understood in terms of both actions (ways of thinking and inquiring) and objects (physical tools, such as magnifiers and graph paper, and science concepts, such as gravity), is especially crucial when teaching science in today's diverse classrooms. Science has its own culture, with particular actions and objects derived from relatively modern, Western patterns of thought. It is valuable to recognize that a scientific worldview will seem more familiar to some students and stranger to others. For many students from non-Western, non-European backgrounds, the culture of science can seem foreign and unusual.

As science teachers we are responsible for helping our students to understand the actions and objects of science, familiarizing them with the norms of thinking, acting, and talking scientifically. With this broadened conception we can reinvent science teaching from the stereotype of dispensing information and replace it with an approach wherein the teacher helps students navigate science as a culture. Only by making science a clearly human pursuit can we expect a wider variety of students to willingly engage in it. The benefits of such a shift extend beyond issues of mere motivation. Interest translates into persistence, which in turn promotes heightened self-confidence. These are powerful foundations on which a teacher can build a science teaching agenda that opens students to a wide array of life's options.

Chapter Summary

- Thinking in a scientific manner draws on several natural mental habits of humans. However, science has unique ways of thinking that distinguish it from other ways people come to understand the world. These habits of mind include having curiosity and skepticism and being open to new ideas.

- Our views about teaching and our expectations for the role we will take as teachers are shaped by a combination of our experiences as students and messages received from the media. Because these impressions are so subtle yet powerful, we may need to reconsider certain assumptions, such as the feeling that teaching is a performance, and replace those with beliefs that will be more suitable for thinking about teaching science to diverse populations.

- Scientific literacy reaches beyond acquiring scientific knowledge to include the need to develop the thought processes involved when someone engages in science. These intellectual tools expand career options, advance the intelligence of the voting public, and give individuals the resources to use to make informed decisions as voters and in their daily lives.

- Although science education was once seen as a way to supply the future scientist pipeline, the current goal is viewed as "science for all." This "all" includes every student who attends school and does not exclude participation in science because of gender, native language, cultural background, physical impairment, or cognitive ability.

- The goal of "science for all" requires that the profession closes the achievement gap. Discriminatory practices of the past, such as excluding women, people of color, and special needs populations, still reveal themselves in science achievement. Even though our path to overcoming these inequities is not completely clear, we recognize that teacher expectations have the potential for reversing these tendencies.
- A cultural perspective can provide science teachers with a fresh way to think about the subject and their role in helping their students to learn it. As with all cultures, science is distinguished by its objects and actions. The goal of scientific literacy requires having students become participants within the science culture.

Key Terms

Actions (of a culture): ways in which participants in the social group think and interact with each other.

Culture: shared views of a group of people about their values and traditions that are united by a common language, physical location, shared history, or belief system.

Culture of science: includes both the objects of the culture (its physical tools and accumulated knowledge) and the actions of the culture (the commonly held patterns of thought and patterns of behavior).

Deficit mentality: the inaccurate belief that many learners come to school without the prerequisite skills, knowledge, and abilities needed to learn science and that until deficiencies are corrected in the learners or the learner's lives, then academic learning is not possible.

Objects (of a culture): the physical tools and the knowledge that accompanies those tools shared by a social group.

Scientific habits of mind: the values of science that influences the way in which individuals participating in the culture of science think and act. Components of this value system include curiosity, openness to new ideas, and skepticism.

Scientific literacy: the goal of science education as described by current science education reforms. The components of scientific literacy include being familiar with the natural world, understanding the key concepts and principles of science, being able to employ scientific ways of thinking, recognizing that science is a human enterprise, and using scientific knowledge and ways of thinking to make informed decisions.

Self-fulfilling prophecy: the prevalent pattern throughout all of education that says if teachers expect students to be high or low achievers, students then act in ways that will cause this expectation to become a reality.

A Favorite Science Lesson

The "Fabric" unit designed by the Full Option Science System (FOSS as it is known to classroom teachers) is a wonderful entry point for science in kindergarten. The entire module is full of activities that are deceptively rich in science. One favorite is the "Soiling and Washing Fabric" activity. Each child receives a square of muslin cloth that he or she is to deliberately stain. The class goes outside so students can rub dirt and grass on the fabric. In the classroom they add more stains using the same household products we see in laundry detergent commercials. The students then try to remove the stains using scrub brushes and water. They discover that adding soap makes a big difference in removing the stains. The reason this activity is so powerful is that it introduces children to fundamental chemistry concepts: solubility, properties, and evaporation. In addition, fabrics are a key feature of many cultures, so students from diverse backgrounds can see connections between school and their homes. Activities include weaving, sewing, and dyeing. Finally, the children's literature connections tap into the rich collection of fabric-related stories from around the world.

Suggested Readings

Engblom-Bradley, C., & Reyes, M. E. (2004). Exploring native science. *Science and Children, 41*(7), 25–29.
During a summer camp experience, students learned about the connections between science and Native Alaskan cultural traditions. One example of such integration was an experiment comparing the insulation of wolf fur with caribou fur. Students gathered data and interpreted them to show that caribou fur is the superior insulator.

Melber, L. M. (2003). True tales of science. *Science and Children, 37*(7), 24–27.
This article describes going directly to the sources to obtain an accurate view of the work of scientists. Through a variety of nonfiction books, students can read entries scientists made in their notebooks and journals as they went about their research. The benefits of this strategy is that a teacher doesn't have to rely on what he or she has to say about what scientists do—students can learn this information directly through nonfiction texts written by scientists.

References

Aikenhead, G. (2000). Renegotiating the culture of school science. In R. Millar, J. Leach, & J. Osborne (Eds.), *Improving science education: The contribution of research* (pp. 245–264). Buckingham, UK: Open University Press.

American Association for the Advancement of Science. (1989). *Science for all Americans.* New York: Oxford University Press.

Annan, K. (2004, February 13). Science for all nations. *Science, 303,* 925.

Ayers, W. (1995). *To become a teacher: Making a difference in children's lives.* New York: Teachers College Press.

Center for Applied Linguistics. (2002). *Immigrant education.* Retrieved from http://www.cal.org/topics/immigrant.html

Cole, T. J. (2003). The secular trend in human physical growth: A biological view. *Economics and Human Biology, 1,* 161–168.

DeBoer, G. (1991). *History of ideas in science education: Implications for practice.* New York: Teachers College Press.

Dewey, J. (1944). *Democracy and education.* New York: Free Press. (Original work published 1916)

Fenimore-Smith, J. K. (2004). Democratic practices and dialogic frameworks: Efforts toward transcending the cultural myths of teaching. *Journal of Teacher Education, 55,* 227–239.

Garcia, E. (2001). *Hispanic education in the United States: Raices y Alas.* Lanham, MD: Rowman and Littlefield.

Gay, G. (2000). *Culturally responsive teaching: Theory, research, and practice.* New York: Teachers College Press.

Good, T. L., & Brophy, J. E. (1994). *Looking into classrooms* (6th ed.). New York: Hill.

Goodlad, J. L., Mantle-Bromley, C., & Goodlad, S. J. (2004). *Education for everyone: Agenda for education in a democracy.* San Francisco: Jossey-Bass.

Goodnough, A. (2005, January 23). Survivors of tsunami live on close terms with sea. *The New York Times,* section 1, p. 6.

Hardy, L. (2000). *What's ahead for your schools* [*Education Vital Signs,* supplement to *American School Board Journal*]. Retrieved from http://www.qeced.net/ed/Stand/FutureSch.htm

Labaree, D. F. (2000). On the nature of teaching and teacher education: Difficult practices that look easy. *Journal of Teacher Education, 51,* 228–233.

Labaree, D. F. (2005). Life on the margins. *Journal of Teacher Education, 56,* 186–191.

Lee, O., Fradd, S. H., & Sutman, F. X. (1995). Science knowledge and cognitive strategy use among culturally and linguistically diverse students. *Journal of Research in Science Teaching, 32,* 797–816.

Lortie, D. C. (1975). *Schoolteacher.* Chicago: University of Chicago Press.

Lynch, S. J. (2000). *Equity and science education reform.* Mahwah, NJ: Lawrence Erlbaum.

Merton, R. (1948). The self-fulfilling prophesy. *Antioch Review, 8,* 193–210.

National Center for Education Statistics. (2003). *The nation's report card: Science 2000.* Washington, DC: U.S. Department of Education.

National Research Council. (1996). *National science education standards.* Washington, DC: National Academy Press.

National Science Foundation. (1994). *Women, minorities, and persons with disabilities in science and engineering.* Arlington, VA: Author.

Newkirk, T. (2005, October 12). Brain research: A call for skepticism. *Education Week, 25*(7), 15.

Nieto, S. (1992). *Affirming diversity: The sociopolitical context of multicultural education.* New York: Longman.

Palmer, P. (1998). *The courage to teach: Exploring the inner landscape of a teacher's life.* San Francisco: Jossey-Bass.

Postman, N. (1996). *The end of education: Redefining the value of school.* New York: Vintage.

Secada, W. G. (1995). *Recommendation for the science education of Hispanic students.* Background paper prepared for the Equity Blueprint Committee. Washington, DC: American Association for the Advancement of Science Project 2061.

Torres, H. A., & Zeidler, D. L. (2002). The effects of English language proficiency and scientific reasoning skills on the acquisition of science content knowledge by Hispanic English language learners and native English language speaking students. *Electronic Journal of Science Education, 6*(3). Retrieved from http://unr.edu/homepage/crowther/ejse/ejsev6n3.html

two
Observe, Infer, and Classify
Basic Science Process Skills

Chapter Highlights

- Process skills represent the active doing of science and provide benefits to the classroom that extend beyond science learning. You should learn how to have all students observe, infer, and classify to engage in the actions of the science culture.

- Observing is the most fundamental of the basic science process skills and includes sight and the other senses. Students are to learn that observations should be unbiased and valued for their factual basis.

- Inferring is an attempt to explain the reason or cause for what has been observed. You should understand how to help students appreciate that inferences are judged by how sensibly they explain observations.

- When classifying, scientists organize objects into distinct categories. The keys to an effective classification system include using observable properties and always separating objects into only two categories at any one time.

- The culture of science involves very special actions that have formalized as it has been practiced. Recognize that teaching students includes helping them appreciate that scientific thinking is not automatic or natural but instead one group's way of viewing the world.

- Teachers should reserve teaching about the integrated science process skills for students who are in upper elementary school or middle school. The basic science process skills provide a foundation for students and teachers who are ready to tackle integrated process skills such as manipulating variables and posing operational definitions.

Teaching All Features of Science

Far too many people regard science as a collection of facts and formulas. As important as scientific explanations are to science, studying science requires more than just learning about the products of science. Teachers who are unaware of the actions of science hold an incomplete view about the science learning their students should experience. Presenting science to students as an accumulated body of knowledge addresses only one aspect of the broad culture of science and will give students an inaccurate and limited view of the discipline. Teaching science with too much emphasis on the content would be like teaching language arts by providing students with a few nouns but no verbs—and expecting them to construct sentences. Likewise effective science teaching incorporates a healthy balance of concepts and skills.

Scientists are not often attracted to the science profession because they want to memorize the theories and discoveries of other scientists. Instead people are drawn to science because of the things they get to do: the actions of science that lead to scientific discoveries. The appeal for those who become science enthusiasts is the opportunity to inquire about their world. Emphasizing inquiry as an essential component of the actions of science is particularly important when teaching in diverse settings. By allowing students to inquire about the world in or around the classroom, teachers accomplish several important educational goals.

Teaching students to inquire is fundamental to helping them become participants within the culture of science. However, the unique features of the scientific inquiry process are not immediately apparent to all students. Furthermore, not all students enter the classroom with the same cognitive, behavioral, and physical abilities to participate in inquiry. Although inquiry is a centrally important feature of the actions of science, careful support is required to help students become successful within these actions. To begin understanding how to help students to inquire, we will focus on a set of specific actions, called the **science process skills,** which lay the foundation for scientific inquiry.

Benefits of Process Skills

Achieving an appropriate balance is one of the secrets of becoming a professional. For example while a group of American Indian college students were preparing to become social workers, nurses, and psychologists, they were challenged to balance their cultural perspectives with Western, scientific perspectives (Weaver, 2000). Being successful in courses meant that they needed to learn a different way of thinking. But to be effective when working with American Indian clients, they needed to balance this new thinking with their native culture.

Duffy (1998) compared teaching to maintaining one round stone on top of the other—a balancing act that requires constant attention and frequent adjustments. Teachers, in terms of supporting their students' science learning, are challenged to achieve a balance between science concepts and process skills. Too much content can stifle student interest, whereas paying too much attention to the process skills can distract students from learning the substantive ideas within science. You might imagine the pull in opposite directions: to one side is the attraction of having students actively involved in working with materials while the other side is the desire for students to master essential scientific concepts. As classroom teachers, we have to find a way to avoid pulling too far in one direction or the other.

There are several reasons why science process skills should be present within elementary and middle school science lessons. We identify these reasons because teachers can feel pressure to not spend too much energy on having students use the science process skills. For example students are more active and talkative when they are using the process skills than when they are reading from a textbook. Sometimes people confuse active learning with messing about, and there are instances where this may be the case. But when the use of science process skills has a clear purpose, to the teacher and to the students, then they aren't a matter of playtime. What follows are several justifications that support having students engage in the science process skills as a regular component of science instruction and as a necessary feature of science learning.

Sense-Making Tools

One key to closing the academic achievement gap is to make certain that students are learning both the content and the processes of subjects (North Central Regional Educational Laboratory, 2004). Frequent and increasingly challenging uses of the science process skills support students in developing their efforts at scientific inquiry. This is important because increased intellectual development diminishes students' dependence on the teacher in the classroom. As the students become more skilled and confident with doing science, they begin to make connections for themselves. The teacher is still an important resource to the students but is no longer the source of all knowledge. As a consequence the students develop the power to become more independent learners. Simply learning the process skills does not magically cause this to happen. Instead students need to actively engage science process skills as tools to effectively expand their understanding of science. With each use of the tools, and with increasingly sophisticated application of the tools, students are better able to make sense of the natural world.

Supporting Language Development

Science process skills also support the development of student language because, as a part of using these tools, students are simultaneously called on to engage in discussions with others. The need to communicate what is being seen or to describe ideas to another person challenges a child to articulate his or her thoughts. For English language learners, the opportunity to practice oral communication in the context of actual science activities is a powerful way to develop fluency (Amaral, Garrison, & Klentschy, 2002; Linik, 2004). The same support of language fluency applies to young learners. The need to provide descriptive words and complex ideas creates the need to find specific and elaborate ways of using language. Students can practice the same skills when they communicate to each other about what they have read, but there is a heightened sense of purpose when students are more actively engaging process skills and communicating ideas about real materials. As a result students develop greater control over their abilities to communicate and are less dependent on the teacher for their learning. More detailed information about strategies for supporting process skills development is in the chapter by Maatta, Dobb, and Ostlund (2006) in the book *Science for English Language Learners* by Ann Fatham and David Crowther.

Creating a Community of Learners

Science process skills also provide the opportunity to create a community of learning within the classroom. Students are engaging science process skills when they are working with materials, ideas, and other people. In other words, this practice replicates the social aspect of a professional scientific community: information is exchanged, explanations are ventured, and understandings are negotiated. In the previous chapter we identified three myths about teaching, and here we see a way to undercut and replace all three. Because instilling a collective effort to understand science makes the class less dependent on the teacher, the teacher no longer needs to meet the demands of serving as the full-time expert (Dawes, 2004). Through shared experiences, individuals from an array of backgrounds can jointly participate in lessons rich with the science process skills.

Fostering Natural Curiosity

A final justification for relying on the science process skills is the potential to make use of students' natural curiosity. When people are intrigued by equipment or an artifact from the natural world, the challenge of motivating them is almost solved. It's hard to envision elementary or middle school students asking, "Why do we have to learn this?" when they are engaged with materials and using science process skills. Truthfully, the materials can be a source of distraction when the teacher tries to shift the students' attention to important information. But this is a much more solvable problem than trying to engage students in the first place. Although words such as *enchantment* and *wonder* seem almost too dreamy to apply to science teaching, the opportunity to engage with science through direct experiences does seem to have a somewhat magical quality. Not all children will be motivated to the same extent for every activity. Yet the motivation to learn is more likely to come from inside the students when they are using process skills than when they need to rely on someone else to communicate information to them.

Observing

Several years ago a few educators tried to emphasize the active dimension of science by turning it into a verb. Even though the word *sciencing* hasn't persisted, the idea was a good one. If we want science to become more accessible to a wider spectrum of students, we need to make it clearer that science study requires doing science, not simply learning about science.

We suggest using the verb form for each of the basic science process skills. We prefer ***observing*** to *observations*. Observations have already been done; observing is something that we can and will do ourselves. Commonly, observing means using our eyes to make observations, and that is true much of the time. However, scientists make observations with their other senses, and students should be guided to recognize when they are using their senses while observing. For students with particular physical limitations, the teacher will need to make appropriate accommodations. This includes allowing the student with poor vision to listen to the sounds of different types of powders as they are poured into a container or to use his or her sense of touch to observe the texture of rock samples. In a similar vein, the varied ways of observing (seeing, tasting, touching, listening, and smelling) are important to employ with students with limited cognitive capacities. Relying on multiple modes of observing allows individuals to build a more complete understanding of their experiences. Furthermore, encouraging students to use of a variety of senses while observing benefits English language learners. With more opportunities to use the language, they have increased opportunities to develop and expand their vocabulary.

As we advance the notion that observations can make use of all of our senses, we have the major challenge of avoiding the urge to interpret the significance of observations too quickly. Observing should focus on telling "what it is" and "how it is" but not "why it is." We have found it convenient to regard observations as facts. This means that observing shouldn't differ depending on who makes the observation. Observing in science is an active endeavor and should be done with care. Two people, one carelessly looking about and one carefully observing her surroundings, may be seeing the same thing but not noticing the same features. Sherlock Holmes demonstrates in the following dialogue the distinction between seeing and observing. When one person makes a careful observation, such as the number of steps in a stairwell, and another person can confirm that she can witness the same thing, then we are talking about the process skill of observing.

Sherlock Holmes and Watson discuss the difference between seeing and observing (from "A Scandal in Bohemia" by Arthur Conan Doyle [2004]):

Watson: And yet I believe that my eyes are as good as yours.

Holmes: Quite so. You see, but you do not observe. The distinction is clear. For example, you have frequently seen the steps which lead up from the hall to this room.

Watson: Frequently.

Holmes: How often?

Watson: Well, some hundred times.

Holmes: Then how many are there?

Watson: How many! I don't know.

Holmes: Quite so! You have not observed. And yet you have seen. That is just my point. Now, I know that there are seventeen steps, because I have both seen and observed.

Differentiating Fact From Opinion

Before proceeding we need to clarify the role of opinion within science. As will become apparent, such traits as creativity and intuition are very important to science. We don't want to dismiss the role of individual insights, because they are absolutely necessary for transforming information into understandings. Nevertheless, we need to help students regulate the use of their opinions while they are doing science. Facts and opinions are distinct yet interdependent ideas. To a large extent scientific inquiry relies on facts, gathered through observing, as its starting point. When we interpret facts too quickly, we may neglect other observations that could be significant—and, in turn, prematurely come to a conclusion that is incorrect. By emphasizing the idea that observing leads to facts, we want students to avoid the danger of allowing preconceived ideas from influencing what they notice.

In reality it's impossible to expect scientists, either as professionals or as students, to do all their observing first and then make the switch to explain these facts. But a distinction needs to be made between observing and explaining. To aid students in this distinction, ask, "Which of your senses did you use to make that observation?" If they cannot identify a sense, then the statement is likely an inference.

Observing as Paying Attention

There is a legend about zoologist Louis Agassiz and his strategy for teaching his students about observing. Agassiz founded Harvard's Museum of Comparative Zoology and apparently had the habit of putting his new students in front of a preserved fish and telling them to observe (Menand, 2001). Then he'd leave them with neither tools nor hints about how to proceed. Nathaniel Shaler, who would eventually become a professor of paleontology at Harvard, recounted one version of Agassiz's teaching technique:

> When I sat down before my tin pan, Agassiz brought me a small fish, placing it before me with the rather stern requirement that I should study it, but should on no account talk to anyone concerning it, nor read anything relating to fish until I had his permission to do so. To my inquiry, "What shall I do?" he said in effect: "Find out what you can without damaging the specimen: when I think that you have done the work, I will question you." (Shaler, 1946, p. 213)

Ultimately, after Shaler spent many hours observing and documenting, Agassiz was sufficiently pleased by his efforts. Another of Agassiz's students, who eventually distinguished himself with a career as an insect expert, related his story about observing a fish as part of his training:

> In ten minutes I had seen all that could be seen in that fish, and started in search of the professor, who had, however, left the museum. … Half an hour passed, an hour, another hour; the fish began to look loathsome. I turned it over and around; looked it in the face—ghastly; from behind, beneath, above, sideways, at a three-quarters view—just as ghastly. I was in despair; at an early hour, I concluded that lunch was necessary; so with infinite relief, the fish was carefully replaced in the jar, and for an hour I was free.
>
> On my return, I learned that Professor Agassiz had been at the museum, but had gone and would not return for several hours. Slowly I drew forth that hideous fish, and with a feeling of desperation again looked at it. I might not use a magnifying glass; instruments of all kinds were interdicted. My two hands, my two eyes, and the fish; it seemed a most limited field. I pushed my fingers down its throat to see how sharp its teeth were. I began to count the scales in the different rows until I was convinced that that was nonsense. At last a happy thought struck me—I would draw the fish; and now with surprise I began to discover new features in the creature. Just then the professor returned.
>
> "That is right," said he, "a pencil is one of the best eyes." (Scudder, 1879, p. 450)

We don't want to give the impression that good teachers should make students learn how to observe by forcing them to stare at a dead fish for, at least with some of Agassiz's students, days at a time. The reason we present these stories is to illustrate that observing is much more involved than many people realize. One needs to observe with great care and attention to details, ideally writing or drawing what is witnessed. These two future scientists both remarked that as a result of this experience, they came to look at something ordinary with a fresh perspective.

NSES Content Standard B: As a result of the activities, all students should develop an understanding of properties of objects and materials.

Observing With Minimal Bias

Observations are supposed to be free from bias. This means that *what* one expects to observe shouldn't have much influence. By taking steps to avoid allowing our own opinions to obscure what we observe, we are approaching **objectivity.** What can be done to help improve the quality of observations? One way is to have multiple people make observations and compare what is found. If we know our observations will be checked against others' observations, we will probably be more careful because we'd rather not find that the statements once thought to be observations are in reality just opinions.

In other words, it is likely that observations will be more reliable if others check them and that they will be less influenced by personal prejudice if a large number of people are recording them. Ideally we would be able to reperform certain experiments with more people making observations and then check to see whether the results are the same. This desire to eliminate prejudice in observations ties into the scientific habit of mind of skepticism. Think about watching a magician as she performs a sleight of hand trick. When we can't believe our eyes, one of our inclinations is to want to see the trick again. It's as if we doubt that what we witnessed really happened. The same idea applies with regard to repeating observations.

Observing Within Learning

We have given the impression that students' use of the science process skills should begin with observing. However, observing is not simply the first step, and its use isn't over after making observations. Observing is like breathing: you can't do it only once. When put to effective use, the process skill of observing continues, just as with breathing, throughout all subsequent activity. This should reinforce the value in having students learn to make unbiased, multisensory observations: they will continue to rely on this skill during all phases of the science lessons and activities.

> Observation exists at the beginning and again at the end of the process: at the beginning, to determine more definitely and precisely the nature of the difficult to be dealt with; at the end, to test the value of some hypothetically entertained conclusion. (Dewey, 1910/1991, p. 77)

As John Dewey explained, observing is put to use at different times within scientific activity. Students will observe specimens and materials when they are first introduced to them, they will continue to observe as they note patterns, they will make observations as they modify the conditions, and they will observe yet again to determine whether their expectations have been met. None of the process skills can be treated as items on a checklist that can be marked off once they've been used. Younger students can refine their observing by relying on multiple senses and attending to distinctive features, whereas older students can begin to employ tools to aid in their observing while seeking patterns and regularities as well as unique characteristics (Harlen, 2000).

Inferring

If observing is the beginning of scientific investigation, then inferring follows very close after. It is a challenge for students to keep facts separated from opinions because students can be very quick to explain what happens. Without having made thorough observations, by being in too big of a hurry to explain, students can overlook details that might be crucial. Think about observing as the first stepping-stone in your path of scientific inquiry. Inferring represents the second step. When anyone neglects observing, they bypass the first stepping-stone. Quite literally this describes "jumping to conclusions." One of the most powerful aspects of helping students learn the actions of science is in teaching them how to not jump to conclusions. Careful, detailed, and even written or illustrated observations are key prerequisites to making inferences.

The philosopher John Stuart Mill claimed that inferring is "the great business of life" and each of us is constantly trying to make sense of the world. It's rare for humans to be willing to let the facts stand on their own. Especially when we observe something that is unusual, we almost can't help ourselves from trying to explain what we have witnessed. Rushing to conclusions can cause us to miss key features and, consequently, make inferences that are insufficiently supported by facts. Or one might make an inference that proves to be a dead end—and then need to make more observations to reach a new conclusion anyway. Starting with extensive observations increases the chance the resulting inferences will be justified and accurate.

To draw inferences has been said to be the great business of life. Every one has the daily, hourly, and momentary need of ascertaining facts which he has not directly observed; not from any general purpose of adding to his stock of knowledge, but because the facts themselves are of importance to his interests or to his occupations. (Mill, 1884, p. 5)

Our definition of **inferring** is developing an explanation that is based on and supported by valid observations. Synonyms for *inference* include *speculation, suggestion, supposition,* and *hypothesis.* Unlike observations, inferences are drawn from experiences and ingenuity. Someone who is skilled at inferring is able to take observations and then generate reasonable explanations for them.

The Criteria for Judging an Inference

Observations, which are based on use of the senses, can be evaluated by considering whether they represent facts. The test of an inference is much less obvious than the criteria for judging an observation. An inference is an attempt to explain, it is a claim about why something is the way that it is. Inferences are not facts but opinions informed by facts. Unlike opinions, which we can judge based on whether we agree with them, judging an inference forces us to rely on the supporting facts. Deciding whether an inference is appropriate requires a judgment call, and learning to make useful inferences is again an essential action of the culture of science. We must learn to judge the quality of an inference based on how well it is supported by the observations.

You might use a courtroom as your mental model. The prosecution and the defense express their particular inferences. Both try to convince the judge or jury that their inference makes sense, and they use evidence to support their claim. Pieces of evidence, in the form of photographs, weapons, or tape recordings, are equivalent to observations. Everyone has access to those facts and pieces of data. The job of the lawyers is to use those pieces of evidence to create explanations that are compelling and convincing. The better inference is the one that makes the best sense in explaining the greatest number of observations.

NSES Content Standard A: Use data to construct a reasonable explanation.

There are many ways in which this analogy between the legal process and science is insufficient. First of all, in science there aren't necessarily two inferences in opposition to each other. In science we may have multiple inferences or hypotheses that need to be considered. Within science there isn't a single judge to decide what inference is correct. Instead science relies on a large, seemingly quarrelsome community that determines the correctness of knowledge claims. The best inference is the one accounting for more of the observations than any other.

In science there isn't only one occasion to make a decision. In our legal system a person cannot be forced to stand trial a second time if someone doesn't like the results of the first trial. Unless things are complicated by appeals, the outcome of a trial is the final decision. In contrast (remember openness to new ideas as a scientific habit of mind?) scientific inferences are ALWAYS open to reevaluation by the broader community of science. When more evidence has been gathered, it can be used to test whether the current inference is still sufficient. Alternatively, a scientist can propose a new inference, and it always remains as a possibility that the old inference can be discarded because the new one does a better job of explaining the data.

Another problem with the courtroom analogy is the inevitable appeal to emotions. In a courtroom, attorneys will often attempt to sway opinions by trying to take advantage of people's sympathies, by taking pity on either the victims or the accused. In judging inferences we must teach students to rely on the quality of the observations for their decision. In addition, students must learn to resist being influenced by such things as the personality of the individual who champions an inference.

One way to avoid allowing biases to interfere with the consideration of an inference is to try to detach the claim from the person making it. An inference is an idea that is held out for everyone to consider. It should withstand a comparison with the available observations. When an inference is judged to be unreasonable or unacceptable, it shouldn't be seen as a reflection of the person who proposed it. An inference doesn't have feelings, and so there should be no worries when one is rejected. This is particularly important to model for your students.

NSES Content Standard A: Think critically and logically to make the relationships between evidence and explanations.

A teacher should make it clear to his or her students that all inferences need to be carefully examined, even (or especially) ones proposed by the teacher. By doing this the students will learn to understand that part of the actions of doing science is to critically examine inferences. Polite critique of an inference is not a sign of disrespect but a central and defining feature of the scientific culture. As such, questions such as "How do you know that?" or "What is your evidence?" should be commonplace in a classroom. Furthermore, these questions ought to be posed by teachers and students. Such questions will feel more natural for some students than for others, because many cultures are taught that questioning an adult is inappropriate. Because asking "how we know" in science is such an important scientific action, explicit conversations and repeated modeling are necessary to help students recognize the value. In addition, the teacher must provide support and enthusiasm for students when they pose such questions. Over time, the need to support all knowledge claims with convincing evidence can become a natural part of a vibrant classroom culture.

So What's the Right Answer?

Because scientific explanations always have the potential for being replaced by newer, better explanations, it is never accurate to say that a particular inference has been proved. Even though many people anticipate that science will provide the right answers and that the answers will hold true for all time, in actuality scientific explanations may be replaced. There are a host of examples of this happening throughout the history of science. For example biologists once thought that the number of predators, such as foxes, controlled the number of prey, such as rabbits, in an area. This made sense because the changes in rabbit and fox populations seemed to be related. But after a great deal of study of these animal populations, scientists found that rabbit populations were influenced by the amount of available food and that this in turn influenced the number of predators that could survive in the area. This is an example of an inference re-formed because of a fresh interpretation of observations.

This changing of explanations is another example of the culture of science. Scientific explanations are always reasonable enough for the length of time that the community accepts them. But it would be a strange strategy to try to trap a scientist into saying whether he or she is 100 percent confident in an explanation, because the concept of certainty in scientific knowledge is foreign to the culture of science. The current debate about the "greenhouse effect" is a recent example. There may never be sufficient data to claim, with absolute certainty, that the burning of fossil fuels is changing the earth's temperature and climate. However, gathering and analyzing data can lead scientists to make stronger inferences that, in turn, could give greater credence to either side of the argument.

The professional scientific community evaluates inferences based on the strength of the supporting data. So too will students in the classroom be expected to supply observations in support of the inferences they propose.

For Reflection and Discussion

The scene illustrated in Figure 2.1 is an open field of snow. The dark marks seem to be tracks made in the snow. Generate a list of statements about this scene. Some of these statements should be observations and some should be inferences. Write these as statements, but without including a form of the word *observe* or *infer* in those sentences. Ask someone to identify which they regard as observations and which they suspect are inferences. What were the criteria they used to help them to decide?

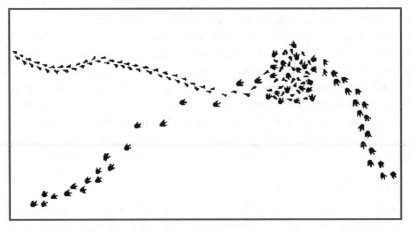

FIGURE 2.1. This drawing of animal tracks allows you to practice observing and inferring.

Science as a Creative Endeavor

In his book *How We Think,* John Dewey described how inferring connects to observing. He wrote that thinking requires us to take the facts that have been gathered and then make a leap to try to explain the facts. The facts, our observations, are what we use in science as the bases for building observations. A person who is creative is more likely to propose many inferences compared to someone who takes things at face value. Scientific study benefits by having many inferences to consider, because multiple inferences provide more options that may lead to a very powerful explanation. Being creative doesn't mean that any idea is acceptable. There are certain guidelines that must be followed, one of the most important being that one must rely on observations to support inferences. Yes, it is useful to remain open to all ideas, and we shouldn't be too eager to discard inferences prematurely. But after the wild speculation has run its course, we must sort through the assorted inferences to determine how well each is supported by our observations.

Another key to proposing inferences is to avoid allowing one's biases to interfere. John Dewey identified the move from what is known (observations) to what is not yet known (inferences) as being "peculiarly exposed to error." He went on to identify possible causes for these errors: previous experience, self-promotion, strong opinions, false expectations, and good old mental laziness. If those doing science, and this includes professional scientists and elementary school and middle school students, remain attentive to these dangers, then they can use their creativity to help sort through what might otherwise be a confusing jumble of observations. Ideally a teacher would elicit a wide variety of explanations and then guide students to evaluate the viability of these inferences based on the available data. Those inferences that will become the most compelling will account for the greatest number of observations. Although that may not lead to the "right" answer, the process of sorting weaker inferences from stronger ones is important to demonstrate and make obvious to students.

Classifying

We have established that the culture of science anticipates that there are patterns existing in nature. The goal of scientists is to uncover those patterns, beginning with organizing observations. Unless observations are organized, the task of identifying patterns is difficult. **Classifying** is the process of organizing objects into groups based on observable properties. Through classification, patterns that may not have been apparent when objects were viewed as a large group can become evident.

Before going further, we want to reinforce the idea that classifying and all the other science process skills are activities in which we want students to engage. If you hear the word *classifying* and have visions of how living things are organized (e.g., kingdom, phylum, genus, species) then you know only part of the story. While existing classification systems are important to scientific literacy, it is also important for students to learn *how* to construct classification systems. In elementary and middle schools, it is valuable for students to become acquainted with classification systems for clouds, landforms, and vertebrates. Beyond helping students make conclusions, the process of classifying allows them to appreciate how current systems for classification came into existence.

Part of the problem with the way that classification is commonly presented in classrooms is that it is too often treated as an end product rather than as something that can provide insight into the actions that led to its production. Students should be taught that any current classification system is only the most recent in a prolonged process of pattern seeking and sense making. In other words, knowing *how* to classify and having ample opportunities to develop classification skills are as important as knowing *about* classification.

Classification in Daily Life

All students should be given the opportunity to build their science knowledge on their personal experiences. The differences among students in a classroom, whether cognitive, cultural, or linguistic, need to be appreciated by the teacher. This means more than simply recognizing that all children are special in their own ways. For every student to become skilled in science, students need to connect their everyday lives with the study of science. This is not to suggest that some children have weaker backgrounds than others, but the reality is that every child comes to school with a rich set of life experiences. Good teachers will recognize those experiences as important foundations for science learning. Too often a teacher will assume that his or her experiences parallel those of his or her students. For example a colleague was teaching a science lesson in an inner-city school. In an attempt to describe kinetic and potential energy, he tried using the analogy of a waterfall. Having grown up in the country and traveled extensively, he had a strong image of waterfalls. When his explanation failed to advance his students' understandings, he realized that his students did not share that experience, and he failed in his choice of examples. For teachers who embrace the value of student diversity, they will need to work a little harder to uncover what represents "everyday" for students. In this way, science instruction starts with objects and actions with which the students are familiar and comfortable. Starting with the familiar makes it much more likely the students will become comfortable with the objects, actions, and ideas of science.

Life is very complicated, so we try to organize it. We organize our clothes by some system, maybe sorting the dressy clothes from those that are more casual. Likewise we rely on classification systems that others have created to make our lives easier. For example stores are organized so that certain products are all in one section. These are examples of classifying. Essentially there are a bunch of objects that are placed into groups based on selected properties.

The items in a grocery store are classified, in part, by the type of container: canned goods in one section, fresh fruits in a different section, and so on. Interestingly, there are many ways to classify the products in a grocery store. Going to a new grocery store is often a challenge, because you don't yet know their particular classification system (where do they keep the cornstarch?). Once you understand the rules that have been used to classify, then you have no problem locating the products you need. To a large extent, the science process skills are based on very natural human behaviors. We observe our surroundings and try to make sense of what we notice by generating inferences. When we are faced with an assortment of objects, we may try to manage the confusion by creating a system for organizing: junk mail versus personal mail, junk food versus healthy food, reality shows versus documentaries—all of this involves classifying. In this way, learning to classify builds on thought processes students may bring from home. We can expect that studying science will refine and expand students' general classification abilities.

The process of classifying allows for considerable personal choice, yet there are certain standards that make some systems better than others. In what follows, you will learn guidelines for creating effective systems of classification. You might think of these guidelines as a system for separating the good from the weak when it comes to classifying. Nevertheless you can exercise a great deal of flexibility, creating several classification systems for a set of materials. If the guidelines are adhered to, each classification system should be equally effective.

Relying on Observable Properties

When classifying, you need to organize the objects or events based on properties that can be observed. We will refer to this as Guideline 1. Color, shape, weight, and composition are observable properties and are acceptable classification criteria. Inferences do not have a place in classifying. In the scientific culture, we don't classify according to whether objects are funny, scary, or boring. We may classify movies this way, but in science we focus our classifying on the materials as they are, not what we feel about them. Likewise you should not classify according to the usefulness of an object. The process skill of classifying reinforces the need to make observations that are factual, and the best properties to be used for classifying are those that are unambiguous, obvious, and based on observations—not inferences.

Dividing Into Two Subgroups

A second guideline for classifying involves the number of groups created with each property. A property that follows Guideline 2 should divide objects into only two groups and should be specific enough to avoid the danger of some objects being classified in both groups. Guideline 2 insists that we not use a single property to subdivide a group into more than two subgroups. To accomplish this, we use a rule for separating the objects that is clear and does not require us to make a judgment call. You can think of classifying as a process of walking down a path with many branches. At each branch you can go to the left or to the right—you just have to choose one or the other. In our classifying path we never come to a fork in the road that has three possible routes.

It seems that a Venn diagram would be useful for classifying. Venn diagrams are visual guides for organizing information and are used in elementary and middle school classrooms (Moore, 2003). Venn diagrams provide teachers with another tool for clarifying their instructions and students with a guide for organizing their thinking. Typically Venn diagrams consist of circles to show the relationships between different objects. Figure 2.2 shows three possible arrangements of Venn diagrams for representing two sets. However, in the process skill of classifying, only one of these Venn diagrams is appropriate. The Venn diagram to the left sorts objects into one of two alternate groups, ensuring that an object will always be classified in one category or the other. The other two Venn diagrams don't allow for the either–or approach that is required by the second guideline.

Imagine that you dump the contents of your book bag onto a table. In trying to classify these objects, you could use countless properties. In keeping with Guideline 1, you should sort them according to properties such as color or label. But you shouldn't use a possibly undetectable property such as cost (unless everything still carries a price tag) or origin (unless a label designates where the object was made)—sorting by these properties might require inferring. For students who struggle with using Guideline 1, it can be useful to tell them to pretend to not know what the objects are or how they are typically used. That way students will be more apt to

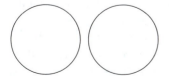 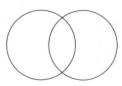

FIGURE 2.2. According to Guideline 2, only the left Venn diagram represents how objects are sorted into two groups.

focus on the physical properties of the objects rather than on their purpose. If you are uncertain whether a property is effective as a classifier, consider the criteria we used for judging an observation. Properties that are based on factual observations and don't require any judgment or opinion are the best.

Our goal becomes identifying the properties that clearly divide the contents of your book bag into one group or the other. If a quality such as color is used, it is better to divide objects according to one color (i.e., whether it is a specific color) rather than a variety of colors. Recall that Guideline 2 is about dividing into one of two categories. But you need to make some distinctions to make the either–or practice clear. If you choose to classify objects according to color, then you probably should use a flexible system that dictates something like "contains some yellow" versus "contains no yellow."

Size can also be an effective property for classifying objects, but your parameters for doing so should be as clear as those we just discussed for separating objects according to color. For example dividing objects into two groups of "big" and "small" might seem to fulfill Guideline 2—except that it creates problems with Guideline 1. Is your textbook big or small? It's big compared to a car key but not compared to a car. To avoid such problems, you should standardize the classifying property size. For example you could divide objects relative to the size of your hand. In this case, a book is big, while a car key is small. Alternatively, the property of size could be based on an actual measurement (e.g., "taller than 15 centimeters" or "less than 100 grams"). Such measurable properties are not open to debate (Guideline 1) and clearly segregate the object into one of two opposite categories (Guideline 2). Now it's your chance to practice both of these.

Figure 2.3 shows an overlapping Venn diagram. We labeled the left circle "white shapes" and the right circle "square." The labels communicate observable properties and seem to be OK according to Guideline 1. However, some objects in the diagram could be sorted into both circles, violating Guideline 2. So you will need to identify a new property according to which to divide these thirteen objects. A good way to start is to redraw this Venn diagram so there are only two circles and they do not overlap at all. There could easily be a dozen different ways to classify these objects in ways that meet the criteria for both classifying guidelines.

The Endpoint of Classifying

Guideline 3 states that the classification process is complete when each object is in its own group. Starting with four objects, we must first divide them into two groups and then further divide the subgroups by other criteria. The property that we use to sort the objects might initially divide them into groups of two and two or three and one. The goal of a complete classification system is to continue the sorting until every object is by itself. For the shapes exercise in Figure 2.3, this would require dividing by a series of properties until each object is in a separate category. How many times would the objects need to be divided? The answer is the number of objects you have less one. For the thirteen shapes shown in the figure, you would need to divide and subdivide the objects twelve times for each object to be by itself.

If you follow the three guidelines, you will find classifying to be a very powerful tool for organizing and thinking about a set of objects. Creating a classification system for a collection of leaves, stones, or kitchen utensils requires close observing of details. Along the way, patterns that were previously unnoticed may appear. Classifying is a process even very young children can use. Although we would not expect kindergartners to be pushed to follow Guideline 3, we could reasonably expect them to learn about Guideline 1 and perhaps Guideline 2 by having them engage in a game of Guess My Rule using a jar of buttons. In summary, classifying dictates that one must divide objects into clear and observable properties.

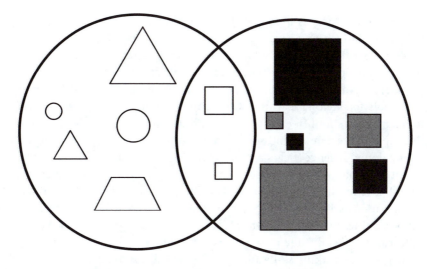

FIGURE 2.3. The basic unit of a tree classification diagram identifies the property and two opposite descriptions.

Point–Counterpoint

Using science process skills with science instruction has been a common theme for over four decades of science teaching and learning. However, process skills do not seem to have achieved universal application in American elementary and middle school science classrooms. In response, some might suggest that the push for process skills should be increased. Yet others question whether process skills are actually that appropriate in every situation. So in response to the question "What are the benefits of the science process skills?" we consider two differing opinions.

Science Process Skills: Tools for Everyone to Become Lifelong Learners (and Lovers) of Science

Cynthia A. Lundeen

Science Teacher Educator at Florida State University and Former Elementary School Teacher

Educating young children in science is a particularly slippery slope for teachers who often must negotiate time and talent for teaching this often elusive subject. Content or process? Seeing or doing? Best practice or least path of resistance? Hands on or off? Clean classroom or messy classroom? If truth be told, science process skills are largely underrepresented in many science lessons and classrooms, despite abundant research supporting their benefits.

Why this unfortunate fact? Attitude! Just say the word *science* in an open forum and watch people recoil. Many people view science as an intimidating mass of facts, figures, symbols, and substances beyond comprehension. This pervasive view of science as an encyclopedia of content just may be stunting our national growth in science achievement. Raising yet another generation of "science haters" reflects not on the product but on the teaching processes responsible for yielding poor achievement and poor attitudes. Attitudes toward a subject can be as important as the subject itself! Far too many teachers approach science teaching as a body of knowledge to be memorized (and scorned!) by students. Without attaching a meaningful connection to what is learned, students easily lose ground in learning science content and concepts. Science content meaning comes from connecting action, or science processes, to concepts.

So what is the value of the science process skills in teaching and learning science? To provide tools for lifelong learning! Changing attitudes and achievements in science education demands action! In early through middle childhood, *science* should be viewed as a verb as opposed to a noun. Introduced and practiced as a way of thinking and acting, "learning by doing" science yields a more meaningful understanding while promoting positive attitudes about science. I believe that one of the most significant goals of meaningful learning is teaching students, all students, to think and problem solve through active participation and application. Science teaching can contribute to this goal by maximizing opportunities to manipulate the physical world through the science process skills. These skills can enable all students to process new information through concrete experiences by sharpening thinking skills and building new understandings.

The notion of teaching science through an emphasis on process skills is not new. According to the National Science Teachers Association, a "reasonable portion" of a science curriculum should emphasize science process skills. We know that in early childhood years, children begin to build understandings and beliefs about the world around them through physical manipulation and personal experiences and interactions as they continuously attempt to build more complex understandings of their world. Capitalizing on this critical learning time means teachers need to link science concepts to children's lives through methods uniquely associated with the process skills. In addition, young students develop a healthy skepticism about their environment as they grow, integrate, and actively negotiate their world. Teaching and learning through the science process skills maximizes the potential of every child to learn (and love) science!

Just How Universal Are Science Process Skills?

Malcolm Butler
Science Teacher Educator at the University of South Florida and Former High School Science Teacher

One day while sitting in my office preparing a lesson on the basic science process skills for a group of twenty-five young ladies soon to become elementary teachers, my mind began to wonder (as it often does). This time, I wondered about a possible connection between what we had done in a previous class on working with students from diverse backgrounds and the use of science process skills for understanding the natural world. Since the days of BSCS (Biological Sciences Curriculum Study) and SAPA (Science: A Process Approach) elementary science curriculum in the 1960s, all elementary school science teachers have been inculcated to believe that science is a set not just of facts but also of skills and scientific habits of mind. But lately I've begun to wonder.... .

The process skills are considered universal. Along with the universality of the process skills is the commonly accepted idea that all children can learn. Inherent in this idea is that teachers must be able to teach students from diverse backgrounds, teaching them science in a way that is meaningful to them. There are several resources available to assist teachers in connecting the process skills and students' cultural background. For example Bazin and

Tamez (2002) and the Exploratorium Teacher Institute have a set of activities that address the process skills from a multicultural perspective. So to think that there could be some aspects of the process skills that are inconsistent with some students' way of thinking and seeing the world could be heresy. Could it be comparable to being a member of the Flat Earth Society (Russell, 1997)? Could I be hanged for considering that there are some cultural issues that the teaching of process skills doesn't necessarily address?

But wait a minute. What about the kid who is struggling with the idea of classifying? Could it be that for this student, the idea of putting items in groups according to some characteristic goes against his home culture's belief that we should see the oneness of the world and all things? To take it one step further, consider that a dichotomous key proposes that either an item has or does not have some property, which forces one to have a maximum of two groups. Could this idea of separating one from many be difficult for students who think monolithically?

One more example about the possible disconnect between culture and the process skills comes to mind. Recently I was observing a group of first-grade students inquiring into magnets. As a diverse group of four students tried to figure out how magnets work, one of them suggested that the group try to test the strength of the magnet by measuring its length. Her reason for suggesting the idea was that her family had taught her that the taller a person is the stronger he or she is. Height is a sign of authority in this child's family. Now how would most teachers deal with this girl's train of thought? I think we would probably take the student's preconception (indeed, misconception) and move the student away from the idea that length equals strength and authority to the more accurate conception, without asking the question of why. So even though the child may come away with an understanding of what determines a magnet's strength, will she internalize the new concept or will she continue to hold onto a tenet of her family life?

It seems that we must admit that the process skills are a Western phenomenon. While the Western origins and universal acceptance of process skills do not eliminate them from universal utility, we need to recognize that they can be more difficult for some students to grasp because they are incongruent with the students' cultures. While in the past we've viewed process skills as this universal pathway for all students to move into science, I suggest that teachers need to consider the potential cultural baggage that travels with the process skills.

Oh well, enough wondering for this day. Maybe tomorrow I'll take a closer look at the geocentric view of the universe and the learning cycle. ...

Creating Visible Classification Systems

When the classifying of a group of objects is completed, then the outcome needs to somehow be recorded. From a teaching perspective, this is necessary so you can assess how well each of your students understands how to classify. In addition, translating ideas about how to sort objects into a written or inscribed form reinforces and clarifies understanding in the mind of the person who is developing the classification system. Finally, once a classification system is completed, it can serve as a tool for others. Having it recorded on paper makes it possible for others to apply the system to objects with which they are unfamiliar.

Classifying With Dichotomous Keys

The most common method of creating a visible classification system in science is the **dichotomous key.** A key is a tool for identifying something that is unknown—think of it as an answer key. The word *dichotomous* simply means that the key is based on the rule of dividing, and subdividing, into only two groups. Dichotomous keys are very common in field guides. These reference materials are useful for helping us to identify birds, trees, or rocks. The procedure is pretty straightforward. You start with the first pair of descriptions and decide which statement applies to your unknown object. Then you follow the next step. If it says "Go to ... ," then you jump down the key to that place, even if that means skipping other paired statements. When you reach a dead end, then you have identified the object. Here's an example of a dichotomous key that can be used to identify dried beans.

Dichotomous Key for the Contents of a Soup Bean Mix

1a	Bean shape is round	**Garbanzo bean**
1b	Bean shape is not round (oblong)	Go to 2
2a	Bean is dark in color	Go to 3
2b	Bean is not dark in color	Go to 4
3a	Bean color is solid	**Kidney bean**
3b	Bean color is speckled	**Pinto bean**
4a	Bean is entirely white	**Navy bean**
4b	Bean has a dark spot	**Black-eyed pea**

With a garbanzo bean, sometimes known a chickpea, in front of you, it would be possible to immediately identify it by reading the first line of this dichotomous key. Instead imagine you had a bean-shaped object that was brownish with dark spots. You would use the dichotomous key by reading the first statement pair and deciding which of the two statements described the object. Because of the bean's shape, line 1b is the better description, and it directs you to statement pair 2. Here you are to focus on the color. Because the bean is dark, you are sent to statement pair 3. Between those two statements, line 3b describes your object, which you now know is a pinto bean. Had you tried to identify a black-eyed pea, you would, as always, have begun at statement pair 1, which would have sent you to pair 2 because of the bean's shape. Here you would be directed to "go to 4," so you'd skip over and ignore pair 3. Because line 4b is the better description, you would now confirm the identity of your bean.

Looking back through the bean dichotomous key we can recognize the existence of all three classifying guidelines. First of all, because all properties are observable (color and shape), it is unlikely that any inferring would be required. This is consistent with Guideline 1. Next, this system follows Guideline 2, because every set of properties is an either–or situation, as shown by the statements as always in pairs. Last of all, if we assume that we began with five types of beans, then each object would result in its own category, which is in keeping with Guideline 3. Notice that to completely classify all five beans, our key needed to sort the objects by a number of properties equal to one fewer than the number of objects. Now if you were going to have students classify jelly beans, as Dave Crowther described in a *Science and Children* article (see the Suggested Readings section near the end of this chapter), and you started with twenty different types, students would need to create nineteen statement pairs to develop a complete dichotomous key. Maybe this will reinforce why it may be best to begin with a much smaller group of objects.

Classifying With Tree Diagrams

Another way to produce a visible classification system is to create a tree diagram. Although it looks very different from the dichotomous key, the way it functions and its adherence to the three guidelines are consistent. The key components of a tree diagram are an oval and two labeled arrows, such as what you see in Figure 2.4. The oval specifies the property you want to focus on—ignoring all possible others. Refer back to the first line of the bean dichotomous key. What property goes into the oval? Yes, it is shape. This alerts the person who is trying to identify a bean to which feature to pay specific attention. Shape, rather than color, size, or anything else, has been identified as the distinguishing characteristic.

The arrows are used to indicate which pathway to follow. Notice that there are only two pathways, never more than that. Because the choice is between only two pathways, it is clearest to label the arrows with characteristics that are opposite of each other. Again using the bean dichotomous key as a reference, we would label one arrow "round" and the other "not round." Using "oblong" as the second characteristic might not be clear enough. We have now translated the first line of the bean dichotomous key into a basic tree diagram.

A tree diagram is a graphic representation of the first statement pair in a dichotomous key. Some people are more comfortable using the tree diagram as a classification system because it is so visual. The benefit of the dichotomous key is that it takes up less space on the page. You may have a preference for one over the other, and that's fine. Both rely on the same classifying thought processes and are consistent with the three classifying guidelines. You should be able to understand both ways of representing the completed classification system and be able to move back and forth between the two without much difficulty.

Figure 2.5 represents a complete tree diagram that relies on the same properties and characteristics as the dichotomous key for the beans. You can double-check the tree diagram to compare its consistency with the dichotomous key. We can imagine that the ovals in the tree diagram could be labeled with the line numbers from the dichotomous key. Meanwhile, the arrows would be identified with "a" or "b." Using either system, that is, the original dichotomous key or this tree diagram, someone would be able to identify a dark red, bean-shaped object as a kidney bean and confirm that a spotless white bean is a navy bean.

Classifying and Cultural Norms

The process skill of classifying can be challenging, because it's much more complicated than making an observation or creating an inference. There are also cultural assumptions

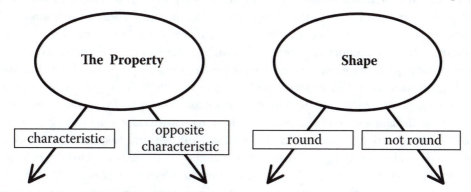

FIGURE 2.4. This classification system fulfills Guideline 1 but not Guideline 2.

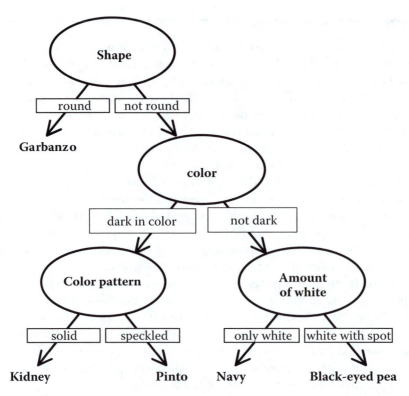

FIGURE 2.5. This tree diagram is conceptually identical to the soup bean dichotomous key.

that are tucked within the three guidelines and that, for those who hold a worldview that doesn't mesh with the guidelines, contribute to the difficulty of classifying. Sometimes students struggle with classification systems for reasons that extend beyond their inability to comprehend the goal. Even adult students sometimes express frustration with making a classification system. It's almost as if the thought processes required when classifying, which is obviously based in the science culture, are a way of examining the world that is unusual for some people. Consequently, we find that teachers may very much need to treat classification, particularly as it is a process of science, as a foreign culture. Teachers may need to give additional guidance to some students. An effective way teachers can provide this guidance is to move those students back and forth between their ways of thinking and the science culture's ways.

Modern science emerged out of traditions that are clearly Western. It seems that the process of sorting into either–or categories can be traced to ancient Greek thought. The process of organizing objects according to whether they have or do not have a particular property, with no intermediate category, is sometimes called Aristotelian (Bowker & Star, 1999). This very formal approach to classifying, unlike the version of classifying we might use in everyday living, makes no allowance for fuzziness. It is important to recognize that thinking scientifically is not natural or automatic. Indeed learning to perceive the world in ways consistent with this dichotomous, observation-based perspective is something we must learn. For some of us, this may seem to be very natural. In actuality it is an extension of the cultural traditions within which we were raised. Classifying is an example of a very particular way of thinking that teachers must introduce to students to familiarize them with the culture of science.

Here is a very specific example comparing people from two cultures. Researchers presented study participants with proverbs that seemed to contradict themselves, such as "Beware of your friends, not your enemies" (Peng & Nisbett, 1999, p. 744). This proverb suggests we should be cautious about the people we have grown to trust. Such contradictory proverbs, along with non-contradictory proverbs, were presented to college students in the United States and to similar-age students in Taiwan. The American students showed a dislike for contradictory proverbs, whereas the Chinese students preferred them. This suggests that a Western view favors ideas that are internally consistent, whereas an Eastern view is comfortable with such ambiguity. The bottom line is that Western thinking favors either–or categories, whereas Eastern thinking accepts less clear-cut divisions. This illustrates how cultural background may complicate the classification guidelines for some students and make the guidelines more difficult for such students to grasp.

A challenge we have as science teachers is finding the right balance between the culture of science and the cultures of the students. Even though many individuals have made contributions to science, the culture of scientific thinking is, for better and for worse, not an approach that makes sense to all cultures. This becomes an opportunity to reinforce that culture is much more than simply a student's family life. In addressing the broad challenges of classifying, researchers have recognized that learning to classify is complicated by culturally bound ways of thinking: "Categories are learned as part of people's membership in communities of practice in that categories are tied to each community's particular usages and practical requirements" (Vosniadou, Pagondiotis, & Deliyianni, 2005, p. 118). The implication in the science classroom is that learning to formally classify is not simply something students must absorb. Instead classifying in a scientific fashion is part of a very specialized culture that can be odd to those who have not been enculturated into either–or mind-sets.

The culture of science reveals itself in the classification guidelines. First, science places a great deal of emphasis on facts—little tolerance is given to knowledge claims that can't be supported by data. When a team of scientists claims to have made a new discovery, no one pays much attention unless the scientists are able to provide data to support their claims. Even then, other scientists will conduct similar experiments to see whether the same data can be gathered. This is apparent within classifying Guideline 1, which makes no allowance for inferring within a system of classification. Second, the actions of science leave little room for shades of gray. Thinking scientifically requires a worldview that is largely dichotomous. These cultural norms of science (i.e., the demand for facts and the either–or mentality) can be in conflict with other ways of thinking about the world. This competitive spirit, the appeal for either–or thinking, which seems so much a part of American culture, is very much at odds with many non-Western cultures. In this regard, creating a classification system may be unnatural for individuals who don't view their world in such a competitive fashion.

How do we negotiate such a cultural conflict? What can a teacher do when students appear to struggle with classifying and are seemingly resistant to the process? One approach is to believe that some students can learn how to classify while others cannot—and we are NOT recommending this tactic. A far better approach is to think about the situation as an opportunity to help a person from one culture learn about another culture. This means making the cultural norms, the ways we think in a culture, very explicit.

Imagine science as a special cultural neighborhood in your community—a place where students may not have visited. Your goal is not to make them sacrifice their own culture but instead to make them aware of and appreciate a different culture. In preparation for your "science-town" field trip, you explain to the students how to act so they aren't perceived by the locals as being disrespectful. You need to tell them what is appropriate, perhaps even writing down the behavioral norms and posting them around the room for all to read. Learning how to classify is similar to a cross-cultural field trip. As students present the classification systems they've developed, you should explain the norms again, referring to the charts posted around the room, and help students understand the underlying reasons for these norms. This disposition toward teaching children how to classify—how to move toward this scientific action—is much healthier than saying that "some kids don't think that way" and more likely to be effective.

For Reflection and Discussion

Consider the value of balancing the content of science with the process skills of science. What would it be like if an elementary school science curriculum emphasized content to the exclusion of process? In contrast, what would be some drawbacks of a science curriculum that focused only on process skills and spent little energy on teaching children science concepts?

Process Skills and Students With Cognitive Limitations

Just as the actions of science are unfamiliar to students from non-Western backgrounds, so too are these actions difficult for students with cognitive limitations. It is important to recognize the cultural backgrounds and linguistic capabilities our students bring to school, and it is equally essential to become familiar with the cognitive abilities students carry with them. For some students, process skills such as classification represent a substantial intellectual challenge. As teachers we need to understand the level of cognitive challenge that is appropriate for the students in our classroom. This understanding should be based on an assortment of information sources.

Credible sources of data include insights from the parents, discussions with special education teachers, results of past testing, and our observations of student performance. However, the inferences we make about students' cognitive abilities must be understood as tentative. This is because a student's participation in the actions of science can help them move above their current capabilities. If a student enters our room at the beginning of the year having great difficulties with the prospects of creating a classification system, this should not suggest that he or she can never have success with this process skill.

The desire to help all students develop their science process skills is crucial, but desire, hope, and good intentions are not enough. As teachers of science, we must know the actual strategies we should employ to help all students achieve their highest potential. This involves not only giving the students time and opportunity to practice and refine their use of the process skills but also appreciating the emotional, social, and behavioral dimensions of classroom tasks. Teaching the science process skills places demands on students that extend beyond the cognitive aspects of observing, inferring, and classifying.

Maroney, Finson, Beaver, and Jensen (2003) suggested that helping students, particularly students with learning disabilities, to succeed in classroom science should begin with the teacher's careful analysis of the various skills required for completing a science activity. Within the context of a science activity, teachers should consider these categories of performance: classroom behavior, social skills, group coping, academic skills, science process skills, and scientific inquiry. In advance of a science activity, the teacher should closely analyze the various kinds of skills involved in an activity to decide the relative difficulty of the various skills and to determine if the activity is appropriate for all the students. If it is not, then the teacher can use the chart presented as Appendix A to inform modifications of the activity for some of the learners in the classroom. (See Appendix A for an example of a rubric to aid in this analysis.)

Then as the students work on an activity, the teacher can gather information about particular students in terms of their abilities on each of the categories of performance. By looking at these charts over time, teachers then have a sense of the students' development. What is as important is that such analysis of the demands of a task can also remind the teacher that teaching science process skills cannot be separated from the other demands students face, especially those students whose cognitive abilities are below the norm for their age group.

When carefully selected activities are employed, that is, those that challenge students' abilities in one or two of the categories of performance, but not all four, students can develop their competence. If the process skill to be developed is classification, students should be initially asked to observe and make inferences about a variety of materials, such as an assortment of buttons, shells, or screws. This can be followed by having students examine and use others' classification systems and creating and refining their own classification systems. As students make progress with the activities, teachers should limit other aspects that special education students might find difficult, such as allowing those students to work alone if social skills and group coping skills are particularly challenging. The challenge for teachers is to be aware of the challenge they provide for students and to make conscious decisions about the number of challenges a student can be expected to meet. Through a progression of activities, all students can become proficient with process skills, such as classifying in a genuinely scientific fashion—even though it might take some students a little more time to reach that point. Growth and improvement should be the goal for each of our students, particularly for those students challenged by special cognitive limitations.

As teachers of science, not only must we recognize that we need to give the students time and opportunity to practice and refine their use of the process skills but also we have to appreciate the emotional, social, and behavioral dimensions of classroom tasks. One of the reasons that science can be so powerful for students with cognitive limitations is that the subject can provide the context that is so necessary for learning. Process skills supply this context because the students are in direct contact with the subject matter (Patton, 1995).

Scientists' Use of Process Skills

A reasonable question about the science process skills is whether emphasizing their use by elementary and middle school students represents authentic science. Are professional scientists really involved in the processes of observing, inferring, and classifying? Or are process skills an oversimplified attempt to have children engage in scientific activities? A rare and revealing peak into the thought processes of a scientist can reveal the obvious value of process skills such as observing and inferring.

Richard Feynman won a Nobel Prize for his work on quantum electrodynamics, and even if we wanted to explain this field of science to you, we really can't. We thought it might be interesting to have a glimpse into his mind. Rather than try to understand his ideas regarding photons and matter, we'll draw on an earlier example of his investigative thinking. Writing about his life as a scientist, Feynman described, in the following passage, his curiosity about ant behavior:

> One question that I wondered about was why the ant trails looked so straight and nice. The ants look as if they know what they're doing, as if they have a good sense of geometry. ...

The moment the ant found the sugar, I picked up a colored pencil I had ready (I had previously done experiments indicating that the ants don't give a damn about pencil marks—they walk right over them—so I knew it wouldn't disturb anything), and behind where the ant went I drew a line so I could tell where his trail was. The ant wandered a little bit wrong to get back to the hole, so the line was quite wiggly, unlike a typical ant trail.

When the next ant to find the sugar began to go back, I marked his trail with another color. (By the way, he followed the first ant's trail back, rather than his own incoming trail. My theory is that when an ant has found some food, he leaves a much stronger trail than when he's just wandering around.)

The second ant was in a great hurry and followed, pretty much, the original trail. But because he was going so fast he would go straight out, as if he were coasting, when the trail was wiggly. Often, as the ant was "coasting" he would find the trail again. Already it was apparent that the second ant's return was slightly straighter. With successive ants the same "improvement" of the trail hurriedly and carelessly "following" it occurred. I followed eight or ten ants with my pencil until their trails became a neat line. … It's something like sketching. You draw a lousy line at first; then you go over it a few times and it makes a nice line after a while. (Feynman, 1989, p. 79)

Here, in the words of one of the leading scientists of his era, we can witness the process skills being put to actual use. We notice how he uses pencils to assist with his observing. We also can detect his efforts to infer the reasons for the ants' behaviors. All in all, without any fancy scientific terminology, a scientist demonstrates his craft and does so in a way that makes the science process skills evident.

More Than Basic Science Process Skills

Within this chapter we've devoted attention to the first three of six basic science process skills. In the next chapter, we will present the balance of the list: measuring, predicting, and communicating. In total, the six basic science process skills form an important basis for an elementary school science program. We can realistically expect students from kindergarten and the higher grades to actively engage in science through their use of these six skills (Padilla, 1990). However, as they mature, students will have the cognitive abilities to learn even more complex science process skills. We present them here only so you are aware of their existence. On the basis of our experiences, as well as our work with classroom teachers, we are very cautious about expecting students to be proficient at the integrated process skills before age eleven years or thereabouts.

The **integrated science process skills** build on the fundamentals provided by the basic process skills. What makes this new list of skills "integrated" is that to undertake them requires integrating or combining the basic science process skills (Rezba, Fiel, Funk, & Okey, 1994). For example to make a graph, which is one of the integrated science process skills, a student needs to be skilled at observing, measuring, classifying, and communicating. Making a graph involves combining all of these into an integrated whole. The reason younger children should not be expected to master the integrated science process skills is that, typically, their minds have difficulty coordinating the thinking required to perform these tasks. It's almost as if younger brains don't have the capacity to manage the integrated skills—much like when a toddler attempts to carry more toys than he or she is capable of holding. At best, children in the primary grades require a great deal of support and guidance by their teachers to master an integrated science process skill. Before children are eleven years old or so, it is probably not worth all of the effort (Kuhn & Dean, 2005). But by the time children are in fifth or sixth grade, their minds seem to be able to handle the complexity required to use the integrated process skills.

There is no single, standardized list of integrated science process skills. As a result, we have chosen to follow the lead of others (e.g., Duschl, 1990) and use the list that was part of a science program in the 1960s and 1970s called Science: A Process Approach. The developers of this program identified five integrated science process skills, and we provide an explanation and example for each.

Defining Operationally: Explaining how a factor was measured within a certain experience; in other words, it is a temporary definition that is operationalized for the purpose of a very specific situation. Example: an operational definition is the use of the amount of time it takes an object to reach the bottom of a ramp to clarify what is meant by "how fast" an object rolls down a ramp. Other ways of describing "how fast" can be used, but choosing just one is what is involved when someone is defining operationally.

Controlling Variables: Identifying the factors that might influence the outcome of an experiment and then ensures that as many of those are kept as constant as possible. Example: if a comparison is being made between the speeds of different objects as they roll down a ramp, the only variable is the object. Constant factors include the length of the ramp, the angle it is raised, and the manner in which the object is released.

Stating Hypotheses: Describing the anticipated outcome of an experiment. This is seemingly the same as a prediction, but when someone is stating a hypothesis, he or she has to make a specific reference to the variables being studied along with an indication about the measurements that will be gathered. Example: someone can predict that smaller cans of soup will roll down the ramp in a shorter amount of time than larger soup cans, because their lesser weight will translate into less inertia. The challenge of keeping all variables and constants in mind is often why stating hypotheses is too much for younger science learners.

Reading and Making Graphs: Translating lists of quantitative data into visual representations, including making wise choices about which graphs are the most appropriate to use. For example a bar graph is a good choice to show comparisons of the speeds with which objects traveled down a ramp, whereas a pie chart is not as useful or informative.

Designing Experiments: Combining all of the process skills, both basic and integrated, for the purpose of testing an investigable question. Example: taking all of the previous integrated science process skills with the goal of conducting a fair test of the difference in speeds of rolling objects, collecting and interpreting the data, and analyzing the accuracy of the original hypothesis are all required within an experiment.

Experimenting as we define it is not something that can be realistically expected to occur on a regular basis in elementary and middle school classrooms. This is because experimenting requires using all of the basic and integrated process skills, much as one would use for a science fair project. Even though many people use *experimenting* as a synonym for any science activity, such as when a child asks, "Are we doing experiments today?" we view experimenting as much more involved and ambitious. Our preference is to use **investigating** as our catchall phrase to describe science activities. The integrated process skill of experimenting is probably best reserved for those activities where older students are given almost complete control over the investigation of a question. In later chapters, we will expand on this idea when we describe open inquiry. But if you substitute *investigate* for *experiment* then you will prevent further confusion down the road.

Chapter Summary

- The science process skills supply us with the actions that complement the concepts of science. The process skills describe the things students should do in science and not just experience by hearing about others doing science. While becoming skilled users of the science process skills helps students gain entry into the culture of science, they also support the development of language fluency and contribute to the development of a coherent classroom community.

- Observing and inferring are intermingled actions: observing involves gathering facts, whereas inferring attempts to explain those facts. Considering how closely the statement is to being an indisputable fact allows us to assess the quality of an observation.

- Inferring involves posing a statement that is intended to explain observations. Inferences are evaluated by considering the strength with which they account for what has been observed.

- Classifying allows scientists and students to sort through observations and organize them by following specific guidelines. Key guidelines include the absence of opinions and the reliance on categories that sort objects into one of two opposite subgroups.

- Science process skills are a cultural norm of science. These norms may conflict with other cultures' views of the world. In particular, the either–or and bias-free properties that are used within classification are representative of a certain worldview that may not be self-evident to those who are familiar with contrasting perspectives.

- Experimenting is considered an integrated science process skill and involves a collection of skills normally not accessible to students until they are in the upper elementary grades. The six basic process skills can be used, to varying degrees of complexity, from kindergarten through middle school.

Key Terms

Classifying: a basic science process skill involving the organization of objects into a comprehensible framework based on observable properties of those objects.

Dichotomous key: common tool of classification that allows the user to identify some item in the physical world. Such keys are constructed by dividing all groups of items into one of two parts, so that the use of keys consists of a series of choices, one choice for each step, leading to the proper identification of the item.

Inferring: one of the essential science process skills, involving generating explanations based on valid observations. In the culture of science, better inferences are always considered possible.

Integrated science process skills: the complex actions appropriate for use starting in the upper elementary grades. The skills are: defining operationally, controlling variables, stating hypotheses, reading and making graphs, and designing experiments.

Objectivity: a characteristic of scientific actions in which personal biases are minimized, often through the process of limiting the role of inference in the collection of scientific observations, allowing for a more straightforward portrait of the physical world.

Observing: one of the essential science process skills, it involves the active use of the senses to make direct descriptions of some aspect of the physical world.

Science process skills: discrete but essential actions of science that are used to conduct scientific inquiries. Process skills include observing, inferring, classifying, measuring, predicting, and communicating.

A Favorite Science Lesson

The "Habitats" unit was created for use in grade-two and grade-three classrooms and was developed by the Education Development Center. This is an environmental awareness unit, and it allows students to appreciate the complexity of nature and their roles and responsibilities as stewards of the environment. The "Exploring Other Habitats" follows prior learning experiences where students identify how the needs of living things are met within the neighborhood. In this particular activity, students use careful observations as they study a small plot of land. Using a plastic hoop, students create an inventory of all the life-forms they can observe within their hoop. In addition to observing, students are to make inferences about how the needs of the living organisms are met within the microhabitats. Classroom activities that supplement this outdoor activity reinforce the need for careful observing. In addition, students participate in games that focus their attention on the properties that can be used to classify the minibeasts they discovered within their hoops.

Suggested Readings

Crowther, D. T. (2003, October). Harry Potter and the dichotomous key. *Science and Children, 40,* 18–23.
>   Dave Crowther teaches elementary science methods in Reno, Nevada, and he created a clever way to teach classification. He relies on a learning cycle lesson plan, something we will address later in this book, to help children classify jelly beans. More than just cleverly using candy, Crowther illustrates very effective planning and a memorable approach to making dichotomous keys.

Wood, J. (2005, April/May). Discovery central. *Science and Children, 42,* 36–37.
>   Rural teacher Jaimee Wood explains how centers are used in a rural classroom. Even though the students are very young, Wood has kindergarten students rely on all the science process skills during a unit involving plants.

References

Amaral, O. M., Garrison, L., & Klentschy, M. (2002). Helping English learners increase achievement through inquiry-based science instruction. *Bilingual Research Journal, 26,* 213–239.

Bazin, M., & Tamez, M. (2002). *Math and science across cultures: Activities and investigations from Exploratorium Teacher Institute.* New York: New Press.

Bowker, G. C., & Star, S. L. (1999). *Sorting things out: Classification and its consequences.* Cambridge, MA: MIT Press.

Dawes, L. (2004). Talk and learning in classroom science. *International Journal of Science Education, 26,* 677–695.

Dewey, J. (1991). *How we think.* New York: Prometheus. (Original work published 1910)

Doyle, A. C. (2004). *The adventures and the memoirs of Sherlock Holmes.* New York: Sterling Publishing.

Duffy, G. G. (1998, June). Teaching and the balancing of round stones. *Phi Delta Kappan, 79*(10), 777–780.

Duschl, R. (1990). *Restructuring science education: The importance of theories and their development.* New York: Teachers College Press.

Feynman, R. (1989). *Surely you're joking, Mr. Feynman: Adventures of a curious character.* New York: Bantam.

Harlen, W. (2000). *The teaching of science in primary schools.* London: David Fulton.

Kuhn, D., & Dean, D. (2005). Is developing scientific thinking all about learning to control variables? *Psychological Science, 16,* 866–870.

Linik, J. R. (2004). Growing language through science. *Northwest Teacher, 5*(1), 6–9.

Maatta, D., Dobb, F., & Ostlund, K. (2006). Strategies for teaching science to English language learners. In A. K. Fatham & D. T. Crowther (Eds.), *Science for English language learners* (pp. 37–59). Arlington, VA: National Science Teachers Association.

Maroney, S. A., Finson, K. D., Beaver, J. B., & Jensen, M. M. (2003). Preparing for successful inquiry in inclusive science classrooms. *Teaching Exceptional Children, 36*(1), 18–25.

Menand, L. (2001). *The metaphysical club: A story of ideas in America.* New York: Farrar, Strauss and Giroux.

Mill, J. S. (1884). *A system of logic, ratiocinative and inductive; being a connected view of the principles of evidence, and the methods of scientific investigation.* London: Longmans, Green & Co.

Moore, J. E. (2003). The art of sorting: Using Venn diagrams to learn science process skills. *Science Activities, 39*(4), 17–21.

North Central Regional Educational Laboratory. (2004). *All students reaching the top: Strategies for closing academic achievement gaps.* Naperville, IL: Learning Point Associates.

Padilla, M. J. (1990). *Research matters to the science teacher: The science process skills.* Retrieved from http://www.educ.sfu.ca/narstsite/publications/research/skill.htm

Patton, J. R. (1995). Teaching science to students with special needs. *Teaching Exceptional Children, 27,* 4–6.

Peng, K., & Nisbett, R. E. (1999). Culture, dialectics, and reasoning about contradiction. *American Psychologist, 54,* 741–754.

Rezba, R. J., Fiel, R. L., Funk, H. J., & Okey, J. R. (1994). *Learning and assessing science process skills.* Dubuque, IA: Kendall-Hunt.

Russell, J. B. (1997). *Inventing the flat earth: Columbus and modern historians.* Westport, CT: Praeger.

Scudder, S. H. (1879). The student, the fish, and Agassiz. In *American Poems* (3rd ed.). Boston: Houghton, Osgood and Co.

Shaler, N. S. (1946). The autobiography of Nathaniel Southgate Shaler. In H. Peterson (Ed.), *Great Teachers* (pp. 213–215). New York: Vintage Books.

Vosniadou, S., Pagondiotis, C., & Deliyianni, M. (2005). From the pragmatics of classification systems to the metaphysics of concepts. *Journal of the Learning Sciences, 14*(1), 115–125.

Weaver, H. N. (2000). Balancing culture and professional education: American Indians/Alaska Natives and the helping professions. *Journal of American Indian Education, 39,* 1–18.

three

Measure, Predict, and Communicate
Basic Science Process Skills

Chapter Highlights

- Students use tools to measure and to extend their observing. Measurements numerically express observations of objects and events.
- As students become more experienced with measuring, their proficiency improves. Giving students time to use rulers, balances, and other measuring tools will help them become comfortable with the metric system.
- The human desire to overcome uncertainty makes predicting a powerful skill. Predictions are powerful, however, when they are correct or incorrect. When students make incorrect predictions, their improper assumptions become explicit and identify where more thinking is required.
- Students communicate throughout the school day. When communicating is connected to their use of observing, inferring, or any of the other process skills, the communication becomes a science process skill.
- Activities that do not involve at least some of the process skills do not qualify to be called science.
- A joint productive activity in which students and teachers participate together in science activities represents an effective pedagogy for diverse learners.
- Viewing the world from a science perspective is an important ability. However, there are other ways of perceiving our surroundings that are legitimate ways of knowing even though they are not called scientific.

The science process skills describe the actions within the culture of science that students can develop through practice. Previously we considered three basic science process skills: observing, inferring, and classifying. In this chapter, we will examine the process skills of measuring, predicting, and communicating. As in the previous chapter, we will define each process skill, demonstrate how each is a component of the culture of science, and discuss where teachers need to pay special attention to students with differing cultures, home languages, or cognitive abilities.

Actions of Science as Essential

It is a common misperception that process skills are somehow less important than the science content we expect students to learn. Our contention is that separating content from process, or disconnecting the objects of science from the actions of science, is not a good idea. First, nothing will more quickly destroy students' natural interest in science than teaching only information without allowing them to actively participate in it. Second, developmental psychologists have demonstrated that elementary school students think in concrete ways; if science is taught in the abstract, it's not going to be useful to the students. Third, even though our attention is often drawn to the concepts when we consult state or national standards for science, the process skills are present in some form within these documents. Fourth, to teach content without adequate attention to process skills is an incomplete and erroneous representation of science as it is performed by professional scientists. Were we to teach without developing students' abilities to use the process skills, we would be teaching not science but actually some other odd subject that has little relationship to the culture of science. Finally, when we consider teaching science to students with diverse cultures, languages, and cognitive abilities, we must develop shared experiences, language skills, and conceptions. In summary, including process skills within science instruction will assist us in our goal of making science accessible to all learners.

Measuring

As is true for all six of the basic science process skills, measuring is a skill that students need to perform and not just learn about. *Learning to measure* takes on greater significance and serves a higher instructional purpose than *learning about measurements*. Measuring is a special example of observing. When we observe we rely on our senses to gather information about the environment. Observations can be divided into two groups: if a number is somehow used to describe what is noticed, then we can label those observations as **quantitative.** In contrast, observations that do not make use of numbers are **qualitative.** To keep these two ideas straight, notice that the first term hints at the quantity of something whereas the second term suggests the quality of what's being observed.

It would be inappropriate to suggest that quantitative observations are superior to qualitative observations. Both are very important and have a place within science, because each way of observing has its own strengths. To describe the intensity of sunlight, we might use a light-sensing tool to quantify the brightness. When we are making observations of the moon, we describe its shape—which represents a qualitative observation.

The process skill of **measuring** is a special type of quantitative observation. This is because measuring requires the use of some tool, such as a ruler, to assist our observing. There are quantitative observations that contain numbers that are not measurements because those observations aren't compared to a standardized measuring tool. Counting is the best example of this. In observing this page of text, you might count the number of times the letter "e" appears. This would not require you to use a measuring tool such as a ruler. Counting the almost three hundred times that letter appears on this page is an example of quantitative observing but not an example of measuring.

Extending Your Senses

Because measuring involves using a tool, it is a special form of observing quantitatively. The tool is a standard against which objects can be compared. Although you might be able to look at a crayon and a pencil and visually determine which one is longer, a ruler can assist the observing by refining what you see. You can think of the ruler as a measuring tool that extends your sense of sight. When people are measuring, and this holds true for professional scientists and students, they use a tool that has been calibrated with a standard unit of measure. As a result, it makes the comparison of observations more precise. Instead of saying that a leaf is big, we can use a ruler to find the length and width of the leaf. If someone else observes the same leaf, they may not agree that it is big. If they measure the leaf, their observation should be the same.

NSES Content Standard A: Employ simple equipment and tools to gather data and extend the senses.

Our senses are very useful to us, but they can be fooled. Tools that measure are not so easily deceived. Think about the cylinders you see in everyday life: a soup can, a paint can, a long potato chip can, a tennis ball can, and a fresh piece of chalk. Consider which would be the closest to having the same height as its circumference. Using your sense of sight you could compare the cylinders' height and circumference. It's hard to tell for sure. However, you can extend your sense of sight by relying on a measuring tape to compare the height and circumference to "see" what the right answer is.

Science Tools for Special Needs Students

It would be very natural for us to think about ourselves if we were learning science where our teacher was using the process skills. But as we develop our sensitivities to diverse populations, we will recognize the value in thinking about how those who are not just like us would respond. For example we might appreciate that learning to use a graduated cylinder would be a challenge for an elementary school student. In addition, we should consider the additional challenges a child who has a physical or visual disability might face when learning such a skill. The act of pouring a liquid into a narrow container and then using one's eyes to decide how many milliliters of liquid are present is a feat for anyone. But we are advocating for all students to participate in science. How might it be possible for students with physical limitations to perform something like the action just described?

Fortuitously, the staff at the Lawrence Hall of Science at the University of California, Berkeley, has created science tools to address these needs. The special but inexpensive pieces of equipment are part of a curriculum program called Science Activities for the Visually Impaired/Science Enrichment for Learners with Physical Handicaps. The shorter name is usually much easier to verbalize: SAVI/SELPH (pronounced as "savvy self"). Figure 3.1 shows pictures and descriptions of some of this equipment from the SAVI/SELPH Web site.

We are not suggesting that as a new teacher you must obtain this specialized equipment or else visually impaired students will not be able to participate in science. But these images show that such materials are available, and you as a teacher may be able to access funds for purchasing such materials for special needs students. Beyond that, we hope this illustrates that with ingenuity and forethought we can engage all students in science. A physical impairment is not a sufficient cause to exclude children from the excitement of doing legitimate school science.

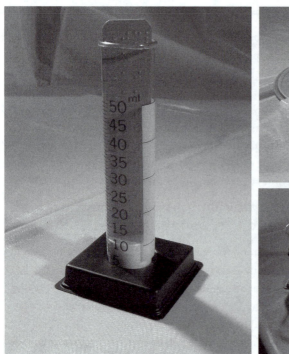

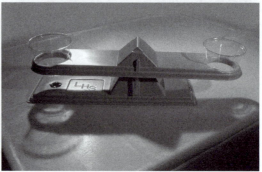

FIGURE 3.1. This equipment allows students with visual impairments to measure volume, mass, and temperature. Photos courtesy of Lawrence Hall of Science at the University of California, Berkeley.

Reducing Sources of Bias

What we notice about our surroundings is influenced by our previous experiences. A toddler might point to the moon and notice how brightly it shines. Someone with more experience might notice its phase and position in the sky. The different backgrounds people have will cause them to note different features. Another example: people can be seated in the same room, and some will complain how cold it is while others are quite comfortable. The difference is because of the temperatures the various people are accustomed to and find comfortable. Again, each individual perceives the environment in his or her own way.

Using measurements can help us avoid having our biases interfere with our observations. You can use a thermometer to augment your sense of touch and find the temperature of the room in terms of a standard unit of measure. Whether 20°C is comfortable is a personal preference, but this measurement will be the same no matter who does the measuring. Thermometers and other measuring tools are immune to the opinions of others. You may be likely to agree with grandmother when she asks, "Isn't it cold in here?" but measuring tools are less prone to the powers of suggestion.

Developing Measuring Proficiency

To become proficient with measuring, we have to develop several abilities. First, we need to learn how to properly use the measuring tool. For example, when using a ruler to measure length, you have to check to make sure that the zero part of the ruler is at the end of the object you're measuring. You cannot just slap down the ruler and read the number. Before finding the mass of an object, you need to first make sure that the balance or scale reads zero when nothing is on it. One part of developing measuring skills is knowing the proper way to use the measuring tools.

NSES Content Standard A: Use appropriate tools and techniques to gather, analyze, and interpret data.

Related to knowing how to use measuring tools properly is recognizing the proper tool to use to make the measurement. You compare heaviness with certain tools, and you compare height with another set of tools. Knowing that different tools provide different information becomes relevant when there is a question about which thing is bigger: what tool you use to compare pumpkins or apples depends on what type of measurement you're interested in studying. If "bigger" is to be decided by heaviness, then a scale or balance is needed. If "bigger" implies the girth, then something like a measuring tape should be used.

For Reflection and Discussion

Measuring requires that we use a tool to extend our senses and assign a quantitative value to the observations. A ruler extends our sense of sight, but measuring tools for the other senses may be less obvious. What are tools that can be used by scientists (or in everyday life) to extend the other senses of taste, touch, hear, and smell?

In addition to knowing the ways of measuring, you also should recognize which tool is most appropriate for making those kinds of measurements. A bathroom scale is not going to help determine which apple is the heaviest. A pocket ruler is not the best tool to use to measure the length of the hallway. A diet scale may not be appropriate for comparing the heaviness of shoes, and a stopwatch is not the right tool for measuring the amount of time that elapses between one full moon and the next. One way to help students choose the best tool for a particular measurement is to provide them with many opportunities to use a variety of measuring tools. Sometimes the teacher may provide some advice and guidance, but there may well be times to allow students to make their own measuring decisions. After students have a few instances of making less than useful measurements, the discussion of the most appropriate tool takes on a whole new significance. The choice of measuring tool becomes more than a matter of being told by the teacher—the students know from their experiences when to select one tool or another.

Metrics in the Science Classroom

What about the metric system? What place does it have in the school science curriculum? Here are two answers to these questions. The first is philosophical: the metric system is the way that scientists around the world make their measurements. Even scientists who collaborate only with other scientists in the United States use grams to record mass, meters to record length, and degrees Celsius to record temperature. This suggests that having students learn the metric system should be part of becoming scientifically literate. For students who have immigrated to the United States from other countries, our use of inches and pounds instead of centimeters and kilograms is going to seem odd. A teacher who is reluctant to use the metric system might need to overcome that reluctance to support the learning of students for whom the metric system is familiar and comfortable.

But the second response to the question about using the metric system is much more practical and depends on the local science standards. Are the students expected to understand centimeters when they take their standardized tests? If they are, then teaching the metric system to them is your obligation. Are the students supposed to know the metric system when they reach later grade levels? If high school science teachers expect the students to walk in the door with a familiarity with grams and meters, then, as an elementary school teacher, you probably don't want to hear that your former students were confused because they had never used those units of measure within your science lessons.

The reality is that the metric system is not especially difficult to learn if students have multiple opportunities to use it. Teaching how to convert back and forth between measurement systems is not a good use of time and energy. Instead your goal, when it comes to metrics, is that the students learn to switch from one system to the other as easily as some people switch between languages. People fluent in multiple languages don't translate every phrase in their mind—they just speak. Inches and centimeters are simply different units of measure that we'd like students to be able to represent using their hands (can you show an inch with your thumb and finger on one hand and a centimeter with the other hand?). But memorizing the formula to convert Celsius to Fahrenheit really has no place in elementary and middle school science.

Perhaps the biggest barrier to learning the metric system is attitude. In this regard, learning science is similar to learning a second language. If a person feels as if he or she is required to learn, whether it's metrics or Spanish, for example, then the depth of understanding is not as deep. However, if learning the new material is regarded as not only useful but also interesting and valuable, then the rate and quality of learning is greatly enhanced. Students will notice if their teacher is resistant to or afraid of the metric system. Positive dispositions are contagious.

Most of us can remember, as high school or college students, where we lost points on an assignment or quiz because we didn't include proper units of measure. At the time, this rule seemed arbitrary and unfair. After all, you might have thought, if the calculations were correct and the numbers turned out right, then what difference does it make whether the answer includes centimeters or grams or whatever? Perhaps at the root of such disputes is an incomplete understanding of the purpose of the assignment. If our task was to calculate how much water would be needed to cool the total volume to 40 degrees, then a number like "120" really has no meaning. Here are parallel examples of insufficient information:

Question: How much baking soda should we add to banana bread?
Answer: 10.

Question: How much fertilizer should be added to the plants?
Answer: 25.

Question: How much of your hair should be trimmed?
Answer: 1.

Does this make the importance of including units of measurement more relevant? This is the same issue that scientists and teachers have with including units. Otherwise the answer is less than incomplete—it doesn't make much sense.

If students are allowed to develop skills at measuring, in multiple contexts and for multiple purposes, then some of the struggles we associate with measuring, including the metric system, will fall aside. Frequent opportunities to conduct measurements, numerous occasions to select among tools for measuring, and abundant instances in which measurements are included within small group and whole class discussions all make measuring a natural part of the students' repertoire of science process skills. As a result, the habit of recording and reporting units of measure will begin in the lower grades and will be significant to the students' efforts. This is much more likely to produce long-lasting understandings than following a rule such as "always include units" and reminding student with red marks and frowning faces on their papers. It is in the light of such experience that the need for units becomes intelligible.

Predicting

Uncovering patterns in nature is the goal of the work of scientists. In many ways, finding the patterns makes life easier because many of us take comfort in knowing there is regularity to the universe. Substitute teachers are well aware of students' desire for regularity. They are almost always faced with students who point out "that's not the way our teacher does it." Routines, traditions, and predictability are important to humans.

Predicting involves making a statement that forecasts what will happen in the future. The expectation with predictions is that we will be able to test their accuracy. In this way we create a cycle of pattern seeking: we observe an event, we infer a pattern, we predict what will happen, and then we observe to see if the prediction turns out to be accurate. The goal is not simply to make good predictions but to find patterns that allow us to decide whether our observations, and the inferences we made from these observations, make sense.

Testing Our Understandings Against the World

Predicting is a science process skill we rely on within our daily lives. A wind begins to kick up from the south, and we grab an umbrella as we head out the door. There's a long weekend coming up, so we buy gas in advance because we expect the prices to rise. The professor always has more than enough to keep the class busy until the last minute, so you don't expect there's much chance you'll be dismissed early. We use what we know to anticipate what's going to happen, and we find out whether our prediction is correct.

Beyond the comfort that comes with identifying patterns, there's money and success to be made in making accurate predictions. Stockbrokers and real estate speculators try to predict human actions and reap the financial benefits when they're correct. Police detectives predict criminal behavior, physicians predict the spread of disease, engineers predict the strength of a structure, and teachers predict the behaviors of their students. Predicting is not exclusive to the culture of science.

However, there is a way that predicting is unique to science. When we predict in science, we are not simply making a guess. Whenever we predict in science, we rely on the patterns that we have observed or even measured. Rather than guess what phase the moon will be on your birthday (Why? Maybe you're contemplating a midnight party?), you could use what you know about lunar cycles as a pattern for predicting if the moon will be full that night. When we guess, we don't always have much basis for that statement, but when we predict, we have to have some underlying rationale that is based on observations and previous experience.

For Reflection and Discussion

Suppose you were going to introduce the process skill of predicting to students. Before you begin the lesson, you want to share with the students how the process skill of predicting is important. How many professions or occupations can you list in which predicting, and predicting well, is an important aspect of the job? Think broadly, and don't restrict yourself to scientific careers.

Benefits of Making Mistakes

We are recipients of the phrase "we learn from our mistakes" when we've really messed up and someone is maybe trying to make the best of the situation. As a result, most of us don't like to hear the phrase because it usually comes right after we've been told that we were wrong. However, if we distance ourselves from the sting of the phrase, we may recognize its value when it comes to the science process skill of predicting.

Here's a scenario: a teacher is doing a demonstration for the class. The teacher holds a dry paper coffee filter over her head and releases it; the class observes as it falls to the ground. Producing a stack of ten coffee filters, the teacher asks, "What do you think will happen if we compare the falling of one coffee filter to ten—which do you predict will reach the floor first?" Students speculate out loud, and the teacher directs them to write their predictions in their notebooks. And then they observe as the investigation continues.

Suppose a student made a prediction that turned out to be correct, but the reasons used to make the prediction were wrong. How might that individual construe what was observed? His or her expectations were reinforced and, as a result, the understandings of the situation remain incorrect but even stronger than before. In contrast, suppose an individual made a prediction that turned out to be wrong. How might this student respond? We hope she or he would not dismiss what had been observed as some trick. Instead the student would need to reconsider the reasons for the prediction. Ideally the thinking would lead to generating a new pattern, because the old pattern failed to stand up to the test.

Which of these would you prefer to happen in your classroom? Many of us are concerned about the possibility that our students will become confused during our lessons, and we shudder at the notion that they will become discouraged. However, another danger is that students will be highly confident in their knowledge even when they are incorrect. How can we alter the situation so all the students are confident and correct?

Jean Piaget provided us with a way out of this dilemma—even though we may not have recognized it until now. Learning is a multifaceted activity. It can entail simply incorporating new information into our existing mental frameworks; Piaget's term for this was **assimilation.** A second type of learning happens as a person encounters ideas that do not fit into his or her existing views. He or she must reorganize the existing mental frameworks. Piaget identified this as **accommodation.** Assimilating is akin to adding a new book, compact disk, or sweater to a shelf where others have already been stored. Accommodating means rearranging the entire cabinet to make space for the new item. Assimilating is easier to do than accommodating. Accommodation describes a more profound mode of learning. Students who make a prediction that ends up being incorrect and then rethink their ideas are accommodating their observations. They must revise their current ways of thinking to make room for an incompatible piece of information.

Accommodation is an important aspect of learning. The alternative involves little more than students plugging new words and ideas into what they already believe to be true. However, when events don't match expectations and students feel off balance, they can overcome that discomfort by reconsidering what they thought they knew. To engage in a struggle to get back in balance, students must experience **disequilibrium.** The feeling of unease that accompanies disequilibrium becomes the impetus to make things right, to figure things out, and to accommodate the new idea.

The classroom climate must be sufficiently open so students do not fear ridicule when their ideas don't work out. Each member of the class should recognize that being uncertain is an important catalyst for learning. Overcoming the discomfort and frustration associated with disequilibrium pushes the individual to reconsider assumptions. True learning happens when students realize that they don't understand something (such as when a prediction is incorrect) and then, because of the uncertainty, figure out a better way to think about the situation. This is the link between incorrect predictions and accommodation.

NSES Content Standard A: Recognize and analyze alternative explanations and predictions.

In the classroom we shouldn't avoid having the students in a state of disequilibrium. The quest for student comfort short-circuits the possibilities for real learning. In other words, having students in disequilibrium is not only OK but beneficial to their intellectual growth. We have to place some faith in students' capacity to make sense of their world and trust that they will be able to work through their uncertainties. You are probably familiar with toys that rock back and forth when you tip them over until they are back in an upright position. Students' cognitive disequilibrium is like that, but instead of gravity being the force that pulls the object back into balance, the students' internal drive to satisfy their curiosity is the force pushing them to accommodate the new ideas and get their minds back into balance with the natural world. As Piaget noted, that internal drive toward equilibrium is a fundamental force for learning, one that needs to be nurtured in the science classroom.

For Reflection and Discussion

When a child moves to the United States and the school expects him or her to be assimilated, what does that suggest about the school's regard for the student's cultural background? In contrast, when schools accommodate new students, what happens to the culture those students brought with them? Use these ideas as a metaphor to explain the learning of new concepts using Piaget's ideas about assimilation and accommodation.

Teachers should remain aware of the role of disequilibrium, and the discomfort that accompanies it, in students' learning. This seems almost counterintuitive, particularly in dealing with students who already seem burdened with the need to learn a new language or students who are operating with a cognitive restriction. However, it is important to recognize that all children need to experience disequilibrium and the discomfort that accompanies it if they are to learn in a meaningful manner. The conscientious teacher must establish a classroom climate that is comfortable and welcoming enough so that students can accept a cognitive challenge. In a supportive classroom, all students can rise to the occasion, moving past their current skills and knowledge.

Communicating

The sixth and final basic science process skill is certainly the most broad. Although there are very specific examples of the previous five process skills, along with criteria that sort the proper form from the improper form, communicating is not nearly as restrictive. This doesn't mean that anything qualifies as communicating, but there are many options. The process skill of observing includes more than observing with the eyes—listening, smelling, and touching can also lead to important observations. Similarly, the process skill of communicating extends beyond the use of written text. Students can communicate their observations through their drawings or models, their verbal inferences, and their measurements in the form of a graph. These are examples of the appropriate use of communication as a process skill.

Communicating and the Other Process Skills

It is difficult to imagine how communicating can be separated from the other five process skills. After all, observing would reasonably lead to sharing that information with others. Classifying promotes the recording of properties or the oral explanation of the rules used to divide objects into two groups. Even when the audience for communication is oneself, such as when recording measurements or predictions for later reference, the act of communicating seems tightly bound to the other process skills.

Then why do we list communicating as a separate process skill? One reason is that communicating reinforces the social dimension of the science culture. Scientists rarely work in isolation—they communicate with others. Scientists must gather evidence to combat skepticism. Scientists rely on their writings, sketches, graphs, and so on to help them recognize the patterns in nature. **Communicating** as a science process skill is necessarily connected to the other process skills.

In our professional opinion, we should not consider every act of communication by students as an example of their use of this science process skill. Our preference is that teachers connect communicating with another specific process skill before they claim that their students are doing science. In other words, if students are writing or drawing but they are not basing those acts on other process skills, then we argue that their action shouldn't be considered science. Science has its limits, and even though many of us perceive the potential for science all around us, that doesn't mean that everything *is* science—including communicating.

NSES Content Standard A: Communicate scientific procedures and explanations.

What Qualifies as a Science Lesson

If science has its limits, does that mean that we are opposed to integrating science with other subjects? Absolutely not. However, we foresee problems when a teacher believes the students are doing science when they actually are not. We will devote more space later in this book to curriculum integration. But for right now, we want you to consider this claim:

> Students must be using the science process skills for us to claim that they are doing science.

This provides a clear way to distinguish science from lessons in other subject areas. Too many people associate school science with reading textbooks and doing worksheets—and that's all. We wish to emphasize that science requires students to engage in science through their use of the process skills. We resist any claims that students can learn observing, inferring, and predicting just by using a book. We urge teachers to apply process skills, as much as is feasible, to objects being studied. In most instances, using the process skills with the actual materials is preferable to just reading about those objects. Even though not every science topic can be studied through direct observation (the solar system and dinosaurs come to mind), students should study actual objects and not just pictures and stories.

When students are learning all of their science without using the process skills (such as by reading a chapter and answering questions at the end), it's not clear what label to give to that subject. In such a case, students are becoming familiar with some of the objects of science, or its explanations, but that learning is incomplete. Furthermore, if students are doing a hands-on activity but they're not using science process skills, such as when they follow the steps in a procedure without any sense of purpose, then their work wouldn't qualify as science either. In this case they are participating in actions but not clearly the actions of science. One of the central goals of science is to come to an understanding of the natural world. If students are "doing" but without having a clear purpose, then these actions are not legitimately actions of science.

Let's find our way back to the process skill of communicating. There are many ways in which students can use communicating within the context of science, but it's a science lesson only when the other process skills are involved. Does this mean that students can create posters, present a skit, or perform a dance as part of science? Can they communicate in these ways and still be considered to be doing science? Not automatically—there has to be a clear connection to the other process skills. If the basis of their understandings comes from phenomena they are observing, inferring, classifying, and so on, then what they are doing would legitimately count as the science process skill of communicating. Students' direct experiences with food chains, moon phases, or rock erosion that are translated into creative representations of their understandings should be included in the actions of science.

Communicating as a Tool for Learning

Lev Vygotsky claimed that before a person can internalize knowledge, he or she must first share that idea with others. Within his theory, learning happens within two planes: the social plane and the internal plane. Obviously, language can be used to communicate ideas between individuals. Perhaps less obvious is the view that language is tightly bound to the thoughts of the individual. Vygotsky's hypothesis was that ideas had to be exchanged within the social plane before the understanding of those concepts would migrate to the internal plane.

You may have experienced this when trying to understand something you do not fully grasp; you may try to express that understanding to someone else. You would have witnessed this when someone said, "I don't know if I get this so let me try to talk it through." This is an example of language being used in the social plane. By expressing ideas and getting feedback from someone else, a person internalizes the knowledge. Does this mean that all knowledge that you have began in a social plane? That's still open for debate. But it seems that to comprehend complex ideas, people need to discuss them with others before the ideas can be fully understood. This theory has direct connections to our current focus on communicating.

Because our shared purpose is to help students to learn science, we ought to draw on as many resources as we can to help make that goal a reality. Assuming that Vygotsky's theory is accurate, and the scientific habits of mind urge us to remain open to new ideas, we can see the value in communicating as one of the science process skills. It is important to remember that the act of representing observations, inferences, and so on not only allows students to communicate but also can contribute to students' understandings of the science topics they are investigating.

Communicating and Cultural and Linguistic Diversity

The action of communicating within science is a central one to focus on when teaching science to students from diverse backgrounds and particularly students who are learning English. Closely observing students' efforts to communicate can allow a teacher to discern what a student is learning—if one is vigilant. Communicating is a very important tool for learning, but it requires teachers to move beyond an overdependence on writing as a primary means of communicating. This expanded notion and appreciation of communicating has positive effects beyond building students' vocabulary and fluency. Having students draw, model, and even role-play ideas allows students who are acquiring basic literacy skills to engage with the content in a meaningful manner and express what they know.

For Reflection and Discussion

Communicating can sometimes be regarded as sharing what you know, whether by writing, speaking, or using some other form. But it also has been reported that the act of explaining ideas helps a person to learn. How has the process of expressing your ideas, such as when you are asked to "write a reflection," assist you with clarifying what you know?

We acknowledge that we are setting high expectations for teachers. They must design experiences so that students use their process skills in the quest for scientific understanding even as they learn to communicate those understandings to others. For English language learners and students with cognitive disabilities, the teacher should not stop there. As students communicate ideas through alternative means, the teacher should step in and model for students what their explanation might look like when expressed in a traditional, written manner. This could involve something as simple as the teacher writing a brief explanation on an overhead projector or on colorful charts posted around the room. Through these activities, English language learners are offered another opportunity to acquire English as they are learning science. Also this approach assists students with cognitive disabilities who will be more likely to encode or remember scientific ideas. Teachers need to model more formal means of communicating ideas for students but only after students have arrived at these notions themselves—an idea we will revisit throughout this book.

Point–Counterpoint

There is considerable appeal to the ideas of multiple intelligences and learning styles, although there is a growing controversy. Proponents regard the concept of learning styles as a very useful tool for thinking more broadly about students' capabilities. But others worry that learning styles may actually interfere with high-quality teaching. So in response to the question "How useful is the concept of learning styles?" we provide two contrasting views.

The Problems and Misuses of Learning Styles Information

Marcy Driscoll
Professor of Psychology and Dean of College of Education,
Florida State University

"He's a visual learner." "She's an auditory learner." "He's a right-brained dominant learner." When I overhear teachers making statements such as these about the students in their classes, I cringe. Don't get me wrong. These teachers' hearts are in exactly the right place.

They know that today's classrooms are very diverse places. Children come to school with a wide range of knowledge and skills, representing different races, ethnicities, and cultures and having had a multitude of different home experiences. There is no question that students have different learning needs, and it is up to the teacher to determine what those needs are and then attempt to meet them.

However, there being different student needs does not mean teachers should use learning styles to guide their instruction. The notion of "learning styles" is so intuitively appealing that it has been transformed into a big business. Web sites, reference books, and other sources offer questionnaires to identify learning styles and instructional strategies to accommodate to learning styles. But as much as I support the value in teaching students as individual learners, I have some problems with the learning style movement.

Learning style is defined as the way a learner prefers to take in and process information. Proponents argue that mismatches between student learning styles and instructional strategies can lead to student boredom, problems with motivation, and lack of achievement. Many researchers have experimented to see whether matching instructional style with learning styles improves learning. Most of these efforts have failed to show any advantage of matched instruction over mismatched instruction. Time and again, researchers, using one kind of student characteristic or learning style after another, consistently find no difference between groups. There simply is very little empirical evidence to support the construct of learning styles.

The authors of a recent research article describing a learning styles inventory cautioned about its use, and their comments echo my concerns. The use of learning style inventories doesn't point to particular strengths or weaknesses regarding a student's ability to learn. Too often, learning style information leads to labeling students as certain types of learners. In addition, teachers may use learning styles as a justification for providing students with activities simply because of the supposed preferences. This is not the intended use of learning style inventories, but it seems to happen quite often. Although a learning style framework is meant to encourage teachers to use a variety of strategies, too often it seems teachers restrict their efforts because they perceive some students can learn only through methods that match a particular learning style.

Designing effective instruction should be an important goal for any teacher. I agree. But trying to design effective instruction based on learning style preferences has been proved over and over not to work. Rather, it is more important for all students to be exposed to a variety of ways for representing and processing information. In other words, learning styles should promote a wider range of teaching strategies. The more connections students can create in their memory and the more senses they use during learning, the more durable will be the knowledge and skills they acquire. We do know that research shows that effective instruction consists of three strategies: communicating to the students what they are expected to learn, helping relate the new material to what the students already know, and designing instruction that touches on issues the students care about and see as relevant. These are the guidelines that teachers can follow to assist their students' learning. Knowledge of these principles will help teachers to meet their students' needs. But knowing about students' learning styles will not.

Kathy Manning
Middle School Science Teacher in Shaker Heights, Ohio

Do not train students to learning by force and harshness; but direct them to it by what amuses their minds so that you may be better able to discover with accuracy the peculiar bent of the genius of each.

—Plato

As a middle school science teacher, I love the first day of the school year. I welcome each student at the door, smiling and doing the best interpretation of Mary Poppins I can muster. Each hormonally propelled adolescent begins with a clean slate, and I hold no preconceptions about their strengths and weakness. On the first day, every one of my new students is a creative and intellectual genius. But on the other hand, I really don't like the first few weeks of school because I know nothing about my students. Even though everything seems possible on the first day, it takes me awhile to develop a good sense about how much to push and how much to back away. Developing healthy relationships with my students allows me unbelievable freedom. I can convince them that studying is worthwhile, that thinking is something they can do, and that it is good to learn science. But first I must learn who my students really are.

One tool I use for gaining insights about my students is a learning styles questionnaire I have created. I spend a few minutes preparing them for the "test." They groan and roll their eyes, but their attitudes change when I explain how I will use the information the questionnaire will provide. I tell them that the information will be used to help plan activities, assignments, and assessments that will match their areas of strength. Their honest responses to the questionnaire will help make me a better teacher. After they complete the inventory and we score it, we discuss the significance of the scores. For many, I suspect they want to hear the answer to important questions such as "am I normal?" or "am I stupid?." The scores show that each person is different and that this uniqueness is worthwhile and something to build on.

Using my learning styles questionnaire lets my students know that I am interested in helping them to be successful in science. This information also reminds me that my teaching must rely on an array of strategies so each student can succeed. I use a wide variety of teaching and learning strategies I have gathered over the years. I don't fall into the trap of teaching each student according to his or her learning style. Instead, I use a wide range of approaches because I know that one student's success can create a ripple effect. The learning of one individual extends my reach by helping to advance the learning of others.

One interesting discovery I made about using my questionnaire was the reaction by the parents, which is very positive. I believe part of this is because they appreciate that the teacher is willing to try to get to know their child. Rather than acting as if their child was just one of the hundreds of students I teach, I reveal a genuine interest in the particular qualities of their child. I use the information when I have parent conferences, and they seem to respond well. I'm not sure that the learning styles information is all that important to them, although they are intrigued to fill in the questionnaire themselves. What I think is more powerful is the idea that a science teacher is not only interested in the content. They seem relieved and comforted by my interest in my students.

Finally, by far one of the strongest reasons I've discovered for using the learning styles strategies is that they help identify many reading and learning disabilities or challenges that would otherwise go undetected by me as an untrained learning disability specialist. As a science educator, I am confronted daily with the need to cover more and more content with greater depth. Knowing my students and their ways of learning gives me the insight I can use to provide them with the best possible approach. Though I've never "seen" a million dollars, I know it exists (just not in my bank account). Though the research may not yet prove that learning styles is a perfect education theory, I have other pieces of evidence that support its use. I see with my own eyes the effect it has on my students, the attitudes of the parents, and my appreciation for their uniqueness. I think Plato would approve.

Process Skills With English Language Learners

As part of our commitment to teaching science to all students, we must pay attention to the particular learning needs of those students whose first language is not English. At the moment we are emphasizing the teaching and learning of the science process skills. Perhaps a natural question would be whether there is anything especially important to keep in mind when providing process skill instruction to English language learners. It might be tempting to suggest that there is nothing different we should do when using process skills with these populations. However, we are reluctant to propose that this is a one size fits all situation. The reason for this caution is that it may lead us to disregard the need to differentiate science instruction at all. To avoid that fate, we will turn to research studies concentrating on subject matter learning in multilingual classroom settings.

The Center for Research on Education, Diversity, and Excellence (CREDE) originated with the goal of guiding those students who face the challenges of culture and language differences, race, and poverty to attain their maximum academic potential. CREDE included very useful information about science education to researchers and teachers (e.g., Warren & Rosebery, 2002). The CREDE organization developed a set of *Five Principles for Effective Pedagogy* toward the goal of educational excellence for diverse students. We will use these five principles as a reference point in our discussions of the science learning of diverse student populations. We briefly introduce all five principles here, and for our immediate purpose we will focus on the first principle only. The other standards will be examined at appropriate places in other sections of this book.

Principles for Effective Pedagogy

The CREDE group has organized a quintet of instructional approaches for teaching diverse student populations how to achieve educational excellence. More than simply techniques, the five principles describe a set of guiding approaches. Although some people might claim these standards are indicators of "just good teaching," our perception is somewhat different from this ordinary assertion. As we illustrated early in this text, there are inequities in our current educational system that, in pure and simple language, are unfair to some students. Although the exact causes are not definitive and obvious, there exist achievement gaps in science corresponding to gender, cultural background, native language, and family economic factors. In light of these disparities, it seems a certain level of urgency and earnestness needs to be assigned to the identification and implementation of strategies that will reduce, if not eliminate, such inequities. For those who prefer to treat the five principles as simply recipes for good teaching, we still support their efforts to employ the principles in any classroom. Yet for those students who, both historically and currently, have been inadequately served by mainstream education, the five principles represent an educational imperative. Either way, these *Five Principles for Effective Pedagogy* (Dalton, 1998) are worth learning by those who teach science in the elementary and middle school grades.

1. Joint Productive Activity: Teacher and Students Producing Together
2. Developing Language and Literacy Across the Curriculum
3. Making Meaning: Connecting School to Students' Lives
4. Teaching Complex Thinking
5. Teaching Through Conversation

Each principle constitutes a suite of instructional approaches and embedded assumptions, and it would be too much to try to describe all of them here. Instead, we will return to each principle in separate chapters to interweave the complex ideas inherent in each principle with the relevant aspects of science teaching and learning.

Joint Production of Understanding

The first principle of effective pedagogy for diverse learners describes a situation in which the teacher purposefully works side by side with the students to understand scientific ideas (see Table 3.1). In this case, the teacher is seen as the expert learner and the student is an apprentice to those ways of thinking, doing, and knowing (Rogoff, 1990). By teacher and students working to resolve a practical problem or achieve a shared goal, the work becomes a joint effort. The beauty of this principle is the creation of a common experience within the context of the science classroom wherein the teacher and students are coconstructing scientific understandings. Despite differences in individual cultural backgrounds, the joint work not only assists students' learning of science but also can support communicating skills and encourage the appropriate use of academic language (LAB at Brown University, 2002). A distinguishing feature of this principle is recognizing the teacher as an active member of and participant with the community of science learners.

The implications for this principle become somewhat clearer when we examine actions teachers could take that would support the joint production of understanding. On the surface, this principle may seem to simply reinforce the idea of group work. However, there is more nuance at play as the teacher joins in—not just in a playful sense but in a genuine engagement—with the problems, questions, or activities. Furthermore, by engaging in productive

TABLE 3.1. Joint Productive Activity and the Appropriate Teacher Actions

The teacher plans learning activities that promote collaboration toward a shared goal.

The time allotted for a joint productive activity is sufficient to complete the tasks.

The seating of people encourages individuals to work and talk together.

The teacher joins in the activity with his or her students.

Grouping occurs in a variety of arrangements: friendships, mixed academic abilities, blended language fluencies, and matched individual personalities—in short an array of efforts to support interactions.

The teacher instructs the students about the social skills required as part of working in groups.

The teacher structures the access to materials and monitors time (e.g., efficient transitions, allowance for cleaning up, etc.) to facilitate joint productive activity.

Note. Adapted from Dalton (1998).

activities, the teacher creates a mechanism that supports language development, all the while in the context of authentic activities. In other words, in the midst of doing science, the teacher is modeling more formal ways of communicating that students can perceive as an example they can follow. As a result, students' language use becomes richer and more sophisticated.

Let's bring this idea of joint productive activity back to our preceding discussion of the basic science process skills. As further support of our efforts to discard the myth of "teachers as experts," engaging with students in science activities seems appropriate. Actually, for a teacher to take a seat with a group of students as they observe, predict, measure, and so on with a group of interesting objects (pinecones, seashells, cereal box labels) not only is okay but represents good teaching. To the uninitiated, the thought of a teacher joining in with his or her students during a hands-on activity seems charming. But the savvy educator will recognize this action as much more substantive. In talking with students about their work, the teacher models effective communication, encourages the voicing of ideas, and creates a forum in which all children, and especially English language learners, can enhance their facility at oral communication.

By now you should be developing a sense about the power and utility of infusing science teaching with the basic science process skills. A key theme is the necessity of giving students many opportunities to apply these process skills firsthand through their study of actual objects. But here we are not talking about activities that the teacher steps back and allows the students to perform; rather the first principle of effective pedagogy in terms of diverse student populations is the value of the teacher's joining in during productive science activities. There is even clear evidence not only that a focus on science process skills is appropriate for students with various cognitive disabilities but also that such an emphasis is actually beneficial to the learning of such students (Mastropieri & Scruggs, 1992). Before concluding our formal consideration of the basic science process skills, we will devote some attention to the way the process skills are inherent within the *National Science Education Standards*. Also, before the chapter is over, we will address the concerns sometimes expressed about teaching elementary and middle school science using the science process skills.

Process Skills and Science Standards

With all the emphasis placed on the science process skills, you might expect that they would have a prominent place in standards documents. However, if you obtained a copy of the *National Science Education Standards* (National Research Council, 1996), you might be surprised to not find "process skills" in the index. Process skills first became a substantial feature of elementary and middle school science and teaching learning forty years ago. The reason for the shift four decades ago was the response to the Russian launch of the Sputnik satellite. This event, which signaled a threat to America's scientific, educational, and military superiority, was used to leverage changes in science teaching, especially through the development of an innovative science curriculum.

One common goal of the elementary and middle school science programs of the 1960s was to shift from traditional, textbook-based science materials to more active, hands-on activities. The reformers imagined that science instruction should not occur with students sitting quietly at their desks and taking turns reading from their textbooks. Instead, the students would be working with equipment, talking with each other, and experiencing science in ways consistent with how science was actually done. This shift in student activity was accompanied by a shift in science curriculum. Books are an ideal way to push scientific vocabulary. However, activities are not as obviously linked to vocabulary enrichment. Within this new approach to science instruction, an emphasis was placed on the science process skills.

One of the more well-known curriculum projects of the 1960s and 1970s was "Science: A Process Approach," also known as SAPA. SAPA was developed under the aegis of the American Association for the Advancement of Science (AAAS) and ultimately contained more than one hundred activities within its K-6 program. The structure of the activities, the presence of a considerable amount of equipment, and the absence of text materials sent a clear message to teachers: learning scientific facts in elementary school was not nearly as important as comprehending the processes used by scientists. This was tightly connected to the belief that science learning should happen by actually doing science, not simply reading about it. For a variety of reasons, partly financial but also political, the SAPA program was unable to sustain itself. In the 1980s, several researchers (Bredderman, 1983, 1985; Shymansky, Kyle, & Alport, 1983) evaluated previously published studies of SAPA and other programs of the post-Sputnik era and found that these materials were at least as good at helping children learn as teaching science from textbooks alone, and in most instances they were better. Measures of the students' creativity and science process knowledge were higher for students who used this activity-based program than for students who did not use it. But there was still much left to be desired, an issue we will return to in chapter 9 when we examine more recent kit-based science programs.

Process Skills: In Context and With Content

What is the reason for this history lesson? In part it shows how science teaching and learning is continually changing. This means that the way you approach teaching science at the start of your career will not be the same as the way that you were taught science in elementary and middle school. In particular, standards and accountability are much more influential nowadays than even just a few years ago. One lesson is to recognize that education is in a constant state of flux. The other lesson is to prepare yourself for those who might question the emphasis placed on science process skills. It seems possible that the resistance to building science teaching around process skills is an overreaction to the emphasis given to process skills in previous generations of science curriculum. However, that's only our speculation. Closer to the truth is probably the view that students really can't and shouldn't learn science by mastering the process skills in isolation from science content. In particular, the authors of the *National Science Education Standards* have made it clear that they see science learning as necessarily combining the learning of science process skills with science content:

> The new vision [as presented in the *Standards*] includes the "processes of science" and requires that students combine processes and scientific knowledge as they use scientific reasoning and critical thinking to develop their understanding of science. (National Research Council, 1996, p. 105)

This desire is strengthened as shown in a diagram (see Table 3.2) within the *National Science Education Standards* in which the old ways of science teaching and learning are indicated as being something to which we should be giving less emphasis (the left-hand column) and the preferred ways of going about science teaching are indicated as things that deserve more emphasis (the right-hand column).

There is much in this diagram that we support. Specific to our immediate concern is the third line down that highlights a shift we endorse: science process skills should be used within the context of learning significant science content. However, we feel the next line down in the table is perhaps too idealistic by claiming that individual process skill use should be de-emphasized. First of all, it makes good educational sense to present students who are new to learning science with clearly defined process skills. We can see a danger in students using only one process skill

TABLE 3.2. Changing Emphases for Inquiry as Identified Within the *National Science Education Standards* (National Research Council, 1996)

Less Emphasis On	More Emphasis On
Activities that demonstrate and verify science content	Activities that investigate and analyze science questions
Investigations confined to one class period	Investigations over extended periods of time
Process skills out of context	Process skills in context
Emphasis on individual process skills such as observation or inference	Using multiple process skills—manipulation, cognitive, and procedural
Getting an answer	Using evidence and strategies for developing or revising an explanation
Science as exploration and experiment	Science as argument and explanation
Providing answers to questions about science content	Communicating science explanations
Individuals and groups of students analyzing and synthesizing data without defending a conclusion	Groups of students often analyzing and synthesizing data after defending conclusions
Doing few investigations to leave time to cover large amounts of content	Doing more investigations to develop understanding, ability, values of inquiry, and knowledge of science content
Concluding inquiries with the result of the experiment	Applying the results of experiments to scientific arguments and explanations
Management of materials and equipment	Management of ideas and information
Private communication of student ideas and conclusions to teacher	Public communication of student ideas and work to classmates

at a time. But we aren't fearful that you or most other teachers are going to take such a narrow path. Also the ways in which students should be expected to learn science do not necessarily have to be identical with the ways in which scientists do science (Millar & Driver, 1987). Perhaps in previous generations, where science education was seen as a site for nurturing future scientists, this would be appropriate. However, this perspective is much too limiting. Our new challenge is to make scientific literacy a possibility for all students. Viewing the science process skills as an integral feature of the actions of the scientific culture, although not as all there is to science, we have become convinced that teaching with an eye toward science process skills is an appropriate entry point for beginning elementary and middle school teachers.

We have found that the science process skills serve as a very important way for new teachers to learn about science teaching. Everyone needs to start learning somewhere. We accept the claim that science process skills alone are not enough, and we are not saying they are enough. But every new teacher needs a place to begin, and any book about how to teach science must start somewhere. From our professional experiences, and from the feedback we've received from former students who return to us for graduate studies, the science process skills serve as an excellent jumping-off point. The list of basic science process skills is fairly easy to remember (you can invent your own mnemonic device if you want to memorize all six), and it is not especially difficult to find opportunities to incorporate them into almost any hands-on science activity. Even though you will discover that science should not simply begin and end with the process skills, they are a powerful foundation on which you can build the other knowledge and skills for teaching science.

We suggest that you put the science process skills at the very core of your science teaching repertoire. We will show you how to add another layer around this nucleus: how to plan lessons. On top of this we will add layers to help you improve your use of discussions and skill at asking questions. Later you will develop more knowledge about other curriculum materials, assessment strategies, and educational technology. At the middle will always be the science process skills—they aren't enough on their own, but there is so much we can build around them once you recognize their value, simplicity, and power. Did the authors of the *National Science Education Standards* exaggerate their concern about the presence of the science process skills? Perhaps, but because they did so many other things well in that document, we won't complain over the neglect of the process skills.

The Scientific Worldview

The culture of science represents a way of thinking, knowing, and being in the world that all students should learn. Teaching science to children is powerful because you can provide your students access to the culture of science—and all the political, monetary, societal, and other types of power it can provide. We have presented the six basic science process skills as components of the culture of science that are accessible to all students from kindergarten to the higher grades. Knowing how to use the science process skills can be an important framework for assisting students to engage in genuine scientific study. When process skills are used in the context of scientific information, they will support the students in their acquisition of scientific content knowledge. In short, the process skills provide all students with access to the scientific worldview.

One approach used by science methods instructors to drive this home is to assign their preservice teachers to participate in a moon investigation (e.g., Abell, George, & Martini, 2002). When we use this assignment in our methods course, we ask our students to maintain a "moon diary" for one month. We ask them to draw the moon's shape each night, note its location, pose questions that come to mind, and keep track of their thinking along the way. At the end of the four weeks, they are to write a summary paper in which, among other things, they report their use of the science process skills. Often to their surprise, they discover that they have used all six science process skills. For example by characterizing the moon's shape as oval or more like a watermelon rind, they have classified. Through classroom discussions, they also develop conceptual understandings of moon phases, eclipses, and other fairly abstract ideas. Consequently, these future teachers develop a scientific worldview.

Despite the power of a scientific worldview, it is limiting. Other worldviews are equally important and can help us be well-rounded human beings. There are many aspects of being a person and posing questions about our surroundings that science cannot adequately address. Science is of very little help when it comes to arts, spirituality, and justice, to name a few features of the human experience. This is all an effort to advocate for science as an important part of the elementary and middle school curriculum. However, despite our passion for the subject, we must acknowledge that other worldviews are important. An illustration of this is the following poem by Billy Collins (1998). Notice that although he is not relying on a scientific worldview, he quite adeptly captures in his poem a way of understanding the moon that relies on a different collage of perspectives.

"Invention" by Billy Collins

Tonight the moon is a cracker,
with a bite out of it
floating in the night,
and in a week or so
according to the calendar
it will probably look
like a silver football,
and nine, maybe ten days ago
it reminded me of a thin bright claw.
But eventually—
by the end of the month,
I reckon—
it will waste away
to nothing,
nothing but stars in the sky,
and I will have a few nights
to myself,
a little time to rest my jittery pen.

The worldview of poetry is an alternative to the worldview of science.

Experiencing the Scientific Worldview

Recognizing that it is quite limiting to only talk about a scientific worldview, we are providing you with an activity that requires only very basic materials. The pendulum was a tool that Galileo used during his studies of objects in motion. Its simplicity makes it an excellent object for reinforcing a worldview that is consistent with the culture of science. You can perform this activity by yourself, but we encourage you to find someone else to collaborate with on this project.

A pendulum is an interesting object to investigate in collaboration with someone else. To make a pendulum you need a piece of string (at least thirty centimeters long) and some object you can tie to it that is heavy enough to cause the string to hang straight. Tie the object to one end of the string, hold the other end of the string so it is well anchored and won't move, and push the object to make it swing from side to side. Don't contribute any force to the pendulum once it starts swinging. When released, the weight should have all the impetus needed to keep swinging. If your anchor hand twitches and wiggles, then the pendulum will slow down prematurely. Keep the anchor steady. Now find a way to keep track of time while counting the number of swings the pendulum makes.

Count the number of times your pendulum swings in fifteen seconds. Try it a few times, without changing where you hold the string or anything else, until you obtain consistent results. Because you now have some experiences, you are going to predict (and not guess) what will happen to the pendulum when you change the conditions.

1. If you change where you hold the string so the anchor point is closer to the weight, do you predict that the number of swings in fifteen seconds will increase, decrease, or stay the same? What does your coworker predict? Use the materials to check your predictions.

2. What will happen if you change the height from which you release the weight? In other words, if you raise the weight so the angle the string makes is larger, will the number of swings increase, decrease, or stay the same? Does your coworker's prediction match with yours? After discussing the possibilities and deciding on your prediction, see what happens.

3. Find another weight you can add to the string. What do you think will happen if you keep everything about the pendulum the same (same length, same angle, etc.) but have a heavier weight on the end: will the number of swings increase, decrease, or stay the same? Does your coworker agree with you? Once again, see what you find out by actually testing the pendulum.

What you notice and how you attempt to explain these facts reflect your ability to observe and infer. When you wonder about the behavior of the pendulum and are puzzled by the data, then you're experiencing the habits of mind of curiosity and skepticism.

It isn't uncommon for the investigation of pendulums to produce surprising results. There is something counterintuitive about the results. We often expect more factors to be the cause of differences in the swing rate of a pendulum than we end up discovering. When our expectations are different from the experimental results, we find ourselves in disequilibrium. In a way, the puzzling results are similar to the actions of the pendulum. Essentially, you perturb the pendulum system by lifting the weight and releasing it. In much the same way, having data in front of you that doesn't align with your expectations is also perturbing. The pendulum's response to being perturbed is to swing from side to side until it stops in a stable position. Likewise when your thinking is perturbed, you may find yourself puzzling over an explanation and perhaps developing or acquiring an explanation that puts you back into balance. This is when your mind is going through accommodation. Along the way, you've veered into the culture of science and come into contact with elements of the scientific worldview. Perhaps you've even noticed that this experience has given you renewed interest in what it's like to learn science.

Chapter Summary

- Measuring is a special form of observing through the use of a tool that extends our senses. Measurements represent quantitative observations and are based on accepted standard units.

- Proper use of various measuring tools and proficiency with the metric system are largely a matter of familiarity. The more frequently these tools are used, the simpler they seem to be.

- Predicting allows students to test their ideas by forecasting what will happen. By posing predictions and then testing their accuracy, students and scientists can begin to uncover patterns. On those occasions when predictions turn out to be incorrect, the cognitive disequilibrium that is produced becomes a motivation for understanding what was really happening.

- Communicating is directly connected to the other science process skills. Whenever communicating occurs without being tied to any science process skills, the communication is being used for some purpose other than science.

- The process skills not only represent how science is done (what we have taken to calling the "actions of science") but also become tools for enhancing student learning. Measuring helps to focus and refine observing, predicting encourages the seeking of patterns, and communicating leads to the clarification of individual's understanding. In each case, the ideal situation is one in which these process skills are being used with actual objects and not simply representations (pictures or texts) of objects.

- The science learning of all students, but especially those who are not yet fluent in English, benefits by the teacher's becoming part of the learning community. By teachers working jointly with students as everyone applies the process skills, the shared participation strengthens understandings of content and language.
- Science is one approach for understanding our world and should not be regarded as superior to any other worldview. Nevertheless, by becoming fluent within the culture of science, students have access to forms of power that can give them more control over their lives.

Key Terms

Accommodation: learning that occurs as a person encounters ideas that do not fit into his or her existing views, and he or she must reorganize the existing mental frameworks.

Assimilation: learning that occurs as new ideas are simply incorporated into a person's existing views.

Communication: the broadest of the scientific process skills and involves the transmission or exchange of ideas through a wide range of media, including verbal means, written text, drawings, and graphs.

Disequilibrium: the feeling of discomfort that occurs when one encounters new ideas that do not fit into her or his existing views. It is a feeling that a person can overcome by reorganizing his or her existing mental framework to accommodate the new idea.

Measuring: a science process skill in which a person makes a quantitative determination of the physical world through the use of standard comparison tool such as a ruler.

Piaget, Jean (1896-1980): a Swiss learning theorist whose most profound contribution was the notion that what people can understand from an experience depends in large part on the prior knowledge they bring with them. He coined the idea that a learner's understandings must adapt in the face of new information, through either assimilation or accommodation.

Predicting: a scientific process skill that involves making a statement based on some scientific knowledge claim that forecasts what will happen in the future. Predictions are often thought to be a useful means for testing the utility of scientific knowledge claims.

Qualitative: a qualitative observation is a form of observation in which numbers are not employed.

Quantitative: a quantitative observation is a form of observation that incorporates the use of numbers such as by counting or measuring.

Vygotsky, Lev (1893–1934): a Russian psychologist whose work emphasized the roles of historical, cultural, and social factors in thought and learning. He said that before a person can internalize knowledge on the internal plane, he or she must first share that idea with others on the social plane.

A Favorite Science Lesson

The "Changes of State" unit developed by the Education Development Center was designed for use in grades four or five. It presents students with the key ideas associated with the water cycle. The activity "Melting: How Fast Can Ice Change State" is characteristic of the high quality of learning experiences provided in this unit. Students are challenged to design an investigation that measures how quickly an ice cube can be made to melt. As their work gets underway, the students are to keep records by writing what they observe and recording the temperatures. Each group could be studying something different, and the postactivity discussion is a time to lead students to recognize that warmer surrounding temperatures and smaller pieces of ice will melt the fastest. Along the way, students are using all of the basic science process skills. They maintain qualitative and quantitative observations, predict the results, classify their findings, and so on. Even though watching ice cubes melt may not seem like something students would find interesting, the design of the lesson encourages them to conduct careful investigations and pay attention to the results.

Suggested Readings

Hoffman, J., & Strong, J. (2002). Electric connections. *Science and Children, 40*(3), 22–25.
>   These two teachers describe the use of predicting and the many other aspects of basic electricity. What is key to this collection of activities is that the students are prompted to evaluate the accuracy of their predictions once the materials are put into use.

Phillips, S. K., Duffrin, M. W., & Geist, E. A. (2004). Be a food scientist. *Science and Children, 41*(4), 24–29.
>   Teachers reinforced the connections between math and science with an emphasis on food preparation with their fourth and fifth graders. The extended unit of food science proved to be an excellent way to build students' skills at a wide array of measuring approaches.

References

Abell, S., George, M., & Martini, M. (2002). The moon investigation: Instructional strategies for elementary science methods. *Journal of Science Teacher Education, 13,* 85–100.

Bredderman, T. (1983). Effects of activity-based elementary science on student outcomes: A quantitative synthesis. *Review of Educational Research, 53,* 499–518.

Bredderman, T. (1985). Laboratory programs for elementary science: A meta-analysis of effects on learning. *Science Education, 69,* 577–591.

Collins, B. (1998). Invention. *The Atlantic, 282*(6), 92.

Dalton, S. S. (1998). *Pedagogy matters: Standards for effective teaching practice.* Washington, DC: Center for Applied Linguistics.

LAB at Brown University. (2002). *The diversity kit: An introductory resource for social change in education.* Providence, RI: Brown University.

Mastropieri, M. A., & Scruggs, T. E. (1992). Science for students with disabilities. *Review of Educational Research, 62,* 377–411.

Millar, R., & Driver, R. (1987). Beyond processes. *Studies in Science Education, 14,* 33–62.

National Research Council. (1996). *National science education standards.* Washington, DC: National Academy Press.

Rogoff, B. (1990). *Apprenticeship in thinking: Cognitive development in social context.* Oxford, England: Oxford University Press.

Shymansky, J. A., Kyle, W. M., & Alport, J. M. (1983). The effects of new science curricula on student performance. *Journal of Research in Science Teaching, 20,* 387–404.

Warren, B., & Rosebery, A. S. (2002). *Teaching science to at-risk students: Teacher research communities as a context for professional development and school reform.* Santa Cruz, CA: Center for Research on Education, Diversity, and Excellence.

four
Approaches to Science Instruction

Chapter Highlights

- Teaching science using a discovery approach is very unstructured. Students directly engage with materials and use their natural curiosity to guide their learning.
- Students require support while they participate in inquiry-based activities. Teachers adjust the level of support depending on the purpose of the inquiry and the abilities of the students.
- Teachers who use inquiry-based instruction must incorporate the five essential features: a question to study, data to gather, evidence to use to form explanations, connections to make to other sources of science knowledge, and explanations to communicate to others.
- Conceptual change instruction aims to have students replace incorrect ideas about the natural world with more scientific explanations. Making students' ideas explicit is a significant first step of conceptual change instruction.
- Teachers of science base their teaching decisions, in part, on their philosophical beliefs. Their ideas about how children learn and the ultimate goals of science education influence their instructional practices.
- When discovery and inquiry science teaching are implemented, a teacher may not necessarily attend to students' background experiences. In contrast, a teacher implementing conceptual change instruction has an explicit focus on the students' prior knowledge. As a result, conceptual change instruction is better predisposed toward use with diverse populations.

A Variety of Science Teaching Approaches

The focus of this chapter is on a trio of contrasting approaches to science teaching. None of these approaches requires the teacher to follow a strict instructional sequence. Instead each represents an underlying philosophy about science and learning. It is from these philosophies that the three teaching models emerged. We present these three models sequentially, but that does not mean that the oldest model has been completely replaced by its successors. The truth is that all three approaches are still used to teach science. An effective classroom teacher should recognize the strengths and limitations of each model.

Teaching Science Through Discovery

The **discovery approach,** perhaps the oldest of the three, is a model of science teaching that places great confidence in children's ability to make sense of their world. In a discovery activity, the teacher provides students with access to plenty of materials and time to explore those materials. This is consistent with the ways in which scientists work. Direct contact with the natural world is seen as the necessary initial step to discovery learning. From there, it is thought that science learning naturally falls into place.

A substantial push to teach science by discovery began in the 1950s. After World War II the United States experienced a severe shortage of scientists. This was not because so many scientists died in combat but because the demand for technicians and scientists grew so rapidly. The general belief was that the scientific innovativeness of the United States was the deciding factor in the winning of World War II and that if the nation was to remain strong militarily speaking, there was a need for more scientists. This need for scientists prompted a desire for dramatic improvements in how science was taught in high schools, which translated into changes in the earlier grades as well. The successful launch of the first orbiting satellite by the Soviet Union, rather than by the United States, prompted President Eisenhower to sign a $1 billion allotment for the National Defense Education Act (Rudolph, 2002a).

In the fall of 1959, thirty-five individuals attended a ten-day conference at Woods Hole Oceanographic Institute. The purpose of this meeting was to discuss how science might be taught so more students would enter scientific fields. The person organizing the conference was Jerome Bruner, a Harvard psychologist—indeed, it is noteworthy that over a fourth of the attendees were psychologists. Two people in attendance were from the education field, although one was from a testing company. The rest of the group members were predominantly from the sciences (biology and physics) and mathematics. Women were barely represented.

As professionals in fields other than teaching, the people at the Woods Hole Conference viewed the world from the vantage point of their scholarly positions. They were passionate about their specialty areas and wanted to instill that same enthusiasm in students. Jerome Bruner captured the appeal of teaching science through discovery in his book *The Process of Education,* which serves as a written summary of the conference. Read the following paragraph carefully, because we will use it to examine the beliefs of those who endorsed a discovery approach.

The Appeal of Teaching Science Through Discovery

Mastery of the fundamental ideas of a field involves not only the grasping of general principles but also the development of an attitude toward learning and inquiry; toward guessing and hunches, toward the possibility of solving problems on one's own. Just as a physicist has certain attitudes about the ultimate orderliness of nature and a conviction that order can be discovered, so a young physics student needs some working version of these attitudes if he is to organize his learning in such a way as to make what he learns usable and meaningful in his thinking. To instill such attitudes by teaching requires something more than the mere presentation of fundamental ideas. Just what it takes to bring off such teaching is something on which a great deal of research is needed, but it would seem that an important ingredient is a sense of excitement about discovery—discovery of regularities previously unrecognized relations and similarities between ideas, with a resulting sense of self-confidence in one's abilities. Various people who have worked on curricula in science and mathematics have urged that it is possible to present the fundamental structure of a discipline in such a way as to preserve some of the exciting sequences that lead a student to discover for himself. (Bruner, 1960, p. 20)

Attitudes Within Discovery Learning

Given the predominance of scientists at the Woods Hole Conference, it is remarkable that they perceived the value in developing student attitudes. This suggests that these scientists had reflected on what had attracted them to their respective fields and were seeking ways to use those attractors to draw a new generation of students into science. Simply learning the subject matter was not enough; in their view the study of science should also lead students to understand how to solve problems without any interference from a teacher. Although Bruner didn't use the phrase "process skills" in his writings, he did endorse the importance of doing science as a means of developing healthy and positive attitudes toward the subject.

In addition to improving students' attitudes about science, the Woods Hole conferees also wanted to enhance students' self-confidence in their abilities to become successful in science. Bruner and his colleagues believed that with the right combination of experiences and materials, students would comprehend their surroundings in ways similar to those held by scientists. The students' discoveries would lead them to identify patterns in the natural world. An outgrowth of these events would contribute to an increase in confidence about being able to learn and do science. As a psychologist, Bruner was certainly drawing on Jean Piaget's ideas of disequilibrium and accommodation, but he went even further by suggesting that processes can lead students to place greater trust in themselves. Central to all of this was the deep belief in the power of discovery.

In the 1960s the steps toward improving American science education were not seen as starting with a list of science concepts for students to learn. Instead the attendees of the Woods Hole Conference described the value in instilling positive attitudes about science in students. When Bruner wrote, "An important ingredient is a sense of excitement and curiosity," he was capturing the value of student affect (interest and emotion) as a tool for enhancing science teaching. Discovery learning was viewed as a method for making this happen.

The Structure of the Scientific Discipline

Another common belief that gained support among science education reformers in the years immediately following the Woods Hole Conference was the importance for teachers and students to understand "the structure of the discipline." This phrase was meant to indicate that students of science must be led to understand the most fundamental ideas of science. This is not the same as the "back to basics" movement in education. Indeed we might even think of these two as opposites. The word *basic* can mean the same as the word *simple*. The basics of chemistry might be atoms, and the basics of botany might be plant cells. The building blocks of these scientific fields, for those who support a back to basics approach, are the important ideas that students must master before anything else, almost as if these ideas are the bricks that will be used to build a footpath.

In contrast, the word *fundamentals,* which is what the structure of the discipline was meant to emphasize, is not as concerned about having students master the basics. Instead the goal was for students to understand a small number of powerful ideas essential in explaining particular events. For scientists of the time, including and beyond those at the Woods Hole Conference (as this idea continues to be reflected in current science education reform efforts), science curricula needs to teach students about the major themes of science so they can appreciate the big picture. Bruner and others felt that the structure of the discipline could be taught in an intellectually honest way that was also appropriate to the developmental level of the students.

Within the *National Science Education Standards* (National Research Council [NRC], 1996), remnants from the Woods Hole Conference are evident with the "big scientific ideas" now labeled as "unifying concepts and processes" that the authors of the *Standards* indicate "can be the focus of instruction at any grade level" (p. 104). Their unifying ideas are as follows: (1) systems, order, and organization; (2) evidence, models, and explanation; (3) change, constancy, and measurement; (4) evolution and equilibrium; and (5) form and function. Obviously a classroom teacher would benefit by some indication about specific topics within these themes. Nevertheless, from the time of the Woods Hole Conference until today, there are those who remind us that part of learning science is recognizing the big conceptual picture.

What is in common across the following scenarios: a mirror that becomes fogged in a bathroom, the white lines that form behind a high-flying aircraft, and the ring that a cold beverage leaves behind on the table? From a back to basics perspective, we might want children to identify that these are examples of condensation. In contrast, a structure of the discipline advocate would want the child to be able to explain what happens at the molecular level that causes condensation. The goal of having students understand the structure of the scientific discipline was to work hand in glove with the discovery approach. By giving students the freedom to discover key scientific ideas through their own messing about, advocates felt that more students would be drawn to science. In other words, the **structure of the discipline** philosophy was that students would learn science best when they came to appreciate in ways similar to how scientists think about science.

We can detect in Bruner's paragraph from *The Process of Education* the enthusiasm for having students learn science as if they were actual scientists. He described clear parallels between laboratory science and classroom science (e.g., a physicist and a young physics student). How could science curriculum be designed to accurately represent the structure of the disciplines? Who should bear the responsibility for ensuring that the science curriculum emphasizes the fundamentals of science in genuine ways? The consensus was that this should be the work of those most closely connected to the discipline, namely, professional scientists. This assertion seems entirely predictable given the professions represented at the Woods Hole Conference and is consistent with the post–World War II confidence in using engineering principles to overcome educational problems (Rudolph, 2002a). It is interesting, using what we now know about educational reform, that teachers and teacher educators did not play a significant role in this conference. It is also perplexing that, given the United States's recent reengagement with the world at large by means of World War II, participation in the Woods Hole Conference was engineered without demographic diversity in mind. But such was the mind-set of the time—an almost singular dependence on the knowledge of scientists to craft educational change. We discuss the implications of these decisions in the following sections.

The Targeted Audience

Just as the participants at the Woods Hole Conference were products of their professional cultures, they were also influenced by mainstream society. Like all of us, they were products of the cultural norms of their time. One largely unspoken assumption of this period in American culture was that scientific careers were best suited for men. It is more than a literary convention that explains why only male pronouns appear in the Bruner paragraph quoted earlier. Science was a masculine field, and young men were assumed to be the students who would be most successful in those careers. Indeed ten years after the Woods Hole Conference, only 8 percent of physicians were women. Likewise given that this conference occurred before the civil rights movement gained prominence in the United States, there was the belief that most of those to occupy scientific careers would be White, an understandable assumption given the history of the profession in the United States—indeed, to this point, most scientists and engineers were White men. Given this assumption, curricula were to appeal to a relatively narrow subset of the population: White boys. Little attention was paid to who would be excluded by such an approach to science education, as the goal was not so much to provide science for all but to create and nurture the next generation of scientists. Thus the curriculum that was designed targeted the needs and abilities of a particular demographic—and poorly served other populations of students.

Today our ambition for science is much more inclusive and aims to attract and effectively educate students from across gender, cultural, and linguistic spectra. Today, instead of the goal being to create more scientists, the agenda of science teaching is to assist all students to understand science so they can recognize how it applies to their lives. The goal, if it can be achieved, is for every student to become scientifically literate and to appropriately use the knowledge of science to make wiser and more informed choices in their lives.

Teaching Science Through Inquiry

Perhaps the major shortcoming to teaching science using the discovery approach, aside from its overly narrow student focus, was the unrealistic expectation that students would enter the culture of science and learn science just by messing about with materials. Another issue with teaching in such an open-ended way is that students are not being explicitly guided into the culture of science. Thus this approach may prove to be more productive for children from homes or backgrounds congruent with the norms of science. But for children whose backgrounds or homes are not congruent with science and those who do not share in the culture of their teachers, this approach leaves too much of the actual teaching and learning of science to chance. Unless a teacher provides specific guidelines that give students access to the science culture, there is a very real danger that many students will not recognize and learn the accepted standards of those individuals who are capable participants within the culture of science. For students from backgrounds congruent with those of science, such learning is much more natural and easily engendered. Although we admire the considerable faith placed in students to learn science on their own within an unstructured atmosphere, our belief is that for students to become competent within the science culture, they must be assisted to learn those skills and dispositions—and this is particularly true for those students who have the most to learn in terms of entering the culture of science. The discovery approach fails to supply this vital guidance.

It seems possible that the scientists who advocated the discovery approach held romanticized memories of their childhood experiences and were nostalgic about their youth and how they had learned science. Or it is possible that these scientists came from homes and backgrounds in which science already played prominent roles, so their learning of formal science seemed "natural." Regardless, many argue that discovery is not a fruitful approach if scientific literacy for all students is our goal. In contrast to the relaxed and free-flowing nature of the discovery approach, teaching science through inquiry, the approach that we will examine next, provides more structure while continuing to support the belief that children can learn science by participating in it. Sometimes inquiry is called "guided discovery" (e.g., McBride, Bhatti, Hannan, & Feinber, 2004) to clarify the influence of the teacher on the activities undertaken by the students.

Components of Scientific Inquiry

Joseph Schwab was an educational theorist who was a key player in the development of inquiry curriculum in the 1960s and 1970s. He was influenced by the somewhat novel recognition that science was more than just a collection of information, a view depicted by the science textbooks of the time. Schwab (1960) was concerned that students were learning about the end results of scientists' work without also constructing an understanding of the thought processes the scientists had used to achieve those ends results. The thought processes used by scientists are labeled *inquiry*.

In Schwab's view the role of a teacher was quite different from the more traditional source of scientific knowledge. To help students appreciate scientific inquiry, the teacher was to use activities and discussions to emphasize three components: posing questions, gathering data, and interpreting results. It was believed that students who were taught by teachers using this approach would understand by means of scientific inquiry (Shulman & Tamir, 1973). Schwab understood the need to provide specific support to students as they learned science, and his inquiry approach, unlike discovery science, was crafted to provide this support. Advocates felt that students who were studying science in a classroom where the inquiry approach was being implemented needed to be given the question to investigate, told how to gather the data, and guided in their attempts to interpret the data. The students were to be progressively given more freedom within the three components of inquiry as their competence improved.

NSES Teaching Standard B: Teachers of science guide and facilitate learning. In doing this, teachers encourage and model the skills of scientific inquiry as well as the curiosity, openness to new ideas and data, and skepticism that characterize science.

Scientific inquiry as taught to students was translated into four different levels, as shown in Table 4.1. At Level 0, the lowest level of inquiry, there was a great deal of teacher control over questions, methods, and interpretations. At Level 1, the students were given the freedom to interpret their results while the teacher controlled the questions to be answered and the methods used to answer them. In Level 2, the only component provided to students was the question they were to investigate, and the students controlled the rest. At Level 3, the students essentially had complete control over each of these three components. This provided a useful framework for teachers as they planned the science activities for their students. The idea of gradually turning control over to the students was easier to accept by many teachers than the largely unstructured discovery approach. Especially at the high school level, inquiry was better received than discovery.

TABLE 4.1. Levels of Openness Within the Inquiry Teaching Approach

	Source of the Question	Ways to Gather Data	Interpreting Results
Level 0	Given	Given	Given
Level 1	Given	Given	Open
Level 2	Given	Open	Open
Level 3	Open	Open	Open

The Many Varieties of Inquiry

Just as for many popular educational terms, the term *inquiry* has suffered from overuse. In fact so many people have used *inquiry* with different purposes in mind that it's hard to uncover the intended meaning. Indeed we aren't going to be able to provide you with the single, correct meaning of *inquiry*. What we will do is describe the different varieties of inquiry. As a result you will be able to sort through the meaning when you read or hear *inquiry* in different contexts.

Inquiry can be divided into two major categories. The first is the meaning, used by Schwab and his contemporaries, of scientific inquiry as performed by adult scientists. This type of inquiry describes the work that scientists do. The *National Science Education Standards* described the first category of inquiry in this way:

> Scientific inquiry refers to the diverse ways in which scientists study the natural world and propose explanations based on the evidence derived from their work. (NRC, 1996, p. 23)

When *inquiry* is used in this way, it suggests that inquiry in the classroom could be very similar, if not identical, to the inquiry done by scientists. Imagining children to be junior scientists with smaller bodies and less sophisticated knowledge would align with this inquiry. The second category describes inquiry about the natural world within the context of instruction. Someone speaking of inquiry in this way is thinking about the inquiries students will perform as they learn about science. The inquiry by students describes something slightly different from adult scientists' inquiry:

> Inquiry also refers to the activities of students in which they develop knowledge and understanding of scientific ideas, as well as an understanding of how scientists study the natural world. (NRC, 1996, p. 23)

Because our interest is science teaching and learning, our use of *inquiry* throughout this book will reflect this second description. Elementary and middle school students process the world in different ways than adults do. In other words, there are more profound differences between adults and children besides body size. The implication for teachers is that the inquiry of adult scientists can't realistically be applied to students. Certainly there can be some parallels, but important distinctions remain. We acknowledge that not everyone feels as we do about this, instead perceiving the inquiry by scientists as perfectly acceptable as a model to apply to classroom inquiry by children (Barman, 2002; Martin-Hansen, 2002). We do support the idea that students can inquire about their world. It's just that the focus of the inquiries by elementary and middle school students should recognize their developmental abilities without lowering our expectations of them.

Types of Inquiry-Based Teaching Approaches

Alan Colburn (2000) identified three forms of **inquiry-based science teaching**, and we will connect those to Schwab's levels of inquiry. Colburn, following the tradition of other science educators, used the phrase **structured inquiry** to identify learning activities where the teacher provides the students with the question to be investigated and the methods of gathering data. What the students will learn as a consequence of doing their activity may not be immediately obvious to the students, but the teacher is there to guide them toward an expected conclusion. Despite variations in the data that different students gather, the teacher will assist them in interpreting the information so everyone understands the implications of the results. Structured inquiry is equivalent to Schwab's Level 0.

At the other extreme of inquiry-based teaching is **open inquiry,** which aligns with Schwab's Level 3. In consultation with the teacher, the students are in control of their decisions for each component of their inquiry. A science fair project is a good example of open inquiry: the student develops a question that he or she can investigate, decides the procedures necessary to collect data, and is responsible for interpreting the findings.

Finally there is **guided inquiry,** which is a label for activities within Schwab's Level 1 and Level 2. As the students become more competent at doing science, the teacher will provide activities in which results interpretation and data-gathering methods will gradually be turned over to the students. This is directly connected with the students' abilities to perform the process skills. Once they understand the procedures and the decisions involved in measuring, they will be prepared to make wise choices about how to gather and record data.

Using the Same Materials for Different Inquiries

The kinds of science equipment that a teacher has available should not dictate the form of inquiry they use with their students. The same collection of equipment can be used for structured, open, or guided inquiry. The teacher should choose, on the basis of his or her knowledge of the students and the nature of the content to be taught, how to have the students engage in inquiry. Let us illustrate this with the idea of pendulums.

Imagine a drawer of science equipment that contains string, washers, rulers, and stopwatches. The process of tying a washer to one end of a string, holding the other end so it will swing, and counting the number of swings is the essence of this activity. However, the teacher needs to decide how much guidance to provide to students. If the teacher knows that the students have had experience conducting experiments, he or she might opt for an open inquiry lesson. To be capable with this mode of inquiry, students would need to understand variables and constants; have practiced creating hypotheses; be skilled in collecting, organizing, and graphing data; and be proficient at interpreting results. The teacher's directions for an open inquiry might be, "Find out what factors influence the behavior of a pendulum and be sure to have evidence to support your claims." That is all that is required to introduce an open inquiry.

NSES Teaching Standard B: Teachers of science guide and facilitate learning. In doing this, teachers focus and support inquiries while interacting with students.

For a structured inquiry activity, the teacher identifies in advance the variables that the students would investigate and specify the methods to be used to investigate those variables. The teacher provides a record sheet (such as the one shown in Table 4.2) that students can use to record their data. The students work individually or in pairs to collect their data without much interference by the teacher. Finally, when students are finished with the activity, the teacher takes a central role in interpreting the results. Referring to the Schwab framework, we see that all three components of inquiry are considered closed because the students aren't left to make decisions about the type of questions, the forms of data, or the interpretation of their results.

If the teacher feels the students are sufficiently skilled to make some decisions on their own, then a guided inquiry about pendulums would be appropriate. This determination is based in part on student skill level and in part on the complexity of the investigations. This pendulum activity is rather straightforward given the materials that are available. Thus moving toward guided inquiry seems reasonable for the objects and actions in this experiment. The teacher can start the lesson by having the class brainstorm potential variables (string length, number of washers, angle of release, etc.) and then allow each group to choose the variable they wish to study. Each group will likely have different data, so the students will have to interpret their results. This allows the students to develop the skills needed to eventually do open inquiry while receiving support from their teacher.

Inquiry-based teaching, even though it became fashionable in the 1960s, never became a staple of instruction throughout the United States, perhaps because it is still so different from the traditional, didactic, teacher-centered approach to science instruction (Abrams & Southerland, 2007). But it has not faded away, perhaps because inquiry is so basic to scientists' understanding of their work. Indeed given its prominent role as a centerpiece of the current science education reform documents (NRC, 2000), it seems to be experiencing a revival. Fortunately, teachers are being provided with a more refined way for thinking about the different ways of having their students do inquiry (as detailed in Table 4.3). This revised inquiry framework gives science teachers a better understanding of how we can modify and improve our teaching practices.

TABLE 4.2. Experimental Design Diagram (After Cothron, Giese, & Rezba, 2000)

	Prediction:		
	Length of Pendulum		
	15 cm	30 cm	45 cm
Trial	1.	1.	1.
Trial	2.	2.	2.
Trial	3.	3.	3.
Average			
	Number of swings in 30 seconds:		
	Constants:		

TABLE 4.3. Essential Features of Classroom Inquiry from the *National Science Education Standards* (NRC, 1996)

	Variations			
	More <– – – – – – Amount of Learner Self-Direction– – – – –> Less Less <– – – – – – Amount of Direction from Teacher or Material– – – – –> More			
Essential Features	**Level 4**	**Level 3**	**Level 2**	**Level 1**
1. Learner engages in scientifically oriented questions	Learner poses a question	Learner selects among questions, poses new questions	Learner sharpens or clarifies question provided by teacher, materials, or other source	Learner engages in question provided by teacher, materials, or other source
2. Learner gives priority to evidence in responding to questions	Learner determines what constitutes evidence and collects it	Learner directed to collect certain data	Learner given data and asked to analyze	Learner given data and told how to analyze
3. Learner formulates explanations from evidence	Learner formulates explanation after summarizing evidence	Learner guided in process of formulating explanations from evidence	Learner given possible ways to use evidence to formulate explanation	Learner provided with evidence
4. Learner connects explanations to scientific knowledge	Learner independently examines other resources and forms the links to explanations	Learner directed toward areas and sources of scientific knowledge	Learner given possible connections	
5. Learner communicates and justifies explanations to others	Learner forms reasonable and logical arguments to communicate explanations	Learner coached in development of communication	Learner provided broad guidelines to sharpen communication	Learner given steps and procedures for communication

Essential Features of Classroom Inquiry

As a follow-up to the publication of the *National Science Education Standards,* the NRC issued another document focusing exclusively on inquiry-based teaching (NRC, 2000). In this document, the three components of inquiry from the 1960s were expanded to five essential features. In addition, the designation of open versus closed was discarded in favor of a continuum of learner self-direction.

We will return to this framework in later chapters, but for right now we want you to be aware of its existence and recognize how it builds on preceding ideas about inquiry. You might recognize that if a science activity was at the far left portion of this framework across all five essential features, then that would accurately describe students engaged in open inquiry. But a teacher could also use this framework as a guide to make successive approximations of this highest level of inquiry-based teaching.

Teaching Approaches as Solutions to Problems

Each approach to teaching science is a response to a problem. For example the discovery approach came about in reaction to dissatisfaction with students learning science solely by reading books and listening to the teacher. It wasn't as if somebody started advocating for the discovery approach for no apparent reason. Instead, groups of educators and scientists became increasingly troubled that science in the schools was being represented as little more than a reading topic. The problem of students passively experiencing science was viewed as potentially solvable by moving toward science activities based on a discovery approach.

The discovery approach certainly solved the problem of student inactivity during science. However, it became apparent that activity alone was not sufficient to prompt science learning by children. After all, students can be active when studying with a microscope, but they are also active when they are arbitrarily mixing powders and liquids with one another. Educators became sensitive to the importance of students being productively active more than simply messing about with materials. Put another way, the new problem that emerged once the student passivity problem was fixed highlighted a new problem. That new problem was the challenge of identifying the differences between doing activities in the service of science learning instead of engaging in activities for nonacademic purposes. The difference between engaging in scientific activity and messing about with nonscience activity was to be reduced through the use of the inquiry approach.

Inquiry was distinguished from other forms of activity by the pursuit of questions, the gathering of evidence, and the interpretation of results. This could be regarded as Schwab's legacy: differentiating activities that represented science activity from other forms of activity that were not science. As a result, curriculum developers and science teachers could find some comfort in the mess, noise, and seeming chaos of hands-on activities because they could perceive that the students were participating in inquiry.

Up until this point we have solutions to two problems: (1) the problem of passive student learning, which was solved by the shift to discovery, and (2) the problem of differentiating science from what might be regarded as playtime, which was resolved by the move toward inquiry. The inadequacies that arose in the process of solving one problem were addressed, at least in theory, by the next approach. However, yet another new problem emerged. Upon careful examination it became apparent that the students were not learning what their science teachers and the curriculum developers had intended. In effect the mistaken notions the students brought to the classroom, despite considerable exposure to concrete materials and the extended involvement in science inquiry, remained unaffected. While the students were supposedly learning the science they were being taught, they still held on to their nonschool ideas about how the natural world operates. This situation was not immediately obvious, because students could provide correct answers to teachers' questions in the classroom. But outside of that setting, many students continued to rely on their nonscientific ideas. It was as if the students had two compartments in their minds for science: one compartment held "school science" knowledge and the other held their "real world" knowledge.

This was not simply a learning problem with younger students. When scientific misconceptions were found to persist for physics majors (e.g., McDermott, 1984), then the problem became a genuine concern—and it was a problem that inquiry seemed unable to solve. Inquiry wasn't necessarily wrongheaded; in fact it was quite to the contrary. We might have to admit that if it wasn't for the inquiry science agenda, we may not have ever reached the point where scientific misconceptions, and their clear persistence among who should be the most knowledgeable science students, factored into the goal of helping students become scientifically literate. However, there is overwhelming evidence from thousands of such studies within the educational research literature that scientific misconceptions are very persistent. (For a summary of the misconception literature, see Carmichael et al. [1990]; Pfundt & Duit [1994]; and Wandersee, Mintzes, & Novak [1994].) An example illustrating these difficulties can be found in the NRC's *Science Teaching Reconsidered* (1997, pp. 27–28):

> A familiar example from elementary school is students' understanding of the relationship between the earth and the sun. While growing up, children are told by adults that the "sun is rising and setting," giving them an image of a sun that moves about the earth. In school, students are told by teachers (years after they have already formed their own mental model of how things work) that the earth rotates. Students are then faced with the difficult task of deleting a mental image that makes sense to them, based on their own observations, and replacing it with a model that is not as intuitively acceptable. This task is not trivial, for students must undo a whole mental framework of knowledge that they have used to understand the world.

Much of the difficulty students have in learning science does not result from their *lack* of understanding. Rather students regularly bring preconceived notions about natural phenomena into classroom discussions of science topics. However, students' everyday ways of thinking are often at odds with the scientific explanation being promoted in the classroom. The difficulty then becomes changing or shaping students' previously held conceptions. Such changing or reshaping becomes difficult, as these explanations have served the students adequately for a number of years, so discarding this useful (although unscientific) notion becomes difficult for most students.

The proposed solution to this newly defined problem, as one might come to expect from science educators, was a different combination of instructional approaches and curriculum materials. More than having students working with materials (i.e., a discovery approach) or using materials as they think like scientists (i.e., the inquiry approach), the new solution took the form of the conceptual change approach. As the name of the approach suggests, the focus was on changing students' science conceptions with the goal of having students discard or reshape their nonscientific explanations of natural phenomena in favor of the explanations accepted within the scientific community.

Conceptual Change Approach to Science Teaching

What are the differences between the mind of a professional scientist and the mind of a student? Is it the size, the number of brain cells, or the amount of information? Perhaps, but there is more than quantity that explains the differences. The ways in which those minds function are very different. Although the advocates for discovery and early inquiry approaches recognized this, even as they made reference to Piaget, they didn't take this difference into account as they created curriculum.

There is a great deal of selecting involved before an individual ultimately becomes an expert in a particular field. Sometimes this involves self-selection where individuals choose to follow a certain ambition. In other cases selection happens because all the aspirants are competing against each other and some are eventually eliminated. Consider the number of girls who attend gymnastics programs and camps and how many of them will actually qualify for the Olympics. Planning for science instruction using professional scientists as role models is unlikely to lead to an inclusive science program. If our goal is to teach science so every child can develop scientific literacy, we can't rely on plans where many more would be eliminated than would be allowed to advance.

Limits to the Novice/Expert Perspective

One problem with attempting to apply the novice/expert perspective to educational settings is that it ignores individual differences. We cannot study a masterful chess player and then claim that we know how to convert a novice into an expert. Even after identifying the very clear differences between the decision-making process for novices and experts, we won't have the formula for creating new experts. The current experts all rose to the top from among thousands of other novices. What happened to all the others? They found something else that interested them more than chess or were drawn to activities in which they seemed to be more skilled.

A third approach to science teaching, conceptual change, came about in response to studies of how children learn science. The discovery and inquiry approaches have as their starting points the ways in which scientists do their work. These approaches treat professional science as the goal of science learning, and the teaching and curriculum that accompany the approaches are designed to move students, regardless of starting points, toward that goal. However, connecting the dots between a student of science and the professional scientist has proved to be not quite that simple. The flaw is in using the expert as the model for all students. It's as if we could re-create a new generation of experts by using the biographies of the experts as our road map. If this held true, then designing curriculum would be easy. To teach children math all we'd have to do is ask the experts to recall what it was that they liked about math when they were young. For history, we'd ask the historians to remember what they experienced that made them want to study history for the rest of their life. All that would be required is for the schools to provide the same experiences that propelled professionals into their careers.

Inside the Mind of a Child

Students have ideas about the world that are very different from the ideas scientists have. At one point in time, we might have dismissed students' explanations as simply wrong. But by carefully listening to how children explain their understandings, science educators have found that there are certain logics to the students' ideas and concluded that it is inappropriate to dismiss their thinking as errors that simply need to be corrected.

Rosalind Driver (1989) devoted her career to cataloging the variety of student conceptions, trying to understand what led them to these ideas and then working to develop teaching methods that would move students away from their initial ideas so they became aligned with accepted scientific explanations. This approach, called "conceptual change teaching," reflects the desire to have students discard naive concepts about the world in favor of explanations that are more scientifically accurate. Students are not deliberately resistant to new explanations but are also unlikely to readily discard the ideas that have served them well. Also we do not wish to imply that we are shifting belief systems. We regard "knowing" and "believing" as different realms. **Conceptual change** represents shifts in what an individual knows and not an effort to undo what they may believe.

The first step in teaching with a conceptual change approach is to bring to the surface the ideas the learners possess. This makes hidden ideas apparent to the students and the teacher. For the next step, students participate in an activity in which their current ideas come into contact with evidence that contradicts what they know. In this way, their current knowledge shows that it is insufficient for explaining what is observed. Students propose new explanations to account for what they observed in the activity. After students attempt to explain this new situation, the teacher introduces the scientific explanation. With a new explanation in hand, students apply the idea to new situations and materials. Finally, they compare their new conception with the one they started with to see which one seems to better explain the natural world. As a result students restructure their conceptions, exchanging their initially limited ideas for explanations that have broader application. The sequence shown in Figure 4.1 is based on Driver's pioneering work (Driver, 1988).

An Example of the Conceptual Change Approach: The Seasons

A fourth-grade teacher has decided to apply the conceptual change approach as she teaches her students about the cause for the seasons. She begins by having students work in groups of three to create posters showing how they would explain the changing seasons. As she anticipated, most of the posters revealed a belief that the earth's orbit controls the seasons. According to the students, when the earth's orbit brings it closer to the sun, the season is summer, and when the earth is farther from the sun, the season is winter. This is a common misconception (Settlage, 2002). The shortcoming of this conception is that it doesn't explain why the seasons are the opposite in the northern and southern hemispheres.

At the start of the next science lesson, the teacher points out the students' posters from the previous lesson, which are displayed on one classroom wall. To summarize the ideas depicted on them, she draws a diagram that shows the earth orbiting the sun and allows the students to explain that the orbit is not a circle but really more of an oval. Because the sun is not at the cen-

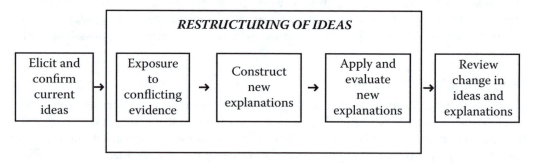

FIGURE 4.1. Basic Framework for Conceptual Change Science Teaching (Driver, 1988)

ter of the orbit, the earth is closer to the sun at certain times of the year. The teacher confirms that astronomers have measured the distance to the sun, and the earth does move in a slightly elliptical path.

The teacher has by now confirmed the explanation that the students currently feel makes sense, and the students are quite aware of their explanations. She then introduces three activities they will perform over the next week. The activities are designed to help students recognize that their current explanations for the seasons are insufficient. For their first activity, they work in pairs to examine photographs taken of the sun at various times of the year. Using the measurements of the sun made from the photographs, the students infer from where along the elliptical orbit the pictures were taken. At some point in this activity the students learn that when the sun appears to be the largest, which, by their understanding would be when it is the shortest distance from the earth, happens to be in January. Likewise when the distance from the earth to the sun is the greatest, and when the sun seems to be smallest, coincides with July.

In the second activity, students are provided with monthly temperature data from a few unidentified cities. Upon graphing this data, the students notice that the peak temperature month is not always the same. For some cities, the highest temperature is in August, whereas for other cities the graph shows that the temperature is the lowest in August. And in the graphs for two cities, there is no detectable difference in temperatures across the twelve months.

The third activity requires students to determine the surface area of the light spot created by a flashlight. Holding the light at the same height every time but at different angles, the students trace the light spot onto a piece of graph paper. Counting the number of squares inside each spot shows that as the angle increases, the size of the light spot also increases.

After the several days necessary for the students to complete these activities, the teacher orchestrates a whole class discussion. Referring to the record sheets the students used to keep track of their work, the teacher guides them to consider an alternative explanation for the seasons. One issue she raises is the discrepancy between the distance to the sun and the time of year. The students' original posters suggest that in summer the sun would be the largest because of its closeness to the earth. But their photographic data show that this is not accurate. Another issue is the recognition that the distance from the sun will not explain the seasonal difference on different places on the earth.

The teacher uses a globe to show how a light beam spreads across the surface more when it shines at a glancing angle compared to when the light shines squarely onto the surface. Gradually the class begins to pull the pieces together. They know the earth is tilted, which would cause the directness of the light rays to vary. When the northern hemisphere leans toward the sun, the light strikes there more intensely than on the southern hemisphere. The teacher guides the students to recognize that the tilt of the earth has more influence on the temperature of the earth than its proximity to the sun.

The teacher then shows her students information about the solar system from a NASA Web site. The students discover that other planets in the solar system have seasons. They learn that the earth's orbit is very close to being circular, not the exaggerated ellipse shown in textbooks. They also discover that other planets experience seasons and, just like on earth, it is summer on one part of the planet when it is winter on the opposite side.

On the last day of this unit, the teacher directs the students to reexamine their original posters. She prompts them to identify why they thought the distance to the sun caused seasons. Several children give examples where you feel warmer when you are close to hot objects (a lightbulb, a toaster, a campfire) than when you are farther away. But they also remind themselves that even though this is true, it is an insufficient explanation for having opposite seasons at the same time on different parts of the earth. The teacher summarizes the shift in the students' explanations. Using the evidence they gathered from their hands-on activities, the teacher reinforces that their earlier theory about the seasons was incomplete. By looking at a variety of evidence, the students reorganized their thinking to develop an explanation for the seasons that does a much better job of explaining the facts.

For Reflection and Discussion

Locate a hands-on science activity that requires more than just a couple of pieces of equipment. A few possible sources are the Exploratorium's Web site (http://www.exploratorium.edu/science_explorer/), the Activities for Integrating Math and Science Foundation's Web site (http://www.aimsedu.org/), or even *Science Activities* magazine, which is available at many libraries. Choose an activity that seems like it would be very entertaining to students and might keep them occupied for more than fifteen minutes or so.

Imagine how you could redesign this activity to incorporate the three approaches to science instruction described in this chapter. This is a complex task, so find one or two other people to help you to think this through.

1. How would you introduce the activity if you were going to follow the discovery approach? What guidelines or directions would we provide to the class?

2. Next consider the implications of doing the same activity with an inquiry approach. What additional structure would you provide for the students?

3. Finally, discuss how this activity might fit within a conceptual change approach. How would this instructional sequence be different from the others, especially in terms of the starting and ending points?

Appropriateness of the Conceptual Change Teaching Approach

It is important to recognize that most students in a classroom will hold conceptions about phenomena that are at odds with those of science. These explanations are not religious beliefs and may not even represent ideas drawn from students' cultural background. These conceptions are often the result of the students' trying to make sense of the world, although some of these ideas are generated during instruction. In fact, because the students' explanations are based on observations, they do possess scientific characteristics, and some science educators prefer the term "alternative conception" rather than "misconception." This label suggests that students are using evidence to support their explanation and in that way is consistent with the actions within the culture of science. The problem is that another scientific explanation exists that better explains the data. As such, the objects within the culture of science (i.e., the concepts accepted within the scientific community) are not fully understood by the students who rely on an alternative conception. In other words, if students' alternative conception is evidence based, they are part of the way toward thinking scientifically. The other piece that is also important is knowing which of the many ways of explaining phenomena is considered acceptable by members of the science community.

In a second-grade classroom that was studying weather, children explored air by making pinwheels, viewing soap bubbles as they blew around the playground, and watching as their teacher demonstrated air's properties (Settlage, Madsen, & Rustad, 2005). One day, the students were discussing wind and a teacher asked them to describe the connections between air and wind. Many children thought that the two were different and used evidence from their previous activities to support their claims. One distinction they made was that air is still but wind is moving. Another was that wind can knock you down but air cannot. Although our first inclination is to smile at these darling ideas, we recognize a problem when we think about how to replace this view. We have to accept that the students do have evidence to support their ideas. In this regard, these ideas are not based on beliefs. Instead the students have interpreted evidence in a way that differs from how a scientist would explain the observations. If we hope to overcome this alternative conception, we need to use additional evidence to show the shortcomings of the current idea and then present another explanation, namely, that wind is air on the move, as a more useful idea for describing the observations.

Having students arrive at their own scientific explanations for a phenomenon, as described previously, certainly requires a significant amount of time and energy. Is all that work necessary? Can't students simply hear or read about the scientific explanation to achieve the same results? The short answer, gathered from a vast amount of research into student science learning, is "no." Science education researchers Jim Wandersee, Joel Mintzes, and Joe Novak (1994) reviewed hundreds of research studies of student learning. Their research repeatedly showed that an individual's alternative conceptions are very difficult to change. A considerable amount of effort is required to help students recognize the shortcomings of their own ideas and the strengths of the scientific alternatives. Without considerable effort, which includes a great deal of time to contemplate and consider ideas and alternative explanations, most students will hold on to their original ideas, even after instruction. If the goal of science instruction is to help students discard their naive ideas in favor of more scientific explanations, then a great deal of time and effort and a variety of activities are required to support this accommodation.

Point–Counterpoint

The theory of conceptual change explains why students are seemingly resistant to discarding personal ideas in favor of scientifically acceptable explanations. Some teacher educators see conceptual change as the key to instilling scientific concepts that are enduring. But others are somewhat less than convinced about the utility of conceptual change, especially within a "science for all" climate. So we have two conflicting outlooks in response to the question "How powerful is conceptual change within science teaching?"

Conceptual Change Teaching Is the Engine Transforming the Experiences of Inquiry Into Student Learning

Lee Meadows
Science Teacher Educator at the University of Alabama and Former High School Science Teacher

Remember that science class when you just couldn't understand the idea the teacher was trying to get across? Maybe it was the idea of inertia when you were in middle school. Perhaps it was balancing chemistry equations in high school. Maybe even now you're struggling with ideas in a college-level science class because you don't understand the main ideas. Sure, by now you probably know how to survive a science class—you know how to memorize your way through the test—but you also know that you do not really understand.

If this is your experience in science classes, then you're absolutely normal! The large body of science education research on student misconceptions clearly shows that most students really don't understand scientific ideas, even after instruction. Traditional approaches to science teaching, particularly text-based readings and teacher-centered lectures, don't cause the fundamental changes in students' thinking needed for strong content understanding. This research has led me to implement a conceptual change approach within my inquiry-based lessons, and I'm finding that the combination is powerful for helping students truly understand science.

Inquiry and conceptual change teaching let me use the ABC approach to science teaching. ABC stands for "Activity Before Content." Students need concrete experiences on which to build their abstract ideas. That's the power of inquiry-based investigations. Remember a science class where all the ideas were so abstract that you couldn't get a handle on them? Probably you didn't start that lesson with a concrete, hands-on experience. You had nothing concrete to hang the ideas on. The ABC approach is quite different. For example to get my students to grasp the abstract concepts of frequency, amplitude, and wavelength, I started them with a guided inquiry using Slinkies. I followed their hands-on work with a conceptual change debriefing in which I guided them to recognize how the abstract concepts explained well their lab experiences. During the debriefing, I led students to link the abstract ideas, such as wavelength, with their concrete experience, such as measuring the wavelengths of the Slinkies.

Inquiry and conceptual change also allow me to implement the classroom discourse necessary for kids to really understand science. Honestly, I can't change kids' ideas. They have to argue themselves into new ways of thinking, and that process requires a lot of classroom talk of different kinds. Students can pair and share and talk in their cooperative groups. I will engage them all in large-group discussions, get groups to talk to other groups, and even get each student to talk with herself or himself through reflective logs. Throughout all that talk, I envision myself as an orchestrator of discourse, which is consistent with the *National Science Education Standards*. I'm the conductor, but they're the ones making the music of learning. During all that talk, I consistently insert conceptual changes strategies into the dialogue to move their ideas forward, and I always get them to base their talk on the evidence collected from their inquiry. If they're still hanging on to a misconception, I remind them of evidence that confronts their wrong ideas. If they're moving forward in conceptual change, I have them reconsider what they saw in the lab so that they have the confidence that they're on the right track. At the end of the lesson, I have them look back with metacognition on how their new ideas are better explanations of their evidence than their original ideas.

Conceptual change is the engine within inquiry that gets kids to really learn the science concepts. The inquiry investigations capture their interest and generate for them evidence about the natural world; conceptual change helps them master the scientific ideas that explain the evidence from their inquiries. Inquiry combined with conceptual change is better than any other approach I know for science teaching, mainly because students actually restructure their knowledge. Better than hands-on science, conceptual change guides students to build knowledge after the experiment is over. Better than discovery learning, conceptual change requires that students discover improved knowledge that moves them closer to the understanding of scientists. My students were tracked; I had very few who were motivated academically or interested in science. Yet they learned science well. When inquiry is combined with conceptual change, students learn the ideas of science in a memorable fashion because the solid ideas in their heads are attached to real experiences in their lives.

Mark Olson
Science Teacher Educator at the University of Connecticut and Former High School Physics and Math Teacher

As a high school physics teacher, I was an enthusiastic advocate for conceptual change teaching methods. I was (and still am) fascinated by the ways my students made sense of natural phenomena and the ways in which I could facilitate their learning of science. In particular, I found teaching for conceptual change to be a tremendously useful model for organizing and structuring teaching. And most important, as noted in the chapter, it helped focus my attention as a teacher on how my students were making sense of ideas in science.

Despite its success as an instructional model, despite its influence on a generation of science teachers, and despite the fact that I think you should use it, there is a small problem.

It's wrong.

You might be thinking, WHAT?

How can it be wrong? Why is it so important and influential if it's wrong? And more relevant to you, why is it in this book? Please let me explain. It's not wrong in a bad way—in fact I like to think of the conceptual change approach as being productively wrong (Anderson, 1995). As I will soon show, being productively wrong is actually an important part of science and not such a bad thing after all! And after this discussion I certainly hope you will still consider the conceptual change approach a worthwhile teaching method for your classroom.

So how can something be wrong and yet still productive?

Maybe an example from science can help. The Bohr model of an atom says that atoms have a hard, little nucleus with even smaller electrons orbiting around it—much like the planets moving around the sun. Everyone learns this atomic model in school, and it is very helpful for thinking about atoms. But atoms aren't that simple. Electrons don't orbit around the nucleus—at least not like planets do around the sun. So why do we continue to teach this model of the atom in schools? The answer is that the Bohr model of the atom is productively wrong. While it might not be accurate, it remains very useful (i.e., productive) as a way to think about what atoms are like.

Likewise the conceptual change approach is wrong because it's also too simple. If you look at the stages in the approach, it talks only about ideas and explanations. Although both are undoubtedly at the core of what it takes to learn, there are other things left out—such as the motivational goals, classroom context, and cultural backgrounds of kids. Some kids are motivated by grades alone, whereas some believe that school won't benefit them. Other kids may have cultural backgrounds that don't encourage arguing with the teacher about ideas. And many studies have shown that boys are encouraged to argue about ideas, whereas girls are taught to be quiet and take good notes. Anyone who has spent time with kids in real classrooms knows that real classrooms are full of complexity. This complexity isn't dealt with in the conceptual change approach.

So with all of these challenges, why even use it? If it's so simple, why not find something that is more complex? This is where the idea of productivity comes in. When the conceptual change approach was being developed in the 1980s and 1990s, teachers were absolutely thrilled with their results. The learning effectiveness for topics that students had previously learned with 0 to 25 percent success rates using traditional approaches often doubled. That's quite an improvement! Hopes were high that conceptual change approaches might enable all students to learn science. However, it eventually became clear that success rates never approached 100 percent (perhaps you can guess that it often worked best with upper-middle-class students—that is, the same students who are already generally successful in school). The productive result was this: people began to think more carefully about how students actually make sense of science in real classrooms with real kids.

So the conceptual change approach is productive because it helps teachers to focus on how their students are making sense of science, and it is wrong because it doesn't work all the time. But as a teacher you can benefit from this approach because you will begin to see how to build on the conceptual change approach to create additional learning opportunities for each of your students. And perhaps you'll even help develop new approaches to teaching so that all students can be successful in science!

Discovery, Inquiry, and Conceptual Change Teaching Within Diverse Classrooms

All three approaches to science instruction hold promise for being useful in diverse settings, and each approach involves students interacting with physical phenomena. The conceptual change approach also emphasizes the understandings the learner brings into the classroom as a basis for teaching. The focus on physical experiences and students' existing conceptions makes these approaches appropriate for teaching students of cultural, linguistic, and cognitive diversity. Although these approaches show promise, they must be carefully applied in a diverse classroom. In many cultures and even different economic classes, children are not raised or allowed to ask questions, as is so common in White, middle-class homes. Instead many children are raised to not question figures of authority. For children with this form of upbringing, the practice of adults asking question of children for which the adult already has the answer can create confusion and discomfort. The exotic nature of questioning aside, inquiry, discovery, and conceptual change approaches to science teaching are particularly difficult for students who are learning English and students with cognitive disabilities. Often the explanations generated are discussed orally by the class, and texts, if used, serve as only as a reference.

NSES Teaching Standard B: Teachers of science guide and facilitate learning. In doing this, teachers recognize and respond to student diversity and encourage all students to participate fully in science learning.

It is important that we recognize the potential difficulties the inquiry, discovery, and conceptual change approaches can hold in classrooms where there is a diversity of cultural backgrounds. However, it is also important to be mindful of our goal to make all students feel familiar, comfortable, and competent when working within the culture of science. With this goal in mind, teachers should adapt lessons to meet the particular needs of students in diverse classrooms. For such adaptations, you will find it useful to review the work of Okhee Lee and her colleagues, who work with English language learners being schooled in south Florida (Fradd, Lee, Sutman, & Saxton, 2002). They suggested that for diverse learners, such approaches to science teaching and learning will require the teacher to be especially clear about explaining the cultural actions of science. This provides students with a great deal of experience in becoming familiar with such actions. Put another way, making it explicit to students how and why questions will be posed becomes part of the teacher's duty to provide access to science. In this way students do not feel as if they are outsiders to the classroom's scientific community, and they grow to believe they are legitimate participants in the science culture.

When attempting to shift, replace, or shape students misconceptions, you should acknowledge Moore's (1999) description of science as a way of knowing. As we will discuss in more detail in chapter 8, scientific knowledge and scientific inquiry have particular characteristics that set them apart from other ways of understanding the world. As we approach students with culturally based conceptions that are at odds with the explanations provided by science, we must acknowledge that science is one way of knowing about the world, a way that operates on particular assumptions and methods. Thus the explanations produced through the actions of science are different from those produced through other ways of knowing the world. In science we discuss scientific explanations, and in science class our goal is for students to construct scientific explanations, but this suggests that such explanations are not inherently "better" than other cultural beliefs but more "scientific." This discussion is an important one and is grounded in a robust understanding of the nature of science—a discussion we have in chapter 8 of this volume.

There are basic strategies that can be employed in discovery, inquiry, and conceptual change instruction to help provide students with access to the explanations constructed. For instance in the conceptual change teaching example described earlier, the teacher, at the end of each lesson, should summarize in a written format, such as on an overhead projector or the board, what was discussed as a class. For students struggling with substantial language or cognitive barriers, providing these summaries in advance will reduce the amount of cognitive effort students are required to spend in class, and they will be better able to concentrate on what is said. With most activities, students should be placed in heterogeneous groups so that they can hear and participate in the group construction of ideas. Providing simple and clear reading passages describing the explanation of the data will provide a way for students to learn the language and better remember the explanations, especially with activities that are complex and bring the class into contact with abstract concepts. By introducing explanations and text after the activities, the teacher can help students build cognitive frameworks that make effective use of their personal interests, which in turn increases the likelihood they will comprehend what they are reading. Adapting inquiry, discovery, and conceptual change lessons to meet the needs of cognitively, linguistically, and culturally diverse students is possible. Such adaptations become a reality only when teachers are committed to bringing all their students into the culture of science.

English Language Learners and Approaches to Science Teaching

In the previous chapter we introduced the Principles for Effective Pedagogy developed by the Center for Research on Education, Diversity, and Excellence (Warren & Rosebery, 2002). These five principles describe a combination of commitments and techniques that increase the likelihood that students from diverse populations will be successful in science. In the previous chapter we introduced the first principle of joint productivity activity. Now we will consider the second principle, which describes language fluency.

Language Development Within Science Lessons

Developing fluency in language does not occur out of context. Language lessons on tapes or CDs provide a scenario for using the language. For example the learner is supposed to imagine needing to know how to find his or her way to the center of town or to buy a train ticket. Similarly

TABLE 4.4. Developing Language Across the Curriculum and the Appropriate Teacher Actions

The teacher attends to conversations among students about their family and community;
makes adjustments to the direction of instruction in response to questions students ask and comments they express;
acts respectful of diverse styles of communicating: taking turns, using eye contact considerately, overlapping talk, and so on;
gives students opportunities during instructional activities to interact with other students and the teacher; and
makes allowances during activities to promote students' use of first and second languages as they communicate.

Note: Adapted from Dalton (1998).

students who are still developing English fluency should be expected to find ways to make the new language their own by using it within the context of learning subject matter. Rather than expect students to absorb accurate vocabulary and proper phrasing, the second principle for effective pedagogy advocates for teachers to make a conscious effort to incorporate language development even as scientific ideas are being discussed and science process skills are being used. Table 4.4 lists instructional moves teachers can apply to support language development within the course of classroom activities.

The subtle message we should receive from this list is that teachers need to be more receptive about and willing to be responsive to students' efforts to develop their English language skills. Such recommendations for the teacher about the need to listen, respond, interact, and encourage are indicators that teachers must be attentive to opportunities to support language development. This requires being aware of the need for and open to opportunities to appropriately respond when the situation presents itself. However, there are ways teachers can be deliberate and proactive to support language development. Such strategies include modeling the use of new vocabulary within the flow of discussions, supplying visual cues (pictures, drawings, symbols) to supplement oral language, and using simpler sentences when conveying essential information (Dalton, 1998). No one can be expected to use all of these strategies within every science lesson. Instead teachers of students who are developing English fluency would be wise to incorporate a disposition toward supporting language development as an integral part of science instruction.

Special Needs Populations and Approaches to Science Teaching

Although progress has been very slow, more and more educators are recognizing the value of science for students who might not have been viewed as capable in previous generations. One possible reason for this shift is the appreciation that science is not all about language arts: reading for comprehension, spelling words correctly, and mastering vocabulary do not necessarily define success in science. In the approaches described in this chapter, there is room at the science table for students with cognitive disabilities. The message becomes more than the ambitions of "science for all" but has actually been shown to be possible, with some modifications, for special needs students.

NSES Program Standard E: Science education policies must be equitable.

Shirley Magnusson and Annemarie Palincsar (1995) were inspired by the idea of "guided inquiry," which, for these researchers, involved students in investigations organized around a guiding question, information gathered during work with materials, findings reported to the group, evidence used to consider the alternatives, and new explanations proposed for everyone to consider. When this idea was implemented in a real-world context, impressive effects were noted for students with learning disabilities (Palincsar, Collins, Marano, & Magnusson, 2000). Rather than describe this in generalities, we will follow the researchers' example by describing the impact on a specific child.

At the time of their study, Don was a fourth grader who was categorized by the school psychologist as profoundly learning disabled. This designation was based on his difficulties with reading and comprehending texts and problems with fine motor skills (i.e., writing). And yet when he participated in science taught in the manner described previously, Don was quite successful. The researchers acknowledged that Don continued to require explicit teaching to make his reading and writing stronger. But in terms of his science performance, Don did not seem encumbered by anything we might label as a learning disability. Although the samples of Don's science notebook provided in the research report (Palincsar et al., 2000) are a challenge to decode, the researchers described his performance with science as follows:

> He was a close observer, paying more attention to the details in this investigation than was typical of his peers. Also, he capably met a number of the cognitively demanding aspects of this instruction, such as thinking about the relationship between the claims he wished to make and the evidence that he had for those claims, or thinking about evidence that would be convincing to others. Another strength was that he demonstrated metacognitive awareness as he checked his dictation for its clarity and coherence and revised his entry when he recognized limitations in his initial attempt. (Palincsar et al., 2000, p. 250)

The implications give credence to our belief that special needs students can and should be involved with science in elementary and middle school grades. First, because Don and his class were participating in a research study, individuals who focused on science learning were able to notice Don's science success. The researchers disclosed that a teacher who knows the subject matter and the type of thinking characteristic of science is much more likely to recognize learning gains in students—gains that might escape notice by someone who is not paying as careful attention. We regard this view as consistent with our push for future teachers to think about science as a culture.

Another inference the researchers recognized was the significance of social interactions as a means for supporting and encouraging Don's science learning. In a setting where students work in groups and engage in a collaborative effort to understand science, a student like Don will be more successful than when interpersonal communication is restricted to interactions between the teacher and a lone student. The final proposition was that teachers should create opportunities for students to actively participate in science activities to help them realize their full capacity. If Don's ability to learn was viewed too narrowly and the adults equated his struggles with language arts as true for all subject areas, then they might not have given him the chance to show what he could accomplish in science. To be sure, this student's reading difficulties did not go away—but they also were not a justification for lowering expectations. A broader view of what it means to be a learner caused those who worked with Don to indicate, "His reading comprehension placed him at the beginning of first grade; however, it was clear that he was capable of handling the demands of cognitively challenging instruction at the fourth-grade level" (Palincsar et al., 2000, p. 250). We see this as a cause for hopefulness and optimism about the prospects for all children, including the Dons of the world, to be provided opportunities to participate in science alongside their peers.

For Reflection and Discussion

Suppose you are a teacher who intends to teach the pendulum activities described in this book. In your heterogeneous classroom, you have students who are English language learners, other students who are new to the United States but otherwise adept in English, and students with cognitive disabilities. What are some strategies you can employ to allow all students to be successful in this activity? Also what are some of the various ways you should consider defining "success"?

Chapter Summary

- In a discovery approach to science, which is philosophically based on the working habits of scientists, the teacher provides students with access to an array of materials and time to explore those materials to construct their own, scientific explanations of natural phenomena.

- In inquiry-based teaching, students rely on a combination of questioning, data collecting, and conclusion generating to come to describe and understand the natural world. Inquiry-based teaching is distinct from discovery in that different forms and levels of teacher support are employed to help students become progressively successful in this process.

- Inquiry-based teaching approaches can be categorized according to the level of teacher support and student decision making. Teachers should select an appropriate level for inquiry based on the skill level of the students and the nature of the content to be learned.

- Teaching based on a conceptual change approach is structured around the premise that students carry unscientific but intuitive ideas into the classroom and that they may have applied these ideas to make sense of their world for a number of years. For students to consider and ultimately accept the scientific explanation for phenomena, they must recognize their preexisting explanations, be made aware of the limitations of their explanations, and consider the usefulness of a scientific explanation for accounting for observations. Only when students are aware of their own ideas, recognize the limitations, and appreciate the greater strength of the scientific counterparts will they accept and use the scientific explanation.

- Each of the three approaches to science teaching (discovery, inquiry based, and conceptual change) is based in underlying philosophies. These include the perceived similarities (or discontinuities) of children learning science compared to the work of professional scientists, the goal of science teaching (to produce scientists versus to foster scientific literacy in all children), and the nature of learning (as a natural process stemming from observations of the natural world or requiring a rigorous process of conceptual change).

- Each of the science teaching approaches addressed in this chapter is potentially useful in a diverse classroom. However, steps must be taken to ensure that students are aware of the particular actions of science (questioning, data collection) and to make sure that the objects of science (the explanations it provides) are accessible to English language learners and students with cognitive limitations.
- When employing the conceptual change approach to science, teachers should be careful to explain that students' naive conceptions for natural phenomena may not be the same as their scientific counterparts but not to denigrate or dismiss these cultural ways as inappropriate ways of viewing the world. Instead conceptions that are a part of the culture of science are the scientific explanations but not the only explanation for any natural phenomena.

Key Terms

Bruner, Jerome (1915–): an American psychologist who was a major proponent of discovery learning in science curriculum.

Conceptual change: a model of science teaching that begins by helping the students to become clear about their own ideas on a scientific topic, followed by having students participate in an activity in which their current ideas are not adequate to explain so that students recognize the shortcomings of their current explanations, after which the teacher introduces the new more scientifically appropriate explanation and students explore the strengths of the new idea. Finally, the students compare the new ideas with their original explanations.

Discovery approach: model of science teaching that is consistent with the ways in which scientists work and that emphasizes children's ability to make sense of their world. Advocates felt that science learning would naturally occur through children's contact with physical objects.

Driver, Rosalind (1941–1997): a British science educator whose work was groundbreaking in the identification and classification of student misconceptions and explaining their role in science learning

Guided inquiry: a semistructured approach to inquiry in which students may have control of the methods used to pursue answers and the interpretation of their results. Such forms of teaching are considered to be Schwab's Level 1 or 2 inquiry.

Inquiry-based science teaching: a science teaching technique intended to echo the activities of scientific work and actively involve students in the use of five essential elements of inquiry.

Open inquiry: This extreme version of inquiry-based science teaching places students in control of their decisions about each component of their inquiry: the question, the procedures, and the interpretation. This is considered Schwab's Level 3 inquiry.

Schwab, Joseph (1909–1988): an American educational theorist who was instrumental in establishing the importance of inquiry into science classrooms.

Scientific inquiry: the varied approaches scientists use to investigate the natural world and the evidence-based explanations they propose as a result of their investigations.

Structure of the discipline: the collection of unifying ideas characteristic of science and felt by some to be the ultimate goal of science education.

Structured inquiry: a guided form of inquiry-based science teaching in which the teacher provides the students with the questions to investigate and the methods to use to gather data. This is considered Schwab's Level 0 inquiry.

A Favorite Science Lesson

As a way to help students understand experimental design, the Full Option Science System, or FOSS, developed the "Variables" unit, which may be the one of the best resources available. The unit was written for use in grades 5 and 6. The activity titled "Plane Sense" is one that is memorable for students. The plane that students use is a rubber-band propeller attached to a soda straw that slides along fishing line. Students are challenged to identify variables affecting the motion of the plane along the guide string. Instead of seeing who can create the fastest plane, students adjust variables including thrust, load, and incline to have the plane fly exactly halfway along the four-meter (twelve-foot) string. Without any teacher involvement, this could easily be considered a discovery lesson. However, by guiding students along the way, focusing them on the features of inquiry, and providing several authentic assessment tasks, a teacher can guide students beyond simply messing about and actually teach them a great deal about variables and designing experiments.

Suggested Readings

Holliday, W. G. (2001). Critically considering inquiry teaching. *Science Scope, 24*(7), 54–57.
    Within just four pages, Professor Holliday summarized forty-plus years of transition from discovery to inquiry-based science teaching. He identified several areas of debate and confusion, urging those in science education to pay attention to the descriptions of inquiry provided in the *National Science Education Standards.*

Kang, N., & Howren, C. (2004). Teaching for conceptual understanding. *Science and Children, 42*(1), 28–32.
    This article describes a collaboration between a science education professor and an elementary school teacher. By applying the conceptual change framework of Rosalind Driver, they were able to successfully address student misconceptions about the solar system.

Lindgren, J., & Cushall, M. (2001). You can always tell a dancer by her feet: Integrating science and math through pressure investigations. *Science Scope, 24*(4), 12–16.
    In a refreshing twist, these authors relied on dancing and dancers to reinforce physics concepts. Using a modification of the conceptual change approach, teachers challenge students to describe the changes that will happen when they weigh themselves on two bathroom scales with a foot on each one. The results are not what the students expected, and the teachers lead them to recognize the need to weigh the evidence.

References

Abrams, E., & Southerland, S. A. (Eds.). (2007). *Inquiry in the classrooms: Challenges and opportunities.* Greenwich, CT: Information Age Publishing.

Anderson, C. W. (1995). Teaching content in a multicultural milieu. In S. Hopmann & K. Riquarts (Eds.), *Didaktik and/or Curriculum* (pp. 365–382). Kiel, Germany: Institut für die Pädagogik der Naturwissenschaften (IPN).

Barman, C. R. (2002). How do you define inquiry? *Science and Children, 40*(2), 8–9.

Bruner, J. S. (1960). *The process of education.* Cambridge, MA: Harvard University Press.

Carmichael, P., Driver, R., Holding, B., Phillips, I., Twigger, D., & Watts, M. (1990). *Research on students' conceptions in science: A bibliography.* Leeds, UK: University of Leeds.

Colburn, A. (2000). An inquiry primer. *Science Scope, 23*(6), 42–44.

Cothron, J. H., Giese, R. L., & Rezba, R. J. (2000). *Students and research: Practical strategies for science classrooms and competitions.* Dubuque, IA: Kendall-Hunt.

Dalton, S. S. (1998). *Pedagogy matters: Standards for effective teaching practice.* Washington, DC: Center for Applied Linguistics.

Driver, R. (1988). Theory into practice: A constructivist approach to curriculum development. In P. Fensham (Ed.), *Development and dilemmas in science education* (pp. 133–149). London: Falmer Press.

Driver, R. (1989). Students' conceptions and the learning of science. *International Journal of Science Education, 11,* 481–490.

Fradd, S., Lee, O., Sutman, F., & Saxton, K. (2002). Promoting science literacy with English language learners through instructional materials development: A case study. *Bilingual Research Journal, 25*(4), 479–501.

Magnusson, S. J., & Palincsar, A. S. (1995). The learning environment as a site of science education reform. *Theory into Practice, 34*(1), 43–50.

Martin-Hansen, L. M. (2002). Defining inquiry. *The Science Teacher, 69*(2), 34–37.

McBride, J. W., Bhatti, M., Hannan, M. A., & Feinber, M. (2004). Using an inquiry approach to teach science to secondary school science teachers. *Physics Education, 39,* 435–439.

McDermott, L. C. (1984). Research on conceptual understanding in mechanics. *Physics Today, 37*(7), 24–32.

Moore, J. (1999). *Science as a way of knowing.* Cambridge, MA: Harvard University Press.

National Research Council. (1996). *National Science Education Standards.* Washington, DC: National Academy Press.

National Research Council. (1997). *Science teaching reconsidered: A handbook.* Washington, DC: National Academy Press.

National Research Council. (2000). *Inquiry and the   A guide for teaching and learning.* Washington, DC: National Academy Press.

Palincsar, A. S., Collins, K. M., Marano, N. L., & Magnusson, S. J. (2000). Investigating the engagement and learning of students with learning disabilities in guided inquiry science teaching. *Language, Speech, and Hearing Services in Schools, 31,* 240–251.

Pfundt, H., & Duit, R. (1994). *Bibliography: Students' alternative frameworks and science education* (4th ed.). Kiel, Germany: Institute for Science Education at the University of Kiel.

Rudolph, J. L. (2002a). From World War to Woods Hole: The use of wartime research models for curriculum reform. *Teachers College Record, 104,* 212–241.

Rudolph, J. L. (2002b). *Scientists in the classroom: The cold war reconstruction of American science education.* New York: Palgrave.

Schwab, J. J. (1960). Inquiry, the science teacher, and the educator. *The School Review, 68*(2), 176–195.

Settlage, J. (2002). Seasons change and conceptions shift—But not always as expected. In D. Tippins, T. Koballa, & B. Payne (Eds.), *Learning from cases: Unraveling the complexities of elementary science teaching* (pp. 103–109). Needham Heights, MA: Allyn & Bacon.

Settlage, J., Madsen, A., & Rustad, K. (2005). Inquiry science, sheltered instruction, and English language learners. *Issues in Teacher Education, 14*(1), 39–57.

Shulman, L. S., & Tamir, P. (1973). Research on teaching in the natural sciences. In R. M. W. Travers (Ed.), *Handbook of Research on Teaching* (pp. 1098–1148). Chicago: Rand McNally.

Wandersee, J. H., Mintzes, J. J., & Novak, J. D. (1994). Research on alternative conceptions in science. In D. Gable (Ed.), *Handbook of research in science teaching* (pp. 177–210). New York: Macmillan.

Warren, B., & Rosebery, A. S. (2002). *Teaching science to at-risk students: Teacher research communities as a context for professional development and school reform.* Santa Cruz, CA: Center for Research on Education, Diversity, and Excellence.

five
The Learning Cycle as a Model for Science Teaching

Chapter Highlights

- Teaching students to learn any subject involves helping them grasp the bits of information and the broad ideas. Planning to teach requires careful decision making about the sequence of the parts and wholes.
- When teaching a topic starts with the main ideas and then moves to specifics, it is labeled *deductive*. In contrast, when teaching begins with an analysis of the parts and subsequently moves toward the whole, it is called *inductive*.
- Teacher support of student learning is gradually reduced as confidence and competence increases. Learning should ultimately result in students having independent control over their work.
- Learning cycle instruction begins with hands-on activities and then moves to the formal presentation of concepts. Following these two stages within the learning cycle, students apply their new ideas to fresh situations.
- Every variation of the learning cycle contains the same key elements. In this text, the model consists of five phases: Engage, Explore, Explain, Extend, and Evaluate.
- Students with a wide variety of backgrounds can learn science through the learning cycle. Background experiences are the starting point that connects every learner to the content.
- Students are expected to master one central science concept after passing through a single learning cycle. This allows students to apply their newly acquired ideas before the teacher moves on to the next concept.

In the preceding chapter we examined three approaches to science teaching. Each approach originated in response to a perceived challenge within science education. The discovery approach provided students with activity-centered lessons, inquiry-based teaching allowed students to participate in the thoughts and actions of science, while conceptual change instruction took its cues from the need to ensure that teaching is actually contributing to students' learning of science concepts. However, it is our view that none of these options provide sufficient detail about how a teacher would actually implement any of these approaches in an elementary or middle school classroom as a central aspect of science instruction. Of even more importance, however, is our view is that none of the approaches pay particular attention to student diversity. Our aim within this chapter is to provide a model of science teaching that resolves these problems.

Within this chapter you will learn about a powerful model of teaching science called the learning cycle. This instructional model is a by-product of the science curriculum heyday of the 1960s and 1970s. Over the years this model has been revised to its current form that we will present to you. There is considerable research demonstrating that this instructional model is a powerful tool, not only for advancing the quality of science instruction but also for potentially fulfilling the goal of "science for all" without excluding any group of students. The phases of the learning cycle are interconnected and interdependent. A teacher who is using the learning cycle effectively has to pay attention to the central science concept and to the details that become important during each phase. Because this approach is so effective at helping children develop solid understandings of the objects of science (scientific explanations), it is important for teachers to understand the learning cycle model and learn to use it in ways that allows them to make it their own.

Models of Teaching

As you know from your time as a student, there are many ways in which a subject can be taught. The teacher might lecture, the students might work in groups, individual students might do independent projects, and so on. Each approach has its own assumptions and purposes. As someone matures into his or her role as a professional teacher, he or she should be masterful at using a variety of teaching models and know the underlying philosophy for each.

We can simplify teaching and learning by reducing it to two components. One component is the central idea that is to be learned. This is the big picture or one concept the teacher intends for the students to understand. The other component is the collection of examples, experiences, and evidence that supports the one concept. Activities that fall into this second component include book excerpts, video clips, Web sites, field trips, hands-on work, and so on.

One component of learning is the "whole," and the other component is what constitutes the "parts." For science learning to happen, a student needs to comprehend both components and be able to explain the ways those components relate to each other. In music the "whole" might be learning an entire song whereas the "parts" would include the melody, harmony, lyrics, and rhythm. Likewise a jigsaw puzzle can be understood in terms of both the individual pieces and the image that appears when all the pieces are properly assembled.

Imagine you are responsible for teaching a group of students with a variety of science and linguistic abilities about simple machines. You are provided with several models of simple machines, some basic equipment (pulleys and gears) in sufficient quantities for every student to investigate, a class set of trade books that describes simple machines in action, and a video that shows the use of simple machines in everyday life; these are the "parts" the students will experience. For the "whole" you have a teacher resource book that provides you with lots of background information about simple machines. You are given the freedom to design your own lessons to teach the students. Where might you begin?

Deductive and Inductive Approaches

One possible approach to teaching simple machines is to orient the students with what they will be studying. This includes providing a quick overview of simple machines. The teacher might explain that simple machines move objects by using a device that makes the work easier. All simple machines function under the same principle: to reduce the force required to move an object, the machine must exert effort over a longer distance. That's the one concept you intend for the students to learn. All of the equipment and other resources are then used over the next several science lessons (including hands-on activities, reading activities, discussions) to reinforce that concept in the minds of the students. An appealing aspect of this approach is the variety of materials that accommodate the various kinds of learners in the class. For the topic of simple machines, some students would respond to working with actual gears and pulleys, others would respond to animations and video clips of simple machines in action, whereas others would learn best by reading nonfiction texts.

In this scenario, what is the sequence of parts and wholes? The learning began with an emphasis on the global idea of simple machines followed by exposure to various examples. When teaching is organized in this way, that is, by starting with the whole and moving to the parts, it is called a **deductive approach** to instruction. Beginning with the general idea and then going to the specifics is a very common way of teaching, and it is probably the most common approach you experienced in your own science learning. A deductive way of teaching has many strengths. A deductive approach is an important tool within a teaching toolbox, especially when the big concept is very specific and can be reduced to a precise sequence.

However, the deductive approach is just one method of teaching (see Figure 5.1). For people who know only the deductive approach, their teaching toolbox is very limited. There is a saying that applies here: "To the person holding a hammer, everything looks like a nail." Obviously there are times when a hammer is exactly the right tool for a particular task, and when used properly a hammer can be an elegant and efficient tool. But in the construction trades there is never a person whose only job is hammering—knowing how and when to use other tools is important. As useful as deductive teaching is, we need other teaching tools to select from.

Another way to plan for teaching is the **inductive approach.** The key feature of an inductive approach is that learning begins with the parts and ultimately leads to the whole. The teacher gives the students experiences with many examples and activities without explaining how everything fits together. Eventually the teacher guides the experiences so the students come to understand how they all fit into a nice and complete whole.

To teach simple machines with an inductive approach, the teacher would begin with the activities. The teacher might have the students first spend a lesson or two working with ramps and inclined planes. They would use spring scales to measure the amount of force needed to pull objects up a ramp. Then the students might work with pulleys and explore what happens to the

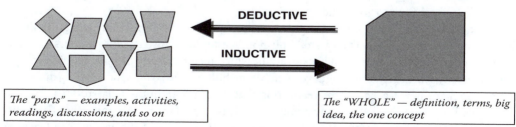

The "parts" — examples, activities, readings, discussions, and so on

The "WHOLE" — definition, terms, big idea, the one concept

FIGURE 5.1. The relationship between parts and whole is how inductive teaching and deductive teaching are defined.

amount of force when multiple pulleys are used. Later they would explore the gears and how those work.

After all of these activities, the teacher would introduce the concept of simple machines. In explaining simple machines, the teacher would help students recognize how all their previous investigations share characteristics that are united under this big idea. The students have developed familiarity and comfort with the equipment, and they are probably finding some patterns in how the materials operate. The teacher's task is to help them to generalize from their varied activities.

We must acknowledge that this inductive approach flies in the face of this old-fashioned notion of teaching: "Tell them what you're going to teach them, tell them while you're teaching, and then tell them what you taught them." This doesn't mean that an inductive approach is a free-for-all. In fact, the teacher has to be especially thoughtful about the activities the students will do so they provide an adequate foundation for the big idea. No activity should be selected simply because the students will have fun. This would be as odd as having a jigsaw puzzle in which the manufacturer threw in some extra pieces just because they were pretty. In short, all of the parts should fit together to build the whole.

For Reflection and Discussion

In what ways have the authors used an inductive approach to introduce the concept of deductive? Similarly, how have the authors made use of a deductive approach to present the concept of inductive?

Student Benefits From Inductive Teaching

Because inductive teaching may not be an approach you've ever experienced, we'd like to give you some reasons to consider using it other than for its novelty. We also want to emphasize that inductive teaching isn't an all-purpose tool; it has its limits. But there is also a great deal of research supporting the use of inductive teaching within elementary school science instruction to support student learning.

In your teacher education courses, you may have heard that an effective teacher is one who starts where the children are. This means that for learning to occur, particularly in diverse classrooms, it must build upon what the students bring to the situation. No matter how young they are, what country they are from, or what language they speak, when children walk into a classroom they already hold many ideas about the world and the way that it works. Anyone who has spent more than a few moments with a child and believes that children are blank slates is not really paying attention to the child. You cannot and should not assume that everything you will teach is completely new to your students.

When we use *diverse,* we aren't using that term in a politically correct way to signify Black, low income, or urban. We don't mean to imply non-White either. Instead, *diverse* refers to a mixture of students who have different backgrounds, which include family income, ethnic heritage, skin color, physical ability, first language, mental capabilities, and so on. One startling discovery for far too many new teachers is the realization that the children in their classroom are not all the same. Instead they vary in many, many ways. It is important to recognize that these differences hold substantial implications for student learning and thus the appropriate teaching approach.

Our particular concern, and the motivation for developing this book, is the persistent science achievement gaps as reported in research and the popular press. From our perspective, these data clearly indicate that some students are in greater need of effective science teaching than others. We anticipate that schools that are more desirable because of sufficient resources, adequate facilities, and other factors known to support student learning will rarely have difficulty with recruiting teachers. However, students in less fortunate circumstances also require teachers, and these teachers must possess an especially potent mix of information and strategies—and commitments—to advance those students. In actuality, when we speak of diverse we have in mind those students who might otherwise not be adequately served by an educational system that is blind, indifferent, or simply incapable of responding to the challenges and opportunities represented by these children. Balanced against this is our firm understanding that it's really hard to know where your students are coming from in terms of their background experiences. In our highly mobile society, you may have students in your class who regularly visit relatives in another country, but you could also have students who have never traveled more than a couple of miles from their home. Some families may set aside one Saturday each month to visit local cultural sites (zoos, museums, concerts, and the like), whereas other families spend the weekends with their extended family. As a teacher of science you have this dilemma: you should begin with the students' experiences, yet they all have had different experiences! In many classrooms the students may have more in common with each other than with the teacher.

The simple fact is that having a teacher who does not live in the same neighborhood as the students can be a source of incongruities. You may not know about the annual summer street fair. You may not be aware of the city park where the children play in their free time, the stream that cuts through a local block of land, or the community garden that many of them frequent. You may not know about the after-school programs held at the community center. Without this knowledge, you will have a harder time coming up with examples from the students' lives to reinforce the concepts you are teaching to them. What can you do? You understand teaching is more effective if you start with the students' previous experiences—but their lives are so varied that you're worried (and rightly so) about making unwarranted assumptions about what they do and do not know about the world. You may harbor the fear (again, rightly so) that you're going to disadvantage some students because you incorrectly assume they have experienced something that you want to use as the basis for an entire lesson. The reverse is also possible. If some of your students have limited English fluency, you may overlook the wealth of knowledge they bring from their lived experiences or schooling outside of the United States. In each of these cases, it is easy to misjudge students' background knowledge. Beyond missing opportunities to connect school science to your students' lives, you can reduce your effectiveness with responding to student behavior and create communication barriers between you and the families of your students.

The Power of Shared Experiences and Inductive Teaching

One solution is to involve all of the students in the same activity at the outset. By doing this, everybody has a shared experience they can all relate to. When the class begins to discuss their ideas, nobody is left out because they are unfamiliar with the scenario. This doesn't mean we neglect or ignore students' prior experience or knowledge. But by beginning with a common experience, there is less chance of some students making connections between the science lesson and their own lives and others being utterly confused because they cannot relate to the discussion. Too, the value in this approach goes beyond just common experiences. For students learning English, such concrete and shared experiences are an excellent **scaffold** to which they can attach their growing English vocabulary.

Scaffolding describes the assistance a teacher provides to students to help them accomplish something that they would not be otherwise able to accomplish. The process of scaffolding is more than the teacher simply providing help. Rather the scaffolding a teacher creates is gradually removed as the student's skills improve. Helping can be thought of as a ramp to move a child from one level to the next—but this ramp will always need to be there. In contrast, scaffolding is a temporary support that is meant, from the outset, to be gradually removed as the assistance becomes less necessary. Lev Vygotsky's **zone of proximal development** (ZPD) demonstrates how scaffolding applies. There is a zone that describes what students can accomplish and it's within this zone that they can function with the support of a teacher's hints, suggestions, and assistance. Scaffolding occurs as the students work with the benefits of this support. The goal is for the students to become skilled in their ZPD and for the teacher to shift responsibility to the students by dismantling the scaffolding. As a result, the range of things students can accomplish on their own expands. Ideally, the teacher would offer learning experiences in which all the students are continuously functioning within their ever-expanding ZPD.

Research has shown that students' reading comprehension and vocabulary development are increased when they are first provided with direct experiences. By beginning with such experiences and *following* with explicit treatment of the terms to be learned, students learn the vocabulary more quickly, tend to remember the vocabulary better, and are more likely to appropriately use the vocabulary in their writing and speaking. Likewise for students with learning disabilities, such initial, concrete experiences are incredibly important in allowing them not only to understand the objects of science but also to be able to retrieve those ideas when needed from their memory. The point we are making is that even though common sense might suggest that students need to be taught terminology first, a host of research indicates that the strongest foundation for learning science is provided by concrete experiences followed by formal vocabulary instruction. We recognize that this approach feels different, as most of us didn't experience science in this manner. But given what we know about how students learn, is it clear that experience followed by analysis of concepts is the most effective way to teach and learn science.

NSES Program Standard B: The program of study in science for all students should be developmentally appropriate, interesting, and relevant to students' lives; emphasize student understanding through inquiry; and be connected with other school subjects.

Teachers and those who are preparing to become teachers should be cautious about treating their childhood experiences as ones that all children have. Yes, each of us should dearly hold on to our family traditions and special events. But thinking that our personal experience is normal leads to the danger of our treating others' experiences as not normal. Even something as basic as tending a vegetable garden or swimming in a backyard pool may not be an experience you can assume all children have had. This may be true not only for students living in the city but also for students who live in prestigious suburban communities. In addition, many people take advantage of the fact that teaching positions are available in many parts of the nation. But after moving to a new community, teachers are often surprised that the local culture can be just as different as are the changes in climate or topography. As a result, what was normal in one setting can prove to be an unhelpful reference point in a new place.

Instead of assuming that every child has had a chance to plant seeds, mix substances, or take care of animals, it would be better to make those experiences the starting points for science instruction. Communities and cultures are built around shared experiences, and if we think of a classroom as a learning community, then providing opportunities for the members to have an experience they all share has great unifying potential. From a socialization perspective, shared experiences are important and should be a regular aspect of science. Certainly, having a shared experience is no panacea for eliminating differences in students' backgrounds and conceptual lenses. However, if the explanation section of the learning cycle is handled effectively, then these differences can be analyzed, compared, and made sense of, allowing for students to understand the concepts more deeply.

From a learning perspective, providing an initial and shared experience makes good sense. Instead of making guesses about the experiences students bring to the classroom (and undoubtedly not knowing with certainty for each and every child), the teacher can start with an experience and build on it. No students are left behind because the teacher assumes too much about what they already know. From a learning and teaching of science perspective, the direct experience is an essential feature of quality science teaching.

Although we have high regard for an inductive approach to science teaching, particularly in diverse classrooms, we must acknowledge that this approach represents particular challenges for some of the students in our classrooms. It is important to remember that asking questions about ideas, experiences, other learners, and the authority of the teacher is a very unfamiliar practice for many students. Some of your students may come from cultures and homes in which young people are not expected to ask questions, and for these students asking questions may seem disrespectful. At the very least, asking questions may be a little used skill for these learners. Because some of your students may not come to you equipped or comfortable with questioning skills, you need to allow for the development of such skills, perhaps by modeling such questions, explicating the need for questions in the doing and learning of science, allowing for lots of opportunities for students to question each other, and rewarding these efforts. Through such actions, teachers can help construct a culture of questioning in their classroom, something all students can benefit from.

Experiential Education

Using experiences within science teaching seems to be a way to move away from the drudgery of traditional instruction. We might begin to believe that direct experience for students is what will make all the difference in their science learning. However, experiences alone are not enough—even sitting at a desk listening to a lecture is an experience for the student. Maybe it's not an exciting experience and maybe it's not an experience that has any positive and lasting learning benefits, but it qualifies as experience.

How can a teacher decide which science experiences are likely to help students learn? How can a teacher determine if a particular activity is nothing more than fun and may not contribute to improved scientific understanding? The legendary educator John Dewey wrote about this issue in his 1938 book *Experience and Education*. Dewey tried to differentiate "traditional" teaching from "progressive" teaching—two opposing forces that are a source of tension in education even today.

What Qualifies as an Educational Experience

The quality of any experience has two aspects. There is an immediate aspect of agreeableness or disagreeableness, and there is its influence upon later experiences. The first is obvious to judge. The effect of an experience is not borne on its face. It sets a problem to the educator. It is [the teacher's] business to arrange for the kind of experiences which, while they do not repel the student, but rather engage are, nevertheless, more than immediately enjoyable since they promote having desirable future experiences. … Wholly independent of desire or intent, every experience lives on in further experiences. Hence the central problem of an education based upon experience is to select the kind of present experiences that live fruitfully and creatively in subsequent experiences. (Dewey, 1938, pp. 27–28)

Apparently Dewey saw a problem with simply rejecting traditional approaches to teaching. For all the right reasons, a teacher might vow to never teach in a traditional way. But Dewey noted that a teacher is not left with a new strategy or philosophy simply by discarding the one that exists. The statement "I'll *never* do that in *my* classroom" doesn't tell us (or the person who says it) what he or she will do instead. When it comes to experience, Dewey gave some guidance: the experience must be enjoyable and it must have connections with subsequent experiences. In other words, a science experience that is simply fun will not be sufficient. What is also required is that this experience continues to inform the students' understandings long after the materials are put away.

From Philosophy to Practice

As we discussed in the previous chapter, leaving students to freely explore (the discovery approach) is limited in its ability to support student learning. In the 1960s there was an explosion of science curriculum reform as the National Science Foundation provided considerable financial support for the development of new science education materials, many of which were inductive in nature. One of the elementary grade programs was called the Science Curriculum Improvement Study or SCIS. This is where the **learning cycle** was born.

The original learning cycle, designed by Robert Karplus, included three phases. In the first phase, students worked individually or in small groups with scientific materials as they pursued a problem or question. In the second phase, the entire class gathered together and the teacher orchestrated a discussion where the scientific concept was introduced. The third phase was an opportunity for students to apply this newly formed concept to different materials.

The learning cycle is still alive today, and we see it as an incredibly powerful model for teaching science (See Figure 5.2). Over the years there have been modifications to the Karplus model, but it remains essentially the same. Direct experiences occur before concepts are taught. Presenting the concepts to the students is not enough—the students need to apply their ideas to see how well the concept and their understandings of it will transfer somewhere else.

If you do a search of "learning cycle" on the Internet, you will find a great deal of information, some of which will differ from what we present here. This is because the learning cycle has become almost a living thing, and in different environments, such as the business world, it seems to change its form. Regardless of the number of phases in a learning cycle (and we use a version consisting of five phases), the model is fundamentally the same. Later in this chapter we will describe the learning cycle's appropriateness for teaching science to a wide variety of students. When Karplus was creating science materials, there was not much emphasis on multicultural education. We feel that the modifications to his original design can make this an effective approach for all students. Let's begin with the basic ideas and components of the learning cycle.

Phase One: Engage

The first phase of a learning cycle lesson is similar to many other approaches to teaching: you need to obtain the students' attention and orient their thinking toward the science they are

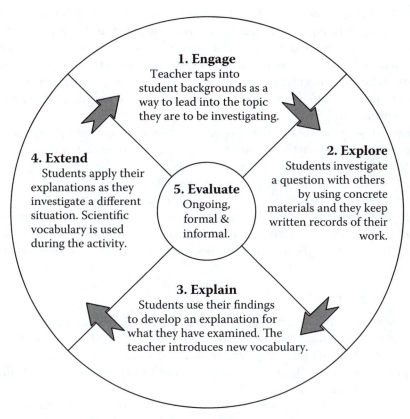

FIGURE 5.2. The learning cycle teaching model.

about to study. If the students are working on another subject, the Engage phase helps them shift mental gears. If the students are returning to their room from another activity or entering from another classroom, then the Engage phase allows them to settle into science mode.

There is not a single technique that you will always use during the Engage phase. For a lesson that is a follow-up to previous lessons, the Engage phase could be in the form of a quick review of the activities the class has been doing. This review could be entirely under the teacher's control, or it could begin by inviting students to recall the previous lessons.

NSES Teaching Standard C: Teachers of science engage in ongoing assessment of their teaching and of student learning.

If this is the first lesson in a much larger science unit, the Engage phase is the teacher's initial opportunity for the students to begin making connections between their backgrounds and the science concept. In this case, the teacher could pose a question to students that taps into preexisting knowledge. For example imagine a unit that deals with basic chemistry, a very common part of many elementary school science programs. On the first day of this unit, the teacher would want to connect his or her students' experiences with the topic. A way to begin would be to ask, "I want to start today by having you think about a time where you've watched somebody mixing a powder with a liquid. This could be when someone is cooking or doing laundry or lots of other things. But I want you to think about what happens when someone adds a powder to a liquid."

It is difficult to imagine the child who cannot think of an example of this phenomenon: adding sugar to a drink, pouring powdered detergent into a washing machine, mixing flour with water, putting fertilizer into a watering can, and so on. The intent of asking this question during the Engage phase is to honor students' personal experiences and use those as building blocks for the lesson. When teachers begin science lessons this way, there is a greater likelihood the students will be motivated to participate in the activity and that the subject matter will seem relevant and worthwhile.

Even if we tried, we could not list all the potential ways of doing the Engage phase. But here's a sample: displaying an object that is intriguing or playing a video clip that captures the students' attention. While students engage with these, invite them to talk about what they are noticing and what they are thinking. As is particularly appropriate in diverse classrooms, record these ideas using simple, straightforward words on a word board, an overhead projector, or some other central place in the room where these words and ideas can remain. The intention is for the teacher to allow the students to identify something that they already know or have wondered about and use that as a springboard into the science activity, as well as an entry point into the language of science.

Phase Two: Explore

The purpose of the Explore phase is to provide the students with firsthand experience with the science concept they are to learn. There is a delicate balancing act to this phase. We don't want to leave this open ended as if it's discovery learning, because we intend for this activity to connect with subsequent experiences. On the other hand, we don't want to make this so highly structured that it turns into a cookbook activity.

It is important to note that in the Explore phase, just like in the more structured types of inquiry, the teacher supplies some structure to the activity as a way to support the students' investigations. This includes pointing out the safety considerations, even if it were as simple as cleaning spills or not looking at the sun with the magnifier. In addition to such practical issues, the teacher should provide a challenge, problem, or question to guide the students as they explore.

Another indispensable way to provide structure is to give the students a record sheet. In working with teachers who use the learning cycle, we have seen that students' memories of the Explore activity are much weaker when they don't use the record sheet. This shouldn't be a fill-in-the-blank worksheet; it ought to provide places for students to record their observations. This could be as simple as "write three things you discovered when you mixed the powder in the water." The record sheet could also include a blank chart or table where the students enter their measurements. There could be a place where they are to draw what they observe. A record sheet is also a good way to encourage students to make inferences and predictions. For English language learners, it is helpful to have these worksheets written in English and their primary language. It is very common in school systems that serve a substantial population of nonnative English speakers to have translation services provided for students in need. Also current curriculum materials often include handouts written in Spanish. Finding access to such services or establishing other community-based resources (e.g., bilingual members of the community willing to contribute time) at the outset of the school year will be an essential component of structuring successful experiences for English language learners. Having these students record their thoughts in their primary language and in English is an important way to help them to learn the content. For students struggling with linguistic or cognitive barriers, drawing can be an excellent way of activating what they know and what they are thinking about the material. The point here is to create record sheets as vehicles for sponsoring student thinking in whatever way seems appropriate.

Point–Counterpoint

From the perspective of everyone who seems to have an official position about science teaching, inquiry seems to be the universal key. However, there are some who feel the definition of *inquiry* is so broad and vague that it's hard to determine what would not count as inquiry. In contrast, there are others who've witnessed teachers implementing inquiry and, despite the challenges, see the value to the students in those classrooms. So in response to the question "How useful is inquiry in real classrooms?" we have slightly divergent perspectives.

Integrating Inquiry Into the Classroom: A Suspicious Construct?

Eleanor Abrams
Science Teacher Educator at the University of New Hampshire

Reform efforts tout inquiry as the way to learn science (American Association for the Advancement of Science, 1990; National Research Council, 1996, 2000). In fact, I feel that inquiry in the classroom has achieved such popularity with the so-called experts in science education that it makes other instructional techniques seem inadequate in helping students learn or, worse, makes it appear that all other approaches stifle students desire to learn science. However, as a science teacher educator, I have some nagging questions that need to be answered before I jump wholesale into advocating the use of inquiry into the teaching practices of science teachers: What does inquiry look like in the classroom? What teaching goals are enhanced by using inquiry as a pedagogical approach? What do you need to know as a teacher to integrate inquiry in the class effectively? How do you prepare and support your students to succeed during an inquiry-based project? These questions are left unanswered, or worse the answers we get are often so vague they aren't of any help.

Take for instance the strategic way the National Research Council (2000) defined inquiry in the classroom. They outlined inquiry in terms of five components: who asks the questions, who designs the experiment, who manipulates the data, who draws the conclusions, and who communications the results. These components are placed on a continuum from teacher directed on one end to guided inquiry in the middle to student generated on the other end. We can score our curriculum, our approach, or our assessment on how inquiry oriented it is. This approach reflects the complexity of trying to integrate inquiry into the classroom. However, it leaves me unsatisfied on the definition of inquiry because it seems that every piece of curriculum, every instructional methodology, and every assessment can be fit into this understanding of inquiry. If inquiry is everything, how can the notion of inquiry guide my science teachers' practice in the science classroom as they struggle to meet the very concrete and defined state science standards and high-stakes testing?

I think one of the pieces of information science teachers will need to integrate more inquiry-oriented approaches into the classroom is a "thick" description of when is it and where is it appropriate to use inquiry. When are other methodologies more effective in creating equitable, caring learning environments where all students can be successful learning science? The reform documents imply that teachers should strive to create an inquiry-based, student-oriented classroom for all learning situations. I am still waiting for the research evidence that says that inquiry is the only way to help students learn effectively.

There are other obstacles besides not being able to find a definition of inquiry or knowing when to use the technique to stimulate student learning. Teacher preparation courses, including my own, teach about inquiry, but most students have not experienced open-ended inquiry in their own science preparation. So I watch my teachers struggle to do what they have not seen modeled. Working in the dark, they take a leap of faith and integrate inquiry into the classroom knowing they are responsible for the very real demands of teaching content to their students. Some of my teachers have successful experiences and feel successful in the ways they do use inquiry in the classrooms. Others do not feel their students learn enough for the amount of time it takes, so they shun inquiry.

One of the unknown factors that determines the success of my teachers is whether their students are prepared and supported during the inquiry. Not a lot is written about what kinds of knowledge or skills students need and how that varies the kind of inquiry that is used. The little that is written indicates students resist the change from more teacher-directed approaches to more student-oriented methodologies because they don't know the rules for success. I think it takes a determined teacher to give the necessary information and skills to the students at the right time before and during the inquiry process, support the students' emotional needs as they experience inquiry for the first time, and articulate the benefits of this approach to parents, administrators, and other colleagues—while feeling uncertain that inquiry will yield the benefits in learning foretold by the science education experts like myself.

I argue that the science education community needs to become more sophisticated in its ability to define inquiry in the classroom, discern the appropriateness of the use of inquiry as compared to other pedagogies, and gather rich examples of how inquiry works so that science teachers are able to adjust their curriculum, support their students, and articulate why they are using inquiry in the classroom. Otherwise, teachers can look upon this notion of inquiry only with suspicion.

Inquiry-Based Science Can Be Done

Margaret Blanchard
Assistant Professor at North Carolina State University and Former Middle School Science Teacher

I can tell you this from my time in classrooms and working with teachers: not only can inquiry-based science be done but it is being done, beautifully so in some cases.

My dissertation was a study of secondary science teachers who were translating a field-based research experience to their classrooms. The teachers had a level of confidence born of the support they garnered through a research experience with other teachers. Each attended a five-week-long marine ecology program, in which they not only conducted science inquiry but also developed a lesson that modeled their learning into pedagogical practice.

What were these teachers' obstacles when they returned to the classroom? They varied. For one teacher, it was letting go of the notion he had to cover his wave lesson as efficiently as he did last year. For another, it was learning how to build a water rocket launcher and figuring out how to assemble enough supplies for four class periods of students. For yet another teacher, it was expanding her notion of what special education students were capable of (a lot more than she had expected!). Letting go of some of her class control was a struggle for a teacher whose middle school students conducted an inquiry lesson on light and color.

What set these teachers apart was not some mystical abilities or extreme levels of competence in subject matter. These teachers took the time and had the motivation to try something new in their classrooms. In some cases it was an extreme makeover, in others it was a new twist on an old version of the same content lesson. What happened when they did it? The students seemed more enthused with the lessons, the teachers found their time to be less rote and more stimulating, and the classroom power shifted. I remember getting goose bumps while listening to the quality of student questions asked following a presentation on a water rocket investigation. In my research, I found that inquiry fostered higher-order questions on the part of students and tended to shift the role of the teacher to a supportive role in the learning rather than as the dispenser of knowledge. For students to excel on high-stakes testing, their answering questions that ask them to think and solve problems and having experiences in inquiry-based learning seem essential.

Inquiry-based science teaching is not only possible but also essential if we are to teach about the processes of science instead of the usual products that are discussed in textbooks and traditional science lessons. I think that the National Research Council's definitions of inquiry make the process clearer than any other document I have ever seen. They give us outwardly observable behaviors that are a litmus test for who owns the learning in that classroom.

Does inquiry-based teaching require support? Yes. Time is essential: time for learning and planning on the part of teachers, and time for thinking, designing, and experimenting on the part of students. Institutional support is needed for this and for materials. But can it be done? Should it be done? Absolutely!

Phase Three: Explain

This third phase of the learning cycle has two parts. One part is the students communicating with each other about what they did, and the other part is the teacher identifying the concept that they have been studying. Both of these constitute the Explain phase. The students explain what they have found, and the teacher explains what to call it.

Because the students work in small groups or even by themselves, the Explain phase is important so they can learn what others have found. Inductive teaching is happening when the separate pieces of experience are pulled together into a unifying whole. In some instances it might make sense for the teacher to provide different materials to each group during the Explore phase. A plant unit that begins with the study of seeds might involve providing various fruits and vegetables to different groups of students. The Explain phase is the time in which students then compare and contrast materials. This initial aspect of the Explain phase is important for diverse learners, and the way in which groups are organized becomes very important. When your classroom includes English language learners, consider grouping pairs of them with able English speakers. Likewise organize students with cognitive limitations in heterogeneous groups. Such colearning has been found to be a fundamentally useful manner in which to learn both science concepts and language.

The teacher's role during the Explain phase is to connect the students' learning to broader ideas. If the activity has provided enough structure, the students will have encountered the science concept at hand during the Explore activity. The teacher then attaches the label to the concept. What we are trying to avoid is thinking that the terminology is the same as the concept. The teacher isn't withholding anything by waiting to introduce the science term. The learning cycle allows the teacher to begin to convey the concept to students without burdening them with too much emphasis on correct vocabulary too early in the lesson. This is essential in everyone's learning of science, including English language learners and students with cognitive limitations. It's similar to a situation where you are familiar with someone or something but you don't know the right name for it. Although it's nice to know the name, the understanding of the person or object is not completely dependent on the name. And once you are familiar with the person or object, remembering the name is so much easier and more meaningful. In this way you should anticipate that the understanding and the label come together during the Explain phase.

NSES Teaching Standard B: Teachers of science guide and facilitate learning. In doing this, teachers orchestrate discourse among students about scientific ideas.

In diverse classrooms, it is particularly important, at the end of the Explain phase, to move beyond simply discussing explanations or ideas as a class. Because some of the students may not have followed all the parts of the class discussion or reading assignments, perhaps because of language barriers or the cognitive complexity of the ideas, it is important to record the understandings the class has constructed and make them apparent and available to everybody. Multiple representations—charts, drawings, role playing, bilingual signs, and straightforward explanations in English—all should be considered and employed to optimize students' science and language learning. Again, using a variety of ways to communicate the objects of science allows English language learners a better opportunity to understand the science and the methods to communicate it, and it allows students with cognitive limitations to better understand and remember what has been said.

Phase Four: Extend

This is the point where deductive teaching takes over. The students understand a scientific concept built during their recent activities, and they now even have a label for this concept. Their task during the Extend phase is to apply this understanding to a new situation. The parts from the Explore phase contributed to the whole from the Explain phase—that's inductive. Now in the Extend phase, students take this whole idea and test it against a new experience, which represents deductive thinking.

Moving From Induction to Deduction

While induction moves from fragmentary details (or particulars) to a connected view of a situation (universal), deduction begins with the latter and works back again to particulars, connecting them and binding them together. The inductive movement is toward discovery of a binding principle; the deductive toward its testing confirming, refuting, modifying it on the basis of its capacity to interpret isolated details into a unified experience. (Dewey, 1910/1991, pp. 81–82)

For whatever reason, teachers often feel tempted to push the Extend phase into new conceptual territory; that's not the right thing to do. Even though the teacher might be ready to move on to something new, the students are not yet there. During the Explain phase, the teacher points out the similarities across the Explore activity discoveries and uses scientific terms in describing the concepts. However, although a teacher will certainly have mastered the concept, the students will still need to invest time and experience to reach the same point.

NSES Program Standard D: Good science programs require access to the world beyond the classroom.

During the Extend phase students take their new knowledge and apply it to another situation. Suppose that during the Explore phase of an activity, students mix water with salt, baking soda, and sand. During the Explain phase they would share and compare their results, while the teacher would introduce the term *solution* and use the students' own findings to reinforce the concept. Likewise during this phase the students would be expected to show that they could use the word *solution* correctly as they investigate new substances such as sugar, pepper, and powdered drink mix. The expectation is that this activity will reinforce the appropriate use of the vocabulary. What is of equal, or more, importance is the Extend activity should strengthen the students' grasp of the concept.

Phase Five: Evaluate

This last component of the learning cycle is a little bit different from the others because it can happen at several points within the learning cycle. Researchers have looked at the previous four phases and found that when the sequence of these phases is changed, the students learn less well than when the sequence of phases occurs as we've described (Abraham & Renner, 1986). In contrast, the Evaluate phase can legitimately occur at several places within the learning cycle.

NSES Assessment Standard C: Students have adequate opportunity to demonstrate their achievements.

For right now, let's treat the Evaluate phase as the last in the sequence of learning cycle phases. This is the place and time in which the teacher evaluates what the students have learned. It also can become a way to inform the students about how well they understand what's been studied. This should somehow be formalized. Evaluation might not be as formal as a written, multiple-choice test, but it shouldn't fall to the other extreme and be based on casual observations of the students as they work. Teachers must be attentive to the type of the evaluation they use in order to minimize the tension between getting at what students understand and optimizing their opportunities to express what they genuinely know. Think in terms of multiple modes of communication, and carefully consider drawing, acting out, graphing, and writing as well as trying more standardized measures.

For Reflection and Discussion

How might the teacher's interactions with the students be different during the various phases of the learning cycle? What is the teacher listening for? What sorts of questions might the teacher ask? What is the goal of the teacher during the different phases?

As with all types of assessments, the Evaluate phase should closely align with the information students have been given and the activities in which they have been participating. Expecting students to respond to a written quiz can be appropriate as an Evaluate phase activity if it requires them to employ the same thinking processes, scientific vocabulary, and process skills they have recently been using. However, an Evaluate phase activity that is a dramatic cognitive departure is not appropriate within the learning cycle. Additional details regarding assessment will appear in a later chapter. But for the time being, let's position the Evaluate phase at the end of a chain of learning experiences.

Appropriateness for All Students

The learning cycle came into being around the time that discovery learning and inquiry were in vogue. Our sense of the limitations of those two approaches doesn't apply to the learning cycle. First, the learning cycle begins with an emphasis on the children and the act of guiding them to think scientifically, rather than having the scientist as the starting point. This approach avoids the danger of excluding students because of any unexamined assumptions about the types of kids who can and should do science.

Another benefit of the learning cycle is that in the Engage phase it makes a deliberate effort to connect with students' prior experiences. Also, in a classroom where the teacher is not completely aware of each child's family background and cultural traditions (which means almost every classroom), the Explore activity provides a shared experience. Then as the students talk about their science notions, they have something in common. No one is left out because the example being used is foreign to his or her experience. And although the students may have a different interpretation of the experience given what they bring into the classroom in terms of their background, the Explain phase should be structured in such a way to make these differing interpretations explicit through comparison and discussion—providing another opportunity for students to refine and deepen their understandings.

A third aspect of the learning cycle that makes it suitable for use with all students is the manner in which learning takes place. Instead of the information coming directly from the teacher, the students are able to test their ideas as they converse with their classmates. Some students have a difficult time asking questions of teachers—this can be because their culture regards the questioning of adults as disrespectful. By creating a classroom culture where students are often working with their peers, questions are raised and debated without the danger of confronting authority. This sort of interpersonal communication is especially prominent during the Explore and Extend phases as the students work on activities.

The fourth aspect of the learning cycle that makes it suitable for diverse learners is inherent in the combination of inductive and deductive approaches. Encouraging inductive reasoning from the outset allows students to gain experiences with which to associate terminology, a definite plus in terms of how people learn. The deductive aspects provide another opportunity to consider these ideas and to further link the experiences to the scientific explanations—again a benefit in terms of enhancing the learning of all students regardless of their English fluency or cognitive abilities.

Extending Science to All Learners

We continue examining the Principles for Effective Pedagogy proposed by the Center for Research on Education, Diversity, and Excellence (Warren & Rosebery, 2002) for their application to science teaching. The third of the five principles is "making meaning: connecting school to students' lives," and it continues to foster the notion that teachers can help all students be successful in science. The basis of this principle is that teachers' backgrounds are often very different from those of their students. As a result, students from diverse populations may have difficulty recognizing the connections between the content presented in school and the realities of their personal lives. For English language learners this challenge is compounded because of the lack of language in which students and teacher are mutually fluent. The teacher's challenge in making connections is to unearth, appreciate, and make effective use of the students' sources of knowledge.

TABLE 5.1. Connecting School to Students' Lives and the Appropriate Teacher Actions

The teacher:

uses what students already know from home, family, and neighborhood to shape the activity;

uses local community norms and knowledge sources to design meaningful learning activities;

guides students to relate and use what they've learned in their home community; and

varies activities in structure to accommodate student preferred forms of participation: collective versus individual and cooperative versus competitive.

Note: Adapted from Dalton (1998).

Connecting the World of Students to School Science

In examining Table 5.1, which lists approaches to building connections between school and home, you may recognize the overlap with the learning cycle. The first teacher action in the list parallels the Engage phase by starting with ideas already familiar to the students. As we've expressed before, this principle, as well as the others, seems appropriate for all students, and not just those who are developing English fluency. Nevertheless, it is necessary to provide students with opportunities to make these connections. Leaving such learning opportunities to chance gives no assurance that they will happen. In addition, such strategies give substance to the claims a teacher might make about being genuinely interested in his or her students. It's one thing to say "I care," but it is much more convincing when the actions of the teacher reinforce such statements.

The other components of this, the third principle for effective pedagogy, provide further justification for the learning cycle as an appropriate mode of teaching science to students who are English language learners. In particular, the Extend phase seems to be a rich opportunity to take knowledge acquired in the classroom and find ways to apply it to the neighborhood. In fact, all of the strategies listed for this third principle seem to mesh with the use of the learning cycle. The acts of finding ways to make meaningful links between academic science and the students' communities and modifying activities to allow for cooperative or individualized activities are well within the bounds of the appropriate use of the learning cycle. Such a synthesis would contribute to increases in the science learning of English language learners, with the potential for reducing the achievement gaps.

Key Features of the Learning Cycle

The learning cycle is an approach to teaching that fosters strong student understanding of science concepts. In a science unit, the second learning cycle should build on its predecessor. For a science unit that consists of multiple learning cycles, we can envision a stack of learning cycles where the information in one provides the foundation for the next. This method of curriculum design has been called a **spiral curriculum,** which describes the path that the teacher and students take as they move upward through a growing stack of learning cycles. The expectation is that information is not simply learned once and left behind. Instead, as students move through the spiral, they circle back to previously learned information and skills, but in more complex and meaningful ways. This is a very important way of crafting the science experiences to enhance learning in classrooms with diverse students.

NSES Program Standard A: Curriculum frameworks should be used to guide the selection and development of units and courses of study.

Another significant feature of a learning cycle is that only one concept is addressed within all five phases. Too often teachers feel they need to move forward and begin to present new concepts partway through. This is counterproductive. The desire to push ahead and move on is based in an old notion of content coverage. In too many situations teachers have been told that they have to cover an overly ambitious number of pages in the science book by a deadline. They have been told that if they don't keep up with all the other teachers, then the next year their students will be behind all the others.

The consequences of this folly are numerous. Students can become discouraged because they don't have enough time to really understand the material or gain the opportunity to express what they know. Teachers become anxious about keeping a good pace, and they transmit this as impatience toward their class. When this is the case, students don't have the chance to truly comprehend the important science concepts because the amount of time needed to struggle with and resolve ideas is never allowed.

We have made several interesting discoveries after making international comparisons of science teaching and learning. One that was widely reported in the media was that many countries have higher science achievement than the United States. Let's imagine for a moment that the comparisons weren't between the best students in other countries and typical U.S. students. What do you predict the textbooks of those other countries would look like? A logical way to think is that better test scores would mean knowing more material, which would be reflected in larger and more detailed textbooks. After all, wouldn't you expect that you'd gain more knowledge from a thick text compared to a slim volume?

If that was your prediction, then you would be wrong. The science textbooks in other countries where student achievement was higher were consistently and substantially shorter than the textbooks in the United States. In looking at the content of the textbooks, researchers discovered that in the United States, there is a great deal of information covered in every grade level but with only a surface treatment. In fact many of the same concepts were being taught from one year to the next. In contrast, the slimmer books used in other countries covered less material but in much greater detail. Furthermore, there was very little redundancy from one year to the next. One way to characterize this is to describe the science curriculum in the United States as "a mile wide and an inch deep." This situation has seemingly contributed to our students learning less science.

Fortunately the current science standards produced through reform movements in the United States have much greater depth while avoiding the tendency of too much breadth. For the most part it seems that individual states have followed that practice as they have adapted their own state curricula to these national reforms. In elementary and middle schools, there is less of a push to cover an entire textbook in one year. Students are expected to experience three to eight science units, and these units are not the same at each grade level.

This brings us back to the learning cycle. Because each learning cycle can address only one science concept and because it may take several class sessions to make one pass through the learning cycle, the amount of science material that can be covered in any one year is greatly reduced. With the learning cycle approach, the students spend more time developing deeper understandings and communicating what they are learning, even though they may not cover as much material. Fortunately the science education standards are consistent with this teaching approach. Rather than having the relentless drive to move from one chapter to the next in rapid succession, the science standards and the learning cycle have the potential to work in concert with each other.

Variations on the Learning Cycle

The most widely recognized form of the learning cycle is typically associated with science educator Rodger Bybee (1997, 2002). Just as with the learning cycle we presented, Bybee's consists of five phases, each of which starts with the letter "E." When you hear or read about the "Five E" model, you should give appropriate acknowledgment to Bybee's promotion of this variety of the learning cycle. However, this shouldn't lead anyone to believe that all learning cycles have five phases.

The original learning cycle attributed to Robert Karplus was a three-phase model: exploration, concept introduction, and concept application (Atkin & Karplus, 1962). Even at its inception the exploration of materials by students clearly preceded the formal teaching of scientific concepts, and this in turn was followed by subsequent activity in which students applied these concepts to new situations. Just as with Bybee's learning cycle, the Karplus version served as the guiding instructional approach for a science program called the Science Curriculum Improvement Study (Karplus & Thier, 1967), which is still commercially available.

Another version of the learning cycle consists of four phases and is best illustrated with the Insights curriculum developed by the Education Development Center (EDC). As described within its materials, the EDC learning cycle proceeds from getting started, exploring and discovering, processing for meaning, and extending the learning experience (EDC, 2003). The distinction from the Karplus model is the addition of a preexploring phase, and the difference from the Bybee model is the evaluation phase. However, the EDC authors don't ignore evaluation: their preference was to infuse it across all phases of the learning cycle and not force it into a separate phase.

Recently, another variation of the learning cycle has been proposed. Eisenkraft (2003) inserted an Elicit phase before Bybee's Engage phase and appended an Extend phase after Bybee's Evaluate phase. The creator of the 7E model freely acknowledged that his model is built on the legacy of its predecessors. And he pushed toward seven phases in response to findings from cognitive research that stress the value of making students' initial ideas explicit (i.e., with the Elicit phase) and the necessity of having students apply their understandings to new scenarios (hence the Extend phase). It is admirable that Eisenkraft uses his learning cycle within the *Active Physics* curriculum he has created. A comparison of these models appears in Table 5.2.

Special Needs Populations and the Learning Cycle

To the best of our knowledge, there has yet to be an educational research study that specifically examines the effectiveness of the learning cycle for special needs populations. Although there's no evidence the learning cycle would not work, there isn't a study we can point to that says it is better than other approaches. But there is no cause for despair, because there is considerable evidence that the underlying philosophy of the learning cycle and the manner in which this model is implemented in the classroom does correlate with demonstrably successful methods of teaching science to students with a range of cognitive abilities.

The research that has been conducted investigating special needs students in the context of science has been the specialty of Margo Mastropieri and Thomas Scruggs. In their extensive

TABLE 5.2. Despite Variation in the Number of Phases, All Learning Cycles Have a Shared Structure

Karplus and Thier	Education Development Center)	Bybee	Settlage and Southerland	Eisenkraft
—	—	—	—	Elicit
—	Getting started	Engage	Engage	Engage
Exploration	Exploring and discovering	Explore	Explore	Explore
Concept introduction	Processing for meaning	Explain	Explain	Explain
Concept application	Extending the learning experience	Elaborate	Extend	Elaborate
—	—	Evaluate	Evaluate	Evaluate
—	—	—	—	Extend

review of research of the science educational experiences of special needs populations, they summarized their field with these encouraging comments:

> Accommodation of individuals with special needs in science classrooms does not necessarily conflict with current thinking about science education and may, in fact, be very compatible with several aspects of such thinking. The aspects including emphasizing general principles and overall themes over separate facts and vocabulary, deemphasizing text; providing more focus on less content; including concrete examples and hands-on activities; [and] promoting cooperative group solutions to scientific problems. (Mastropieri & Scruggs, 1992, pp. 404–405)

While these recommendations are not based on specific investigations of the learning cycle, we recognize key features of this instructional model that apply to special needs students. For example the emphasis of general principles coincides with the "one concept" rule. The preferred focus on more in-depth exposure to fewer topics is consistent with the admonition to provide sufficient time to move through all of the phases. Concrete experiences and hands-on lessons are at the core of the Explore and Extend phases. Finally, the recommendation for having students work in groups is a defining feature of the learning cycle. On a point-by-point basis there are clear indications that the learning cycle is an appropriate teaching model for helping special needs students to become successful at science.

Connecting the Learning Cycle to the Three Science Teaching Approaches

In the previous chapter we presented you with three approaches to science teaching, whereas in this chapter we introduced you to a specific instructional model. A reasonable question one might ask is where are the connections between the approaches and this model. The confusion is understandable because, within discussions and writings about science teaching, people use the same term to signify very different philosophies, and people might be relying on different terms when they are in fact speaking of the same idea. Not everyone is aware of this mixture of meanings, and we are grateful to Bill Holliday (2001) for bringing this situation to the attention of a wider audience.

In an effort to help clarify what is meant by *inquiry* and how it contrasts with the discovery approach, Holliday recommended reading the *National Science Education Standards* and the supplement the National Resource Council published that concentrates on inquiry (National Research Council, 1996, 2000). But, as Holliday (2001) explained, "neither book presents a clear picture of the meaning of inquiry" (p. 55). He went on to speculate, "Perhaps this is because the term is increasingly fraught with different meanings" (p. 55). We see this as an open invitation to make the relationship between the three teaching approaches and the instructional model clearer.

We regard the three approaches as general schemes for presenting science to students but without necessarily specifying how this might be accomplished. In contrast, the learning cycle is much more specific about the delivery of instruction. Perhaps a sporting analogy will help make this clearer. In preparation for a basketball contest, a coach might decide to approach the next opponent with a great deal of intensity in an effort to establish a fast-paced game. Although that's a logical approach, it does not dictate how the players are to perform (beyond being intense). The strategies to actualize the approach might be to use a full-court press on defense and run a fast-break offense after every basket by the opponent and defensive rebound. The approach is rather general, but the actual strategy is quite specific. This is how we imagine the relationship between inquiry and the other two science teaching approaches and the learning cycle as an instructional model: the former describes the ambition whereas the latter identifies the ways it will be put into action.

Admittedly, it seems difficult to connect the discovery approach with the learning cycle model: discovery is characterized by its lack of structure and very little teacher directedness. However, both the inquiry and conceptual change approaches lend themselves to the learning cycle. Initially, the instruction builds on an inductive plan where experiences are used to build toward a significant concept. Subsequently, this concept is deductively applied to new situations. The difference between these applications is that the inquiry approach emphasizes the five essential features whereas the conceptual change approach concentrates on uncovering students' preexisting notions and then deliberately displacing those ideas that are not aligned with scientifically acceptable explanations. The learning cycle does not dictate which approach (i.e., inquiry vs. conceptual change) is used. In fact, the learning cycle could be appropriately used for a variety of inquiry approaches from structured to guided to open (Colburn, 2000).

A Cautionary Note

When we've had this discussion with practicing teachers and when we've discussed the need to acknowledge, build on, and address the very different understandings that students bring into the classroom, we've had teachers occasionally throw up their hands and say "that's too hard," "that's impossible," or "that makes teaching too complicated." Indeed we've both experienced these feelings in our own teaching. But we must acknowledge that actually helping students learn science in deep, useful ways is complicated. If learning depends on what the learner already knows (and it does), then teaching becomes a very difficult task. It is hard. It does take time. And, as we will discuss in chapter 14, despite the enthusiasm we have for the learning cycle, we understand there is no single "right way" to help students learn. But by using of some of the metacognitive strategies (which we will describe in chapter 11 on interdisciplinary teaching) and by paying close attention to students' discussions during their explorations of phenomena, teachers can gain access to some of their students' thinking—then use that knowledge to better shape their instruction. One of the things we find so useful about the learning cycle is that it provides opportunities for teacher listening—as we understand that care paid to student ideas is an essential component of the teaching of science.

Chapter Summary

- Teaching involves addressing the major ideas and specific examples of those ideas. When preparing for science instruction, the teacher must recognize the need to include both details and generalizations and decide the most effective sequence for their presentation.

- A deductive approach to learning begins with the major idea followed by the specific examples. The specific details are used to support the general ideas because the generalities are followed by the examples. In contrast, an inductive approach starts with the students working with particular examples that eventually lead to the major idea.

- By beginning a science unit with direct experiences, teachers provide all learners with a scaffold for supporting their developing ideas. The shared exposure to a situation ensures that all students have something concrete on which to hang their conceptions. As their understandings become stronger, the scaffold becomes a less necessary tool. The shared experience allows students to construct more systematic, detailed, and useful understandings of concepts than is often possible through instruction that emphasizes vocabulary.

- The learning cycle combines inductive and deductive approaches to science teaching. Each trip through the learning cycle focuses on a single yet important science concept with a mix of direct experiences and whole class discussions and explanations of the scientific phenomena in question.

- Despite variations in the number of phases and the labels given to the components, all learning cycles share the same overall structure. The five-phase model used in this chapter reinforces the inductive and deductive components of effective application of this model.

- An inductive approach to science teaching supplies every student in the class with the same foundational experiences. Because they have shared experiences, students with divergent backgrounds and experiences have less of a disadvantage when the teacher begins describing the science concept.

- Although we see the learning cycle as an almost ideal approach for teaching science to diverse populations, it is important to recognize that even this approach has its limitations. Teachers need to recognize that questioning ideas or teachers comes more naturally to some students than to others. Thus it is important to slowly construct the culture in the classroom where students learn to question and teachers support such questioning.

- It takes time for students to learn important science concepts! Consequently, the learning cycle is intended to concentrate on the same concept through all phases. It is inappropriate to introduce new concepts partway through the learning cycle in an attempt to cover more standards.

Key Terms

Deductive approach: a common approach to instruction in which the lesson begins with a general idea or concept and progresses to more specific instances of the idea or concept.

Inductive approach: an approach to science instruction in which the lesson begins with presentations of the part of an idea or concept, typically through examples or activities but without explaining how the parts are related, and progresses to the teacher guiding students to understand how the examples and activities are related to a more general idea or concept.

Learning cycle: an instruction model that originally consisted of three phases: (1) students working with scientific materials to pursue a problem or question, (2) a class discussion in which scientific concept is introduced, and (3) an opportunity for students to apply this newly formed concept to different materials.

Scaffold: the temporary assistance a teacher provides to students to assist them to accomplish something that they would not be otherwise able to accomplish alone.

Spiral curriculum: a method of curriculum design that consists of multiple learning cycles, where the information addressed in one learning cycle provides the foundation for the next. The spiral describes the path that the teacher and students take as they move upward through a series of learning cycles.

Zone of proximal development (ZPD): describes the difference between what a student can do or understand on his or her own and what he or she can understand.

A Favorite Science Lesson

A very common unit within most elementary and middle school science programs is the study of basic electricity. There are many good examples of such materials that provide students with direct experiences with batteries, bulbs, and motors. But the people at the EDC have created an exceptional grade four or five unit titled "Circuits and Pathways" that makes effective use of the learning cycle so it is explicitly and appropriately built into the curriculum. A good example is the "Series Circuit," which occurs approximately halfway through the unit. Students are challenged to connect multiple lightbulbs and batteries using wires such that multiple bulbs glow. Students trace the path of electricity through the devices. The teacher identifies those circuits where there is a single pathway along which the electricity flows as series circuits. This is an example of using an inductive approach, because students explore materials and then the teacher provides labels to the broader concept they have developed.

Suggested Readings

Cavallo, A. M. L. (2001). Convection connections. *Science and Children, 38*(5), 20–25.

> Within this article the author provides two exemplary learning cycle sequences. In the first sequence, students learn about convection currents in air, while the second sequence builds understandings of water convection currents. This demonstrates how one learning cycle can contribute to the learning that will occur in the next cycle.

McCarthy, D. (2005). Newton's first law: A learning cycle approach. *Science Scope, 28*(5), 46–49.

> Newton's First Law of Motion is about inertia: objects at rest tend to stay at rest, and once they are moving, the object continues to move in the same direction unless another force interferes. All of this is embedded within this Louisiana teacher's use of the learning cycle. This author's version of the learning cycle consists of four phases: elicitation, exploration, invention, and application.

References

Abraham, M. R., & Renner, J. W. (1986). The sequence of learning cycle activities in high school chemistry. *Journal of Research in Science Teaching, 23,* 121–143.

American Association for the Advancement of Science. (1990). *Science for all Americans.* New York: Oxford University Press.

Atkin, J. M., & Karplus, R. (1962). Discovery or invention? *The Science Teacher, 29*(5), 45–51.

Bybee, R. W. (1997). *Achieving scientific literacy: From purposes to practices.* Portsmouth, NH: Heinemann.

Bybee, R. W. (2002). *Learning science and the science of learning.* Arlington, VA: National Science Teachers Association Press.

Colburn, A. (2000). An inquiry primer. *Science Scope, 23*(6), 42–44.

Dalton, S. S. (1998). *Pedagogy matters: Standards for effective teaching practice.* Washington, DC: Center for Applied Linguistics.

Dewey, J. (1938). *Experience and education.* New York: Collier Books.

Dewey, J. (1991). *How we think.* New York: Prometheus. (Original work published 1910)

Education Development Center. (2003). *Insights: An elementary hands-on inquiry science curriculum.* Newton, MA: Author.

Eisenkraft, A. (2003). Expanding the 5E Model: A proposed 7E model emphasizes "transfer of learning" and the importance of eliciting prior understanding. *The Science Teacher, 70*(6), 56–59.

Holliday, W. G. (2001). Critically considering inquiry teaching. *Science Scope, 24*(7), 54–57.

Karplus, R., & Thier, H. (1967). *A new look at elementary school science.* Chicago: Rand-McNally.

Mastropieri, M. A., & Scruggs, T. E. (1992). Science for students with disabilities. *Review of Educational Research, 62,* 377–411.

National Research Council. (1996). *National science education standards.* Washington, DC: National Academy Press.

National Research Council. (2000). *Inquiry and the* National Science Education Standards: *A guide for teaching and learning.* Washington, DC: National Academy Press.

Warren, B., & Rosebery, A. S. (2002). *Teaching science to at-risk students: Teacher research communities as a context for professional development and school reform.* Santa Cruz, CA: Center for Research on Education, Diversity, and Excellence.

six
Questioning Strategies and Leading Discussions

Chapter Highlights

- Questioning strategies can be understood using behaviorist theory. The teacher's question is the stimulus, the student's answer is the response, and the evaluation by the teacher is the feedback. Teaching that uses questions can also be understood through two different views of learning, both individual and social constructivism.

- Constructivism provides two rather similar views about learning. When learning is viewed as something that happens as a person interacts with materials, then individual constructivism explains the process. In contrast when learning is viewed as something that happens in an individual or a group but largely as a result of social interactions and sense making, then it is best understood through social constructivism.

- When teachers ask questions, they use different techniques depending on the learning goals at that moment. As a lesson progresses through the learning cycle, the questions teachers ask and the ways in which they respond to students' answers will adjust depending on the phase.

- The power of questions to support student learning can be amplified through the use of the powerful questioning strategy called Wait Time. Wait Time requires teachers to be momentarily silent. Teachers are using Wait Time when they ask a question and allow a pause before calling on a student and after a student answers.

- Science discussions are very important episodes within science teaching. The instructional conversation framework is a collection of ten strategies that together describe an effective way to incorporate English language learners into whole class conversations.

The science lessons described to this point suggest that a great deal of student talking occurs within the classroom. Such an interactive classroom should be viewed as acceptable, because science is an inherently social enterprise, with scientists necessarily communicating within the process of advancing scientific understandings. Because we intend for school science to mirror, although in developmentally appropriate ways, the actions of science as done by the professionals, we would expect interpersonal communication to dominate within science classrooms. Learning to participate in the give-and-take of questioning represents a valuable action within the culture of science. Having students ask questions is a key action within the culture of science, and it is an important part of having students participate in science inquiry. However, the emphasis within this chapter will be on the teacher's use of questions. We will focus on the types and ways that teachers use questions as they guide students' science learning. In addition, discussions among students are necessary for learning to occur. This is true for all students and is especially necessary for English language learners. In this chapter we will consider ways a teacher can use questions to encourage students to think. Knowing how and when to pose questions is a powerful teaching skill. This chapter will also describe a framework for organizing whole class discussions such as would take place during the Explain phase of science instruction. We start by examining ways to pose questions to individual children and then expand our repertoire to consider ways to encourage a class science discussion that invites participation from everyone.

Behaviorism and Questioning

The most dreadful stereotype of a science lesson is one where only the teacher does the talking while the students are expected to absorb what is being told to them. Admittedly there are occasions when such direct instruction is a very efficient way to teach students. For example a teacher might use a direct instruction to teach a class about procedures for evacuating the building in the event of an emergency. In this situation there is very particular information the students need to know and leaving the procedure open to individual interpretation is inappropriate, although even such direct instruction must be followed by assessment activities to be sure that what the students understood about the explanation mirrors the meaning the teacher had intended.

The theory underlying direct instruction is **behaviorism,** which can be represented as a feedback loop:

Stimulus → Response → Feedback

This technique can be used for many purposes. We can teach a goldfish to swim to the surface of an aquarium when we hold our fingers above the water. This process involves a combination of rewards for the fish and patience on the part of the trainer. More complex tricks can be taught to animals by offering them rewards each time they execute a correct behavior. Teachers can use behaviorism to train students as part of their classroom management policy. We use *train* in this circumstance because the learning intended is fairly straightforward: do what the teacher expects and you will be rewarded.

Within academic instruction, teachers often draw on behaviorist principles to good effect, even beyond classroom management. Very simply, a teacher poses a *question* to a class, asks a student to *respond,* and then *evaluates* the correctness of the answer. This **QRE sequence** is distinctly behaviorist:

Question → Response → Evaluation

When behaviorist philosophy is used as a guide for teaching and not simply as a tool for managing behaviors, the underlying goal is the broadcasting and reception of knowledge. The purpose of instruction that uses this notion is to ensure that the information is being taken in just as it was presented to the learner and that the information is organized in an appropriate fashion. The expectation is that the information reported back to the teacher is very similar, if not identical, to that which was originally taught. Students who are "better" at doing this are those who can more quickly absorb and recall that information. Under these circumstances, knowledge is treated as a commodity: the teacher distributes the goods and the students are expected to be able to demonstrate that they possess those goods on demand.

For the QRE technique to effectively promote learning, the connections between each part of the sequence must be very tight. Quickly informing the student about whether the response was correct or incorrect is an essential dimension of this way of teaching. If there is too much delay between the response by the student and the evaluation by the teacher, then the learning will not be as efficient. Thought about in a different way, the gap between each phase of this feedback sequence must be very brief because the longer the delay, the less efficiently the information will be learned. For students who are working to master English at the same moment they are trying to learn the science content, or for those students who would benefit by receiving immediate reinforcement, quick feedback is often an important technique.

This way of teaching is not necessarily bad, and admittedly has its place within the larger universe we could label as learning. Students typically know when and how they are to participate and can learn how to act accordingly. Perhaps because of this dependability, the QRE technique is often seen as much as a tool for maintaining classroom control as for imparting knowledge. However, it is important to recognize that there are many limitations to the QRE technique. First, given its familiarity to both teachers and students, it is too often regarded as the only way of asking students questions, which can make lessons dull and routine. Second, it is most suitable for teaching material that is simple and has definite right and wrong answers but is not as useful when ideas are more complex. Third, the pace of instruction becomes very rapid as one QRE sequence is joined to another in a rapid-fire chain, a situation that can frustrate students who are still developing their English language fluency.

This way of teaching lends itself to a particular type of teacher questioning, namely, the use of **convergent questions**. Convergent questions have a limited number of correct responses and are sometimes termed close-ended questions. When a teacher asks students a convergent question, he or she has a particular answer in mind and evaluates the response a student gives based on that expectation. The goal of convergent questions is not to prompt discussions; the purpose is for the teacher to determine whether a student knows the right answer.

In contrast are **divergent questions**, also known as open-ended questions. When using divergent questions the teacher does not have a specific response he or she is seeking and so welcomes a variety of answers from the students. By their very nature, divergent questions are not used as part of the QRE approach, because it is not necessary to evaluate students' answers to divergent questions. Indeed such evaluations work against the openness of divergent questions. As much appeal as divergent questions might hold because they can foster creative thinking, they are incompatible with a behaviorist-oriented teaching method.

This should lead you to recognize that teacher questioning can serve multiple purposes. Hearing a teacher claim he or she uses lots of questioning in the classroom may not reveal much about the sorts of questions being asked, the kind of learning taking place, or the overall climate that exists in the teacher's classroom. In the next section we explore how questioning strategies are included with constructivist philosophies of teaching.

Individual Constructivism

One of Jean Piaget's contributions to education is the idea that people are actively involved in making sense of their world. Piaget found that children capture information from the outside world and attempt to fit it into what they already knew instead of absorbing what they were told. The odd little ideas we hear from children, such as a belief that wind is caused by the swaying of trees, make some sense when you consider the world from their perspective. A child's suggestion, for example, that rain happens because the clouds tip over and the water they are holding spills out—as amusing as this may seem—shows that children take what they already know, use what they notice, and try to make it all fit together. This is known as **individual constructivism.**

Maybe an analogy will reinforce this elusive idea. Rather than treating the mind as a photocopier or scanner that duplicates what is put into it, as is the case with behaviorist understandings of learning, let's imagine that the mind is an ongoing construction project. This construction project consists of blocks or sticks or whatever toy pieces are familiar to you. The point is that new pieces are being introduced all the time, and they have to be connected to what already exists. New information can come from watching television, reading a book, doing an activity, talking with someone, and so on. Unlike a sponge where information is simply soaked up, the mind of a child is continuously working to make the pieces connect together.

Information Versus Knowledge

Perhaps this is a good place to distinguish between information and knowledge. Information is simply data, whereas knowledge is the product of putting all the information together. Computers can be used to access and store information. But knowledge can exist only within our minds. We can accurately say that the Internet has contributed to the information explosion. However, because information and knowledge are not the same thing, it's inaccurate to suggest that there is a simultaneous knowledge explosion. Data and understanding are not the same. Information is out there, but knowledge requires the extra step of converting that information into understandings.

Every learner enters the classroom with a wealth of prior knowledge. Educational psychologists (people who study learning) describe knowledge as being organized into **schema** or scripts that help the learner make sense of the world. Because every learner has different experiences, each learner has different schema he or she has built and use to make sense of subsequent experiences. Learning becomes a process of fitting new ideas and experiences into the existing schema. Because learners possess different schema, students can come away from the same lesson with very different understandings.

Applying a constructivist understanding of learning, teachers use questions as tools for checking the students' schema, in a way similar to stepping on a sheet of ice to test its strength or pushing at a stack of objects to see whether it will stay upright. The questions that teachers pose are for the benefit of both the individual student and the teacher. The question a teacher asks obliges the student to consider whether his or her understanding of the concept is sufficiently solid to explain a range of situations. The teacher can rely on questions to assess which students have genuinely grasped the material and which have not fully integrated the topic into their schema.

The questions used within a constructivist view of learning should move beyond simple recall. If you recollect **Bloom's taxonomy,** you will remember that knowledge-level questions are at the lowest level of understanding. Questions that tap into the knowledge level prompt students to list, name, and label; the students' responses are at a very basic level. Too often we confuse a student's use of a scientific term as an indication that he or she understands the science concept. Teacher questions that rise above the knowledge level allow students to reveal the depth and complexity of their understandings.

Here's a situation to consider: at the end of the school year, a teacher provided his third graders with disposable cameras. He asked the students to take pictures of science in and around their homes, including pictures of themselves doing science. One girl who had done very well in science all year had her mother take two photographs of her holding a candle, one with the candle lit and the other with it blown out. When asked how this picture represented science, Cecily said it showed evaporation: first the flame was there and when she blew on it, it was gone. Apparently the teacher had not asked sufficient questions during the water cycle unit to see if Cecily's understanding of evaporation was accurate.

Obviously Cecily's photographs revealed how she had constructed her understanding of evaporation. However, because her teacher had been satisfied by her use of the term during the unit on the water cycle, he mistakenly assumed that she really understood the concept. Imagine if the teacher had asked Cecily **higher-order questions,** that is, at Bloom's levels of comprehension, application, analysis, and so on. This would have pushed Cecily to think beyond simply remembering the word. If the teacher had also asked Cecily to apply her knowledge of evaporation beyond the simple class activities, perhaps her thinking would have included more than the "disappearing act" notion. By not using questions to prompt his students to think beyond knowledge and recall, the teacher incorrectly assumed that his teaching had been effective.

Social Constructivist Learning

We typically associate Lev Vygotsky's name with the philosophy of **social constructivism,** just as we connect Piaget with individual constructivism. As the labels imply, individual constructivism focuses on the learning by each separate child, whereas social constructivism takes into consideration the learning as it is influenced by interactions with and influences of social groups. Vygotsky put a much higher value on interactions among people within the learning process. The difference is that Piaget's form of constructivism can draw on interpersonal communication, although it was not necessary. But Vygotsky's social constructivism requires the give-and-take among people for learning to occur.

Without putting too fine a point on this issue, we would expect from the individual constructivist perspective that all learning takes place within the individual mind. In contrast a social constructivist would claim that learning first occurs within a group setting as thoughts are exchanged and then become incorporated into individual minds. The social constructivist philosophy would have clear implications for how science teaching should be organized: the teacher cannot be at the front of the room using her or his own voice and a variety of resources to dispense scientific knowledge into the gaping minds of the students. Instead the teacher needs to offer opportunities for students to propose their ideas within a social environment that allows for testing, revising, and discussing. The teacher's role is to initiate and sustain conversation, and that requires the wise use of questioning strategies.

NSES Teaching Standard D: Student understanding is actively constructed through individual and social processes.

Teacher Questioning Strategies

As we begin examining various types of questions and the responses teachers can make to the students' answers, you should avoid thinking that some strategies are right and some are wrong. Teaching is rarely that simple. Instead whether a type of question a teacher asks or the reaction to a student's response is appropriate depends on the situation. Earlier in this chapter we presented the differences between convergent (closed) questions and divergent (open) questions. An effective teacher knows how to use both questions and knows when is the right time to ask each type of question. In this section we will consider when these two question types are appropriate to use.

How can a teacher determine if his or her use of questioning is appropriate? The answer resides with the unspoken reason for using a question. Within the learning cycle the purpose of questions shifts as the learning progresses from one phase to the next. In an effort to further clarify how to teach science using the learning cycle, we organize questioning strategies according to the phases.

Questions During the Engage Phase   Within the Engage phase, the teacher is seeking information from the students about their previous experiences and existing knowledge. We expect the teacher to pose divergent questions during this phase; for example "What are some things you know about seeds?" and "What are some objects around your home that use batteries?" There are typically no right or wrong answers for engagement questions, and certainly no single answers, and the teacher may genuinely not know what sorts of answers the students may give. But that's OK: the purpose of a divergent question during the Engage phase is to invite a variety of views and perspectives.

If someone regards teaching as just a performance before an audience, then the value of questioning may not be apparent. We should think about teaching as an effort to stimulate individuals to learn on their own. Put another way, for learners to begin constructing understandings, it helps if there is an internal drive to find answers and a desire to make sense of the world. Encouraging children to take charge of their own learning can be enhanced by making good use of their natural curiosity. The questions teachers ask during the Engage phase are intended to raise students' awareness of possibilities and to instill a small measure of perplexity. With these goals in mind, the effective teacher will pose questions that propel and compel the students to want to know more.

Questions During the Explore Phase   The questions the teacher asks during the Explore phase also tend to be divergent. However, the reasons for asking questions during this phase are somewhat different from those for asking questions during the Engage phase. During the hands-on activity of the Explore phase, the teacher has a sense about the discoveries the students should be making. As a result, what seem like divergent questions can also have a somewhat more defined purpose. In other words, a teacher might pose a question that will be perceived as an invitation to the students to explore, but it is also the teacher's way of guiding the students to shift their attention to something that might otherwise go unnoticed.

Here's an example: a teacher involves the students in an Explore activity that is intended to give them some exposure to surface tension. Students are using eyedroppers to add water to the surface of coins. Their record sheets include a data table where they are to record the number of drops that different types of coins will hold. Because of the surface tension of water, if students are careful they can easily put twenty or more drops onto a penny.

As the teacher moves about the room, she overhears a group of students who have noticed that the water is acting as a magnifier: the numbers and letters on the coins are much larger when viewed through a water drop. Although this is an important discovery and not one the teacher wishes to trivialize, the students are not only failing to record the data onto their record sheets but also simultaneously not observing the piling up of water. The teacher poses this seemingly divergent question: "What do you notice about the water when you look at the coin from the side?" The students slide from their chairs and look across their desks at the coins—and they notice the hump of water. The teacher has not diminished the students' enthusiasm for their discoveries but has been able to alert the students to a significant feature. This was accomplished through the use of a well-timed and carefully posed divergent question.

Questions During the Explain Phase   The Explain phase is the debriefing that occurs after students have worked in groups during their explorations. During the Explain phase, the teacher's first task is to have the students communicate their findings to their classmates. This is not a time when just any response is acceptable. When the teacher asks, "What did your group discover?" the expectation is that the answers will be based on what had actually been noticed and ideally written onto their record sheets. On the surface this question appears to be divergent, but in actuality the teacher wants the students to describe specific findings. The teacher may not have a certain answer he or she expects, but at the same time a student cannot merely share an opinion. The "rightness" of the students' answers should be based on the work they did during the Explore phase. In that sense the teacher wants the answers to come from the groups' work. To accomplish this the teacher has posed a convergent question.

But even during the Explain phase the teacher might ultimately pose more divergent questions. After having students present their findings to the rest of the class, the teacher will lead the students to look for patterns in the information. If the teacher had designed an Explore activity where some groups had one set of materials and other groups had slightly different objects, then an appropriate divergent question would be "How might we classify the observations from the different groups?" Having established some patterns or generalizations about the information, the teacher can appropriately use another divergent question that includes a process skill; for example "What kinds of inferences can you make about our data?" Within the Explain phase, the teacher could pose convergent questions at the start and then move toward questions that are more divergent.

For Reflection and Discussion

Sometimes when a teacher asks a question, he or she expects a certain response. At other times a teacher asks questions without having specific answers in mind. What are some things a teacher might say or do to signal to the students that he or she is asking divergent questions or convergent questions? How might this help the students to know which form of question they are hearing their teacher ask?

Questions During the Extend Phase   Convergent questions predominate during the Extend phase, because the purpose is for the students to apply what they have been learning to another situation. Students are not expected to make new discoveries during this phase. Instead this is the time when they are to show if they can **transfer** what was learned about one set of materials to another set of materials. Transfer describes the mental process where students are refining what they know. As a result their knowledge can be useful in a variety of contexts beyond the specific situation where they first encountered this new idea (Wagner, 2006). The teacher expects to hear students using the scientific term presented during the Explain phase as they work with different materials. Often this requires the teacher to intervene with a convergent question phrased something like "What do we call this?" as a way to impress upon the students that they need to be using the new terms. The goal of the Explain phase is not to foster creativity or promote speculation among the students. There is a clear purpose at hand, and that purpose is for the students to practice their understandings of the one concept, including the use of the terminology.

How to Ask Questions

Up until this point, we may have given the impression that effective teacher questioning is simply a matter of asking divergent and convergent questions. Although this addresses *when* to ask questions and *what types* of questions to ask, we now need to consider *how* to ask questions. This leads to one of the most potent teaching techniques you can master. Even though this technique originated in science education, it can be used across all subject areas. Perhaps the most peculiar aspect of this strategy is that it requires the teacher to *not* do something.

Wait Time One

Mary Budd Rowe (1974/2003) was studying science teaching in different elementary schools when she noticed that the quality of discussions was highly varied across classrooms. In some teachers' classrooms, there was widespread participation in discussions with many students contributing ideas, whereas in other classrooms this wasn't happening. There were many potential explanations for these differences: the number of students in the room, the depth of the teachers' scientific knowledge, the availability of curriculum materials, the ages of the students, or the geographic location of the schools. None of these predictions were sufficient. When she grouped the classrooms into categories to test each hypothesis, she did not find a pattern that explained the variation in discussion quality—there had to be something else that would explain the differences in the classroom discussions.

Rowe then noticed that the pace of teacher questions was much more rapid in some classrooms. The QRE sequence occurred in certain classrooms at a dizzying rate. The amount of time that a teacher gave a student to respond to a question was, on average, one second. What was taking place within these lessons was an interrogation, where the teacher rapidly fired questions. When a student did not begin to answer within one second, the teacher repeated the question or called on another student to answer.

However, in those classrooms where bona fide science conversations were happening, Rowe noticed how the teachers were giving their students more time to think. The pause between the moment when a teacher asked a question and the student began to answer was the factor that explained the differences she had observed—not teacher science knowledge, not student maturity, not class size. This pause, which we now call *Wait Time One*, was crucial for fostering classroom science discussions. What was contributing to better science discussions was simply the teachers' willingness to give the students time to think, and it was a matter of only three to five seconds. The fundamental difference was what the teachers did not do: they did not say anything during those few seconds and provided the students with the time to formulate their responses.

One difficulty new teachers sometimes having with using Wait Time One is that they are so accustomed to talking. The constant stream of teacher patter is almost an addiction—but it is a habit that can be broken. To pause and allow silence to prevail, even for just a few seconds, is an odd experience at first. It seems unnatural to some teachers. For students who have been acculturated into a classroom where questions and answers rapidly cycle, this pause can be puzzling. They might feel lost without the familiar, rapid sequence of question, response, and evaluation.

However, once students realize the teacher is pausing so thinking can happen, and not because someone is at the receiving end of a teacher stare, then the students begin to genuinely think about their responses. The pause that signifies Wait Time One may have to be used many times over several class sessions before everyone starts becoming comfortable with this new thinking space. But eventually it will become a defining feature of science discussions and the classroom's culture of learning.

NSES Teaching Standard D: Teachers of science design and manage learning environments that provide students with the time, space, and resources needed for learning science. In doing this, teachers create a setting for student work that is flexible and supportive of science inquiry.

When you use Wait Time One for the first time, you might find that you approach it with a little uncertainty. Instead of staring at the clock for three to five seconds, try holding up your hand to signal that no one is to speak, and inside your head say, "If I wait three to five seconds, my students will give me better quality answers." Saying this little phrase takes three to five seconds. Then call on a student. After a few attempts, you will notice that the students are giving better quality answers, and that should be all the incentive you need to continue using Wait Time One.

Responding to Student Responses

There is more involved with using questioning strategies than simply asking divergent questions and using Wait Time One. If the teacher intends to use divergent questions to foster student contemplation, a judgmental response by the teacher to a student's answer sends a conflicting message. To the student, it might have sounded as if the teacher was seeking a range of possible answers—but the teacher's response clearly shows that he or she had something different in mind. In a similarly confusing fashion, a teacher who is too quick to comment on a student's answer or in some other way rushes forward also sends mixed messages. Knowing about appropriate ways to respond to student answers is as important as the manner in which the questions are posed.

Wait Time Two

The key to Wait Time One is for the teacher to resist talking, thereby giving the students more time to think. *Wait Time Two* is another example of the teacher pausing, but the pause in Wait Time Two occurs after the student has responded. With Wait Time Two the teacher provides a pause of just a few seconds instead of providing an immediate commentary about a student's answer. As with the first Wait Time, this pause does not have to be painfully long. Although it seems minor, this pause has multiple benefits.

One consequence is that students' confidence in their answer increases because the teacher isn't disrupting their responses. In typical classrooms, teachers give students they perceive to have more ability longer time to answer questions, whereas the opposite is the case for students for whom teacher expectations are not as high. When this occurs, more capable students perceive that the teacher believes they are up to the challenge of composing an answer, and less able students recognize that the teacher feels the need to rescue them from their own inabilities. Consequently, the teachers' responses send a very clear message (a message we find very troubling): some students can achieve more whereas others don't need to expend the energy. The

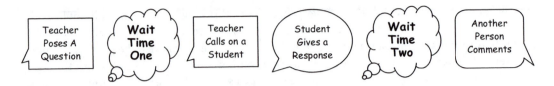

FIGURE 6.1. The occurrence of Wait Time One and Wait Time Two within a questioning sequence.

Wait Time Two pause sends a message to the students that the teacher believes in their ability to give a good answer, and the teacher demonstrates this by not cutting off their response before they are done speaking.

Figure 6.1 shows how Wait Time One and Wait Time Two fit within teacher questioning as an alternative to the QRE sequence. It is worth repeating that this is a very uncommon way of asking questions and responding for the teacher and the students alike. The benefits of Wait Time will not magically appear the first instance when it is used within a science lesson. However, as the students begin to recognize that the teacher will not only pause before calling on someone but also provide a pause that allows time to finish expressing ideas, then the benefits that Mary Budd Rowe uncovered will reveal themselves.

Classrooms Where Wait Time Is Used

A **self-fulfilling prophecy** describes a situation in which the expectations a person holds for a situation shape his or her interpretations of the event. What is expected is often what is observed, and this in turn reinforces the original expectation. A negative self-fulfilling prophecy occurs when someone expects things unpleasant to happen. Regardless of what follows, this expectation treats the events as reinforcing the person's fear, resentment, or disappointment. In contrast a positive self-fulfilling prophecy describes a hopeful disposition toward an event. Even for the same situation, this person would interpret what happens in a much more positive light. In either case, the expectations shape perceptions, which in turn influence future expectations.

Wait Time can guide a teacher toward a positive self-fulfilling prophecy. One consequence of Wait Time is that students will begin to give better answers. Rowe (1974/2003) was able to define "quality answers" as follows: students provided longer responses, declined to respond on fewer occasions, had greater confidence in the tone of their responses, and more frequently used evidence to support their statements. This is an impressive list of reasons for using Wait Time. With this expectation, you may find that the students' responses are just as we have described, and this will in turn reinforce the value of Wait Time in your mind as a questioning strategy.

After Rowe's discoveries about teachers who generated superior classroom discussions, she worked with other teachers to develop their skill at using Wait Time. After a year of gathering data in several classrooms, she found that the teachers who were using Wait Time posed fewer questions to the class (which makes sense because students in Wait Time classrooms give longer responses) and that the types of questions these teachers were asking tended to be of a higher level.

In addition the teachers participating in this research reported that their use of Wait Time improved student responses, particularly among those students the teachers had thought of as the lower achieving individuals in the classroom. Giving the entire class time to ponder, and again this is a matter of only three to five seconds, was associated with higher-quality student contributions from all students. As a result teachers heightened their expectations of students who they had previously felt were not especially good in science. This exemplifies a self-fulfilling prophecy: the teacher communicates higher expectations of the student (by giving him or her time to compose a response), the student gives a richer and more complete response (because there was more time to generate a full answer), and the teacher recognizes that the student's capabilities in science have justified providing more Wait Time.

Another outcome of the use of Wait Time was in the nature of the students' responses. In classrooms where Wait Time is often used, the students provide longer, more thoughtful, and more complete answers to their teacher's questions. The students' responses also tend to include more inferring and use evidence as support of their ideas. Furthermore, students tend to provide more speculative statements as a consequence of Wait Time.

NSES Teaching Standard A: Teachers of science plan an inquiry-based science program for their students. In doing this, teachers select teaching and assessment strategies that support the development of student understanding and nurture a community of science learners.

Finally, Wait Time Two leads to wider participation in whole class discussions. In the classrooms Rowe studied, teachers noticed that more students were contributing (and these were appropriate contributions) even though the teacher had not explicitly called for more responses. Because of their teachers' use of Wait Time, the students viewed the pauses as opportunities to share their ideas, whether to support what had already been said or to offer other possibilities. As a result the strategy acknowledged student diversity and improved the equity of the classroom climate. Communicating equitable expectations to all students goes beyond pronouncements such as "I believe in every one of you." By doing something as straightforward as pausing before calling on students and withholding comment as they complete their responses, teachers put into action the intentions of equity.

For Reflection and Discussion

Suppose that you are determined to try to use Wait Time One the next time you teach a lesson. What can you do to help yourself to avoid calling on students too soon? What sorts of reminders can you put in place so that even though you're deep in the middle of the teaching, you don't neglect giving a pause before expecting a student to speak? As for Wait Time Two, what are some measures you might take to remind yourself not to jump in too quickly as a student responds to your questions?

What Kinds of Questions to Ask

Because teachers who use Wait Time ask fewer questions of the class, they need to adjust the types of questions that they ask. Rather than asking low-level questions where students are expected to recall information, the teacher may begin to use higher-level questions (see Table 6.1). Teachers can ask students to speculate more, press them to give reasons for their responses, and encourage them to pull together several bits of information into a larger and coherent whole.

TABLE 6.1.   Types and Examples of Higher-Level Questions Teachers Could Ask

Type	Purpose	Example
Interpretation	Students are asked to explain data, results, or other information.	What do you think is the reason the water is absent from one container but not the other?
Analysis	Students are to break a bigger idea or situation into component parts.	How are the different parts of the water cycle happening within our terrarium?
Application	Students take their knowledge from one scenario and extend it to another.	How can you use what you know about pendulums to predict the behavior of a swing?
Critique	Students evaluate a situation and appraise it based on certain criteria.	What are the strengths of this science fair project, and how could it have been even better?
Speculation	Students are challenged to hypothesize about future events.	What might be some of the effects of building a shopping center in this natural area?

The Reasons That "Why?" Is a Problem

Asking a student or an entire classroom a question that begins with *Why* may seem innocent enough. After all it's one of the six journalism prompts (*who, what, where, when, why,* and *how*). For some reason, however, asking students questions that begin with *why* makes them guarded and defensive. We can offer two possible explanations.

First, a *why* question suggests there is an ultimate and correct answer; for example "Why is the sun important to us?" or "Why did the litmus paper change colors?" or "Why does the mass stay the same even though we changed the shape?" The way these questions are phrased does not invite speculation but suggests a definitive answer. If the intent of the question was to limit thought and emphasize a single answer, then this type of question is appropriate. But if the teacher hoped the students would propose many possible answers to such a question, he or she would be disappointed by the results. The *why* signals the students to try to give the right answer.

The other reason *why* questions should be avoided within science teaching is their use in everyday language. Often a *why* requires someone to justify his or her behavior. Questions such as "Why are you running in the hall?" or "Why didn't you finish your assignment?" aren't the kinds of questions that are meant to promote contemplation. These are managerial questions that seek the individual's motivations for some action and call for a change in the individual's behavior. These questions are often followed by a penalty or punishment for not following the rules. Because much of student discipline begins with a strongly worded question, when students hear a question that begins with *why*, they may feel that they are being asked a disciplinary question. The bottom line is that the innocent use of *why* by the teacher may have the effect of limiting student thought instead of encouraging it.

A simple solution is to attach a little phrase after the *why* to signal the students that a variety of responses is desirable. That phrase is "do you think... ," and if you plug that in to the *why* questions in the previous paragraph, you can see how the question has a very different feel. How would you answer the question "Why *do you think* the sun is important to us?" Doesn't it seem that there may be many reasons possible and that it's okay to suggest several? These are the subtle shifts in questioning that can influence the sorts of responses we hear from our students.

Instructional Questions Versus Managerial Questions

Questions are used for different purposes in different settings, and you cannot apply the same guidelines for question asking all the time. We advocate for the belief that during science, teachers should be asking questions that encourage students to think before answering. This is implicit within divergent questions, Wait Time, and "why do you think" strategies. Nevertheless it is important to recognize that an effective teacher will use questions in the classroom for other reasons. Sometimes questions will require the students to give the correct answers to convergent questions.

When describing safety procedures, a teacher can rely on questioning. During a unit on microorganisms, there are some health issues related to this kind of work, and the proper disposal of materials is important. A teacher may demonstrate how to seal a container that holds a culturing medium. Having shown the proper procedure, the teacher may pose questions (even *why* questions) to reinforce the need to follow particular steps and to rehearse those steps. Open-ended questions don't apply in such circumstances.

Another example where contemplation is less important than compliance is when teachers are using questions as part of classroom management. For instance we've all been in classrooms where the teacher calls on students who are passing notes or otherwise unengaged in the class activities. In such a situation, the teacher will use questions to signal students to attend to the lesson. It is important to recognize that such use of questions may not always be effective. Lisa Delpit (1996) found that using questions such as "What do you think you should be doing?" might quicken the pulse of many middle-class American students, but students from other cultures do not necessarily interpret this in the same way. She reported that in many homes, the parents will tell the children what to do rather than offer them what might sound like a choice. Rather than saying, "Do want to start thinking about going to sleep?" parents may provide clear instructions: "Put away your toys, change into your pajamas, brush your teeth, and get into bed." Delpit attributed this to different communication styles that seem so obvious to those who operate within those traditions but seem so unusual to those whose traditions are different.

Delpit discovered that teachers are sometimes frustrated in their efforts to discipline children from cultures other than their own because the learners may not recognize the intent of what is being asked of them and so fail to respond in the appropriate manner. Although this might be interpreted as the child's being disrespectful, or at least disruptive, in actuality the student is simply failing to pick up on the teacher's intent. Even though you might be accustomed to the role that questions might have in discipline, you cannot assume that questions will have the same effect on all students. Otherwise you and your students might become aggravated with each other.

Point–Counterpoint

Helping students to learn requires teachers to be supportive. What is somewhat unclear is the appropriate type of support that should be provided. On one hand, students should become independent learners but that should not translate into releasing them from our care too swiftly. The feedback or praise teachers provide to their students is a topic of some disagreement. So to answer the question "How should praise be used in the classroom?" we can consider the opposing stances of two teachers.

Barry Golden
Science Teacher at Maclay School, Tallahassee, Florida

Upon first setting foot in my classroom, I was eager to unleash my secret weapon: praise. I knew that teachers too often reprimanded students instead of giving them the praise that nurtured their participation. Therefore all that was needed was the avoidance of the negative haranguing, combined with the use of praise. However, my experiences quickly disabused me of the perceived magic inherent in praising students. Despite my best intentions, I found my students learning some things that I had not intended to teach.

One problem that resulted from my overuse of praise was that some of the high achievers in the classroom found that they could get this praise by giving less than an all-out effort. If little Susie is rewarded for pretty good thinking, she will not necessarily strive for excellent thinking. Therefore the overuse of praise actually hindered her progress!

The problem that most concerned me is that the praise became the currency within the economy that was my classroom. Students would often strive toward this praise, but an implicit tally was kept as to who was getting the most or the least of it. Therefore this lends weight to the "teacher's pet" paradigm. Mr. Golden likes Timmy best; he always likes what he says! On the other side of such transactions, students who have not been praised very much were patently aware of having the least capital in the class. And if the teacher forgot to praise somebody who probably deserved it, that student often felt neglected. I also found that when such positive reinforcement became the currency of the classroom, it was difficult to ensure that the shy students received appropriate praise. Even when they received the praise, they very often felt punished for being singled out!

Implicit within the current move toward increasing classroom praise is the notion that self-esteem is constantly in need of boosting. Some recent research finds that students' self-esteem is much higher than imagined and that it is quite possible to have too much self-esteem!

I am not claiming that praise should be avoided. I consider praise to be an essential part of the modern classroom. However, teachers should use it judiciously. As we have seen, there are some problems inherent in a praise-rich environment. So throttle down the praise! Praising little Jennie and Robbie a bit less will not destroy their self-esteem and might just nudge them in a more productive direction anyway.

What Does a Student Gain by Being Praised?

Mark Johnson
High School Physics Teacher

I have been a high school teacher of the physical sciences since 1989. While I was taking my science methods courses in 1988, my education professor strongly emphasized the need to praise kids every time they give an answer. She even gave us a printed sheet of phrases that could be used to praise students. My recollection of the purpose of praising student responses was for the purpose of encouragement. I agree with this in principle, and I suggest as humans our egos need to be validated. This validation can be effectively achieved by the admiration and acceptance of others, and particularly those we look up to and respect.

Although I believe that our emotion and ego are what makes us distinctly human, these same things are a liability in the sense that they often cause us to question our esteem. For that reason I argue that we need to be bolstered or validated by praise. Although I cannot say that I have used every adoration on that list in the past sixteen years (some of those phrases coming from my mouth would be transparently artificial, as I am simply not a flamboyant person), I do keep the principle behind that list in mind and take active steps to use praise in my classroom every day.

What does praise allow kids to do? From my experience, praise encourages students to continue their efforts. It congratulates them for something that they have accomplished and encourages them—by appealing to their ego—to continue on in the cognitive process. If a child is not engaged, praise will appeal to his or her sense of conscience to consider participation. During discussions if a student answers a question, I will acknowledge the response in some way. If it is a good response in the sense that it shows insight or understanding, I will praise the student. If the answer is not totally correct but shows some thought, then I will still praise the student—however, in this case I will likely come back with some kind of convergent question that is meant to steer the student in another direction of thought. If the student's response is incorrect, then my answer will usually be just "no that is not right," but I'll use an empathetic gesture and tone. The follow-up is usually a rephrasing of the question and Wait Time. Every opportunity is given for a correct response and that cherished praise that follows. Remember, the point is to encourage correct thinking and participation by appealing to the emotion and ego.

I understand that there is a danger in frivolous use of praise. That is, once students receive the praise that they are looking for, they may disengage from further thought on the subject at hand, having already received their reward. For that reason I maintain eye contact with students for a short time as discussion continues to help to maintain their focus. I feel that the praise of students is one of the tools a good teacher uses, and uses to everyone's advantage.

Alternatives to "Good Job"

For those who have not experienced a teacher who uses Wait Time, it may seem this would be a very unnatural teaching technique. After all, isn't it necessary to honor each student's correct response? Isn't positive reinforcement of correct responses the way students learn from question sessions? Within the context of a classroom science discussion, we would answer no. To always give praise to correct answers is to fall back into the behaviorist mode. In settings where individuals always expect to be rewarded for appropriate behavior, their motivation to learn is controlled by external, or extrinsic, factors.

The trouble with extrinsic sources of motivation is that when these sources are taken away, students stop performing the behavior. A recognizable example is giving students candy as a reward for helping clean the classroom. This works well, and you might have students standing in line to help. But when the candy supply is exhausted, students often stop offering their assistance. In contrast for sustained changes in behaviors, students must find an intrinsic benefit to the practice such as a sense of achievement or pride. Although it seems contradictory, by not praising each and every right answer, teachers can foster the development of intrinsic motivation within students.

There is a subtle yet substantial difference between praise and feedback (Faber & Mazlisch, 1995). **Praise** is restricted to compliments for appropriate behavior (e.g., "good job," "nice work," and "super!"), whereas **feedback** informs the individual about how his or her response aligns with expectations. For example in a classroom where the teacher is encouraging students to include process skill vocabulary within their responses, it is worth commenting on the presence of *predict* or *infer* instead of simply indicating if an answer is correct. All of this may make you wonder: if a teacher is not supposed to immediately react to students' answers (in keeping with Wait Time Two) and if a teacher is not supposed to praise every correct answer, what should the teacher do? You can find the solution by recognizing that the goal of discussions is to facilitate genuine conversations among all people in the classroom, and this can be accomplished by breaking the QRE cycle.

One way to react to a student's response is a technique called **probing.** Probing involves asking the respondent follow-up questions to dig deeper into the original answer (Brown & Wragg, 1993). Probing questions are very productive when used in response to a student's very quick and correct answer to a very complex idea. The goal of probing is to bring to the surface, for both the individual student and the whole class, the thought processes that led to the correct answer. Some ways to probe include asking, "How did you come up with that?" or "What sorts of evidence do you have that supports that idea" or "How does that connect with what we have been exploring?" The probe is meant not to put the student on the spot but rather to uncover the background information and underlying thinking that contributed to the response.

Too often in the flurry of a discussion, the questions that teachers ask don't lead to the kinds of responses they are seeking. This becomes apparent when a student response is nowhere near what the teacher was expecting. When that occurs, one might assume that the student was simply not engaged. However, the problem could be because of the question. If this is a possibility, then **rephrasing** is appropriate. When rephrasing, the teacher poses his or her question in a slightly different way. The teacher can preface the question by saying, "Okay, let me ask this again but using different words. I think maybe I was confusing you the first time." This prevents the students from feeling defensive about their response while still allowing the teacher to communicate high expectations as she or he pushes toward a more scientific idea.

Another questioning technique that will support science discussions is **redirecting.** Redirecting occurs when the teacher designates another student to respond to what someone else had just offered. For instance a teacher has posed a question, paused, called on a student, heard a response, paused again, and then redirected the question: "So Teisha, what do you think?" This invites the second student to provide his or her own interpretation of the questions or to comment on the response by the first student. In either case, the climate reinforces the idea that everyone should feel welcome to contribute. In addition, it reinforces the expectation that everyone can and should participate in the discussion.

In contrast to probing, rephrasing, and redirecting, repeating answers that students offer is a sure way to strangle a discussion. Although it seems that repeating simply helps all students to hear the comments, by doing this, the teacher removes the need for students to listen to their classmates. If each time a student shares a comment and all the students expect the teacher to repeat what was said, there really is no reason to attend to the student who was speaking: the teacher will always say it again. There are lots of reasons teachers might justify repeating answers. But if the teacher holds true to the desire of encouraging a discussion, then the practice of repeating answers can be seen as a way to undercut that very desire. Restating what a student contributed (e.g., "Marta, let me see if I understand what you said by saying it in my own words.") might be an occasional tactic. However, we prefer that the teacher obliges the speakers to make themselves heard (e.g., "Marta, Stuart didn't hear you. Could you repeat what you said?") and expects everyone else to focus on the speaker (e.g., "Remember class, Marta is speaking.").

Using Questions to Encourage Discussions

Think back to the three-step QRE sequence and consider who is talking at each turn. In a lesson consisting of a string of QRE events, the script becomes Teacher → Student → Teacher, Teacher → Student → Teacher, and so on. For every time a student speaks, the teacher speaks twice. Even if everyone in the classroom has the chance to talk, one voice is heard more than any other. Can you think of other nonschool situations where the script works in this way? The ones that come to mind are not very conversational: applying for a job, talking to a police officer, and speaking with a clerk. This is not the sort of arrangement that qualifies as a discussion.

In contrast with the QRE participation sequence, a discussion encourages students to respond to each other's comments. This should not suggest that a science discussion is the same as a party conversation, for there is a learning purpose in the classroom. But from a social constructivist outlook, it is necessary for individuals to test their ideas and have their ideas tested through conversation. If you can envision a science discussion in a classroom where the teacher maintains some control without completely dominating, then you are ready to learn some strategies for encouraging discussions.

Creating a Discussion-Friendly Climate

Generally the view of questioning is that the teacher asks, a student responds, and then the teacher evaluates. When appropriate questions are used, this can be an effective teaching strategy. You might envision this scenario as one where the teacher tosses the question as if it's a ball; the student catches it and tosses it back. The teacher can then toss the ball back to that student or choose someone else.

Teacher → Student → Teacher → Student (same or different one)

Suppose that instead of the permission to talk always going back and forth between the teacher and the class as a whole, the talking was more inclusive. Again using the ball analogy, we are proposing a situation where instead of the ball being returned to the teacher, it goes from one student to the next. Now, we don't want to have multiple balls in the air because that would be chaotic. But what if the path of conversation (and ball tossing) was more ambling and less like a relay race:

Teacher → Student → Another Student → Still Another Student → Teacher → A New Student

The nature of the students' contributions could vary. Students might voice their responses to the question their teacher originally posed. Or their contributions might build on what others have said, even giving alternate interpretations or sharing different experiences. The teacher's task is to initiate the discussion, with a thoughtfully designed question, and then to ensure that the talking stays related to the subject. The goal is not to have the science discussion become a classroom equivalent of a large family dinner, because the underlying instructional purpose should be evident.

NSES Teaching Standard E: Teachers of science develop communities of science learners that reflect the intellectual rigor of scientific inquiry and the attitudes and social values conducive to science learning. In doing this, teachers structure and facilitate ongoing formal and informal discussion based on a shared understanding of rules of scientific discourse.

Leading discussions is not only useful within science instruction. Those who have an interest in teaching reading may also wish to break the dependency on the QRE cycle. Their studies of reading instruction in ethnically diverse classrooms caused Robert Rueda, Claude Goldenberg, and Ronald Gallimore (1992) to develop a framework they called **instructional conversations.** Instructional conversations are classroom discussions in which all class members work toward achieving a broader understanding of a specific topic. As with Rowe's work with Wait Time, the idea of instructional conversations arose from the analyses of classrooms where productive discussions took place. By teasing out the elements of such quality discussions, the researchers were able to identify the effective techniques used by teachers. Although these elements were generated through the study of discussions surrounding a reading passage, these strategies are equally appropriate for science.

The Conversational Elements

Researchers have identified ten elements characterizing instructional conversations. The first five address the strategies for generating discussions. In other words, these are the techniques a teacher should use to initiate and maintain a classroom culture where instructional conversations are commonplace.

1. *Provide a challenging but nonthreatening atmosphere.* This element describes a necessarily delicate balance. On one hand the students must feel their ideas are valuable and that sharing them will not open them to ridicule. On the other hand, there should be a tone of intellectual challenge so the students are pushed to engage with the topic. In this way, an instructional conversation has a higher level of academic expectation than a casual conversation. The teacher creates a climate where the students are pressed to think at a level slightly beyond what they can accomplish without much effort.

2. *Show responsiveness to student contributions.* Even with a clear sense of purpose in mind, the teacher makes allowances for alternative ideas and interpretations offered by the students. This aspect of instructional conversations is consistent with the strategies we examined earlier about responding to students' answers, especially Wait Time Two. To tell students their answers are right or wrong is likely to cut a conversation short. It is far better to redirect or probe the students' responses, thereby opening the door for others to contribute.

3. *Promote discussion.* The teacher needs to move beyond asking questions where there is a single known answer. Asking divergent questions that leave room for multiple and reasonable responses will promote much wider participation in the discussion. This goal is consistent with the higher-level questions and Wait Time One.

4. *Foster connected discourse.* An instructional conversation should foster a wide participation in discussion where ideas are connected to each other. You can probably imagine a situation where many students are sharing their ideas without apparently hearing what anyone else has said. On the surface we might look at this situation and be pleased by the level of participation. However, unless the teacher guides the students to maintain some focus, then learning is not going to happen. Not only should students connect with each other's ideas, but they also need to connect with the topic under examination. In other words, a science discussion must refer to the recently completed hands-on activity or science concept to be connected.

5. *Encourage general participation.* In the QRE system the teacher has almost complete control over who has the opportunity to speak. In contrast, an instructional conversation is open for everyone to control. No, this doesn't mean that students can call out whatever thought flutters through their mind, and they are not to shout their ideas above the din. But everyone should feel that it is acceptable to share their ideas, and no one should be discouraged from volunteering.

The first five elements of instructional conversations describe the tone and techniques required to support discussions in which all students feel welcome to contribute. There is little in these five elements that is specific to reading or science discussions. Indeed we expect a teacher who can lead a reading discussion by applying these five elements would be equally effective at using the same elements for a science discussion.

For Reflection and Discussion

Imagine you are having a conversation with a professional (e.g., during a visit to a physician) where the other person uses some version of Wait Time during the exchange. What might that technique say to you about the other person's opinion of your views and ideas? What might be the parallels for elementary school students in which their teacher uses Wait Time during science lessons?

The Instructional Elements

The second five elements are the instructional dimension of discussions. Here we are taking what was originally created for use in reading instruction and translating it for use in science. The starting point for a reading lesson that uses an instructional conversation is a written text that all the students have read. The discussion entails the teacher selecting a particular theme (e.g., friendship) and guiding the group to discuss the text with this theme in mind. In contrast a science instructional conversation builds on a science activity experienced by all of the students. The teacher again has a particular topic in mind for the discussion (e.g., evaporation) and uses it to focus conversation among the students concerning the activity.

Just to reiterate: an instructional conversation is not simply a discussion where everyone tosses into the mix any idea that occurs to him or her. Instead the focus of such conversations in science must be on the shared experience of a science activity. The goal is to sort through the array of ideas and interpretations to arrive at an explanation fitting the evidence that the students have collected. The next five elements describe teaching strategies that enhance students' science learning from such discussions.

6. *Keep thematic focus.* The purpose of a discussion is not simply to encourage all students to contribute. Rather the goal is for their contributions to relate to the understandings the teacher wants them to learn. This requires the teacher to initiate the discussion with a clear sense of an instructional purpose. As the instructional conversation develops, the teacher may occasionally have to steer the students' attention back to the concept or theme that is at the center of the lesson.

7. *Activate and use background knowledge and relevant schemata.* It is important to help students to recognize how their in-class science activities connect to other experiences, including their nonschool lives. Teachers should take advantage of occasions in which they can connect the current topic to others that the class has considered.

8. *Practice direct teaching.* Teachers do need to provide explicit instruction to the students. It is important for the direct teaching to develop as a natural outgrowth of the discussion. If the instructional conversation is a prelude to the formal presentation of information by the teacher, then direct teaching is appropriate. But if the teacher allows the discussion to proceed as if he or she is preparing to launch into a lecture, then the discussion may be intellectually impoverished.

9. *Promote more complex language and expression.* For students to learn science, they need to have opportunities to fully express their ideas and to rehearse their use of scientific terms. The

teacher's use of Wait Time Two can facilitate this. In addition, the teacher will sometimes ask students to clarify their meanings when they use vague terms such as *it*—especially when there are process skills or science concepts the students are expected to have mastered.

10. *Promote bases for statements or positions.* Scientific explanations are to build on observations and other forms of evidence. During instructional conversations, teachers should encourage students to buttress their comments with supporting information. The teacher should encourage students to use texts, pictures, data, and reasoning to support their ideas.

Pulling Together the Pieces in a Diverse Classroom

In diverse classrooms, teachers can find it particularly tricky to orchestrate effective science discussions. There is evidence that students from varied cultural and linguistic backgrounds or with varied cognitive abilities can learn very well from inductive teaching methods. In addition students from a range of backgrounds and abilities benefit from whole class discussions because they are able to participate in the development of scientific understandings. Nevertheless the nature of discussion may not be familiar to many students because it can represent a substantively different way of conversing from that with which they are familiar. The taking of turns, the types of questions, and the tones of voices may be so unique to some students that they may feel uncomfortable and struggle to participate.

Bryan Brown (2006) studied science learning in urban environments and suggested that the unique features of scientific communication have a profound influence on students' sense of having access to science. More than just a matter of unfamiliarity, the use of language within science represents a substantially different form of discourse. The implication is that science teachers must make deliberate efforts to help students bridge the culture of home with the culture of science, and this includes explicitly describing the features of science as a way of communicating. The unique ways that scientists communicate, such as the insistence on evidence to support knowledge claims, are very subtle. We can't simply hope that students will somehow absorb these understandings. Instead it is valuable to frequently announce to students when these ways of communicating occur—in what they read in a textbook, what they hear on a video, or what actual students say during a class discussion. For instance during a class discussion, a teacher could quickly jump into the conversation by asking, "Remind us, what was your evidence for this idea?" These moments don't need to take long or distract from the flow of the lesson. Think of them as little pop-up menus that remind students about the culture of science within the context of the activities they're doing and the concepts they are learning.

Hampton and Rodriguez (2001) found in their study of English language learners that when science discussions were conducted only in English, many students faced a double struggle: the cognitive demands of the science content plus the linguistic demands of a new language. In a similar way, students with cognitive disabilities may have difficulty participating in class discussions. In a diverse setting, the complexity of the content combined with the struggles to translate thoughts into oral language requires additional preparation by teachers to make such discussions useful for all students.

Given these issues, the challenge becomes how to craft science discussions so they are instructional for all students. Some of the general strategies we've already discussed are very important. Wait Time One and Two allow students to compose their thoughts and consider ways of expressing their ideas to the entire class. A teacher's use of probing, rephrasing, and redirecting also are of great value, because they move the discussion beyond low-level questions and simplistic answers. But when we attend to the variety of learners who populate a classroom, we need to move beyond a belief that "good teaching is good teaching," because this effectively denies the uniqueness of individuals.

The apparent remedy for the need to generate successful discussions and instructional conversations among diverse students is to devise ways to pose questions that are more than simply verbal. This requires being sensitive to the variety of ways in which your students think and communicate. This might involve pointing to science words written in students' native languages during your question. You might display the materials they had used as a cue about the context for your questions. Remind students of their work by displaying their drawings, graphs, and so on to provide visual clues to the focus of your questions. As a teacher, these are minor adjustments; to students who are facing multiple challenges (e.g., science content and a new language), these are significant aids to their understandings.

Reducing Complexity Without Lowering Expectations

The adjustments teachers make to accommodate the language challenges faced by their students should not translate into asking simpler questions. To do this would work against the desire to guide all students to think deeply. The types of words used in a question can be relatively simple (and this might compel the teacher to be even more clear in his or her word choice) but still address less than simple ideas. A discussion of challenging ideas, such as the cause of the seasons and the sources of seeds, does not require the use of technical terms—but that doesn't mean the ideas are simplistic. To illustrate this, consider the following as spoken by a teacher:

> Imagine that you are outside on a hot and humid day. To cool off, you are drinking a cold beverage from a can. Have you ever noticed that the outside of the can will become wet? How might you explain the appearance of this moisture?

As you read this passage, you could probably relate to the situation being described. Yet for someone who is trying to master the English language, this seemingly ordinary situation is made exceedingly complex because of language issues.

As an alternative, imagine how you might respond to the same situation if it was explained in this way:

> This is a cold can of soda. Touch the outside. Can you feel the water? Where do you think this water is coming from?

Through simpler language and direct exposure to the events, the teacher encourages students to think about condensation. By relying on actual objects and giving students concrete experiences, the teacher asks a question that is more obvious without giving anything away or somehow diluting the instructional purpose.

One reason for posing questions to students is to encourage them to solidify their understandings. By being challenged to articulate their ideas, students are encouraged to take their fuzzy and disconnected ideas and piece them together so that they make sense. But this does not necessarily mean they must explain their ideas directly to the teacher. English language learners can improve their conversational skills during science by expressing their ideas with classmates. The strategy called "think-pair-share" pretty much describes how to make this happen. After hearing a question, students are to (1) think individually, (2) pair up to compare ideas, and then (3) share their ideas with the whole group when called on by the teacher. This strategy provides all the students with the chance to express the ideas in a way that is less emotionally intimidating compared to speaking in front of everyone. It also gives them a venue to rehearse their delivery even as they clarify their understandings of the science concepts. When students are paired with another person who speaks their native language, they are able to first sort through the science in a language in which they have fluency and then make the translation to English.

One goal for science discussions that may not be immediately obvious is the need to have all students involved—and this involvement doesn't mean that some are simply listening as others speak. A teacher ventures into treacherous terrain when he or she doesn't engage particular students (i.e., English language learners and those with cognitive challenges) in discussions. What seems to be a kindness may in reality send a message of lowered expectations. In his or her mind the teacher might rationalize, "I'm not going to embarrass those kids by making them struggle to share their ideas. They'll be just fine and less stressed that way." But in the minds of those students, they may think, "¿Por qué no me hacen preguntas? Deben creer que no soy muy inteligente?" (Translation: "Why don't they ask me any questions? They must think that I'm not very smart.") As a teacher, you might feel you are protecting a student from the embarrassment of speaking in class. But when everyone else is expected and allowed to talk, the teacher's not providing equitable opportunities can send a message of lowered expectations. When a student struggles to respond to a question and the teacher decides to give someone else a chance to respond, the unintended message the student receives is that the teacher really didn't believe he or she would be able to answer.

NSES Teaching Standard B: Teachers of science guide and facilitate learning. In doing this, teachers recognize and respond to student diversity and encourage all students to participate fully in science learning.

This is where the teacher's tool kit for diverse learners becomes especially important. Imagine a teacher who asks an English language learner the question "What are some examples of mammals?" and the learner responds with a puzzled look. If the teacher says, "That's OK" and moves on to another student with the same question, then the first student is sent the message that the teacher really wasn't expecting a correct answer. However, if the teacher responds by pointing to the English–Spanish word pair for *mammal* posted in the room or allowing another bilingual student to rephrase the question, then the likelihood of a proper response is increased and the student feels both challenged and successful. The goal here is to find the appropriate level of challenge for each student and then to provide support so students can achieve at that level. It is important to recognize that by frequently asking a simplistic question or always moving along with diverse learners, although it looks and feels as though the teacher is striving to protect those learners, the teacher actually works against the goal of helping those children to learn science.

For Reflection and Discussion

If you are interested in learning about your use of questioning strategies within your teaching, what might you listen for if you tape-record yourself while you are teaching a science lesson? How might you assess your effectiveness at asking questions of a wide variety of students?

Special Needs Students and Science Discussions

As part of the global desire to communicate appropriate expectations to all students, all types of students should have the opportunity to contribute during science discussions. This translates into the value of the teacher asking questions of all students, regardless of their backgrounds or abilities—including students with learning disabilities (Jarrett, 1999). Not giving such students access to the science discussions compromises their ability to learn the material. In addition not posing questions to students with learning disabilities suggests they are not capable. Guidelines for teaching science that are patently more inclusive are consistent with the more general strategies described throughout this chapter:

> Students should be given ample time to respond to questions and teachers should not interrupt or redirect too soon, but work to improve students' responses by prompting students or rephrasing the question. Teachers should respond to questions or statements from students with learning disabilities as thoroughly and with as much positive affect as they would respond to other students. In this way, teachers model respect for the dignity and diversity of all learners. (Jarrett, 1999, p. 17)

It is important to recognize that students with disabilities may be able to pick up on cues when the questions they are asked are slightly altered. Scruggs and Mastropieri (1994) suggested that open-ended questions can be modified to sound more directive. They suggested the teacher be more specific (e.g., "Drop the tablet into the water and describe what you observe") rather than ask a much less structured question such as "What happens when you work with these materials?" Within the context of a science discussion, a teacher can support students' contributions by supplying a little more in the way of structure to guide them in formulating their responses.

Teaching English language Learners Through Science Conversations

Another of the Principles for Effective Pedagogy advanced by the Center for Research on Education, Diversity, and Excellence describes how English-language learners can develop their fluency by engaging in conversations within science lessons (Warren & Rosebery, 2002). This principle is derived from the instructional conversations framework presented earlier in this chapter. Dalton (1998) reduced the instructional component to the three ideas of clear goals, assessment, and assistance and the conversational component to the ideas of responsiveness, inclusiveness, and balance (see Table 6.2). Used in combination, the process of engaging students in meaningful conversations about science is yet another force for supporting development of English language fluency.

TABLE 6.2. Using Conversation to Instruct and the Appropriate Teacher Actions

The teacher:

guides conversation by articulated subject matter goals;

ensures that student talk occurs at a higher rate than teacher talk;

guides conversations to include students' views, using texts and other substantive support;

ensures that all student preferences influence how they are included in the conversation; and

uses questioning, restating, and encouraging to support students' learning via conversation.

Note. Adapted from Dalton (1998).

Science Conversations as Instructional Events

Understanding is actively built as individuals engage in conversations about the matters at hand. Although the teaching community has often viewed conversation as an off-task classroom behavior, conversation, albeit on academic matters, is a powerful tool for advancing students' science understandings and fostering English language proficiency.

The instructional conversation framework and the associated principle of effective pedagogy describe situations in which students are actively challenged to use their developing language skills to express ideas and to provide evidence to support what they claim. Teachers are to use a variety of questioning strategies and follow-ups to students' responses. All of this takes place within a supportive and encouraging classroom climate. Along the way, the value in having English language learners express their ideas, even if necessitated by explicit prompts by the teacher, will assist both their scientific understandings and their fluency in a new language.

Chapter Summary

- The cycle of Teacher Question → Student Response → Teacher Evaluation is a classroom application of behaviorist principles. The fast pace and the anticipation of single, correct answers have their place within instruction but not as all-purpose teaching techniques appropriate for all learners.

- The individual constructivist philosophy associated with Jean Piaget claims that a learner independently builds understandings of his or her world. The social constructivist philosophy attributed to Lev Vygotsky emphasizes the importance of students' spoken communication as essential to making sense of their experiences. The talk between individuals leads to incorporating those ideas into one's own understandings.

- The types of questions a teacher asks will vary depending on the purpose of the particular portion of the lesson. Divergent questions are appropriate when students are first being engaged with and exploring a concept, while convergent questions are better used as the information they are to learn is much more specific.

- Wait Time One is defined as the pause a teacher allows after asking a question and before calling on a student to answer. The brief interlude of silence allows students to contemplate and compose a response. Similarly Wait Time Two serves as a quiet moment to give students extra time to complete their thoughts and verbal contributions.

- Instructional conversations consist of ten elements that serve as strategies for supporting science discussions. The elements were created as a tool for supporting English language learners but are beneficial to all students' science learning in the context of science.

Key Terms

Behaviorism: a theory of learning that focuses on observable behaviors; mental aspects of learning are not addressed through this theory. Within this theory, learning is defined as the acquisition of a new behavior.

Bloom's taxonomy: created by Benjamin Bloom, a classification system for questions based on the level of abstraction.

Convergent questions: also known as close-ended questions, these have a limited number of correct responses.

Divergent questions: also known as open-ended questions that do not have a singular, predetermined answer but allow for a variety of appropriate responses.

Feedback: a teacher comment that informs the student about how his or her response aligns with teacher or classroom expectations.

Higher-order questions: typically refers to questions at the higher levels of abstraction in Bloom's taxonomy (i.e., evaluation, synthesis, analysis).

Individual constructivism: a theory of learning, typically associated with Piaget, in which all learning occurs through the lens of previous knowledge, thus individuals are thought to use and reconstruct their preexisting mental models to make sense of new experiences.

Instructional conversations: classroom discussions in which all class members work toward achieving a broader understanding of a specific topic.

Praise: a form of teacher comment to students that is restricted to compliments for appropriate behavior (e.g., "good job," "nice work," and "super!").

Probing: asking the respondent follow-up questions to expand the original answer in more depth.

QRE sequence: a sequence of classroom interactions in which a teacher poses a question to a class, asks a student to respond, and then the teacher evaluates the correctness of the answer.

Redirecting: when the teacher indicates to another student that he or she should respond to a comment another student just offered.

Rephrasing: when the teacher asks a follow-up question wherein the original question is slightly modified.

Schema: a term from educational psychology that refers to scripts in which a learner's prior knowledge is organized, and these schemas are used by the learner for sense making.

Self-fulfilling prophecy: a mind-set in which what a person expects to notice influences his or her perception and, as a result, the original expectation is reinforced.

Social constructivism: a theory of learning, associated with Vygotsky, that describes that learning first occurs within a group setting as thoughts are exchanged and only then are these ideas incorporated into individual minds.

Transfer: a form of thinking in which a person refines what is known so this knowledge can have application to a variety of situations and contexts.

A Favorite Science Lesson

The Education Development Center grade-six unit called "Human Body Systems" takes a learning cycle approach to a topic that is normally taught in a very deductive fashion. Instead of introducing students to the concepts and then having them do activities to reinforce what the teacher provided, this unit and the activities begin with students' questions. A very effective use of teacher questions occurs within the activity "What Happens When You Exercise" that serves as one of the unit's culminating activities. Leading up to this lesson, students have learned the anatomy and physiology of breathing, digestion, and blood flow. During this particular activity, students jump rope and apply their scientific understandings to explain what is occurring in the various body systems. The debriefing that follows their investigation provides a wealth of questions for the teacher to pose to the students: How do your results compare with your predictions? How did the needs of your body change when you exercised? What does it feel like when your cells need more oxygen than you can supply? Because the students have been studying separate body systems over the preceding weeks, this activity allows them to pull together their understandings to explain something they have directly experienced.

Suggested Readings

Beisenherz, P. C., Dantonio, M., & Richardson, L. (2001). The learning cycle and instructional conversations. *Science Scope, 24*(4), 34–38.

Emphasizing the Explore phase of the learning cycle, these authors describe and give examples of the questioning strategies teachers can use to support students' science learning.

Martens, M. L. (1999). Productive questions: Tools for supporting constructivist learning. *Science and Children, 36*(8), 24–27.

Building on constructivist theory, this author offers general categories of questions that will encourage productive efforts by students. The question categories are attention focusing, measuring and counting, comparing, action, problem posing, and reasoning.

Worth, K., Moriarty, R., & Winokur, J. (2004). Capitalizing on literacy connections. *Science and Children, 41*(5), 35–39.

The authors describe a professional development program they implemented with practicing teachers. Their goal was to guide teachers to integrate language arts literacy with scientific literacy. The article describes four approaches for successful integration: science discussions, science notebooks, formal scientific reports, and reading expository text.

References

Brown, B. A. (2006). "It isn't no slang that can be said about this stuff": Language, identity, and appropriating science discourse. *Journal of Research in Science Teaching, 43,* 96–126.

Brown, G., & Wragg, E. C. (1993). *Questioning.* New York: Routledge.

Dalton, S. S. (1998). *Pedagogy matters: Standards for effective teaching practice.* Washington, DC: Center for Applied Linguistics.

Delpit, L. (1996). *Other people's children: Cultural conflict in the classroom.* New York: New Press.

Faber, A., & Mazlisch, E. (1995). Praise that doesn't demean, criticism that doesn't wound. *American Educator, 19,* 33–38.

Hampton, E., & Rodriguez, R. (2001). Inquiry science in bilingual classrooms. *Bilingual Research Journal, 25,* 417–434.

Jarrett, D. (1999). *The inclusive classroom: Mathematics and science instruction for students with learning disabilities.* Portland, OR: Northwest Regional Education Laboratory.

Rowe, M. B. (2003). Wait-time and rewards as instructional variables, their influence on language, logic, and fate control. *Journal of Research in Science Teaching, 40,* S19–S32. (Original work published 1974)

Rueda, R., Goldenberg, C., & Gallimore, R. (1992). *Rating instructional conversations.* Washington, DC: National Center for Research on Cultural Diversity and Second Language Learning. Retrieved from http://www.ncela.gwu.edu/pubs/ncrcdsll/epr4.htm

Scruggs, T. E., & Mastropieri, M. A. (1994). The construction of scientific knowledge by students with mild disabilities. *Journal of Special Education, 28,* 307–321.

Wagner, J. F. (2006). Transfer in pieces. *Cognition and Instruction, 24,* 1–71.

Warren, B., & Rosebery, A. S. (2002). *Teaching science to at-risk students: Teacher research communities as a context for professional development and school reform.* Santa Cruz, CA: Center for Research on Education, Diversity, and Excellence.

seven
From Activity to Inquiry

Chapter Highlights

- For an activity to be qualify as inquiry based, a teacher must determine if the five essential features are present.
- We can place too much confidence in hands-on materials as instructional tools. The equipment doesn't do the teaching. The activity doesn't do the teaching. Instead it is the thinking and talking about the activity that allows students to understand a concept. The teacher must organize activities around a question that the students are to investigate.
- For students to obtain evidence that allows them to answer a scientific question, they must collect, organize, and interpret their observations. Teachers will need to provide structure for students as they develop skills and confidence in working with evidence.
- The move from evidence to explanation in an activity parallels the move from observation to inference in science. Knowing the difference and providing students with the support to distinguish between them is an important teaching skill.
- The connection of student explanations to scientifically accepted explanations is a fundamentally important feature of inquiry-based teaching. Having students generate their own explanations is insufficient unless they also connect their ideas with scientific concepts. Again this parallels what happens in science as scientists must connect their ideas with the other ideas of science.
- In science, students must develop explanations that are supported by evidence. Knowledge based in evidence is a defining feature of the culture of science.

- Teachers who translate "fun" hands-on activities into inquiry-based experiences must remain mindful of all five essential features if their activities are to become effective learning experiences.
- Science taught in ways consistent with inquiry should not exclude diverse populations. Teachers need to recognize that some students will require additional support as they move toward the actions and objects of science as found in inquiry. Students from home cultures that are very distinct from the culture of science may need explicit instruction to recognize the centrality of inquiry to the culture of science.

The purpose of this chapter is to guide future teachers of science to think beyond purely activity-based lessons. To assist us, we return to the essential features of inquiry-based teaching. Having students participate in hands-on science activities is several steps above simply reading a textbook. But often hands-on activities, although appealing, fall far short of genuine science learning. So much more is possible in terms of developing students' scientific literacy if the teacher knows how to transform interesting activities into quality learning experiences. This requires the gradual but deliberate transfer of control from the teacher to the students.

The Allure of Hands-On Activities

Moving beyond a dependence on the textbook is a valuable step toward effective science teaching. Because students need to actively use process skills to develop proficiency with them, it seems that using hands-on activities is a logical teaching decision. This is consistent with the use of manipulatives within math teaching. However, hands-on activities in science and manipulatives in math are not the complete solution to student learning—just an important first step.

Deborah Ball (1992), a university professor, studied children's learning by regularly teaching math in schools. Her insights into manipulatives match our views about the limits of hands-on activities. In both subject areas, educators will often advocate that equipment can act as a substitute for books and that the equipment or activity carries meaning like a text. The idea seems to be that the shortcomings of written text, with the implication that reading is a passive way to learn, can be solved by allowing students to engage in relevant classroom activities. As much as many teachers and schools would be thrilled to receive a shipment of new science equipment, this stuff will go only so far in helping students to learn. The challenge that remains is effectively implementing the equipment within the classroom setting. Ensuring the students engage with the materials and use the process skills is an appropriate goal. Even better is to also draw on inquiry as an organizing framework.

> Creating effective vehicles for learning mathematics requires more than just a catalog of promising manipulatives. The context in which any vehicle—concrete or pictorial— is used is as important as the material itself. By context, I mean the ways in which students work with the material, toward what purposes, with what kinds of talk and interaction. The creation of a shared learning context is a joint enterprise between teacher and students and evolves during the course of instruction. Developing this broader context is a crucial part of working with any manipulative. The manipulative itself cannot on its own carry the intended meanings and uses. (Ball, 1992, p. 18)

Revisiting Inquiry-Based Instruction

In chapter 4 we presented information from the *National Science Education Standards* (National Research Council, 1996) about classroom inquiry. The developers of this framework identified five essential features of the inquiry in which students could engage as they participated in science lessons. For each essential feature there is a range of possibilities from more teacher direction to more student control. We are going to examine the five essential features of inquiry-based instruction in succession. When we first introduced the essential features, we didn't provide much detail about how to put them into action. In what follows we will provide much more guidance about how to make decisions about using these features in the context of activity-based lessons.

Questions With a Scientific Flavor

Children can be full of questions that can signal teachers how to connect school with students' interests. Yet because of the limitations of science, not every question that a student will raise can be answered through science. This doesn't make such questions any less important; science will never corner the market on worthwhile information. But teachers often need to help students to reformulate their questions before data gathering can begin.

A question that a student can try to answer through the use of scientific thinking is termed an **investigable** question. As the name suggests, questions that lend themselves to science are those that students can investigate. An investigable question that is well formulated will suggest how one would go about finding an answer. It will probably come as no surprise that the best investigations allow students to use many of the science process skills. Questions that would lead to investigation include the following: What can we put onto the ground that will keep the snails away from our plants? Which type of eye shadow is the best bargain? What happens to the weight of a pumpkin if we allow it to decompose?

NSES Content Standard A: Students should develop the abilities to ask a question about objects, organisms, and events in the environment.

There are other questions that cannot be investigated. This doesn't mean that these are unimportant questions, but they do demonstrate the limitations of science. Questions that science is not able to answer include the following: Why do there have to be wars? What happens to people when they die? Who will I become when I grow up? These types of questions, when posed by children, deserve to be considered. From a science perspective, process skills or inquiry cannot solve these questions. When we conceive of investigable questions, our narrow interest is in those questions that have the potential for being addressed within the culture of science. These are the challenges that we can use our teaching wisdom to shape into investigable questions.

Where should investigable questions originate? Is it the teacher's duty to supply these for students? Or is it reasonable to expect students to propose them on their own? The answer is that the teacher may have to steer the students when they are first learning how to develop questions they can investigate. As the students' confidence and skill at scientific questioning improves, the control over questions can be gradually turned over to them.

Control Over Scientific Questions

Table 7.1 shows the first of the five essential features of inquiry-based teaching and addresses scientific questions. When there is the least amount of learner self-direction, at Level 1, then the question the students pursue is given to them. Rather than burden them with developing a question to investigate, the teacher provides a question. Alternatively the question can come from other sources such as books, Web sites, and so on. In either case, the question provided to the students is phrased so it is clearly one that can be investigated using the physical and mental tools of science.

Moving toward the left side of the table we see that the students are provided with incrementally more control over their science questions. At Level 2, the learner begins with an idea supplied from outside and then makes slight modifications so it becomes investigable. In other words, the teacher or some instructional materials supply the general idea of what to investigate but the student has control about the exact question. At Level 3, the student is given several possible questions to investigate and selects the one that holds the most interest. And at Level 4, the student has complete control over the question he or she will be investigating. These describe the valuable but uncommon circumstances in which the student is provided very little guidance about the sort of question he or she will study.

This framework was designed to highlight the range of teacher and student control over the features of inquiry, but this should not be seen as some form of scoring rubric. Rather than being tempted to push students to function at the level in the far left column, teachers should see that each student has the opportunity to participate in all variations of scientific questioning. Perhaps the goal should be for every student to show how he or she can function at all levels of learner self-direction, including situations where they have complete control over the question they investigate. But to make Level 4 the goal of every science lesson is overly ambitious and developmentally inappropriate and would prove frustrating for both teacher and student.

Developing Investigable Questions

It is difficult to define the characteristics of investigable questions and to differentiate those from questions that are not investigable. The types of questions that students could most readily use to structure an investigation are those that allow them to adjust one factor to see how it influences a

TABLE 7.1. Using Questions Within Inquiry

Essential Feature	More ← Amount of Learner Self-Direction → Less			
	Level 4	Level 3	Level 2	Level 1
1. Learner is engaged in scientific questioning.	Learner is expected to pose a scientific question.	Learner selects from among several provided questions.	Learner sharpens or clarifies question provided by teacher or other source.	Learner engages in question provided by teacher, materials, or other source.

Note: From National Research Council (2000).

situation. In other words, questions that seek to uncover cause-and-effect relationships are most likely to be investigable. Questions that take the form of "what will happen to X when we change one variable" are almost assuredly going to be investigable.

Somewhat more broadly, student questions that begin with *why* are often difficult to use to design an investigation. When children ask "why" they are often looking for the purposes of certain phenomena (e.g., "Why are there mosquitoes in the world?"). There is very little about this question to suggest how it could be investigated. However, if the question could be sharpened so it proposes a link between two factors, then it could be investigated. For example the question "What does temperature have to do with the presence of mosquitoes?" is closer to being the starting point for an investigation.

Defining the traits of an investigable question is difficult because the reasoning processes are circular: the investigable questions are questions that someone can investigate. Okay, that may not seem very helpful. But it points out that the way to test if a question is investigable is to think about how we might begin to find an answer. In other words, by thinking about the procedure for testing a question, the teacher and students can determine if the pursuit will provide the necessary insights. It's almost as if one needs to take one step past the question to see if it leads down a fruitful path. The discussions and considerations of issues surrounding questions are important to model for students so they become more adept at analyzing questions on their own.

NSES Content Standard A: Students should develop the abilities to use data to construct a reasonable explanation.

Before striking out on an investigation, students must consider certain issues: what information will be gathered, how will that information help to answer the question, and how convincing will the explanation be if the gathered data are used as supporting evidence? By weighing these questions before starting the actual investigation, students may be able to determine if the question they have posed is investigable. Meanwhile, the degree of structure or freedom the teacher provides to the students for addressing these issues becomes the focus of the remaining essential features of inquiry-based teaching.

Collecting Evidence

Closely linked to the types of questions posed are the kinds of information to be gathered to answer the question. The culture of science is unique in its insistence on evidence as support for every knowledge claim. To be persuasive in a science discussion, one must use evidence, not appeals to emotion or other efforts to sway others' opinions. The quality of the evidence is what holds power in the scientific culture. We often hear the term **data** in discussions of scientific evidence. The term refers to something as basic as an unbiased observation. Measurements, as special types of observations, are often considered compelling forms of data, because they seem less likely to be influenced by individual biases than other kinds of evidence. When multiple observations and multiple measurements reveal consistency about a certain situation, the evidence is considered stronger.

Helping Students to Value Evidence

In a disagreement between individuals where both sides insist that they are right, they may draw on many resources to prove their point. They might use physical force to exert their will. They might claim someone in authority would support their stance. They might invoke the fear of divine intervention. Or they might attempt to use a superstition to win their position. But in

TABLE 7.2. Collecting Appropriate Evidence

Essential Feature	More ← Amount of Learner Self-Direction → Less			
	Level 4	**Level 3**	**Level 2**	**Level 1**
2. Learner gives priority to evidence in responding to questions.	Learner determines what constitutes evidence and collects it.	Learner is directed to collect certain data.	Learner is given data and asked to analyze them.	Learner is given data and told how to analyze them.

Note: From National Research Council (2000).

the culture of science, none of these tactics are too influential. Because science teaching is, in part, a process of familiarizing students with the actions of science, students must be guided to appreciate the value of evidence in science because that evidence may not hold the same status in everyday life.

Understanding the difficulty students may have with recognizing the necessity and quality of evidence, teachers should provide a great deal of direction to them as they participate in inquiry. Table 7.2 indicates that when the greatest amount of structure is being imposed, the students are supplied with the data and instructed about how to make sense of it. At its most basic, the analysis of data simply requires that the observations or measurements be organized in some way that one can see if any patterns exist.

Imagine a science activity where students dropped different kinds of balls and counted the number of bounces. Simply listing everyone's data onto a chalkboard might be an important strategy. But the blizzard of numbers on the board could be confusing. Although the students would have evidence in front of them, it would not be in a form that would be informative. As fundamental as it seems, to organize this data (such as putting all the observations for soccer balls in one group) is an important strategy for students to learn as part of data analysis. The next step is to suggest generalizations about what was observed.

Creating columns of data for the different types of balls may reveal some patterns. Often it is useful to reduce a string of numbers to a single, representative number that we would identify as "typical." Instead of listing all the values of the soccer balls' bouncing, it would be more convenient and informative to be able to identify a single value representing the typical number of bounces for this kind of ball. A familiar way to do this is to calculate the mean or average for the data. However, it is important to recognize this might be a very weak way to represent a typical value.

Suppose we have seven measurements from an event. There are three different methods for determining the typical value for these numbers. A very quick approach is to arrange the numbers in order and choose the number that's in the middle of the sequences, in this case the fourth number on our list (statisticians call this the **median**). If we had an even number of measurements, say eight, then we would split the difference between the fourth and fifth measurement after they'd been sequenced. Not only is the median a convenient way to determine typical, it also does a nice job of dividing the data: about half the measurements are higher than the typical value and the rest are lower than it.

A second way to determine typical is to scan the data to see which measurement occurs the most often. If an observation occurs more times than any other, then this number represents the **mode**. The difficulty with trying to use the mode as typical is that there can be a tie for the most frequent measurement. Another issue is that the mode could be at one extreme of the full range of data, and it seems strange to claim that this is typical because it doesn't necessarily appear in the middle of the data.

The third way to determine typical requires arithmetic. First you total all the measurements and then divide the total by the number of observations made. This number is the **mean.** There are two problems with automatically using the mean. One issue is that the process of calculating can be confusing and distract teachers and students from the overall purpose of the analysis, namely, to uncover patterns. The other issue is that the mean can be heavily influenced by a very high or especially low single measurement. If you had a very oddball piece of data, then the mean might be pulled to one extreme and not really seem to fall close to the middle of all the data. In this case, the mean would not be so typical.

For Reflection and Discussion

For the following list of data, determine the mean, median, and mode: 2, 21, 5, 3, 10, 2, 6. Beyond the challenge of sorting, calculating, and counting these data, which result would appear to be the best representation of "typical" for this list? What makes the other two ways of summarizing the data less useful, at least for these data?

Having gathered the data and reduced its complexity by determining the typical for each group of data, students should begin to look for patterns. They might notice the number of bounces of one type of ball is considerably different from the rest. It is also possible there will be no substantial differences among the different pieces of data. Representing the typical values by creating a graph can be another helpful way to analyze the data. Quite simply, the measurements appear along the vertical axis of the graph, and the categories (e.g., "type of ball") are distributed along the horizontal axis. The height of each column in this bar graph represents the typical value. A completed graph provides a visual display of the actual measurements and allows for a more straightforward analysis of the evidence.

What Counts as Evidence

As obvious as it seems, the evidence that is gathered must address the question being tested. Sometimes the question has to be modified because of limitations in the way data can be collected. For instance an experiment about batteries might begin with a question such as "What kind of batteries are best?" Comparisons could be made by measuring the brightness of flashlights powered by different brands of batteries. In this example, the definition of *best* needs to be clarified, because data are restricted to bulb brightness. Other data sources, such as how long the battery produces light or how fast a motor spins when powered by each brand of battery, rely on other definitions of *best*. If bulb brightness is the data to be collected, then the question should be revised to reflect the specific design of the experiment. This could be something like "What kind of batteries produce the most light in a flashlight?" Notice how much more specific this version of the question is than the original.

In addition to ensuring that the data and the question align with each other, we need to consider other features of evidence. One feature is that the process of gathering data is as free of bias as possible because we wish to avoid having our own expectations of the results influence the data. An experiment where **objectivity** is in place is an experiment where essentially the same evidence will be collected regardless of who collects that data. Even though what we observe can be influenced by our experiences, the goal in designing an experiment is to prevent our desires from influencing the results. In the example of the batteries, one way to reduce bias might be to have an outside observer, someone who is not directly involved in designing the investigation, measure bulb brightness.

Another characteristic of high-quality evidence is replication of the experiment. This permits others to evaluate the credibility of the evidence so the results can be confirmed or refuted. Unless other scientists or students are able to gather data under similar conditions, the original experiment's results are not very reliable. Credible evidence depends on our ability to eliminate any doubt about the scientist's biases influencing, whether intentionally, the design of the experiment and the data that were collected. Having several student groups perform the same experiment is an example of a way to ensure that an investigation is replicable.

Generating Explanations From Evidence

This brings our discussion to the third essential feature of inquiry-based teaching: the transition from evidence to explanations. A notion about the actions of science that people are commonly mistaken about is that once a scientist has gathered the data, the explanation is immediately obvious. As neatly packaged as this idea seems, it misrepresents how science really occurs. In some ways, the transition from evidence to explanation is parallel to the leap from observations to inferences, a challenging situation we first encountered during the introduction to the science process skills.

The mental jump from evidence to explanations is where people can make their mark in science. Because scientific explanations are only as good as the evidence that supports them, creativity doesn't mean that any wild speculation is acceptable. Rather by being creative we portray a person who can examine a collection of bits and pieces of data and propose how it all fits together into a coherent whole. Having "really good" data is not going to be enough, even though possessing evidence that aligns with the initial question is important. The process of making sense of the data still remains, and proposing explanations for evidence is a vital skill within the culture of science. John Dewey placed a premium on people's being able to make many suggestions to explain observations. For our purposes, we use Dewey's words to explain how different people may respond to information. The light that Dewey described is what we are referring to as evidence (or data or observations). How a person responds to this light is what we regard as explanations of the evidence.

> As the metaphor of dull and bright implies, some minds are impervious, or else they absorb passively. Everything presented is lost in a drab monotony that gives nothing back. But others reflect, or give back in varied lights, all that strikes upon them. The dull make not response; the bright flash back the fact with a changed quality. (Dewey, 1910/1991, p. 35)

It is inappropriate to suggest that the "dull and bright" as used by Dewey is equivalent to "dumb and smart." The meaning we are using is an individual's ability to propose a plentiful and varied supply of explanations. Dewey provided this idea in a chapter about relying on personal resources to train people to be thoughtful. Our interpretation is that these resources cannot be reduced to some measure of intelligence but may have as much to do with personal attitudes. A willingness to consider alternatives, the capacity to propose fresh ideas, and the desire to think beyond the immediately obvious are examples of Dewey's brightness. This has less to do with a person's cognitive abilities than with how many ideas their minds can generate. We can readily imagine people who are so determined to have the correct answer, with little tolerance for ambiguity or creativity. No matter how intelligent such individuals might be, if they are unwilling, as opposed to unable, to propose many explanations for a body of evidence, then Dewey would place them in the dull category.

Students need guidance to develop an ability to generate a wealth of explanations. Fortunately there are significant role models we can use to demonstrate such a disposition. A real-life example of this is Mary Anning, who became one of the leading paleontologists of her time. Her story is told in a children's literature book that is appropriate for elementary school students (Anholt, 1999). Her life's work began as a child when she walked along the seashore gathering strangely shaped rocks that the locals called "curiosities." These odd formations were familiar to many people in the area, but no one had recognized their significance. Anning explained these rocks in a fresh light: they were bones of ancient living things. The whole concept of fossils was not something anyone else had considered. And yet when examining the same stones others had observed, Anning saw them in a fresh light. Initially she raised money for her family by selling the fossils but you may have already known that the tongue twister "she sells seashells by the seashore" refers to her entrepreneurship. Anning's insights into these rocks as being much more than strangely shaped stones became the starting point for modern paleontology and contributed to our understandings of extinction.

Supporting Students in Forming Explanations

As with the previous essential features, a teacher can provide varying levels of self-direction to the students. At Level 1 of Table 7.3, students are given considerable assistance with creating explanations, whereas the descriptions appearing to the left show progress toward higher amounts of freedom. Students become more competent with the actions of science as the teacher models the transition from evidence to explanations. As students have more experiences with forming explanations from evidence, even if they are simply witnesses to the process, they are likely to internalize the characteristics of a good scientific explanation: simplicity, accounting for all the evidence, and ending with logical conclusions. Over time, the teacher shifts the amount of direction he or she provides to students, and they move toward more self-direction. Gradually students are allowed to create scientific explanations from the evidence with little guidance from the teacher.

Connecting With Scientific Knowledge

Although students need to learn how to construct explanations based on evidence they have collected, they should connect these explanations to the scientific knowledge developed by professional scientists. This is a delicate situation for many reasons. Teachers shouldn't abruptly discard the explanations the students worked hard to develop. On the other hand, having students become scientifically literate implies that they can grasp scientifically accepted explanations.

Another way to think about this challenge is to recognize that school science should accomplish much more than simply giving students opportunities to practice the science process skills. There is a body of knowledge included in the objects of science that students should acquire. It is the expectation of parents and society that students will complete their schooling with solid understandings of scientific ideas and the ability to use these understandings to make sense of their lives. The standards in place for science, based on national standards and then translated into state guidelines, are meant to clarify what objects of science students should understand. The challenge is to use students' own inquiries as a step toward accomplishing the science standards.

TABLE 7.3. Formulating Evidence From Explanations

| Essential Feature | More ← Amount of Learner Self-Direction → Less | | | |
	Level 4	Level 3	Level 2	Level 1
3. Learner formulates explanations from evidence.	Learner formulates explanation after summarizing evidence.	Learner is guided in process of formulating explanations from evidence.	Learner is given possible ways to use evidence to formulate explanation.	Learner is provided with evidence and explanations.

Note. From National Research Council (2000).

TABLE 7.4. Making Connections to Science Knowledge

| Essential Feature | More ← Amount of Learner Self-Direction → Less | | | |
	Level 4	Level 3	Level 2	Level 1
4. Learner connects explanations to scientific knowledge.	Learner independently examines other resources and forms. links to explanations.	Learner is directed toward areas and sources of scientific knowledge.	Learner is given possible connections.	(nothing specified here)

Note. From National Research Council (2000).

TABLE 7.5. Communicating and Justifying Explanations

| Essential Feature | More ← Amount of Learner Self-Direction → Less | | | |
	Level 4	Level 3	Level 2	Level 1
5. Learner communicates and justifies explanations to others.	Learner forms reasonable and logical arguments to communicate explanations.	Learner is coached in development of communication.	Learner is provided with broad guidelines to sharpen communication.	Learner is given steps and procedures for communication.

Note: From National Research Council (2000).

Although our desire is for students to recognize that science is a dynamic intellectual endeavor, it is acceptable to provide scientific explanations and science concepts to the students rather than hope they will stumble across them on their own. However, the need for efficiency must be balanced against the value of students grappling with ideas. For students to construct a solid understanding of science concepts, they need to have the time to wrestle with them. As a consequence the variations of the fourth essential feature of inquiry suggest that teachers make wise decisions about when to give students more or less latitude in connecting to the objects of science (see Table 7.4). In some cases it may make sense to provide Web sites or readings that supply the students with widely accepted scientific explanations for what they have been studying. You may have noticed we are indicating that readings should be introduced after the students have explored the material. This is consistent with the learning cycle, because reading material can be introduced in the Explain and Extend phases. There should also be opportunities, perhaps based as much on the quality and availability of supporting texts, for students to do their own digging to uncover what scientists say about the concepts. We will further discuss this in chapter 10 as we consider the challenges of integrating science with other curricular areas.

Justifying Claims and Explanations

Addressing the fifth essential feature of inquiry involves two challenges. First, students need to recognize that the best explanations are those supported by the evidence. Appeals to emotion are not useful. The other challenge is for students to be told (and reminded) that scientific arguments are about ideas and not about the people who propose them. As a result one idea may win out over all its competitors, but not so it criticizes a person's thinking or character.

The word *argument* has several different meanings, most often invoking a situation full of emotional turmoil. An argument is sometimes viewed as a disagreement between individuals who resort to emotions as they try to get their way. In contrast a scientific argument is a dispute between explanations, with data being used to justify each position (see Table 7.5). In a scientific argument, most commonly thought of as a scientific debate, the controversy focuses on how data were collected, what data can or should be included, and what inferences can be made based on a set of evidence. The focus here, ideally, should be placed not on the persuasive power of the scientists but on the strength of the experimental design, the evidence, or the explanations based on this evidence.

Making the Leap From Activities to Inquiry

When teachers first become concerned about teaching science, the kinds of things they worry about are very practical: Will we have enough equipment? Can I keep the students on task? Will the classroom remain reasonably quiet? But being a good teacher is more than simply managing a classroom. Furthermore, being a good teacher goes beyond keeping the students contentedly busy. The expectation is that when teachers teach science, the students learn science. In far too many classrooms there is an unspoken arrangement between the students and the teachers: the teacher won't push the students too hard, and the students won't make life too difficult for the teacher. This sort of truce does create a congenial environment, and Robert Fried (2001) called this the game of school. This arrangement can be especially harmful when the students are enrolled in schools where expectations for achievement are already low. But it also fails to support the level of learning that will take place in a more rigorous atmosphere. Very little of the learning that we've described to this point will happen within a room that is in disarray. But we want you to never forget that the true test of a teacher's effectiveness is the students' learning, not whether the room is peaceful.

At some point, and we hope this happens very soon and not years from now, we want you to recognize that activity-based science is not sufficient by itself. The resources seem to be stacked against those of us who would rather rely on inquiry-based teaching rather than on mere activities. Libraries and bookstores are full of science activity books, and the Internet is choked with exciting activities parents and teachers can use to make science fun. But you will not often find resources clearly describing how an activity is consistent with inquiry-based teaching, and you will seldom find explanations for how to go from doing the activity to helping students learn. The good news is that you aren't stuck—good activities can be converted into inquiry-based teaching if you rely on the essential elements of inquiry to make adjustments that will promote science learning.

The following is a classic science activity (that means it's been around so long that every science teacher should know it). By using very simple materials, a student can investigate a very interesting phenomenon. If you've never seen this activity, you should try it for yourself.

Creating a Cartesian Diver

What You Should Do   Take a drinking glass and a plastic soda bottle and fill both with water. Pull water into an eyedropper by squeezing the rubber bulb while the tip is submerged in the drinking glass. Then release the dropper to see if it floats or sinks. Adjust the amount of water inside the dropper so it is barely floating but not sinking. When the dropper is just floating in the drinking glass, carefully place the dropper into the soda bottle. Put the lid on the bottle and screw it on so it is tight. Squeeze the bottle's sides, and watch the dropper descend. When you release the bottle, the diver will return to the surface.

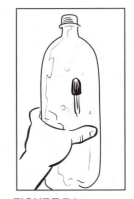

FIGURE 7.1

Why This Happens   This is a demonstration of buoyancy. An object is buoyant when the weight of water it displaces is greater than the weight of the object. When pressure is applied to the bottle and the size of the air bubble within the dropper is reduced, the dropper becomes less buoyant and begins to sink. The dropper displaces less water when the bubble is compressed, and when the amount of water it displaces is less that the dropper's weight, the dropper sinks. Fish can control their depth in the water by adjusting the size of their swim bladder. Just as with the dropper, the fish goes down when the gas inside the bladder is compressed. When the gas in the bladder is allowed to expand, then buoyancy causes the fish to rise.

The Strengths and Shortcomings of This Activity

It may not be an overstatement to claim the behavior of a Cartesian diver is captivating. Knowing the scientific explanation does not detract from the pleasure of making the diver rise and fall without actually touching it. That it uses very simple materials only adds to its charm. But although using this activity as written makes it fun, it does not necessarily support the development of scientific inquiry. For this activity to accurately represent the culture of science, students must have opportunities to become involved in science's objects and actions. This means that science concepts and the appropriate use of process skills must be embedded within the learning.

What are the shortcomings of this activity that, in its current form, prevent it from qualifying as an inquiry activity? For one thing, there is not a question guiding an investigation. Also the students aren't encouraged to gather any information or to make inferences based on their observations. In short this is an activity that will work if the students follow the directions—but this won't promote inquiry.

Point–Counterpoint

Teaching science through inquiry is complex, and teachers can be assisted by guidelines or heuristics that they can refer to. However, the use of heuristics can create difficulties. Some educators who work with future teachers of science worry that the details of the heuristics will prevent the novice teachers from paying attention to the larger picture of student learning and scientific literacy. In contrast other educators believe the heuristics provide exactly the level of detail new teachers must pay attention to even though there is limitless flexibility. So in response to the question "How can guidelines about using inquiry influence new teachers?" we provide two competing viewpoints.

Don't Let the Details of Inquiry Obscure Its Purpose

Julie M. Kittleson
Assistant Professor in Science Education, University of Georgia

Inquiry, as a way of doing science and as an approach for teaching science, is complex. When you begin thinking about how you're going to teach science, you'll likely find that there are a lot of things you have to keep in mind. Many textbooks written for future science teachers (like the one you're reading now) include descriptions of how to organize inquiry-based science lessons. For example in this book you read about essential features of inquiry. The authors described the nature of scientific questioning, the nature of evidence and how it is used in science, the ways in which evidence is used to formulate explanations, and so forth. Authors of other texts present strategies such as driving questions to describe how to align science teaching with the tenets of inquiry. All these descriptions provide a platform teachers can use when they are developing inquiry-based science lessons. These descriptions of inquiry can be thought of as heuristics, and as heuristics, or "rules of thumb," they help to simplify some of the messiness associated with inquiry.

In a science methods class I taught, I presented two heuristics for teaching inquiry. On one hand, this may have been a poor pedagogical strategy, because I think it prevented our class from thoroughly exploring one approach to inquiry-based teaching. On the other hand, I found that students did not connect the words and details to wider issues of science teaching and learning but rather tended to get caught up in the terminology and details associated with each heuristic. I tried to convey to students that although authors who write about inquiry sometimes use different terms to describe their approaches to teaching, they often have similar goals in mind. That is, there are some core ideas associated with inquiry-based science. I wanted students to understand the core ideas rather than the specific terms attached to the different aspects of inquiry. In addition I wanted students to think about how the different approaches were similar in terms of the ways in which they made links between scientific knowledge and scientific investigations.

Using heuristics to teach about inquiry can be helpful for highlighting ways in which the various aspects of inquiry can be pulled together into a coherent whole. Heuristics are useful because they incorporate important aspects of the nature of scientific knowledge, the nature of scientific investigations, and the links between the two. Pulling the pieces of inquiry together is important if a teacher is to develop meaningful learning experiences for her or his students. Although heuristics can be helpful, I think it is important not to focus too closely on the details—such as the terms or the steps—presented in the heuristic. That is, don't let the details of inquiry obscure its purpose. Ultimately, the thing that seems more important than the details is recognizing how the elements of inquiry relate to broader issues related to the nature of scientific knowledge.

Making Inquiry Work for Your Classroom—It's All in the Details!

Danielle J. Ford
Science Teacher Educator at the University of Delaware

Julie Kittleson pointed out that the core ideas within inquiry heuristics are common across many models of inquiry—they just often have slightly different names. When you look across models of inquiry, you see common components similar to those outlined in this chapter (questions, evidence, explanations, connections, justifications). All models go well beyond a single hands-on activity to achieve real learning with students.

If you make sure you cover all five features, will that mean you're doing inquiry? Not quite. In reality, implementing authentic inquiry requires attention to the details—the specifics about your classroom, your students, your curriculum, and your community. It's these details, the unique conditions in which any instruction takes place, that make inquiry truly meaningful—and truly authentic—for you and your students.

No two classrooms and activities should look the same, even when engaged in the same content area and same investigation. Why? Because each classroom has its own set of learners with their own sets of interests and their own local contexts with which to make learning meaningful. Some classes will need more structure, because they're newer to inquiry or less familiar with a particular content area. Some classrooms will need less structure, because they can draw on their own understandings or familiarity with content to go further on their own. Sometimes inquiry requires you to backtrack through the features—to move back to further refinement of questions when evidence is surprising or different or to skip forward to justifications before a complete explanation has been formulated. The power of a heuristic is that it isn't the stereotypical lockstep "scientific method" where every kid in every classroom follows the same checklist to completion. (You might remember learning the step-by-step approach called the scientific method, in which missing a step meant messing up an experiment. That's not inquiry, and it's not how scientists work.)

Instead inquiry is infinitely flexible. The beauty of the heuristics outlined in this chapter is that, although sharing common features, the employment of these features, the order, and the need to go forward or backward or skip around are all up to you as a teacher. The power of the heuristic lies in its ability to support customization. And this in turn allows inquiry to be not just a caricature of the scientific method but also a dynamic and customizable tool that allows teachers to move within the framework to fit their particular needs.

Of course it's important not to stray too far from the heuristic. Students must eventually engage in all five features, or they won't have experienced inquiry. The sequencing of the features needs to be thoughtful, and not too scattered, or students won't grasp the important relationships between features, such as gathering evidence and using that evidence to evaluate a question or strengthening an explanation through justification to others. It's important to realize that there are touchstones within inquiry—the five features discussed in this chapter—but instruction at each feature requires a reflective analysis to help determine what happens next. Attention to the details about your particular instructional context—the children, the content, the curriculum, and you—is what makes inquiry work.

Translating Hands-On Activities Into Inquiry Lessons

There is not an all-purpose formula that will translate a fun activity into something that will develop students' scientific literacy. However, a guide we can use takes the form of the essential features of inquiry. Ultimately the original lesson could mature into a component of a learning cycle. But first things first. Let's uncover opportunities for building inquiry into this activity.

There are many activities that have been published that may not work in a classroom. For example in a third-grade science textbook, we found directions for making a giant thermometer. A two-liter bottle was to be filled with colored water and then sealed with a piece of clay that had a soda straw running through it. The illustrations showed how the change in temperature would cause the liquid to rise and fall within the straw, just like in a commercial thermometer. This is a very appealing activity because it would allow students to create a tool for measuring the temperature of their classroom, the playground, and so on. But as written, it doesn't work—the soda straw is just too wide to detect any change in the liquid level.

It's a pity this activity is such a dud. It would be exciting to build your own thermometer. But what's even worse is the idea of a teacher having gathered all the necessary materials (think about acquiring and storing enough bottles for every student!), generating some enthusiasm in the students, and then having the activity fall completely flat. A successful activity, that is, one that will teach students science, will often allow us to look beyond the mess (wet clay and colored water). But when an activity bombs, the residual mess only adds to the frustration and embarrassment.

The first rule in planning a science lesson is to make sure that the activity works by trying it out ahead of time. Even the Cartesian diver is not free of problems. For this activity we found that glass eyedroppers work great but plastic ones are not dense enough and you have to add some extra mass to weigh them down. This is not a major problem unless you take it on faith that the materials will work according to the written plan.

Having established that the materials will cooperate, the teacher can invest thought into how to make the activity more inquiry based. We cannot assume that simply because students are engaged in an activity with concrete materials they are participating in inquiry. You may recall this as a flaw of the discovery approach. We must reach for a delicate balance between telling the students everything we want for them to learn and putting all our trust in their innate curiosity to lead them to make great conceptual leaps on their own. So how can we reach this balance with the Cartesian diver activity? The five essential features of inquiry can be very helpful to us in the planning stages.

A Question to Explore (the First Essential Feature)

As it was written, the Cartesian diver activity did not include a question to stimulate students' thinking. The first essential feature of inquiry identifies a range of supports a teacher can provide to students for forming questions; highlighting any of these would be a step toward making this activity more inquiry based. Given this particular activity, it seems appropriate to provide a large amount of teacher control. Remember the goal is not for every activity to be fully open ended or to be situated at the higher levels of the essential features diagram. And for this activity, it really doesn't make a lot of sense to leave the students to come up with their own question. In fact to give the students the materials and ask them something like "See what you can discover with the eyedropper, bottles, and some water" feels more like a game than an opportunity to learn. The purpose is not to have them stumble upon how to build a Cartesian diver but to use the equipment to help them to learn about buoyancy. A teacher isn't giving anything away by showing them what they will create.

In reference to the Cartesian diver, it is fine for the teacher to pose a question to the students to guide their investigation. Referring to the first essential feature, this activity is evidently pitched at Level 1. The teacher would have a working Cartesian diver system already created as an example for the students and could demonstrate what can be done to make it rise and fall. The question posed to the students would be "I would like you to work with the equipment that I will provide to you to build a Cartesian diver. The question for you to answer is, 'What does it take for these materials to cause the diver to rise and fall?' " Certainly this isn't leaving the students with much latitude for posing their own question, yet it will guide their explorations without telling them what they are going to uncover.

Collecting Evidence (the Second Essential Feature)

The second essential feature of inquiry conveys the importance of gathering and analyzing data, observations, and evidence (we can treat these as synonyms). The variations on this essential feature once again refer to the amount of teacher control versus student control. With complex equipment or challenging data, it makes sense for the teacher to assert more control and have students functioning at Level 2 of the essential features diagram. We've found this is especially true when the evidence is in the form of quantitative observations because learning to manage measurement data is often confusing for students. Faced with potentially complex data, students can avoid unnecessary frustration with the support the teacher.

However, because of the relative simplicity of the Cartesian diver activity, there is less need to provide students with much structure for their observations. Our inclination is to move more toward allowing more learner direction, sliding far to the left within the essential feature (see Table 7.2), perhaps to Level 3, the "learner is directed to collect certain data" variation. Giving students a record sheet for recording their observations might be sufficient. Even more structure can be provided with a record sheet where the students are guided to propose inferences based on their observations or even predictions that they can then test. If the teacher leaves students to simply record their observations and inferences within personal science notebooks, this activity would be at Level 4 of the second essential feature ("learner determines what constitutes evidence and collects it").

There is an interesting chain of cause-and-effect relationships that takes place within the Cartesian diver system, some that have a bearing on the actions of the diver and others that do not. For example squeezing the sides of the bottle may cause the water level in the bottle to rise. Although this is an artifact of the applied pressure and does accompany the rise and fall of water levels inside the eyedropper, the change in the bottle's water level doesn't contribute to the diver's motions. This becomes an observation students might notice, but it fails to supply any useful evidence about the diver; learning to sort relevant observations from those that aren't useful for forming explanations is a good thing for students to experience.

Creating Explanations for the Evidence (the Third Essential Feature)

Because the behavior of the Cartesian diver is so accessible to the students, a teacher is justified in turning over the control for forming explanations to the students. Had we used this activity as written, the explanation would have already been given to the students even though they made observations on their own. By requiring the students to make written observations of the Cartesian diver system, as part of the previous essential feature of inquiry, they will have much of the information they need to help them to generate explanations.

The relationship between explanations and evidence is a defining aspect of the actions of science. There are many decisions that we make in our lives that aren't based in evidence, such as choosing what is an appropriate gift to buy for someone. However, when we're involved with the actions of science, evidence absolutely must be used to support all explanations. For the Cartesian diver system, the cognitive jump from collecting evidence to making an explanation may seem rather obvious. After all, the explanation provided within the activity makes it seem quite simple. However, it is important to appreciate that the transition from evidence to explanations, or from information to understandings, is not quite so simple. Great scientific discoveries are often made using data that have been around for a while. Simply having a nice collection of data is not enough—it takes creativity to make sense of the observations. What made Watson and Crick so famous, and somewhat controversial, was that they used data others had gathered to figure out how the pieces that make up DNA are put together. The evidence was there, but it took creativity to figure out the now-well-known shape of the DNA helix.

There are two implications of this situation for inquiry-based science teaching. First, it is unreasonable to expect students to easily make the leap from evidence to explanation. Not all of the observations that students might make of the Cartesian diver are relevant to explaining the diver's movement. In this way, doing science is like having a puzzle where you have more pieces than you really need. Second, recognizing that evidence does not immediately lead to explanations is part of understanding the nature of science, which we will address in more detail in the next chapter.

Connections With Scientific Knowledge (the Fourth Essential Feature)

A big part of learning new material is realizing how different ideas are connected to each other. In some ways, helping students to recognize that different experiences have some underlying similarity is a big leap. As part of science, students are expected to learn about ideas such as solids, liquids, and gases; cumulus, cirrus, and stratus clouds; igneous, metamorphic, and sedimentary rocks; and, stars, planets, and moons. Noting the similarities and differences so they can put observations into groups (sounds like the classify process skill, doesn't it?) is one aspect of connection making.

In addition, as teachers we are responsible for helping our students to connect their experiences with the knowledge of the scientific community: the objects of science. In other words, as powerful as it can be to have students participating in and controlling their own inquiries, we are obligated to assist them to understand that their discoveries relate to those of scientists.

The fourth essential feature of inquiry describes how much control the teacher exerts over the processes students use in making the connections.

The Cartesian diver activity, in its current form, makes a useful connection for the students. Because eyedroppers and soda bottles are not a part of the natural world, it seems useful to identify an analogous system. Fish have used buoyancy to their advantage for millions of years. The text within the Cartesian diver activity provides that connection for the students: the experience is explained for them through the printed word. This is a very efficient way to build conceptual bridges between classroom science and the real world. Nevertheless we need to be aware that students need practice in making their own connections. If the teacher always makes the connections for the students, they will never develop skill at doing this on their own. At Level 4 of the essential features diagram, we can read that the students are to consult resources to create their own connections. Does this seem like a purposeful use of the Internet?

Although we didn't expect to find much by typing "Cartesian diver" into an Internet search engine, we found three intriguing connections. Finding this information helped us to better understand what happens within the Cartesian diver system and also reinforced the value of helping to make connections between our firsthand experiences and the knowledge held by the scientific community.

One Web page had the title "How Do Fish Rise and Sink in the Water?" and was part of the "How Stuff Works" Web site (http://science.howstuffworks.com/question629.htm). Here we found an extensive explanation of the science behind fish buoyancy, along with information concerning several related topics including submarines, blimps, and helium balloons. We also learned that because sharks do not have a swim bladder, they must use their fins to rise and sink within the water.

Another Web site, which is part of the Exploratorium online museum, describes how to make Cartesian divers using ketchup packets and soy sauce pouches (rather than an eyedropper) (http://www.exploratorium.edu/snacks/condiment_diver/). If the packets are filled so they just barely float in a water-filled soda bottle, they will rise and fall just as the Cartesian diver does.

Another Web resource we found, an article from *Science News* (http://www.phschool.com/science/science_news/articles/leashing_rattlesnake.html) (Milius, 2003), tells about William Mackin, a biologist at the University of North Carolina at Chapel Hill who studies birds' diving behavior. The shearwater bird goes below the ocean surface to obtain food. Mackin dusted the inside of plastic tubes with powdered sugar, sealing one end while leaving the other end open. When attached to a shearwater's leg, water will rise in the tube in proportion to the depth it dives. By measuring the amount of sugar rinsed from the tube's inside, Mackin learned that shearwaters reach a depth of seven meters (about twenty-three feet) in their dives. The water in Mackin's tube is pushed upward, just as when we squeeze the soda bottle to push water into the Cartesian diver.

NSES Teaching Standard B: Teachers of science guide and facilitate learning, encourage and model the skills of scientific inquiry, as well as the curiosity, openness to new ideas, and skepticism that characterize science.

Communicating and Justifying (the Fifth Essential Feature)

The last of the five essential features combines the process skill of communicating with the goal of having students justify their scientific explanations. Translating what they did and the thought processes they used during their investigations not only reveals what was accomplished but also assists the students in recognizing what they've learned. This essential feature is consistent with the social aspects of science—scientific discoveries must be carefully and critically examined before they are accepted by the scientific community. How might this be accommodated in an elementary or middle school classroom? Students can present their observations to the class and propose explanations for what they observed. Students can venture a defense of their explanation relative to other explanations. It is important for these to occur with other students as the audience to reinforce the social aspect of the science culture.

In a similar way, students need to be able to share their scientific discoveries and understandings with others. A teacher may first ask students to do this orally and then put those ideas onto paper. But if the students are relatively new to this sort of thinking, the teacher can provide specific directions (such as at Level 1 for this essential feature) for generating explanations.

Evaluating a Science Activity

Inquiry activities are substantially different from regular hands-on activities, and the five essential features provide a framework for promoting inquiry in elementary and middle school science classrooms. But there are other criteria that probably should be used to evaluate whether an activity is appropriate for classroom use. In this section, we will describe a rubric teachers can use for this purpose.

In her article "Activity Selection: It's More Than the Fun Factor," Carolyn Jeffries (1999) advocated for using activities that go beyond being fun. She urges teachers to select activities that are interesting and help students to learn science. One criterion she indicated as important in selecting an activity is the possible application of the activity. This is particularly relevant, because activities can be appropriately used at several places with the learning cycle. For example activities are used to engage students at the beginning of the learning cycle. Second, they help students to develop science process skills, which would be appropriate at several places in the learning cycle—probably most strongly in the Explore and Extend phases. Third, as detailed in this chapter, activities can be used as a basis for student inquiry. Finally, activities can be an opportunity to assess students—an idea we will explore in greater detail in chapter 11.

Jeffries (1999) suggested, within her criteria, that we examine potential activities in terms of the content and the pedagogy. For the former, this requires deciding if the activity is appropriate to the developmental level of the students, if it encourages the use of the science process skills, and if there is background information provided for the teacher that explains the underlying content in an understandable and accurate way. Under pedagogy, we would consider the clarity of the activity's goals, the potential for promoting inquiry, the availability of the necessary materials, and the efforts to elicit explanations from the students. In a sense, Jeffries supplied a rubric we can use for evaluating any science activity.

For Reflection and Discussion

Locate a science activity that you might consider using in your teaching. Decide where it would fall along each of the essential features if you used the activity just as it was written. What changes might you make to the design of the activity so it moves one or two blocks to the left for each essential feature?

Moving Toward Inquiry in Diverse Classrooms

One of the more important issues to consider when you move toward inquiry in diverse classrooms is the notion of **congruence**. Lee and Fradd (1998) encouraged approaching science instruction so it draws on and resonates with the lives, languages, and patterns of thoughts of the students (which might be very different from that of the teacher, the text, or even the broader culture of science). Instruction that is more congruent with learners and their ways of thinking will be more effective in helping students of all backgrounds and abilities learn science. Central to this idea of congruence are the sources of the ideas upon which the inquiry is built. We are talking here not about the concepts an activity is supposed to address (in the previous activity it was buoyancy) but about the substance of the activity (here, the Cartesian diver). All too often in science classes, the activities are drawn from abstract examples, unrelated to the lives of students. This runs counter to the desire to establish instructional congruence between the curriculum and the students' experiences. We will spend more time within chapter 14 with this issue as we consider the need for teachers to negotiate multiple communities.

For instance a chemical reaction involving acetic acid and sodium bicarbonate, although it looks and sounds much like a reaction between kitchen vinegar and baking soda, is interpreted, understood, and remembered much differently by students. If the teacher selects items from students' lives and experience (such as vinegar and baking soda) and refer to them as such (instead of by their complex scientific names of acetic acid and sodium bicarbonate), students, particularly those new to the culture of American schools and the culture of science, will much more likely be interested in these activities. If students are interested, they are more likely to engage with the material, allowing them to construct a deeper understanding of the concepts. Activities allow students to relate the science they learn in the classroom to the science in their lives. For the Cartesian diver activity, the teacher should exert the additional effort to show how buoyancy plays a role in students' lives; for example objects in liquid during cooking, toys in the bathtub, and objects in natural bodies of water (fishing gear, toy boats, etc.).

Another important aspect of congruence is the scientific action of communication. Because learning to communicate scientifically is central to the culture of science, much support is needed to scaffold attempts toward scientifically acceptable norms. As students offer their evolving explanations, teachers should ask (and students in the class should learn to ask each other), "What is your evidence for this?" or "Help me understand your thinking." During these exchanges, teachers should explicitly point out what kind of thinking can be included in science (based on evidence) and what kind of thinking cannot be included (based on emotions or beliefs).

NSES Teaching Standard E: Teachers of science develop communities of science learners that reflect the intellectual rigor of scientific inquiry and the attitudes and social values conducive to science learning.

Special Needs Students and Inquiry

It is important to recognize that learning through questions and questioning will come much more easily and will seem much more natural for some students than for others. For students new to this way of thinking and interacting, teachers should begin on the right-hand side of the essential features of inquiry. This will provide support for students as they first become aware of these aspects of the actions of science and science learning. This consideration should be extended to students with cognitive limitations. Movement toward the "student-centered" end of the various continua for essential features of inquiry carries higher expectations for student involvement, decision making, and responsibility.

When the scientific concepts are particularly difficult and abstract, or if individual students operate with cognitive limitations, it is inappropriate to place too much decision-making responsibility for a lesson on the students. Adjustments need to be made by teachers so the requirements of inquiry activities are within the students' grasps, while avoiding an inappropriate lowering of expectations. Teachers should continually reevaluate students' abilities as they participate in inquiry, mindful that such experiences support not only science conceptual understandings but students' inquiry skills as well. By year's end teachers should consistently be operating much further to the left, on the essential features continue placing more responsibility for scientific inquiry on all of the students in a classroom.

None of these cautions and considerations would justify not using inquiry with certain students: "When activity-based instruction is appropriately structured, students with disabilities can master concepts in science that are usually taught in regular science classrooms" (McCarthy, 2005, p. 257). The essential features of inquiry provide a tool to help teachers know how to provide such structure. Otherwise, "structure" might be too narrowly interpreted. Also teachers should recognize that the degree of student or teacher control over the essential features does not create a tension between inquiry and noninquiry science. Instead this framework defines real inquiry as experiences and activities involving all five features. The amount of teacher control describes varying degrees of guided inquiry or open inquiry. But the research suggests, and our own experiences confirm, that it is appropriate to hold inquiry as a goal for all students. The challenge is with finding an appropriate balance of structure across the five essential features.

Challenging English Language Learners to Apply Complex Thinking

We have reached the last of the five principles for effective pedagogy that the Center for Research on Education, Diversity, and Excellence proposed as being necessary to promote learning of English language learners (Warren & Rosebery, 2002). As with the others, we are relying on these principles to fortify our repertoire of science teaching practices. Encouraging students to apply more complex thinking (see Table 7.6), the core of this principle, runs in contrast to the typical approach used for teaching second-language learners. All too often the presumption is that those who are not fluent in English must first learn the fundamentals before they should be expected to engage in more complex thinking (Dalton, 1998). As a result far too many students have been victims of basic skills development through worksheets, repetition, and other strategies that discourage students from achieving.

TABLE 7.6.   Complex Thinking, Challenging Expectations, and the Appropriate Teacher Actions

The teacher:
  ensures that students comprehend the big ideas and the constituent parts for each concept;
  promotes standards that are appropriately challenging to all students;
  supports student comprehension by the thoughtful selection of activities and assignments;
  uses previous success as a basis to encourage students to move toward more abstract
    thought and complete understandings; and
  communicates to students how their performance aligns with standards by supplying timely
    and explicit feedback.

Note: Adapted from Dalton (1998).

Teaching to Encourage Complex Thinking

There are many reasons that teaching for complex thinking is an appropriate tactic to use with English language learners. First, the challenges of complex thinking are often more motivating than instruction that emphasizes rote memorization and low-level knowledge. Second, complex thinking requires the use of complex language creation, which creates a mutually supportive framework. Academic thinking requires more sophisticated uses of language that in turn support the need for increased English fluency. Finally, having complex thinking as an explicit goal promotes higher expectations of students. Students who are given appropriately challenging activities develop greater confidence, a resource that will benefit them as they face additional challenges.

NSES Content Standard A: Students should develop the abilities to think critically and logically to make the relationships between evidence and explanations.

Complex thinking has a tendency to encourage students to pay more attention to their thought process. This **metacognition,** which is defined as being consciously aware of one's thinking, helps English language learners, and all other students for that matter, to monitor the ways they approach circumstances that are cognitively challenging. In a sense, the goal of complex thinking and expecting high standards for student performance go hand in hand. The goal of promoting more complex thinking has implications for teachers, as it requires selecting activities and adapting lessons for the promotion of genuine, higher-order thinking. As a reminder, this approach is useful for all learners. But it takes a concerted effort to combat traditional notions of the capabilities of English language learners and what we can reasonably expect them to accomplish. The ambition of promoting complex thinking is not a cure-all to the science achievement gap, but it does a great deal to encourage students of science (and their teachers) to expect a little bit more and to open themselves up to the additional possibilities when ambitious standards and high expectations are achieved.

Chapter Summary

- Hands-on science activities are widely available but rarely provide for inquiry-based teaching. However, using the essential features of inquiry as a framework, the conscientious elementary or middle school teacher can translate a fun activity into an opportunity for genuine student learning.
- Too much faith is often placed in the power of equipment for supporting students' science learning. One important adjustment that will promote an activity to being truly inquiry based is to use a question as the starting point for student investigation.
- When answering scientific questions, students must know that the role of evidence takes precedence over all other factors. As students mature in their ability to participate in inquiry, they will need help with deciding which forms of evidence are more credible.
- By compiling and summarizing a collection of evidence, students have transformed their data into material that will assist them with making explanations. The creativity involved in moving from explanations to evidence is akin to the transition between observations and inferences.

- Classroom-based inquiry does not end when students have generated personal explanations for the evidence. It is also necessary for students to build explanations between their ideas and the accepted knowledge from the scientific community.
- Within inquiry activities, students should be expected to communicate logical explanations based on their evidence and information gathered from other credible sources. These actions are consistent with the unique cultural norms of science.
- Translating an activity that is fun into an inquiry activity requires teachers to incorporate the five essential features and to decide the degree of teacher control required within each feature.
- Adjustments for language differences, comfort with ambiguity, and other issues related to student diversity must be considered during the planning and implementing of science inquiry. Within these efforts teachers should not permit themselves to believe that a certain segment of the student population is incapable of engaging in inquiry.

Key Terms

Congruence: refers to the degree of alignment between the concepts, patterns of communication, and required habits of mind employed in school settings and the students' own language, cultural experiences, and thought processes.

Data: information obtained using unbiased observations.

Investigable question: a question that a student can answer through investigations using scientific thinking and process skills.

Mean: a statistic regarded as one way to characterize a group of numbers, calculated by adding each of the numbers in a sample together then dividing the total by the amount of numbers in that sample. Also referred to as the average of the sample.

Median: a statistic, regarded as one way to characterize a group of numbers, determined by finding the middle value in a sample in which the numbers are arranged in ascending or descending order.

Metacognition: an awareness of one's personal thought processes. It describes an explicit awareness of the ways one thinks through a situation.

Mode: a statistic, regarded as one way to characterize a group of numbers that is the number that appears most frequently in that sample. Sometimes referred to as the norm of a sample.

Objectivity: a characteristic of scientific actions in which personal bias is minimized often through the process of limiting the role of inference in the collection of scientific observations, allowing for a more straightforward portrait of the physical world.

A Favorite Science Lesson

A module by FOSS (the Full Option Science System) designed for grades one and two called "Solids and Liquids" gives students firsthand experience with chemistry concepts at a level they can comprehend. The "Liquids" activity seems very basic but proves to be quite rich for primary grade students. With clear and unbreakable containers holding household liquids (e.g., corn syrup, vegetable oil, fabric softener, etc.), students recognize the similarities and differences of these liquids. Rather than memorizing the idea that liquids take the shape of the container they are in, students actually develop this idea from their own investigations. Along the way, normally complex terms such as translucent and viscous become real to the students, because these words help to describe what is being observed. This information about liquids is then applied when the students later mix solids with liquids to see which solids will dissolve. As with other hands-on activities, there is immense potential to build real inquiry into what the students are doing. The resources listed within this unit help make connections to science using a variety of books and the Internet.

Suggested Readings

Cavaness, D. (2004). SPF 30: Exposing your students to science inquiry. *Science Scope, 27*(8), 12–17.
There is much to admire and appreciate about this article. First of all, it makes creative use of specially designed plastic beads that change color when exposed to sunlight. These objects become tools to measure the protective properties of sunblocks. Also this author describes how she guides her students to recognize how to devise questions that lend themselves to scientific investigation.

Galus, P. J. (2002). Snail trails. *Science Scope, 25*(8), 14–18.
On the basis of her teaching experiences, this author describes how snails are used to support the development of students' science inquiry. She describes everything from introductory activities to help students become familiar with land snails and several experiments that can be done to investigate snail behaviors.

References

Anholt, L. (1999). *Stone girl, bone girl: The story of Mary Anninng*. New York: Orchard Books.

Ball, D. (1992). Magical hopes: Manipulatives and the reform of math education. *American Educator, 16*(2), 14–18, 46–47.

Dalton, S. S. (1998). *Pedagogy matters: Standards for effective teaching practice*. Washington, DC: Center for Applied Linguistics.

Dewey, J. (1991). *How we think*. Amherst, NY: Prometheus Books. (Original work published 1910)

Fried, R. L. (2001). *The passionate teacher*. Boston, MA: Beacon Press.

Jeffries, C. (1999). Activity selection: It's more than the fun factor. *Science and Children, 37*(2), 26–29, 63.

Lee, O., & Fradd, S. H. (1998). Science for all, including students from non-English language backgrounds. *Educational Researcher, 27*(4), 12–21.

McCarthy, C. B. (2005). Effects of thematic-based, hands-on science teaching versus a textbook approach for students with disabilities. *Journal of Research in Science Teaching, 42*, 245–263.

Milius, S. (2003, September 27). Leashing the rattlesnake: A behind-the-scenes look at experimental design. *Science News, 164*(13), 200.

National Research Council. (1996). *National Science Education Standards*. Washington, DC: National Academy Press.

National Research Council. (2000). *Inquiry and the National Science Education Standards: A guide for teaching and learning*. Washington, DC: National Academy Press.

Warren, B., & Rosebery, A. S. (2002). *Teaching science to at-risk students: Teacher research communities as a context for professional development and school reform*. Santa Cruz, CA: Center for Research on Education, Diversity, and Excellence.

eight
The Nature
of Science

Chapter Highlights

- The nature of science is central to its actions, so to deeply understand the culture of science, students must come to understand the nature of the knowledge it produces.

- Students need to learn that science is a distinctive way of knowing, because it demands the availability of evidence to support knowledge claims. Other worldviews may not require such an emphasis on empiricism, so teachers need to make those distinctions apparent.

- Students may not recognize that creativity is as essential to science as it is to other ways of knowing. Teachers should reinforce the value of creative thinking throughout the scientific processes (not just within the design of experiments).

- Scientists attempt to identify how their opinions and biases can influence their observations and explanations. Although it is impossible to become completely objective, teachers need to inform students about the need to identify and reduce the influence of bias within science activities. However, it is important to acknowledge that the background knowledge scientists bring with them into the doing of science is also a source of insight that allows sense making. Scientists' prior knowledge both allows them to make sense about what they are focusing on but it also places constraints on their thinking.

- Teachers should disabuse students of the idea of *the* scientific method. Although there are particular activities characteristic of doing science, these activities are not constant and do not occur in a fixed sequence, as is too often portrayed in science textbooks.

- Students should come to recognize that the collaboration involved in their science learning echoes the social nature of science for practicing scientists. Just as professional scientists do, students should present their work and ideas to others as part of the science community.

- Teachers should reinforce to students that scientific explanations are tentative. Scientific knowledge has advanced because old ideas are replaced by better explanations, and students should be taught that their ideas might be usefully replaced with more scientifically acceptable ideas.
- Students' sophisticated understanding of the nature of science is a key to making science accessible to all students.

To this point we've examined several dimensions of elementary and middle school science education. First, we considered the idea of the culture of science, with culture consisting of both actions and objects. Then we spent time looking at the actions or verbs of science in the form of the science process skills. Next we examined the implications for our teaching to emphasize the actions and objects of the culture of science: the learning cycle, questioning strategies, and inquiry-based instruction. We will now more closely examine the culture of science. As a part of our desire and responsibility to develop science literacy within students, we must understand in greater depth not only the knowledge that science produces (its objects, such as photosynthesis or Newton's law of motion) but also the processes that help us arrive at such knowledge (the actions of science that are employed in scientific inquiry). The manner in which we conduct scientific inquiry gives shape to the knowledge it produces. In other words, we can divide the culture of science only temporarily and artificially—the objects and actions are as interdependent as nouns and verbs in a paragraph. Examining the interaction of product and process, of object and action, along with the implications for teaching science in diverse settings, is the focus of this chapter.

Explanation of the Nature of Science

We can find ourselves facing a flurry of seemingly contradictory scientific information. For example here are scientific statements related to nutrition: "A low-carbohydrate diet helps you lose weight and control cholesterol levels"; "A low-carbohydrate diet is unsafe because it is often high in fat and places too much stress on the kidneys"; "Eat high amounts of grains and fruits and a minimum of meats and dairy for a well-balanced diet"; and "Eat a limited amount of grains and a high amount of meats and other protein for a well-balanced diet." How can scientists produce these contradictory messages? Isn't there some data that can resolve these contradictions? Shouldn't scientists all say the same things? The goal of this chapter is to scrutinize how scientific knowledge is produced and to focus on how its production shapes that knowledge. By improving your understandings of the nature of science and scientific inquiry, you will better understand how to become a wise consumer of scientific knowledge. Ultimately your deeper understandings will shape your science teaching and, in turn, benefit the understandings of your students.

In the midst of doing their work, scientists may not attend to the grander ideas of their profession—but then neither do most professionals. Scientists have to worry about if their equipment is in working condition, if their schedule allows them to gather the data they need, and if the data they are collecting will help them to solve the questions they are investigating. Because they are so involved, scientists may not often sit back to think about how their research connects to the bigger picture. Consider the work of other professionals such as a nurse, police officer, or cook. Each profession has its own global concerns (health, justice, and nutrition), and those have the power to subtly shape what the individuals do as they go about their work. But as a nurse gives a patient a shot, as a police officer interviews a witness, and as a cook goes about measuring and sifting flour, they probably aren't focused on the big picture. But if you asked, they probably can explain how they see their tasks connecting to something bigger and more important than just these mundane activities. So it is with the professional scientist.

The phrase the **nature of science** describes the underlying tendencies and unspoken assumptions that guide the actions of scientists, as individuals and as part of a larger cultural group, in shaping the knowledge science produces. As a result of these traditions, the knowledge that is created retains these embedded characteristics. The phrase "scientific inquiry" refers to actions involved in scientists' pursuit of knowledge; that is, the manner in which they seek explanations of natural phenomena. It is difficult to clearly distinguish concepts related to the nature of science and scientific inquiry because the two interact and shape one another. We will discuss both in tandem to provide a coherent portrait of the culture of science.

It is difficult to list the components of the nature of science just as it is challenging to summarize the parts of any culture. If you've wondered about how to effectively teach science to a particular category of students (e.g., girls, children with hearing disabilities, students who are not fluent with the English language), then you can appreciate why it's hard to quickly and accurately define the nature of science. Just as it is impossible and perhaps unwise to reduce any of these groups of students to a list of specific characteristics (e.g., girls like to work in groups, children with disabilities don't like to be singled out, English language learners will need particular help in the sciences)—as there is so much variability and complexity within these groups—it is very difficult to reduce the knowledge about science to a specific list of characteristics. So why should we try? Think about it this way: if you were trying to explain your cultural traditions to an outsider, you would need to help them recognize some major themes of your culture. Knowing the timing of special events, knowing the kinds of food that are eaten, and knowing the special phrases that are used are only surface features. A genuine cultural tradition consists of much more than its rituals.

Traditions have their bases in underlying beliefs and norms. When outsiders focus on just the surface feature of a culture's tradition, they fail to recognize the significance of those traditions for the members of the culture. To study science without an understanding of the nature of science is to become familiar with the surface features of that culture and to never really understand, be comfortable with, or be able to work within the culture of science. What we will try to accomplish in this chapter is to give you a sense of what is included within the nature of scientific knowledge and how it is shaped by the practice of scientific inquiry so you can construct a better sense of the culture of science. The short-term goal is strengthening your understandings of the nature of science, and the long-term goal is to ensure that your teaching about science is consistent with and expilcibly reinforces the nature of science.

Unpacking Students' Ideas About the Nature of Science

When we ask students "What is science?" we often receive the same sorts of responses whether they are elementary school, middle school, high school, or college students. Students point to a biology book and say, "That is science." Or they may give a list courses such as physics, biology, and chemistry. With additional probing, they'll cite the scientific method as an explanation of how science is done. When we prompt them to draw a picture that answers the question "What does a scientist look like?" we again receive similar messages from students across the grade levels. Students tend to draw a befuddled, wild-haired man in a white lab coat. As we spend even more time discussing these matters, students (again from across the age and grade spectrums) explain that science is a large body of very sure facts, facts that are "discovered" by objective scientists as they study all aspects of the world, a study that is sometimes described as "prying open" the natural world as if the answers are hidden inside like a prize. These scientists are often viewed as "lone rangers" who work in isolation and surprise the world with their discoveries after long hours of diligent work.

For Reflection and Discussion

If you were asked to draw or describe a scientist without thinking about it too deeply, what characteristics would you include? If elementary or middle school students held the same views of scientists similar to yours, how might that influence their desire to become participants in that culture?

How do we develop our ideas about science and scientists? It is notable that students' responses are very similar across ages. This suggests that these ideas are first learned early in life and little occurs that diminishes these perceptions. Elementary schooling might contribute to this situation. But it is unfortunate that not many students actually study science during their elementary careers. So where do these ideas come from? It seems that much of what students "know" about the culture of science comes from the media—the news, movies, cartoons, and so on. Think about the scientists you've seen on television and in movies, fictional stories, and educational programs. What do many of these scientists have in common? They are usually seen as White men with wild hair who are just a bit different from all the others around them. Unfortunately, even programs supported by the National Science Foundation for educational purposes, such as *Bill Nye the Science Guy*, reinforce the stereotypes.

Few experiences in daily life accurately portray science as it is actually performed by scientists. The stereotypical versions of science, although comical, send a clear message to students that only certain people can become scientists. These misperceptions of science may actually cause students to believe that science is not something they can do or would want to do. Our working hypothesis is that if students' mythical notions are unpacked, if we can help teachers and students to understand the actual nature of science and scientific inquiry and who does it, then more students will understand that they can be capable science learners.

Just as stereotypes of the physical appearance of scientists are portrayed in movies and television, and students develop misconceptions about the work of scientists through these media. Thus students will enter their formal studies of science class holding many perceptions about the nature of science. In the following section, we will describe the most relevant aspects of the nature of scientific inquiry for elementary and middle school students. As we examine the nature of science concepts, we will point out the common myths held by students (and far too many people from the general public). Next we will address those concepts that are potentially the most pertinent for effectively teaching science in a diverse setting. Finally we will provide suggestions about infusing the nature of science concepts throughout classroom science instruction.

The Empirical Aspect of Scientific Knowledge

By now we can probably agree that the ultimate purpose of science is to understand and explain the physical world. The actions of science include the scientific tasks of collecting information (data or evidence) about that world, and the objects of science are the constructed explanations. As we have discussed, science involves both processes and products, and its culture can be understood only through studying its actions and objects. One defining feature of the actions of science is that they center on a process of inquiring into the physical world. That is, at some level the actions of science can never stray too far away from the world surrounding us. Given that a central goal of science is to develop useful understandings of the physical world, its methods are inherently **empirical.** This term describes knowledge that is grounded in observations and experimentation not in opinions and sensations. If a biologist wants to empirically understand the behavior of snails along a coastline, at some point she will need to collect data about these behaviors (e.g., where are they during different times of the day, what they eat, how quickly they move) and data about a variety of other environmental factors (such as salinity, water temperature, ambient temperature, presence of edible plants, and potential predators). All these data may allow the biologist to construct an explanation that allows her to accurately describe and predict snail behavior. If the explanation she constructs is helpful to her and to other scientists in predicting accurately the behavior of the snails, then this explanation is regarded as a useful piece of scientific knowledge.

NSES Content Standard A: All students should be able to think critically and logically to make the relationships between evidence and explanations.

This discussion might be familiar to you. The work of scientists is powered by the desire to understand the physical world. Its actions center on collecting data about the natural world, so it is empirical. However, the empirical aspect is only part of the portrait of science. There are other very dynamic aspects of doing science. Yes, science is empirical, but it is also many other things.

The Creativity of Science and Scientific Knowledge

As we have indicated, the goal of science is to produce explanations of the physical world. Where do these explanations come from? In part they begin as careful observations of nature. But you should recognize that the making of explanations entails creativity on the part of scientists. In contrast to the well-recognized empirical character of science are three aspects of the creative nature of science and scientific inquiry. These aspects are as follows: (a) explanations are generated from evidence, (b) personal bias influences the creative process, and (c) science benefits from creativity. In the following sections, we will illustrate some of the creative aspects of the culture of science.

Explanations Are Generated From Evidence

Doing science is much more creative (and interesting) than simply stringing together pieces of data to create an explanation about what's been studied. For example a scientist may watch the steam rise from a boiling pot of water and explain that the heat from the stove was transferred to the water, causing the water molecules to speed their motion, take up more space and thus become less dense than the surrounding air, and then rise. The evidence is the water vapor rising from the pot on the stove. The explanation involves the relationship between heat, molecular movement, and density. Andy Anderson of Michigan State University suggests that the core of scientific inquiry is the cycle between evidence and explanations (Anderson, 2006). By this he meant that the opportunity for creative thinking within science is embedded within making the leap between what has been empirically described (the evidence) and a reasonable description about how things are as we have found them (the explanations).

Another example comes from the biological world. Imagine a potted plant that is wilting. After giving it a generous watering, you are impatient to see if it recovers. However, the plant doesn't seem to perk up very much. You touch the surface of the soil to reassure yourself that it is damp. You provide the plant with fertilizer and even several hours later the plant fails to be as healthy as you expect. You peer into the dish under the pot to see if there is any water there, and you are startled to see roots poking out of the pot's bottom. When you lift the plant out of its pot, you discover that there are so many roots that they have grown into the exact shape of the interior of the pot. This evidence of tangled roots leads you to the understanding (and explanation) that the wilting is because the roots are too tightly packed and that you need to put the plant and a liberal supply of soil into a larger pot. Once the plant returns to its vigorous and unwilted shape, you become convinced by your explanation that the wilting of the leaves had something to do with the roots' inability to take up water. The evidence were your observations that the leaves were wilting, the roots were filling the pot, and that the behavior of the plant changed once the plant was placed into a larger container. The explanation has to do with the movement of water through the vascular system of the plant.

Anderson's claim that inquiry involves the cycling between evidence and explanations (see Figure 8.1) can be challenging to understand. This might be because many of us believe that the work of scientists involves uncovering nature—taking the lid off the natural world to see what's happening inside. Many people see the actions of science as simply a set of procedures that must be followed. Using this view, these people feel that generating the objects or explanations of science becomes the process of simple description, as though the physical world is waiting to tell the scientists how things work, so that the evidence is seen as synonymous with the explanation. To those individuals, Anderson's suggestion that creativity is essential to science may seem odd. But the reality is that scientists must be creative in their work.

Creativity includes not only designing experiments for testing a hypothesis but also thinking about the data after they have been gathered. Being able to interpret the data to develop a reasonable explanation demands creative thinking. This connects to a quote from earlier chapters about the leap from observations to inferences. In the following quote you can read how John Dewey thought about this transition. Yes, a scientist's role is to describe nature, but from those descriptions and those observations, they need to generate inferences to develop ideas based on those descriptions. The objects of science are the explanations based on the evidence scientists collect. As such, evidence and explanations are closely related and interdependent.

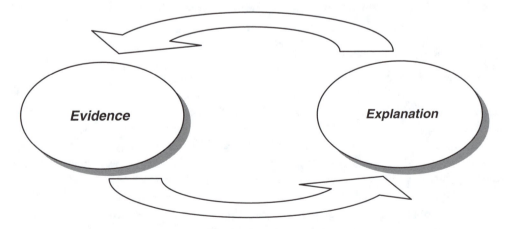

FIGURE 8.1. Evidence and explanation influence each other.

But the process of reaching the absent from the present is peculiarly exposed to error. … The exercise of thought is, in the literal sense of that word, inference; by it one thing carries us over to the idea of, and belief in, another thing. It involves a jump, a leap, a going beyond what is surely known to something else. … The very inevitableness of the jump, the leap, to something unknown, only emphasizes the necessity of attention to the conditions under which it occurs so that the danger of a false step may be lessened and the probability of a right landing increased. (Dewey, 1910/1991, p. 26)

By now we hope you are beginning to appreciate the role of creativity in the doing of science. Far from being a mindless and mechanical gathering of evidence, the work of science benefits from personal creativity and the ability to shift from data to explanations. In the process of generating explanations, a scientist's prior thinking comes into play. Because scientists must interpret evidence, their biases and background knowledge become important.

The Subjective Nature of Science

Scientists can become impassioned about their work and genuinely excited about creating explanations of the world. It is reasonable to imagine that their eagerness might cause them to view scientific evidence through hopeful, biased, and thus subjective eyes. **Subjectivity** refers to the role that a person's individual perspective plays in shaping what the person perceives. Because scientists are human, we accept the role that their preconceived ideas will have in influencing what they notice. Perhaps a key difference between the culture of science and other fields is the desire and effort to remain as objective as possible and to limit the impact of a scientist's bias in the meaning he or she makes. To amplify the impact of the empirical world on the sense science makes of it, scientists take measures in the actions of science (particularly the social aspects of scientific inquiry) to reduce the influence of bias within their work so they can better "see" what is there.

We acknowledge that bias shapes the construction of scientific knowledge. What a scientist already knows influences what he or she finds out in an investigation. Background knowledge affects what sorts of questions are posed, the kinds of data collected, and, as we saw in the preceding section, the interpretation of those data. Scientific knowledge progresses because of an ever-increasing supply of explanations. Scientists rely on previously constructed explanations as they examine the evidence they collect, making the actions and objects of science slowly build on themselves. Without background knowledge or knowledge of previous explanations—some sort of "theoretical bias"—scientists couldn't begin to understand the meaning of the data they collect, and they would not be particularly effective in collecting such data. In short, the reliance on preceding work influences scientists' subsequent efforts.

One example of the impact of bias on scientific explanations can be found in the stars, through the work of two astronomers, Tycho Brahe and Johannes Kepler. Brahe was a well-established astronomer in the 1500s, and the instruments he employed allowed him to make the most detailed observations of planetary motions available at that time. Using his scientific instruments, Brahe collected incredibly detailed data about planetary motion that he used to construct an explanation of the solar system; his explanation placed the earth at the center. Brahe's model was similar to models of the universe commonly accepted at the time, and he used his data to support the geocentric world.

Kepler, using the same data, proposed an alternative explanation for planetary motion, one based on a model that positioned the sun in the center with the planets orbiting around it. The knowledge that shaped Kepler's views was different from that held by Brahe, and Kepler was willing to consider the possibility that the shape of orbits could be an ellipse—

unlike Brahe, who strictly adhered to the idea of circular orbits. Brahe and Kepler used the same set of data describing planetary motion, yet these two scientists constructed different explanations from these data. This example illustrates the role of bias in the actions and objects of science. Brahe's biases (i.e., his background knowledge and beliefs) prevented him from seeing the potential of a sun-centered universe. Looking back, it seems reasonable for Brahe to have organized the universe with the earth at the center. After all, that was the conventional wisdom—although his resulting model for predicting planetary motion was exceedingly complicated.

Because of the subjective nature of science and the role of bias in shaping the nature of science and the nature of scientific inquiry, the varied background experiences of scientists benefit discovery. One example of how the knowledge produced through science is different when new scientists with fresh perspectives begin to participate can be found in biology's explanation of the process of fertilization. For years it was understood that the sperm cells were active participants in fertilization whereas the egg was relatively passive. The standard scientific explanation was that a sperm cell had to swim vast distances (relative to the size of a cell), compete with other sperm, locate an egg cell, and penetrate the egg by releasing enzymes that digested the covering of the egg. In this characterization, the sperm is seen as the active participant. In other words, the explanation was that the sperm did all the work whereas the egg simply waited to be fertilized.

As more women scientists began studying the process of fertilization, a very different portrait of this event was produced. It was recognized that the egg actually "grabbed" the sperm, in effect pulling it in. It was also shown that the enzymes released by the sperm were not active until they interacted with another secretion from the female. Thus the updated and generally accepted explanation is that the sperm and the egg are both active agents in fertilization. Although some evidence leading to this new explanation for fertilization was made possible by the development of new instrumentation (the electron microscope), other bits of evidence have been around since 1919; the relatively male-dominated science field was not yet ready to recognize them.

There is an unavoidably subjective nature to the construction of scientific knowledge, as science is a creative human activity. Because of the role of bias in creating explanations, scientific explanations benefit through the participation of scientists with varied backgrounds.

NSES Content Standard G: All students should develop understanding of science as a human endeavor, the nature of science, and the history of science.

Creativity in the Methods of Science

Like the creativity used to construct explanations based on evidence, creativity is an essential aspect of the scientific inquiry process. Sadly, there is a long-standing myth in science that appears in far too many science textbooks and that makes it seem that creativity is unimportant within the doing of science. What we need to do is recognize that creativity is essential to doing science despite this fictional icon: the Myth of The Scientific Method.

In the 1940s a man by the name of Keeslar wished to describe the different elements of scientists' work. He began by generating a list of all the things he imagined scientists did: carefully making measurements, maintaining detailed written records, defining a research problem. This list was used as the basis of a questionnaire that he sent to professional scientists. They were asked to indicate which of the activities were part of their scientific work. This list was then turned into a questionnaire and distributed among many professional scientists. Keeslar took the returned questionnaires and tallied the items according to how often scientists selected the different activity descriptions. He organized the items receiving the highest rankings into a sequence that seemed logical and published these findings in an education journal (McComas, 1998).

Keeslar was simply reporting on scientists' uses of different thinking strategies, but his report was interpreted as describing a nice neat sequence of how science is performed. A science textbook writer saw Keeslar's list and turned it into The Scientific Method—touting it as *the* way science proceeds. Indeed there is really no such thing as a singular **scientific method,** and this list doesn't accurately portray the work of scientists. Because this list of the steps of the scientific method is based on an inappropriate interpretation of Keeslar's study, there is very little that is factual about it. One could reasonably wonder what teachers are trying to portray by drilling students on the scientific method.

The Scientific Method Myth*
  1. Define the problem
  2. Gather information
  3. Form a hypothesis
  4. Make relevant observations
  5. Test the hypothesis
  6. Form conclusions
  7. Report results
     *Note: This really is a myth!

Indeed in checking with scientists, we discover that The Scientific Method is a gross oversimplification of the process of scientific inquiry. Kesslar never intended for his work to be used in this manner. A problem with the Scientific Method Myth is the implication that there are particular steps that must be followed in science and that scientists progress through the steps in this specific order. Maybe it's more comfortable to imagine that scientists are such logical individuals. But the life of a professional scientist is not quite so neat and orderly, and it is much more creative. Turning the work of scientists into a strict sequence is as full of problems as trying to reduce other complex activities to a to-do list. Try to imagine putting your family's preparations for a celebratory meal into a neat little sequence.

  1. Construct a list of materials you will need for the meal, and purchase them from the local grocery.
  2. Twenty-four hours in advance, thaw out the avian protein, and cook the vegetables for inclusion in later casseroles.
  3. Early in the morning of the event, the avian protein is placed in a covered pan and placed in the oven for a time to be determined by its weight.

And so on. As official and logical as these steps seem, the reality is much less tidy and allows for much greater individuality. To turn the preparation of a meal into such a sequence is inaccurate and misleading; it also shields us from appreciating the creativity involved in the process and the significance of the final product. The same criticism applies to using The Scientific Method as to using this recipe to prepare a great meal. Creativity is not simply allowable within doing science but it is necessary.

Just as each of us has slightly different or very different actions in the process of participating in a cultural event, scientists have slightly different or very different actions in the process of participating in the culture of science. A biologist discussed previously goes about her work much differently than the astronomers (Brahe, Kepler) of yesteryear or even the astronomers of today. There isn't a single scientific method that encapsulates the work of scientists even within a single discipline (physiology, evolutionary biology, ecology) much less between disciplines (biology, chemistry, physics, geology). Even within biology, some professionals focus on describing body structures (anatomists) or behaviors of a species (ethologists). In these cases, close descriptions are required. Other biologists may focus their work on systems that have already been closely described, and their work often focuses on explaining how things work, such as the physiologist who performs experiments on organisms to investigate the biochemistry of muscular movement. Each of these endeavors represents science, but each employs very different approaches to scientific inquiry.

Imagine for a moment that you are required to do a science fair project as part of your science teaching methods course. Your instructor is open to letting you study anything of interest to you as long as you employ The Scientific Method. Look at the steps presented earlier and think about how you might proceed. According to the guidelines you are supposed to start at item 1, then move to item 2, and so on. Feeling frustrated, overwhelmed, or irritated? So would we. The reality is that you might well start at item 4, then go to item 2, then go back to item 4, and eventually get around to item 1. And guess what: that's what scientists do. The Scientific Method is not the golden staircase to scientific enlightenment. It's just one way of many, many pathways describing how scientists can go about their work. Just as scientists must be creative in posing explanations to account for the evidence they collect, they must use creativity to develop ways to gather evidence.

Within this discussion about the nature of science, we are emphasizing the creativity possible within doing science. We want to dispose of The Scientific Method because it is inaccurate and it perpetuates a noncreative view of doing science. If we throw the myth of the scientific method out of the proverbial classroom door, how do we replace it? What is a science teacher to do? Think back to the pendulum study in which we were testing to see what influenced the swinging rate. It would be quite natural for someone to begin studying a pendulum by first doing some test swings. This could lead to the person creating some ideas about what makes a pendulum swing faster or slower. Ultimately, after considerable inquiry, the person might find that the length of the pendulum is the single most relevant variable. But this knowledge would not be the result of following the strict sequence of the scientific method. Perhaps a way to begin thinking about the scientific method is as one method of scientific inquiry and as just one pathway an individual can take in solving a problem. Once students have experienced such a method and become comfortable with the actions of science, then other questions can be pursued, with a classroom conversation establishing the logical sequence of actions and comparing those steps with those originally introduced. The point here is to emphasize to students that this list is one way of pursuing a question but certainly not the only one.

Science as a Social Enterprise

Given that so much of science involves making that creative leap from evidence to explanation, as well as creating appropriate ways to collect evidence, a significant part of the actions of science is convincing others in your field of the value of your ideas and methods. The exchange of ideas among scientists is included within the actions of science. As a direct reflection of this, a recent issue of the journal *Science* had an average of over four authors per research article. That means these individuals worked together in writing the report, in gathering data in the lab or field, and in formulating the research design in the initial discussions. Although the mass media often depicts science as a solo endeavor, in reality working in isolation is not an accurate or honest portrayal of the actions of science.

The entire process of sharing and debating scientific ideas and methods—core actions in the culture of science—must occur within a social setting. Conferences are held so scientists can share their ideas with other scientists who, in turn, question if those ideas make sense in terms of the data. One of the most valuable ways scientists check for the influence of bias on interpretations of data includes having numerous scientists conduct and analyze the same experiment or having different groups of scientists with different theoretical biases study the same problem. In part science needs to be social to ensure that scientists are making the best explanations of the physical world, and this is done through the comparison and debate about findings. Before a scientific article is published in a journal, it must be reviewed and critiqued by knowledgeable colleagues who determine if the work attains the standards of that scientific community. Even without face-to-face conversations, the ways in which scientific knowledge is generated, evaluated, and distributed is necessarily situated within a social sphere.

A common caricature of a scientist is someone working in almost complete isolation. The cartoonish view of a scientist is a person who is painfully awkward in social settings—suggesting that scientists are awkward because they are rarely around other people. With this common stereotype is it any wonder that many students fail to see any appeal in the prospects of becoming scientists? We need teachers to assist us with debunking the myth of the lone scientist and the scientific method if students are to develop robust understandings about how science is done. They need to see that science is a social enterprise and understand the role debate, discussion, and other forms of communication play in scientific culture. By emphasizing the social aspect of the doing of science, teachers can better emphasize the community aspect of the learning of science. Just as is true for scientific inquiry, important aspects of the learning of science come from talking, debating, and writing about the sense students are constructing in the classroom. Just as these activities are important in doing science, they are important in learning science.

The Tentative Nature of Scientific Knowledge

To this point we have portrayed science as a process of creating explanations from evidence gathered in the physical world. In addition we have illustrated how science is a creative process influenced by the backgrounds and biases of scientists. Third, we have described an image of science as a social activity for debating the validity of the evidence and the explanations constructed based on that evidence. Because the production of scientific explanations involves many creative processes, it should not be surprising to recognize that scientific knowledge can change. Students and adults often think that once science produces knowledge and once a scientist offers an explanation of some aspect of the physical world (like our snail-studying biologist mentioned at the outset of this chapter or Brahe's description of an earth-centered solar system) and this explanation is accepted by the entire scientific community, that knowledge will never be modified. Using this line of thought, science textbooks can be expected to grow only larger as knowledge is added. If scientific knowledge does not change, one would never expect science books to be revised or rewritten. However, the explanations scientists create about the physical world are always open to revision, and scientists recognize this as part of the culture.

Consider this idea: the west coast of Africa looks as if it might fit very nicely with the east coast of South America. Figure 8.2 is a geographer's attempt to show what it might look like if we could push the American continents against Africa and Europe. A drawing such as this was published in 1858, but geographers had noticed this possibility before 1600. From this angle you can see how South America seems to snuggle very nicely against Africa. But there was little evidence that continents could actually move around the globe: what would push them?

The conventional wisdom among scientists up until the early twentieth century was that volcanoes created new mountains and that erosion wore them away. There wasn't any evidence the continents might actually move, and the apparent matching of the continent's edges was regarded as a coincidence. Indeed in 1915 Alfred Wegener, a geologist, suggested that the earth's continents were once connected, and as a result his colleagues in the scientific community ridiculed him (Smith & Southard, 2001). Over the years more evidence has accumulated. As new instrumentation was invented, scientists were able to map the floor of the ocean. They expected it would be fairly smooth and covered in a deep layer of sediment. After all, the erosion of millions of years should amount to substantial accumulation. However, their predictions weren't correct.

First, the sediment layer wasn't nearly as deep as they had expected. There should have been much more there than was found. Second, the floor wasn't smooth at all: running along the middle of the Atlantic Ocean floor is a giant mountain range, and a massive trench was found along the bottom of the Pacific Ocean. It was almost as if new rock was being added to the continental plates in the Atlantic and then submerged and melted in the trench along the floor of the Pacific.

Other bits of evidence emerged. Volcanoes and earthquakes seemed to exist in only certain regions. The idea was that different continental plates rubbed against each other as they moved. The volcanic and earthquake events took place where these seams occurred. It was suggested that the events occurred as seams of the continental plates rubbed against each other. Furthermore, there were fossils that were found only in places that were separated by large distances. It is interesting that the fossils' locations matched the places where the Africa and South America puzzle pieces touched, as shown in Figure 8.3.

It wasn't until the 1960s that science textbooks finally began to describe "plate tectonics" as a legitimate scientific theory, finally vindicating the ideas Wegener had ventured decades earlier. Geologists have identified thirty plates that make up the solid crust and documented the melted mantle just below that crust. As this liquid mantle flows, it pushes the massive plates (both continents and ocean floors are part of these plates) and they move about, at a maximum speed of two inches per year. At times these plates collide with one another. The Himalayan Mountains are an example of plate collisions. Although moving very slowly, the India plate is "slamming" into the Eurasian plate, creating the tallest mountains on earth—at least among those mountains that aren't underwater.

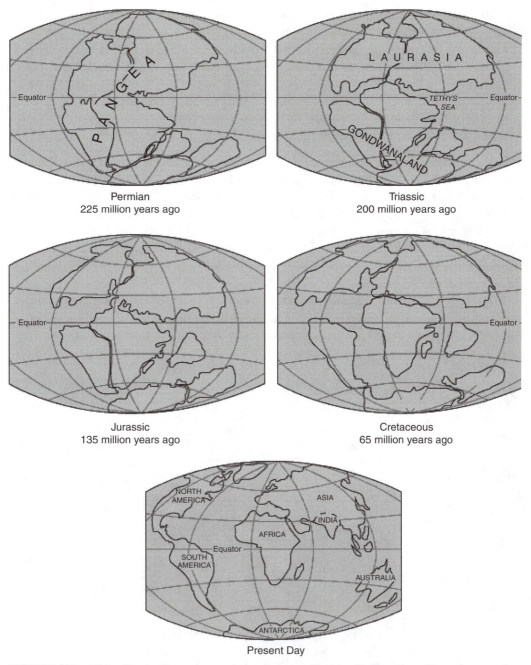

FIGURE 8.2. This illustration shows how the continents fit together like pieces of a puzzle. Source: U.S. Geological Survey.

Although Wegener's ideas help us make sense of a great many physical features of the earth (mountains, basins, patterns of volcanic activity), this doesn't mean that the story is completely solved. Indeed according to the United States Geological Survey, there are still some unresolved questions in terms of the earth's physical features. The following paragraph reinforces the dynamic and changeable aspect of science:

Plate tectonics has proven to be as important to the earth sciences as the discovery of the structure of the atom was to physics and chemistry and the theory of evolution was to the life sciences. Even though the theory of plate tectonics is now widely accepted by the scientific community, aspects of the theory are still being debated today. What is the nature of the forces propelling the plates? Scientists also debate how plate tectonics may have operated (if at all) earlier in the earth's history and whether similar processes operate, or have ever operated, on other planets in our solar system. (United States Geologic Survey, 1999)

It is important to note that when we say that scientific knowledge is **tentative,** we do not mean that the current scientific theories are especially flimsy or undependable—far from it. Indeed the currently accepted scientific explanations are based on a great deal of experimental and observational evidence. But the actions of science are structured so that if another idea comes along that is better at explaining all the available data, then that new idea could replace the current ideas that scientists rely on. This portrait of a robust, useful but tentative, scientific knowledge allows students to see the actions of science for what they are: dynamic, changing, and so interesting.

The tentative nature of scientific knowledge is readily apparent as news programs, newspapers, and the Internet provide fresh stories about scientific debates and changes in scientific knowledge. The tentativeness of science is in large part connected to the creative aspects of science. In science there is always another question to ask, another piece of information to collect,

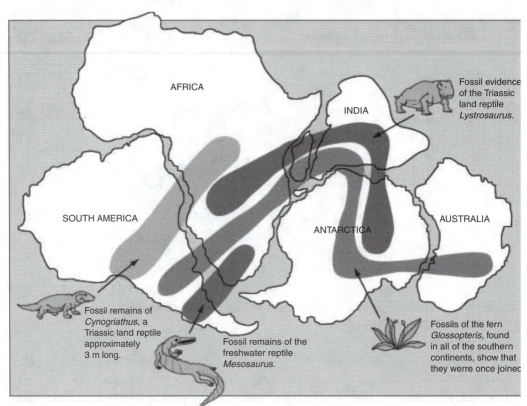

FIGURE 8.3. This map shows how fossil evidence supports the explanation of plate tectonics. Source: U.S. Geological Survey.

and another way to interpret the evidence. But the social nature of scientific inquiry is responsible for the mechanisms responsible for changes (the scientific actions of replication of investigations, review by colleagues, and scientific debate). If students are not aware that the scientific explanations are supposed to be tentative, then they may misinterpret these debates and become dismissive of science (i.e., "Why do I have to learn this if it is going to change?"). The alternative is that if they see science as unchanging, with the exception of the occasional discovery, science can seem boring, as if all of the real discoveries have already been made. Instead, by helping students see examples of how scientific explanations can and do change, they can appreciate the debates, arguments, and changes in explanations produced by scientists that are the defining features of the actions of science. Learning the culture of a dynamic and ever-changing enterprise is more attractive to many students than a culture centered on the memorization of past discoveries. Emphasizing the tentative nature of science not only allows students to interpret the science as it is played out in the media but also this component of the culture of science allows science to feel more interesting and engaging within the classroom.

Scientific Theories: The Power of Science

Sometimes you may hear the phrase "it's only a theory." People tend to use this phrase when dismissing an idea or when suggesting that an explanation is weak. Indeed that science can and does change seems to support this notion of scientific theories as flimsy guesses. Yes, science is tentative and scientific explanations do change. But, paradoxically, it is because of this tentative nature, the idea that as explanations are tested they are revised, that the actions of science produce such durable and dependable explanations. The tentative nature of science contributes to its durability and utility. So where do scientific theories fall into this?

In our everyday lives we have often said things such as "I have a theory about ..." or "The reason the washing machine broke is ..." (or why the cat is losing weight or why the car makes a bizarre noise). By this use of theory we mean we have a good guess about some phenomenon (the washing machine, the cat, or the car). This is very, very different from the way scientists use the term *theory*. Scientists tend to reserve the term **theory** for their best, most powerful, and most supported and accepted explanation for natural phenomena. In science, explanations achieve the status of theory only after many scientists have investigated them and found the ideas able to explain a wide range of evidence. In science to say "it is only a theory" is nonsensical. It is akin to saying "it's only a million dollars" or "it's only the best explanation anyone, anywhere has ever generated to explain this situation." A scientific theory is our best attempt to explain how something happens, based on empirical evidence, logical explanation, and much debate. Keep in mind that the goal of science is a set of explanations about the physical world, and these explanations are articulated as theories.

This understanding of theory becomes important in the event that someone wants to dismiss controversial scientific ideas by saying "that's only a theory." When that happens, we need to remind him or her that theories are the best, most powerful objects that science can produce. One of the fascinating aspects of the biological world is the immense variety in the types of objects that are considered living. To explain the cause for biological diversity, we can rely on the process of natural selection. Too often this explanation is attacked because evolution is a theory. The criticism of evolution often focuses on the theoretical nature of evolution, without understanding (or perhaps deliberately ignoring) the intended meaning of *theory*. There are other scientific theories, including the theories of photosynthesis, atomic structure, inheritance, and plate tectonics. Like evolution, these explanations are tentative; by definition, all scientific theories are explanations open to debate and possible modification. But also like evolution, these explanations are widely accepted in the scientific community and represent the best, most useful explanations scientists have been able to construct. Theories are not simple guesses or flimsy conjectures. Even though theories are viewed as open to change and tentative, they provide the very foundation for science. Even though scientific explanations may change, theories are not likely to change until there is considerable contrary evidence.

How do theories as specific products of science compare to other well-known products such as laws and hypotheses? A common myth regarding the nature of science is that theories, once proved, will turn into laws. In this myth, laws are regarded as unchanging, indisputable, and the most important piece of scientific knowledge. In reality scientists think of laws as specific, straightforward, and simple descriptions of patterns in nature, such as the law of universal gravitation. The role of laws is to describe common patterns in the physical world; they don't explain those patterns. For example the law of universal gravitation doesn't explain gravitation, it just describes the effects of gravitation between two objects. Although laws are durable and they enjoy a great deal of empirical support, their role is not explanation: laws are descriptive. Using this line of thought, it becomes obvious that theories, however well supported, cannot be promoted to become laws. Instead theories and laws have different uses within the culture of science, one explanatory and one descriptive. In contrast, hypotheses are very tentative, exploratory ideas scientists develop to focus and structure their inquiries. Hypotheses will be refined as scientists test them against data that support or refute them. Hypotheses are initial attempts to explain, but they are trial explanations whose fates are determined by the tests of more data.

Point–Counterpoint

The nature of science appears to be a valuable component of science education. Yet there is some uncertainty about whether nature of science ideas can and should be fully revealed to students. For example the tentativeness of scientific knowledge can be held as a way to push open the door to science to a wider variety of students. However, others wonder whether emphasizing the tentativeness may serve to confuse students and distract them from comprehending the widely accepted scientific theories. So in response to the question "How should the nature of science be taught in schools?" we are treated to two diverse stances.

Emphasizing the Tentative Nature of Science in the Classroom

Adam Johnston
Physics Educator at Weber State University

I often ask myself what it is that we really want our students to understand about science in the long run. Do I want them to know something about forces and motion? Something about how research is done? Maybe we should all find application of science in our everyday lives? Yes. All of these are valid, but none of them are sufficient. What we really need is to give children—our future citizens, voters, decision makers, and so on—a grander view of what science is and how it works, a sense of ownership in the scientific process, and, perhaps more than anything, a sense of wonder for the natural world.

Science is a way of knowing that the world is both powerful and limited, and I want my students to deeply understand how this is and what it means. I want students to see what science can and cannot do for them. Too often, the "answers" of science are overstated, and similarly too often the "answers" of science are dismissed out of hand. If our students are to understand anything about science and the knowledge that it produces, they need to understand the tentative nature of the knowledge it produces.

The fact that the knowledge of science is tentative is foundational to what science is. Science will never end, for there will always be another question to ask, another rock to turn, another explanation to propose. Because all of science's knowledge must be testable, it must always be tentative. Even the most known piece of science knowledge—for example the explanation that all stuff is constructed from atoms—is continually open for further investigation. If it weren't for this philosophy and attitude, science would stop. If we stopped asking questions and testing what we know, our knowledge would become dry, tasteless, and stale. But with an ongoing quest for explanation, we have a science that is always fresh, even if the universe stays the same.

At the same time, this ongoing quest and testing of our understandings makes science durable. For me, this is an exciting irony. The philosophy that our knowledge is always subject to testing and change allows us to feel that it really has been legitimately probed, and if we are wrong about something, we're eventually going to find a way to make corrections. We rely on Newton's laws not because they are in a textbook but because they have been put through the ringer. We are always using these ideas, seeing how they apply, and searching out their limitations. This makes science something that we can lean on to give us useful, reliable information.

Tentativeness also points to the different levels of scientific knowledge. We collect data, and certainly there is always more data to collect, but if this were all that science was about, we wouldn't think any more of science than we would of stamp collecting. Even more interesting and useful than our data is our set of creative explanations. To make science mean anything, we have to try to create an understanding for ourselves that we can communicate to others. These creations of explanation are always based on the data, but they are creations nonetheless. Clearly, we should always ask ourselves if we have these explanations right, and continually test them against our data. For students to see this interaction between the facts of the natural world and the explanations of these facts is invaluable, for it shows exactly how creative an endeavor the scientific process is.

I want students to embrace this creative science, because, besides representing science for what it truly is, the creative science is an open invitation to all students. One of my biggest frustrations with science education is that students come to view science as being unapproachable. If we let entities such as science books present science, it is a bunch of static facts and equations that simply sit there, waiting for the user to turn to page 735 to look up the atomic mass of nitrogen. However, if science is not so much a book of facts but a pursuit of new, dynamic explanation, then suddenly the entire landscape is changed. Only when students view science's knowledge as being tentative can they see that there is room for a new question, a new investigation, and a new answer. This is the science that I want my children to have in their classroom, and it is the science that I want citizens to embrace. If they see science as static, then they will misinterpret facts as dogma. If they miss the point that science is always being tested, then they can take any scientific claim and consider it ludicrous.

Finally, I like science for many reasons, but most of all because it makes me say things such as "ooh" and "wow." The tentative nature of science is something that fits hand in hand with the ideals of inquiry, trying out new experiments, asking new questions, and looking at things in new ways. This is exactly what I want my classroom to look like. If science is not tentative, then there really isn't anything to do. If my students come to class with the hopes that I will give them the next correct answer from out of the back of the solutions manual, then they aren't getting what science is really all about. I want my students to come to class every day with the possibility that they're going to ask the next question that needs to be asked. Emphasizing the tentative nature of science emphasizes this openness to the inquiry process and the learning goals that I envision for my students.

Possibilities of Degrees of Tentativeness of Science in the Classroom

Scott Sowell
Science Teacher Educator at Cleveland State University and Former Middle School Science Teacher

As has been mentioned, an extremely important part of a sophisticated nature of science (NOS) understanding is recognizing that scientific knowledge is tentative. Indeed we know that successful participation in science requires addressing the common misconception that science is about discovering or unearthing a preexisting set of certain and absolute truths. Learning science is much more than the rote memorization of vocabulary terms in the textbook chapters. However, for those of us teaching science in K-12 classrooms, there may be practical reasons to not emphasize that all scientific knowledge is equally tentative in all circumstances.

Elby and Hammer (2001) questioned the either/or way we think about students' tentative views about the nature of science: either naive or sophisticated (e.g., either students correctly describe scientific knowledge as created or tentative or they incorrectly describe it as discovered or fixed). Rather than relying on generalities about what students do or do not know, Elby and Hammer made an eloquent argument for paying attention to the contexts and nuances of both practicing scientists' and non-scientists' NOS understandings. In particular they make the distinction between the correctness and productivity of a NOS understanding. Although believing that science is about discovering objective truths may be incorrect (in terms of the science education community's best understandings about NOS), it may be productive for a student to work to understand a scientific explanation through a classroom activity. The "correct" beliefs about science expressed by practicing scientists and other academics may be different from the "productive" beliefs that assist in students' learning.

It is important to recognize that not all knowledge is equally tentative, and it is not productive for practicing scientists (or even students) to even think so. For example Elby and Hammer mentioned how the degree of tentativeness varies when considering two different scientific explanations: the round shape of the earth versus the theories of dinosaur extinction. Or consider how the degree of tentativeness differs between the knowledge presented in an introductory biology textbook and the knowledge being generated by biologists working in a tropical rain forest. When we consider that the work done at the leading edges of science is more tentative than many of the basic theories and principles that underlie such work, it becomes more sophisticated to attend to context and nuance, and this sophistication makes us consider degrees of tentativeness. For example when working with students on an understanding of how today's genetic research explores human biology, there may be a need for students to grasp that, although not written in stone, our models about the double-helix structure of DNA are less tentative than our explanations concerning the links between genes and certain disorders. Therefore rather than being limited to either–or ways of talking about students' NOS understandings (sophisticated = tentative and evolving versus naive = fixed and absolute), we might want to consider the value in using Elby and Hammer's terminology of sophisticated tentativeness versus naive tentativeness.

Although I want my students to have a strong appreciation about the tentative nature of science, I would be wary of instances in which individuals might hide within extreme relativity and view science as simply a set of continually evolving stories or creations. This may be especially true when considering more controversial theories in science, such as evolution, that may tempt some students to engage in discrediting the findings of science on the grounds of its tentativeness. Therefore discussions about tentativeness need to be couched within conversations about how the culture of science creates durability as its findings, explanations, and theories are strengthened through peer review and professional debate.

This conversation forces us to ask if there are instances in which younger students, or students in introductory science courses, benefit from viewing the science they encounter as fixed truths rather than as evolving human constructions? Does this perspective better assist them in situating the science content within their own lives released from teh burden of struggling to view it as a constantly recreated invention? Should we be asking our students to think about the degrees of scientific tentativeness rather than merely having them reject science as a set of discovered truths? Although these questions have yet to be resolved, the work of researchers such as Elby and Hammer push us to think beyond our current understandings of tentativeness in the science classroom. We need theoretical arguments such as this to recognize the possible limitations of our current practices and to search for better ways to teach science. In other words, it helps us to see our own teaching practices as tentative and evolving.

Science as a Way of Knowing

To this point we've described how science can be useful for understanding the physical world by virtue of the way scientific inquiry shapes the knowledge it produces. In an attempt to best encapsulate this conversation, we find it useful to use Moore's (1999) description of **science as a way of knowing.** By this he meant that scientific knowledge and scientific inquiry have particular characteristics that set it apart from other ways of knowing the world. Characteristics of science as a way of knowing include the empirical, creative, social, and tentative dimensions. The notion of science as a way of knowing acknowledges that the actions of science are based on a particular set of assumptions. Assumptions of the culture of science include that the best explanations are emperically gorunded, logical and straightforward and do not employ supernatural forces or agents. This brief description acknowledges that science is simply one way of knowing and distinguishes science from other ways of knowing the world, ways such as the arts (whose standards do not require logic or evidence) or traditional belief systems that have assumptions in direct conflict with those of science (such as the religious belief in supernatural agents). We wish to be quick to indicate that there is no implied hierarchy to these "ways of knowing." Rather each of us relies on a range of strategies for understanding our world. We live in complex worlds, and although science can help us to think through some things, there are other circumstances where science is of little use. We must rely on other ways of knowing that allow us to consider the interpersonal and the internal, the just and fair, the patriotic and the rebellious.

While the characteristics of scientific inquiry and the assumptions underlying those inquiries make science a powerful way of knowing the world, these assumptions of the action of science also limit what can be understood scientifically. As pointed out by Poole (1996), there are occasions when a scientific account may provide an inadequate, even inappropriate, approach to a topic:

> The scientific study of a work of art, say a picture, may give an exhaustive account of the chemical constitution of the pigments, the wavelengths of the light they reflect, their reflection factors, masses and physical distributions. But such a scientific account has hardly begun to say much of interest to the viewer or to the artist. Aesthetic considerations, issues of meaning and matters of purpose are of far greater importance. A sociological study of the influences on artists' work will have similar limitations. It is not that pictures cannot be described in terms of chemicals, or mental activities in terms of brain functions—they can. What is wrong to assert (for it cannot be demonstrated) that these scientific accounts are the only valid ones there are. (Poole, 1996, p. 165)

Given that scientists begin their work by making various assumptions, the teacher's role is to help students become aware of these assumptions to help in determining what kinds of questions can be pursued scientifically and what kinds of questions cannot be reasonably investigated using this way of knowing.

NSES Content Standard A: All students should be able to recognize and analyze alternative explanations and predictions.

As described by Mike Smith and Larry Scharmann (1999), who have closely examined issues of science and religion in the classroom, it is important for students to understand that science as a way of knowing is very helpful in understanding some aspects of their lives but is nearly useless for understanding others. As such although it may seem that science contradicts or refutes other ways of knowing, this idea is based on the narrow view that science claims to be the only way of knowing the world. Smith and Scharmann claimed it is valuable for students to recognize that science does not assert that there are no supernatural forces, and it does not refute the existence of God. Instead one feature of doing science is that one may not invoke supernatural or metaphysical explanations in constructing a scientific explanation. Scientific explanations must instead rely on logic, observable evidence, and testing. That is not the same as saying that unobservable, nonphysical forces do not exist but that in doing science we cannot resort to the power of nonempirical agents. If the metaphysical or supernatural must be used to construct an explanation, then that explanation violates the assumptions of science and so is considered nonscientific. This is a crucial distinction. The fact that an explanation is not scientific does not make it a weak or flawed explanation—it is simply a nonscientific explanation. That same explanation may be useful for a great number of people in understanding their lives, but that explanation is simply not consistent with science as a way of knowing.

To help students understand, Smith and Scharmann suggested it is useful to present a number of questions to discuss how to place these questions on a continuum between more and less scientific. This list can include the following things: Is it wrong to keep porpoises in captivity? How was the earth made? Do ghosts haunt old houses at night? Am I in love? Is there a god? Through discussing these and other questions, students may begin to recognize that science is particularly good at helping show what is clearly outside of the scope of scientific investigation. Once we begin this conversation in the classroom, we begin to understand that there are important aspects of our lives that are out of the boundaries of scientific investigation (religious beliefs, interpersonal relationships, morality, and so on), because they rely on the supernatural or metaphysical or because they are not empirical. But just because these things are out of the bounds of science does not prevent them from playing a huge part in our lives.

Why is this discussion of science as a way of knowing so important to have in a classroom? In the past century, American culture has become so enamored with the products of science (antibiotics, jet engines, computers) that it seems that our society has treated science as the best way of knowing. Because science and the technological by-products have proved so amazingly powerful in almost every aspect of our daily lives, the American culture has begun to view science as perhaps the only legitimate way of knowing. Many scientists and science teachers have become dismissive of ideas generated outside the culture of science. This is unfortunate because as they dismiss nonscientific ways of knowing, they also dismiss students who hold alternative perspectives. Within the classrooms of the past century, it was common for science to be presented as the only real way of understanding the world. Far too many students may have felt as if they had to reject science because it was so contradictory to their family traditions or cultural beliefs. When science is presented in this uncompromising way, it seems reasonable to expect that students from non-Western families or students with strong religious or spiritual convictions will be intimidated, discouraged, or disenfranchised. The consequence may well be that the students in diverse classrooms come to view science as a powerful and alienating way of knowing the world.

As teachers we must recognize that it is hard for students to concentrate in a classroom in which a large part of their lives doesn't belong or is devalued. Who among us would want to participate in a culture that is dismissive of much of who we are? Helping students to recognize science as one way of knowing the world becomes necessary when teaching science in diverse classrooms. Allowing students to understand the power, as well as the limitations, of science fosters powerful classroom conversations. By treating science as another culture, teachers and their students are more likely to recognize other important, but nonscientific, aspects of students' lives.

For Reflection and Discussion

Gather the following materials: several ceramic mugs, a metal spoon, sources of hot and cold water, and an almost endless supply of powdered hot chocolate mix. When making a mug of hot chocolate, we can observe an interesting and not-easily-explained phenomenon. After stirring the hot chocolate mix into the water, tap on the bottom of the cup and you will notice that the tone produced is a relatively low pitch, but gradually the tone rises in pitch as you keep tapping. Stirring the hot chocolate again will restore the lower tone, but as you continue to tap with the spoon, the tone will again rise. As you continue to mess about with these materials, consider these questions: are you doing science and, if so, what is there about your efforts that can be considered scientific?

Nature of Science and Diverse Classrooms

Our portrayal of science is as follows. It is a way of knowing the world. It is tentative. It is limited in its scope and use. It is increasingly performed by a variety of people. It is situated in a community populated by individuals with varied background and biases. It is accomplished through the use of a range of methods. It is the consequence of individuals working together to create theories that explain evidence collected from the physical world. We argue that working from and toward such a portrayal of the culture of science is necessary when teaching science in diverse settings. Why? This portrayal is dynamic and intriguing, emphasizing a culture based on a recognition of the need for change and placing a premium on scientists with diverse knowledge and backgrounds. Science becomes more inviting than our traditional characterization of science as a solo activity in which ideas are gathered and recorded and for which the bulk of the real creative work and important discoveries have already been accomplished.

The central idea to the nature of science is that science is a way of knowing, a way that differs from others, a way that is powerful, but also a way that is limited in the kind of knowledge it produces because of the nature of inquiry it employs. By emphasizing science as a way of knowing, students can begin to understand that just because another way of knowing is nonscientific does not mean it is flawed but simply that line of thought differs from science. Such realizations permit students to understand that schools, schooling, and schoolteachers do value things other than science and so value a large portion of these students' lives. Such knowledge is essential for demystifying the culture of science, making it far less threatening and far more inviting for students.

Who Does Science? Who Can Do Science?

When students are asked to draw pictures of scientists, they often portray scientists as men in white lab coats working in a chemistry laboratory. Clearly, if students see science as an activity in which only White men participate, many students will direct their interests elsewhere. Thus both science (which could benefit from the contributions of scientists with varied backgrounds and biases) and the learners (who will need scientific knowledge to negotiate their lives) lose out. Over the years, this stereotype seems less evident in children's drawings, indicating that this notion about science is gradually fading away. Even in television and movies, scientists are becoming a bit more diverse. We see more women and people of color in the roles of scientists—a change we applaud and hope intensifies. Teachers can support this change by pointing out the limitations in the portrayal of scientists in popular culture (teaching their students to ask questions such as "Why is the lead scientist always a White man?") and bringing in many alternatives for students by emphasizing the contributions of non-Westerners, people of color, and women to the scientific enterprise.

But beyond the more obvious barriers that we can observe on television are more subtle but persuasive barriers to students' access to science that may be created or supported by parents and teachers. Parents often may dismiss their child's efforts in science, saying, "I was never good at it, so I can't expect her to be," or "She'll probably never really need this stuff." Women teachers might shy away from teaching science or show uneasiness or squeamishness through playful squeals or yelps when the more "icky" aspects of the natural world (i.e., worms, snakes, mold) come up as they so often do when students engage in science. These seemingly harmless comments and humorous gestures are soaked up and internalized by children, just as they mimic behavior of characters in their favorite films. Subconsciously some students begin to think that they cannot do and cannot learn science.

If you want to help students become comfortable working with the culture of science, a common component of your classroom culture must be to have high expectations of the science learning of all students regardless of gender, ability, or background, and these expectations and your reasons behind them must be conveyed constantly to the children and to their parents. And you must remember that as their teacher, you have become one of their role models. So for them to become comfortable working in the culture of science, you must show that you are comfortable in the culture of science.

NSES Teaching Standard B: Teachers encourage and model the skills of scientific inquiry and the curiosity, openness to new ideas, and skepticism that characterize science.

There is a wealth of research on the teaching and learning of the nature of science that demonstrates that the more traditional approaches to teaching about the culture of science—having students read about it, having students do science—are insufficient if we desire for students to grasp the nature of science (Abd-El-Khalick, Bell, & Lederman, 1998). The educational research has revealed that instruction that explicitly addresses nature of science concepts and encourages learners to be aware of their nature of science ideas and reflect on their ideas and how they change is essential for students to learn about the nature of science (Akerson, Abd-El-Khalick, & Lederman, 2000). For students to come to understand the culture of science, they not only have to be actively involved in it but also need to explicitly think and talk about the nature of science and focus on how their own ideas about the nature of science have changed during instruction. Crafting such an explicit, reflective, activity-based approach to the nature of science is a difficult thing for teachers, but it is essential if students are to become familiar and comfortable operating in and understanding science.

Chapter Summary

- To increase the likelihood that all students will engage in the culture of science, they and their teachers must have a better appreciation of the nature of science. The stereotypes of scientists are more than inaccuracies and may actually discourage students from wanting to be successful in science.
- Because of its demand for evidence to support any and all knowledge claims, the culture of science is distinct from many other worldviews. Unless ideas are supported by data, they are unlikely to be given any consideration within the scientific culture.
- Using creativity is acceptable and desirable within the culture of science. Suggesting explanations based on the available data is necessary for scientific knowledge to advance. The valuing of creativity is a feature the culture of science shares with many cultures.
- Objectivity is a goal of science, even though it is generally understood that biases and preconceived ideas can influence what scientists perceive and propose. Reducing the influence of bias is something scientists strive to achieve within their work.
- A common myth is that scientists follow particular steps toward a scientific discovery. The reality is that science is not nearly as linear and sequential as the scientific method suggests.
- The work of individual scientists must ultimately be presented to a larger scientific community for evaluation and possible acceptance. The social feature of the culture of science is often in contrast to the stereotype of scientists working in isolation.
- The tentativeness of scientific explanations accepts the possibility of theories and laws being modified as new data are gathered and different interpretations of the evidence are proposed. Despite the tentativeness, scientific theories are based on reliable data and are very useful within the work of science.

- In making "science for all" a reality within diverse classrooms, teachers must educate students about the nature of science so they can recognize how to function within the culture of science and realize they can be successful within this culture.

Key Terms

Empirical: information based on data and evidence not on opinions or beliefs.

Nature of science: specific characteristics of the knowledge produced through science, characteristics that are influenced by the practices and beliefs specific to the culture of science.

Science as a way of knowing: perspective about the world that relies on empiricism and, though distinct from other worldviews, should not be regarded as superior to other ways of knowing or as providing the sole pathway to the truth.

Scientific method: while often presented as a fixed sequence of steps followed by scientists, is a myth that is based on an incorrect interpretation of the nature of science. When "the scientific method" or "methods of science" are viewed as a combination of thought processes that do not necessarily occur in certain sequence, this is a more accurate representation of the ways science proceeds.

Subjectivity: interpreting the world through the filters of one's own perspectives.

Tentative: an idea or explanation that is considered accurate for right now, but has the potential for being modified as more information becomes available.

Theory: an explanation that is based on well-documented evidence and is accepted by the scientific community as the most scientific way to make sense of a phenomenon. A theory is not merely a guess but the best-substantiated explanation agreed on by a group of scientists.

A Favorite Science Lesson

Many of the most effective nature of science lessons are activity based and allow for studens to recognize their own, beginning conceptions about the nature of science. Through discussion of the activities accompanied by a reflection on how their reconceptions fail to adeqately explain what happens in the activity, students are more prone to change their conceptions. This activity addresses the conceptions that science is tentative, partly because science is a human activity. In the activity, students manipulate sealed "mystery" boxes (which contain a moving ball and fixed barrier or two). The key to any nature of science activity is for studens to be asked to be explicit at the outset about how they think science works, and following the acitivity, the teacher leads the students to reflect on the utility of their ideas. Afterwards the more current description of the nature of science can be effectively introduced. (See http://www.indiana.edu/~ensiweb/lessons/mys.box.html)

Suggested Readings

McComas, W. (1996). Ten myths of science: Reexamining what we think we know..., *School Science & Mathematics*, 96, 10–16.

   In this article, the author identifies and explores the most prominent misconceptions regarding the nature of science held by students presented in a very accessible form. Knowledge of these misconceptions may be very helpful in crafting appropriate nature of science lessons for students.

Reeves, C., & Chessin, D. (2003). Did you really prove it? *Science Scope, 27*(1), 23–26.

> The authors situate the challenges of teaching students about nature of science within the context of student science fair projects and lab activity reports. Within the article they describe characteristics of the nature of science in a clear, straightforward fashion.

Smith, M. J., & Southard, J. B. (2001). Exploring the evolution of plate tectonics. *Science Scope, 25*(1), 46–49.

> In this article the authors summarize in very clear ways the changing explanations about the movement of continents. The article also is a nice illustration of the historical shifts in scientific explanations. In addition this article is an example of the "science content" articles sometimes appearing in National Science Teachers Association publications.

References

Abd-El-Khalick, F., Bell, R. L., & Lederman, N. G. (1998). The nature of science and instructional practice: Making the unnatural natural. *Science Education, 82,* 417–436.

Akerson, V. L., Abd-El-Khalick, F., & Lederman, N. G. (2000). The influence of a reflective activity-based approach on elementary teachers' conceptions of the nature of science. *Journal of Research in Science Teaching, 37,* 295-317.

Anderson, C. W. (2006). *Teaching science for motivation and understanding.* Unpublished manuscript available online at http://www.msu.edu/~andya/

Dewey, J. (1991). *How we think.* Amherst, NY: Prometheus Books. (Original work published 1910)

Elby, A., & Hammer, D. (2001). On the substance of a sophisticated epistemology. *Science Education, 85,* 554–567.

McComas, W. F. (1998). The principal elements of the nature of science. In W. F. McComas (Ed.), *The nature of science in science education* (pp. 53–70). Dordecht, the Netherlands: Kluwer.

Moore, J. (1999). *Science as a way of knowing.* Boston, MA: Harvard University Press.

Poole, M. (1996). For more and better religious education. *Science and Education, 5*(2), 165–174.

Smith, M., & Scharmann, L. (1999). Describing versus defining the nature of science: A pragmatic analysis for classroom teachers and science educators. *Science Education, 83,* 493–509.

Smith, M. J., & Southard, J. B. (2001). Exploring the evolution of plate tectonics. *Science Scope, 25*(1), 46–49.

United States Geologic Survey. (1999). Historical Perspective. Retrieved from http://pubs.usgs.gov/publications/text/historical.html

nine

From Lessons to Units
Science Curriculum

Chapter Highlights

- Any time teachers are supporting students' science learning, they are using science curricula. It is important to recognize that curriculum includes more than just a science textbook. Curriculum includes everything from the instructional strategies used by teachers to the methods used to assess student learning.

- Teachers should make use of their creativity even while implementing a formal science curriculum. The official curriculum adopted by a school system allows many opportunities for teachers to use their creativity. Adjusting the formal curriculum so it accommodates the needs of students within specific classrooms requires considerable care, creativity, knowledge of students, and the local context.

- The learning cycle provides a mechanism for building a curriculum that emphasizes the development of students' science concepts. As students move from one learning cycle to the next, the concepts build on one another to create a spiral curriculum.

- Most activity guides are not the same as a full curriculum because they commonly neglect the features of inquiry. However, many kit-based materials, especially those that have been field-tested in classrooms and revised based on this information, are potentially very useful curriculum for addressing a broad range of student learners. Teachers need to closely examine kits and guides, looking past the packaging and accessory materials, to determine how useful they may be.

- Three kit-based curriculum programs are available in modules and are appropriate components of elementary and middle school science programs. All three programs have their particular strengths, and their different features should be familiar to everyone who teaches in elementary school and middle school.

■ Kit-based curricula make use of the very approaches that have been repeatedly shown to be effective for use with special needs students and culturally diverse students. The defining features of these programs closely align with the findings of science learning by a wide variety of students.

Within this chapter we step back from the specifics of teaching and use a broader perspective to think about science units and science curriculum. If you've had the opportunity to teach science, you recognize the incredible number of decisions arising during a lesson. Being able to attend to the details while remaining mindful of the big picture is challenging yet necessary for you to become an effective teacher of science. Included within the big picture is the ability to recognize how each science activity is a component of a larger science unit. Science lessons combine to form science units, and science units are gathered to create an entire curriculum. This chapter will provide you with conceptual tools for thinking about the issues and ideas related to science curriculum.

The Source of Science Curriculum

Curriculum refers to the subject matter that is taught in schools and that the children are expected to learn. Just as with science, curriculum is constantly changing and being refined. It is unreasonable to expect that we will ever reach the point where science curriculum is done, because improvements and modifications will always be possible. These changes are more substantive than simply updating the photographs, and more is involved than revising the scientific information. Education researchers are gradually expanding what we know about helping children to learn, and those improved understandings are often translated into curriculum design.

Developing curriculum is a fascinating process and involves everything from tinkering with existing materials to attempting to create spectacular new materials that exploit the latest educational technology. People who develop curriculum represent a range of professions, including anyone from the teacher who creates a unit for use in the classroom to large publishing houses that develop complex, multimedia units. Curricula are changed in response to issues large and small. Over the years, as fresh science discoveries are made, that information in curriculum must be updated. But curriculum can also be changed in response to pressures from outside the school.

Anytime there is a shift in the content emphasis or revisions in the ways in which the material is to be taught, those changes require adjustments to the curriculum. The continual revising of curriculum is more than simply an effort by companies to generate revenue. As with all things related to American education, science teaching is subject to shifts in social, political, and other external forces. This is a feature about education that many citizens may not realize: schools (and curriculum) are under constant change because society is always changing, and this is not a new phenomenon but a long-standing historical tendency (Zimmerman, 1999). If we choose to view the perpetual changes in education as evidence that nobody can get it right, we will be continually frustrated. If instead we accept the revision process as an immutable feature of education, then we are better able to respond to these inevitabilities, whether to curriculum or any other part of schooling. Later in this chapter, we will propose how a teacher might appropriately respond to changes so the students are not placed in jeopardy.

Unlike most nations that employ a unified science curriculum for all schools, the United States has a curriculum that varies so greatly that it has been pejoratively referred to as "splintered" (Schmidt et al., 1997). With the lack of a single science curriculum in the United States, comparisons to other nations' curricula can be very revealing. For example fourth-grade science

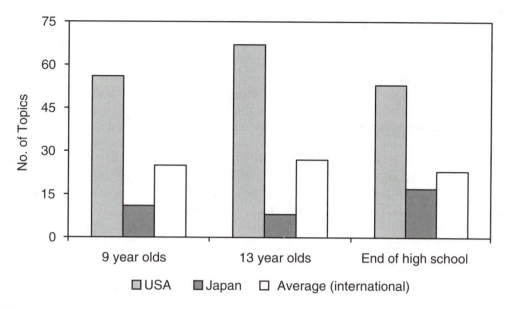

FIGURE 9.1. This figure show the number of topics covered in science textbooks (National Research Council, 1999).

textbooks in the United States average nearly 400 pages in length whereas the international average is only 125 pages (Schmidt & Valverde, 1998). Also, as Figure 9.1 shows, the amount of material that U.S. schools address in science is much greater relative to what other countries address.

There are many interesting implications of these data. First, the data suggest that science achievement is not directly related to the scope of a curriculum. Covering a wider array of science topics does not translate into better student learning. Second, this information has, to a certain extent, prompted shifts in the science standards at the state level. The suggestion that more is not better has provided evidence that the science content to be covered within each grade level should be reduced. Finally, this information suggests that curriculum should not only be less expansive and broad but provide ample time for students to study topics rather than quickly move from one to the next. Useful science curriculum is not designed with the purpose of content coverage.

How is science curriculum developed? This is not a singular process, but it occurs in the midst of many demands. For a curriculum to be useful, it must attend to state policies and national standards. It ought to be based on what is known about effective teaching practices. The curriculum should also attend to the equipment necessary to make the teaching effective. These are some of the pieces that go into a science curriculum. Ideally the sequence of curriculum development should not be purely linear. The wisest of curriculum developers plan for the field-testing of their materials and then make revisions based on those evaluations. But within the reference text *Designing Mathematics or Science Curriculum Programs,* the National Research Council (1999) acknowledged that the manner in which science curriculum should be developed is not the way it usually happens. As a result, everyone involved with science education needs to assume the role of a careful consumer and approach adoption and purchasing decisions with a level of care and attention to detail that exceeds what most people invest when they are shopping for a car.

Curriculum and Textbooks

For quite a long time, elementary and middle school science curriculum and textbooks were one and the same. Until recently teachers and administrators didn't talk much about curriculum, because it was simpler to talk about where the students were in their science books. The problem with teaching science from a book is that it is too often the only way that science is taught. Even the best publisher would have a hard time building all the features we've considered within the preceding chapters into the pages of a hardbound book. Process skills and the nature of science are nearly impossible to understand if a student only reads about them. Learning science exclusively through written text is developmentally inappropriate and educationally unacceptable. Even though we recognize that there is something ironic about using a science methods textbook to advocate for learning by experience, we feel we've been consistent with our messages. You can't learn to teach science by only reading about how to do it. If your teaching preparation program is well designed and if science methods instructors had their druthers, you would be experiencing science teaching and learning firsthand, not by reading a chapter first and answering the questions at the back.

For Reflection and Discussion

What do the schools in your area use as their science curriculum, and how closely are the teachers expected to follow this curriculum? If you were a teacher in this school system, how much opportunity would exist for you to be creative as you planned for and delivered science lessons?

It is important to think about curriculum as being more than following the chapters in a text. For one thing, textbooks are written for a national audience, which means they cannot be customized for every state's or district's science standards. Also, unlike in other countries, the United States does not have a national curriculum. There is a legend about the scheduling of lessons in other countries where every child in the same grade is on the exact same page at any given moment. The American tradition of local control makes such a scenario highly unlikely—and that's something many of us appreciate. Except in rare instances, future teachers don't want to teach directly from a manual. They want to allow their own interests, excitement, and experiences to influence their science lessons. Following a set of published instructions is what we associate with manufacturing, not something as human, complex, and exciting as working with children and all their diversity. Teaching is appealing because it allows us to be creative, and this is as true for science as for any other subject area.

Relying on Your Creativity

One feature of good teaching is the ability to be creative. Many of us were attracted to teaching because we were looking for an outlet for our creativity. Being creative by making something new and unique is rewarding—but being creative requires time, something no teacher feels he or she can ever have enough of. Although creativity can sometimes happen in a flash, more often creative projects require advanced preparation. You can't rely on sudden inspiration, no matter how creative you are, as your daily method of designing lessons. If your students are going to learn, then you must invest preparation time before the lesson begins. You're going to need to find a balance between two extremes. At one extreme you could act like a technician and simply follow a script written by someone else. At the opposite extreme you could create every lesson, assessment, and assignment on your own. Obviously there are problems with either extreme, but we also acknowledge that creativity in response to your particular teaching context should be part of who you are as a teacher.

Using existing materials and modifying them for a specific situation is an example of creativity. It is unreasonable to expect for a science activity right off the shelf to work perfectly, even if you follow the directions exactly as published. You might need to adjust the focus to address your state's science standards, or your students may already have enough background that you can make the activity more open ended. You might decide to modify the lesson because the equipment you have available is slightly different or extend the time devoted to the activity to give the students more space to work and think. You might even elect to integrate the activity with other subjects. These are all examples of creativity. Of course this assumes the original activity you are adapting is useful and worthwhile. But we'll get to that in a little bit.

The point is that creative teachers do not begin with nothing. First of all, an elementary school teacher is responsible for teaching not only science but also math, social studies, reading, and so on. It is impossible to invent creative lessons for every subject for every day. Second, it is not only efficient but also wise to rely on others' expertise. Isaac Newton wrote, "If I have seen further it is by standing upon the shoulders of giants." His point was that he made his discoveries because he relied on the previous work of such scientists as Kepler and Galileo. No one is going to question the creativity and genius of Newton. Finally, when you're a novice in a profession, it's very difficult to be as creative as someone with much more experience. Although we might agree that a child can create a watercolor painting, it would lack the sophistication of an experienced painter's work. Choosing to build on the expertise of others who have spent years teaching science makes good sense. You still will rely on your intuition, inspiration, and creativity to translate this material for your own classroom use, but relying on others' expertise is just good sense.

Spiral Curriculum

Learning a certain concept such as "molecules" requires more than just a single exposure to the idea. If a student is going to remember a science concept, he or she should experience it multiple times and in various contexts. That is one of the strengths of the learning cycle: the students have direct experience with the concept, then they talk about it, and then they have even more direct experience. Reading, watching videos, and listening to others' thoughts contribute to a more solid understanding of the concept. This suggests more than repetition. Each event allows the student to examine the concept from a different perspective. Ultimately this will lead to a substantive, useful understanding of the complexities and nuances of the concept.

If we visualize a learning cycle lesson as a physical object, we can imagine it as a disk. One trip through the learning cycle is equivalent to one complete trip around the disk. This might involve specifically connecting the end of the last phase of the learning cycle to its beginning. The teacher would finish the learning cycle by having the students look back on the ideas that they came up with during the engage phase. Taking this analogy a little further, we suggest that the subsequent learning cycle is represented by a second disk resting on top of the first. A science unit might consist of eight, twelve, or even twenty learning cycles that would be represented as a stack of disks. Moving up through the stack symbolizes a progressively greater understanding of the material.

Imagine a stack of dinner plates representing a connected series of learning cycles. Now shrink yourself so you are small enough to walk along the surface of the plates, just as if you were moving through the phases of the learning cycle. After you make one trip around the bottom plate, you crawl up to the plate above and move in a circle around it. Each time you return to the starting point for one plate, you ascend to the next one. From a distance your journey would trace a spiral. This approach, where one cycle of instruction is built on another, is referred to as a **spiral curriculum.** A unit about a major science topic such as the water cycle, electricity, or sound would be a spiral curriculum if the lessons consist of a connected series of learning cycles where the students' experiences and understandings accumulated, one building on top of the other.

A spiral curriculum can also describe a science program that is spread across several grade levels. For example fossils should be a part of all students' science learning. But so is plant growth. Does that suggest that they learn this material each year? No, because that would mean teaching all the key science concepts in every grade level. Imagine what science textbooks would look like if our goal were to teach the same topics each year. In fact some educators who have compared science textbooks in the United States to those from other countries have accused us of having a science curriculum that is "a mile wide and an inch deep." Fortunately the science education standards at the state and national levels are pushing science curricula in the right direction by identifying when the science ideas are to be taught.

Standards and Curriculum

The science units you will be teaching fit into a larger picture, namely, an entire school district's curriculum. The majority of districts base their local curriculum standards on those published at the national level. Because every district is a little bit different, we are going to use national standards in our examples. Even though your local standards will not be identical, the underlying philosophy will be the same. So let's think about fossils and how to teach about them to elementary school students.

Students can learn a little bit about fossils over several years. This becomes an example of a spiral curriculum that is spread across grades. Suppose there's an earth science unit in every elementary grade as one of maybe five or six science units in each year. When it comes to fossils, here are the understandings we can reasonably expect children to attain:

Grade 1: Some living things that were once on earth no longer exist. There are others that are like them that are still around.

Grade 3: Fossils are evidence of the types of living things that were around and of the environment that existed at that time.

Grade 5: Living things can become extinct when they are unable to survive changes in their environment. Extinction is very common; most of the species that have been on earth have gone extinct.

In this scenario, students wouldn't learn about fossils every year but when they did study fossils, they would be building on the knowledge acquired in previous years. In this way, science learning is an example of a spiral curriculum: students revisit fossils every couple of years, all the while building increasingly stronger understandings. Perhaps you can begin to see how a science unit is a combination of learning cycle lessons and one component of a larger curriculum. The learning cycle lessons combine in a spiral to form a science unit. In turn the science units combine across grade levels to form a spiral throughout a student's science learning career. The result is the opposite of the "inch deep" learning that we are avoiding. In its place each child develops a very deep understanding of the most important scientific concepts.

Moving Beyond Textbook Science

Even though textbooks continue to dominate the science curriculum, they aren't the only option available to those of us involved with science teaching. Many school districts make use of kit-based programs that provide teachers with enough structure to teach science in a manner consistent with the approaches we've been describing. Instead of relying on a teacher edition of the student book (the difference is that one has the answers printed in the margins), a **kit-based program** emphasizes involvement of the students in inquiry. This can be accomplished because the kit includes the equipment needed to do the hands-on activities. But before going into detail about these curricula, let's make a distinction between activity guides and curriculum.

NSES Program Standard A: Curriculum frameworks should be used to guide the selection and development of units and courses of study.

In chapter 4 we examined three different approaches to science teaching. The discovery approach is an unstructured way of teaching that is based on the belief of "learning by doing." Despite its appeal, open-ended methods are not all that successful—yet people are often drawn to the idea that doing activities is all that is required for good science teaching. You should know that kit-based programs are not simply activity guides. **Activity guides** are not curriculum even though they are sometimes interpreted to serve those purposes. These guides should not be regarded as curricula because they emphasize activities while the concepts and skills the students are to learn are often pushed into the background. The term *activity-mania* reflects the naive overexcitement of having children doing science (Moscovici & Nelson, 1998). Although firsthand experiences are crucial for students' science learning, in and of themselves they are not sufficient. Students must talk, think, argue, and write about what they've been doing, as is described by social constructivism (as we discussed in an earlier chapter and will revisit in chapter 10). All of these activities are necessary for students to construct a meaningful understanding of science. As we have been emphasizing throughout this book, the culture of science involves the objects and actions of science that lead to students' becoming active participants in not only the information but also the ways of thinking that are distinctive to science.

We should be careful about criticizing science activity guides. The materials are relatively inexpensive, and the activities are admittedly quite engaging for students. For this reason many teachers will swear by their science activity guides, often defending them by claiming, "The activities are really fun and the kids love them!" We don't dispute the fun kids have while messing about with bubbles, doing crime scene investigations, or testing paper towels. For that reason we agree that activity guides are interesting supplements that might be perfect for a Celebrate Science day or some other event where developing an appreciation for science is the goal. However, there are two major problems with many activity guides that make them much less powerful than kit-based science programs.

First, the essential features of inquiry are not evident in activity-based materials. In part this is understandable, because inquiry such as described by the essential features wasn't the goal for the developers of such resources. The original intent was that the activity guides would serve as supplements. Is it possible for a thoughtful teacher to infuse the missing inquiry features into these fun activities? Probably. But that creates more work. In fact it adds so much more work that a teacher may neglect these features in the midst of all the other challenges associated with managing an equipment-intensive activity. Consequently one problem with activity guide science is that even with the enjoyable activities, a teacher still must invest a great deal of extra planning to ensure that the students are participating in inquiry and learning science.

The other shortcoming of activity guides is that often the goal is mainly for the students to have fun. Now before you become irritated with us because we seem opposed to making learning fun, give us a moment to defend ourselves. We are not against the idea of children enjoying school. Our worry is that when fun becomes the primary goal, it can distract us from the true purpose of school: helping children learn. Do learning and fun go hand in hand? Oftentimes, but learning is a somewhat higher goal than fun. If our target is fun, then we may not be aiming high enough. Our stance is that if learning is relevant to the children's lives, if it taps into their natural curiosity, and if the effort they exert has a pay-off in terms of greater understandings, then it will also translate into fun. When students obtain satisfaction and have a sense of accomplishment as a consequence of their hard work, then often this represents fun. In other words if teachers set as their goal having their students actively participating in genuine scientific inquiry and the children believe that the learning is of value to them, then fun is an automatic by-product. We are unconvinced that the opposite would happen: when participating in enjoyable activities, there is no assurance that real learning will be the result. By aiming toward the more ambitious goals of engagement, relevance, and the construction of conceptual understandings, then fun (admittedly less ambitious and easier to achieve goal) will also be attained. Fun is an inappropriate goal for science curricula; instead intrigue, personal significance, and conceptual understandings are far more appropriate.

For Reflection and Discussion

How is the goal of making learning fun an example of extrinsic motivation? What problems might develop in terms of students' perspectives about science if there is a constant emphasis on fun?

The reality is that activity guides were not intended to be the science curriculum. When they were first developed, they were meant to be supplements to textbooks. In this regard there is much to admire about the activity guides. They focus on a single topic and provide students with interesting hands-on experiences. But there are so many holes in activity guides that schools and teachers would need to do a considerable amount of extra work to convert them into actual science curriculum. Fortunately, there are curricular materials that fall in between the activity guides and textbooks. On one hand the activity guides are very experiential, but they don't supply the tools for assessing learning or accommodating individual differences. On the other hand textbooks are unable to be as kinesthetically engaging but provide material in a logical sequence. If we had a resource that could act as our science curriculum and take the best features of these two, then we would have the kit-based programs, which we will spend much of the rest of this chapter examining.

Contents of Kit-Based Curriculum

In this section we will describe three kit-based science programs. All are commercially available, and the federal government funded their development. There are differences among these programs but they share common characteristics. One commonality is that they do not rely on student texts as information sources. Instead each program has a very detailed teacher guide and a substantial supply of science equipment. A traditional textbook curriculum consists of a classroom set of textbooks, a teacher guide, and a binder of ancillary materials (e.g., overhead transparencies, posters, assessment ideas). In contrast a kit-based program consists of a large teacher manual and containers of science equipment in sufficient quantity to allow the entire class to regularly do hands-on activities.

Another common feature of kit-based programs is that they are packaged as **curriculum modules.** Each module emphasizes a particular science topic such as plant growth or rocks and minerals. As a result school districts have the ability to assemble their science curriculum by combining several modules. This is an improvement over textbook programs because every state has somewhat different science requirements. Because textbooks are written for a national audience, publishers cannot customize the material to each district's specific needs. However, the modules permit districts flexibility, so teachers are freed from the obligation of covering everything in the textbook in the sequence in which the information is presented. Instead a district can create a spiral curriculum by plugging a module for liquids (a good introduction to basic chemistry) into second-grade classes and having fourth-grade classes use the module on changes of state (solids, liquids, and gases). Modules provide the customization not easily accomplished with traditional science textbooks.

The developers of kit-based curriculum created modules that require six to twelve weeks of instruction. Instead of skimming over the surface of the material, students have the opportunity to delve into the important science ideas. One erroneous complaint against kit-based programs is that the time required to finish them prevents teachers from covering all the material required by their state science standards. Because the *National Science Education Standards* (National Research Council, 1996) has advocated for more depth of study and less breadth, and because state standards are based on the national standards, the number of science topics addressed within each grade level is much smaller than it was several years ago. Most states have standards that require somewhere in the range of three to seven major science ideas within a given grade level. Consequently the modules of kit-based programs match quite nicely with state science standards.

The Need for Teacher Creativity

Earlier in this chapter we presented the idea of teacher creativity. One point we were trying to make was that you could be a creative teacher even when you start with materials developed elsewhere. We are returning to that idea now, because using kit-based science programs does not eliminate the need for teacher creativity. This was a mistake made by curriculum developers in the 1960s and 1970s. Back then professional scientists and education psychologists thought it was possible to create **teacher-proof curriculum,** which meant that the materials would be so brilliantly designed that all that was required was for the teacher to follow the directions. The science education community has learned from that mistake. The way in which someone teaches science is so tightly bound to the material being taught that the two cannot be separated. To have a curriculum that will be taught in the same way no matter who is in charge of the classroom is unrealistic.

As you learn more about the various kit-based programs available to elementary and middle school teachers, you should understand that none of them are perfect. Each has its strengths, yet none would serve as an all-purpose solution to all the science teaching challenges. This is where the teacher becomes so important. If you do have the opportunity to use a kit-based program, you should recognize that you will need to make some slight adjustments based on your local circumstances. For example some materials contain student handouts written in English and in Spanish. As helpful as this could be in some settings, it may not be enough in other places. First of all, even though the Spanish-speaking population in American schools is large, Spanish is not the only language that falls within "English as a second language"—you won't find handouts written in Arabic, Serbo-Croatian, or Hmong. Also it is not always correct to assume that a child who speaks Spanish is also able to read that language. Furthermore, some politicians are trying to prevent anyone from teaching children in a language other than English. The point we're trying to make is that even the best curriculum will benefit from the caring and creative efforts of a classroom teacher.

Development Process for Kit-Based Programs

The three kit-based programs we will present in this chapter were developed with funds provided through the National Science Foundation (NSF). The development of these programs was financed with tax dollars, but the final products materials are commercially distributed. This is one way in which curriculum development efforts of the 1960s and 1970s differ from current ones. Back then NSF did not require developers to negotiate marketing and distribution plans with publishers. It should not be surprising that few of those curriculum projects survive until today—there was no push to ensure that what was being created could actually be sold to schools.

A requirement for each kit-based program was that they be **field-tested** in schools. Although this might at first seem like common sense, in actuality it is very rare in curriculum development. A field test takes a lot of time because it adds a great deal of extra work to the process. First, the curriculum developer has to write what he or she believes is the absolutely best curriculum possible: the activities need to be interesting, the equipment should be easy to obtain, the directions need to be clear, and the format should be obvious to the teacher. After spending a great deal of time doing this, the developer turns his or her work over to a field-test team who recruits teachers willing to try the materials in their classrooms. After the field test, the curriculum developer is expected to change the original materials to make them better for the next field test. This can be agonizing, because the developer must accept the fact that some of his or her best ideas just didn't make it when put into the hands of real children: the handouts may have been confusing, the materials may not have generated much excitement, the teacher guide may have contained poor question-asking strategies, and so on. After the revisions, the materials are field-tested again.

For Reflection and Discussion

The phrase "steak versus sizzle" describes the challenge of distinguishing between real features and perceptual features. What are some of the features you might seek in a science curriculum that would help you to differentiate a resource that simply looked good versus a resource that might actually help your students to learn science?

Why would curriculum developers go through all this trouble? Because it increases the likelihood that the final product is appropriate for classroom use. Watching the materials being used by children and receiving feedback from teachers gives the developers input that ultimately creates a curriculum program that has proved itself. You might expect this is the same process used for all curricula, including textbooks, but it is not. The expression "time is money" applies to curriculum development. Because the kit-based programs had federal support, developers could invest the time (and dollars) into creating, field-testing, and revising the materials. Textbook publishers cannot always afford to make that kind of investment because the profit margins are becoming smaller each year. On the other hand the kit-based programs are not especially pretty compared to textbooks. Kit-based programs, because of the money spent on the development process, do not have the budget to include lots of photographs, illustrations, and other features that make textbooks visually appealing. When you first encounter a kit-based program and start flipping through the teacher guide, you should be aware that the reason it's all in black and white and there are very few photographs is a matter of cost. But the benefit of kit-based programs is in the field-testing. We have much greater confidence in curricula that have been revised and improved based on their use by real teachers and students.

Point–Counterpoint

When science lessons, objectives, and assessments are combined into a unified whole, then we have a science curriculum. Some science educators perceive that the curriculum field-tested and developed by experts is an excellent starting point for a local science program. However, others see commercial curriculum as too narrow and limiting. So in response to the question "How appropriate is it to rely on commercial science curriculum?" we have two opposing views.

Emphasizing the Value of Commercially Developed Science Curriculum

Suzanne Broughton
Doctoral Candidate at the University of Nevada at Las Vegas and Former Sixth-Grade Teacher

Galileo made it possible for others to view the universe without having to go through all of the steps necessary for reinventing the telescope because he did the work for them, and others benefited from his expertise. In much the same way, commercially developed science curriculum allows teachers like me to present organized and thorough lessons without having to recreate them on my own. There simply is not sufficient time to research and plan daily science lessons that are as innovative and complete as those already in existence.

When I first started teaching sixth grade, I spent an incredible amount of time searching for science lesson ideas. I was calling my former professors, looking through old class notes, searching the Internet, and checking huge piles of books out from our local library. Then it dawned on me that my energy should be invested in the things I was good at: organizing a classroom and teaching my students. The curriculum developers were the experts in the content, so it was okay to leave that work to them. They had the in-depth understanding of the scientific concepts and the overall picture of what students need to learn. I could translate their expertise about content and sequence into lessons I knew would be appropriate for my students.

A commercially developed curriculum follows a cohesive sequence, removing the need for me to struggle to know when to introduce a concept. As an undergraduate I had learned about the learning cycle and knew there were good and not so good times to present information to students. Units are designed logically, proceeding from fundamental ideas to more complex concepts. This benefits my students because they acquire background knowledge with which to connect the to-be-learned information, one step at a time. There is a wealth of research supporting the view that learning is most effective when students can connect new information with their existing knowledge. Commercially designed curriculum does this in ways I could not because I didn't have sufficient time to think through every detail.

Commercially developed curriculum helps to align science instruction schoolwide. Students within a particular grade level will be learning the same information on the same days. Teachers benefit by collaborating with each other about the activities. Students are able to exchange ideas and insights on what they are learning with students from other classrooms. In addition setting up the materials for some lessons requires extra time and space. Within my team the three sixth-grade teachers were teaching the same lesson within a day or two of each other. We were able to set up the materials and rotate through the science resource room to present lessons to our classes. By having a shared curriculum guide that had been created commercially, we saved set-up and clean-up time.

There are some people who worry that commercially developed curriculum does not work in real classrooms with real students. However, from my experience participating in the field test of a curriculum under development, I found that the opposite is true. Each unit is tested in classrooms and teachers provide the developer with information on what actually works for students before the curriculum is released to the public. As lessons are taught, the curriculum developer is in the classroom observing and interacting with students to analyze and refine presentation of concepts and how they align with meeting the learning objectives. I can tell you that the developers take this work very seriously. I felt bad when a lesson didn't go the way the authors had planned. But they were grateful and almost always indicated the cause of the problem was their plan, not my implementation.

Teachers can spend a large amount of time creating materials lists, shopping for supplies, and assembling the tools for students to use for just one lesson. In an attempt to alleviate the cost of supplies, many teachers ask for donations from parents. However, this too takes time, and there is always the possibility that the donated supplies will be incomplete. Commercially developed curriculum units provide teachers with the necessary tools and supplies. Often the equipment is preassembled, which again saves teachers preparation time. Teachers can read through the materials list provided in the lesson, go to their storage closet, and gather the appropriate supplies.

Using a commercially developed curriculum also provides opportunities for students to acquire a working knowledge of science process skills. I strongly believe in the power of learning science through hands-on, inquiry-centered approaches. The adage "We learn by doing" applies quite well to science. These curriculum units emphasize research-based instructional methods that ensure the students are involved in the processes of science. The lessons help students see themselves as scientists—because they are.

The Perils of Relying on Commercial Curriculum Materials

David Moss
Teacher Educator at the University of Connecticut

Beginning teachers share a fear: standing in front of a class with nothing to say. The seconds seem like hours as we fumble. Our fragmented ideas, somehow first rate the night before, are completely insufficient. In these moments the siren song of commercial curriculum is luring indeed. "Ready to go" lessons with all the bells and whistles may seem ideal. But nothing could be further from the truth. Although everyone can appreciate the desire for a curricular safety net, prepackaged, glitzy materials undermine the very nature of our profession. Yes, teaching is a profession, not a mere job where we leave our talents, compassion, and intelligence at the classroom door each morning. Writing lessons is a fundamental precursor to effective and engaging teaching.

Although my personal opinion of commercial curricula is that they tend to be poorly developed and bland, I offer a more substantial argument. First, all teaching is contextual. If you were to visit a thousand classes, you would witness many different learning communities, each with its special circumstances. The best advice I can give to the young professional is to know your students as individual learners. As such you are afforded with the unique opportunity to develop and facilitate curriculum that will maximize the learning of your students. To abdicate this responsibility to so-called experts is nothing short of professional misconduct. What do they know of you and your class? In addition your school is located in a geographic area that affords you and your students the opportunity to explore real science issues facing the community. Regardless of whether your school is in an urban setting, sits in the midst of suburban sprawl, or is isolated in rural America, your students will come to class with authentic questions about their environment. Why ignore these in favor of a one-size-fits-all approach? Your students' questions are the key. Leveraging their authentic questions into curriculum will have an added benefit. It will proactively address classroom management issues that arise when bored students ask the age-old question, "Why do we have to learn this?" As you examine your state science standards and associated assessments, you'll see they offer only broad guidelines of what concepts to cover. They don't tell you what to teach each day—and neither should anyone else. Trust in your ability to easily cross-reference student-generated topics with what the standards call for at your grade level, and you'll be surprised how routine this really is.

Second, commercial curriculum endeavors to be all things to all people. Ironically, it marginalizes many of our students. The increasing diversity of our student population demands we address issues of language and culture in our classrooms. National curriculum tends to ignore the richness of our classrooms in favor of a fictional typical classroom. When we consider the generic examples used to fortify the tedious laundry list of concepts and the same-old, same-old role models presented for our students, we see a glaring and tragic disconnect between the prepackaged curriculum and who students are and how they think of themselves. You must ask yourself, "Do you believe that schooling is teacher proof?" Commercial curriculum developers do. They think that they can supply our classrooms with all the answers and that your job is to merely convey a vast array of science content. I suppose the more progressive programs provide inquiry opportunities for students. But in the overwhelming majority of cases, the questions they pose for our students are irrelevant and of no clear personal consequence.

If we are to truly treat our students as scientists, as many reformers suggest that we do, we must be prepared to meet our students on their own cognitive turf so we can lead them toward a scientifically literate future. At its core there is a power struggle at play. If you want to succeed as a teacher, and not just exist, you must be prepared to take risks. Forego the safety net and trust that your professional preparation empowers you with a host of meaningful, creative things to say in front of the class as you facilitate your lessons. Experienced teachers will tell you it's not about running out of things to say in class but about finding the time to address all of the wonderful things we want to.

TABLE 9.1. Three Leading Kit-Based Science Programs

Title	Developer	Publisher	Number of Modules
Insights	Education Development Center	Kendall–Hunt Publishing	17 for elementary grades
FOSS (Full Option Science System)	Lawrence Hall of Science	Delta Education	26 for elementary grades, and 9 for middle school
Science and Technology for Children (STC)	Smithsonian Institute	Carolina Biological Supply	24 for elementary grades, and 8 for middle school

Three Kit-Based Science Curriculum Programs

In describing the three specific kit-based science programs (see Table 9.1), we think it would be ideal if you had the actual programs available to examine. Because these materials have been on the market for several years, there is a good chance that you will see examples in the local schools. Also your college curriculum library might have samples of these materials. You can view portions of these kit-based programs on the Internet, but there's nothing quite like having the opportunity to hold a teacher guide in your hands and flip through the pages.

Insights

The Education Development Center (EDC) in Newton, Massachusetts, developed the Insights curriculum materials (see Table 9.2). The EDC has been involved with science curriculum development for years. In the 1960s this organization developed the Elementary Science Study materials, which are perfect examples of the thinking of the time: pure discovery. Just as with the current kit-based programs, the Elementary Science Study materials were field-tested in classrooms. The discovery approach was the central idea, and by the mid-1970s there were eighty (!) units available. The developers of the Elementary Science Study were advocates of discovery-based learning. However, the authors of Insights were much more closely connected to learning issues, and the materials reflect that sensitivity.

Of the three kit-based programs, Insights makes the most effective use of the learning cycle. Each module begins with a pretest called the Introductory Assessment that is to be administered prior to doing any teaching about the unit. This provides the teacher with information about the students' preexisting ideas and stimulates the students' interest in the topic. The Insights curriculum refers to the lessons as learning experiences, and each explicitly identifies the phase of the learning cycle (their version consists of four phases: Getting Started, Exploring and Discovering, Process for Meaning, and Extending Ideas) and describes the students' and teacher's

TABLE 9.2. Titles of the Modules From Insights

Grade Level			
K–1st	**2nd–3rd**	**4th–5th**	**6th**
Living Things	Growing Things	Circuits and Pathways	Human Body Systems
Balls and Ramps	Lifting Heavy Things	The Mysterious	There Is No Away
Myself and Others	Habitats	Powder	Structures
The Senses	Rocks, Minerals, and	Bones and Skeletons	Music to My Ears
The Weather	Soil	Changes of State	
	Sound	Sun, Earth, and Moon	
	Liquids	Reading the	
		Environment	

actions within each phase. Insights modules were designed to give some flexibility across grade levels. For that reason, the modules are grouped for K–1st, 2nd–3rd, 4th–5th, and 6th grades.

FOSS (the Full Option Science System)

Another kit-based science program is the Full Option Science System, usually called by its much shorter name FOSS (see Table 9.3). FOSS was developed by scientists and educators at the Lawrence Hall of Science, University of California at Berkeley. The Lawrence Hall of Science has a history of developing innovative science curriculum. From the mid-1970s until the mid-1980s, this group created a program called SAVI/SELPH (short for Science Activities for the Visually Impaired/Science Enrichment for Learners with Physical Handicaps). They invented and field-tested science equipment for students who had visual impairments or physical handicaps. What they discovered was that the modules they developed were also quite useful for students who had different abilities. As a result, several of the SAVI/SELPH modules and equipment pieces became centerpieces of the FOSS program.

As is the case for Insights, each FOSS module consists of a teacher guide and containers of hands-on science equipment. FOSS modules are divided into three to six investigations that focus students on a particular topic over multiple science class sessions. Unique to FOSS are specific modifications teachers can make to the lessons for students with special needs, including specially created equipment for students with physical impairments. The FOSS kit is also unique in that in contains a teacher preparation video that shows teachers how to use the equipment and includes classroom footage of the materials being used. FOSS provides student handouts in English and Spanish. Although the front matter in the FOSS materials indicates that the learning cycle is used, it is not as explicitly embedded in the lesson as in the Insights materials. However, the FOSS materials cover a broader range of science topics and do a much better job with earth science concepts than does Insights.

Science and Technology for Children

The Science and Technology for Children (STC) kit-based program is the third and final one we will be examining (see Table 9.4). Just as with Insights and FOSS, STC materials were developed with support from the National Science Foundation. The group responsible for these materials is the National Sciences Resource Center within the Smithsonian Institute. Unlike the other two programs, STC does not have a long history. The modules are not adaptations of materials previously developed for other purposes. When you examine the titles of the modules, you will see that there is much topic overlap with the other two programs.

The STC materials are packaged in much the same way as the others. At the core is a detailed teacher guide and a bin of hands-on equipment. The STC distinguishes itself in two ways. First, it includes a student activity book that contains reading material and activity sheets. This feature appeals to those who feel the need for children to have books to accompany their science lessons. Second, the STC materials are the most scientifically intensive of the three programs. The modules appear to contain much more in the way of vocabulary and technical information for the students. To some, this makes the upper-grade materials superior to the other two programs.

However, the STC materials have their shortcomings. One is that there is a much higher vocabulary demand than for the other programs. Even with the students doing a great deal of hands-on activities, the developers place a fair amount of emphasis on terminology. But perhaps the biggest drawback is that the learning cycle is not consistently used. This is unfortunate, because the developers seem to know about the learning cycle because they described a four-phase version within the teacher guide. But as you look through the lessons, more often than

TABLE 9.3. Titles of the Modules From FOSS (the Full Option Science System)

		Grade Level		
K	**1st–2nd**	**3rd–4th**	**5th–6th**	**6th–8th**
Animals Two by Two	Air and Weather	Earth Materials	Environments	Chemical Interactions
Fabric	Balance and Motion	Human Body	Food and Nutrition	Diversity of Life
Paper	Insects	Ideas and Inventions	Landforms	Earth History
Trees	New Plants	Magnetism and Electricity	Levers and Pulleys	Electronics
Wood	Pebbles, Sand, and Silt	Measurement	Mixtures and Solutions	Force and Motion
	Solids and Liquids	Physics of Sound	Models and Designs	Human Brain and Senses
		Structures of Life/Water	Solar Energy	Planetary Science
			Variables	Populations and Ecosystems
				Weather and Water

TABLE 9.4. Titles of the Modules From the Science and Technology for Children (STC) Curriculum

			Grade Level			
1St	**2nd**	**3rd**	**4th**	**5th**	**6th**	**7th–8th**
Organisms	Life Cycle of Butterflies	Plant Growth and Development	Animal Studies	Microworlds	Experiments with Plants	Catastrophic Events
Weather	Soils	Rocks and Minerals	Land and Water	Ecosystems	Measuring Time	Energy, Machines, and Motion
Solids and Liquids	Changes	Chemical Tests	Electric Circuits	Food Chemistry	Magnets and Motors	Human Body Systems
Comparing and Measuring	Balancing and Weighing	Sound	Motion and Design	Floating and Sinking	The Technology of Paper	Properties of Matter
						Organisms—From Macro to Micro
						Earth in Space
						Light
						Electrical Energy and Circuit Design

not the sequence takes a deductive approach. For example lessons sometimes have the teacher introducing vocabulary before the students have had the chance to explore. In other cases, the exploration is not followed by discussions where the teacher introduces and labels concepts. This is not to suggest that the STC materials are of little value. In fact they do provide some novel experiences such as watching caterpillars develop into butterflies right in the classroom. But some of the features of effective science teaching that we've been describing within this book are not present, and the materials would require a fair amount of modification by the teacher.

Availability of Kit-Based Programs

Despite all the strengths of kit-based programs, you shouldn't expect to see them being used in every elementary and middle school classroom you visit. One reason is that these programs aren't as heavily marketed as textbooks. Another reason is that there are still many people who equate science curriculum with textbooks. It's difficult for such people to imagine how children could learn science unless the class is reading about it. A third reason is the concern about test performance. Because science tests hold so much value for districts and administrators, it is challenging to convince some people that a well-taught kit-based program is just as valuable as textbook and worksheet science. Old traditions are often hard to put aside.

Most criticisms of kit-based programs are based on incomplete information. For example some complain about the costs: one module can cost $600 and would be only one of the four to six needed to fill a school year. However, if a budget person would compare the cost of kit-based programs with the cost of a classroom set of textbooks, he or she would find that the textbooks are actually more expensive. But for certain people there's something comforting about a shelf full of textbooks that bins of science equipment don't provide, at least for those who think that reading science is the most efficient way for children to learn.

Admittedly, kit-based programs create challenges that textbooks do not. Using equipment requires more preparation and clean up time than when teaching science from books. While students work with equipment, they tend to be noisier than when they are reading. The teacher is not always at the front of the room or at the center of attention during activities. While working in groups with science materials, children may exhibit more emotions (from joy to frustration) that are not as evident when there's a book in front of them. Homework assignments that build on hands-on activities are not as straightforward as when children are assigned to answer questions from the back of the chapter. Kit-based programs generate a very different classroom climate. Compared to instruction based on textbooks, kit-based programs have a very different look and feel (and sound and smell!). But that does not automatically mean these are insurmountable barriers for a dedicated teacher.

NSES Program Standard A: Support systems and formal and informal expectations of teachers must be aligned with the goals, student expectations, and curriculum frameworks.

Having students performing hands-on activities is not sufficient for those who buy into the goal of having all children learn science. If the goal is for your student to have fun doing science, then you will be failing them. As a teacher you are expected to help children learn, and that means you sometimes have to push them to exert more effort than we would associate with free play. Sometimes this will require that you push them to record their observations in their notebooks. Kids will normally resist because they'd prefer to keep working with the equipment. But it is reasonable to expect them to pick up their pencil to make a quick sketch of their findings and to jot down a sentence or two. Your job is to teach them science, and their job is to learn science. That doesn't require that you be mean. It simply implies that you express and enforce expectations that are higher than if you're content with your students merely having fun.

NSES Program Standard A: Responsibility needs to be clearly defined for determining, supporting, maintaining, and upgrading all elements of the science program.

Our experience in working with many teachers as they implement kit-based science programs is that the role of the teacher is pivotal. Despite having the kit of science equipment and science lessons that are the products of considerable field-testing, these programs do not teach themselves. There is no script the teacher can follow even though the curriculum authors developed rather detailed lesson plans. Despite suggestions in the teacher guide for accommodating a variety of learners, it is within the teacher's control to decide how to accomplish this with the students inhabiting their classroom. In short, kit-based curriculum programs can provide valuable support and guidance—but the ultimate success depends on the classroom teachers' thoughtful implementation of the curriculum.

What to Do in the Absence of Kit-Based Programs

As we have already indicated, it seems likely that these kit-based programs may not be present in most elementary and middle schools. Does that mean that without these curriculum programs it becomes impossible to teach science in ways we've been promoting? No, this isn't an all-or-nothing situation. There may be other ways to move toward the goal of science literacy for all students, such as using kits developed by other groups or creating similar materials at the local level. But our view is that any alternative to these three kit-based programs involves some level of compromise. It is unfair to compare a local curriculum, no matter how cleverly designed, to kit-based programs that have been the recipients of millions of dollars, thousands of hours of development, field-testing in hundreds of classrooms, and the culmination of thirty or more years of refinement. Although still not perfect (as if that's even a reasonable standard for science curriculum) these three kit-based programs represent the most potent foundations for elementary and middle school science teaching and learning.

Rather than recommend that teachers find ways to create their own curriculum, our suggestion is that time and energy be invested in obtaining individual modules. The worst case scenario is for a teacher to use his or her own money to purchase a $500 kit. However, in our experience there are other ways to underwrite these costs. For example the local parent–teacher organization might be willing to provide support. Local businesses, especially those who are perceived as being science related, may be willing to sponsor the purchase of the program. It is possible that the central office of the local school district already has some of these materials, provided by a commercial distributor as complimentary samples. We've even had success at approaching a building principal and asking that he or she buy one kit with the understanding that it will rotate among all the teachers at a particular grade level.

On the other hand, on too many occasions we've been in schools where science kits have been purchased and are stored unused. Sometimes the teachers have not been trained on their use, so there is hesitancy about jumping in. Other times we've found the very kits we've described stacked in a basement storage room that teachers don't even know exists. Rather than feel outraged by such situations, we prefer to treat them as opportunities. At the very least, even partial kits provide some of the equipment that would allow a teacher to implement a kit-based program. But you should also recognize that when schools spend thousands of dollars on kits, it doesn't mean they will be used in the ways that they were originally intended. And yet for those of us with sufficient ambition and drive, there are often the resources necessary to accomplish our goals.

What Is in and out of Curriculum

Elliot Eisner (1994, 2002) has written extensively about curriculum, and his perspectives are worth mentioning during our consideration of science curriculum. One powerful point he has made, and others have championed, is the distinction between what the curriculum is intended to do and how that curriculum is actually put into play within the classroom. The differences between the intended curriculum and the enacted curriculum are a source of considerable frustration for many in the education field. First of all, curriculum developers hold on to the expectation that teachers will use the curriculum in ways consistent with how they were designed. Second, those in charge of curriculum for an entire school, district, or state would legitimately anticipate some fidelity between the structure of the curriculum and the ways in which it is used. But there are many examples showing the lack of alignment between the official curriculum and actual curriculum, everything from the attitudes and assumptions of teachers (Brantlinger & Majd-Jabbari, 1999) to the mismatch between the curriculum materials and various accountability measures such as local standards and achievement tests (Settlage & Meadows, 2002). There is a fine distinction between differentiating or accommodating curriculum so it is more appropriate for the students within a classroom and straying too far from the curriculum developers' original purposes.

Eisner has boldly argued that the information neglected from what is taught in schools is part of the curriculum. These gaps, these silences, and these omissions are the **null curriculum.** Although he has gone to considerable lengths to decry the absence of arts within schools, we should recognize how the concept of the null curriculum has implications for teaching science in diverse classrooms. When particular information is left out of the curriculum, students receive clear messages about the missing content. For example failing to include women and minorities in discussions of scientists can embed in students' minds beliefs about who is, and is not, capable of being successful in science. In a similar way, failing to include certain topics such as environmental issues also sends a signal to students that such ideas may not be important. In this regard teachers must be vigilant about the null curriculum. Although we might want to believe that we avoid biasing students by not saying anything negative, by failing to say anything positive, we are also sending messages to them that may undercut our stated intentions.

For Reflection and Discussion

What information did you learn in college or outside of your formal education that might be considered the null curriculum of your schooling? What was your reaction toward your precollege education when you reached this realization?

Curriculum and Cultural Responsiveness

Near the beginning of this book, Gloria Ladson-Billings described her attempts to fulfill a seventh-grade science assignment in which she was to create a leaf collection. Unfortunately, her teacher's view of what constituted a legitimate leaf was not especially clear but nevertheless had a powerful influence on how the assignment was graded. Living in a part of Philadelphia where the only outdoor leaves came from sycamore trees, Gloria was resourceful in obtaining a variety of leaves from a greenhouse where a friend of her family worked. But because a leaf carefully collected from a lemon tree was not seen as equivalent to a maple leaf that another student may have found in his backyard, Gloria's teacher failed her on this project.

What went wrong in this situation? Apparently Gloria and her mother reinterpreted the assignment in a way that did not resonate with the teacher's expectations. Also the teacher not only seemed to have a restrictive view of leaf legitimacy but also somehow failed to communicate his perspectives to all of his students. The lesson to be learned from Gloria's story is not simply that we should have a broader view of what is acceptable as a leaf or that we need to be more explicit in communicating the guidelines for assignments, even though this is not a bad idea. The broader and more powerful interpretation of this study is that when implementing the science curriculum, a teacher must be sensitive to the local contexts in terms of students' access to resources, their cultural perspectives, the language differences, and so on. All of these are captured within the idea of being **culturally responsive.**

The term *culturally responsive* describes a stance about education that regards student diversity as a resource for education. Rather than treating language differences as a barrier for students learning science, a culturally responsive teacher would view Spanish as a resource. For example, the Spanish translation of *frog* is *rana,* which happens to also be the scientific name for a genus of frogs. In fact because the classification of organisms is based in Latin, many scientific names may seem less foreign to students who are native Spanish speakers. A teacher who is not culturally responsive would not recognize how being fluent in Spanish can enhance students' science learning. A culturally responsive teacher, in contrast, would be almost automatically finding ways to make the connections between the curriculum and his or her students' backgrounds.

The leaf-collection project was part of the official science curriculum at Gloria's school. However, as it was implemented, it was not culturally responsive. The material the students were to learn was not congruent with the lives of all the students. The teacher seemed unaware of the unique culture of science and did not recognize his role in helping to give children access to the science culture (Parsons, 2000). In the leaf-collecting scenario, we hear only Gloria's voice, and we point this out because it seems likely that others students were similarly frustrated by this curriculum. A culturally responsive approach to science education has demonstrable benefits in terms of academic achievement that is more than the value of making students feel as if they belong in a classroom and can become successful in science. Okhee Lee (2003) reported, "Recent efforts to provide culturally congruent science instruction indicate that when linguistic and cultural experiences are used as intellectual resources, students from diverse backgrounds are able to engage in scientific practices and show significant achievement gains" (p. 473). For multiple reasons, implementing a culturally responsive approach benefits students.

Traits of a Culturally Responsive Teacher

For at least two reasons it is probably too much to expect a science curriculum to be fully culturally responsive. First, it is immensely challenging to anticipate every potential cultural connection for the wide variety of children attending schools across the country. In this regard we can appreciate why curriculum can fulfill only part of the promise of cultural responsiveness. Even the best curriculum materials will require fine-tuning to respond to the particular nuances of local circumstances. The other reason it is unreasonable to expect the curriculum to be culturally responsive is the potential gap between the intended curriculum and the implemented curriculum. A cynic would suggest that even the very best culturally responsive science curriculum can be completely undone in a classroom where the teacher fails to ascribe to this belief system. In other words the intentions and actions of the teacher represent the most crucial link in the chain of events determining whether a curriculum is culturally responsive. What would be the characteristics of an elementary or middle school science teacher who provides a culturally responsive science curriculum to his or her students?

Villegas and Lucas (2002) identified six characteristics of culturally responsive teachers, and although they were not speaking specifically about science, the connections are not at all hard to perceive. First, such teachers are *socioculturally conscious,* which describes those who recognize that the way in which people process information and interact with the world is the product of their ethnic background, their native language, their cultural heritage, and so on. This consciousness applies to teachers' awareness about the ways they think, act, and believe as much as it applies to recognizing the role of these factors among the students. Related to this is the second trait, which describes teachers as holding *affirming views of student diversity.* More than being accepting and tolerant of students' backgrounds, an affirming teacher will assist students to become skilled in the culture of mainstream society without the expectation that they will reject their backgrounds. This trait is consistent with the view that science should be treated as a culture that students can understand and access.

The third trait of culturally responsive teachers is that they accept that they are responsible for contributing to efforts to *make schools more equitable.* In addition to recognizing that schools can treat diverse students in inequitable ways, this third trait highlights the value of teachers making efforts to improve the situation. More than creating a culturally responsive climate, teachers should advocate for greater equity for their entire school. Fourth, culturally responsive teachers view *learning as a process of knowledge construction* within the minds of the students rather than as the acquisition of information. The related piece is the teacher's belief in his or her ability to be able to promote the construction of knowledge by all students under his or her care.

The fifth trait of culturally responsive teachers is that they are *well informed about their students' lives.* This knowledge about students is more than informational and should inform instructional decision making. In addition to knowing students is to continually update that knowledge by remaining in contact with the families of the students. Finally, culturally responsive teachers communicate high expectations and *challenge students to extend themselves* beyond familiar information. Beyond developing a broad repertoire of instructional strategies, which certainly makes for a more adept teacher, the sixth trait also describes teachers' ability to create a classroom environment that supports and encourages all students. This discussion will continue in more detail in chapter 14.

NSES Program Standard A: Teaching practices need to be consistent with the goals and curriculum frameworks.

When considered all at one time, these six traits are quite ambitious—and yet we've already made steps in the right direction. The reason these ideas appear within the chapter on curriculum and not somewhere else is because we want to emphasize the pivotal role of the teacher in the science curriculum. Whatever science curriculum is in place, even if it is the very best kit-based program we can envision, the degree to which these materials will advance the science literacy of all students is largely under the control of the teacher. We view the combination of a quality curriculum and the determination of a culturally responsive teacher as the key to moving closer to the goal of science for all students.

Balancing Curriculum and the Standards

Despite negative, unintended consequences of accountability, it does not seem appropriate for teachers, administrators, or schools to act irresponsibly when it comes to addressing science standards. Students' interests will not be served if the science curriculum ignores the local, state, and national standards. We can deceive ourselves if we pretend that the standards are irrelevant because the results of tests, rightly or wrongly, are used to determine who is admitted to the next level of education. However, this does not give license to teach only what is included in the standards. Time and again, educational officials explain that the standards represent minimum competencies that most, if not all, children are expected to exceed. In the analogy of a race, the goal isn't to get to the finish line; to have finished, let alone win—the person (or horse, car, or whatever) must go over the finish line.

The dilemma we face as teachers is finding an appropriate balance between helping students to attain the standards and making sure that this doesn't simultaneously force them to discard their personal and cultural identities. From one direction teachers receive memos and attend meetings emphasizing the need to pay attention to the standards. From the opposite direction teachers are encouraged to teach all children and pay attention to individual differences. Rarely are these sets of messages in harmony with each other. This is unfortunate because the conscientious teacher would agree with these goals and would like to find ways to strike that balance, but in response to the appropriate and reasonable questions about how to do this, there is little more than silence. Rather than feel hopeless, we can make productive use of the activist spirit of others who are determined to improve schools.

Author Jonathan Kozol has written several books about educational challenges with urban school systems. His most recent book (Kozol, 2005) contains many stories of the difficulties teachers face when trying to struggle against bureaucratic decisions that are made with other than the best interests of students in mind. Within his reporting about changes in urban schools tied to the current accountability movement, Kozol occasionally stepped away from his discouraging reports and offered us some encouragement. He proposed a philosophy teachers can use when confronted with curricular demands that run counter to the goal of providing equitable opportunities to learn. Although some might suggest that he is advocating for insubordination, it is probably more accurate to say that he would support teachers who are able to negotiate external mandates so the needs of children are not sacrificed. This requires knowing when to follow along and when to deviate from the official proclamations.

> Many good teachers make use of these principles and concepts [from the official curriculum], but they do so with an artful flexibility and a degree of sensible irreverence that enable them to gain some benefits from what appears to be a good and innovative notion without letting it become another orthodoxy that defeats the purposes for which it was intended. (Kozol, 2005, p. 331)

With that ambition in mind and recognizing the need to combine teaching with instructional materials, we think it is appropriate to describe ways for evaluating curriculum. In the following section we discuss some hows and whys of evaluating curriculum that might be adopted for use in elementary and middle school science situations.

Evaluating Science Curriculum

What do we expect of an effective elementary or middle school science curriculum? The obvious answer is that such a curriculum will provide guidance about the activities and supply the necessary information to support the learning of all students. The challenge is to find out which curriculum fits this standard before a curriculum is purchased and implemented. Almost any teacher can decide if a curriculum is working after it has been used or even while it is being used. But to make this determination before it is ever used represents a genuine problem. Fortunately, there are various tools for evaluating elementary and middle school science curriculum, and we've provided one such example here.

Curriculum Evaluation Tool Developed by the EDC

Content
- appropriate to designated age?
- significant and relevant to students lives?

Instructional Design
- scientific investigation taught, modeled, and practiced?
- materials actively engage students to help them understand the content?
- sufficient opportunities for students to discuss their science ideas?

Organization of Teacher Materials
- adequate and clear background information?
- guidelines clearly support the teaching of all part of the lessons?
- structure and format easy for teacher to follow?
- special equipment and facilities required?

Assessment
- assessment tools included?
- variety of formal and informal assessments?

Equity
- material free of bias (ethnic, gender, ability, age, etc.)?
- strategies are appropriate for special and diverse students?

Alignment with Standards
- aligns with local and state content standards?
- aligns with local and state inquiry standards?

Much of this curriculum evaluation system is self-explanatory. Nevertheless, it is worth noting some key features. Even though there are several categories to consider, there is an emphasis on how all the pieces fit together. For example the content section emphasizes the value in paying attention to the developmental appropriateness of the subject matter and reminds us to consider how the curriculum relates to students outside of the school. Similarly the instructional design section addresses issues of content, student participation, and personal relevance. All in all, these criteria emphasize the importance of curriculum coherence.

NSES Program Standard B: Science content must be embedded in curricula that are developmentally appropriate, interesting, and relevant to students' lives.

When you have the opportunity to evaluate a science curriculum program, as part of a course assignment or within the context of a district adoption decision process, this evaluation system helps reinforce the holistic aspect of curriculum. Curriculum is not just a part of science education that can be plugged into an existing system. Rather curriculum is influenced by the local situation and also has the potential for changing what occurs in classrooms. Many factors must be taken into consideration during the deliberations about which curriculum to adopt. Unfortunately, these decisions are too often made on a ridiculously tight schedule and are made only once every few years. At the very least, this list of curriculum evaluation criteria can be a resource when it is suddenly necessary to decide what curriculum to use in an elementary school or middle school.

Science Curriculum and Diverse Populations

As with every dimension of science education, if we do not pay attention to the variety of students and their unique needs, then we will be unable to achieve the goal of scientific literacy for all students. Such is the case with curriculum. One might reasonably wonder if curricula such as the kit-based programs we've described are adequate and appropriate in all settings. Recognizing that no curriculum is perfect and that all will require moderate adjustments to address local and specific circumstances, we still have reasons to support kit-based curriculum for all science learners. Helping students connect the science learned at school with science-based issues within the community is an important action for teachers.

Kit-Based Curriculum and Special Needs Students

To discern if kit-based curriculum programs are appropriate for students with cognitive and physical disabilities, we return to the expertise of Mastropieri and Scruggs (1992), who we've relied on in previous discussions. Their recommendations for special needs populations are the implementation of science experiences that stress "general principles and overall themes over separate facts and vocabulary; providing more focus on less content; including concrete examples and hands-on activities; promoting cooperative group solutions to scientific problems; and developing science process skills" (pp. 404–405). In the context of this quote, these authors were not describing the use of kit-based science curriculum—but they may as well have been. Each of these emphases are central and defining features of the kit-based programs.

To our knowledge there are no published research studies specifically examining the use of the kit-based science programs described in this chapter with special needs populations. Rather than wait for that data to be collected, analyzed, and distributed, we're obliged to make curricular decisions with the knowledge currently available to us. One such example (Mastropieri et al., 1998) suggested that the approaches we've been advocating and the curriculum we have been describing are appropriate with special needs populations. Researchers have found that students with disabilities may be perfectly capable learners when kit-based materials are being implemented:

> The results of the present investigation provide further evidence concerning the effective inclusion of students with disabilities in science classrooms. In the present case, students with disabilities not only participated on an equal basis, but achieved comparably to their peers in the activities/inclusion class, and superior to average peers in the textbook classes. (Mastropieri et al., 1998, p. 178)

Not only do kit-based programs promise to be useful bases for science curriculum for special needs populations but there are also many reasons to expect similar success in using these same resources when teaching in culturally diverse settings.

Science Curriculum and Culturally Responsive Ambitions

Here we return to the concept of culturally responsive science teaching to provide one more challenge to you. Many of us recognize the importance of displaying sensitivity toward different cultures and gradually appreciate the role of that disposition within the context of science teaching and learning. One additional challenge in developing a commitment to cultural responsiveness is recognizing that culture is not only out there but also something we carry inside ourselves.

We readily admit that culturally responsive science teaching is a simultaneously worthy and demanding goal. To make progress toward that goal requires developing knowledge about the cultures of the students in your classroom: their traditions, their communication styles, their belief systems, and so on. For those of us who grew up in rather homogeneous settings, there is a great deal of knowledge that must be generated. But such knowledge is insufficient.

As we have mentioned before, the success of any curriculum, even the most potent kit-based program, relies on the qualities of the teacher as he or she implements them in a classroom. For a curriculum to be culturally responsive, a teacher must translate it to address the six characteristics proposed by Villegas and Lucas (2002). What often goes unrecognized are the demands this places on the teacher. The following comments were in response to the efforts to implement a new curriculum in an urban setting:

> A closer look reveals that what is more important for culturally relevant teaching are the ways in which teachers understand who they are racially and culturally … and how they have learned to view human beings who are racially and culturally different from themselves. … It requires opportunities for individual teachers to work in settings that allow them to examine their own thinking and reflect on their teaching practice as a political, rather than neutral, aspect of their being. This is a painful and unsettling process for teachers. (Shujaa, 1995, p. 200)

The implications for this quote are substantial. Even if we have the sincere desire to implement a science curriculum in ways that can be viewed as culturally responsive, such efforts will be compromised if teachers don't accept the fact that their cultural perspectives play a significant role in the ways that they react to their students. Until teachers recognize that they are products of their culture and understand how those perspectives color everything they do, then their efforts to create a classroom that is culturally responsive, from the types of teaching strategies used to the manner in which the curriculum is implemented, will always be limited. This is neither an easy accomplishment nor a comfortable realization. Nevertheless, more and more educators are beginning to comprehend the underlying truth, even though it can be a source of uneasiness.

Chapter Summary

- The information students are expected to learn and the manner in which it is to be taught describe a science curriculum. In the past, the textbook was used as the entire curriculum, but now science curriculum includes standards, equipment, and specified activities.
- Although there can be a perception that a formal curriculum restricts teacher creativity, it is not necessarily the case. Teacher creativity may be better used to modify an existing curriculum rather than to invest energy in creating a new curriculum.
- A science curriculum consisting of a collection of learning cycles is an example of a spiral curriculum. With each pass through a learning cycle, and with one concept building on the others, student understanding builds on prior knowledge.
- Sometimes science activity guides are thought of as curriculum. However, because these resources rarely include important aspects of effective science teaching, such as the features of inquiry, these materials are not sufficient as stand-alone science curricula.
- Kit-based programs developed through extensive field-testing can become powerful components of elementary and middle school science programs. These materials are not teacher proof but rely on teachers to use their professional judgment to ensure that the curriculum is appropriate to the students in their classroom.

- In the absence of research that has specifically examined the role of kit-based curriculum with special needs and ethnically diverse populations, we find ourselves looking at research that describes the characteristics of science that are effective with these groups. There is a very consistent pattern: the structure of kit-based programs is reflective of science teaching practices for a wide variety of learners.

Key Terms

Activity guides: booklets describing a variety of interesting hands-on activities that can serve as a supplement to the science curriculum.

Culturally responsive: educational approaches (i.e., curriculum, management, instruction, etc.) that use students' cultural and linguistic backgrounds as resources, and not barriers, to support students' success in school.

Curriculum modules: Curriculum modules are discrete sections of a broader curriculum included in a kit-based program. Each module emphasizes a particular science topic, which might take anywhere from six to twelve weeks to complete.

Field-tested curriculum: instructional material that has been revised and redesigned based on the feedback from teachers who employed original versions of the curriculum in their classrooms.

Kit-based programs: a vehicle for delivering science curricula that provide teachers with the structure necessary for teaching science through student-centered activities. The kits include directions thoroughly describing the teaching approach, the specific directions for the activity, and the equipment needed for the activities.

Null curriculum: material that is deliberately or subconsciously left out of the formal curriculum but, by its absence, reinforces subtle messages through these omissions.

Spiral curriculum: a method of curriculum design that consists of multiple learning cycles, where the information addressed in one learning cycle provides the foundation for the next.

Teacher-proof curriculum: the goal of curriculum developers in the 1960s and 1970s, now considered to be a damaging one. The idea was for curriculum to be so well designed that teachers simply had to "follow the directions."

A Favorite Science Lesson

The grade-three and grade-four unit of FOSS titled "Earth Materials" begins by having students examine a mock rock. What they don't know is that the teacher used a recipe from the teacher guide (ingredients include sand, flour, aquarium gravel, salt, oyster shells) to make the rocks the students are investigating. Although these look very much like real sedimentary rocks, they are soft enough for the students to take apart using a nail as a chisel. They find inside the rock a piece of shell and almost always claim they've found a fossil. They then put the leftover ingredients in a jar of water, shake up the mixture, and let it sit. A day later, they discover the layers that have formed. The liquid on top is poured off to evaporate, and they discover crystal formation. By the time the teacher pulls out the real rocks, students are enchanted by the idea that they are geologists. May be one of the best geology units we've seen.

Suggested Readings

Jeffries, C. (1999). Activity selection: It's more than the fun factor. *Science and Children, 37*(2), 26–29, 63.
This article begins with the sentence "Many people assume that if an activity is published or popular, it is a good one." The author then provides a rubric teachers can use to differentiate science activities that are fun from those that also provide great learning potential.

Schiller, E., Joseph, J., & Konecki, L. (2004). A handle on hands-on. *Science and Children, 41*(9), 30–32.
One persistent challenge of teaching science is dealing with equipment and materials. These experienced science educators outline strategies for storing, organizing, ordering, and budgeting so that a teacher and school can spend more time teaching and less time dealing with the stuff that kids will use.

References

Brantlinger, E., & Majd-Jabbari, M. (1999). The conflicted pedagogical and curricular perspectives of middle-class mothers. *Journal of Curriculum Studies, 30,* 431–460.

Eisner, E. W. (1994). *Cognition and curriculum reconsidered* (2nd ed.). New York: Teachers College Press.

Eisner, E. W. (2002). *The educational imagination.* Upper Saddle River, NJ: Merrill-Prentice Hall.

Kozol, J. (2005). *The shame of the nation: The restoration of apartheid schooling in America.* New York: Crown.

Lee, O. (2003). Equity for linguistically and culturally diverse students in science education: A research agenda. *Teachers College Record, 105,* 465–489.

Mastropieri, M. A., & Scruggs, T. E. (1992). Science for students with disabilities. *Review of Educational Research, 62,* 377–411.

Mastropieri, M. A., Scruggs, T. E., Panayota, M., Sturgeon, A., Goodwin, L., & Chung, S. H. (1998). "A place where living things affect and depend on each other": Qualitative and quantitative outcomes associated with inclusive science teaching. *Science Education, 82,* 163–179.

Moscovici, H., & Nelson, T. H. (1998). Shifting from activity mania to inquiry. *Science and Children, 35*(4), 14–17, 40.

National Research Council. (1996). *National Science Education Standards.* Washington, DC: National Academy Press.

National Research Council. (1999). *Designing mathematics or science curriculum programs: A guide for using mathematics and science education standards.* Washington, DC: National Academy Press.

Parsons, E. C. (2000). Culturalizing science instruction: What is it, what does it look like and why do we need it? *Journal of Science Teacher Education, 11,* 207–219.

Schmidt, W. H., McKnight, C. C., Raizen, S. A., Jakwerth, P. M., Valverde, G. A., Wolfe, R. G., Britton, E. D., Bianchi, L. J., & Houang, R. T. (1997). *A splintered vision: An investigation of U.S. science and mathematics education.* Dordecht, the Netherlands: Kluwer.

Schmidt, W. H., & Valverde, G. A. (1998). Refocusing U.S. math and science education. *Issues in Science and Technology, 14*(2), 60–66.

Settlage, J., & Meadows, L. (2002). Standards-based reform and its unintended consequences: Implications for science education within America's urban schools. *Journal of Research in Science Teaching, 39,* 114–127.

Shujaa, M. J. (1995). Cultural self meets cultural other in the African American experience: Teachers' responses to a curriculum content reform. *Theory into Practice, 34*(3), 194–201.

Villegas, A. M., & Lucas, T. (2002). Preparing culturally responsive teachers: Rethinking the curriculum. *Journal of Teacher Education, 53,* 20–32.

Zimmerman, J. (1999). Storm over the schoolhouse: Exploring popular influences upon the American curriculum, 1890–1941. *Teachers College Record, 100,* 602–626.

ten

Integrating Science With Other Subjects

Chapter Highlights

- Teachers who organize instruction around themes must guard against neglecting specific subject areas. Too often thematic units fail to effectively address science as so much of the teacher's and learners' attention is focused on multiple subjects.
- Literacy strategies can effectively combine with science teaching in ways that support student learning. As a result reading and writing can both support and be supported by effective science lessons.
- Teachers should apply the philosophy of inductive teaching when integrating reading with science. The best approach is for students to first engage in science activities and then access books or other materials to enhance and consolidate their science understandings.
- Students need to receive explicit instruction about how to write in a scientific style. They also require assistance with reading informational texts. Both strategies rely on language arts to reinforce the culture of science.
- Writing within the context of science learning is not restricted to composing sentences. A broader definition of writing embraces concept mapping and graphing as forms of literacy. These modes of written communication support students' learning and mirror the ways in which scientists communicate.

Interdisciplinary science teaching attracts considerable attention. The authors of science education reform documents emphasize the need to connect science across disciplines (i.e., biology, earth and space science, and physical science) and to other fields such as mathematics, history, and language arts (American Association for the Advancement of Science, 1994). We might imagine that it would be most efficient to rely on a single lesson to cover more than a single subject. After all when a week of instruction is scheduled so that a fixed number of minutes is designated for reading or math, science is often squeezed out. Integrating lessons would allow a teacher to include more science in a crowded schedule. All of this might lead us to accept interdisciplinary units as a healthy approach to teaching science. Within this chapter we will examine the promises and problems of teaching science in an interdisciplinary fashion. With this knowledge, you can decide for yourself how much interdisciplinary teaching you are willing to undertake.

The Interest in Thematic Units

For many adults, there is an appeal to a classroom organized around a captivating theme. It is hard to ignore the creative energy emanating from such a classroom. A second-grade room that features pictures of butterflies, shelves full of butterfly books, a window looking out to an outdoor butterfly garden, butterfly graphs plastering the walls, and colorful butterfly art dangling from the ceiling is an environment many new teachers would like to duplicate. It seems obvious from looking at the various displays that the children have used the butterfly theme in art, reading, mathematical estimation, and scientific observation. Indeed it might even seem natural to teach with such themes. But as you may be growing to realize, almost all ideas related to teaching, even when they appear "natural," are open to misuse.

Thematic units are not necessarily bad, and interdisciplinary teaching is not misguided. But there are reasons for caution. Thematic teaching and learning can be fun, to a large extent because it represents a departure from traditional curriculum. In addition doing something creative and novel seems to generate its very own energy (we know, this is scientifically impossible—but it's nice imagery). A classroom decorated with symbols of a unit's theme would appeal to all but the sternest curmudgeon. Keep in mind that a classroom should serve a grander purpose than entertaining its occupants. The distracting nature of thematic units is perhaps their single biggest danger. The rubber stamps and reward stickers that are consistent with a theme are far at the edges of the central purpose of schools and what they were created to accomplish.

Integrating Science Without Diluting It

Our surroundings are not science. Instead science occurs within our attempts to understand our surroundings by using particular ways of thinking. When someone reduces science to objects such as apples, penguins, or the sun, then an incomplete and incorrect understanding of science becomes evident.

We should recognize that when a creative teacher finds ways to link science to other subjects using a certain theme, it does not mean that thematic connections are the most effective ways for students to learn science. Kathleen Roth, a teacher educator at Michigan State University, has voiced concerns about the thematic teaching of science (Roth, 1994). As part of her typical workday, she taught in a fifth-grade classroom at a school near her campus. Some years ago, she worked with other teacher colleagues to design a thematic unit around Columbus's arrival in the new world in 1492. This ambitious unit was designed to focus on social studies, science, art, and literature. As an aside, we feel obligated to mention the problems with teaching with a Columbus theme or any other "great discoverers" theme. At some point, every teacher should be aware of the hidden problems with such themes. Take a look at the book *Rethinking Columbus*, edited by Bill Bigelow and Bob Peterson (1998), to become aware of the pitfalls of an explorer theme.

Although the Columbus theme unit intrigued her, Roth found that the students developed superficial understandings about science. At one point during the unit, students were supposed to focus on diversity in humans in the new world (for social studies) and the local plant life available to those groups. The students were not guided to understand important science concepts such as ecosystems, food chains, or the cycling of matter. According to *Benchmarks for Science Literacy* (AAAS, 1994) students are to understand the following by the time they complete fifth grade: "For any particular environment, some kinds of plants and animals survive well, some survive less well, and some cannot survive at all." This would have been a logical and worthwhile way to bridge the theme with the science. Sadly, for the science portion of this unit, students and their teachers never went beyond describing the plants that could have been found alongside local populations of American Indians.

What could have been done that would have allowed this thematic unit to do justice to the science? One problem was that the science concepts were supplements to the theme rather than the core of it. This would have required immersing the students in central science concepts over more than a single lesson. Also, and by now you should expect to hear this, there must be opportunities for students to personally apply science process skills and the five essential features of inquiry. As reported by Roth, none of this happened. Instead the students touched only on some science vocabulary and ended the unit with weak scientific understandings. What was the cause of this neglect of science? Roth seemed to feel that the teachers began with a theme and subsequently identified science topics that might fit. Unfortunately, this resulted in selecting science concepts that weren't logically connected to the students' experiences. The scientific ideas were not selected because they served a purpose beyond a clever fit within the broad theme.

Science will not be automatically neglected whenever elementary or middle school teachers organize their curriculum around a central theme. But from Roth's example, as well from our experiences working with teachers, too often the science within a thematic unit is weak. The tendency is for the science to be diluted because too much attention and energy are invested in the theme. It is truly difficult to keep in mind all the components of effective science teaching and learning (e.g., core science concepts, process skills, inquiry thinking, the learning cycle). But when these are absent, the science that students experience is much less than it could and should be. If students are led to believe that hearing a story about bats represents science, then is there any surprise that they don't see science as something that they can do?

Roth suggested that teachers approach thematic teaching with great caution. Identifying a central idea around which lessons are designed is very wise. For reasons we do not fully understand, when the central idea for a unit is a theme, the tendency is for the science to play a supporting role rather than a central part. On the surface an interdisciplinary approach makes sense. Instead of having all disconnected pieces of content, an interdisciplinary unit supports a more holistic plan. As such the students learn that knowledge is not divided into neat chunks where science is separate and disconnected from other fields. But interdisciplinary curriculum often creates artificial and forced connections—and the science almost inevitably suffers as a result.

Themes With Concepts at Their Core

The common starting point for a thematic unit is to identify a central organizing idea. This theme is chosen with the expectation that it will connect various subject areas into a unified whole. A curriculum that combines the study of a major idea from the perspective of assorted disciplines (e.g., science, math, history, literature, etc.) represents an **interdisciplinary curriculum.** An interdisciplinary curriculum at a high school would require teachers from multiple subject areas, such as science, social studies, and literature, to coordinate their teaching so they are each addressing an agreed on organizing idea. For example one could imagine an interdisciplinary curriculum about space exploration: in science the students could be taught about planetary motion, in social studies they could examine the cold war's influence on the mission to the moon, and in literature they could read classic science fiction stories about space travel. Just as the planets orbit around the sun, the different subject areas and their representative teachers would circle around a central topic.

Here are some practical issues an interdisciplinary curriculum will supposedly solve (Jacobs, 1989). One issue is the ever-increasing amount of information that students are intended to master, while another issue is the fragmented schedule within the day. A third issue that interdisciplinary curriculum advocates believe they can solve is the persistent teaching material that seems to have little relevance to the interests of the students. The suggestion is that teaching subjects in an interdisciplinary fashion will allow the students to discover the relevance of their school studies to their everyday lives. Unfortunately, interdisciplinary curriculum doesn't seem able to fulfill all these promises. It's difficult to explain this phenomenon, but it is quite real. We could speculate that those teachers who are uncomfortable with teaching science might be drawn to interdisciplinary approaches as a way to reduce their anxieties. However, what tends to happen is that the science is often forgotten in the flurry of language arts activities.

Time and again interdisciplinary curriculum units fail to accomplish the task of using different disciplines to allow students to understand a central idea. From our perspective, the science is often neglected. Perhaps this is because the teachers involved hold an incomplete understanding of science as a culture—one of our reasons for writing this book. And while although this is a much more global issue, it is especially grating when one claims to be covering science by absorbing it into an interdisciplinary approach. Indeed one of the faults we find with some aspects of interdisciplinary teaching is that teachers can then say "we've done science," even if the science is taught in a superficial or tangential fashion.

If we've done our jobs as science educators, you will now recognize that science lessons should involve students in the process skills. In addition you should recognize that science is not only content and not only process. Instead science can be viewed as a culture with certain traditions of communicating and viewing the natural world. We understand that this is a lot to ask of elementary and middle school teachers. Our worry is that because these are necessary components of good science teaching, the science becomes diluted when someone is trying to balance those demands against the additional challenge of attending to a theme. When this happens the students are no longer being provided with the opportunities to learn the science they deserve.

Does this mean we want to hold science as a subject separate from all the others? We can understand why you might come to that conclusion, but that is not our intent. However, we are cautioning you against losing hold of the important distinctions of a scientific way of thinking. In the next section we will illustrate how science and language arts can be combined in ways that meet our primary goal of helping students to learn both domains. Our challenge as teachers of elementary and middle school science is to navigate between two dangers. On one side is the problem of thematic units in which the science is diminished or even lost. On the other side is the danger of segregating and insulating science too much. We see a path in between these two, and the way to accomplish this is to understand how to realistically combine science with language arts in ways that are mutually beneficial.

Language Arts at the Center of Science Learning

The possibilities of combining science with language arts are quite different from the traditional thematic approaches to science and reading and writing. An example of an inappropriate meshing of language arts with science is a lesson in which the teacher reads a book about some natural organism or phenomenon and then claims that science and language arts were both covered. Imagine dropping into a classroom during this lesson: the teacher reads the story *Stellaluna* (Cannon & Cannon, 1993) to the class. This is followed by a short discussion about bats, which then leads to students writing their own story or poem about bats. We claim this is not science teaching. For one thing, inquiry is not clearly evident in this example. Another problem is that the students aren't using science process skills. Is this a bad way to teach? No, this could be a marvelous language arts lesson. But the claim that this is a science lesson is what troubles us.

We want you to think about connecting language arts and science in a very different way. Rather than believe that reading and writing about natural phenomena represent an integration of language arts and science, let's return to our understandings of culture. Within every culture, language plays a central and defining role, and the culture of science is no different. As teachers of science, we expect all students to participate in the culture of science and to develop a reasonable level of scientific literacy, and this includes becoming proficient at using the specific language of science. Just as with learning any other language, becoming fluent is much more than simply acquiring vocabulary. We use this chapter to further reinforce the benefits of thinking about science as a culture, even as we consider how to effectively integrate science with the language arts. By "effective" we mean that students will enhance their skills in the language arts at the same time they learn both the objects and the actions of science.

For students to gain access to the culture of science, we as teachers need to attend to the students' cultures and the science culture. It is important to simultaneously honor individual abilities, experiences, and voices even as we present them with the objects and actions of science. Science instruction must accommodate those students for whom English is a new language, but not in a way that neglects the importance of students learning to use the specialized language of science. Language is an essential component of participation within a culture. When we treat science as a culture, we can appreciate the importance of guiding students to learn to communicate in ways that allow them to become members of the science culture.

As teachers of science and as teachers working in diverse classrooms, we should understand how reading, writing, and speaking are essential to the actions of science. These actions include the ways we speak when doing science, the manner in which we write as we participate in science, and the processes we use as we take meaning from science texts. These are the characteristics and norms associated with the language of science, and teachers are responsible for guiding students to become familiar with them. Certainly, given the nature of science and scientific inquiry, what we include within the actions of science must include the features of the language of science and how it is used as members of a culture communicate with each other.

Science and Reading: A Healthy Relationship

We have advocated for an inductive approach to science teaching in diverse settings, and we continue to rely on this approach as we begin connecting science with communicating. Fortunately, we aren't inventing contradictory ways of thinking about teaching science. There is a natural role for reading about the objects of science, in both the learning and the doing of science. We have pushed aside the traditional notion of science teaching, so we don't feel that learning should begin by introducing vocabulary. Now we use the same rationale as we plan to integrate textual material with studies of science.

Teachers who are uncertain about how to integrate reading with science can rely on the simple phrase "do first, read later," as was coined by Larry Yore (2004, p. 88). This means reading in a science classroom isn't the starting point for science learning but can play a very important supporting role. The use of text materials should be reserved until after a student has established a personal need to read. In other words reading can satisfy the desire for an answer to a question. Thinking back on the learning cycle, we see that this use of reading would occur after students have worked with science materials during the Explore phase. In this way the exploration of real materials will generate questions. The questions arising in students' minds serve as the driving force for them when they dig into the books.

The conventional wisdom seems to be that reading about a topic is necessary to supply a mental foundation for the learner. We want to be clear that we are not opposed to allowing students to read to learn about science. However, reading researchers have identified ways of helping students to become engaged with text, and we recommend using these methods. Children are going to become more involved with their reading and more likely to comprehend the material when there is a clear purpose to their reading. The activities used within the Engage and Explore phases of the learning cycle allow students to connect with the topic. Along the way their explorations compel and propel them to enter into their reading to make sense of their experiences.

Just in case it hasn't been obvious what we've discussed up to this point, we want to make it clear that direct experience and hands-on activities are an absolute necessity for much of science learning, and this applies to all types of learners. This is not to suggest we can rely on activities to do the teaching for us, but they are often a necessary starting point. Interestingly, researchers have found that direct experiences also promote better reading comprehension. Nancy Romance and Mike Vitale (2001) found that when students have direct experience with a science concept, their subsequent comprehension of reading material improves. The activities not only hook students into participating in reading but also lead students to better comprehend what they later read.

Reading is usually considered necessary for students to comprehend science concepts. However, it is becoming increasingly apparent that intrinsic motivation is key to individual engagement with and understanding of written material. To a large extent we can improve students' reading skills and scientific knowledge by following Larry Yore's guidance. Starting with activities involving real objects and then using reading as a way to resolve questions both supports students' scientific understandings and improves their reading comprehension. Students' initial experiences with materials play an important role in shaping their comprehension of text as they read to make sense of those experiences. In this way doing science promotes better reading comprehension, which in turn contributes to the construction of better understandings of the science. The essential part of this cycle is to have the students begin with direct experiences.

The interrelationship between reading and experiences becomes especially vital when we are teaching science to nonmainstream students and those who struggle to read because of language differences or cognitive barriers. Beginning with concrete objects and then moving toward abstractions (i.e., the printed word) is a sound instructional practice. This inductive approach relies on direct experience to build a foundation and then reading material to strengthen the students' understandings. In this way reading supports science learning. Beyond this, the "do first, read later" sequence also supports reading skills of diverse students: the exposure to equipment, objects, and other stuff promotes greater interest in the reading material, thus encouraging students to engage in reading for meaning.

For Reflection and Discussion

Think about how the "do first, read later" approach to learning has applied to you. What things have you learned best by experiencing them first and then reading about them later, and how might this experience translate into your teaching of science?

Texts as Resources for Science Learning

Reading can play a powerful supporting role for students' science learning. Once a teacher appreciates the interrelationship between science and reading, an entire world opens up in terms of what counts as texts and how they are used. Textbooks, informational trade books, newspapers, and Internet-based materials all become excellent resources for helping students to better understand the phenomena they are investigating. Students can rely on narrative and informational storybooks to try to make sense of their explorations. Nevertheless, as teachers we must avoid believing we can exchange texts for hands-on, physical experiences as the starting point for science learning. This is because to initiate science instruction with the use of texts may be successful only for students who are already comfortable and familiar with traditional ways of schooling. To reserve the use of reading until after direct experiences is beneficial to every student.

NSES Teaching Standard D: Teachers of science design and manage learning environments that provide students with the time, space, and resources needed for learning science. In doing this teachers identify and use resources outside the school.

Using texts is central to the work of professional scientists. The implication for science teaching should be clear: accessing written information is a vital part of the culture of science. Do not think that if students are using texts that they are violating the actions of science, because the opposite is true. Creating a classroom community where the culture of science is alive and well means that there are times when students should be reading. Helping students to become skilled at accessing scientific information through reading is something we should not neglect. It is not accurate to believe that scientists derive explanations solely from empirical evidence. What this ignores is that scientists rely on the work of other scientists, often by accessing the writings produced by others.

Beyond analyzing the evidence they have personally collected, scientists participate in the actions of science as they examine what other scientists have written. The questions they ask, the methods they employ to answer those questions, and the inferences they make based on evidence are actions of science that are informed through accessing the work of other scientists. Reading is not something scientists do only occasionally. Digging into the material that others have written is a vital part of the work of scientists. In a similar way students must become skilled at going to texts to inform their thinking. Once again the culture of science in the classroom can parallel the culture of science as enacted by professional scientists, and this includes reading what has been written by others.

Using Texts to Inform Student Explorations

As part of acquiring the culture of science, students should become skillful at using texts to understand their explorations. At a very basic level, this requires that students have easy access to an abundance of texts. It helps to have a classroom filled with books of all sorts (informational trade books, storybooks, picture books) and the Internet accessible to students. Veteran teachers often have a substantial collection of texts. A newer teacher should consider raiding the school library in preparation for a new science unit. If that is not a possibility or if your school library is not especially prosperous in terms of science books, visit your public library. There you can obtain a variety of titles and types of texts related to the science content to be studied. Children's librarians can be quite helpful if you go in and say, "I need every book you can give me that talks about X," where X is the next science unit. You might be able to gather these materials on your own, but often librarians are more resourceful than even the best search engine.

With a classroom supply of a wide assortment of texts, it becomes natural for students to learn to access a variety of text sources to generate explanations for the questions emerging from their Engage and Explore activities. By being readily accessible, a teacher can guide students in the search for explanations. This avoids the tendency to view the teacher as the sole source of knowledge. Students can compare explanations from different sources, a practice that not only emulates the actions of scientists but also encourages deeper involvement with the ideas. All of this increases the likelihood the students will genuinely understand the science concepts, because they are able to pursue and resolve questions that hold considerable personal significance. Equally important, students acquire the skills to independently access information and become capable of comparing information from various sources—both of which are profoundly important literacy skills.

The language of science as it appears in a written form can frustrate many students, because it is so unique. Authors of informational texts use language in ways that are substantially different from the ways language is used in other genres of writing. This form of writing challenges many students, in part because the style is not familiar. But the use of language is also very different from what most students would have been exposed to. As adults we recognize some writing styles as being more technical than others. You can sense that the following sample is the type of writing characteristic of an informational text:

> Humans can change the water cycle by their actions. When a road or parking lot is built, water cannot flow into the ground. Instead the rain that falls there evaporates or runs off. Humans are not the only ones who change the water cycle. In this picture, you can see a pond made by a beaver's dam. The water cycle was changed by the beaver. Trees were used to build the dam. Water that used to flow now stands still. The actions by the beaver changed the water cycle in this area.

Scientific writing often uses a passive verb tense instead of an active voice. In this example, the author used the passive voice with the sentence "The water cycle was changed by the beaver." If this were written in the active voice, it would have appeared as "The beaver changed the water cycle." Although the meaning is pretty much the same, the style may seem very odd to students. But the oddness of informational texts does not imply that teachers should avoid using such texts within their classrooms. In fact the opposite is true. Understanding this genre is the key to comprehending the material and contributes to improved science learning. Furthermore, children actually enjoy reading informational texts, even though common sense suggests that developing readers prefer stories (Dreher & Voelker, 2004). Informational texts should not push storybooks out of the way—there ought to be room for a greater array of texts in classrooms for the purpose of extending children's science learning (Duke, 2000).

Becoming comfortable with reading informational texts is key for improving elementary and middle school students' science learning (Bernhardt, Destino, Kamil, & Rodriguez-Munoz, 1995). This requires that teachers guide students to make sense of informational texts. More than simply sounding out words, students learn to interpret informational texts by mastering new literacies. In storybooks the illustrations provide a visual reinterpretation of the words. The illustrations in informational texts are essential to understanding the authors' meaning. Storybooks have a plotline that is sequential. In contrast informational texts can be practical and useful even when the reader just jumps into the middle. Storybooks rely on narrators, whereas informational texts do not. For these and other reasons, the genre of informational texts can be unusual for novice readers. But by making the strange familiar, teachers can help their students to make appropriate switches in their reading strategies (e.g., between when they are looking for information within *The New Way Things Work* [Macaulay & Ardley, 1998] as compared to their reading a Harry Potter book). This is not to judge one as important and the other as trivial. What is becoming increasingly clear is that as teachers we should make room for informational texts on classroom bookshelves and that the use of books ought to extend beyond the time designated for reading within the school day.

Selecting Informational Texts

Each year a group of educators are appointed by the National Science Teachers Association to review science information texts written for the K-12 audience. This review panel's work leads to the announcement of the annual list of Outstanding Science Trade Books (http://www.nsta.org/ostbc). The following criteria used for evaluating the candidate books provide us with a rubric for conducting an independent evaluation of books.

Science content is substantive
Clear and accurate information
Information is not overly simplified so it becomes misleading
Generalized comments are supported by facts
Material is free of bias (i.e., gender, ethnicity, etc.)

The books from the most recent list of Outstanding Science Trade Books are presented in the following categories: archaeology, anthropology and paleontology, biography, earth and space science, environment and ecology, life science, physical science, and technology and engineering. Each year's winners are selected from books published in the previous calendar year, and only those books that are submitted for evaluation are considered. As a result there may be books that never reach the review panel. Our suggestion is to consider how to use the National Science Teachers Association's criteria as you skim through books in your library.

Using Read-Alouds Within Science Teaching

Reading should not always occur as a solitary activity. When a teacher presents an informational text to his or her students, he or she makes reading a public activity by reading aloud and inviting comments along the way. This read-aloud strategy shares the information from a text with the class and encourages the group to join in conversations that support scientific meaning making. Read-alouds allow students to practice their use of languages: the language of science and the English language. As described by Christine Pappas, Maria Varelas, Anne Barry, and Amy Rife (2004), including whole class discussions while a teacher reads an informational text allows students to pose questions, offer information, and explore ideas. In turn the teacher models and supports those activities. What makes such discussions any different from other classroom conversations? These discussions center on the reading of an informational text. More than simply providing information to the students, the teacher uses the read-aloud to introduce students to the specific language of science. As a result they are learning science concepts (objects of science) and ways of behaving (actions of science) that are consistent with becoming participants in the culture of science.

Conducting whole class read-alouds serves purposes within science teaching beyond providing students with new information. Read-aloud discussions provide a forum for operating within the culture of science as students become familiar with *talking science,* meant in its broader sense of communicating scientifically (Lemke, 1990). The work by Pappas, Varelas, Barry, and Rife suggests that as students participate in read-aloud discussions about informational texts, they not only pull scientific explanations from the text but also begin to incorporate the scientific patterns of communication employed in the text into their own ways of speaking. Because the teacher supplies the scaffolding for informational text discussions, she or he provides a safe and familiar space (i.e., the teacher reading to the class) in which students can practice using the language of science. To develop competence with the culture of science, students need opportunities to practice their use of the language.

Read-alouds of informative texts become defining moments within science instruction. Within the essential features of inquiry discussed in chapter 4, students are to connect their personal ideas to scientific knowledge. Toward the teacher-centered end, this essential feature describes the students being provided with possible connections. When this strategy is appropriate, and for certain situations it is, the teacher will build the bridge that relates informational text to students' recent explorations. As the amount of teacher control is relaxed, the students are directed toward informational texts as sources of scientific information. When informational texts are in sufficient supply and students have become skilled at independently locating relevant information and using that to form deeper connections, then they are operating at Level 4 of the essential features continuum (shown on Table 4.3). The take-away message is that using informational texts has the potential for fulfilling a key part of inquiry, namely, the connection making between personal experiences and the larger body of scientific knowledge.

Even as read-alouds connect students to new sources of scientific information, the students are also exposed to and ultimately able to participate in the distinctive language of science. Texts carefully selected by the teacher will address the phenomena students have been exploring. The students should be encouraged to discuss the contents of the text and compare the text to information from other texts and from their firsthand experiences. The students are able to collaborate with others as they construct shared explanations for what they have been investigating. Although this may require considerable teacher direction for young readers or those who are still developing fluency in English, the thoughtful teacher can guide his or her students as they try out the patterns of communication characteristic of the culture of science.

Reading in Diverse Classrooms

When integrating reading into science lessons, teachers use texts as tools that support students' sense making but don't drive that learning. Using texts in this manner is particularly useful for students who are learning English or students with cognitive limitations, as the learning experiences are **multimodal.** One mode is to learn by reading. Another mode is to learn by listening. Yet another mode is to learn by physically manipulating objects. When science learning relies on multiple modes, reading can be seen as one of many pathways that support students' science learning. With this more prudent approach for reading, where texts are seen as simply one source of knowledge, teachers should be willing to use texts as one of several varied sources of information. Through multiple modes, students have a variety of ways to interact with and think about the materials and events they have been exploring.

Reading informational text such as textbooks is a much different activity from reading narrative picture books (Yore, 2004). Because informational texts are essential to the doing of science, all students need to be taught how to read such texts. This implies that teachers need to supply instruction about using reading strategies as the students approach informational text. Here are some guidelines. When reading informational material, the student should first scan the text to answer the following questions: What question do I hope to have answered by reading this text? What are the headings telling me? What information is included in the graphs, charts, and illustrations? After scanning the text, the student should carefully read it as he or she asks, "How does what the text is saying compare to what I already know and what I've read elsewhere?" This process of reviewing the book, asking questions, then thoroughly reading the text assists comprehension of the material. This approach also enhances the meaning students construct from their reading. These reading strategies need to be explicitly taught within the context of science and not left to chance.

In addition to developing appropriate reading strategies in the science classroom, teachers should pay careful attention to the needs of students learning English, students who may have some cognitive disabilities, or students who, for whatever reason, have been unable to acquire the knowledge necessary to make sense of informational texts. Our advocacy for inductive instruction, always moving from the concrete to the abstract, increases the likelihood that students will comprehend informational texts. By choosing to begin with the students having direct physical experiences with materials, a teacher is helping his or her students to build the cognitive structures necessary to better comprehend text. The explorations provide a foundation and raise questions. Texts are potential sources of answers to those self-generated questions. To further optimize the learning of all students, the teacher might find it helpful to employ other adaptations as well.

Selecting Appropriate Text Resources

As teachers gather texts to be used in concert with their science teaching, they need to consider the individual learners in their classroom. In addition to locating texts addressing the targeted science concepts, we should be taking into account the reading level of each book. If the content of a book is valuable but the reading level appears too advanced, then the students may require complementary readings, that is, texts that use more straightforward language to convey meaning. However, there is a tension to recognize here—second-language learners require texts that use simpler sentence structure to convey information but that don't water down the meaning. For instance, as authors of the book you are reading, we felt it was important for us to write in a style familiar to you as college students. For that we have tried to use everyday language wherever possible. Although many of the ideas we have discussed originated within educational research articles, we have avoided duplicating the dense vocabulary used by the research community. This community also tends to include extensive citations of other authors' work within the text. In our effort to make our ideas more accessible to you, we have tried to keep that practice to a minimum. This is not to say that we've simplified what you are reading. Instead we have deliberately chosen a writing style that serves the needs of our readers: those who are learning to become effective teachers of science.

The goal when selecting texts is to find a balance between simplicity of expression and complexity of content. This is the challenge of incorporating reading with science for English language learners. For instance some teachers of students learning English elect to provide science texts pitched at lower grades. However, the conceptual level of such texts is often lower as well. Though such texts will still help developing readers gain literacy skills, they reduce scientific knowledge to a more simplistic level. For example a sixth grader who is reading at the second-grade level needs a text that is simply written but addresses concepts appropriate to his or her age. Although textbooks from earlier grades may be seen as useful reading resources for English-language learners, these texts need to be augmented with other texts that convey the concepts at the appropriately challenging age level. This is why having a wealth of texts accessible in a classroom is so vital. Nevertheless, for students with cognitive disabilities, very basic texts may be an ideal resource, because they provide an entry point for formulating explanations of scientific ideas.

Providing texts written at the appropriate reading level that also provide scientific explanations at a suitable cognitive level will be a persistent challenge for teachers. You will almost certainly find yourself asking questions such as "Why can't anybody write a science book about light and sound that my ESL students can handle?" One approach to consider is to recruit the assistance of bilingual individuals to create supporting texts. Although this might involve classroom aides, having other students create these materials might serve multiple purposes. Constructing such classroom texts can prove useful as a learning opportunity for both the students helping to produce it and the students consuming it.

The increasingly common use of a word wall by teachers also supports the integration of reading with science. Quite simply a word wall is an area where particular words are written on cards for students to consult. We all have had that experience when a name, title, or word won't come to mind. The word wall is a place where teachers and students contribute to an ongoing display of important words and, as such, becomes another source of textual support throughout science lessons. For example during the Explore phase portion of the learning cycle when students are creating written observations, as well as during the Explain phase when students are transferring oral explanations into writing, the word wall helps students choose the right words, and it provides the correct spellings. Posting the major words included in the scientific explanation for a phenomenon can support students as they transfer what they are beginning to understand into a written format. Word walls can include translations of terms to languages other than English, not only as a way to support students' understandings but also as a clear way to honor students' home cultures.

For Reflection and Discussion

Not everyone in education endorses the use of word walls. Such critics view these displays as crutches, a complaint that parallels the issue of calculator use in math lessons. How might the conscientious teacher explain to students and parents that resources such as word walls actually support children's learning rather than function as shortcuts to avoid learning?

Writing to Show and Writing to Learn

Scientific writing gives students a way to express scientific explanations. But the value to learning science that comes from writing goes beyond the final product. Scientific writing is much more than a journal entry or paragraph summary. We write to express our understandings and to understand. In this way writing about science is about the products and the processes. Students or scientists can use writing to express what they discover—this is a product of their studies. But from a learning perspective, what is even more powerful is the struggle to create a written explanation that may not yet be fully formed. The writing of the idea actually helps to clarify understanding, and this is where writing becomes a process for learning science. That said, we write within science to learn how to write scientifically and to refine the scientific action of communication. Writing is vital to students' science learning, because it supports their developing understandings and refines their scientific communication skills.

Perhaps the least appreciated benefit of writing is that it can foster **metacognition.** Metacognition describes an individual's conscious awareness of what she or he knows. Questions such as "Do I understand this?" "Does this make sense?" and "What do I still need to know?" are metacognitive questions. Put another way, *cognition* describes what you know, whereas *metacognition* describes what you know about what you know. The act of writing can encourage students to think metacognitively. As their teacher, you can help to make them aware of this. As students think about what they are attempting to write, they can recognize the development and refinement of their understandings. The result is that the students are writing what is known, writing to help clarify what is known, and thinking about their knowledge as they go about their writing. All of this helps them become more successful in their science learning. Writing is particularly important in inquiry science, as students need to keep track of what they know, what happened, and what they still need to learn.

Writing Strategies Within Science Instruction

Throughout this section, when we discuss "writing," we include any means of inscription by the student—written words, drawings, graphs, and so on. Students in elementary school and middle school sometimes have difficulty writing in the traditional format. It is challenging to express observations and explanations with words. In addition other forms of inscriptions are simply undervalued within science teaching. Because the process of writing helps an individual to learn, having multiple ways of writing means there are a variety of pathways toward understanding. If we, as teachers of science, rely on writing only as an end product, as in a form of assessment, then we are not using writing to its appropriate advantage. Fortunately, there are many ways to employ writing to enhance students' science learning. What we present next is a handful of strategies that can support an atmosphere in the classroom of writing science to learn science.

One-Minute Takes

In this writing task students are provided sixty seconds to write a response to a particular prompt. An uninterrupted opportunity to write allows students the mental space to establish their current thinking about a phenomenon. Because the task is only one-minute in duration, there is not too much pressure on the students to write a great deal. There is also no suggestion that they need to produce the right answer but to simply write about what they are thinking right now. A **one-minute take** begins with a question that is focused on a specific situation but phrased in a very open-ended way:

- How would you explain what happened to the water that was in this jar?
- Should bats be classified as mammals or birds? Explain your thinking.
- Consider a tree; what is the source of the material that makes up the wood?

The teacher can speak these prompts, but in diverse classrooms the teacher also needs to post them in a written format. Even better is to include appropriate visual cues in the prompts, such as a simple sketch of the phenomenon, to assist students' thinking. The goal of these prompts is not evaluation. Instead the goal of one-minute takes is for students to pull together their ideas, solidify their thoughts, and then provide the teacher with a view of this construction process. The teacher can invite students to share what they wrote. Or the teacher can gather the papers on which the students have written the one-minute take to read and consider as he or she prepares for subsequent science lessons.

Understandably, there are teachers in diverse classrooms who may hesitate to make such assignments, because English language learners are often not confident with their writing. This also applies to students with cognitive disabilities. But to these teachers we say that one-minute takes should be viewed as tools for helping students to learn and not as methods for assessing the correctness of knowledge. Each of us has been in a situation where there is so much information coming at us that we wish we could press a pause button so we could gather our thoughts, which is what a one-minute take provides to students who are learning English or who often struggle in science. Avoiding tasks such as the one-minute take fails those students who require extra time to pull together their thoughts. Once the anxiety of being expected to write is diminished, and this happens simply by frequently using one-minute takes, the students have a wonderful opportunity to construct ideas.

The brief and focused work involved with composing a one-minute take supports individual student metacognition. The writing helps them to formulate their ideas and to recognize what they know. Offering ideas orally is intimidating for culturally and linguistically diverse students and for those with cognitive limitations. Clarifying thinking, transferring those still-forming thoughts into words, and then speaking out loud to a waiting audience can be terrifying. This struggle may not even help them to learn science, because they are so overwhelmed by the pressure to perform in the moment. By giving the students time to write out their ideas, the teacher offers everyone a sheltered space to think. The time, the quiet, and the anonymity permit all students, regardless of their English fluency, cultural background, or cognitive abilities, to generate a personal response to a prompt. One-minute takes do not have to be in the form of written words. Very important ideas may be communicated with illustrations. But making a decision about allowing students to draw rather than to write should be for the purpose of helping them to make their understanding clear not to allow them simply to draw. The goal is not for every student to create something to share. The purpose is to push students to translate their ideas into a written form that can be shared or assessed by others.

In some settings allowing students to talk about their thoughts before they write them down can enhance the usefulness of the one-minute takes. This is akin to the cooperative learning strategy called "think-pair-share." A teacher can provide the students with a prompt (orally and in text), invite students to silently and individually think about it, then direct them to discuss the prompt with a partner, and finally request that they write their ideas down. This is an expanded version of the one-minute take. For many students it is less threatening for them to offer a jointly produced idea than simply their own thoughts. The conversation with a partner gives the students the time to rehearse the expression of their ideas. As a modification of the think-pair-share from cooperative learning, speaking with one's peers helps students to articulate their ideas. This also allows them to become more aware of other perspectives. When it comes time to share their thoughts with the whole class, the students have already had time to rehearse the phrasing of their ideas. The result is more widespread participation and more substantive contributions within a nonthreatening class discussion.

Concept Maps as an Alternative Form of Writing

Concept maps are another way in which students can use writing to solidify their science ideas. Unlike traditional ways of inscription and the one-minute takes we have already examined, concept maps are less closely tied to a student's literacy skills. This is because concept maps provide a visual way to represent understandings (see Figure 10.1). Freed from the linearity of sentences, students can use concept maps to show the interrelationships among concepts as a multidimensional representation. In addition because concept maps are not constrained by the rules of grammar and sentence structure, the process of writing a concept map allows for a more natural outpouring of ideas. Not having to worry about punctuation, capitalization, and so on reduces the need to edit thought while creating a concept map. The result can be a concept map that is a more accurate representation of a student's thinking than would be possible in a more traditional written format. That said, we must acknowledge that learning to produce a concept map is a skill. There is an admitted investment of training time that must be given so students become skilled with creating concept maps. As with most other intellectual skills, the more frequently the skill is used, the more proficient individuals become at using them. But first we will provide some details about concept maps and suggestions about how to construct them.

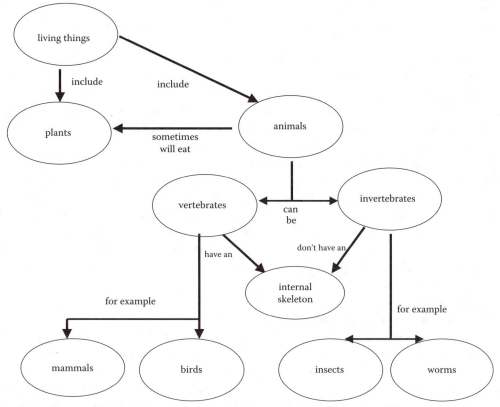

FIGURE 10.1. This figure shows a sample concept map about animals.

You may be familiar with word webs in which an idea appears in the center and other associated ideas radiate outward. Concept maps are distinct from word webs in a very significant way. In word webs, two ideas are simply connected with a line. In contrast a concept map uses arrows to connect concepts, and those linking arrows are labeled with a word or phrase. The result is that each pair of concepts, along with the linking words, creates an understandable combination in the form of a phrase.

Concept maps represent an individual's understandings about a concept and its relationship to other concepts. A concept map, as described by Joseph Novak (1999) and Jim Wandersee (1990) and others, is a schematic (a visual representation) showing how concepts are related to each other. In these maps all concepts must be related to others in ways that specify the nature of the relationships. Some researchers advocate for the map being organized in a hierarchy, with the most general concept at the top, moving toward the more specific ideas and examples at the bottom. By producing maps in this way, students begin to analyze how concepts are related to one other, moving beyond memorized definitions. But unlike other word maps or spider charts, concept maps require that students follow certain design rules to produce one.

Teaching Students to Create Concept Maps

To create their first concept map, students should work from a list of terms with which they are familiar. The teacher can supply the terms, and the list shouldn't be longer than ten terms. Students write these terms on index cards or sticky notes so that they can move the terms around as they create connections between ideas. At this point the teacher models for the class how to create a linking phrase that sensibly joins two terms. There are a few guidelines. First, the phrase involves only two terms and the linking phrase. There is no incentive to string together several terms into a long sentence. Second, the linking words should be brief. The connections between one term and another might be words such as "is an example of," "is also called," or "happens after," and so on. Finally, the connection between terms has a direction (and this is a major difference from word webs). The arrow shows the sequence of the phrase: first term, then linking phrase, then the second term. After thinking about how to create combinations of two terms and a linking phrase, the students can begin the real construction of the concept map.

The sticky notes or index cards are attached to a larger piece of paper. The relationships between terms are shown with an arrow, and the linking words are written on this arrow. Sometimes this may create a concept map that looks like a string of beads, and that's OK. But when a concept map has many connections between the terms and looks more like a net, it shows that the maker of the map is aware of the multiple relationships between the terms. If the resulting map is accurate (the connections are sensible) and the format is correct (the terms and their linking words create an understandable phrase), then complex maps are generally viewed as superior to linear maps.

All concept maps should be regarded as works in progress. As we become more knowledgeable about a topic, the organization and complexity of our understandings improve. A concept map is likely to show that change. Your initial response to concept maps is likely that you will love them or hate them. Your reaction probably has a great deal to do with how well you feel that this form of writing accurately represents your understandings. Put another way, you may like concept maps if you imagine that your thinking is organized in that way. In contrast if you are skeptical about concept maps as a way of writing, it may be because you don't feel it is an accurate way of showing how your thinking is organized. It is likely that your students will have similar reactions, although in general it seems that concept mapping is more quickly embraced by children than by adults.

Your Chance to Make a Concept Map

John Dewey (1938) wrote in his book *Experience and Education,* "Growth depends upon the presence of difficulty to be overcome by the exercise of intelligence" (p. 79). The difficulty we are creating for you is the challenge of making a concept map. According to Dewey you can overcome this difficulty through the use of your intellect—and this represents your growth. If you find this exercise frustrating, then your growth will be that much greater once you figure out how to construct the concept map. The following is the list of terms to include in your concept map. Your task is to show how you understand the connections between these terms. If you wish to add additional terms, you may. But you must use all of the terms in this list.

APPLE	BREAD	CARBOHYDRATE	CHEESE	MILK
EGG	FRUIT	OATMEAL	ORANGE JUICE	PEACH
PEANUT BUTTER	PROTEIN	SYRUP	TURKEY	YOGURT

You should begin by deciding which concepts are more important or inclusive and move them toward the top. Then you should decide how to connect pairs of terms with appropriate linking words. Recognize that there is a sequence to how the combinations are read. The result should be a phrase that makes sense when read out loud. See what you can invent for these combinations:

PEANUT BUTTER _____ BREAD
CHEESE _____ MILK
PROTEIN _____ TURKEY

Don't worry about guessing the right answer. Instead use linking words to create a sensible phrase that accurately represents your thinking. Continue selecting pairs of concepts and develop directional linking phrases that join the concepts to each other. There is really no limit to the number of combinations you can generate.

Now you are ready to create a concept map. You can copy these words onto sticky notes, or you may be bold enough to just start writing directly onto a blank sheet of paper. Place the concepts from the original list inside ovals and then draw arrows from one term to the next. Remember to write the linking phrases on arrows so they create meaningful phrases. Do not try to invent very long combinations, such as oatmeal with apple and a glass of milk has lots of carbohydrates and protein—your concept map consists of many paired terms, not long strings.

You will probably notice that your concept map quickly becomes a web of connecting links. Don't let that worry you. At first you should focus on showing how terms are related to each other, no matter how messy your work becomes. At some point you may notice that certain terms can be moved to a more central location or even to the very top of the map if they are more important or more inclusive concepts. That is how you can revise your map. The connections will stay the same, but you will just move the pieces around.

When you have finished, compare your concept map with other people's maps. See if you can understand their thinking by reading their map. Even though their work may be different from yours, you will probably see some consistency. You may notice that even though their way of thinking is different from yours, you can still understand their thought processes by examining their concept map.

Usefulness of Concept Maps

Concept maps can become an excellent metacognitive tool for students. By taking their ideas and trying to represent them on paper, the students can begin to recognize just how it is that they think. The realizations that come with knowing what it is that you know, the definition of metacognition, help students to become more empowered about their learning. After all when we are aware of the gaps in our understandings, we gain added incentive to pursue the information that will fill those gaps. Concept maps aren't intended to show students how little they know. Instead the process of creating a concept map can clarify an individual's understandings. As a result concept mapping can serve as a very powerful tool to support a student's learning of science.

Another useful aspect of concept maps is the way in which they can inform teachers about their students. Once students develop their skills with correctly using all of the key features of concept maps (e.g., always labeling the links), they can create maps that reveal to the teacher their understanding of a science topic. Imagine how much more confident you will be about your teaching if you know from the outset what your students already understand and the parts of their science learning that are incomplete. Sometimes teachers use a prewriting activity to assess their students. Concept maps can serve a similar purpose, and this is why we treat concept mapping as a form of writing. By having students create concept maps on a specific topic, the teacher can obtain a clear sense about their prior knowledge.

To this point we've emphasized concept mapping as a tool for gaining insights into students' thinking at a particular point in time. The term *preassessment* should, in turn, suggest the idea of a postassessment. Concept maps can also be an activity students perform at the conclusion of a science unit. There are several reasons for doing this. For one, the students can compare their initial and final concept maps to become aware of the evolution of their thinking. Perhaps you can imagine what it would be like to be an elementary or middle school student and have the opportunity to see the changes in your thinking by comparing maps before and after a unit. Talk about metacognition!

As much as we want to believe that students learn everything we try to teach, we must admit that we aren't perfect as teachers. In fact recognizing our fallibility is one characteristic that Haberman (1995) suggested separates great teachers of diverse students from those teachers who are just adequate. Recognizing that you can make mistakes as a teacher and constantly strive to recover from those failings is significant. If you use preconcept and postconcept mapping exercises with your students and you discover that some of the gaps appearing at the beginning persisted until the end, then you have a couple of ways of responding. One thought that too many teachers invoke is that the kids were lazy and didn't care. But for teachers who are able to accept their potential fallibility, the disappointment about the results translates into clearly identified areas for improvement. As odd as this may sound, when you suspect that you have the potential to improve your teaching, assessment results can help clear up any confusion about where you might begin to make changes.

At some point you might wonder about judging or grading students' concept maps. After all it seems that you'd be very subjective in deciding whose map is accurate and whose might not be that good. There are some methods educational researchers have developed for assigning a numerical score to concept maps (Novak, 1999). However, what is useful information from a researcher's perspective may not be all that useful to the classroom teacher. Some researchers have been quite clear in saying that a sophisticated concept map scoring system may be too complicated to be practical from a teaching perspective (Rice, Ryan, & Samson, 1998). What we find interesting is that researchers have compared different ways of scoring concept maps. In some instances very specific rubrics were used to determine point values, whereas other rubrics relied on holistic grading where scorers assigned a point value based on a sense about the entire concept map. Using a detailed rubric is much more time-consuming but sometimes seems to be more objective than deriving scores based on intuition. It turns out that analytic grading versus holistic grading leads to about the same scores. As a consequence it doesn't seem necessary to use a complicated method to create a fair and dependable score for a concept map (McClure, Sonak, & Suen, 1999). Given the finite amount of time teachers have for grading, we cannot in good conscience recommend that teachers regularly use a complex rubric to derive scores for concept maps. We will provide in the next chapter a more comprehensive discussion of assessing students' science learning.

Finally, the greatest utility of concept map is the benefit it provides to the mapper—the person producing the map. It allows the mapper to organize his/her thoughts and allows for metaorganization. All these benefits are lost when students are asked to complete predrawn maps. These predrawn maps, found in many science textbooks, actually become fancy fill-in-the-blank exercises, and are of little use for either knowledge organization or metaorganization.

Science Notebooks: Journals for Science Knowledge

Individual science journals are a prominent form of writing within the work of scientists. Professional scientists write in their journals for the purposes we associate with classroom science writing. The journals serve as a record of what is known and are an opportunity to try to make sense of what is not completely understood. Many researchers in education promote science notebooks as deserving a prominent role in today's science classrooms. The rationale is that when students maintain science notebooks, their understandings of the science improve even as their writing skills are strengthened. Furthermore, keeping a science notebook is consistent with the culture of science as practiced by those who are making a career of science.

Science notebooks are not universally used in elementary and middle school classrooms, and a teacher needs to give careful thought to how these will be used. One basic decision the teacher must make, and then act on, is to determine when the students are to write in their science notebooks. At the very least it seems that students would be expected to record observations in their science notebooks. But for teachers who see value in having their students reflect on what they are thinking, they must provide time during class for this writing. This sends the message that says, "Reflecting and writing about what you know is so very important that we are going to devote some of the precious time we have in class for this kind of activity." Students will quickly catch on to the value you, as their science teacher, place on writing. If you reserve reflective writing to homework or study hall, then you are inadvertently sending the message that other tasks are more valuable than reflection.

If students are to go beyond using their science notebooks only as a record book for their investigations, then the teacher will need to provide guidance for their writing. Being able to think deeply about activities and their significance is not something that teachers can leave to chance. Learning to write in ways that support science inquiry will benefit students by providing a framework that will scaffold their writing. Toward this end, the *science writing heuristic* can provide some assistance (Wallace, Hand, & Yang, 2004). A **heuristic** describes a teaching method or technique that guides students to make sense of information on their own. Think of a heuristic as a road map or tip sheet that students can refer to when they need help with remembering the steps of a procedure. A writing heuristic gives students hints about how to create an appropriate piece of writing. A science writing heuristic provides the guidance to assist students to write in a scientifically appropriate way. In this way the following *The Science Writing Heuristic* (Wallace et al., 2004, p. 357) provides a scaffold for students as they learn to write in a way that is consistent with the culture of science:

The Science Writing Heuristic (Wallace, Hand, & Yang, 2004)

1. Beginning ideas—What are my questions?
2. Test/experiments—What did I do?
3. Observations—What did I see?
4. Claims—What can I claim?
5. Evidence—How do I know? Why am I making these claims?
6. Reading—What do my ideas compare with other ideas?
7. Reflection—How have my ideas changed?

Although we might recognize a piece of writing as being scientific, it doesn't mean we understand how to write in that way. The same applies to students. The *Science Writing Heuristic* so helpfully provides prompts to address and questions to answer that will lead to an effective piece of writing. It is no coincidence that the *Science Writing Heuristic* leads students (and their teacher) to address all of the essential features of inquiry. Best of all we don't leave the students to figure out on their own or by trial and error how to write in scientifically appropriate fashion. The *Science Writing Heuristic* makes it quite clear the sorts of information and insights that are necessary. It even supplies the appropriate sequence for providing that information.

By following the *Science Writing Heuristic* as they write, students will recognize that inquiry activities are not cookbook recipes. Instead they will appreciate the necessary components of an effective inquiry and the relationships among those components. Although not reinforcing the myth of the scientific method, this approach will reinforce the standards of scientific practice. This includes the need to provide evidence to support every claim. In addition data must be gathered in a systematic fashion. Also the inferential jump from evidence to explanation must be logical—wild explanations have no place if no data exist to support such ideas. The final questions in the *Science Writing Heuristic* encourage students to become metacognitive about their knowledge. Through the use of the *Science Writing Heuristic,* students not only construct more robust scientific understandings but also become more conversant (writing, thinking, and talking) with scientific communication. Consequently, they express themselves in a manner consistent with the conventions of the culture of science. Finally, the metacognition required by such work makes students explicitly aware of their knowledge growth and provides a clearer sense that the scientific knowledge is tentative and open to revision.

Earlier in this book we described an inquiry activity involving pendulums. Imagine that we wanted to extend this activity and use it for a writing exercise. Let's consult the *Science Writing Heuristic* as we consider how to apply that technique to this particular activity. There is no single best way to approach this task, but we'll propose one that we've used as one possibility. For the sake of discussion, we are going to assume that a class has already performed a study about pendulum behavior and entered their data onto a record sheet. Using the *Science Writing Heuristic*, a student would be expected to generate a piece of writing such as the following. We have inserted numbers corresponding to the prompts from the *Science Writing Heuristic*.

Our question for this experiment was about pendulums. 1. We were trying to see if the length of the string made a difference in the pendulum swinging. I thought that making the string shorter would make the pendulum swing a little bit faster. 2. What we did was measure the string and let it swing for thirty seconds. We did it three times at 15 cm and did it the same way except for a longer string for 30 cm and 45 cm. 3. We observed that the pendulum was speedier when we had a short string. 4. So we concluded that when the string is longer the pendulum goes slower. 5. Our evidence is our data in the chart. All the 15 cm measurements are close together. This is when we had the most counts in 30 seconds. We did it more than once just to be sure. Every single time we made the string longer, we didn't count as many swings. 6. On the Internet we found something about the pendulum in old clocks. When they want to make the clock run slower, they make the pendulum longer. 7. That's just like what we found out except we were using a string and a washer. This is pretty much what I expected. Except the length made a bigger difference. The longer string really didn't have that many swings in 30 seconds. But my ideas were right.

The idea of having children use a science notebook can be intimidating to a new teacher. You might wonder if this is too ambitious for very young students. Or you might have some uncertainties about trying to use science notebooks with English language learners. Although we appreciate these concerns, the reality is that many teachers have used science notebooks in extremely diverse settings, even with kindergartners. Obviously a five-year-old won't be able to use the *Science Writing Heuristic*, but you should be able to make an instructional decision about this situation. If you are committed to helping every student, regardless of background or cognitive ability, to learn science, then you are interested in finding ways to make this happen. As we've described in this chapter, reading and writing play exceedingly valuable roles in science learning. The decision you need to make specific to science notebooks is not about if students are capable of writing in science notebooks. There is plenty of evidence that they can. The decision you need to make is about how you are going to try to use the notebooks as a central piece of your science teaching.

Here are some guidelines that will help with your decision making about science notebooks. One guideline is that you must be clear to students about the style of writing that you expect for them to include. If you are a teacher who has students using multiple notebooks, then you might want to restrict the science notebook to very specific uses. You may choose to not use the science notebook for creative writing tasks. It is necessary for students to recognize when they are expected to write scientifically and when they are expected to write in other ways. Science has distinctive ways of thinking. A science notebook that reflects the special objects and actions of science can serve as a tangible reminder of the unusual culture of science. Students will not receive as clear a message if they use one notebook for all of their writing, drawing, and so on across all of their subject areas. This is all to say that the teacher must be explicit in how she or he intends for students to write within their science notebooks.

Several years ago Herbert Walberg (1984) conducted a study in which he examined thousands of studies to assess which instructional factors contributed to student achievement. He was able to find data on two different types of homework: homework that the teacher grades and homework that is simply assigned. He found that how students' homework was graded had a very significant influence on their learning. In contrast when homework was assigned but not graded, there was not much benefit. Practically speaking, according to Walberg's research, assigning homework that the students know will not be graded is not worth the trouble. This applies to assigning students to write in their science notebooks. Unless the teacher provides feedback about the writing, the notebooks lose a great deal of power. If a teacher reads but not necessarily grades students' science notebooks, then he or she can guide the development of student writing and scientific thinking. To provide some feedback is necessary should you decide to not assign a grade, but this feedback should be substantive and not just a checkmark or a sticker. The feedback can take the form of questions such as "How did you use your data to come up with that explanation?" or "How well do your conclusions match with what you read in the book?" These prompts reinforce the *Science Writing Heuristic* and guide students to become more proficient at writing (and hence thinking) in ways appropriate to the culture of science. Certainly the use of such notebooks is neither simple nor effortless, but the gains in scientific understandings, patterns of reasoning, and moves toward communicating scientifically can be remarkable.

For Reflection and Discussion

Providing feedback to students, of which grading is just one example, is a burden that those outside of education may not adequately appreciate. However, there is no substitute for a thoughtful comment or well-timed question. What are some strategies teachers can use to ensure that students are receiving regular written feedback on their science notebooks and to distribute the work so it becomes manageable?

Other Means of Inscription

The reading and writing activities we have examined rely heavily on students using words. However, there are occasions when words are simply insufficient to express understandings, including those instances when a student does not possess the basic literacy skills that permit written expression. When teachers want students to communicate other than by writing or speaking, they can assign drawings as a useful method of expression. Having students draw what they know, in place of the written word, can allow a teacher access to students' understandings. We need to remind ourselves that students may know more than they can say or write. A toddler may not be able to say *gorilla* or *elephant,* but they can show through gestures or noises that they recognize these animals in a storybook. Students who are still developing their English fluency but are not yet able to verbalize their understandings may be able to reveal a firm grasp of material through drawings. Interestingly, there are students who we might feel are able to write or verbalize seemingly clear understandings of a concept, but when we ask them to illustrate their understandings, they may reveal an underlying misconception. Thus having students create drawings of what they observe or what they understand, and not just as pretty pictures, provides unique insights into what students understand about a scientific topic. Drawings can be particularly useful for nontraditional students who understand the material but struggle to represent their knowledge through more written or oral means of expression.

Producing and Reading Graphs

Graphs are another form of literacy used to communicate information. Because graphs are so common to science, it is important for students to develop the skills to create and interpret graphs. Knowing how to create graphs is similar to knowing how to create a descriptive paragraph. For both means of inscription, there are traditional standards that are followed. Knowing those standards helps us recognize what the graph is capable of showing. In addition, inasmuch as we wish to guide students to be competent participants in the culture of science, we ought to assist them to not only read graphs but also create them as well. In this regard **graphical literacy** describes proficiency with not only acting as a consumer of graphs but also having some measure of skill at producing graphs. As with English literacy or what mathematicians call *numeracy,* the goal is not for students to simply receive information but for them to be able to produce information consistent with that literacy. The guidelines we will apply to graphical literacy are parallel to other forms of literacy.

NSES Program Standard C: The science program should be coordinated with the mathematics program to enhance student use and understanding of mathematics in the study of science and to improve student understanding of mathematics.

First, learning to communicate requires being exposed to good examples. Exposure to a range of high-quality models helps students to grasp the format and the information, whether it's a paragraph of explanatory text or a graph of experimental data. Graphs will seem to pop up in lots of places once you begin looking for them. Almost every newspaper has graphs associated with the weather, and if you have the time to look at several sources, you will see just how varied the graphs can be, not only in their design but also in the data being represented. Help your students to recognize the wide variety of graphs in the same way as you display colorful book covers. Posting graphs for all to see is a way to draw students into that form of communication.

Second, graphs and texts come in a variety of forms. A graph can be composed of columns, lines, or wedges of a pie. Knowing what each style represents, and when each form is appropriate to use, is also part of becoming graphically literate. Both words and graphs make use of abstractions as shortcuts to represent bigger ideas. In a story the lead character may not be referred to by his or her name—that's where pronouns are brief and welcomed substitutes. Similarly a graph does not necessarily display every single piece of data. Oftentimes graphs display only summaries, in the forms of averages, to represent bigger sets of data.

Third, there is no magic technique for developing graphical literacy. Just as with reading, some students catch on faster than others. Understanding which type of graph to use and being able to interpret what a graph is representing are things that can come only through experience. The experience may begin with very concrete representations, such as when a kindergarten class lines up according to height. This may become more abstract when register tape is cut to the same length as each individual and displayed on the wall. Again, starting with direct experiences lays an important foundation for more abstract and generalized understandings.

Finally, graphical literacy should serve similar purposes to traditional notions of literacy. Graphing should not be done just for the sake of learning how to do it. The graph should be used to help facilitate the communication of ideas, if not the telling of a story. Graphs are no more useful than the extent to which they help in transmitting information and ideas from one person to another. Once students develop their graphical literacy, they will take control of their use and will recognize when a graphical representation of information is superior to any of the other options available to them.

Putting It Together in a Diverse Classroom

We are advocating for a relationship between the language arts and science that is much more powerful than simply another opportunity for thematic teaching. Instead guiding students to communicate within the culture of science is a crucial part of learning science. This is because the work of science is so heavily dependent on writing, reading, drawing, and graphing. Because doing science relies on communication, the science classroom must foster the development of the varied communication skills. As important, by taking part in the act of communicating to create explanations for others, with written words or graphs, students develop deeper understanding of the objects of science. Along the way they become fluent in the actions of science, especially in the particular ways of communicating scientifically. Students should be making presentations and composing written explanations not only to practice actions of science but also to better comprehend science content. We must remember that communication is as much about constructing better ideas as it is about sharing those ideas and learning how to share those ideas in a manner that is fitting within the culture of science.

For diverse learners we are obligated to arrange for our science lessons to become opportunities for them to develop a variety of literacies. A great deal of learning happens through observing models and then learning how to mimic those exemplars. Models can take the form of role models in which a novice notes how experts go about their work. We can learn how to kick a ball, generate a piece of artwork, or create a building by first watching how it is done by those who have been refining their practice for years. Models are also in the form of the products of experts' work: a graceful movement, an inspiring painting, or a solid house—each reflects the expert's skills. This idea of an apprenticeship (Collins, Brown, & Holum, 1991) can be applied to developing students' science learning. Larry Yore's phrase "do first, read later" is a clear message about how this can be accomplished when it comes to integrating science and the language arts.

It is an oversimplification of learning for teachers to claim that the basics must happen first. This is a common mistake that teachers make with culturally and linguistically diverse students. There is an odd assumption that such students cannot be expected to learn science until they have mastered the basics of reading and writing. From what we've described in this chapter, you should recognize that such a mind-set not only excludes students from the opportunity to learn science but also compromises potential avenues for reinforcing English literacy. When we hear a claim that science is just too abstract for children, we cannot help but wonder what makes concepts such as weather, weight, or heat abstract compared to nonscience themes such as friendship, fear, or loneliness. We are urging you to consider the wealth of evidence showing that the language arts and science can actually help support each other rather than compete against each other for class time and students' attention.

English Language Learners and Science Integration

We return to the *Five Principles* for *Effective Pedagogy* we considered in earlier chapters. The Center for Research on Education, Diversity, and Excellence devised these principles to guide the teaching of diverse students about academic subject matter. We have relied on these principles to shape our understandings about appropriate responses for teaching science to students who are English language learners (Dalton, 1998). Although we have already covered the essence of the five principles in previous chapters, we return to those principles to consider their implications as part of the prospect of integrating science with other subjects, especially the language arts.

Promoting English Fluency During Science Integration

Quite simply the means by which students will develop English fluency is by using the language in ways that help them understand the subject matter. In relation to science, second-language learners are encouraged to develop their English fluency as they simultaneously work to comprehend the subject matter (see Table 10.1). It seems to be a kindness to shield English language

TABLE 10.1. Integrating Science to Promote Fluency, and Appropriate Teacher Actions

By having students participate in discussions and communicating through writing, the teacher relies on modeling, probing, restating, and other strategies to sustain development of English fluency.
Using utterances and listening, and reading and writing, the teacher helps students build linkages between the subject matter and their language proficiency.
As students express their ideas and understanding, the teacher promotes the use of specific subject matter terminology.

Note: Adapted from Dalton (1998).

learners from potential embarrassment by not expecting them to participate in science discussion or not requiring them to generate written text. However, such actions, despite their apparent compassion, are in reality detrimental to the students. Not only are the students not held to appropriate academic standards but also because their opportunities to hone their written and oral language are diminished, they are less likely to develop English proficiency.

There is no true secret to integrating science so it supports the language development of students who are not yet fluent in English. The key seems to be for teachers to accept that the supposed goodwill of not holding English-language learners to appropriate standards of written and oral communication is perhaps one of the larger barriers to their potential success. As teachers we must be very cautious to avoid thinking that being accommodating and generous toward students who are working toward English proficiency includes reducing expectations for their written abilities or opportunities to participate in class science discussions.

Chapter Summary

- Thematic teaching is effective only if the theme promotes the learning of fundamental aspects of the academic disciplines. If themes are to be used, they should be selected on the basis of how well they make sense for students to learn content, not by how many activities can be included.

- When science and the language arts are thoughtfully integrated, the study of one can enhance learning in the other. In this way reading and writing can advance students' science understandings and vice versa. Also there are specific features of scientific reading and writing that can be included in the culture of science.

- The sequence of reading activities within science is consistent with the inductive approach used within the learning cycle. Reading should serve as a support for scientific understandings and should be used after students have begun to experience objects and equipment firsthand.

- Science informational texts are sufficiently different from stories that teachers need to scaffold students' access to this form of writing. The writing style of scientific informational texts is just one more dimension of the science culture. Learning to write with a scientific purpose can assist students to become more metacognitive about their science learning.

- Literacy as it is integrated with science becomes more than simply reading about a science topic. Also to be included are opportunities for students to write about their experiences, to create concept maps illustrating their understandings, to generate graphs to summarize their observations, and to participate in conversations in which they rehearse and refine their skills with talking scientifically.

Key Terms

Concept maps: schematic (visual) representations of an individual's understandings about a concept and its relationship to other concepts.

Graphical literacy: the ability to accurately generate and interpret graphs of data.

Heuristic: a tool or technique that guides individuals to complete a task or solve a problem on their own.

Interdisciplinary curriculum: combination of multiple subject areas into an integrated study of a central organizing topic.

Metacognition: an individual's conscious awareness of what she or he knows. Some instructional practices, such as journaling and concept mapping, support the development of students' metacognition.

Multimodal: employs providing for different forms of experiences to support student learning, including reading, listening, discussing, and doing physical activity.

One-minute take: a writing activity in which the learner writes about his or her understandings of a particular phenomenon within a sixty-second interval.

A Favorite Science Lesson

The unit by the Education Development Center called the "Mysterious Powder" is designed for students in grade four or grade five to participate in kitchen chemistry activities. Perhaps the most exciting lesson in this unit is "Solving the Problem of the Mysterious Powder in the School Yard." Having spent several previous lessons learning how to identify powders (baking soda, cornstarch, citric acid, etc.) using a variety of indicators (vinegar, iodine, etc.), students in this lesson are required to use all their prior knowledge to identify an unknown. There is a great deal of equipment involved in this lesson, but it effectively builds on all the other skills and knowledge the students have been acquiring over the preceding weeks. The fictional scenario is that a playground is discovered to be covered with a white powder, and no one knows what it is or where it originated. Using their forensic science skills, the students discover that the powder is actually a mixture of multiple powders and they need to use multiple approaches to figure out the components. (See https://secure.edc.org/publications/prodview.asp?1757.)

Suggested Readings

Akerson, V. L. (2001). Teaching science when the principal says "teach language arts." *Science and Children, 38*(7), 42–48.

> Akerson is a college professor, and in this article she describes how she deals with the interdisciplinary issue within her science methods courses. She describes the need to choose an appropriate theme, the interplay between science skills and language development, and the thoughtful integration of nonfiction books within science teaching.

Vanides, J., Yin, Y., Tomita, M., & Ruiz-Primo, M. A. (2005). Using concept maps in the science classroom. *Science Scope, 28*(8), 27–31.

> In this "how-to" article, the authors provide a practical framework for guiding students to create concepts. In addition they show a variety of concepts that students have created to depict the variety of possible structures. Finally, they supply a rubric to show how concept maps might be evaluated.

References

American Association for the Advancement of Science. (1994). *Benchmarks for science literacy.* New York: Oxford University Press.

Bernhardt, E., Destino, T., Kamil, M., & Rodriguez-Munoz, M. (1995). Assessing science knowledge in an English/Spanish bilingual elementary school. *Cognosos, 4,* 4–6.

Bigelow, B., & Peterson, B. (1998). *Rethinking Columbus: The next 500 years.* Milwaukee, WI: Rethinking Schools Ltd.

Cannon, J., & Cannon, J. (1993). *Stellaluna.* New York: Harcourt.

Collins, A., Brown, J. S., & Holum, A. (1991). Cognitive apprenticeship: Making thinking visible. *American Educator, 15,* 6–11, 38–46.

Dalton, S. S. (1998). *Pedagogy matters: Standards for effective teaching practice.* Washington, DC: Center for Applied Linguistics.

Dewey, J. (1938). *Experience and education.* New York: Touchstone.

Dreher, M. J., & Voelker, A. N. (2004). Choosing informational books for primary-grade classrooms: The importance of balance and quality. In E. W. Saul (Ed.), *Crossing borders in literacy and science instruction* (pp. 260–276). Newark, DE: International Reading Association.

Duke, N. K. (2000). 3.6 minutes per day: The scarcity of informational texts in first grade. *Reading Research Quarterly, 35,* 202–224.

Haberman, M. (1995). *Star teachers of children in poverty.* Indianapolis, IN: Kappa Delta Pi.

Jacobs, H. H. (1989). *Interdisciplinary curriculum: Design and implementation.* Alexandria, VA: ASCD.

Lemke, J. (1990). *Talking science: Language, learning and values.* Norwood, NJ: Ablex.

Macaulay, D., & Ardley, N. (1998). *The new way things work.* New York: Houghton Mifflin.

McClure, J. R., Sonak, B., & Suen, H. K. (1999). Concept map assessment of classroom learning: Reliability, validity, and logistical practicality. *Journal of Research in Science Teaching, 36,* 475–492.

Novak, J. D. (1999). *Learning, creating, and using knowledge: Concept maps as facilitative tools in schools and corporations.* Mahwah, NJ: Lawrence Erlbaum.

Pappas, C., Varelas, M., Barry, A., & Rife, A. (2004). Promoting dialogic inquiry in information book read-alouds: Young urban children's ways of making sense in science? In E. W. Saul (Ed.), *Crossing borders in literacy and science instruction* (pp. 161–189). Newark, DE: International Reading Association.

Rice, D. C., Ryan, J. M., & Samson, S. M. (1998). Using concept maps to assess student learning in the science classroom: Must different methods compete. *Journal of Research in Science Teaching, 35,* 1103–1127.

Romance, N., & Vitale, M. (2001). Implementing an in-depth expanded science model in elementary schools: Multi-year findings, research issues, and policy implications. *International Journal of Science Education, 23,* 373–404.

Roth, K. (1994). Second thoughts about interdisciplinary studies. *American Educator, 18,* 44–48.

Walberg, H. (1984). Improving the productivity of America's schools. *Educational Leadership, 41*(8), 19–27.

Wallace, C., Hand, B., & Yang, E. (2004). The science writing heuristic: Using writing as a tool for learning in the laboratory. In E. W. Saul (Ed.), *Crossing borders in literacy and science instruction* (pp. 355–367). Newark, DE: International Reading Association.

Wandersee, J. H. (1990). Concept mapping and the cartography of cognition. *Journal of Research in Science Teaching, 27,* 1069–1075.

Yore, L. (2004). Why do future scientists need to study the language arts? In E. W. Saul (Ed.), *Crossing borders in literacy and science instruction* (pp. 71–94). Newark, DE: International Reading Association.

eleven
Assessing Students' Science Learning

Chapter Highlights

- Reports of students' progress resulting from assessments are a valuable source of information about a teacher's effectiveness. These data should guide teachers to improve their lessons. Students also benefit from assessment data, because these data clarify for them the soundness of their own thinking.

- Summative assessments are those used at the end of instruction. Assessments used at intermediate points are called formative. An effective assessment plan will make use of both types of assessments.

- Quizzes and tests are considered formal assessments. Performance assessments are also formal, and they assess students by their use of science equipment. When teachers use informal assessments, they are less concerned with determining grades and more focused on obtaining insights about students' learning.

- Aligning the means of assessment with the curriculum the students receive is a vital task. Otherwise students are not being legitimately assessed about what they are taught. If the assessment and the curriculum are not aligned, the teacher cannot use assessments to determine her or his effectiveness, and students cannot gain a sense of the soundness of their own thinking.

- Interviews are powerful assessment strategies because they provide access to student thinking through one-on-one conversations about specific concepts and questions.

- What makes assessing English language learners challenging is differentiating between students' language fluency and their science understandings. Teachers should become knowledgeable about nonstandard spellings and phrasing and recognize that these mistakes can have their roots in a student's native language.

In this chapter we describe assessments with numerous forms and varied purposes. Those entering the teaching profession will benefit by holding a broad perspective about assessment. Assessment extends beyond multiple-choice tests to include a variety of strategies for determining what it is the students know and what they are able to do. The key feature of assessment is that it should be infused with the other aspects of teaching and learning, not solely with some external force imposed from the outside.

Assessment in Broad Strokes

One revelation to many people is that assessment goes beyond giving and grading multiple-choice tests. Assessment can be thought of as the process of checking on performance and then providing feedback. The tests you took to get into college are an example. The test checked on your knowledge (and maybe some thinking skills), and the score served as feedback to you and the committee responsible for deciding who should be admitted to the program. In addition if you're cooking something on the stove, you are also using a form of assessment. If you glance to see if the burner is on or how hot it seems to be burning or glowing, you observe information you can use to make adjustments. The view of assessment as filling in bubbles in a test booklet is too narrow. Such a view ignores the potential benefits of assessment, and an effective teacher needs to have a clear sense about all that should be included within the concept of assessment. Think beyond the bubbles—recognize the value of assessments for how they can shape the quality of cooking and the quality of science learning.

Assessing With a Purpose

Just as assessments can take several different forms, the results they provide can be used for several purposes. Too often assessment is equated with multiple-choice tests, and too frequently the results are used exclusively for calculating grades. Before we begin looking at specific assessment tools, let's consider the varied uses of assessments. Once you recognize the multiple ways in which assessment can be used, you will recognize the value in knowing a variety of ways for assessing.

One common use of assessment is to report about an individual's accomplishments. As obvious as this might sound, too often students may not be aware of their progress within science. Although we might admire the innocence of children who are relatively unconcerned about their grades, alerting them to the quality of their thinking and class work before issuing final grades for report cards makes good sense. Some schools require teachers to give midterm reports about each child's performance. But even when this is not an institutional requirement, the practice of keeping students apprised of their science grades can keep them on track. Furthermore, updating students' progress is a good way to keep parents and administrators informed—both groups, as a whole, don't like surprises. If a student's work is not as good as it should be, the caring teacher won't wait until the end of the quarter, semester, or year to reveal to the child how badly he or she has been doing. A more proactive approach in which the teacher gives students updates about the quality of their work is much more productive. Doing so will encourage those students who are succeeding to maintain the quality of their work. For students who might be blissfully unaware that they aren't doing as well as they should, they are given hard facts about where they stand, along with the gentle but firm expectation that they need to do better.

NSES Teaching Standard C: Teachers of science use student data, observations of teaching, and interactions with colleagues to report student achievement and opportunities to learn to students, teachers, parents, policy makers, and the general public.

Assessing is about more than grade giving. Assessments can give the teacher information to help improve his or her effectiveness. A parallel concept is the speedometer on a car. As a driver goes along, he or she might feel as if he or she is moving along at an appropriate rate of speed. But making an occasional check of the speedometer provides a very definitive measure—and after doing so, the driver may find that he or she needs to slow down to remain within an acceptable speed. In this sense the speedometer is an assessment tool. We don't assign grades based on the speed of a car, although a speeding ticket might be the equivalent of a failing grade. The assessment of speed, with the aid of the speedometer, allows the person in charge to make adjustments. Similarly teachers use assessments to make necessary adjustments to the way they are going about their work.

If you've spent much time in classrooms, you recognize that lessons seldom follow a predetermined script. One child may raise a question you hadn't anticipated, a handful of students might become restless because they've already mastered the material, or an interesting discussion may spring from apparently nowhere—all of which require a teacher to modify the original plans. A teacher shouldn't rely on spontaneous events to guide all science instruction. But the ability to pay attention to the context of the classroom is one of the distinctions separating excellent teachers from those who are simply good. This is how we want you to think about assessments: they can give you a unique glimpse into the minds of your students, which will in turn provide evidence about how to make appropriate adjustments.

Imagine you've just finished teaching a science unit you felt was successful. However, the end of unit assessment reveals several gaps in the students' understandings. This is a painful experience for teachers, and most of us who have had to face this reality have had a mixture of guilt, anger, and despair. A common response to this situation is to say, "The students simply weren't trying" or "They weren't paying attention." But although assessments are often used as a measure of a students' progress, they are also invaluable measures of a teacher's effectiveness. Assessments can serve as a very clear signal that we need to modify what we've been doing. When a substantial portion of your students are still struggling with the unit's main ideas or when most of the class has apparently misunderstood a certain concept, then something must be done differently. This doesn't mean that you reteach the unit in the exact same way using a louder voice. Substantive changes in your actions as a teacher need to be made.

NSES Assessment Standard A: Assessments must be consistent with the decisions they are designed to inform, are deliberately designed, and have explicitly stated purposes.

One way to avoid such disappointment is to not wait until the end of the unit to assess your students. Assessments given at the end of a unit, often as the culminating activity before moving to the next topic, are called **summative assessments**. As the name suggests, such assessments are summaries and final events. These summative assessments, often in the form of an end of unit test, are a nice way to pull together the ideas that have been studied over the previous several weeks and serve as a signal to the class that they will be moving on to a new science unit very soon. This is not a good time for a teacher to discover the students have not been catching on.

In contrast are the **formative assessments** given during the unit rather than at the conclusion (Black, Harrison, Lee, Marshall, & William, 2003). As this name implies these assessments are used to determine the formation of ideas and skills in the students' minds. These are the types of assessments that will help a teacher make adjustments while the science unit is still in progress. Ideally the formative assessments will occur within the context of the science unit and not represent a dramatic departure from the work the students have been doing. But a formative assessment should not occur in an artificial way. In the following section we will present various assessments that will help you recognize the different ways in which formative and summative assessments can be designed.

Types of Assessment

Assessing students can be very deliberate and planned in advance. Or assessing can be unanticipated and unstructured. This is how we distinguish between **formal assessments** and **informal assessments.** With formal assessments the teacher knows in advance how the students will be assessed and has an instrument prepared for that purpose. Formal assessments include the district's end of the year science test, a quiz the teacher designed, and an activity that the students perform. In contrast, informal assessments are not quite as structured but still can provide the teacher with invaluable information about the students and their knowledge and skills. An informal assessment can be a whole class discussion of a science topic on the first day of a new unit. Another informal assessment is when a teacher asks the students to write down what they know about a topic so far and where they still feel unsure. Informal assessing also describes times when a teacher steps backs and observes individuals or groups as they are working in an effort to understand what is going on. Formal assessment is structured and methodical. Likewise informal assessment shouldn't imply the assessing is so casual it is sloppy—rather informal refers to assessing that which is less obtrusive and less confining. In chapter 10 we provided a number of approaches that can be usefully employed as informal assessments.

Formal Assessment

Before getting into specifics, we want to raise some points. First, teachers cannot refuse to give tests. If you're a person who hates testing, you are obliged to set your anxiety and resentment to one side. Within your own classroom, you can rely on tests to inform your students about their progress and inform yourself about the effectiveness of your teaching. In other words tests do not have to always be threats dangling above the heads of students and their teachers. As you consider the various forms of assessment, you may need to envision tests differently from what you've experienced. For starters, imagine a multiple-choice test where students who really participated in class and did all the necessary work obtain a high score whereas those few who were less attentive do not do as well.

Another aspect of formal assessment you must come to grips with is that standards and testing are very tightly connected. Gone are the days when teachers could cover any material they wanted and had completely free reign over the curriculum. The reality is that parents want to know if their child is learning, administrators want to know that every teacher is helping all children to learn, and politicians want to be assured that every child is achieving. Another way to think about this is to recognize that standards are not very useful unless there is some mechanism for measuring the extent to which they are being met. Students are to learn certain material and develop proficiency with particular skills, and the most cost-effective way to do this is through testing.

There are many ways to assess science learning and, as with many things in teaching, there are some benefits and weaknesses with each method. You should know about the variety of assessment approaches available to you so that you can decide when to use them. Because many of us are most familiar with quizzes and tests, we will start there and gradually move to less conventional ways of assessing what students know and can do in science.

Quizzes and Tests

When it comes to quizzes and tests, newer teachers tend to regard them as opportunities for students to demonstrate what they know but not always as a means to show what they can do. As a result quizzes and tests are sometimes written so students can do very well without much effort. Too often the questions on quizzes are so simple that many students would be able to answer correctly even before participating in the science activities. Because assessments ought to provide teachers with some evidence about the effectiveness of their science lessons, a quiz or test that all but gives away the right answers is not going to be very informative.

On the other hand, the questions on quizzes and tests shouldn't reach far beyond what is reasonable for the students to have learned. The types of knowledge and skills students are asked to demonstrate on a quiz should be realistic outgrowths of what they learned during science lessons. This requires a careful balance. The test questions shouldn't be so far beyond what was studied that few of the students are likely to understand, but the questions shouldn't be so simple that they seem trivial. How can this be accomplished? One way is to identify the sorts of knowledge you want a student to demonstrate as a result of a particular lesson or learning cycle. An effective assessment item can be found by your answer to this question: What can my students do after they've worked through this lesson (or set of lessons) that they probably wouldn't have been able to do before? This kind of focus helps us think more closely about the intended impact of our teaching without getting too caught up in a desire to ensure that every child can be successful with a minimum of effort.

Assessment is a circumstance where Bloom's taxonomy becomes relevant and useful to the teacher. Without going into too much detail here, we remind you that Bloom identified six levels of thinking. In his scheme, knowledge is the lowest level, and it describes vthe ability to recall information. The next higher level is comprehension, which allows individuals to show how well they can interpret information. Next is application, which requires showing how to take information and use it effectively in a new situation. Following these first three levels are analysis (taking a larger idea and identifying its components), synthesis (taking separate ideas and pulling them together into a larger whole), and evaluation (using knowledge to judge or critique a situation). Test items that are mainly at the knowledge level are mediocre if overused in assessments, because they won't challenge the students. Whether a particular test item is technically an example of comprehension, application, or analysis is probably not worth worrying about. However, what teachers can do is find ways to extend thinking by asking students to perform such simple tasks as listing, defining, matching, and recalling. We will provide some examples to help illustrate this possibility.

The multiple-choice question shown in Figure 11.1 could be used as part of an upper elementary or middle school unit about mixtures and solutions. Typically in such units students learn how to separate combinations of substances. Different techniques are used depending on the properties of the substances. Separating salt from water requires that the solution be allowed to evaporate. The emphasis of such a unit is not for students to memorize how to separate every possible combination of substances but for them to develop problem-solving skills to figure out which techniques can be appropriately applied to different situations. With that goal in mind,

The equipment in this picture can be used to separate substances. Which of these combinations could be separated into its components using this equipment?

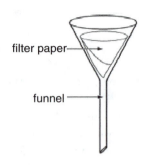

A. a mixture of salt and pepper
B. a mixture of pepper and water
C. a solution of water and oxygen
D. a solution of sugar and water

FIGURE 11.1. This figure shows a sample multiple-choice test item from the Third International Mathematics and Science Study.

consider the kind of thinking a student would be using as he or she contemplated this assessment item.

Realistically a teacher wouldn't expect a student to remember how to separate all the different possible combinations of substances. Instead a student would need to use a little bit of problem solving to come up with the right answer. Maybe you can imagine the thought processes (e.g., "D isn't right because the sugar would dissolve and pass right through the filter paper"). Because the thinking required involves more than simple recall, this test question goes beyond the usual multiple guess. In case you think this question seems much too easy and that B is the obvious choice, you should know that only a little more than a third of all eighth graders who answered this question during the Third International Mathematics and Science Study (TIMSS) selected the correct answer. The TIMSS project is an ongoing, multinational research study that provides the standard by which comparisons are made across different countries to evaluate the quality of science teaching and learning and makes use of an interesting array of assessment approaches (http://nces.ed.gov/timss/).

Assessments are not to be designed to trick students. Instead the information produced should reveal what students know and can do, ideally beyond a simple recall of information. Figure 11.2 shows another multiple-choice item from the TIMSS research requiring a student to do some multistep thinking. In other words a student must take into account several bits of information to finally come up with the best choice. Just to put a little pressure on you, 60 percent of eighth graders were able to identify the right choice. To accomplish this they needed to understand that mechanical energy indicates some form of movement being produced. In addition they needed to know that chemical energy could be thought of as some form of fuel that is consumed (food is an example but so are petroleum products). Even though heat energy is involved in each of the four events, only one of them contains the three forms of energy (chemical, mechanical, and heat) in the proper sequence.

There are many published guidelines describing the features of effective multiple-choice test items. Included in these guidelines is the suggestion that every **foil,** the technical term for each choice, appears equally likely of being the right choice. This means the foils are grammatically correct, of approximately the same length, and clearly not a silly choice thrown in for amusement purposes. The underlying rationale for presenting the choices in this manner is that multiple-choice tests, as an example of science assessments, are designed to uncover what it is the student knows—not to ensure that everyone gets the right answer.

chemical energy → heat energy → mechanical energy (+ wasted heat)

The sequence of energy transformation shown in this diagram is describing which of these events?

    A. a flashlight is turned on

    B. a birthday candle is lit

    C. gasoline burns to power an engine

    D. electric current operates a freezer

FIGURE 11.2. This figure shows another sample test item from the Third International Mathematics and Science Study.

Writing high-quality multiple-choice test items is more difficult than many people realize. Because this form of assessing is one of the quickest ways to judge students' knowledge, it is by far the most common method used when the goal is to assess large groups of students. For this example students who chose the gasoline-powered engine would receive one point, whereas those who chose any other selection would receive a zero. In contrast an essay question could be worth several points because, even without writing a perfect response, the student wouldn't necessarily give an answer that is either completely right or wrong. However, grading essay questions is much more time-consuming.

Every type of assessment involves some compromise. If you worked for a company that created, administered, and scored standardized tests, you would need to take three factors into consideration. One factor is the quality of the test questions, because you want the information being tested to be accurate and you want to use questions that separate the "knowers" from the "guessers." That's the quality issue. A second issue is efficiency. The faster you can score the students' responses and report them back to the districts and states, the happier everyone is with the process. Last of all is the third factor of keeping costs down, which is very important. A paper-and-pencil test is considerably less expensive than a test where students have to work with actual equipment (think back to that earlier option with the funnel separation test item). Understandably, customers want the assessments they purchase to include all three: quality, speed, and low cost. But improving one of these qualities cuts into the others. Those in the standardized testing industry will tell their customers that the only solution is to select two of the three choices, because it's quite impossible to accomplish all three (Henriques, 2003).

Performance Assessments

One complaint about tests and quizzes is that they assess individual learning in a manner inconsistent with the way in which the material is learned. An assessment that is more consistent with hands-on experiences is a hands-on activity. For instance a performance assessment that measures how well students understand how to use a balance to find the mass of an object would entail putting the necessary equipment in front of the students and having them demonstrate their abilities. Sometimes this way of assessing is referred to as **authentic assessment,** because the assessment task is authentic to the way the students learn the concepts and skills.

Even though a performance assessment involves a test that requires students to use science equipment, it is still a formal method. Remember that *formal* refers to an assessment the teacher has designed to determine what the students know and can do. Performance assessments are not all that unusual outside of school, and for good reason. Imagine the value of having performance assessments for students in cosmetology, truck driving, building trades, and dentistry. A written test would not be sufficient, but demonstrating one's proficiency could certainly be used as a formal assessment. Performance assessments provide very high-quality information, but do so at considerable expense and low efficiency. However, performance assessments are the very best way to evaluate students' understanding—and for that reason better teachers find ways to incorporate these methods into their repertoire.

One example of a performance assessment is one used at the end of an electricity unit. During this unit the students would have worked with batteries, wires, lightbulbs, and electric motors. They would have discovered that a battery acts like a pump pushing electricity through a circuit. They would have learned that adding bulbs to a circuit reduces the amount of current that can flow. As each bulb is added to a series circuit, the brightness of the bulbs is lessened. They would have recognized that electricity flows through a circuit in a loop, which explains why a motor spins in opposite directions when the wires connected to it are switched. The performance assessment for this unit would include a small and sealed cardboard box. From the outside all the students would see would be the heads of brass paper fasteners. They would be told that connected to these paper fasteners are motors, batteries, bulbs, and wires, and their task is to determine how this equipment is connected to the paper fasteners.

What makes this an effective performance assessment? For one thing, because the students have used the same science equipment during class that they will use during the performance assessment, the execution of the task is consistent with what they did during the science lessons. Another benefit of a performance assessment is that we don't have to wonder if a student's performance is somehow compromised by his or her reading abilities. Put another way, a student's ability to be successful with this task is more closely related to his or her science understandings and not some other set of skills such as decoding vocabulary. Finally, this performance assessment provides students with a somewhat novel task requiring them to use their knowledge as they apply it to a new situation. Simply being able to recall information is not always sufficient. To be successful at this task, the students must rely on what they know and use it to solve a problem.

For Reflection and Discussion

How much of what you know and are able to accomplish do you think would be better assessed using a performance assessment rather than a paper-and-pencil assessment?

Educational researchers place a great deal of confidence in the validity of performance assessments. For example if we want to compare different approaches to teaching a concept such as the water cycle, we would find the students' abilities to demonstrate their understandings to be much more compelling than administering a written test. When international comparisons of students' science understandings were made, the information gathered included students' competency on performance assessments. The following example is our modification of a task from the TIMSS project. In this fourth-grade performance assessment, students were to test three containers containing hot water to compare how quickly liquids cooled.

For this task, the student was provided with three containers (e.g., a paper cup, a metal can, and a coffee mug), three thermometers, a stopwatch, and a sheet of paper containing the following directions.

Hot Containers Performance Assessment　　Your challenge is to determine which of the three containers will keep a hot drink warm for the greatest length of time. Your experiment will last ten minutes, and you are expected to keep records of your work.

1. Gently place a thermometer in each container, and ask your teacher to pour hot water into them. Measure the temperature of the water in the containers. Decide how you will gather your data, and record it in this table. When you have collected the data for ten minutes, then you are to answer the questions.

Time	Cup A	Cup B	Cup C

2. According to your data, which container will keep a hot drink warm for the longest amount of time? Explain your choice.
3. What is it about this container that explains these results?
4. Which container do you think will be the best for keeping ice cream cold? What is your reason for this choice?

The teacher needs to evaluate each student's work upon their completing this task. When we score a paper-and-pencil test, we rely on an answer key. An answer key allows us to designate right and wrong answers. But for performance assessments it is appropriate to offer students partial credit on items. A **rubric** becomes the tool we use to grade students' work on performance assessments. The following rubric describes in great detail how you would arrive at a score for a student's work on this performance assessment.

Hot Containers Rubric (12 points possible)
 Item 1 *(worth 4 points)*
　A. Use of equipment (1 point possible)
　　Uses thermometer properly and safely without
　　　　any help from teacher . . . . 1 point
　　Needs assistance with using or reading thermometer . . . 0 points

　B. Recording data (3 total points possible, 1 point per criteria)
　　Entire data chart filled in with times and temperatures . 1 point
　　Data gathered over the entire ten-minute period . . . . 1 point
　　Temperature data shows temperature declining over time　1 point

Item 2 *(worth 3 points)*

A. Identifying container (1 point possible)

Choice of container that stays warm the longest
is consistent with data .... 1 point

Data doesn't support choice of container .... 0 points

B. Explaining choice (2 points possible)

Explanation contrasts chosen container with the other two . 2 points

Explanation focuses on only chosen container .... 1 point

No explanation for chosen container .... 0 points

Item 3 *(worth 2 points)*

A. Inference about container characteristics (2 points possible)

Compares composition of all containers and ability
to transfer and retain heat....................... 2 points

Identifies chosen container's characteristics without
comparison .... 1 point

Lack of logical explanation about container's properties .. 0 points

Item 4 *(worth 3 points)*

A. Identifying container (1 point possible)

Selects the same container as was identified
for Item 2 .... 1 point

Selects different container from Item 2 .... 0 points

B. Explaining choice (2 points possible)

Describes how transfer and retaining heat applies
to hot and cold substances .... 2 points

Provides reasonable explanation but without
referring to heat .... 1 point

Explanation not provided or is not sensible .... 0 points

At first you might feel that this rubric is much too detailed. However, when you have many students' work to grade, you don't want to spend your precious time making too many judgment calls. Too, such rubrics allow you to assess a number of papers in a very similar manner, something that your students (and their parents) will expect. The criteria for scoring on a rubric are closely connected to the directions and questions provided to the students. In addition to score full points, students need to not only use the equipment properly but also apply the science concepts (e.g., heat energy) as they generate their answers. Although it seems cumbersome to devise such rubrics, remember that there are a host of materials available on the Internet to support you in their construction. In addition, time invested in designing a rubric will be saved many times over as you use it to guide your grading. The result is a test that will much more authentically assess what each student knows and can demonstrate than will a typical, paper-and-pencil test.

This is not to say that this performance assessment is without its challenges. You need to gather all the necessary materials (and, no, thermometers are not always easy to find, and hot water is not always available in your classroom) and decide how to organize the students so everyone completes the performance assessment in a reasonable amount of time. But despite the extra work, most teachers have much greater confidence in the results from this assessment than they have from less authentic approaches.

Portfolio Assessments

Portfolios represent compilations of individual student work and are intended to reveal their accomplishments over a broad spectrum of knowledge and skills. As with other forms of assessments, portfolios are most useful when they inform the student and the teacher. One thing a good portfolio should not be is a collection of all the works by a person. By featuring significant and representative pieces, a portfolio becomes a showcase, not a container of every piece of work.

A student's science portfolio should be conceived of as an exhibition. If you think about exhibits at an art museum, a science center, or a zoo, you know the materials on display don't simply stand on their own, and they are not expected to speak for themselves. Most of us have had the experience of seeing a very unusual object on exhibit and wondering about its name, its origin, and its significance. This could be some contraption or some unusual beast. When your curiosity is aroused, having a placard nearby that provides a description is appreciated. An effective exhibit consists of a helpful combination of the object on display and the accompanying explanation. In much the same way, a portfolio should consist of work samples and a narrative describing the relevance of each individual piece to the overall project.

The **portfolio artifacts** are the raw materials selected to be included in a portfolio, and the **portfolio narrative** is the written explanation that goes with each artifact. Most commonly the artifacts are samples of a student's written work, although they can be other things such as videos, photographs, or software. The increased ease of use of technology makes it conceivable for students to create electronic portfolios. But whether an individual portfolio is in the form of a Web page or a three-ring binder, the basic elements are the same: samples of work and their explanations. A student might select as an artifact the sheet he or she filled in while doing an in-class science investigation, but he or she also needs to include a written explanation describing why this is a representative piece of work. As with museum exhibits, the narrative connected with the artifacts is essential. Truly any piece of written work a student produces can become part of their portfolio provided there is something significant about the work and a narrative accompanies it.

The types of artifacts to be included in a portfolio are shaped by the purpose of the portfolio. Frequently a portfolio consists of samples of a student's best work. But there may be reasons for the teacher to have in role in deciding what should be selected. A powerful use of a science portfolio is to document changes in students as a way to represent their growth over time. We see this as perhaps one of the more powerful uses of portfolios, because they oblige the student and teacher to take a less atomized view of student learning. In the elementary and middle grades, students' minds are developing very rapidly, and unless everyone involved pays attention to changes, the truly astonishing evidence of growth can go unnoticed. When the goal of a science portfolio is to represent the growth of a student, in terms of their science concepts, their process skills, their understandings of the nature of science, and their ability to work with increased autonomy in science inquiry, then assessing with portfolios provides an often pleasantly surprising view of the student, not only for the teacher but for the learners. Again this assessment process is greatly aided by the use of a well-designed grading rubric, one that you may consider sharing with your students at the very outset of this assignment to guide them.

Informal Assessment

Teachers can use assessments to uncover what it is the students are thinking. With formal assessments a teacher determines in advance the criteria he or she will use to evaluate the students' work. In contrast, the use of informal assessments may not be as predetermined. An informal assessment serves a similar purpose to formal assessments, namely, to uncover children's ideas and skills. But the process is less structured. Informal assessments can provide teachers with useful information but normally not with the goal of assigning students a grade. Informal assessment is a mechanism for a teacher to check in on the formative understandings of students.

You can think of homework assignments as informal assessments. If you regard traditional homework such as reading a chapter and answering questions at the back as inconsistent with what we've been advocating to this point, then you are right. The types of tasks students are expected to perform as at-home assignments should be consistent with the kinds of activities the students do during science class. Homework can also help keep lines of communication open between the school and your students' families. Homework can also give a teacher another way of assessing the students and their abilities related to science.

Suppose you were teaching a science unit about electricity, and you were concerned about your students' abilities to apply the information from class to situations outside of school. You could use homework to do this. Rather than imagine homework as a time for students to practice what they know (which is relatively low on Bloom's taxonomy), you could give students assignments that encourage them to make those connections. How might you accomplish this? Here are some examples from the Insights "Circuits and Pathways" unit. The first Explore activity in this unit introduces students to small electric motors. The "Home-School Worksheet" serves as the Extend phase, because it has the students searching for motors at home: in an appliance that cools, an appliance that heats, and a toy. Much later in this same unit, the students explore simple fuses. Their homework assignment is to recruit an adult to help them locate the fuses and circuit breakers at their house or apartment. The students are to record where they found them, make a sketch of one, and describe what they remember happening when a fuse broke or breaker tripped. All of this is described on a take-home sheet the students fill in and return to their teacher.

As with the better things in teaching, this strategy serves multiple purposes, not the least of which is building bridges between school and home. However, at this stage we want to emphasize the assessment potential. When you assign the kind of homework just described, you have access to all kinds of information about your students. You can see how well they can communicate their ideas. You can see if they can extend classroom ideas to their own world. You can see if they become aware of their surroundings. You can see if they can recognize their capacity to do science without being directly supervised by the teacher. Can you use the information to enter grades in your grade book? Perhaps, but maybe it should simply be a tally of who completed the assignment. The more revealing aspects of this homework are the insights you can glean from what the students turn in. You may discover that within your science lessons, you are not doing a good enough job with the Explain phase because the concepts are not especially clear in your students' homework. You might also learn that the students are making much stronger connections between home and school than you had realized, especially among students who may not be as verbal during science lessons. This might allow you to reconsider how effective the lessons have been and strengthen your resolve to continue teaching science in ways that seem to be reaching all of the students.

Another way of informally assessing in science is through teacher observations. One interesting feature of this type of assessment is that the students aren't doing any writing. Instead the teacher discretely observes students as they work on activities while keeping notes about the students' actions. It is too ambitious to expect a teacher to do this form of assessment for every student during one lesson—choosing three or four individuals during an activity is probably sufficient and will allow a teacher to gather useful information about the entire class in a way that is not overwhelmingly complex. As with the homework, teacher observations are assessments that give insights about the students and the lessons and allow the teacher to determine the effectiveness of the science teaching, without necessarily using every assessment as a mechanism for assigning individual grades.

Observational assessment can also help the teacher to evaluate students' social skills. Because science lessons involve interpersonal communication, conducting an assessment of students' appropriate use of social skills makes good sense. Of course we can't expect students to automatically know how to work well together—these skills need to be explicitly taught to them. As part of cooperative learning, many teachers identify specific behaviors the students should be exhibiting. Social skills such as taking turns, following directions, and making shared decisions do not lend themselves to formal assessment. A teacher can simply jot down notes about students as they work in groups to record how well they are implementing the social skills. One technique is to write on several sticky notes the names of a few target students. As the children work, the teacher can pay attention to those select students and write down evidence about their use of the social skills, perhaps including specific actions or utterances. These can then easily be transferred to file folders that the teacher has created for each student to be used for parent and student conferences.

Another fine way to use observations is to gather more information about individual student proficiency with the essential features of inquiry discussed in chapter 4. Although the essential features are meant to be a template for teachers as they plan for instruction, they can also be used as a tool for assessing students. For a given activity, such as comparing what shape of a boat made of aluminum foil will hold the most cargo (in the form of pennies), the teacher may have intended for the lesson to meet the standards shown in Table 11.1.

Just as with the social skills example shown in Table 11.1, a teacher can keep notes of students as they work and record the extent to which they can function within the essential features of inquiry. As the students participate in the activity, the teacher can note how skillfully they are able to clarify the initial question after having been supplied a general question about possible boat designs (e.g., rafts and canoes). Even though the teacher may have told students what data to collect (the number of pennies each boat can hold before capsizing), the teacher can assess how well students can do this by carefully observing them at work. The general idea for this type of informal assessment is to casually and unobtrusively observe students as they are working and to create anecdotal records about their actions as a way to document their science performance.

TABLE 11.1. Standards for Assessing Student Use of Inquiry

Essential Feature	Expected Outcome	Teacher Direction
1. Learner engages in scientifically oriented questions.	Learner clarifies question provided by the teacher.	Somewhat
2. Learner gives priority to evidence in responding to questions.	Learner directed to collect certain data.	Low
3. Learner formulates explanations from evidence.	Learner formulates explanation after summarizing evidence.	Very little
4. Learner connects explanations to scientific knowledge.	Learner directed toward areas and sources of scientific knowledge.	Low
5. Learner communicates and justifies explanations to others.	Learner forms reasonable and logical arguments to communicate explanations.	Very little

Point–Counterpoint

The accountability era places a unique set of pressures on classroom teachers. The very real possibility that one's effectiveness at science teaching will be measured by a standardized test is a reality for which every elementary and middle school teacher should prepare. So in response to the question "How should teachers of science respond to standardized testing?" we are privileged to receive two related recommendations.

Doing Inquiry in the Classroom Despite Standardized Testing

Omar Morales
Middle School Science Teacher in Miami, Florida

When I think of standardized tests, I think of sinkholes. In Florida the problem is widespread. Houses are swallowed by the earth. What used to be a beautiful neighborhood becomes an area of utter devastation. Sinkholes are caused by the weakening of the limestone foundation on which the houses are found. Water slowly eats away at limestone, causing openings, underground caves that gradually give way under the weight of the burden above. Standardized tests in today's schooling environment work in a similar way. The test undermines the teacher who tries to teach in a way that fosters deep, conceptual learning. The result is utter devastation: kids who know a lot about nothing.

Standardized tests prepare our students for quiz shows, not for the future. Students are tested for breadth and not depth. When tested they are rarely asked to make connections among concepts. Their knowledge is shallow and scattered. Most students are being exposed to various topics at lightning speed because these tests require it. The result is a generation of very confused students. One of my students, when asked on a survey, "Does your science teacher help you or hold you back?" answered, "No, he doesn't hurt me but I think that he takes us through each lesson too fast. Like, first, we'll be talking about space [and the] next thing you know we're discussing cells and genes. I didn't really learn a lot about science. I know most of [science] but didn't understand it really."

What does this student's quote communicate? As I reread it, I think of how these standardized tests have worked against what I try to do in my class, day in and day out. I want my students to learn in a deep, meaningful way, not just through rote memorization. I do this by giving my students the opportunity to discuss concepts and make sense of the ideas by permitting them to test their ideas together. There are benefits to this method of encouraging students to build their knowledge on what they have already experienced.

Some of the drawbacks of not using this epistemology are explained by the writer of the introduction of *Science for All Americans* (AAAS, 1989), otherwise known as *Project 2061*. The authors of this report explain that students who don't think for themselves in school may not think for themselves in their futures out of school. Indeed they explain that learning to memorize ideas out of context will not help students problem solve and think critically later in life.

The present science textbooks and methods of instruction (I would also add standardized tests), far from helping, often actually impede progress toward science literacy. They emphasize the learning of answers more than the exploration of questions, memory at the expense of critical thought, bits and pieces of information instead of understandings in context, recitation over argument, and reading in lieu of doing. They fail to encourage students to work together, to share ideas and information freely with each other, or to use modern instruments to extend their intellectual capabilities.

So what are teachers who agree with AAAS [and the National Research Council] to do? Those teachers need to balance what they know about teaching and learning with the current environment of standardized testing. This means that teachers will set the stage so that deep, conceptual learning is happening more often than not, and inquiry allows for this stage. Teachers must work tirelessly against this undermining effect that testing has on our students. Given our goals as teachers and our hopes for our students, we need to employ inquiry despite the pressures of standardized testing.

Doing Inquiry in the Classroom Because of Standardized Testing

Karen Rose
High School Biology Teacher, Tallahassee, Florida

A common reason I hear teachers give for not incorporating inquiry into their teaching is because of time constraints related to content coverage for high-stakes testing. In the past I worked in a middle school where I felt those pressures. But since escaping this "back to the wall" setting, my ideas on this issue have evolved. This evolution has also coincided with my enrollment in a graduate program and exposure to field-based scientific research experiences through a local teacher development workshop. After these experiences I now assert there is a considerable amount of research that supports the use of inquiry in the classroom. Most educational researchers agree that inquiry enhances students' learning by promoting higher-order questions and thinking. Combined with that, a close read of our state's standardized test shows that many of the questions on this test require higher-level thinking on the part of the student. So over the past two years, I've come to understand that instead of serving as a barrier to inquiry, these tests are the reasons that we as teachers need to employ inquiry in our classrooms. We need to teach through inquiry because of standardized tests.

There is a misconception that using inquiry-based teaching involves an immediate overhaul of one's instruction. Not true! Based on my own experience, I can see that changes in my teaching can be made gradually, one lesson at a time, as time permits. By making my teaching more student centered, I not only facilitate learning but am able to grow as a learner as well. In an inquiry-based classroom, both the students and the teacher are engaged in discussions, collaborating, writing, expressing ideas, and creating. What better way to prepare students for higher-order test questions than through inquiry? What better way to prepare them for life?

Children are naturally curious, so it seems to me that we want to take advantage of that characteristic. Inquiry involves posing questions by the learner, investigations or research, and evaluations of data and explanations. Allowing students to engage in inquiry-based activities fosters creativity, independence, and an appreciation for the scientific process and the skills and attitudes that are basic to the scientific community.

If I reflect on and ponder the ultimate question of "Why do I teach?" then I have to say that I am here to assist parents, the community, and others in nurturing citizens who are productive, independent thinkers and are globally responsible. In "The Pedagogy of Poverty," Haberman (1991) cautioned that if we do not challenge our students to think, then we will never leapfrog them past their socioeconomic limitations. If test scores are the only benchmark, do we not run the risk of holding low-achieving students back, despite our very intentions to elevate them? If independence and true achievement is our goal, then inquiry is a "no brainer" in the classroom. If you think you don't have time for it, think again! You must make time. Given our goals as teachers and our hopes for our students, we need to employ inquiry in part because of the pressures of standardized testing.

Aligning Assessment With the Curriculum

All criticisms of any form of assessment can come down to one major issue. Whether someone is talking about a college entrance test or a final exam, the central problem is one of **alignment.** When an assessment is well aligned, then the material covered in the assessment closely matches what the student was expected to understand. This alignment applies to not only the topic but also the depth of knowledge and levels of thinking. If students are learning the general characteristics of living things versus nonliving things, then an assessment shouldn't focus on the structures of the cell. If students are expected to analyze information, such as graphs showing the motion of objects, then the assessment shouldn't overemphasize definitions.

> **NSES Program Standard A: Assessment policies and practices should be aligned with the goals, student expectations, and curriculum frameworks.**

One reason, at least at the classroom level, that curriculum may be misaligned with assessments is that it is based on a teacher's desire for his or her students to be successful. It is incorrect to believe that making things simple is the appropriate strategy for guaranteeing success. We trust you can see the inconsistency between a science unit that involves the children in direct experiences, group work, and higher-order thinking and an assessment that focuses on recalling information. A teacher who holds genuinely high expectations for his or her students will communicate those beliefs within all they do: in the types of activities he or she provides, in the kinds of assignments he or she makes, in the level of questions he or she asks of the students, and in the ways in which he or she assesses the students. Wouldn't you wonder about an instructor's opinion of your abilities when, after expressing great confidence in your potential as a future teacher of science, she assessed you in a way that failed to reinforce those supposedly high expectations? Elementary and middle school students will notice this as well.

This might lead you to misinterpret our position. We are not suggesting you should set your students up for failure. We believe all students can learn science and become successful at it. But what we want to do is caution you against the all too common desire to make life easier for students, especially when we are talking about student diversity. In all sorts of ways, teachers can send mixed messages to students that undermine their intentions. A teacher who stands before the class and claims everyone is supposed to be successful in science but then does little things that suggest this confidence is shaky undercuts the positive message. You cannot legitimately expect students to believe you when you say you have great confidence in their scientific thinking capabilities and then administer a science assessment that is a vocabulary test. The feature of standardized tests that raises such anxiety and frustration is usually connected to its appropriateness as an assessment tool. If standardized tests really measured student knowledge and did so in a way that distinguished good thinking from lucky guessing, if assessments were unambiguously connected to the curriculum, and if the ways in which students learned science were aligned with the ways in which students were assessed, then most complaints about assessment would be conquered. However, when it comes to large-scale assessments where thousands of students must be tested for their science knowledge, this kind of alignment is hard to attain. That leads us to consider what teachers should do in such an environment.

For Reflection and Discussion

Upon visiting the Web site http://fairtest.org, you are confronted with this statement: "The National Center for Fair & Open Testing works to end the misuses and flaws of standardized testing and to ensure that evaluation of students, teachers, and schools is fair, open, valid, and educationally beneficial." How is this mission consistent with or in conflict with your views of standardized testing?

Interviewing as an Assessment Method

We are unable to get to know somebody in normal, everyday life by asking him or her to take a multiple-choice test. Instead we develop relationships by talking to and working with others. As a result of this information, we develop a sense about who the person is. In effect we are assessing who someone is. It's not a judgment. It's not necessary for us to supply results back to the person. And it's not necessarily an unnatural process. But if we are thoughtful in the questions we ask and respond in a genuine fashion to what we hear and see, we can learn a great deal by talking to someone. This is the basis for interviewing: asking questions, following up on responses, and using the exchange to develop an assessment about what the other person thinks.

In the DVD version of the movie *Pulp Fiction,* Uma Thurman's character interviews John Travolta's character on the occasion when they first meet. This scene provides an unusual yet illuminating approach to interviewing. Each question during the interview is followed by two possible answers. Thurman's character explains, "My theory is, that when it comes to important subjects, there's only two ways a person can answer. Which way they choose, tells me who that person is." To illustrate her theory she claims that someone is either an Elvis person or a Beatles person; no one can like them both equally. At a pivotal point in the interview, Thurman's character asks, "In conversation, do you listen—or wait to talk?" After a five-second pause, Travolta's character confesses, "I have to admit that I wait to talk. But I'm trying harder to listen." There we find perhaps the key to being a good interviewer: trying harder to listen.

When interviews are used for assessment purposes, teachers have the goal of discovering what students know and how they go about thinking within certain situations. The challenge for many teachers is to use the conversational feel of interviews as a time to learn about a student's thoughts and not as an opportunity to provide supplemental instruction. A key ingredient becomes the interviewer's genuine interest in a student's thinking, which is consistent with the portrait of an effective teacher we've been creating throughout this book. If we can reinforce the concept of "teacher as learner," then many of the ideas appearing in previous chapters rise to the surface. When conducting an interview, the person asking questions uses the process skills of observing and reserves the leap to inferring until after the interview has concluded. Asking a student to articulate his or her thinking can be regarded as the time when the teacher as learner is in the explore phase of the learning cycle. Instead of exploring concrete materials, the teacher uses the interview to explore the ideas held in the minds of the students. In addition, the essential features of inquiry are nestled within an effective interview: questions drive the investigation, explanations about what students know are derived from what they say and do, and connections are made to what others have noticed about student thinking. In total, if an interview of a student is treated as an opportunity for a teacher to learn about his or her students, then it is consistent with the traditions we've described for student learning.

Interviewing as Active Listening

Just as we described in chapter 6, the questions we ask and the reactions we make to the answers we hear are crucial if we hope to learn from a conversation. Toward this end, we highly recommend the use of a **semi-structured interview** format. In contrast to a structured interview where the interviewer asks questions that have been written in advance, and no other questions, the semi-structured interview, as the name suggests, balances the use of scripted questions with follow-up questions. Because there is a core set of questions, the conversation between the interviewer and interviewee does not aimlessly ramble. But allowing the interviewer to probe into the student's responses provides opportunities to explore in more depth the underlying thoughts that may not be evident from the student's initial response (Roulston, deMarrais, & Lewis, 2003).

The role model for an effective interviewer is not the police interrogator we see on television who succeeds in extracting a confession from the suspected criminal. Interrogators know what they want to hear: "Yes, I did it!" In contrast, interviewers genuinely desire to hear something about which they do not hold a preconception. This necessitates the use of active listening. Unlike the disposition of someone who is waiting his or her turn to speak, an active listener uses verbal and nonverbal cues to encourage the other person to continue speaking. Nodding, making eye contact, and smiling send unspoken messages, as do encouraging remarks such as "That's interesting." In place of the interrogator role model, we offer the talk show host. If while interviewing a student, you're not sure what to say next, you can ask yourself, "What would Oprah do?" When the goal is to have the interviewees or guests share their thoughts, people use different conversational strategies than if we already hold preconceived ideas about what the suspect or subject will reveal to us.

Water-Cycle Concepts and Interviews

A very productive topic to be used for interviewing students from a wide range of backgrounds, ages, and abilities is the water cycle. Because components of the water cycle are such a common part of everyday experience, with everything from rain falling to towels drying, students inevitably have ideas about the process. Also because the water cycle is the source of such an important array of science concepts such as molecular motion and energy transfer, the scientific explanations associated with the water cycle represent significant learning goals. Last, because concrete examples of the components of the water cycle are so readily available, conducting interviews generates very interesting conversations with students.

For this example interview, we focus on two science concepts: evaporation and precipitation. The questions to be asked to students rely on some hands-on materials: a small amount of rubbing alcohol, a picture of containers holding colored water, and a blank piece of paper and crayons. In Table 11.2 you will find the accepted scientific explanations for each set of questions and examples of student misconceptions we've heard during such interviews. We've provided this information here with the expectation that you readily use it as a guideline for conducting an interview with an elementary or middle school student.

For the prompt "drops of rubbing alcohol," a few drops of rubbing alcohol are dribbled onto a flat, nonabsorbent surface or into the palm of their hand. Students are directed to observe the behavior of the drops. If your supply of rubbing alcohol has a high percentage of alcohol and is not diluted with much water, then the students will easily see the liquid disappearing. The interviewer can begin by asking the students to describe what they are noticing. This ensures that they've seen what you want them to comment on and not something else, like the liquid cleaning the desk. Asking the students to describe what happened to the liquid gives access to their understanding of evaporation. Be very careful to avoid equating whether the students use the word *evaporation* with their real understanding of the phenomenon. We've found that students may use that word to mean that the rubbing alcohol no longer exists. But we've also heard students give insightful descriptions of the alcohol changing from liquid to vapor without ever using the word *evaporate*. Use active listening to uncover what they really understand.

Although it may not be obvious to the interviewee, the second task "containers with and without lids" is also meant to uncover students' understanding of evaporation. In this case, we have used a technique called "interview about events" (White & Gunstone, 1992), which presents the students with an event and then asks them to describe what they notice and how they would explain it. The event we use for this interview prompt is a series of a pair of containers,

TABLE 11.2. Guidelines for Conducting a Semi-Structured Interview About the Water Cycle

Interview Topic, Materials, and Questions	Accepted Scientific Explanation	Sample Alternative Reasons
Drops of Rubbing Alcohol (concrete materials) What happens to rubbing alcohol when a drop is spread on a table?	Alcohol changes from liquid to gas. Heat and wind increase the rate of evaporation. Particles float into the air.	Alcohol goes away, it soaks into the table, it disappears, or it changes to some other substance.
Containers with and without Lids (picture) How would you explain what happened to the water in the containers?	Liquid water changes to vapor and goes into the air. Lid keeps vapor from going into air.	Some person or thing spilled or drank the water. Water just goes away.
Clouds and Rain (conversation and illustration) What causes rain? How does it start? Where do clouds come from? What are clouds made of?	Water vapor in the air is cooled, condenses, and falls as rain. Clouds consist of water vapor.	Water falls out of clouds. Clouds are bags of water, sponges, or bowls. Clouds are made from smoke.

FIGURE 11.3. This is an example of dyed water in two vials shown at different days.

one with a lid on top and the other open to the air. The water inside is dyed to make it easier to see, and photographs are taken at different days. This progression is shown to the students, the time frame is explained, and the students are asked to describe what they notice. Then they are encouraged to offer explanations for the event.

Just as with the previous interview prompt, the interviewer should avoid becoming too caught up in the absence or presence of the word *evaporate* within what the students say. In fact it's not all that unusual in interviews to find that the students don't recognize that this picture sequence and the preceding rubbing alcohol activity can be explained by the same scientific concept. Also no matter how many times we hear students say it, we continue to be surprised when they suggest that someone messed with the materials as an explanation of why the water level went down in one container. Such surprises, however, can prove useful. Knowing about the types of ideas students hold before beginning formal instruction provides the teacher with another key piece of information on which to base instructional decisions.

The third interview prompt allows the students to respond through a combination of writing, drawing, and talking. As with the previous prompts, we are less interested in responses that use scientific terms and more attentive to the display of understandings and explanations. The deceptively simple prompt is to ask the students to describe the cause of rain and explain the role of clouds in the process. By using paper and coloring materials, students can illustrate and explain their responses. We've learned that when the drawings include lines to show movement, the students should be prompted to add arrowheads to show the direction. Also the drawing is much easier to interpret later when labels are added to the pictures. What may seem to be obvious, such as a cloud, sometimes proves to signify something else, such as smoke from a factory. Asking students to write words on the drawing is important. Even though the response to the question is drawn rather than spoken, an effective interviewer will rely on questioning strategies to probe for detail and ask for fuller explanations.

Within an interview the teacher may find it useful to ask a student to react to an alternative explanation. The **counter-suggestion** strategy works by indicating that someone else explained the situation in a way different from what the student had just provided. The student is then asked to evaluate this option. If the student gave an explanation that is not scientific, then the counter-suggestion can be a scientifically acceptable idea. But if the student used a scientifically acceptable explanation, then the counter-suggestion can be in the form of one of the alternatives. This is most effective when the alternative explanation is said to have come from another student. Preservice teachers have found this to be very revealing. In some cases students readily give up on their original idea. However, in other cases they will tenaciously hold to their personal explanation. Very often the manner in which the students respond gives an interesting glimpse into their thought processes.

NSES Assessment Standard C: The technical quality of the data collected is well matched to the decisions and actions taken on the basis of their interpretation. The feature that is claimed to be measured is actually measured. Assessment tasks are authentic. Students have adequate opportunity to demonstrate their achievements.

Assessment Within a Diverse Classroom

Imagine that you are grading a student's test. The question was asking for students to explain the reasons for the prediction made during an investigation. Here is what an actual student wrote during a science activity:

Bicos the las papertall is theeker we thot eet chud be bery stron.

What should a teacher do with such a response? First, many of us are challenged to determine what the child meant to write. Sometimes reading it out loud will help in the decoding. With experience it becomes easier to figure out the intended meaning. In this case the response was meant to be "Because the paper towel is thicker, we thought it would be very strong." Reactions by different people to this type of writing are highly varied: some are troubled, some are amused, and some recognize strengths in the respondent's thought processes.

It turns out that there is much more going on than a simple matter of inventive spellings. In a document prepared by Kopriva and Sexton (1999), we find there are genuine linguistic issues at play in this scenario. Specifically for this English language learner's response, we might be able to appreciate how the native language has influenced the response. There are examples of words that are spelled phonetically (*bicos* for *because* and *papertall* for *paper towel*) and of the influence of specific pronunciations (e.g., *sh* and *v* tend to be pronounced, respectively, by Spanish speakers as *ch* and *b*). Given that the student who wrote this response had immigrated to the United States during the previous school year, the way we judged this response was that it was essentially correct and our only quibble was the failure to use *predict* instead of *thot*. Otherwise in our estimation the student was effectively using supporting information in a way that seemed reasonable—once we figured out what was written on the test.

NSES Assessment Standard D: Assessment tasks must be appropriately modified to accommodate the needs of students with physical disabilities, learning disabilities, or limited English proficiency.

Although it seems obvious, the assessments used within science ought to focus on the objects and actions of science but not on whatever limitations the students might have with expressing their knowledge and skills. In our view even though we appreciate the need to help students develop a written literacy, we don't become overly concerned with grammar and spelling unless it interferes with students' science learning. Once during a study in a third-grade classroom in Boston, we asked the students to write down some questions they had about light. One child wrote, "Who invented the light bulb and was it hod?" It seems inappropriate to quash this curiosity by pointing out the misspelling, especially because when she and her family said the word *hard,* it sounded just as she had spelled it.

For Reflection and Discussion

Visit the Performance Assessment Links in the Science Web site (http://pals. sri.com/) and examine several of the assessments tasks posted there. If these assessments were somehow part of the expectations for your science students, how might that influence the manner in which you go about teaching?

English Language Learners and Assessing in Science

A few of the five Principles for Effective Pedagogy proposed by the Center for Research on Education, Diversity, and Excellence have relevance to this chapter about assessment. Because assessments are effective when built on the practices within the classroom, it should come as no surprise that these approaches were addressed in previous chapters. Two of the approaches appeared when we described the value in challenging students to engage in complex thinking, whereas the other two approaches were first discussed within the instructional conversations principle. Because of the clear mentioning of assessment, we've chosen to highlight them within this chapter.

Principles for Effective Pedagogy Related to Assessment

In the 1970s a book titled *With Objectives in Mind* written by Wynne Harlen was popular among elementary and middle grade teachers in England. Although the actual text is no longer in print, the title evokes a thoughtful stance toward teaching. The essence is that effective science teaching should occur so the teacher is always aware of the ultimate objectives. In a climate where accountability is so important, teachers report feeling uneasy about pursuing teachable moments (Settlage & Meadows, 2002). However, if teachers clearly understand the knowledge and skills the students are expected to develop, that is, they know the standards inside and out, then they will recognize which unanticipated events are worth pursuing and will appreciate how to sculpt the situation so it is aligned with formal expectations.

The approaches for English language learners listed in Table 11.3 emphasize the need for teachers to have clear outcomes in mind. There should be a reciprocal relationship between attending to the students' interests and the assessments the teacher uses. This situation is described by the terms *reflective* and *responsive*. Teachers must absorb information about their students and contemplate the significance, and then they need to use these insights to shape their subsequent instructional decisions.

TABLE 11.3. Assessing Science Understandings, and Appropriate Teacher Actions

The teacher:
  listens carefully to assess levels of students' understanding;

  guides the students to prepare a product that indicates that the instructional conversation's goal was achieved;

  presents challenging standards for student performance; and

  gives clear, direct feedback about how student performance compared to challenging standards.

Note: Adapted from Dalton (1998).

The first two approaches in the table are from the instructional conversations framework. From an assessment perspective, the first statement describes formative and informal assessments of students. Put bluntly, it suggests that teachers must pay attention to what their English language learners are saying when they talk about science. The second approach in this list reinforces the ideal of keeping objectives in mind: science discussions are not meant to be rambling affairs but should accommodate a variety of perspectives while the teacher also guides and nudges the conversation toward the overall learning goals. The latter pair of approaches combines our current assessment conversation with the goal of challenging students to use complex thinking. The first approach reminds us to make performance expectations clear to English-language learners rather than to expect them to anticipate the ways in which they will eventually demonstrate their understandings. The last approach has its origins in the behaviorist principle wherein the feedback provided about a response should be supplied without delay. In terms of English language learners and science assessment, this approach is a reminder to share the results of an assessment event as quickly as possible with the students. In addition this feedback should inform the students about the quality of their performance relative to the expected standards. Timely and unambiguous feedback will contribute to the extinction of inaccurate ideas and reinforce proper understandings. Finally, these strategies are crucial for guiding the science learning of students who are still developing their English language fluency. Using these four approaches within the context of science assessment will benefit all students, especially those who are learning a new language and challenging subject matter at the same time.

Chapter Summary

- Assessment involves gathering information about an individual student or an entire class and using this information to inform students about their progress, to make changes in the pace at which material is being tuaght, and to make decisions about the kinds of teaching strategies being used.

- Assessments can occur near the end of a unit, and these summative assessments are the culmination of the students' learning. In contrast, formative assessments are used in the midst of learning to decide where adjustments might need to be made.

- Formal assessments are planned in advance and are to be designed to assess specific information. These include quizzes and tests but can also extend to performance assessments and portfolios. Informal assessments are more spontaneous and are often used to obtain a sense of students' understandings without expecting them to create a complete picture.

- Ideally the assessment tools will be aligned with the curriculum. The manner in which the students learned the science should be consistent with the ways in which it is assessed. This includes the concepts, materials, and level of understanding. When the assessment is misaligned with the curriculum, the results the assessments create are considerably less reliable.

- By asking a student questions about selected science topics, a teacher can use a one-on-one conversation to assess the thought processes. An interview can yield substantial information because of its intensity and focus.

- Because English language learners may use spellings and phrasings that have their roots in their native language, science teachers should remain attentive to the differences between a nonstandard use of English compared to incorrect understandings of the science concepts.

Key Terms

Alignment: the degree to which the assessment matches what the student is expected to understand. The alignment applies to not only the topic but also the depth of knowledge required of the student.

Authentic assessment: an assessment administered in a manner consistent with the situations in which the material was learned.

Counter-suggestion: an interview technique that works by asking a student, after he or she has given a response, to evaluate an alternative explanation.

Foil: on multiple-choice test items, a choice that is equally likely to be the correct answer.

Formal assessments: designed before the teaching event (i.e., the district's end of the year science test, a quiz the teacher designed, or an activity students perform that the teacher will use for assessment purposes).

Formative assessments: administered during a unit or lesson and not reserved until the conclusion. The goal of formative assessments is to inform the progress of the unit or lesson so that adjustments can be made to enhance student learning.

Informal assessments: employed on the fly of teaching (i.e., class discussions, student's short explanations, observations of small group work), thus not structured or confining but still informative.

Portfolio artifact: a raw material selected to be included in a portfolio (i.e., samples of a student's written work, videos, photographs, or software).

Portfolio narrative: the written explanation that accompanies each and every portfolio artifact.

Rubric: a tool used to assign a grade to student work in which important traits of the assignment are identified and assigned appropriate weights along a continuum of performances.

Semi-structured interview: a form of interview in which the interviewer uses a script of predetermined questions but also asks unscripted follow-up questions.

Summative assessments: administered at the end of a unit or lesson as a culminating activity before moving on to the next topic. Although summative assessments can inform later offerings of the unit or lesson, these assessments are typically used to judge the degree to which students mastered the material.

A Favorite Science Lesson

Teaching students about weather is fairly typical but doesn't necessarily involve much science inquiry. The "Air and Weather" unit produced by FOSS for use in grade one or grade two changes all that. The "Exploring Air" activity introducing the unit is truly exploratory but also provides a valuable foundation for subsequent studies of weather. Students are provided with a large plastic syringe and invited to discover all they can. From there students make all kinds of discoveries about air moving in and out as they pull and push on the plunger. They are then provided with a short piece of aquarium tubing and encouraged to connect one end to their syringe and the other to that of a partner. Now they find that pushing one plunger causes the plunger on the other side to move out. Pulling one plunger out causes the other to move in as if by magic. The teacher simply guides the students to try other possibilities and then orchestrates a postactivity discussion to clarify the students' ideas about air and pressure.

Suggested Readings

Ayala, C. (2005). Formative assessment guideposts. *Science Scope, 28*(4), 46–48.

This author provides several powerful guidelines to assist our thinking about formative assessments. We have two favorites. The first is that formative assessment is about learning, not about deciding about ranking students. The other is a reminder that students should be permitted to make mistakes to help us, as teachers, appreciate their thought processes.

Hammerman, E. (2005). Linking classroom instruction and assessment to standardized testing. *Science Scope, 28*(4), 26–32.

Making the case that teachers are obligated to know the expectations as described in their local science standards to be effective professionals, this article contains a self-check survey. Even though this was designed as a questionnaire to be used for planning professional development, it also can be a way for novice teachers to recognize the sorts of knowledge they should possess before entering an elementary or middle school classroom.

Smith, D. C., & Wesley, A. (2000). Teaching for understanding. *Science and Children, 38*(1), 36–41.

This team, a science education professor and fifth-grade teacher, worked together to prepare for a unit on plants. In looking at the preassessment results, they discovered that many students didn't have the fundamental understandings the teachers felt they should have learned in earlier grades. What results is an example of the value of using assessment data to shape instructional decision making.

References

American Association for the Advancement of Science. (1989). *Science for all Americans: Project 2061.* New York: Oxford University Press.

Black, P., Harrison, C., Lee, C., Marshall, B., & William, D. (2003). *Assessment for learning: Putting it into practice.* Maidenhead, UK: Open University Press.

Dalton, S. S. (1998). *Pedagogy matters: Standards for effective teaching practice.* Washington, DC: Center for Applied Linguistics.

Haberman, M. (1991). The pedagogy of poverty versus good teaching. *Phi Delta Kappan,* 290–293.

Henriques, D. B. (2003, September 2). Rising demands for testing push limits of its accuracy. *New York Times,* p. A1.

Kopriva, R., & Sexton, U. M. (1999). *Guide to scoring LEP student responses to open-ended science items.* Washington, DC: Council of Chief State School Officers.

Roulston, K., deMarrais, K., & Lewis, J. B. (2003). Learning to interview in the social sciences. *Qualitative Inquiry, 9,* 643–668.

Settlage, J., & Meadows, L. (2002). Standards-based reform and its unintended consequences: Implications for science education within America's urban schools. *Journal of Research in Science Teaching, 39,* 114–127.

White, R., & Gunstone, R. (1992). *Probing understanding.* London: Falmer Press.

twelve
Managing a Classroom for Science Learning

Chapter Highlights

- Creating a climate in which students feel safe and free from harm is fundamental to classroom management. Taking action to prevent, monitor, and respond to classroom events helps teachers to maintain a safe classroom environment.

- Addressing safety issues from the outset of science activities should become routine within the planning and introducing of every science activity. Safety concerns are responsibilities to be shared by teachers and students.

- One factor contributing to management challenges in diverse classrooms is that the teacher's efforts may not be consistent with the cultural norms of the students. Efforts to better align behavioral expectations in the classroom with students' backgrounds reduce interpersonal friction and prevent miscommunication.

- Classrooms have their own climates, and those features can be assessed using questionnaires that are administered to students. The results can identify the gaps between the actual and preferred aspects of the classroom climate and provide insights to teachers about adjusting the climate.

- Cooperative learning is a common feature of inquiry-based science learning. This strategy goes beyond organizing students into groups because it includes, among other things, the need to provide specific information to students to advance their social skills development.

At this point we turn our attention to managing a classroom so it supports the science learning of all students. We will begin with a review of Maslow's hierarchy of needs theory, which remains relevant even sixty years after its introduction. We'll then consider the variety of features of a classroom that contribute to a healthful learning climate. We'll consider the physical safety of the students, which is not a small consideration when we engage them in inquiry. We will also present information about making a classroom an emotionally and intellectually safe environment. To assist with this we'll supply a questionnaire teachers can administer to elementary and middle school students to identify their perceptions of the actual classroom environment and the type of classroom environment they prefer.

Meeting Individual Needs

Ideally those we teach will become independent and self-sufficient learners. As teacher educators we expect you to become a competent teacher who is able to take charge of your classroom and to move beyond a dependence on others' expertise. Likewise as much as you may enjoy having students around you, we suggest the greatest reward is for you to see them become individuals in their own right. In a sense the proof of an educator's effectiveness is the extent to which his or her students learn to thrive as individuals as a consequence of what they've been taught.

Such a transformation is not a quick or simple process. Educational psychologists have proposed that humans are motivated by a certain set of needs arranged into a hierarchy formalized by Abraham Maslow (1943). We can think of these needs as appetites that must be satisfied, and the most basic of these needs is physiological. Food, warmth, and water are the needs of all living things, and meeting those is the most fundamental form of motivation. Unless physiological needs are being adequately met, none of the other levels of Maslow's hierarchy have much significance to the individual who is hungry, cold, or thirsty. Put another way, if creature comforts are not being fulfilled, then a person is not going to be motivated by other factors such as a desire to become independent and self-reliant.

When individuals' physiological appetites are satisfied, then their wants shift to the next layer in Maslow's hierarchy: safety. Just as with the physiological needs, it isn't until the needs for safety are met that an individual's motivation will shift to even higher levels. For the record, the subsequent layers proposed by Maslow are love, esteem, and self-actualization. The point we wish to make is this: a student's drive for personal safety while in a school or classroom must be satisfied before he or she can be motivated to learn. Although this brings us close to the very sensitive issues of poverty and hunger, not insignificant issues for far too many students, Maslow's hierarchy has clear applications to science teaching. According to his theory, we cannot realistically expect students to become motivated to learn science if they are not feeling safe. This need for safety is not restricted to being free from physical harm. Safety includes perceptions of consistency and regularity within the school day, the sense of being within an emotionally safe environment, and the feeling of occupying a classroom where intellectual safety is maintained. The need for stability and comfort is essential for each student to feel safe.

> [The child] seems to want a predictable, orderly world. For instance, injustice, unfairness, or inconsistency in the parents seems to make a child feel anxious and unsafe. This attitude may be not so much because of the injustice per se or any particular pains involved, but rather because this treatment threatens to make the world look unreliable, or unsafe, or unpredictable. Young children seem to thrive better under a system which has at least a skeletal outline of rigidity, in which there is a schedule of a kind, some sort of routine, something that can be counted upon, not only for the present but also far into the future. Perhaps one could express this more accurately by saying that the child needs an organized world rather than an unorganized or unstructured one. (Maslow, 1943, p. 377)

The focus of this chapter is on managing a classroom. We are not going to ignore the traditional perception of classroom management, because making sure students behave is clearly one aspect of safety. But keeping students under control is a limiting view. We do not dispute the need for an orderly classroom. Maslow indicated that this is a defining aspect of safety. But we do not want to make classroom control our ultimate goal. Although it seems obvious, we don't hear this idea expressed often enough to convince us that everyone is convinced of it: the purpose of school is student learning, and managing student behavior is a prerequisite for learning, not the goal. There are many varieties of safety that must be satisfied for learning to occur. Physical safety is one, and an orderly and predictable environment is another. In addition we must attend to issues of emotional and intellectual safety for students to be motivated to learn. Broadly speaking, we focus this chapter on creating a safe environment to support the science learning of all students—it's just that we don't regard an overemphasis on behavior management as sufficient to allow us to reach this goal.

An Environment of Physical Safety

We have quite deliberately avoided a discussion of laboratory safety until this point, because we were worried that such concerns might be used as a reason to avoid using hands-on activities that are the basis of inquiry. Aside from getting a paper cut or dropping a heavy text on one's foot, there are admittedly far fewer physical risks associated with teaching science from a book. Our hope was not only to convince you of the power of direct experiences as part of teaching science to all students but also to help you to accept your obligation to take the steps necessary for this to happen. In other words over time you should become more fully prepared to incorporate direct experiences with scientific materials into your teaching. We anticipate that you are now prepared to learn how to reduce the chances of one of your students being hurt during science experiences.

NSES Professional Development Standard D: Teachers of science design and manage learning environments that provide students with the time, space, and resources needed for learning science.

We must be ready to accept the reality that children are accidentally bumped or bruised as part of everyday living. Heads might bonk together during group activities, a tooth might work itself loose, or someone might accidentally poke a hand with a pencil. Despite this inevitability, we should take steps to reduce the frequency and intensity of any harm that might befall our students. We organize our responsibilities regarding classroom safety into three categories: preventative, monitoring, and responsive. **Preventative safety** is a matter of being knowledgeable. For the teacher it means knowing which substances might be harmful, how equipment might be misused, and what steps to take to avoid situations in which an injury might occur. The preventative aspects of classroom safety also include students' knowledge. They too should know about the problems of touching their eyes during an activity, know how they might hurt themselves if they mistreat science equipment, and understand proper procedures to ensure their safety. If this knowledge is couched as if it is part of the larger agenda of making sure everyone is safe, then compliance will not occur out of fear. As teachers we are responsible for educating ourselves about safety issues and transmitting that knowledge to the students.

The next category of safety is making sure the knowledge is actually being applied. Knowing that a stopwatch shouldn't be spun around by its cord is useful knowledge only if nobody does that with this piece of equipment. Safety goggles can be required equipment during a chemistry activity, but the difference between knowing this and using them is what makes all the difference. As with preventative safety, **monitoring safety** is a responsibility that is not exclusively the teacher's. Safety in the classroom is something everybody must work to achieve and sustain.

The final category of science classroom safety is **responding** in appropriate ways in the event something is broken, somebody is hurt, or some other problem arises despite knowing and monitoring. For example, if a test tube or something else made of glass breaks, the inclination to pick up the pieces with one's fingers should be resisted. In addition, putting broken glass into the same trash can as papers might harm an unsuspecting custodian. In science laboratories there are special containers reserved for broken glass. In an elementary or middle school classroom, there is less need for such a container, but the lesson is the same. Broken glass should be disposed of in ways so no one can be accidentally cut. One possibility is to wrap the broken glass in a paper towel and put that inside a plastic cup—and perhaps the teacher will deliver the package to the school dumpster on his or her way to the parking lot at the end of the day.

Most school districts and all state offices of education have published safety guidelines. These normally take the form of long lists of rules, warnings, prohibitions, and procedures. Unfortunately, there is usually so much information and it is presented in such a technical way that it doesn't encourage us to read the material. To a certain extent safety guidelines published by a school are for legal purposes and may sound more frightening than we might prefer. Because you are unlikely to consult your school's or state's safety guidelines on a regular basis, we urge you to locate a copy (maybe you'll be fortunate and find one on the Web) and read it completely, even just once. As an aid for helping you to sort through the safety materials, we are going to describe several categories of safety issues as an advanced organizer for your official safety guidelines reading assignment.

Injuries: Bleeding and Burning

Perhaps the most frightful safety issue is the possibility of students being injured by a piece of equipment such that they draw blood or become burned. Let's return to our three types of safety knowledge. First, consider how to prevent situations that might lead to bleeding or burning. Working with sharp materials such as needles and knives are obvious dangers, but so too are toothpicks and scissors. Reminding students that these materials are potential causes for pokes and cuts is always wise. Remind them that you are most worried about anyone being hurt and much less interested in trying to catch perpetrators. This is not an issue about intention versus accidental harm. The goals are for no one to be hurt and for you to not worry about whose fault it might be if someone is hurt.

Objects that are sharp can cause bleeding, but so can equipment that suddenly becomes sharp during the course of the activity. In other words when something breaks it can transform from being a nice beaker to being an assortment of flesh-tearing pieces. Thermometers are another example: typically we may not think about thermometers as dangerous, especially because mercury thermometers are so rare in schools anymore. But a thermometer that snaps in two because of horseplay or by being dropped instantly becomes a cutting hazard.

Our first instinct when we hear something break might be to ask "Who did that?" when a far better thing for a teacher to say is "Did anybody get hurt?" Being disappointed that a piece of equipment was broken should not overshadow the importance of keeping everybody safe. Students expect an adult to say something right after something breaks. The message you send in that moment can be profound! Imagine a situation where a jar of pond water slips from a sixth grader's hands and shatters on the classroom floor. Here's an appropriate response by a teacher:

Teacher:	"Okay, did anybody get cut by glass?"
Class:	"No."
Teacher:	"Good, let's make sure it stays that way. I need for you to not move. Instead look around to make sure there isn't a piece of glass near you that somebody might accidentally step on. Don't move, don't pick anything up. Just look."
Student:	"Here's a piece by this desk."
Teacher:	"Okay, thank you. Terry, would you please get the dustpan and brush. And take that old coffee can with you. Walk carefully toward that group and have your classmates show you where they see pieces of glass."
Student:	"There's a big piece. And some more over here."
Student:	"What about the water?"
Teacher:	"It is most important right now to find all the pieces of glass. Terry will need to sweep up all the pieces. Carefully put those in the coffee can. After that, then somebody can use some paper towels to clean the water so we don't have a slipping hazard. If your group is not anywhere near the broken glass, then you still have work to do. I'm glad everyone is safe. For Terry and others nearby, please do not touch the glass. Only use the dustpan and brush. I'll be over to check the area as soon as I can. Everyone has a job to do. Get back to work."

Burns will occur only when there are hot materials present with which the students can come into contact. The most obvious preventative measure is to not allow anything very hot to come into the classroom. Safety guidelines published by states and equipment suppliers are usually very detailed regarding flames from candles and Bunsen burners. But in elementary and middle schools, our recommendation is to simply never have flames in the classroom. When a heat source is needed, you might consider using hot plates. Just recognize that this substitution is very much like having several glowing stovetops in your classroom. However, on those occasions when you do need very hot water, we've had fairly good success by simply using an old coffeemaker. Again the best safety guideline for avoiding burns is to avoid allowing hot objects into the classroom.

Even with prevention and monitoring, there may be unfortunate occasions when a student is injured. Except in extreme cases, the major concern is with infection. Unless you have training in first aid for very minor injuries, you should admit to your limitations and send a student to the school nurse. When we consider the issue of infections, we first think about the injured student's wound becoming infected. In addition we must recognize the possibility of infections spreading from the injured student to others. Blood-borne diseases are not merely issues for adults, as children may carry viruses and other infectious agents. Without being alarmist, we think it's probably best to exercise extreme care and caution whenever blood is involved. Checking in advance with the policies for your school and district is a good step toward prevention. Minor scrapes and cuts can be treated in the classroom with an adhesive bandage. This should be accompanied by notifying others who should know what happened; at the very least this includes the student's family and the administrators in the building. Of course this doesn't apply solely to science injuries—it represents professional good sense in the gym, on the playground, or at the bus stop.

Trips, Slips, and Falls

In the prior section we considered injuries resulting from students coming into contact with sharp objects. In this section we discuss injuries that might occur as students move through the classroom. Although we're tempted to use this as an opportunity to present the physics of falling (gravity, friction, and acceleration), that would make light of a serious issue. We are concerned about keeping our students safe while they are in our care. Part of the solution is avoiding situations where movement is hampered to a point where people might trip or where the conditions cause them to slip. Even when people lose their balance but don't actually fall, trips and slips can still cause injuries because of the sudden and wrenching movements and the strain put on muscles and bones as someone tries to catch him- or herself.

An example of exercising prevention and monitoring is to create pathways through the classroom that are free of potential tripping hazards. Tables, desks, and chairs should be arranged so there are obvious paths for walking. Although not really a safety issue, easy access to such items as the pencil sharpener, recycle bin, computers, and bookshelves should be taken into consideration as part of the physical arrangements of the classroom. Imagine the flow of traffic through the classroom, and pay attention to tripping hazards. One important issue is the stowing of book bags and backpacks. Although the idea of having these items close to their owners may be appealing, such items have a tendency to migrate from underneath desks and chairs, finding their way into walking paths. Furthermore, for students who are already dealing with physical challenges and rely on crutches or wheelchairs to move around, the need for clear aisles becomes even more necessary. In general, if students can be trained to monitor if they are maintaining clear passageways, they will help to prevent tripping accidents.

When hands-on activities are about to get underway, the teacher should alert students to the potential for the equipment they are using to become a tripping hazard. For example, this might simply take the form of a reminder not to allow meter sticks to unnecessarily hang over into the aisles. When the equipment being used requires electricity, such as with microscopes, then being aware of the presence of the cords may necessitate reminding the students that they exist. Again the emphasis is not on students' somehow misbehaving but rather on their remaining conscious of potential problems—in this case a tripping hazard.

Slips occur when the surface someone is walking on is other than as expected. The cause for slips within a classroom is almost always spills and not only of liquids. Paper and sand can also change the floor's surface so it becomes slippery. It doesn't really matter that trips are falls forward and slips are falls backward. The effects are the same, even if the causes differ. If we apply our previous guideline of prevention and monitoring, then we may be fortunate enough to never need to worry about having to respond to a classroom situation where someone trips or falls.

Evacuation Procedures

Classrooms should be safe spaces, and we want to imagine the comfort students feel as they enter your classroom. Ideally this sense of reassurance would extend throughout the entire school.

However, there can be times when remaining in a classroom is incredibly unsafe, the most notable example being a fire. Although not necessarily a science education issue, it is important within the context of safety concerns to give evacuation procedures due consideration. In addition, depending on the location of your school, you also should learn the schoolwide routines for evacuation in response to earthquakes or tornadoes.

Fire drills are a common facet of American schools, but this tradition has a tragic origin. In 1908 the heating system in an elementary school in Collinwood, Ohio, caused a fire. The panic among those in the building combined with the fact that the doors opened inward rather than out contributed to the deaths of nearly two hundred children and teachers. This is something to keep in mind whenever a fire drill interrupts the school day. Fire drills are intended to make the efficient evacuation of a building automatic in the unfortunate event that an actual fire occurs. Rehearsing the evacuation of your classroom is a serious event and a lifesaving precaution.

There are two key aspects of evacuation: emptying the school and then ensuring everyone is accounted for. Standard operating procedure is that when the fire alarm signal is heard, students immediately move toward the exits and the teacher grabs the attendance book. Once everyone is assembled at the designated location, at a safe distance from the building, the teacher must take attendance to ensure everyone is present. As a student you may have participated in more than a dozen fire drills over the years. But in your role as teacher, the significance of a fire drill is much more serious. Obviously preventing fires from occurring within your classroom is smart, which is why we suggest never using flames as part of science teaching, even for a demonstration. But knowledge about evacuation is not solely yours. You must share this knowledge with your students, and the fire drills are a way to rehearse those understandings.

We have spoken at great length in this book about culture, and we feel compelled to return to this topic. If you are teaching in a school similar to the type in which you were educated, you may not be fully aware of the traditions, such as fire drills, that you have come to accept as part of what it means to go to school. For something as serious as physical safety, teachers shouldn't leave the knowledge about such cultural practices to chance. As teachers we must formally explain the safety processes from the outset of the school year and remember to incorporate them into whatever orientations are provided to students who are added throughout the year. We want to illustrate the importance of this in the following excerpt. In this story Luis describes his experience as a recent Mexican immigrant attending school in California. In addition to empathizing with his confusion, we trust you will recognize the implications for you as a teacher who will be responsible for children like Luis.

> A day came when I finally built up the courage to tell the teacher I had to go to the bathroom. I didn't quite say all the words, but she got the message and promptly excused me so I didn't do it while I was trying to explain. I ran to the bathroom and peed. … But suddenly several bells went on and off. I hesitantly stepped out of the bathroom and saw throngs of children leave their classes. I had no idea what was happening. I went to my classroom and it stood empty. Nobody. I didn't know what to do. I thought everyone had gone home. I didn't bother to look at the playground where the whole school had been assembled for the fire drill. I just went home. It got to be a regular thing for a while, me coming home early until I learned the ins and outs of school life. (Rodriguez, 2004, pp. 25–26)

Biological Safety: Allergies and Organisms

It is quite natural in science classrooms to have living things as part of the learning environment: seeds sprouting in cups, guppies swimming in an aquarium, and so on. In this section we want to raise your level of awareness regarding biological issues. Teachers must be sensitive to the health of their students. For example allergies are proving to be a condition we may not have given sufficient attention to in the past. More and more children are being diagnosed with asthma for reasons that are not completely understood within the medical community. Being aware of the causes of asthmatic events and taking measures to prevent them are included under the banner of classroom safety. Allergies to dust and other substances may mean you cannot have furry animals in your classroom. Food allergies must also be identified, so you know which students cannot risk exposure to peanuts and other foodstuffs. We also caution you against the practice of culturing molds or bacteria in your classroom unless the school provides you with adequate sanitation equipment.

Even when students have no diagnosed allergies or other health concerns, a general awareness about the spread of germs is especially significant in the realm of science teaching. We urge you to consider how you will have students dispose of objects that they use within science activities and that might spread germs. In terms of causing physical injury, soda straws and balloons may not seem too dangerous. But when we think about the potential for spreading germs as children play with these objects, then we recognize possible safety issues. In general we do not allow our students to leave the classroom with science objects that have been in contact with mouths. A special container, ideally lined with a plastic bag, should be identified as the proper disposal site for everything from cotton swabs to Petri dishes. The chance that germs will spread throughout the classroom always exists. Safe disposal of potential germ sources is a wise tactic. Hand sanitizers, disinfectant spray, and a well-stocked supply of paper towels are good pieces of classroom safety equipment.

Teacher Knowledge Is the Key

There are few published guidelines about laboratory safety that specifically apply to science safety in elementary and middle school classrooms. However, what does exist provides us with useful information. For example when the number of students in a high school or college science lab becomes large or when there is an insufficient amount of space within the lab, the frequency of accidents increase dramatically. Although this has obvious implications for university laboratories, it does reinforce the need for teachers to be aware of physical space and crowding as potential sources of safety problems.

For Reflection and Discussion

Along with the many other responsibilities of a classroom teacher is the often-unaddressed issue of safety. Where do you think a teacher who is new to the profession, or even just new to a school, might obtain all the necessary safety knowledge required for the classroom to be appropriately safe for the students?

Other issues linked to laboratory safety include storing chemicals in places that students cannot access and keeping the supply of chemicals small enough so the inventory is sufficient for just a couple of years. But of all the guidelines summarized in an *Education Week* article about laboratory safety, the one most relevant to elementary and middle school science teaching is teacher knowledge. When teachers are aware of potential safety issues, they are better prepared to anticipate problems compared to those teachers who have received less safety training. The implication is that schools ought to, but teachers have to, be willing to attend to safety issues. This means reading the warning labels on chemicals and the accompanying Material Safety Data Sheets (MSDS). This means remaining alert to local workshops about lab safety. This means taking control of the knowledge about safety, because this knowledge will translate into providing a safer environment for your students.

Starting With Safety

The first few times you try something new, you have to consciously think through each step. You might have a checklist handy that you refer to, or you might try to pull the process from memory. Examples at a child's level include handwriting or even just learning to write the letters of one's name. You might be able to call up the image of a child leaning into his or her paper, tongue poking out one corner of his or her mouth, and reciting the steps involved in writing a capital letter R. A more adult example is learning a new exercise or dance routine. Initially there is very little flow because of all the little hesitations, backtracks, and do overs. What is so hard to recognize in people who do something with skill and grace is the fact that they had to struggle in the early stages of learning their craft. The polish and flow with which experts execute a performance conceal the stumbling efforts that occurred when they were first learning.

We are describing this idea of "practice makes perfect" because of what is involved with becoming an expert teacher. Dealing with safety issues is more likely to be incorporated into the flow of your teaching if it is included now, in the early stages of your professional development. You may already be aware of different teaching styles as you've visited various classrooms, and you are probably wondering what your teaching style will be. Style refers not only to what you say and do but also to the subtle messages you send to your students and colleagues as an extension of how you go about your work.

Identifying for students the potential safety issues within a hands-on activity should become part of your teaching style. Once you have developed an effective way to obtain the students' attention, to explain the expectations for a lesson, and to identify the resources they are to use, then you should include a brief comment about safety issues. We even go so far as to recommend that you include this within your lesson plan. By always mentioning safety issues, the preventative and monitoring aspects, at the start of every hands-on activity during the early years of your career, you will more likely make this a common piece of your teaching style.

We are not suggesting a dry recitation of safety problems. We don't wish for you to become a human warning label. Rather you are to identify possible safety hazards involved with the equipment and its use. Talking about and physically demonstrating how the students are to use the equipment will reduce the likelihood of students being poked, cut, or injured. If the activity requires wearing safety goggles or glasses, then show how that equipment will shield the students' eyes. Identify potential trip and slip problems. Explain, or ask a student to explain, what is to be done to avoid creating a tripping hazard and what to do in case something is spilled. Also explain how you expect the students to dispose of used materials, for example, what to do with the used litmus paper, toothpicks, and paper towels. In addition, plan ways to dispose of materials that do not belong in the classroom trash can or recycle bin. Here we would include soil and plant parts and so on. You don't want to have a hands-on activity become an awful experience because the clean-up process becomes a chore. This is all to say that by addressing these issues at the start of the lesson, at least as many as you can anticipate, you will make the room safer and reduce the distractions that interfere with students' science learning.

Classroom Climate

New teachers repeatedly express concern about creating a classroom climate in which learning can take place, and handling student misbehaviors is often at the very center of this worry. This concern is often exacerbated by the prospects of teaching in a classroom populated by students whose backgrounds are very different from those of their teacher. We feel these concerns are legitimate. When a teacher and his or her students have very different backgrounds, the likelihood for misunderstandings is very high. The misinterpretations of a student's actions or comments may lead a teacher to apply inappropriate disciplinary measures. What has its roots in cross-cultural communication can deteriorate into a very emotionally charged and negative situation.

A trio of teacher educators from Rutgers University (Weinstein, Tomlinson-Clarke, & Curran, 2004) proposed the idea of Culturally Responsive Classroom Management. Their perspective is that when teachers are working with cultural groups of students with whom they have inadequate knowledge, five aspects must be addressed:

1. Recognizing one's ethnocentrism
2. Knowing more about the students' culture
3. Accepting the sociopolitical contexts of schools
4. Having willingness to adopt classroom management approaches that are culturally appropriate
5. Committing to the aim of creating a caring classroom community

We will return to the problems of ethnocentrism in chapter 14 of this book. For now we feel it's sufficient to identify the problem when a teacher views her or his background and experience as being the standard against which all others should be compared. The second aspect of Culturally Responsive Classroom Management (becoming acquainted with students' background cultures) is tightly linked to the first aspect.

The third aspect in this list describes the need to understand that schools mirror the broader community in terms of social and political norms. For example people in a town experiencing an influx of immigrant families might respond with hostility to these events, and local schools may well mirror this response. Patterns of discrimination in terms of gender, race, and social status occur within schools, because those practices and attitudes are parts of the local fabric. Prejudice against certain ethnic groups within the town may reveal themselves in prohibitions against students' speaking their native language (Adams, 1997). The walls of a school do not shield the occupants from the politics of the community. As a classroom teacher you should remain attentive to opportunities to become an advocate for equity and an opponent to all forms of discrimination, even if some students have received different messages from adults in their community.

The next aspect of Culturally Responsive Classroom Management describes a step you can take at this very moment: deciding you need to use classroom management approaches appropriate for the cultural backgrounds of your students. This may be a somewhat abstract notion, because you are unlikely to know the cultural backgrounds of your students. But as will be discussed in chapter 14, a willingness to learn about students' cultures is a key step to running a more effective classroom. Finally, the fifth aspect describes your commitment to make your classroom one in which the climate is distinguished by a shared sense of caring. The desire for a caring environment is not a novel idea, and some trace this notion back to Maria Montessori's work with city children in the early 1900s (Martin, 1995). Perhaps paying particular attention to the value of creating caring classrooms is another artifact of shifting school demographics.

When teachers and students possess a shared heritage, maybe the sense of caring unconsciously arises because of the shared backgrounds. However, in classrooms that include individuals with varied backgrounds, there is a wealth of ways that cultural differences can contribute to a confusing situation. Such diversity in the classroom requires that we explicitly and deliberately pursue the goal of a caring classroom.

Creating a caring classroom is more complex and meaningful than simply being kind to your students. Nel Noddings elevated caring to a higher level when she described an ethic of caring that reflects a deeper commitment to care than merely providing hugs and treats to the class. In Noddings's work, she has moved beyond generalized notions of caring and nominated actions teachers can implement:

> Noddings (1992) suggested that four aspects of teacher behavior are critical for understanding the establishment of an ethic of classroom caring: (a) modeling caring relationships with others, (b) establishing dialogues characterized by a search for common understanding, (c) providing confirmation to students that their behavior is perceived and interpreted in a positive light, and (d) providing practice and opportunities for students to care for others. (Wentzel, 2003, p. 322)

A caring classroom becomes more than a kind and polite space. A caring classroom is one in which the relationships among students are shaped to reflect a caring attitude among individuals and the ways to practice and exhibit care are deliberately fostered by the teacher. In short an ethic of caring is infused throughout the daily routine and is dispersed among everyone. Teachers who show they care for their students are important; teachers who do this and also help students to learn how to act in caring ways toward others are doing much more to create a caring climate.

Student Belonging

A key part of feeling safe in any situation is an individual's perception that he or she belongs. A caring classroom ensures that every student feels he or she belongs, and student belongingness has been the focus of considerable research in schools. Research has shown how middle school students' positive sense of belonging is associated with better academic achievement (Roeser, Midgley, & Urban, 1996), and there are indications that students' sense of belonging is correlated with their respect for their teachers, which may relate to a reduction in negative behaviors such as cheating (Murdock, Hale, & Weber, 2001). Our interpretation of this and related research reinforces our belief that we need to ensure that students feel safe within our classrooms. There are humane reasons for wanting students to feel cared for and as if they belong. There are also practical reasons such as the reduction in classroom management difficulties when students feel as if they belong. But beyond these touchy-feely features, caring and belongingness contribute to students' persistence and self-efficacy and ultimately to their ability to achieve. In a summary of research on school belonging, Osterman (2000) reported this consistent finding from classroom research:

> Students who experienced a greater sense of acceptance by peers and teachers were more likely to be interested in and enjoy school and their classes. These perceptions of school were also reflected in their commitment to their work, higher expectations of success, and lower levels of anxiety. (Osterman, 2000, p. 331)

Student belongingness and a caring classroom environment provide benefits to students' emotional health, the teacher's ability to manage student behaviors, and even students' academic performance. However, we have not discussed how we might evaluate the classroom environment. At best we might suspect that we can accomplish this only by relying on our intuition: do students seem comfortable, is the air free of tension, does it seem like everyone gets along? We do not want to dismiss the value of becoming sensitive to the tone of a classroom. But there are more formal ways for assessing the classroom climate. The usefulness of this resides in the opportunity to uncover hidden problems and then to use this information to make adjustments in how we run our classrooms. In the next section we will focus on the means for assessing the classroom environment and the examples of what we can do in the spirit of data-based decision making.

Point–Counterpoint

Keeping a classroom under control is a common worry expressed by new teachers. In response to this need, many resources are available that claim to be the key to becoming an effective classroom manager. However, there are mixed opinions about the usefulness of these "teaching packages" as advertised on the Web and in countless teaching magazines. So in response to the question "How much confidence can new teachers place in the teaching packages marketed as beneficial to new teachers?" we can consult two informed opinions from very different sources.

Assembly of Your Very Own Teaching Package

Todd Hunter
Secondary School Science Teacher, Austin, Texas

Standardized tests. Faculty meetings. Department meetings. Completion of a portfolio. Professional development courses. Going to the school play. Attending the football game against the archrival. These are just a few of the things a first-year teacher must worry about, and I haven't even mentioned anything that goes on in a class. First-year teachers are easily inundated with the vast array of tasks that teachers are responsible for. With all of the outside pressures, teachers need any help they can get in successfully navigating their first few years. There are several management techniques that can be implemented in a classroom that will make the first years of teaching significantly easier to traverse.

Management techniques promoted by many teachers, most prominently Dr. Harry Wong, are based on the idea of routine. Routine allows the students and teachers to become comfortable with the day-to-day flow of the classroom, and both parties know their roles in relation to each other and to the class. Students know what to do upon entering the class; upon encountering various types of activities such as labs, lectures, and videos; and upon leaving the class. At first glance this may seem childish, but on further investigation we find that routine is in fact very much part of our everyday lives. Most of us take the same route to work every day. If you need to be at work at 8:00 a.m. and you change your route to work every day, can you meet the expectations of being on time with certainty? Probably not. You may be unaware that on an alternate route, there is construction. Signs are generally posted to warn well in advance that construction is coming, and to plan accordingly. If, however, you change the route to work every day, you run the risk of using a route that has construction you do not know about. So we self-impose routines every day. Why should routine then not have a place in the classroom?

Some of the routine techniques advocated by the likes of Dr. Wong include setting up classroom rules, board work, and procedures for different types of activities. When setting up class rules, the teacher should have three to five rules and then allow the class to initiate rules as well. When the students have a stake in the rules of a classroom, then, when a rule is broken, the offender disobeyed not only the teacher but also the entire class. Board work, or warm-ups, helps the students get into the class mind-set and lend ease to starting class. Procedures allow for students to become comfortable with changing activates in the middle of class.

One argument against these strategies may be that they inhibit inquiry. In fact they make inquiry easier. Students become accustomed to starting class on time, so you don't need to struggle to get everyone's attention. Students have a procedure for entering the lab and have set up their own rules governing lab behavior, so you need not fear having them use lab materials. Instead of stifling student questioning and discussion, these strategies enable students to engage each other on various topics, as the rules for such activities were partially created by the students, and the procedure has been established.

I am not favoring strict adherence to the methods laid out. Teachers must pick and choose what works for their own class, and that includes the routines discussed here and many others. If it doesn't work, modify it. If it still doesn't work, get rid of it. However, no one ever entered teaching because he or she wanted to control people. Use of these methods creates an environment where the class controls itself. And it allows the teacher to focus on the more important stuff, like creating great lessons or going to the faculty meeting or the homecoming game under the Friday night game lights.

The Allure of the "Teaching Package"

Mary Burbank
Teacher Educator at the University of Utah and Former Elementary School Teacher

"You too can be a teacher for only $29.95!" and "Ten surefire tips for your Teaching Toolbox!" These provocative titles certainly seem compelling. But are they all they claim to be?

The call to action of many texts on classroom management captures the attention of educators seeking the secrets for effective teaching. Pictures of successful teachers, checklists for setting up a classroom, and maps and diagrams for those who are most successful in the classroom captivate the attention of those hoping to make or break their approach to classroom discipline.

A glance through the table of contents in many of these how-to books reveals basic components of a classroom that will increase management success with the implication that most classrooms will run like well-oiled machines. By implementing these tried-and-true methods proposed in many of these books, teachers will get the results they envision. For many novices and veterans, there is an allure to guidebooks that will help them address the oftentimes overwhelming demands of running classrooms.

Is there merit to the suggestions offered? Without a doubt there are clearly instructional strategies and organizational tools that make teachers' lives more manageable. As with any profession, there are technical elements of one's work that allow for basic competencies related to organization, planning, and communication. However, if the answers to effectively run classrooms were simply a matter of applying the "new and improved" strategy for "managing today's youth," why are educators inundated, year after year, with the new and improved texts for responding to classroom management? If these strategies for discipline work, and if teachers are adept at implementing these tools, why does classroom management continue to rank as one of the primary concerns cited by both novice and veteran teachers?

Educators must look at classrooms, like any complex system, and those inhabiting classrooms more holistically. As educators we must examine the interplay among many variables and ask ourselves why our classrooms operate in a particular manner. As two teacher educators stated so eloquently, "When teachers remark that they've adopted a practice because 'it works' ... we are challenged to ask ourselves whether these actions are morally, socially, and educationally defensible." Furthermore, we must determine whether we are seeking short-term compliance or long-term learning.

Addressing classroom management must include the recognition of the integration of strong instructional practices, a curriculum that is relevant to each student, and a philosophy that values the knowledge students and their families bring to classrooms and schools. Furthermore, we must understand that classrooms reflecting the integration of students, curriculum, instruction, and assessment are not a formula for chaos well. Instead these classroom communities operate in a manner that extends well beyond the minute-by-minute surveillance of the next policy violation.

Assessing the Classroom Environment

To a certain extent teachers are informally able to assess the climate in their classroom. They can develop a sense of how things are working by examining subconscious and subtle clues: the tone of students' voices, their body language when in groups, and who associates with whom when there is free choice. Alternatively teachers formally assess the students' views about the classroom climate by using a questionnaire. Barry Fraser (1986) has made a career of studying learning environments, and he has created several assessment tools for this purpose. One that is especially appropriate for elementary and middle schools is called the "My Class Inventory" (MCI; Fraser, 1994). We included a copy of this questionnaire in Appendix B, and here we will consider possible uses of it.

The MCI uses "yes or no" responses to a twenty-five–item questionnaire to establish scores on five subscales: satisfaction, friction, competitiveness, difficulty, and cohesiveness. One of the most effective ways to use the MCI is to have students fill it in twice. First, they circle their responses based on their perceptions of the actual classroom, and the second time they circle the answers to show how they would prefer the classroom to be. In Figure 12.1 we show the kind of profile a teacher might obtain after giving the MCI to her class.

How do we interpret these data? First, we should focus on those areas where the gap between actual and preferred is the greatest. Even though it might appear cohesion is the highest factor (i.e., it has the greatest degree of concern), we must attend to the subscale where the discrepancy is the largest. This data suggest the teacher has the most work to do to bring the perceived difficulty of the class more in line with the class preference. The distance between the actual score and preferred score is the greatest for this subscale.

This might appear to be strange: students preferring a classroom climate that is more difficult than it actually is. But research by Mark Storz and Karen Nestor (2003) in which they interviewed urban middle schools students revealed that students desire greater challenge from their education. In other words, many students expressed frustration that they were not being held to very high academic expectations. Students enrolled in city schools recognized they were not being expected to learn as much as their friends and relatives attending suburban schools.

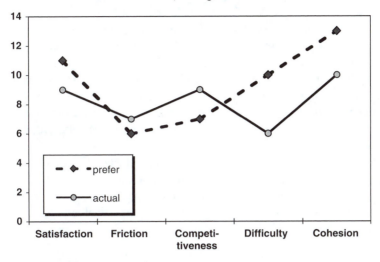

Classroom Results, Average on MCI Subscales

The data below are represented in the graph above

	Satisfaction	Friction	Competitiveness	Difficulty	Cohesion
prefer	11	6	7	10	13
actual	9	7	9	6	10

FIGURE 12.1. This graph shows the class profiles on the "My Class Inventory."

In talking with Storz and Nestor, the urban middle school students indicated they wanted to be pushed to learn more than what was currently being expected. We should not be puzzled when students circle "no" on the MCI for the actual classroom conditions but circle "yes" on the preferred classroom climate in response to statements such as "Most students can do their schoolwork without help" and "Schoolwork is hard to do." For many students, challenging material and high expectations are what they actively seek.

Adjusting the Environment in Your Classroom

Fisher (1986) outlined how to translate an interest in improving your classroom environment into action. The stages he identified are deceptively straightforward; the implications can be quite profound. Stages 1 and 2 are assessing and analyzing the classroom environment, respectively. Fisher recommended that we assess the actual and preferred environments. The version of the MCI we provide in Appendix B can be used for both purposes. You simply indicate on the form, either by circling the appropriate phrase yourself or by having the students do it, which way of thinking they should use as they respond to statements. A clear indication on the questionnaires about actual versus preferred is necessary not only to keep the students on track but also for you to analyze their responses. Creating a graph showing the profile, either for individual students or for the entire class, will help you to visualize where the biggest gaps exist between the actual and preferred classroom environments.

Stages 3 and 4 are the most intellectually challenging and perhaps the most emotionally demanding as well. Stage 3 is the self-reflection phase, and Stage 4 is the intervention phase. You have to take a cold hard look at the data, accept the facts as being actually representative of the students' views, and then decide how you might go about responding to the results. Attempting to fix everything at the same time is unwise. Instead you should focus on the subscale that shows the biggest gap and then reflect, on your own or in consultation with a trusted colleague, on how to respond. You may decide to rely on regularly scheduled class meetings (Charles & Senter, 2005) to increase classroom cohesiveness or reduce interpersonal friction. You may need to consider providing differentiated instruction so students feel appropriately challenged by the work yet satisfied by their accomplishments. There are dozens of ways you can respond. The situation almost demands that you do something. After all when the data in front of you describe the students' views of the classroom environment, as the teacher you are obligated to act on this knowledge.

Stage 5 is where you reassess the students following your efforts to modify the classroom environment. Fisher didn't suggest how long you should wait before asking students to complete the MCI again. Our sense, and probably yours as well, is that the classroom environment is not constant and cannot be quickly transformed. It may not be unreasonable to wait a month or longer to conduct the reassessment.

Beneficial Effects of Adjusting the Environment

You might question if assessing students' perceptions of the classroom environment is worth the investment of time. In a study of the classroom environment and student achievement, She and Fisher (2002) uncovered very solid and positive relationships between these two measures. The students who felt as if they were being asked challenging questions by their teachers, who perceived their teachers as providing more support in nonverbal ways, and who felt most strongly that their teachers were friendly and understanding had higher grades in their science classes. This further reinforces the findings from a review of research conducted several years ago showing students' achievement is higher when they perceive that the classroom is more cohesive, there is a greater sense of satisfaction, and the degree of interpersonal friction is much less (Haertel, Walberg, & Haertel, 1981). The bottom line is that the classroom environment is clearly connected to students' learning.

NSES Teaching Standard D: Teachers engage students in designing the learning environment.

We began this chapter with a quick look at Maslow's hierarchy of needs, indicating that until one level of an individual's appetite is satisfied, he or she is unmotivated to achieve higher levels. In Maslow's framework belongingness is the motivational factor that comes after the satisfying of bodily and personal safety needs:

> If both the physiological and the safety needs are fairly well gratified, there will emerge the love and affection and belongingness needs. ... Now the person will feel keenly, as never before, the absence of friends. ... He [or she] will hunger for affectionate relations with people in general, namely, for a place in his [or her] group, and he [or she] will strive with great intensity to achieve this goal. (Maslow, 1954, p. 89)

Teachers' indications of their positive regard for their students, sometimes described as "pedagogical caring" (Wentzel, 1997), translates into improved academic performance, to say nothing about the emotional well-being of the students.

Cooperative Learning

When people are working together we say they are cooperating, and we regard cooperation as a reasonable social behavior. Among educators, cooperative learning means more than having students working in groups. Extended investigations in classrooms by researchers studying various approaches to group work have revealed the key features of effective cooperative learning.

NSES Program Standard D: The K-12 science program must give students access to appropriate and sufficient resources, including quality teachers, time, materials and equipment, adequate and safe space, and the community.

There are many names that have come to be associated with cooperative learning, but perhaps the best known is the team of brothers Roger and David Johnson. Their work has been sufficiently extensive and enduring that they operate the Cooperative Learning Center at the University of Minnesota (www.co-operation.org). The Johnsons have been admirably generous about sharing their knowledge and expertise. In some ways by providing guidelines about how to think about implementing cooperative learning rather than a particular system a teacher must use, their work has been incredibly useful to the education profession. The most recent edition of their text *Circles of Learning* (Johnson, Johnson, & Holubec, 2002) is an impressive resource for the classroom teacher. In the space we have available, we will focus on the key features as they relate to science teaching.

Components of Cooperative Learning

Within science teaching the idea of cooperative learning has been well accepted. In particular, because good science teaching relies on social learning situations, and here we are referring to lab work or hands-on activities, the Johnsons' approach to cooperative learning seemed suitably aligned with what teachers wish to accomplish. According to the Johnsons, cooperative learning involves five key components: positive interdependence, promotive interactions, individual and group accountability, social skills development, and group processing.

Positive interdependence involves creating relationships in which each member of the groups relies on the talents, insights, and knowledge of others. When this dependence is coercive and students are forced to work with each other, then genuine cooperation will not occur. When the members of a group rely on the others to accomplish an overall goal, positive interdependence is represented. Within science teaching a very common way to address this component is to assign different students within the group to particular roles. Especially for complex tasks, dividing the responsibilities among the group members increases the likelihood the group will complete its assignment. The goal is to oblige students within the group to become accepting of individual contributions.

The second component of cooperative learning is **promotive interaction,** which describes a shared effort in which everyone seeks to support the growth of every individual by encouraging, supporting, and insisting on each person's contribution. This relates to the third component of **individual and group accountability.** One criticism of group work is the fear that some students will allow others to do all of the work. This concern is often used to suggest that classrooms ought to be competitive environments where each individual's strength and determination is rewarded. Cooperative learning advocates are not opposed to the need to maintain appropriately ambitious expectations for every single student, as long as it isn't accomplished in a way that necessitates there be losers and winners. The Johnsons portray cooperative learning groups as support systems: individuals' academic and affective needs are nurtured and advanced within a climate of shared responsibility.

There are many ways a science teacher can encourage both individual and group responsibility. We will mention one practical approach, even though it borders on being viewed as a gimmick. Imagine a classroom where students are working in groups of four on a hands-on activity. For the sake of continuity, let's pretend the science lesson is within the Extend phase of the learning cycle. Students are entering data and answering questions on the record sheets the teacher provided to them. Once it becomes clear that everyone has finished their writing, the teacher instructs them to hold their individual papers in the air. She then moves about the room, randomly taking one or two papers from each group. These will be evaluated to determine grades for individual students. Nobody knew in advance whose papers would be selected, so everyone needed to do the work. Not having a paper graded this time doesn't mean any student was deceived. After all the purpose of doing work in science class is to learn the material, not simply to obtain high marks. In this scenario every student was accountable for doing his or her work. Each needed to support the efforts and understandings of other group members, but there was also the real possibility that the teacher would judge individual effort.

The fourth component of the Johnsons' view of cooperative learning is **social skills development.** In a classroom where students are not often allowed to work with each other, their knowing how to interact with others is not really an issue. However, when elementary and middle school students are obliged to work with others, then their immaturity as social beings can come to the surface. As much as we might like to believe that our students come to us knowing how to work in mutually collaborative ways, the reality is that these are skills that must be learned. Knowing how to work with ovthers is not an inborn talent. In fact learning the appropriate ways in which people work together is part of becoming cultural beings. Just as with manners such as politeness and respect, social skills must be taught to children as part of their maturation process.

Within social skills we include basics such as sharing materials and taking turns. We also should attend to more complex behaviors such as active listening, reaching consensus, and respecting other views. Doing these well is pivotal to creating a climate that is safe for every student and consistent with the actions of the culture of science. Our approach to social skill development parallels our earlier stance regarding process skills. Although skills are rarely used in isolation, we can benefit from developing their use by focusing on them as discrete elements. Observing and inferring often happen simultaneously within our work, but it is valuable to separate them to reinforce their distinctiveness. In a similar fashion we need to isolate social skills to assist novices with recognizing and using them. We cannot realistically expect students to learn multiple social skills simultaneously. By teasing the social skills apart, we can name them, describe them, and help students learn how to use them in the context of cooperative learning activities. The Johnsons have supplied a technique we can use for this purpose (Johnson & Johnson, 1990).

The Social Skills T-chart is an instructional tool a teacher can use to embed social skill development within the context of science cooperative learning activities (see Table 12.1). The T-chart

---

For Reflection and Discussion

Within the business world there is a definite trend toward generating learning communities. How might the skills associated with cooperative learning be beneficial to your students when they eventually enter the workforce?

TABLE 12.1. Social Skills T-Chart Showing What Students Feel Are Appropriate Actions

Respecting Other People's Ideas	
Looks Like	**Sounds Like**
Looking at the person talking	"I think that's a good idea."
Nodding to show you know what they mean	"OK, but how is that better?"

allows us to isolate and emphasize a particular social skill and help students recognize what is involved in its use. For example suppose the social skill for a science lesson is "respecting other people's ideas." This would appear as the title for our T-chart (on a sheet of butcher block paper, the chalkboard, or the overhead projector). The T consists of two headings: looks like and sounds like. The information to be written underneath these headings is to come from the students. After the teacher gives a general description about the need to respect others' ideas, the students are then invited to describe how those would look in action. Here's a typical scenario we've experienced.

Teacher: As you work in groups today, I want you to practice using a new social skill. We are going to talk about it right now before I explain the activity for the day. And then, depending on when we finish, we will come back to this social skill at the end of the lesson or maybe first thing tomorrow. First, what does this look like up on the board?

Student: A gigantic letter T.

Teacher: Yes, this is going to be our T-chart. At the top I'm going to write the title for my T-chart. Who could read this for us—Jess?

Student: "Respecting other people's ideas."

Teacher: Thank you. We've been doing really well working in teams. But I'm worried that not everyone feels like they are able to contribute to the group. I'm not saying anybody has been doing anything wrong. What I am saying is we need to be careful and give everyone the chance to contribute. Why is this important?

Student: So nobody feels left out or like they were being ignored or something.

Student: Just because some people are more quiet doesn't mean they don't have something important to say.

Student: Maybe somebody will have a good idea that nobody else had thought of yet and then we get to hear it.

Teacher: Good, good, good. Now let's think about what will be happening in your groups if you are respecting other people's ideas. Suppose I'm over on one side of the room and I glance at a group clear on the other side. And let's say the group is doing a good job with this social skill. Here is my question: What would it look like if the students in a group were showing respect for other students' ideas?

Student: Maybe when one person is talking, the other kids aren't saying anything. And they are all looking at you when you are saying your ideas.

Teacher: Okay, so I'm going to write on the T-chart "looking at the person talking." We will come back to this "looks like" in just a minute. On the other side of the T is "sounds like," and this is what I would hear when a group is respecting other ideas. Suppose I'm standing next to a group and just listening in to the conversation. What kinds of things would I expect to hear? Kaitlyn?

Student: You could hear somebody say to the other person, "I think that's a good idea."

Teacher: Okay, that's a fine example. Thank you. Who else can suggest other things we could write for "looks like" or "sounds like"?

When cooperative learning is implemented so it is more than simply group work, it has been shown to benefit all students. As with much of what we have described in this book, cooperative learning should be seen not as a goal but as a mechanism for achieving the goal of encouraging every student to learn science. In other words, don't rely on cooperative learning just as a change of pace. Instead recognize and embrace this approach as a powerful option within your teaching toolbox. For example, cooperative learning could be seen as a way to provide additional help to students who are cognitively or physically challenged. Cooperative learning is regarded as an important feature of inclusive classrooms (Fetters, Pickard, & Pyle, 2003), and we can use it to benefit all science learners.

English Language Learners and Managing a Productive Classroom

The Center for Research on Education, Diversity, and Excellence (CREDE) seems to have anticipated this chapter on management within its Five Principles for Effective Pedagogy. The following approaches should reinforce the notion of creating a climate supportive of student learning rather than of communicating a need to control students and their behavior. Advanced planning in terms of organizing classroom space, making effective use of social relationships, and creating structures so time and materials are used in an efficient manner are all part of the larger picture.

Creating Structures to Support Science Learning

For students who are still developing their English fluency, the barrage of oral and written language must feel like an assault on their senses. Not knowing which messages are necessary (e.g., a poster of classroom rules) and which are less essential (e.g., posters intended to inspire) makes sorting through public texts very labor intensive. But reading text in a language where fluency is not yet achieved is only part of the difficulty. Add to this the constant flow of oral information, and one can sympathize with the sensory overload. There are approaches from the five principles of effective pedagogy that correspond to the management ideas presented within the current chapter. These can be thought of as tools to guide English language learners to sort through the constant flow of English so they can focus and become successful within science (see Table 12.2).

The need for social support of English language learners is apparent within several of these approaches. This is accomplished in part by thinking about how to arrange the classroom's physical space to accommodate conversations between students and support discussions between the teacher and small groups of students. There are also social skill development considerations included within the use of group work and cooperative learning. Finally, the classroom can be managed to support the science learning of English-language learners through the creation of routines on which students can come to rely. Included within this are knowing where materials are located so they are available at the instant they are needed and providing guidelines about the time allotments for activities. When these approaches are in place, English language learners are not as burdened by the possible confusion of sorting out the important from the incidental. The reduced cognitive load frees their minds to focus on the science concepts they are to learn while also supporting the development of their language fluency.

TABLE 12.2. Managing a Science Classroom and Appropriate Teacher Actions

The teacher

uses the seating of people to encourage individuals to work and talk together;

organizes groups in a variety of arrangements according to friendships, academic abilities, language fluencies, and individual personalities—in short an array of efforts to support interactions;

instructs students about the social skills required as part of working in groups;

uses physical arrangement of furniture and space to encourage teachers and small groups of students to participate in frequent conversations; and

structures the access to materials and monitors time (e.g., efficient transitions, allowance for cleaning up, etc.) to facilitate joint productive activity.

Note: Adapted from Dalton (1998).

Chapter Summary

- Classroom management includes issues of safety. Attending to possible threats to physical safety needs to be considered part of science instructional decision making (e.g., preventing, monitoring, and responding).

- A significant way to avoid injuries, falls, and so on is to announce sources of those problems at the outset of each science activity. Sharing responsibility with the students for monitoring safety concerns reduces the likelihood of physical harm.

- Teachers may struggle with classroom management if they ignore potential cultural influences on students' actions. Becoming more informed about cultural norms will provide teachers with insights that will increase their effectiveness at creating a classroom environment supportive of students' sense of belongingness.

- Teachers can assess classroom climate with student questionnaires. The data showing gaps between preferred and actual features of the environment, with such measures as competitiveness and satisfaction, provide teachers with insights needed for adjustments in the climate of the classroom.

- Cooperative learning has come to represent a defining aspect of hands-on science activities. More than just group work, cooperative learning relies on teachers to provide students with specific instruction about social skill development.

Key Terms

Individual and group accountability: an important component of cooperative groups in which both individuals in a group and the overall group are held responsible in tangible ways (i.e., grades) for achieving a shared goal. Such accountability allows for students' affective needs to be met within a climate of shared responsibility.

Monitoring safety: the ongoing and shared attention, given by students and their teacher, to potential threats to personal safety during science activities.

Positive interdependence: describes the relationships between members of a cooperative group where each member of the groups relies on the talents, insights, and knowledge of others to accomplish a shared goal. Such positive interdependence is typically not established when dependence between group members is coercive and when students are forced to work with each other.

Preventative safety: the advance knowledge of the teacher and students that will avert potentially harmful situations in a science classroom.

Promotive interaction: an important component of cooperative groups that describes a shared effort in a cooperative group in which everyone seeks to support the growth of every individual; encouraging, supporting, and insisting on each person's contribution fall within this component.

Responding safety measures: comments (assurances of calm and expressions of concern) and reactions (e.g., proper disposal of broken glass) that should occur in the event of a science accident.

Social skills development: an important component of cooperative group activity in which students learn to interact with one another in mutually collaborative ways.

A Favorite Science Lesson

Kindergarten science teaching is not exclusively about playing around, but it also doesn't have to be overly academic. The "Animals Two by Two" unit from FOSS is developmentally appropriate while also providing genuine science for that age. The "Land and Water Snails" lessons involve activities where not knowing the answers is actually beneficial to teaching the students. As the students examine snails moving within the clear plastic basins, eating lettuce leaves, or maneuvering around the small cardboard fences, they will ask questions and make comments a teacher will not have anticipated. It becomes quite natural for the teacher to reply with open-ended questions such as "Why do you think the snail is doing that?" Simultaneously, it is a treat to participate in the investigation of a living thing such as a land snail, especially if you've never taken the time to really observe one carefully. The quality of conversations kindergartners can have about snails can be quite amazing, and all the more so when you are unconcerned about sharing your knowledge.

Suggested Readings

Hand, R. (2004). Creating a fair classroom environment. *Science Scope, 28*(1), 54–55.

> This middle grades teacher reveals some of his management techniques. Even though he thought he was being fair toward his students, they did not perceive he was. In response he developed a few clever approaches that reduce the chances that it appears he was playing favorites.

Roy, K. (2005). Greener is cleaner, and safer. *Science Scope, 28*(6), 50–51.

> This author is chairperson for National Science Teachers Association's Science Safety Advisory Board. He writes extensively about issues related to classroom science. In this article he highlights a movement toward using environmentally safe chemicals whenever possible when teaching hands-on science.

Schulte, P. L. (1999). Lessons in cooperative learning. *Science and Children, 36*(7), 44–47.

> The essentials of cooperative learning are highlighted within this article. The author provides practical advice, including some clever ideas about how to assign roles within groups.

References

Adams, D. W. (1997). *Education for extinction: American Indians and the boarding school experience.* Lawrence: University of Kansas Press.

Charles, C. M., & Senter, G. W. (2005). *Building classroom discipline.* Boston: Allyn & Bacon.

Dalton, S. S. (1998). *Pedagogy matters: Standards for effective teaching practice.* Washington, DC: Center for Applied Linguistics.

Fetters, M., Pickard, D., & Pyle, E. (2003). Making science accessible: Strategies to meet the needs of a diverse student population. *Science Scope, 26*(5), 26–29.

Fisher, D. (1986). *Changing the environment.* Glasgow, Scotland: Scottish Council for Research in Education, University of Glasgow.

Fraser, B. J. (1986). *Classroom environment.* London: Croom Helm.

Fraser, B. J. (1994). Research on classroom and school climate. In D. L. Gabel (Ed.), *Handbook of research on science teaching and learning* (pp. 493–541). New York: Macmillan.

Haertel, G. D., Walberg, H. J., & Haertel, E. H. (1981). Socio-psychological environments and learning: A quantitative synthesis. *British Educational Research Journal, 7,* 27–36.

Johnson, D. W., & Johnson, R. T. (1990, January). Social skills for successful group work. *Educational Leadership, 47,* 29–33.

Johnson, D. W., Johnson, R., & Holubec, E. (2002). *Circles of learning: Cooperation in the classroom.* Edina, MN: Interaction Book Company.

Martin, J. R. (1995). A philosophy of education for the year 2000. *Phi Delta Kappan, 76,* 355–359.

Maslow, A. H. (1943). A theory of human motivation. *Psychological Review, 50,* 370–396.

Maslow, A. H. (1954). *Motivation and personality.* New York: Harper and Brothers.

Murdock, T. B., Hale, N. M., & Weber, M. J. (2001). Predictors of cheating among early adolescents: Academic and social motivations. *Contemporary Educational Psychology, 26,* 96–115.

Noddings, N. (1992). *The challenge to care in schools: An alternative approach to education.* New York: Teachers College Press.

Osterman, K. F. (2000). Students' need for belonging in the school community. *Review of Educational Research, 70,* 323–367.

Rodriguez, R. (2004). *Hunger of memory: The education of Richard Rodriguez.* New York: Bantam.

Roeser, R. W., Midgley, C., & Urban, T. C. (1996). Perceptions of the school psychological environment and early adolescents' psychological and behavioral functioning in school: The mediating role of goals and belonging. *Journal of Educational Psychology, 88,* 408–422.

She, H. C., & Fisher, D. (2002). Teacher communication behavior and its association with students' cognitive and attitudinal outcomes in science in Taiwan. *Journal of Research in Science Teaching, 39,* 63–78.

Storz, M. G., & Nestor, K. R. (2003). Insights into meeting standards from listening to the voices of urban students. *Middle School Journal, 34*(4), 11–19.

Weinstein, C. S., Tomlinson-Clarke, S., & Curran, M. (2004). Toward a conception of culturally responsive classroom management. *Journal of Teacher Education, 55,* 25–38.

Wentzel, K. R. (1997). Student motivation in middle school: The role of perceived pedagogical caring. *Journal of Educational Psychology, 89,* 411–419.

Wentzel, K. R. (2003). Motivating students to behave in socially competent ways. *Theory into Practice, 42,* 319–326.

thirteen
Educational Technology and Science Teaching

Chapter Highlights

- Technology as a tool for learning includes pencils, calculators, and computers. Educational technology specifically refers to computer-based materials used for a variety of educational purposes.

- The current push for increasing the use of computers in schools has parallels with previous generations and the fascination with innovative technologies of each era. One implication of the history of such efforts, however, is that technology is only as good as the teachers and the schools in which it is used.

- For a technology to be innovative, it must address a fundamental need and do so in a unique and compelling fashion. Educational technology can be categorized into four taxonomic groups: productivity tools, communicating ideas and information, tools for investigating, and authoring knowledge products.

- Educational technology can be very useful to teachers as they plan for instruction. Lesson plans are freely available on the Web, and record keeping can be assisted through the use of several types of software.

- A popular and sometimes productive form of educational technology for learning involves uses of the Internet. These uses include WebQuests, partnerships between students and scientists, and virtual field trips.

- Not all educational technology requires access to the Internet. In addition to stand-alone software and data-sensing tools called probes, computers can be pressed into service as assistive technologies for those with physical impairments.

- Educational technology is the cause of some teacher resistance, some of which is the product of individual uncertainty whereas other concerns have more rational bases. One significant issue is the disparity in the access to computers that continues to separate the wealthier students and districts from those that are less advantaged.

- Considerations about the appropriateness of a particular educational technology rely on the same criteria as for other instructional decisions. A focus on the culture of science (concepts and process skills, inquiry and nature of science, etc.) and curriculum standards should be applied with as much rigor to a computer tool as to any hands-on activity.

Within this chapter we will examine the potential for educational technology to support our goal of helping all children to learn science. The rapidity with which technology is changing makes it impossible to consider every classroom possibility. As we will show, some technologies of the past, which were thought to be highly beneficial, proved to be otherwise. Yet there is continued hope for technology to truly transform science teaching. As science teachers we hold a position of skeptical optimism. Our natural reaction to every new technological innovation is caution mixed with interest. Time and again we find the potential value of any technology has less to do with its speed, power, or portability and more to do with the skill with which a conscientious and informed teacher uses it.

Defining Technology

As we begin our discussions about technology as it relates to teaching science to all students, we should begin by clarifying what we include within technology. We need to do this because a definition of *technology* is not obvious. From a historical perspective, technology was once viewed as the practical arts and the methods used to solve problems. In short, technology can be equated with tools and their use. Because our concern is with teaching and learning, the tools with which we are interested should be easy to list. Let's begin: the Internet, e-mail, electronic slide shows, and chat rooms. But is this list too narrow because it includes only computer-based technologies? Probably, so our list of educational tools should also include DVD, CD, and videotape players. Perhaps we can legitimately include overhead projects and calculators. Must we stop there? Can we also include pencils, markers, and chalkboards? What seemed like the simple task of listing educational technologies reveals a considerable variety of options.

> [Technology] once meant knowing how to do things—the practical arts or the study of the practical arts. But it has also come to mean innovations such as pencils, television, aspirin, microscopes, etc., that people use for specific purposes, and it refers to human activities such as agriculture or manufacturing and even to processes such as animal breeding or voting or war that change certain aspects of the world. (AAAS, 1993, p. 43)

It should come as no surprise to find in an article about the history of technology a chronology moving from the Stone Age to the Industrial Revolution to the current information age (Fitzgerald, 2002). For millions of years humans have been using technology, even if in the form of stone tools. (Do you suppose a call for tech support back then involved repairing broken arrowheads?) Although this seems to take the definition of technology to an extreme, it should raise some uncertainty about what is meant when a teacher uses technology within his or her science teaching. We might think we know what is intended, but we can't be sure. To complicate the situation even further, sometimes technology education is advocated as a way to make students aware of engineering careers—for example through such projects as invention competitions. You may have thought a chapter about technology and science education would address the uses of computers in classrooms—and we will reach this point before too long. But first we feel the need to show what we have chosen to leave out of our discussion of technology.

Technology in the Science Education Standards

Because technology seems so prevalent within modern education, we consulted the *National Science Education Standards* to see if this document could illuminate our confusion about technology.

> The central distinguishing characteristic between science and technology is a difference in goal: the goal of science is to understand the natural world, and the goal of technology is to make modifications in the world to meet human needs. Technology as design is included in the *Standards* as parallel to science as inquiry. (National Research Council, 1996, p. 24)

In this context, technology is equated with design in a manner paralleling the connections between science and inquiry. The idea is for students to learn about technology by participating in design. This suggests we should view technology, design, and engineering as processes for attaining the goal of creating a solution to a problem. In contrast the goal of science is building evidence-based explanations and understandings of our surroundings. The path to answering questions beginning with "What is …" runs through scientific territory, whereas questions beginning with "How can we solve or fix …" veer into engineering technology. There are considerable overlaps between technology and science as we have come to appreciate them. But the meaning of technology is not what we plan to emphasize here. Instead our interest is in exploring the uses of technology for educational purposes.

History of Educational Technologies

Before we fool ourselves into thinking that technology for educational purposes is a new thing brought about by computer innovations, try this little exercise. In Table 13.1 are four quotes about particular technologies. We have replaced the name of the invention in each quote with a capital letter. See if you can match the quote with the appropriate technology (notice we didn't include computers as one of the choices).

These quotes and descriptions are drawn from two sources. Todd Oppenheimer (2003) wrote a book in which he questioned the promises being made about computers for revolutionizing education. We borrowed his quotes from three technology advocates who spoke about A, B, and C corresponding to inventions 2, 3, and 4, respectively. The telegraph (1) matches D, and this quote is a description from Tom Standage's (1998) book *The Victorian Internet*. Each innovation was seen as a fantastic invention expected to transform schooling into something beyond anyone's wildest dreams. But from our current perspective, we can see how these aspirations were never realized. We also hear echoes of the current hype about computer-based technology in these antiquated pronouncements.

We use this exercise to highlight why we temper our excitement about the computer. It's as if there is something in human nature causing us to expect a single invention to completely change schools—and this thrill about the possibilities arises from one generation to the next. This is not to suggest we should not be using computers in science education because every so-called revolution in the past has ended up in a dumpster within a decade or so. But given the cycle of propaganda and disappointment, we cannot help but feel as if the teaching profession has had its hopes raised and its wallets raided many times before. But we also accept the inevitability of students needing to know how to use computers, so we work around our own fears and use the technology for their benefit.

TABLE 13.1. Varieties of Technology and Historical Claims for Their Effectiveness

_____ 1. The telegraph (1865)	"I believe that the A is destined to revolutionize our educational system and that in a few years it will supplant largely, if not entirely, the use of textbooks."
_____ 2. The motion picture (1922)	"The time will come when a B will be as common in the classroom as is the blackboard. B instruction will be integrated into school life as an accepted educational medium."
_____ 3. The portable radio (1945)	"The one requirement for a good and universal education is an inexpensive and readily available means of teaching children. Unhappily, the world has only a fraction of the teachers it needs. Samoa has met this problem through C."
_____ 4. The television set (1968)	"D revolutionized the ways countries dealt with one another. The D gave rise to creative business practices and new forms of crime. Attitudes toward everything from news gathering to war had to be completely rethought."

Technology for Instruction and Education

In some places, including the *National Science Education Standards,* technology for the purpose of educating students about science is identified as **instructional technology,** and it is praised because it "provides students and teachers with exciting tools, such as computers, to conduct inquiry and to understand science" (National Research Council, 1996, p. 24). We agree with treating computers as a dominant form of technology within teaching. However, we feel overly restricted by calling this "instructional," because many uses of technology within classrooms are not purely for instructional purposes.

We prefer the label **educational technology** to include the wide range of uses of computer-based tools to support all aspects of science education. More than just using educational technology to present lessons to students, we accept computers as tools for many uses by the teaching professional: keeping records, searching for resources, and communicating with parents. From this point forward we will leave abandon such questions as whether litmus paper or thermometers are technology. For our purposes we use the terms *technology* and *educational technology* to designate the use of computers within science education.

Varieties of Educational Technology

There are many tools that we can use in the classroom for teaching science and that can be considered educational technology. Although we agree a laser pointer or a cell phone can be used to help teach science and admit there is a high-tech component to these items, these aren't the types of educational technology we will address. Some people might dispute our narrow view, but even when we restrict educational technology to equipment and activities requiring a desktop or laptop computer, we are still incorporating a wide variety of tools. Unless we want to devote an entire book to the appropriate use of all forms of computer-chip technologies, we have to set some limits. As it is, by examining only educational technologies involving the computer, we involve an array of possibilities.

New technologies are often described in terms of their fundamental and unique features. A **fundamental feature** describes the central purpose or use of a technology, such as writing a report. A **unique feature** describes the exceptional and distinctive aspects of the technology, such as embedding animation within a final report. Technologies that are successful achieve both categories of features: they fulfill a basic need, and they do so in a way that is by some measure superior to existing technologies. For example mp3 players such as the iPod are used fundamentally for storing and playing music. At a basic level, such a technology is similar to previous generations such as phonograph record players, cassette players, and CD players. At a fundamental level, a gramophone and an iPod are the same: they both play prerecorded audio.

However, not many people own a gramophone because more recent technologies have displaced the old technology even though all are fundamentally music players. More than claiming that an iPod is simply better than a gramophone, we can identify the features that make an iPod unique and compelling. These include portability, sound quality, the ability to jump from one song to another, and the number of songs that can be stored. Why do iPods exist? For two main reasons: first, they fulfill a fundamental purpose (providing music), and second, they have unique features that displace previous inventions but that had served the same fundamental purpose.

We propose a way to think about technology that is more practical than simply becoming enamored by every new toy. Instead of focusing on the variety of tools, we propose a taxonomy of educational technology practices. This is, we believe, an important shift in how to think about educational technology. For the most part, we tend to equate technology with the equipment. The problem with this mode of thinking is that each time a new technology is invented, we are required to add that innovation to our list—and that eventually becomes overwhelming. Having a taxonomy of educational technology practices will not only help us to manage and organize our understanding of new technologies but also guide us in deciding about the suitability of those technologies for classroom use.

Taxonomy of Educational Technology Practices

This taxonomy is an adaptation of four focuses for education described elsewhere (Gee, Hull, & Lankshear, 1996). We have adapted the four focuses to apply specifically to teaching all students in elementary school and middle school about science. The four categories of educational technology practices are productivity tools, communication, investigation, and authoring. We present these categories to illustrate the ways in which educational technology can be implemented within science teaching and learning. The purpose of this taxonomy is twofold: to provide a structure for organizing the wide variety of educational technologies and to provide a mechanism for deciding if a particular technology has practical benefits.

Productivity Tools

Teaching requires considerable stamina, and this extends well beyond instructional practices (Settlage & Wheatley, 2004). Teachers must manage the substantial demands made on their time and energy while still providing instruction to students. There are many aspects of teaching that we could describe as secretarial, such as keeping records, managing inventories, and sharing information with others involved in education. Although these tasks may not seem central to the purpose of helping students learn, they still must be managed as part of the responsibilities of the teaching professional. There is no escaping the need to keep track of attendance and monitor students' progress. Because these are unavoidable demands on a finite amount of teacher time and energy, any teacher would appreciate having ways to accomplish these tasks in a more productive fashion.

Being productive refers to accomplishing a task with greater efficiency. The key to efficiency is reducing the number of minutes and amount of energy that a teacher invests in secretarial tasks. But we can and should consider student productivity as well. Saying that we help students to accomplish tasks should not suggest that we are allowing them to get by with doing less than is expected. Rather the premise of aiding student productivity is that students too have a finite supply of energy and time. Being productive means spending increased proportions of time and energy on activities that will contribute to learning and less time on activities that may be necessary but have less to contribute to student development. Student productivity is improved when students spend more time doing science and less time waiting for materials to be distributed or standing in line.

The fundamental application of productivity tools is to the activities that are a normal part of teachers' and students' lives. Writing is a very fundamental task and is something teachers and students have been doing for hundreds of years. The same is true for keeping track of supplies, organizing information, and so on. The unique and compelling feature of productivity tools is that, by using them, the same tasks can be accomplished more efficiently. For example a daily routine includes determining how many students plan to purchase lunch and transmitting that information to the cafeteria. An educational technology practice that speeds up this accounting procedure, such as having students indicate their choice on the computer as soon as they walk into the classroom, is an example of a productivity tool. The innovation is that by decreasing the amount of time spent on tallying and reporting lunch orders, more time can be spent on learning.

Communicating Ideas and Information

A fundamental feature of science is communicating. It is a basic science process skill, embedded within the essential features of inquiry, and there are particular aspects of communication that are particular to the culture of science. As we've indicated when describing communication as a process skill (in chapter 3) and within the discussions about integrating science with other subjects (in chapter 10), communicating includes the written word and graphs and illustrations. Educational technologies supporting any of these modes of communicating fulfill a fundamental purpose within science learning.

The unique and compelling feature provided by certain educational technologies is the two-way communication of ideas and information. For example communicating information about the local environment can, through the use of innovative educational technologies, allow students and schools to exchange data with others. In less technologically rich settings, information about scientific ideas travel in one direction, namely, from scientists to students through textbooks and television programs. Educational technologies can enrich communication by expanding the scope of the audience. Even something as seemingly ordinary as e-mail affords a way of communicating between schools and scientists.

Investigating With Technological Tools

Investigating involves gathering observations and trying to make sense of the information. Investigating includes studying seeds as they sprout in a clear container and maintaining a written record of the events. There are two interrelated pieces to this investigating: collecting information (e.g., writing in a seed diary, making illustrations, recording measurements of length) and representing this information (e.g., creating a graph of the change in stem length over time). Educational technology tools exist that support this fundamental practice of investigating, and there are many aspects of investigating that some forms of educational technology can accomplish in unique and compelling ways.

We can identify two ways in which educational technology practices can supply fresh approaches to investigating. One of these is through simulations, and the other is through innovative data gathering and representation. In some ways educational technology practices can engage students in the fundamental actions of science. By allowing students to investigate in ways that might not otherwise be possible, educational technologies can serve a unique and innovative purpose. Efficiencies are gained by being able to gather data more quickly and conduct simulated investigations without needing equipment beyond the computer tools and having the capability to redo an investigation without too much effort beyond clicking on a "start over" button on the screen.

Using Simulations for Investigating   Simulations permit students to investigate the world in a manner that would be otherwise impractical because of the constraints of time, expense, safety, and so on. There are many science-specific simulations appropriate for use in elementary and middle school classrooms. Although there is the possibility of these being treated as games, there are approaches that ensure that simulations are truly educational experiences and not purely entertainment. For example, teaching that uses simulations can rely on a four-phase approach as described by Bruce Joyce and Marsha Weil (Joyce, Weil, & Calhoun, 2004): orientation, participant training, simulation operations, and participant debriefing. For those who are preparing to teach using simulations, we can highly recommend the simulations section from Joyce and Weil's invaluable text.

Within the context of education technology practices, we wish to reinforce how simulations not only fulfill the fundamental desire for students to investigate but do so in unique and compelling ways. For example a very common standard within elementary and middle school science is for students to recognize the basic needs of living things. Imagine how this might be investigated. For plants, students can try growing seeds in different environments to uncover the necessity of warmth, moisture, and air. This is not an especially difficult task, but it necessitates waiting a considerable amount of time for the results to become apparent. When we consider investigating the needs of animals, the situation becomes much dicier. Although we might be satisfied to tell students the basic needs of all animals and then challenge them to identify the specifics for a variety of local animals, there seems to be some long-lasting benefits to investigating these needs. But the idea of culturing different living things (even if they are invertebrates such as insects, brine shrimp, or worms) while anticipating that some will not survive when their needs are not sufficiently met makes many of us uncomfortable. Fortunately, students can conduct these investigations using computer simulations. The content is accurate but devoid of the messiness of watching organisms die. An example of such a simulation is the program *SimAnt* in which students attempt to maintain an ant colony in the face of a variety of external pressures. Because simulations have long been a popular form of educational software, many of these programs are available free from the Internet.

Simulations can be used as alternatives to performing investigations that might otherwise be too expensive or messy. Conducting frog dissections with a computer program is a rather obvious example. But simulations can also allow students to conduct investigations that would otherwise be impossible. For example by using the Internet, students can visit the virtual fish tank in Boston's Museum of Science and even design their own fish to see how well it survives in a virtual aquarium populated with other fish.

Investigating with Data-Gathering Tools　Collecting data and then converting them into a sensible display such as a graph are useful skills for students to develop. Moving from evidence to explanations is central to the culture of science. But when students become overburdened by the twin tasks of gathering data and then trying to draw detailed graphs by hand, the tedium can interfere with more important learning goals. In other words, gathering and graphing are fundamental and vital dimensions of science. When educational technology can facilitate these efforts, an important purpose is fulfilled.

Within investigating we see two potential benefits for using educational technology. One of these is graphing software. Imagine that you have a data table that contains the temperature, humidity, and barometer readings over a two-week period. There are countless ways you might choose to summarize this data using various kinds of graphs: there can be a line graph for each aspect of the weather, a pie chart showing the proportion of days that were above average for each aspect, and so on. The procedure required to generate these graphs by hand is quite cumbersome. But when students can use an educational technology to represent the data in a wide variety of graph types with just a few clicks of a mouse, then the significance of the data takes precedence over the mechanics of creating the graphs. Most computers now arrive preloaded with spreadsheet programs for creating graphs. However, because these programs were created for use in the business world, it is sensible for a school to invest in a kid-friendly graphing program that allows generation of bar graphs, pie charts, and line graphs. Such a use of educational technology greatly facilitates student investigation through examination of data.

Another category of investigating using educational technology also involves working with data. Instead of taking data that were gathered elsewhere, students can use computers to collect their own data. Instead of using a thermometer or a meter stick to measure, students can simply use tools called **probes,** which not only can gather temperature and distance data but also can display the measured values on the computer screen. These "real-time" data can be displayed using numerals or shown as a line graph that the probe instantaneously creates based on the data as it senses them. What this means is that instead of reading a thermometer, writing down the temperature, and then making a graph, the probe and computer combination does this simultaneously. The moment the temperature changes, such as when the probe is moved from a cup of warm water to a container of colder water, the graph immediately and automatically creates a graph that shows the drop in temperature.

Authoring Knowledge Products

The fourth and final category of educational technology practices is perhaps the most far reaching. The label suggests the production of written texts, but we envision authoring as including a wide range of outcomes. Independent of the topic or media being put to use, authoring describes the creation of a unique product in which the designer pulls together pieces of information. Perhaps the simplest example is a poster in which a student uses a variety of information sources to create a unified whole. There are two fundamental aspects of authoring. First, the inventor, creator, or designer operates at the highest levels of Bloom's taxonomy by synthesizing information and materials while working to evaluate, judge, or critique his or her learning. Second, the process of authoring strengthens the individual's understanding. In other words not only does the development of the product demonstrate what the individual knows but also the process of creating becomes a learning event.

Educational technology can enhance the process of authoring in several unique ways. Traditional paper reports can be enhanced with computer-generated graphs and pictures, whereas computerized reports can include hyperlinks, which allow the reader to jump from idea to idea.

Authored products can reside on a classroom computer for others to use, be presented to others as a multimedia slide show, or be posted to the Web for anyone in the world to view. The varieties of authored products are limitless in their possibilities. As software allows even beginners to fashion interesting visual effects, create animations, and exploit simple programming, the functionality of authored products is constrained only by one's imagination.

The challenge with authoring is that the fundamental purposes are neglected when teachers and students become so enamored by the unique and compelling dimensions. For example creating a Web page to show the effects of pollution on the environment can contain an astonishing combination of graphics. However, if the process of developing the product neglects the fundamental purpose of synthesizing information to strengthen and extend the developer's knowledge of the topic, then this way of using the technology is questionable. Just as there are criteria proposed for deciding if a teacher should rely on the Internet for a given activity (Chen, Wong, & Hsu, 2003), as instructional decision makers, teachers need to shield themselves (and their students) from engaging in the use of educational technology for its own sake. An educational technology must both fulfill a fundamental need and do so using unique and compelling features. It is this combination that is necessary for a technology to be educative.

Technology is not automatically educational: the role of the teacher is pivotal. For example, we might believe that having students use word processors will enhance their learning. However, the research about the benefits of word processor use is not overwhelmingly positive. Using a word processor improves students' attitudes toward writing and the quality of their writing only when combined with effective teaching practices (Roblyer & Edwards, 2000). Otherwise word processing alone may not be especially advantageous. Such limitations can be readily extended to any authoring task. Unless a teacher provides high-quality support to the students, authoring is unlikely to lead to instructional benefits beyond learning how to use a piece of software. As such, the fundamentals, in this case creating a new knowledge product as a mechanism for strengthening knowledge, must remain at the center of the purpose and attention of the teacher and students.

For Reflection and Discussion

We can organize our individual comfort and expertise with educational technology along a continuum. On the left side are those technologies for which our desired level of knowledge is very near to our level of current knowledge. At the furthest extreme, to the right, are those technologies about which we have the least knowledge and comfort in using. The following is a list of several types of technology you might use as a classroom teacher. Arrange these in a continuum from least familiar to most familiar. What other technologies might be added to this continuum? What are the educational technologies you need to become more familiar with, and what steps might you take to develop your competency with them?

Online grade book	Digital camera	Spreadsheet program graphing
Voice mail	Overhead projector	WebQuest activity
Web page design	Dry erase whiteboard	Electronic slide show (e.g., PowerPoint)
Two-way video conferencing	Online chat room	Data collection with a PDA (e.g., Palm Pilot)
Instant messaging	SmartBoard	Homework posted on the Web

Educational Technology for Teachers and Students

Teachers sometimes report that they use technology more than they allow their students to, and yet there is great deal of overlap in the types of technology the two groups use. Vannatta and Fordham (2004) reported that both teachers and students used word processing software more than any other educational technology. Likewise neither teacher nor students made much use of scanners. Despite these similarities, there were uses of technology that were very different—and this makes perfect sense, because teachers and students have very different roles within a classroom. In the following sections we will describe technology being used for planning and for learning, which corresponds to the work of teachers and students, respectively. Along the way you might consider how each of the technologies fall within the taxonomy we've proposed.

Technology for Planning

A very reasonable way to use a technology for planning is to treat the computer as an electronic file cabinet. Lesson plans, homework assignments, unit tests, and so on can be more compactly stored and easily retrieved from a hard drive than from a file drawer. The possibilities and problems you've experienced using computers as a college student will probably continue when you are a classroom teacher. Here we are talking about the incompatibility between computers at home and computers at school. Districts, just like colleges, are very concerned about the inappropriate use of computers. Software you use to prepare a lesson plan over the weekend may not open on the school's computer. Formatting on pages changes depending on the computer and printer. Furthermore, you will find it can be very hard to load software on school computers because of protective measures such as passwords and firewalls. Although these firewalls are well intentioned and meant to prevent having school computers overloaded with worthless files or infected with viruses, you will not be the first teacher to say to a computer, "All I want to do is load this program!" None of this will be new to you if you've tried to transport files from one computer to another at your college or university. It's just that the problems become more intense. As a college student, the consequence might be a late assignment; at school you may find yourself desperately trying to make the computer work even as you hear the voices and footsteps of your students approaching your classroom.

In many ways computers are very limited, and whatever standards of organization you have in your noncomputer world will extend to your uses of the computer. If you tend to misplace papers on your desk, you will likely carry over the same organizational difficulties into your computer filing. Labeling, organizing, and filing are talents you need to develop whether you are using paper or electronic tools. There is only a small bit of truth to the belief that computers will make you more organized. Unless you develop habits for organizing electronic files, you'll find yourself as lost as ever. This reinforces our global orientation toward technology: it is effective only to the extent that the user knows how to put it to good use.

Sources of Lesson Plans

There are countless sites on the Internet where you can access free lesson plans, and classroom teachers have written most of the plans. To the credit of their creators, these lesson plans usually describe the equipment you will need to conduct any given activity and the cost for these materials is often minimal. Because the lessons are in an electronic format, it is quite easy to search and find lessons on particular topics. In general the plans are not full-blown lessons but creative activities. For elementary schools these tend to emphasize the integration of language arts or craft projects with science. This isn't a criticism of the lesson plans, but it should caution you against expecting to find complete science lesson plans addressing the goals we've described in this book. We've known this is the case, so since the beginning we have been giving you the basic background and necessary skills to transform clever activities into genuinely powerful science learning experiences for all your students. The same suite of instructional decision-making practices is equally valuable whether the source is an activity book you bought at a used book sale or the fanciest Web page.

We have not found on the Internet a collection of science lesson plans for elementary and middle schools that approaches the quality of the commercially available materials we described in chapter 9. Maybe it's unrealistic to expect a lesson plan posted to the Web to be as well tested and clear as those materials sponsored by the National Science Foundation. Yet we are still disappointed when we search through online lesson plan collections and find relatively little about inquiry, the nature of science, the science process skills, or the learning cycle. This is not to suggest the materials from chapter 9 always include all of these features, but lesson plans from the Web rarely include more than one of these four elements. Despite this shortcoming, the Internet can be helpful for planning purposes, but only in terms of providing raw material and not final, polished complete products.

Record Keeping

Maintaining effective records is one part of teaching that many of us do not appreciate. At the most basic level record keeping is necessary to determine students' grades. In addition teachers need to keep careful track of student attendance. There are also inventory issues to consider, such as when distributing textbooks. These are fundamental bookkeeping tasks, and the materials become part of the permanent records of the student and the property of the school. However, record keeping serves other purposes that are less routine: monitoring individual student progress, informing parents and families of their child's performance, and charting behavioral patterns of the students. A parent of a child or two can often do this record keeping in his or her mind; a teacher of an entire classroom of students cannot rely on memory to keep such important and detailed records.

NSES Teaching Standard D: Teachers of science design and manage learning environments that provide students with the time, space, and resources needed for learning science. In doing this teachers make the available science tools, materials, media, and technological resources accessible to students.

There are software programs, anywhere from free to modestly priced, for keeping these records. The more sophisticated versions can generate reports and even make the information accessible over the Web. Although several challenges have been associated with teachers' implementation of electronic grading software (Migliorino & Maiden, 2004), more districts are moving toward their use each year. Because the software programs are so specific, it is unwise for us to try to generalize about them. If nothing else you might want to do a Web search of grade-book programs to see what is available. An even better idea is to visit teachers in their classrooms to see what they are required to use. You might consider asking during your job interviews about the sorts of technology the school uses to maintain students' records.

Other Teaching Resources

Sometimes you just need basic information about a certain science topic. Because you may not have had the time to learn everything there is to know by watching public television, here is a Web site you might want to bookmark or make one of your favorites: http://www.pbs.org/teachersource/sci_tech.htm. This address will bring you to a page that is constantly updated. Typically the opening screen describes a television program or series that is going to be broadcast in the near future. For most of its broadcasts, PBS provides downloadable teacher resource materials that can be used in conjunction with that program. But even if the upcoming science show is not about a topic you are responsible for teaching, you can search the site's index, by grade level and science topic, to call up other science broadcasts.

A further beauty of the PBS Web site are the connections it provides to recently published books and exceptional Web sites. These links are not necessarily related to the particular science television programs, but they do bring to your attention very clear and interesting Web sites that would strengthen your science content background and maybe even give you some ideas for classroom demonstrations.

The Internet is both a marvelous and a frustrating resource for science teaching. For one thing, the Web is being constantly updated, so it acts like a textbook to which the latest ideas and information are being added. On the flip side is the fact that no one is in charge of organizing all the sites on the Web, so even as new pieces are being added, old pieces are sometimes taken offline. The strategies you might have used during your leisurely days as a college student will not work for you once you start teaching full-time. Resources such as the PBS Web site are beneficial, not because they connect you to everything available but because they have selected some of the best materials that are out there and put them into a searchable list.

For Reflection and Discussion

Evaluate each of the following tools according to the taxonomy of educational technology presented in this chapter: drawing and graphics programs; digital cameras and camcorders; presentation software; e-mail and discussion groups; a class Web site; a spreadsheet; a digital microscope; probes and probeware; and word processor.

Into which of the four categories (productivity, communicating, investigating, and authoring) does each belong? You might decide one technology can belong in multiple categories. What fundamental purpose does each of these innovations address?

Point–Counterpoint

Educational technology provokes very strong reactions among educators. On one hand-supporters regard computers as tools that can transform education. Others claim that computers are the latest in a long string of false promises. The truth may reside somewhere between the two. But in the meantime teachers must make decisions about how to respond to the computers that are available in their school. So in response to the question "What should teachers expect from educational technology?" we offer dramatically different outlooks.

Using Technology to Enhance Real-World Learning in the Science Classroom

Marlene Morales

Instructor at Miami Dade College School of Education and Former Middle School Science Teacher

The use of technology in the science classroom is having an unquestionable impact in promoting exceptional inquiry-based instruction. The *National Science Education Standards* insists that inquiry-based instruction allow students to pose questions, design investigations to gather data, and interpret their findings in an open forum. In the past ten years, the Internet has encouraged these types of activities. I believe it can provide real-world applications to enhance science instruction.

The Internet allows for unique and compelling learning opportunities that did not exist previously. For instance, students can engage in quantitative scientific investigations while communicating with experts and students from around the world. In the module "Human Genetics" (http://k12science.org/curriculum/genproj/), students analyze and collect data to see if the dominant trait occurs more frequently than the recessive trait. Students can also access real-time information such as weather images, earthquake data, and hourly air quality readings to examine scientific principles. In "Musical Plates: A Study of Earthquakes and Plate Tectonics" (http://k12science.org/curriculum/musicalplates3/en/), students explore the relationship between earthquakes, volcanoes, and plate boundaries. Students can also retrieve original primary source materials such as letters, sketches, photographs, and maps to make real-world historical connections in science.

In "The Spinning Sun" (http://solar-center.stanford.edu/spin-sun/spin-sun.html), students compare Galileo's sunspot sketches with current telescopic photographs of the sun to estimate the sun's rotation rate as Galileo did in 1612. Furthermore, students can use interactive computer simulations to design and test scientific theories by manipulating variables. In "EngineSim" (http://www.grc.nasa.gov/WWW/K-12/Enginesim/index.htm), students examine jet engines, exploring the effects they have on the speed and range of aircrafts. These types of Internet applications assist in reinforcing the higher-order thinking skills needed to be scientifically literate.

Now more than ever teachers are held accountable for developing productive citizens. Recent studies in educational technology suggest that students who download and analyze data from the Internet and use interactive simulations perform better on standardized tests such as the *National Assessment of Educational Progress,* whereas those who use drill and practice applications perform worse (Wenglinsky, 1998). Therefore it is important for educators to provide technology-enhanced, inquiry-based activities where students can use their critical-thinking and problem-solving skills, organize and critically analyze scientific data and information, and engage in scientific discourse to make sense of its relevance in the real world.

Owen Gaede

Science Teacher Educator at Florida State University and Former High School Physics Teacher

Since I first became involved as a graduate student with the PLATO system at the University of Illinois in 1974, I have been an advocate for the educational use of computers. PLATO was one of the first computer-assisted learning systems. It was a "time-sharing" system in which up to two thousand special terminals were connected simultaneously to a central computer. But for more than thirty years, I have been disappointed at how "technology" has been used in schools.

I put the word *technology* in quotation marks because I feel the term is generally misused. Technology has become synonymous today with computers and the Internet. But more accurately, technology is the application of scientific and systematic procedures toward the achievement of specific goals or outcomes. In the case of educational technology, those goals and outcomes are student learning. Thus technology is a process, not a thing. But by any definition, the use of technology in education has failed to result in fundamental change in the way we teach and the way students learn.

Shortly after the first Apple microcomputer came on the market, I received a phone call from a library-media specialist. She told me she came back from summer vacation to find the principal had purchased five of these new computers, and the boxes were now sitting in her media center. "Help!" she pleaded. "The principal wants me to use these. What in the world do I do with these things?" By today's standards, these computers had the power of a gnat. There was very little software available, and what programs were available had to be loaded off cassette tapes each time the computer was turned on. There were no disk drives, no modems, and no network to connect to even if you had a modem. Yet there was this feeling we had to use this "technology." So what did we do? We taught students to program in BASIC. For years schools that had "computer literacy" courses focused on teaching programming skills (that quickly became obsolete) because there was little else you could do with these early computers.

Well, times have changed. Even the name *computer* is no longer relevant. The power of computers has increased by orders of magnitude, but most of that power is used not to crunch numbers but to process and display information in many formats. And with the simultaneous growth of the Internet, access to information has become almost limitless. From 1983 to the present, hard disk drives have expanded from 10 megabytes to 250 gigabytes, and the cost of magnetic storage has fallen from $2 a megabyte to 7 ¢. We can access, store, process, and display information in ways that seemed like science fiction only ten years ago. Everything is now digital. And we must remember the end is not in sight. Some have even predicted that the rate of increase in computer power will double over the next five years.

So we now have very powerful information tools, and twenty years have gone by since the first computers began appearing in schools. Unfortunately, we are still asking the same question that media specialist who called me so long ago asked: "What in the world do we do with these things?" We have been asking the wrong questions. Instead of asking, "How can we use technology to improve what we do?" we should be asking, "How can technology enable us to do different things?"

Generally speaking, computers and the Internet have been used to supplement and enrich business as usual in schools. It's like giving a new coat of paint to an old car. That old vehicle continues to focus on the process of teaching rather than on student learning. Schooling relies upon the length of time in class as a measure of educational achievement rather than focusing upon whether students meet specific learning outcomes. Time is the fixed variable; achievement varies according to ability. The real power of the today's computers can't be unleashed in a system that emphasizes group, time-based instruction. The information processing and artificial intelligence possible with today's computers can enable us to make learning time the variable and to standardize the outcomes. But that would require major paradigm shifts in schools that we are either unwilling or unable to make.

There are some sectors of society in which "technology" has had much greater success in improving learning. One example is military training, which has made extensive use of sophisticated adaptive learning programs and simulators. The military has the advantage of generally having very clearly defined outcome objectives. The individual is to reach a certain minimum competency in a specific task or skill. Efficiency of training is of concern. The goal is to be sure trainees reach that minimum proficiency level in the least amount of time. So the military really does apply learning technology in the proper sense of the word. That is, they use a scientific and systematic approach to reach a clearly defined goal. Some individuals may take one hundred hours to reach that level; others may take only twenty hours. Compare that with a typical secondary school where it takes fours years to earn a diploma, regardless of the actual level of competency reached.

In visiting schools I often see students using the Internet to locate information instead of going to the library and using books as was done in the past, but the fundamental lesson plan hasn't changed. Students now use PowerPoint instead of posters to make class presentations, but the curriculum hasn't changed. Teachers use electronic grade-book programs to enter grades, but the grades are still determined in the same old ways, often by comparing one student with others instead of against prescribed learning outcomes.

Sadly, not much has changed. And no matter how powerful our "technology" becomes, not much will change until we begin to examine some of the sacred, unquestioned assumptions left over from the past century that form the foundation of today's schools.

Web-Based Technology for Learning

We will begin our examination of the use of educational technology in the service of science learning by first looking at Web-based tools. The financial windfall of the Internet in the 1990s benefited schools in terms of computers and Web access; nearly every school in the United States has Internet access, with a national average of four students per computer in schools (Park & Staresina, 2004). The phrase "technology in schools" usually brings to mind computers, and it also elicits the idea of using computers to access the World Wide Web. Although there are other innovative ways to use technology, we will start by examining a few Web-based educational tools and save the discussion of educational technology that does not require Internet access for the subsequent section.

WebQuests

The Internet is a rich resource of information. Far beyond a bookshelf of reference texts, the Internet's information contains audio, video, animation, and multimedia materials. A WebQuest is designed to connect students with a sampling of these Internet resources in something akin to a guided scavenger hunt. The simplest WebQuests begin with a Web page that describes a task and then provides the links to guide students to answer the questions or solve the problem. One example is a scenario where the child is to develop care plans for four snakes a fictional herpetologist has left behind in the classroom. The WebQuest describes the scenario and then directs the students to several sites to learn vocabulary, create a life-cycle poster, design a holding pen, and decide how to feed the four snakes. All of the necessary information is contained in the dozen links leading from the initial Web page.

You will probably not be surprised to learn that there is a wide variety in the quality of WebQuests. At the lowest level a WebQuest is little more than a workbook where students follow links to fill in the blanks. But when WebQuests provide questions that are engaging to students and that provoke them to think deeply about the task, then they can be appropriate for classroom use. The developers of WebQuest.org have defined what they feel are the necessary components of an effective WebQuest and provide a continually updated list of WebQuests meeting those criteria. One of the people involved with the WebQuest movement has created a rubric he uses to evaluate WebQuests. If you reach the point where you would consider building your own WebQuests, review this rubric, as it provides a guide for the design of a WebQuest you might use with your students (see Table 13.2).

WebQuests use Web-based technology in a way that is very easy for teachers and students to manage. When the directions are clear and none of the links are dead, a teacher can pretty much let students loose on a WebQuest without having to supervise their work very closely. Because most schools have an "acceptable use policy" for allowing children to access the Internet, consisting of a form the parents or guardians sign, and because the better WebQuest sites have been screened by educators, a teacher has few worries compared to allowing students to simply start searching on their own for information. The WebQuests' links point the students directly to another site and don't require the use of search engines, which might lead students to controversial sites.

Our concern about WebQuests relates to their limitations. Even though they can be very impressive as technological tools, their very design means they are essentially language arts activities. From this standpoint we see that WebQuests can be immensely powerful as they encourage students to read for meaning, extract important information, and translate the information into a written product that is not a simple cut-and-paste exercise. But we have yet to see a WebQuest in which the user is involved in collecting and analyzing data. Even though the WebQuest developers claim there is inquiry involved, when we refer back to the essential features of inquiry (chapter 4), we find considerable gaps. One problem is the lack of opportunity for collecting evidence and then generating explanations from the data. Truthfully it's very hard to imagine how this might be accomplished within a WebQuest, and we recognize this difficulty. Nevertheless, we see the same limitations in using WebQuests as in integrating science with other subjects—the core aspects of science learning can easily be pushed aside by the novelty of the technology.

Partnerships With Scientists and Science

In the 1980s the National Geographic Society sponsored an education technology program called Kids Network. The idea was for students to gather environmental data and send this

TABLE 13.2. Criteria for Evaluating a WebQuest Activity (Rubric From http://ozline.com)

Criteria	Low Quality	Medium Quality	High Quality
Engaging opening	It makes no attempt to appeal to learners.	It honestly attempts to appeal to student interests.	It has that something that compels attention.
The question and task	No real question is presented, or it is a fuzzy task. Maybe what's asked for is lower-level thinking or information retrieval.	There is at least an implicit question and task that targets higher-order thinking. All this may not be totally clear.	There is a clear question and task. These naturally flow from the introduction and signal a direction for sophisticated learning.
Background for everyone	It makes no attempt to access prior learning or build common background.	It makes some mention of addressing a common body of knowledge, but it might not happen within the activity.	It clearly calls attention to the need for a common foundation of knowledge and provides needed Web resources.
Roles and expertise	There are no roles or use of perspectives, or the roles are artificial and may lack inherent conflict of interest.	The roles are clear and realistic. They may be limited in scope but do evoke conflict.	The roles match the issues and resources and provide multiple perspectives from which to view the topic.
Use of the Web	The activity can probably be done just as easily without relying on the Web.	Some resources reflect features of the Web that make it particularly useful such as images, audio, interactivity, current information, and so on.	It uses the Web to access at least some of the following: interactivity; multiple perspectives, multimedia, current information, and so on.
Transformative thinking	There is no transformative thinking. (This is not a WebQuest but may be a good knowledge hunt).	It requires higher-level thinking, but the process for students may not be clear.	It requires higher-level thinking for students to construct new meaning. Scaffolding is provided to support student achievement.
Real-world feedback	No feedback loop is included.	The learning product can easily be used for authentic assessment, although this may not be addressed or it happens only in the classroom.	A feedback loop connecting learners to the real world is included on the Web page, and an evaluation rubric is probably provided early on.
Conclusion	There is minimal conclusion, and no mention is made of student thinking or symmetry to the introduction.	It returns to the ideas in the introduction and may sum up the experiences and learning that was undertaken.	It has a clear tie-in to the introduction. It makes the students' cognitive tasks overt and suggests how this learning can transfer to other domains and issues.

information by e-mail to a central location. By having many schools involved in this project, a network of information was created to study trash, solar energy, water quality, and so on. The underlying goal of this project and others like it was to use the emerging technology (this was before the Internet) to allow children to participate in long-distance collaborations of genuine science activity (Kyle, Abell, & Shepardson, 1995). Unfortunately Kids Network did not adapt to the arrival of the Internet, and the project has pretty much faded away. But the idea of having students in geographically dispersed areas collecting and sharing data, as well as working with scientists, is still happening.

A similar program in which students gather and report data using telecommunications is called GLOBE (Global Learning and Observations to Benefit the Environment). Using guidelines developed by scientists, students gather data about the atmosphere, soil, and land in their area and report their information using the Internet. Because schools and students around the world use the same protocols for collecting and reporting data, the data on the GLOBE Web site (www.globe.gov) can be used to create maps and graphs. Perhaps what's most impressive about this project is that the data the students are gathering help professional scientists to do their research. In a genuine fashion, students from around the world are contributors to scientific research.

The GLOBE projects involve actual scientists in the process. One interesting story about soil scientist Elissa Levine reinforces our message about making science available to all students. Her passion for earth science study is based on her belief that it is not an abstract study: all one needs to do is walk out of the school building. As she worked with teachers and students, she became sensitive to the challenges hands-on science presented to children with visual impairments. According to a NASA "Earth Explorers" biography, Levine has been successful in having blind students use **adaptive technologies** (tools modified so people with physical disabilities can use them) to participate in science inquiry. Here is a description of the tools used to do earth science activities:

> The new instruments include two kinds of talking thermometers—one for the air and a "meat thermometer" that can be inserted into the soil. … A graduated cylinder with a floating Styrofoam plug serves as a rain gauge. The plug moves up or down depending on the volume of water and is attached to a plastic measuring scale marked with Braille. (http://www.nasa.gov/audience/foreducators/informal/features/F_Blind_Camp.html)

If you are intrigued by the prospects of your students sharing data with others across the nation or the world, then there are a few other projects you might want to examine. One of the oldest and most distinguished projects is called Project FeederWatch and is organized by Cornell University. A registration fee provides a teacher with a bird identification key and instructions for how to stock a bird feeder, gather data, and submit this information to the project Web site (www.birds.cornell.edu/pfw/). How you might use this data is entirely up to you—but there is some evidence that participating in the FeederWatch project fosters the scientific thinking we'd like to engender in students (Trumbull, Bonney, Bascom, & Cabral, 2000).

Another partnership program linking students and scientists is called Journey North. The following description comes from the project Web site (journeynorth.org):

> Journey North engages students in a global study of wildlife migration and seasonal change. K-12 students share their own field observations with classmates across North America. They track the coming of spring through the migration patterns of monarch butterflies, bald eagles, robins, hummingbirds, manatees, whooping

cranes—and other birds and mammals, the budding of plants, changing sunlight and other natural events.

Our personal favorite is the tulip project. Using standardized techniques, students across North America plant Red Emperor tulips in the fall and then watch to see when they emerge in the spring and then finally open their blossoms. By posting their data to the Journey North Web site, students are adding their findings to a huge database. They can access the maps feature to chart the growth and blooming of tulips as spring makes its journey north. But if you're not into tulips, you and your students can study red-winged blackbirds, caribou, frogs, or lots of other living things whose appearance signals a change in seasons. This is not just a springtime opportunity. There is also a Journey South set of projects, one of which charts the migration of monarch butterflies to their winter refuge in Mexico. We show the data from a recent study of monarch butterfly migration in Figure 13.1.

The Web site for the Journey projects contains a wealth of resource materials and lesson plans. For the tulip project there are more than fifty lesson plans and activities. These are indexed to *National Science Education Standards,* including an emphasis on science inquiry. Even though the Journey North materials are readily available and not tightly regulated, they can serve as a defining component of an elementary or middle school science program. Finally, we see this as an excellent use of educational technology because it would not be possible without computers and it gives all students exposure to genuine scientific inquiry.

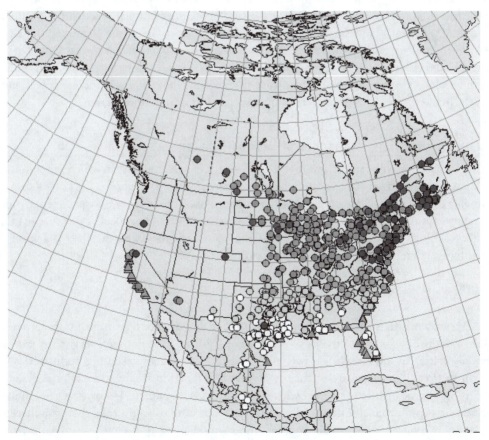

FIGURE 13.1. This figure shows a map of monarch butterfly migrations from the Journey North project.

Virtual Field Trips

The virtual field trip is the last of the Web-based educational technologies that we wish to highlight. Unlike a traditional field trip where students must be loaded into buses or vans and transported to a local nature center, zoo, or museum, a virtual field trip relies on Internet connections to allow students to visit a novel location. There are two Web sites we recommend as starting points. The first will direct you to the home pages of science museums, and the other will allow your students to look at the earth's surface from outer space.

Science museums represent **informal science** in that individuals are able to make their own decisions about what they learn and can learn it at their own pace and in whatever sequence they like. You may be aware of a children's museum or nature center in your community, and maybe you've heard of a major center in a large city such as the Exploratorium in San Francisco or the Franklin Institute in Philadelphia. What many people do not realize is how many science and technology centers exist. To find those nearest to your school, visit the Web site for the Association of Science-Technology Centers (www.astc.org). But also consider using the Web to have your students visit science museums anywhere in the world—there are more than five hundred from which you can choose, and most have online exhibits.

Another way to conduct virtual field trips is to access a NASA educational program called EarthKAM (Earth Knowledge Acquired by Middle school students). This project posts photographs of the earth's surface taken from space. The photographic library began as part of the shuttle missions and has continued through the use of the international space station. A library containing thousands of pictures from space would be very difficult to navigate, so the EarthKAM Web site (www.earthkam.ucsd.edu) has several organizational features. One is called "Themes" and guides you through images of topics such as coasts, deserts, and ice. You can also search for images by geography and look from space at our planet. Because there is text included with the images, you and your students can access a great deal of information.

Technology for Learning—Web Free

Within this section we examine several types of educational technology in which the computers the students are using are not connected to the Internet. Even though this area of educational technology is not expanding as rapidly as Web-based uses, there are two forms of educational technology future elementary and middle school teachers should be aware of to support their science teaching. The first of these is very specific science software, and the other is a set of scientific tools that rely on the computer to display data.

Science Court

As a teacher you will receive catalogs in your mailbox advertising a variety of educational software. Many companies allow for a free trial period so you can see for yourself if the programs will be worthwhile for you to use in your classroom. But we have not seen very many pieces of software written in ways consistent with the strategies we've been presenting in this text. Once again it seems as if tools to learn science by inquiry are something many instructional designers have trouble knowing how to support within the materials they create. However, it's not unusual to receive a memo from a building administrator requesting software titles, because there is a small pool of money that has to be spent by the end of the fiscal year. Here is our recommendation to you: buy *Science Court* published by Tom Snyder Productions (www.tomsnyder.com). We have not seen software as complete and instructionally sound as this collection.

Tom Snyder Productions began with the idea of "teaching in a one-computer classroom." As much as we might like the idea of having a computer for every student, that is not usually the case, and in the two decades since Tom Snyder began his work, he still takes a very practical look at the realities of the classroom. With *Science Court* a teacher uses a single computer (with a projector or with a large monitor) to show segments of an animated program to the class. The program introduces a dilemma, and the storyline always involves someone going to court to try to prove he or she has been wronged. Evidence is presented and evaluated by the students, and ultimately scientific knowledge prevails.

The teacher materials consist of a teaching guide and a CD from which the animation can be played . There is also the option of buying supplemental hands-on materials so students can perform activities. The teaching guide contains background information, instructional strategies, and black-line masters for duplicating and distributing to the students. Let's use the "Water Cycle" program as a typical example. The teacher begins *Science Court* by showing an animated clip—in this case a man slips in a puddle that he alleges was created by a leaking pipe. He decides to sue the pipe manufacturer. In the subsequent courtroom scene, evidence is presented suggesting the pipe was not leaking but perhaps dripping the water that had condensed on it. The program stops automatically, the students are put into cooperative learning groups, and they answer a set of questions. The computer is then used to randomly call on a group (by number designation) and a person (by letter designation) to answer the questions. The program provides immediate feedback, and once all the questions are answered, the students are returned to the courtroom.

There are many features we admire about *Science Court*. First, the technology involved is very simple and easy to use. Second, the science content is accurately portrayed and even addresses, in very subtle but accurate ways, why particular misconceptions are insufficient. Third, the cooperative learning appropriately uses the strategies recommended by the experts. Fourth, the essential features of inquiry are all touched on during the program's use. Finally, the program has what has made animated full-length movies so popular: it is entertaining to children while also amusing to adults.

The original *Science Court* is designed for upper elementary and middle school students and addresses the following science concepts: sound, fossils, living things, inertia, gravity, particles in motion, seasons, soil, electric current, statistics, water cycle, and work and simple machines. The more recent *Science Court Explorations* uses the same approach but are more appropriate for lower elementary grades. Those titles are "Flight," "Friction," "Heat Absorption," "Magnets," "Pendulums," and "Rockets."

There are not enough *Science Court* titles around which to build an entire science program, nor is the sole resource or one approach ever a good idea. But in our experience, there is no parallel collection of educational software that is as easy to implement, instructionally appropriate, and engagingly designed.

Probeware

You can evaluate the temperature of a beverage by dipping your finger into it. This might be accurate enough to let you know whether it's scalding or tepid. A more scientific way to assess temperature is with an ordinary thermometer, and after waiting a few minutes for the red liquid inside to stabilize, you can determine the degrees in Celsius or Fahrenheit. Recently digital thermometers have become available, and you can find these devices in hardware stores. They give readings almost instantaneously, often to the closest tenth of a degree: they are fast, safe, and accurate.

Yet a more advanced way to measure temperature is using a probe—a device you plug into a computer to gather data. Just as with the digital thermometer, the probe displays the temperature quickly and accurately. But the probe works with the computer to create a graph of the temperature. You can move the probe back and forth between two cups of water and watch the graph jump up and down in response to the changing water temperature. Or you can leave a temperature probe plugged in over the weekend and return on Monday morning to see a display of the temperature changes.

One of the most widely used brands of probeware is Vernier. This company manufactures its own probes, writes its own software, authors its own curricular materials, and supplies its own professional development. The Web site (www.vernier.com) provides a wonderful introduction to probeware. Even though probes were first used in college and high school science labs, they are trickling down to middle and elementary schools. Unlike technologies that might be a forced fit, Vernier has simplified its suite of tools (software and hardware) to make the data-gathering and display procedures highly accessible to younger students. Some of their products are too sophisticated for normal use, but we've found the temperature, light, and distance probes to be very useful in the hands of elementary and middle school students.

For Reflection and Discussion

A single educational technology can often be used for multiple purposes. For example, the University of Wisconsin maintains a Web site called "The Why Files" (whyfiles.org). Take a visit to the site, and consider these two possibilities: How might you personally use this Web site to support your planning to teach science? How might you direct your students to use this site within their science learning, especially in terms of the appropriate phases of the learning cycle and the essential elements of inquiry?

Assistive Technologies

People with physical disabilities possess limitations that interfere with their abilities to move or to sense outside information. However, such challenges should not exclude individuals from the freedoms afforded to those who are not physically challenged (i.e., living independently, engaging in fulfilling careers, and being able to completely participate in mainstream educational, social, and artistic facets of American society). Freedoms some individuals take for granted, such as having control over one's life and being able to fully participate in personal, educational, professional, and social pursuits, are matters of federal law, and the legal aspects extend to providing devices for augmenting and supporting individuals with disabilities to function and participate in everyday life, free of the barriers others do not face.

Assistive technology is equipment that helps people with physical disabilities in their movements and sensory perceptions. We introduce the concept because we want to show how educational technology can assist us to extend the scope of "science for all" to include individuals who in previous generations might not have been as likely to fully participate in science activities. Being able to safely manipulate lab equipment, being able to read the display of a measuring device, or being able to use a computer keyboard or mouse are challenges that a wide variety of devices have been built to accommodate. When the types of devices we will introduce to you are made readily available to students, the physical barriers to their participating in science activities are reduced. The largest obstacle that then remains for these students is their teachers' perceptions of their capabilities.

Assistive technologies involving everyday computer use can modify how a person inputs information and accesses information otherwise appearing on a monitor (Brodwin, Star, & Cardoso, 2004). Input technologies include voice-recognition devices, eye-tracking tools, and keyboards controlled by feet and mouth sticks. Output devices include talking word processors, speech synthesizers, and refreshable Braille technology, where text on the screen is translated into a pattern of pins a person can feel through a special device.

A search of the Internet for "assistive technology" will uncover an ever-increasing array of equipment and software, some of which you might never have thought would be beneficial to students with certain disabilities. For example we just discovered a talking color detector. It seems this device can be placed on a piece of fabric, fruit, or any other object and will tell you its color, even distinguishing different shades. On one level we find it amazing such a tool exists. But when we think about our ambition to teach science to all students, becoming aware of this tool makes us realize there are many science activities where being able to detect color is essential. For example, an investigation in which students use litmus paper to test various foods would not be accessible to an individual who is visually impaired or to a student who is color-blind. But now we know of a tool that will allow someone who would otherwise not be able to discern whether he or she was holding blue or red litmus paper to fully participate in a science activity.

Creating accommodations for students with various physical disabilities is being made much easier with the advent of computer-chip-based technologies. A Web site called "Barrier Free Education" (http://barrier-free.arch.gatech.edu/) describes a project that provides college students of all physical abilities access to chemistry and physics laboratories. In addition to information about a variety of assistive technologies, this site describes safety considerations and provides links to many suppliers of assistive technologies applicable to science teaching and learning. In our minds these may be the most powerful benefits to educational technology: providing to individuals with various physical abilities the mechanisms for participating in inquiry-based science, regardless of barriers that might have otherwise excluded them.

Contemplating the Use of Technology

We began this chapter by clarifying that we were most interested in computer technologies, Web-based or otherwise, for use in planning and teaching science to all students. Next we examined the excitement previous generations had expressed about innovative technologies, finding that the hype about the past is very similar to the promises we sometimes hear about current educational technologies. We then examined a sampling of the educational technology resources available to us and that are related specifically to science teaching and learning. We now return to a broader perspective of educational technology to provide an appropriate balance to all the possible benefits we've been describing in the preceding pages.

Teacher Resistance

For those who advocate for the increased use of technology within science classrooms (e.g., Tinker, 2004), the apparent resistance to the more frequent use of technology must feel frustrating. No doubt there are countless policy makers who have voiced concerns to the effect: "We spent all this money on technology but nobody's using it!" How might we explain such circumstances in cases where, even when schools are provided with a considerable amount of educational technology, the electronic tools appear underused?

It turns out the investment in equipment has not been accompanied by a parallel investment in training. Surveys of public school teachers have revealed several barriers to using computers (National Center for Education Statistics, 1999), but the greatest obstacle teachers report is an inadequate amount of time to learn, practice, and plan to use the educational technology. Unfortunately, this trend seems likely to continue: expenditures for staff development dropped by 20 percent between 2002 and 2003. Another issue related to time is the perception by teachers that there is insufficient room within the tight school schedule to devote to allowing their students to use computers. That the use of technology is being squeezed out of daily and yearly schedules because of the accountability and testing movement does not seem to be an outlandish claim.

NSES Professional Development Standard A: Professional development for teachers of science requires learning essential science content through the perspectives and methods of inquiry. Such science learning experiences must introduce teachers to scientific literature, media, and technological resources that expand their science knowledge and their ability to access further knowledge.

Before trying to convince anyone that any innovation is going to benefit students' learning, we must address issues related to knowing about and managing the new demands of an innovation. Until those concerns subside, and it seems staff development is the best way to accomplish this, educational technology may not see the widespread use so many reformers have imagined. Even though schools may continue to invest in upgrading computers, decreasing the number of students per computer, and updating the software, the fundamental concerns of teachers must be appeased if educational technology is going to become a routine part of students' educational experience.

Developmental Considerations

Resistance to progress is not a new phenomenon, and a frequently noted example is a fictional group of defiant people called the Luddites. The tale goes something like this: Nel Lud was an Englishman frustrated by the encroachment of the Industrial Revolution, and in a rage he broke two machines used to knit stockings. Supposedly his anger was directed at the machines, which were displacing work once done by hand. This in turn led others to organize themselves in the early 1800s, and they destroyed textile manufacturing equipment throughout England. This story is full of holes (Pynchon, 1984), but the label remains: anyone who shows resentment, fear, and resistance to technology is tagged as a Luddite, and this is a derogatory reference.

Using the Luddite label may too quickly dismiss legitimate concerns about technology and its appropriateness in educational settings. Especially in conversations about early childhood education, there is considerable debate about the proper role of educational technology. The concerns extend from the lack of evidence showing that educational technology is especially helpful and continue to the almost extreme assertion that educational technology can actually be harmful to children. From a scientific perspective it seems appropriate to seek evidence supporting the push for educational technology and reasonable to ask if computers in classrooms are really all that great of an idea. One group, the Alliance for Childhood, has published two documents that express troubling concerns about computers. Both reports are available on the Web site (www.allianceforchildhood.net) and are titled *Fool's Gold: A Critical Look at Comput-*

ers in Childhood and *Tech Tonic: Towards a New Literacy of Technology.* The following excerpt is from their more recent report:

> The supposed benefits of this techno-revolution for children are relentlessly promoted by high-tech corporations, even though independent research (conducted by those with no financial stake in the outcome) has produced little evidence of lasting, long-term gains. At the same time, the damage being done by immersing children in electronic technologies is becoming clearer. Increasing numbers of them spend hours each day sitting in front of screens instead of playing outdoors, reading, and getting much-needed physical exercise and face-to-face social interaction—all of which, it turns out, also provide essential stimulation to the growing mind and intellect. (Alliance for Childhood, 2004, p. 1)

A tantalizing claim made in this report is that there is little evidence showing educational technologies' supposed benefits to student learning. This claim is accompanied by the implication that studies that have shown benefits are questionable because of the close association between those providing the funds and those conducting the research. But as we look past the potentially lucrative possibilities of doing research on educational technology, we do have to face the reality about careful research in the field—there is no overwhelming evidence supporting the use of computers for instruction (Bayraktar, 2002; Bernard et al., 2004; Weller, 1996). Also a very close examination of computer use in Silicon Valley schools that reveals little success with the technology has been documented in Larry Cuban's (2001) book *Oversold and Underused: Computers in the Classroom.* What can be definitively said about educational technology and science learning is that we are still unable to claim anything definitively about its influence. Where we do have solid evidence is in the form of the computer disparity between schools responsible for educating different demographic groups.

The Digital Divide

Educational technology is not equitably distributed across school districts. Issues such as access to working computers, the quality of the hardware and connectivity, and individual technological literacy create a split along economic lines. The gap in educational technology between different demographic groups is called the **digital divide,** and Figure 13.2 shows one example of the disparity.

The talk surrounding the digital divide bothers us, because we do not feel it is adequately addressing the root of the problem. Inequities in educational opportunity corresponding to family income, cultural background, or ethnic membership are problems we have been criticizing throughout this book. From our perspective the digital divide is not a central issue but rather a symptom of something larger. In some ways we feel the digital divide agenda is a distraction, similar to putting makeup on a bruise rather than looking to the cause for the injury. If inequitable education were a genuine concern to policy makers, then financing an increased number of computers would be seen as only part of a larger and more demanding challenge.

Two researchers from UCLA analyzed data from California teachers and found that 32 percent of the 1,071 respondents indicated they did not have enough texts for students to read outside of school (Oakes & Saunders, 2004). The percentage of science teachers reporting a shortage of books for students to take home was equal to the number indicating the technology available for teaching was fair to poor in quality. Would spending more money on technology fix this problem? No, especially when we compare the relative expense of textbooks to that of computers—not to mention the costs of ongoing upkeep and inevitable software upgrades. To be sure, there are

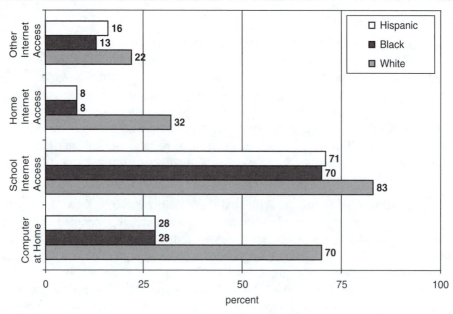

FIGURE 13.2. This graph shows students' access to computers and the Internet, by student race and ethnicity (National Center for Education Statistics, 2000).

substantial problems in teacher quality, financial support, and instructional resources in schools serving lower-income families that are not found in those schools with the luxury of educating less financially strapped communities. The problems are profound, and many feel a certain urgency about doing something to set things right.

We return to the book by Todd Oppenheimer (2003) that we quoted earlier in this chapter. His study of educational technology began by comparing modern promises with those of the past. As Oppenheimer concluded his writing, he returned to the single greatest factor influencing the quality of education in any setting—the teacher. Our enthusiasm for or critiques against educational technology must take into account the strengths or limitations of the adult who serves as guide to a student's learning. Oppenheimer was troubled by our tendency to look for easy solutions and especially troubled about how such tendencies might disadvantage those who are most at risk. We decided to rely on his eloquence on this issue:

> I hope that at some point, the public breaks its habit of amnesia when it comes to promises sold to schools. One would think that adults—all of whom have gone through many difficult years of experience in school and most of whom have children of their own—would pay more attention when politicians and school administrators started buying into quick fixes for education's troubles. ... Education doesn't require the same concentration of thought as would a business, whose failures create oil spills or drops in stock prices. No, the price of education's failures is conveniently amorphous, spectacularly delayed, and of little consequence to all but the poorest among us." (Oppenheimer, 2003, p. 401)

Working Through the Technological Confusion

At this stage it seems we are sending mixed messages. On the one hand we've described a variety of innovative tools for teaching science and making science accessible to students regardless of any physical disability. Yet we have also identified the problems and perils of educational technology such as its questionable effectiveness and its ambivalence toward educational inequities. Where does this leave novice elementary and middle school teachers? Would we advise you to turn away when you hear *technology*? Not necessarily, but we want you to be able to sort through the appropriateness of any given technology given the themes we've presented throughout this book. The following is a list of some questions that are specific to science teaching and learning that you might pose when you find yourself facing a decision about a particular technology:

- Will using this technology assist my students in mastering the science process skills?
- What opportunities for inquiry (i.e., the essential features) will be possible by using this technology?
- Will the technology give my students access to science content otherwise not available to them?
- What types of learning will persist for my students after we discontinue using the technology?
- How might aspects of the nature of science be folded into the use of the technology?
- What measures should be taken to ensure the technology does not exacerbate differences among the students?

It is probably fair to claim most educational technology is innocuous and only beneficial or damaging depending on its use. If the strongest criticism we might make is its dubious effectiveness or its questionable expense, then educational technology is not markedly different from a host of other examples of gimmickry that unscrupulous vendors foist on to educators. However, we cannot reject educational technology out of hand any more than we can embrace every new gizmo that comes along. In addition to using the questions proposed in the previous paragraph, which you can use to sort the promising from the perilous in educational technology, we can also make use of the *National Educational Technology Standards*.

The International Society for Technology in Education has created different sets of standards that are applicable to students, teachers, and administrators. We will not duplicate the extraordinary level of detail associated with technology standards, but we will use the space available here to highlight the foundations of the standards for students. If you visit the Web site (www. iste.org) and follow the links for "Standards for Students," you will find descriptions of the particular skills students should demonstrate in primary, upper elementary, and middle school grades. We feel these guidelines, when combined with our recommendations for science teaching and learning, will help you to navigate the continued flow of educational technology you will no doubt experience throughout your career. The students should be able to

- demonstrate proficiency in basic uses of educational technology;
- display responsible, ethical, and strategic uses of educational technology;
- apply educational technology to extend learning and advance creativity;
- communicate to multiple audiences using telecommunication and multimedia; and
- locate and organize information for problem-solving and decision-making tasks.

In closing we want to stick up for our ambivalence toward educational technology. It is impossible to predict what forms of educational technology will be available to you when you become a full-time teacher. For one thing there are considerable differences from building to building and district to district. In addition we are unsure about the direction technology will take in the future: more exciting tools may be invented or the plummet in financing for technology may accelerate. Because our purpose is to prepare you as a teacher of science, we don't want to risk giving you misleading information. It is unethical for us to advocate for a novel technology and build up your expectations for using it when you take your first teaching position only to find that what we have been promising is not possible. We'd view this as educational malpractice.

Our preference is for you to concentrate on the core ideas for teaching science to all students and not depend too heavily on educational technology. We are confident that when you have clarity about your goals as a teacher of science, you will be effective with or without the latest high-tech equipment. Similarly your effectiveness as a science teacher should not be based on your skill at using educational technology. We expect teachers to be equally effective in teaching all students whether a lesson involves magnifiers and toothpicks or probeware connected to graphing calculators. The greatness has very little to do with the form of technology; it really comes down to the knowledge, skill, and determination of the individual teacher.

Chapter Summary

- An immense array of tools can be considered technology for teaching. In everyday language, however, technology is equated with computer-based equipment and often implies connections to the Internet.
- Technology has often been proposed as a way to improve schooling. The lesson from history is that the current promises are almost indistinguishable from previous generations' expectations of the telegraph, radio, and television. The informed educator will to avoid the possibility of history repeating itself and use good judgment in assessing the appropriateness of educational technology and its role in teaching science to all students.
- A taxonomy of educational technology practices consists of four categories, all of which fulfill fundamental educational purposes and supply unique and compelling features. The four categories within this taxonomy are productivity tools, communicating ideas and information, tools for investigating, and authoring knowledge products.
- One use of educational technology is for teacher planning: accessing outside information, organizing resources, and maintaining records.
- Although not the only uses of educational technology, accessing the Internet to conduct WebQuests, partnering scientists with students, and participating in online field trips are all popular uses of computers within science teaching.
- Within science education, technology can use software programs and probeware that do not depend on an Internet connection. Also educational technology that doesn't require the Web can take the form of assistive technology.
- Many teachers resist the push to integrate technology into their science teaching. Some causes of resistance are based on uncertainties, but there are also legitimate concerns for being cautious about using educational technology. The digital divide is one reason teachers who might otherwise not be advocates of technology might still incorporate it into their teaching.
- A filtering approach by the classroom teacher can assist the process of deciding on the use of educational technology. First, questions about the technology's support of science teaching and learning goals (e.g., process skills, inquiry elements, and equity issues) can be applied. Also standards proposed by educational technology societies can be used to sort the inappropriate uses of technology from those that are appropriate for use with elementary and middle school students.

Key Terms

Adaptive technologies: tools that are modified for use by people with physical disabilities.

Assistive technology: a piece of equipment that helps people with physical disabilities with their movements and sensory perceptions.

Digital divide: the gap in educational technology between different demographic groups.

Educational technology: used to assist in many aspects of the professional work of the teacher, including instruction.

Fundamental feature: the key purpose and central use of a technology, such as making a graph or measuring light intensity.

Informal science: opportunities for science learning in which individuals are able to make their own decisions about what they learn and can learn it at the pace and in the sequence they like.

Instructional technology: used for the purpose of educating students about science.

Probe: a device for collecting data that can be connected to a computer.

Unique feature: attributes of a tool that are unusual and distinguish the tool from other tools that serve somewhat similar purposes.

A Favorite Science Lesson

Being aware of who we are and how we compare with others is a significant part of growing up. The "Myself and Others" unit created by the Education Development Center begins with students' natural curiosity about themselves and their bodies and uses that as the focus for an entire science unit for children in kindergarten or first grade. Along the way a range of experiences with the basic science process skills is included. The "Measuring Height" activity uses actual representations of students' heights to introduce measuring, graphing, comparing, and other thinking skills. With the teacher's help, each child is measured using a strip of adding machine paper or cash register tape. Each child's height is represented by the strip of paper that is identical in length to his or her height. Names are written on the strips, and then these are arranged in order along a classroom wall. Students can appreciate the concepts of "less than" and "more than." This life-size graph is also a powerful display to leave on the classroom wall to share with parents and siblings who visit the classroom.

Suggested Readings

Christmann, E. P. (2004). Probing for answers. *Science Scope, 27*(4), 44–45.
> This article does an excellent job of highlighting the various probeware options available for use in science classrooms.

Davis, D. (2005). Tracking through the tulips. *Science and Children, 42*(7), 28–31.
> Dorothy Davis, a second-grade teacher in Tennessee, wrote this article about her class's participation in the Journey North project.

McNall, R. L., & Bell, R. L. (2004). Discovering flowers in a new light. *Science and Children, 41*(4), 35–39.
> The most innovative aspect of the teaching described in this article is the use of a digital microscope. But even as the students are looking at the tiny structures inside flowers, the instructors are using a learning cycle approach and making effective use of children's literature.

References

Alliance for Childhood. (2004). *Tech tonic: Towards a new literacy of technology.* College Park, MD: Author.

American Association for the Advancement of Science. (1993). *Benchmarks for science literacy.* New York: Oxford University Press.

Bayraktar, S. (2002). A meta-analysis of the effectiveness of computer-assisted instruction in science education. *Journal of Research on Technology in Education, 34,* 173–188.

Bernard, R. M., Abrami, P. C., Lou, Y., Borokhovski, E., Wade, A., Wozney, L., Wallet, P. A., Piset, M., & Huang, B. (2004). How does distance education compare with classroom instruction? *Review of Educational Research, 74,* 379–439.

Brodwin, M. G., Star, T., & Cardoso, E. (2004). Computer assistive technology for people who have disabilities: Computer adaptations and modifications. *Journal of Rehabilitation, 70*(3), 28–33.

Bromley, H., & Apple, M. W. (1998). *Education/technology/power: Educational computing as a social practice.* New York: SUNY Press.

Chen, D., Wong, A. F. L., & Hsu, J. J. (2003). Internet-based instructional activities: Not everything should be on the Internet. *Journal of Research on Technology in Education, 36,* 50–59.

Cuban, L. (2001). *Oversold and underused: Computers in the classroom.* Cambridge, MA: Harvard University Press.

Fitzgerald, M. (2002). The evolution of technology. *Tech Directions, 61*(7), 20–24.

Gee, J. P., Hull, G., & Lankshear, C. (1996). *The new work order: Behind the language of the new capitalism.* Boulder, CO: Westview.

International Society for Technology in Education. (2000). *National educational technology standards for students.* Washington, DC: Author.

Joyce, B., Weil, M., & Calhoun, E. (2004). *Models of teaching* (7th ed.). Boston: Pearson.

Kyle, W. C., Abell, S. K., & Shepardson, D. P. (1995). Using NGS Kids Network as an instructional tool in science methods courses. *Journal of Computers in Mathematics and Science Teaching, 14,* 169–186.

Migliorino, N. J., & Maiden, J. (2004). Educator attitudes toward electronic grading software. *Journal of Research on Technology in Education, 36,* 193–212.

National Center for Education Statistics. (1999). *Public school teachers use of computers and the Internet.* Washington, DC: U.S. Department of Education. (FRSS Document No. 70)

National Center for Education Statistics. (2000). *The condition of education.* Washington, DC: U.S. Department of Education. (NCES Document No. 2000–062)

National Research Council. (1996). *National Science Education Standards.* Washington, DC: National Academy Press.

Oakes, J., & Saunders, M. (2004). Education's most basic tools: Access to textbooks and instructional materials in California's public schools. *Teachers College Record, 106,* 1967–1988.

Oppenheimer, T. (2003). *The flickering mind: The false promise of technology in the classroom and how learning can be saved.* New York: Random House.

Park, J., & Staresina, L. N. (2004, May 6). Tracking U.S. trends. *Education Week, 23*(35), 64–67.

Pynchon, T. P. (1984, October 28). Is it O.K. to be a Luddite? *New York Times Book Review, 1,* 40–41.

Roblyer, M. D., & Edwards, J. (2000). *Integrating educational technology into teaching* (2nd ed.). Upper Saddle River, NJ: Merrill.

Settlage, J., & Wheatley, K. (2004). Key challenges for teachers: Windows into the complexity of American classrooms. In D. M. Moss, W. J. Glenn & R. L. Schwab (Eds.), Portraits of a profession: Teaching and teachers in the twenty-first century (pp. 109-140). Westport, CT: Praeger.

Standage, T. (1998). The Victorian Internet: The remarkable story of the telegraph and the nineteenth century's on-line pioneers. New York: Berkley Books.

Tinker, R. (2004, March). *The science summit talking points.* Paper presented at the Science Summit, Washington, DC, U.S. Department of Education.

Trumbull, D. J., Bonney, R., Bascom, D., & Cabral, A. (2000). Thinking scientifically during participation in a citizen-science project. *Science Education, 84,* 265–275.

Vannatta, R. A., & Fordham, N. (2004). Teacher dispositions as predictors of classroom technology use. *Journal of Research on Technology in Education, 36,* 253–265.

Weller, H. G. (1996). Assessing the impact of computer-based learning in science. *Journal of Research on Computing in Education, 28,* 461–485.

Wenglinsky, H. (1998). *Does it compute? The relationship between educational technology and student achievement in mathematics.* Princeton, NJ: Educational Testing Service. Retrieved August 25, 2006, from http://www.ets.org/Media/Research/pdf/PICTECHNOLOG.pdf

fourteen
Teachers Negotiating Different Communities

Chapter Highlights

- Learning to teach science in effective ways extends beyond mastering the methods of teaching. With culture representing such a central place within our understandings of science and diverse classrooms, learning to negotiate a variety of cultures is central to teachers' learning.

- As a means to help students navigate within the culture of science, teachers should develop ways to make the school experiences congruent with students' language, culture, and ways of thinking.

- A commitment to issues of equity can be mistakenly equated with the need to treat all students the same. A far better approach is to recognize individual differences and make adjustments to standard methods of science to best accommodate the needs and strengths represented by these differences. This requires rejecting the goal of a "one best way" to teach science to all students.

- There are many communities teachers need to negotiate: the students' communities, the school community, and the community of science. Using their knowledge of these different communities, teachers shape the culture of their classrooms.

- Without rejecting their own personal cultural heritage, teachers should make the effort to avoid making their own heritage and culture the standard against which students' cultures are compared. Recognizing the role culture has had in each of our lives can better prepare us to be responsive to the range of cultures represented by the students in our classrooms.

It was the teacher's first day of school in her new position as the only science teacher in a small, rural parish (in states outside of Louisiana, parishes are called counties). Her talks with her principal had provided her with important background information. For instance, she had learned that 75 percent of her students were African American, and 20 percent were Acadian American. The principal had also shared that only 5 percent of her students had their sights set on college. Last school year three science teachers had come and gone. Recognizing that these students were very different from the students in her own White, middle-class educational experience, the young teacher felt the need for an approach that was out of the ordinary. As a White woman with two college degrees, she wondered how well she would connect with her students.

The school in which she would be teaching was in a rural community on the banks of the Mississippi River just north of New Orleans. In contrast to Huckleberry Finn imagery, the local environment was dominated by chemical manufacturing plants. The water was tainted, and the air was stained with the colors and smells of these facilities. Recognizing that students learn best when they are aware of real-life connections to the subject matter, the new teacher decided to begin the school year with an environmental science unit. Her plan was to start by having students construct charts of the cancer rates reported along different stretches of the river. The teacher expected her students to naturally wonder about the causes after analyzing the data. She imagined that they would ask about what cancer does to the body. She anticipated that the students would ask hard questions about how the polluting effluents were harmful to human health and damaging to the local ecosystems. Such an approach, she thought, would address important science content even as it was wrapped in real-world issues. The new teacher envisioned this unit as a way to help her students, beyond learning the subject matter, recognize the application of science to their lives and also to minimize the management problems her predecessors seemed to have had in motivating the students to learn.

By the end of the first week, the teacher felt discouraged. The interactive discussions she had imagined would take place in her classroom did not develop. Instead of becoming enthused about learning, the students showed all the signs of apathy: she could hear it in their voices, and she could see it in their body language. The data, the graphing, and the topic did not elicit a flicker of interest. All of the advanced preparation she had invested appeared to be wasted. After one especially grueling day, as the teacher sat at her desk, her eyes fell on the shelves of environmental science textbooks. These thick books, weighing in at six pounds each, were poorly written and full of terminology. There was nothing in these texts that she thought would be of interest to her students, but her innovative efforts didn't seem to be any better and were consuming a great deal of her time and energy. To teach from the book instead of trying to implement an innovative unit would save the new teacher an incredible number of hours in preparation. Given the lack of responsiveness from her students, it appeared that the activities she was using were hardly worth the trouble. What was going on? The authentic, inquiry activity should have worked like a charm. Was this group of kids simply unteachable?

More Than Just Methods

In the past you may have regarded science learning as a cognitive endeavor, as if students' brains were receptacles for the information provided to them by a book and reinforced by the teacher. Assuming the preceding chapters have prompted a shift in your perceptions, you may appreciate that science teaching is not so simple and that becoming an effective science teacher to all students cannot be reduced to a collection of clever activities. As you reflect on the previous chapters, you will recall many suggestions for teaching in innovative and student-centered ways: process skills, conceptual change, inquiry-based teaching, the learning cycle, questioning strategies, and so on. You might reasonably expect that the pathway to effective science teaching is assured by the skillful implementation of these approaches. However, as this bleak true-life story reveals, approaching science teaching as if the skillful application of methods is all that is required is simply wrong-headed.

Learning is obviously an intellectual activity, but to teach as if that is all there is to it can lead to the difficulties and frustrations experienced by this new teacher. A too narrow view of the subject matter promotes a view of teaching that is full of flaws. We suggest that one of the reasons science teachers have historically done such a poor job of educating a diversity of students resides in part with an overly narrow view of the subject and a way of teaching that reinforces a purely cognitive impression of learning.

At an intuitive level classroom teachers recognize that helping students to learn science must extend beyond a single-minded emphasis on the cognitive. For learning to occur, teachers should pay attention to their students' motivations and perspectives. Learning science is not nearly as logic driven as we might suspect, and research in a variety of settings has demonstrated this reality (Alsop, 2005; Demastes-Southerland, Good, & Peebles, 1995; Strike & Posner, 1992). Students are people who hold particular interests and ambitions. Students are cultural beings whose ways of interacting with others and thinking about the world have been shaped by their cultures. Students learn for many reasons, and not all of these reasons are strictly cognitive. The fact that you are a student of teaching ought to reflect these claims: the reason you chose to become a teacher is far more complex than just a simple logical decision. When it comes to learning science, there are many factors that come into play. Direct experiences and clearly stated explanations provided by the teacher represent only a subset of factors that influence students' science learning (Moje, Collazo, Carrillo, & Marx, 2001; Southerland, Kittleson, Settlage, & Lanier, 2005).

Teaching science to all students, and particularly teaching in diverse classrooms, requires teachers to accept that science learning transcends the purely cognitive. Learning is shaped and supported by many factors, some of which are intellectual and logical. However, other powerful contributing factors include motivation, attentiveness, relevancy, and intrigue. To be effective in supporting science learning for all the students in your classroom, you must begin to attend to all of these. As illustrated in this chapter's opening vignette, a teacher who expects cognitive forces to carry the day is taking a big chance. To rely on this mind-set can cause us as teachers to become overly concerned with finding particular strategies and methods for delivering information. The problem is that a compulsion for the "right" technique can prevent teachers from taking into account the larger picture. Tedick and Walker (1994), second-language educators, articulated the shortcomings of searching for simplistic secrets to good teaching:

> The obsession with "methods that work" reinforces an historically inaccurate belief that teaching methods are the essence of teaching, that all methods work, and that techniques are the tools of teaching. The focus on methods excludes student, context, content and teacher; it assumes that an approach works regardless of who the students are, who the teacher is, what the content is, what the social context is, and why a particular method is appropriate for communicating particular content. In other words the focus on methods emphasizes the how and leaves the what, who and why out of the equation. What is missing in such practices is a sense that all of teaching occurs within a social, historical, and political context and requires that teachers above all consider this context before and while they think about what activities might best meet students' needs. (Tedick & Walker, 1994, pp. 307–308)

There is so much to think about as we approach the task of teaching science. The list is long but ought to include process skills, inquiry-based teaching, local science standards, and scheduling. But attending to only the pragmatic demands is not enough. Admittedly, conversations about science or science education rarely dwell on sociological considerations. After all, one might ask, even if we want to consider the social, historical, or political context of science teaching, where do we begin? Envisioning a classroom that adequately addresses the cognitive dimensions of science seems amply demanding, and any additional consideration of sociological issues seems to be overly complex. How political is it, for example, to teach physical science to sixth graders? To be honest, we thought about science teaching in this way when we began our careers. Our ambition was to guide the students to appreciate the excitement we felt toward science. More than recognizing the science that was included in our texts or supporting resources, we recognized the presence of science within our daily lives. We felt we understood our world better because we knew the underlying scientific explanations and could rely on scientific reasoning to help us make decisions and solve problems, and we wanted the same for our students.

Over the years we have come to accept the inadequacies of this way of thinking. These discoveries about ourselves were not always pleasant, especially when we realized that our supposed acts of kindness were actually having the opposite effect. When preparing to student teach in a middle school in Missouri, one of the authors planned an entire eight-week unit about plants. He dug into the resources in his university's curriculum library, he borrowed equipment from biology professors, and he sketched out the entire scope of hands-on activities onto a large sheet of paper. When the time came to deliver his lessons, things didn't go well. He had not taken into consideration the noncognitive aspects of teaching science. In fact he'd planned the entire unit without ever meeting the students. It required several years of experience teaching science for him to appreciate the problems with his approach. He had focused his classroom management on perceptions of being fair to everyone without acknowledging the diversity of his classroom. His perceptions of science teaching were restricted to a confidence in technical expertise. This is not to suggest that his teaching was a complete failure. But it was far less effective than it would have been if he had recognized that teaching science shouldn't ignore the complexity of human beings, the intricacies of social structure, or the magnitude of culturally based ways of thinking.

A Cautionary Note About Reaction to Difficulties

In many ways we wrote this book as an outgrowth of the mistakes we made as science teachers. We accept the value in learning from experience, and we acknowledge that we learned certain aspects of our teaching only by stumbling and recovering as part of the natural process of learning to teach. We realize that at the very beginning of our careers, we held inappropriate mind-sets about how to think about teaching science. We were so enthralled by the subject matter and we were so insulated within our personal ways of thinking and communicating that we were much less effective than if we had adopted a more inclusive approach to science teaching. Although we might have believed that every child could learn science, and we probably even made statements to that effect, it seems likely that our actions as teachers failed to articulate those goals. We are troubled by our ignorance, and we want to prevent our preservice teachers from having those painful realizations about themselves.

Learning from one's mistakes is a powerful tradition, and we are evidence of that approach. However, the mistakes we made shouldn't be repeated. Within this chapter we will examine some delicate issues. We need for you to believe that you shouldn't feel as if our words are attacking you, and we don't want to cause you to become defensive. Not so long ago we were in the same situation as you are, looking forward to becoming a teacher and feeling anxious about doing it well. You may be so eager to get into a classroom that you are not looking for any advice beyond being provided with a collection of proven hands-on activities. But we remain hopeful that you will persist in your reading and reflect long enough to benefit from our experience and the findings of the research literature. In what follows we will offer advice that would have helped us in supporting our students' best interests if we had known about it when we began teaching. You don't need to accept or agree with everything we describe. However, we honestly believe that we would have been much more effective at teaching science to all of our students if we had been able to move beyond our narrow perceptions of teaching. When you start to feel defensive, please believe us when we say that we are confessing our inadequacies to caution you against following a similar path.

Negotiating a Shifting Terrain

We are moving into territory that is not completely understood. Our specific interest throughout this book has been exploring and strategizing about teaching science to a wide range of students. This is a departure from previous generations where science was viewed as too difficult for all students to master—so the expectation was that not all students would learn it. Because the goal of science literacy for all is a relatively novel undertaking, we, as members of a science teaching profession, are still attempting to determine how to best proceed. However, clearly this is not something we can approach with leisure. The complexion of our student population is quite literally changing with every year that goes by, and we cannot delay our efforts just because we are uncertain. The situation is too urgent. Added to the compelling push to act is the shifting nature of the work. Standards and accountability are in considerable flux right now, even as the nation experiences one of its most massive influxes of immigrants. All of this and more create a science teaching landscape that is constantly changing. It is our challenge and opportunity to find our way—for the betterment of all our students' science learning.

We created this book to support novice teachers who are in the process of preparing to teach science in diverse classrooms. Now is the point in the process where we are forced to confront several thorny issues. Knowing about the issues and having a sense about how to respond will provide teachers with the tools to negotiate the issues when they occur. Each issue presents itself as a dilemma. We will contemplate the current situation, consult what others have written about it, and then propose ways in which elementary and middle school teachers might elect to respond. The three dilemmas are as follows: (1) distinguishing equitable science teaching from an approach to science teaching that attempts to treat everyone equally, (2) differentiating between science teaching that recognizes cultural and ethnic facets of each child and the notion of being color-blind when it comes to differentiating instruction, and (3) negotiating a variety of communities so instructional practices are responsive to family backgrounds and students' interests while still responding to the science standards and the expectations of the science teaching profession.

The Goal of Equitable Science Teaching

We begin with **equitable science teaching,** which describes a situation in which all children have access to the knowledge, resources, and experiences that will contribute to their genuine understanding of the culture of science. The differences among students (cultural background, home language, physical ability, and so on) should not dictate whether they are granted the opportunity to learn the material. Furthermore, simply having a diverse student body in the same room does not equate with equity. Acquiring equivalent expectations and being the recipient of a fair share of teacher attention are also necessary. Independent of the supposed learning styles of individual children, no differences in who they are should dictate if they are allowed and encouraged to participate in all aspects of science lessons. Realistic expectations should not be diminished because of the teacher's beliefs about who is capable of learning science. Any question about which students should be expected to learn the content, skills, and attitudes that we include under the banner of "scientific literacy" shouldn't take place because of unequal access to the knowledge or dissimilar attention from the teacher.

Much of what we will discuss in this chapter owes its origins to the Kamehameha Early Education Program (KEEP), a language arts program specifically designed to serve the needs of underachieving native Hawaiian children. This program, which drew on the work of scholars such as Heath (1983) and Banks and Banks (1993), was one of the first educational programs specifically designed to identify and build strong linkages between students' everyday ways of knowing and the practice of schooling (Au, 1980; Tharp & Gallimore, 1988). Although KEEP was focused on language arts teaching and learning, the lessons educators learned through KEEP have been extended to many content areas (literacy, mathematics, science) and can be found in many of the goals and strategies currently being used to teach in diverse classrooms. In this chapter we will focus on the science education community's interpretations and applications of these lessons.

One step toward creating a genuinely equitable classroom is to rely on pedagogy constructed around students' values and practices (Cochran-Smith, 1995). For students whose backgrounds and cultural practices are similar to those of their teachers, the need to connect school with home may not seem as necessary. But what is deceiving in these situations is that, in a hundred unrecognized ways, the teachers are building those connections—they just seem so natural that no one seems to recognize them. But when circumstances are different and teachers and students have very different life experiences, the absence of those subtle connections has profound influences on learning. References by the teacher to holiday traditions, foodstuffs, vacation spots, reading materials, and even popular culture have the potential for reinforcing the academic tasks at hand. But when teachers are unable to forge those links because their lived experiences are different from those of their students, the quality of the interactions between teachers and students, between the culture of science and the culture of the children, is compromised.

Science educators working in diverse classrooms in Miami have suggested that a useful route to equitable science instruction begins by examining the instructional congruence for the learners in the classroom (Lee & Fradd, 1998). They defined **instructional congruence** as the strength of the alignment between the academic world and the students' language, cultural experiences, and thought processes. The greater the instructional congruence of a lesson with students' lived experiences, the more likely the students will find the content accessible, meaningful, and relevant. Lee (2003) suggested that when instruction is congruent with the students' culture, experiences, skills, and communication patterns, students will be more engaged in science. For pedagogy to have a high degree of instructional congruence, it must be planned and delivered so it is mindful of students' out-of-school lives and ways of thinking and speaking.

Common Barriers to Equitable Science Instruction

Incorporating knowledge about students' backgrounds into instructional decision making is a very wise approach for all teachers. When teachers are less familiar with a particular group of students within a linguistically and ethnically diverse classroom, attempts at creating instructional congruence become even more necessary (Lynch, 2000). However, there is no secret, all-purpose way to accomplish this task. What we must guard ourselves against is treating the facts of diversity and the desire for equity as a problem begging for a solution. To look at the situation in this way places science teachers not as professionals who are choosing wisely but as technicians who are working around a flaw. Too often this results in not remaining attentive to the big picture. Again we rely on others to clarify our meaning:

> There is too much emphasis on consideration of technique and procedure...on the omnipotent method with little attention to awareness and attitude and to the reasoning, the values, and the politics that underlie the social context of teaching. (Tedick & Walker, 1994, p. 308)

This appears to be a rather extreme position. After all, if we believe teachers to be professionals, then wouldn't we expect a more thoughtful approach to linking diversity and equity? Rather than teachers trying to "fix" a "broken" situation, we think it is reasonable to expect that teachers view students' diversity as a resource to draw on, not something that they must work around to get the job done. However, a detailed examination of a program to educate teachers to accommodate diverse learners has revealed the depth of the problem-based approach to diversity.

The Problem With Emphasizing Techniques

Megan Peercy (2004) conducted research with teachers who were receiving ESL (English as a second language) training. What she discovered is that many teachers come to the classroom armed with certain teaching methods and techniques and the feeling that they have been prepared to deliver specified content through a particular process. Just as Tedick and Walker (1994) cautioned, the teachers who Peercy studied were so focused on techniques for instructing ESL students that they neglected other key features of effective teaching: they paid little attention to what the students wanted to know, they overlooked the concepts and skills the students were supposed to be learning, and they did not hold a mental model for considering how their students learned. This neglect of students' ways of "coming to know" is a persistent problem. Whether this negligence is a product of the training the teachers received, the pressures they were feeling, or some other shortcoming is hard to determine. But the consequences were clear: teachers in Peercy's study were unable to bridge the gap separating them from the diverse students. Instructional congruence, when approached as a technical problem, was not being accomplished.

When teaching occurs without teachers factoring in who is being taught, students experience a wide range of success in their learning. Who does an unexamined approach to teaching harm the least? The students who are most like the teacher. A technical approach to teaching typically benefits those students who are being raised as the teacher was raised and who have learned to talk and negotiate within their family and wider social settings in ways similar to those used by the teacher. When teachers approach teaching without sufficient regard for students as complex cultural beings, their teaching resonates most strongly for those who share the culture of that teacher. Meanwhile students whose upbringing differs from that of the teacher are typically underserved by such instruction. When the technical disposition toward science teaching predominates and when instruction is conceived of and implemented as if there is a universal formula, the students who benefit the least are those who often need it the most.

Peercy's (2004) work reinforces the need for instructional congruence as a core piece of equitable science instruction: there simply cannot be a "one size fits all" science lesson. Not all White, middle-class students will learn equally from the same activity, Web site, or discussion. A variety of approaches is required to accommodate the range of approaches to learning. Likewise students whose backgrounds are not the same as the dominant culture are not going to learn equally as well from many of the strategies known to be successful with students from the mainstream culture. Thus equitable science instruction cannot be achieved by providing the same experiences for all learners. Instead equitable science instruction can be accomplished only by providing instructionally congruent experiences for each learner.

Our new teacher in Louisiana was discouraged because she believed very strongly in the value of scientific inquiry. As she thought back on her science learning experiences, she found it hard to have fond memories of listening to lectures. Her hands-on experiences in her college science classes were what she subconsciously used as models for her efforts as a new teacher. The microbiology class where she cultured a bacteria from the environment and then had to identify it, genus and species, was one of the most open-ended science experiences she had. Field biology courses where she conducted insect surveys in the fields just off campus were much more structured because they were part of her professor's research, but it still felt to her like "real" science. Meanwhile her meteorology class, which involved lectures and slideshow presentations, was a waste of her time.

Because inquiry had been such a powerful way for her to learn science, she saw this instructional method as the best way to teach science. Her standard for "effective science teaching" was purely a matter of her own experience as a student. In her mind those methods she felt had helped her learn were likely the methods that science teachers should be using with all students. Her mistake was that as she planned to begin the school year, she hadn't dug deeply enough. By learning about the students' ethnicity, cultural heritage, and post–high school educational ambitions (which were very limited), she had gone only part of the way. She had been incompletely aware of the need to uncover the students' learning histories.

She invited a few students to have lunch with her so they could have some heart-to-heart conversations. In addition to learning more about the students as individuals with full personalities, our young teacher discovered that she was trying to implement an approach to science teaching that was completely foreign to her students. Her predecessors had structured science classes as lectures supplemented by information displayed with the overhead projector. The students' role in this arrangement was to transfer this information into notebooks that were graded for how thorough and neat the pages were. Her teaching methods, everything from urging students to generate questions they could investigate to challenging them to supply evidence to support their ideas, were simply foreign to these students. They weren't sure what was going on in her class or where they stood.

Despite her intentions, this teacher realized she wasn't doing a very good job of explaining to her students why she was using inquiry. For her part the teacher had incorrectly assumed that her goals were understood, even though they were left unstated. The consequence was a complete disconnect between what she was anticipating and what the students thought was being asked of them. Within her science learning history, learning by inquiry was a natural approach. However, to use her background as the standard for her students was a poor assumption. Beyond having different family traditions, her students had experienced ten or more years of schooling traditions that weren't closely aligned with the inquiry method she was trying to use. The mismatch between the students' experiences and her teaching method was a by-product of the teacher's incomplete understandings. She began to recognize that if she wanted her students to participate in science in ways consistent with her college science experiences, it was her duty to start with where her students were right now and then build on their learning backgrounds. This didn't mean that she would try to dismiss her students' community traditions. But it would involve helping them to appreciate the customs of the scientific community.

Equity Cannot Ignore or Deny Differences

The democratic ideal of equity has often included a commitment to treating everyone the same. Americans expect that laws should apply equally, freedom to vote should be extended to all adults, and a reasonable amount of medical care should be available to everyone. Fairness is important in everyday life, and even young children recognize the inequitable distribution of treats with claims of "That's not fair!" When resources such as income are not equitable, the American ideal of **meritocracy** is supposedly at play. This view states that individuals who are able to obtain more advantages than others do so because of their ability and industriousness. For the most part mainstream America holds to a belief that everyone starts out on an equal footing and any person's successes are largely the result of natural talent and hard work. This is what is meant by the "American dream" and is the way many people think about equity.

> **NSES Program Standard E: All students in the K-12 science program must have equitable access to opportunities to achieve the *National Science Education Standards*.**

We can see how this perspective closely links to the concept of the American melting pot. The motto *E Pluribus Unum* (translated as "from many: one") suggests that our society is open to all views, backgrounds, and traditions. Metaphorically new entrants into society are added to the mix so they become part of the overall blend that constitutes America. Toward that end schools have historically been viewed as a way to help families new to our nation to become assimilated. Stories of immigrant children finding their way through school and into successful and rewarding careers have become legends that inspire many of us and reinforce the idea that everyone can succeed if they have that desire. However, these success stories fail to show that individuals must often subvert and even deny their heritage to make their way through the system (Rodriguez, 2004; Rose, 1990). It is as if these individuals had to set aside their identity as members of a particular family with its cultural traditions to move up in the world. To join the melting pot, they had to remove the features that made them different so they could become fully assimilated—often forcing them to disconnect from their families and histories.

The melting pot view of society has some appeal, because it suggests that everyone can succeed if only they try hard enough. However, at some point we should realize that this type of equity usually means eliminating differences and variety. The melting pot ideal generally requires that an individual sacrifice his or her uniqueness to fit into an existing system. The only way to become successful, at least in a socially acceptable fashion (as opposed to becoming a famous gangster), requires developing ways to fit in while giving up on one's cultural background. We use the idea of the melting pot as a way to blend different ingredients, but we should recognize that the result of this melting pot is a homogeneous product wherein distinctive features are diluted. In short the melting pot metaphor reflects a desire for sameness.

The same forces are at play if we claim to not recognize differences in races among people. Although this appears to be evidence of equity, as educational researcher and advocate Gary Howard explained, there are dangers with such a view:

> Similar to the melting pot idea, the declaration of colorblindness assumes that we can erase racial categories, ignore differences, and thereby achieve an illusory state of sameness or equality. The colorblind perspective treats race as an irrelevant, invisible and taboo topic. (Howard, 1999, p. 53)

Teachers should recognize that equitable science instruction cannot and should not be equated with color-blind instruction. A **color-blind** perspective suggests that we can disregard students' differences in terms of language, culture, ethnicity, social class, and so on. Such a stance implies that one cannot be biased if all differences are rendered inconsequential. A teacher subscribing to a color-blind perspective approaches science instruction by denying that student diversity is of much significance. But when teachers conflate equity with sameness, the biases they hold are still present—just concealed. They may believe that their beliefs and actions reinforce equity and fairness. But this interpretation is the opposite of equity:

> "We are all the same" translates as "We are all like me," which is comforting for those who are accustomed to dominance. A White teacher once told me that "God is colorblind," which raised the assumption of rightness to a [much] higher level. I responded, "If God is colorblind, why did she create such a beautiful array of skin tones among the human family?" This produced a blank stare from the teacher so I turned to my African American colleague and asked, "Jessie, if I tell you I don't see color, how does that make you feel?" His response was, "You don't see me." This led to tears from the teacher. Her claim to colorblindness was coming from the goodness of her heart. Her assumption of rightness was well intended, as it often is. It was painful for her to realize that her dearly held belief in the sameness of human beings actually denied the authentic existence of people whose experiences of reality were different from hers. (Howard, 1999, p. 54)

We must acknowledge the intent of a color-blind perspective and praise the desire to combat overt forms of racial bias. The problem is that color blindness is simultaneously difference blindness. When a teacher is blind to the diversity within his or her classroom, there is the unspoken principle, or maybe even a clearly articulated belief, that all students can and should be treated as the same. Related to this is the conviction that we are turning away from a faith in sameness by adjusting our teaching to accommodate difference in culture, language, and so on. But we are making a serious mistake if we assume that all students can be taught in the same way, regardless of heritage, and that there are surefire science teaching methods that will work with all children (Cochran-Smith, 1995). We applaud the desire to overcome bias and preferences based on stereotypes. But a color-blind perspective is not the right way to make this happen.

Equitable science instruction requires teachers to learn about their students' lives, cultures, expectations, and languages. In turn this knowledge should inform day-to-day, moment-to-moment instructional decision making. Given that so much of our students' experiences, cultures, norms, expectations, and languages is tied to racial or cultural identity, ignoring this identity contributes to teachers' ignoring students' out-of-school lives, and it encourages us to engage in practices that ignore the habits and norms that shape the students and their learning. Difference blindness might be thought of as a way to reject racial stereotypes and patterns of explicit discrimination, but it also can prevent teachers from recognizing students' out-of-school experiences, experiences tied to their cultural identities. For that reason equitable science instruction must respond to the patterns of thought, culture, and tradition of the students while simultaneously breaking patterns of discrimination. As teachers working in diverse classrooms, we must not be reluctant to recognize differences; instead in our classroom instruction we must capitalize on those things that make learners different.

For Reflection and Discussion

Each of us has been in a situation where our name might as well have been a number: the person in charge (the instructor in a large lecture hall, the official at the driver's license bureau, or the nurse at the clinic) used our name only to pull us out of the crowd. In what ways is a color-blind perspective going to make a student feel in ways similar to how you felt when you believed the person in charge had very little interest in who you were?

Teachers Negotiating Different Communities

Learning to teach science in equitable ways is not an easy task. In addition to understanding the culture of science, teachers must be aware of other factors: the published science standards, the need to move beyond a belief in a "one best method" of teaching, and the avoidance of a perspective that denies the relevance of individual differences. Teaching science in a way that holds close the principle of instructional congruence requires particular knowledge and expertise. In a sense teachers who are committed to equitable teaching serve as cultural brokers. They are actively helping negotiate the boundaries between the culture of science and the cultures of their students. Just as for a tour guide in an exotic land, the teacher must be fluent in two areas and able to serve as a translator. The teacher must be competent at moving around through the culture of science: she or he can recognize the habits of mind, the science process skills, the nature of science, and the methods of inquiry within science activities. In addition the teacher must be competent at genuinely communicating with the members of the classroom and their families. Essentially the teacher should be competent in the students' cultures and the science culture—and just as important be capable of helping her or his students to learn how to negotiate the borders.

Ann Rosebery, Beth Warren, Cindy Ballenger, and a host of other researchers and classroom teachers, through their work at the Chèche Konnen Center for Science Teaching and Learning, brought the idea of "repertoires of practice" developed in anthropology (Gutiérrez & Rogoff, 2003) into the field of science education. Rosebery (2004), in a talk describing the work of her colleagues within the Chèche Konnen Center, described repertoires of practice as "what people do and what they say about what they do. It is the practices they engage in, what they do as a result of their involvement in particular communities" (p. 2). In terms of science teaching, one part of the repertoire of practice is the culture of science, another is the culture of the classroom, a third includes the culture of the school, and yet another is the broader culture of the teaching profession. Rosebery and her colleagues suggested that teachers of diverse learners must learn to negotiate the repertoires of practice of the community of science, the community of the students they teach, and the communities in which the teachers participate. Our ultimate goals as equitable science teachers are to move among these communities with skill and grace and to develop a rich repertoire of practice.

Our young teacher realized how fortunate she had been as a college student, because she had stumbled into many situations in which she could actually participate in scientific inquiry. She had weighed baby birds in nests, she had used a seine to retrieve invertebrates from a stream, and she had learned to build maps using the latest handheld satellite positioning equipment. Along the way she'd unknowingly absorbed the ways of thinking appropriate to scientists: withholding conclusions until she had sufficient data, holding multiple competing explanations in mind, and designing studies and conducting analyses in which she would reduce the likelihood that her preconceived biases influenced the results. For all intents and purposes, our teacher was pretty good at passing as a member of the scientific community.

The teacher's lunchtime conversations with her students helped her to accept the possibility that she was functioning with an insufficient amount of information about her students. She felt responsible for guiding her students to be successful in science and developing their appreciation for the subject and the thinking skills this field can supply. For her to connect with her students, she needed to know more about them, but not by trying to become their friend. She needed to know more about who they were as learners. For this our teacher sought out the advice of veteran teachers in the building who seemed to be successful in teaching other subjects to her students. This move came about partly by accident. During her planning period, our teacher had walked by a social studies classroom in which the teacher was leading an interesting discussion about the Declaration of Independence. She was startled to see that some of the students who were among the most reserved in science class were actively and articulately engaged in the class conversation. How was this teacher capable of engaging the students that she had so far failed to engage in science? How might she learn to motivate these students to learn and not simply play a game of compliance? A series of after-school discussions with other teachers proved to be very educational for our teacher.

Negotiating the Community of Science

We introduced the objects and actions of science in the first chapter, and we've made an effort to build on this "science as a culture" idea ever since. The desire to create instructional congruence is tightly bound to this view of science. At this point we want to emphasize the actions of science, because this seems to be the more elusive idea for teachers and for students. Knowing how relevant the actions of science are to understanding the culture of science cannot be overstated. As the staff of the Chèche Konnen Center described, "If a teacher has not been prepared to recognize a wide-range of practices as scientific, she may respond to students of color in ways that limit not only their participation and learning but the participation and learning of all her students" (Rosebery, 2004, p. 6). If teachers have a very narrow view about how science produces knowledge (e.g., ascribing to THE scientific method), then opportunities to make connections for the students may be missed.

Students enter the classroom with patterns of thought that can potentially be tied to scientific thinking. The teacher unfamiliar with the "actions of science" fails to capitalize on ways to build bridges between students' natural curiosity and science. There are countless connections that teachers can grasp if they are sufficiently knowledgeable and attentive. When a student who notices the moisture forming on the outside of a water bottle begins to discuss the possibilities with another student, a strategic teacher will use the event as way to connect the conversation to the way in which scientists wrestle to generate explanations based on evidence. Equating ways of thinking and communicating that spontaneously arise in the classroom with the actions of science can happen only for teachers who see themselves and their students as participants in science.

Teaching science to diverse populations is much more involved than helping students to master terminology. Instructional congruence is much more involved than having students define science terms in their own language. As important as this technique can be, a teacher cannot satisfy the need to familiarize students with the culture of science if she or he neglects the actions part of the culture of science. To craft intelligent decisions about what and how to teach one's students, teachers must develop a thorough understanding of the culture of science.

Negotiating Your Students' Communities

Although perhaps the most obvious of the Chèche Konnen Center's recommendations, the suggestion that teachers become familiar with their students is hard to pin down. Teachers should become familiar with the community of science and the histories, ideas, and communities of the students they teach: "In addition to understanding the important ideas and practices of science, teachers need to understand what and why their students say and do what they do; and they likewise need to be able to express themselves in ways their students understand" (Rosebery, 2004, p. 6). Understandable expression is much more involved than projecting loudly, enunciating clearly, and speaking bilingually. "Simply sharing language does not ensure smooth communication" (Helmer & Eddy, 2003, p. 33). The ways of communicating are at least as important as what is being said.

Just because other people can speak our language and share common interests does not mean they know us. If a guy drives the same color, make, and model car that you do, it doesn't mean you really have that much in common. In the same way, knowing how to speak a few words in a student's native language is helpful in showing some sensitivity, but we shouldn't equate this with understanding the student. As real as linguistic barriers can be to communication, recognizing and overcoming these barriers is not the complete solution. An essential feature of understanding students is a focus on common patterns of reasoning, questioning, and explaining employed by the students and their communities. How do your students think through a problem, and how do they explain their ideas? What patterns of thinking and explanation are commonly employed in their out-of-school communities? Teachers must also consider what is valued by students and by members of the students' communities, pursuing questions about the value of science in students' out-of-school communities. Even more fundamental is seeking to understand that the community's perceptions about the purpose of schooling are worth investigating. Each piece of information contributes to understanding students, and their communities provide another step toward teaching science in culturally congruent ways.

NSES Program Standard D: Good science programs require access to the world beyond the classroom.

In terms of interpersonal relationships, teachers need to be aware of patterns of nonverbal communication, such as kinetics (bodily movement such as posture, gesture, eye contact that individuals, and particularly communities, employ for communication) and proxemics (use of personal space between ourselves and others). Such nonverbal behaviors can carry a great deal of meaning, and if these cultural norms are unknowingly violated, the actions get in the way of meaning making in the classroom.

From Ideas to Actions

At this point you may be thinking it would be useful if we could provide you with the rules of thumb for understanding cultural practices and acting appropriately when you encounter various ethnic, racial, or social class groups. Such lists do exist, as businesses and government agencies view these cues as tools for building sensitivity toward diverse clients. But we are not going to supply such a list to you. The reason is that we are genuinely concerned about the potential misuse of such a checklist. We are sensitive to the concerns of our colleagues (Gutiérrez & Rogoff, 2003; Rosebery, 2004), who show these lists reinforce stereotypes. A handout that says something to the effect of, "When working with members of XYZ culture, you should …" conveys a belief that all members of a cultural group think, act, and believe in identical ways. Individuals who share a common language or ethnic membership are not a homogeneous mass; they remain individuals with variations in personalities, learning styles, and motivations.

When we imagine that everyone within a particular social group is the same, we are engaging in a practice called **essentializing.** When we examine a group of stones and describe their similarities, we are identifying their essence, and that is a reasonable aspect of doing science. But to essentialize individuals and to generalize people is not quite the same as doing so with inanimate objects. Generalizations about groups of people may be a matter of convenience, but for something as vital as teaching children, such generalizations are fraught with problems. Consequently, we must actively resist essentializing statements such as "Latinos enjoy cooperative group work," "American Indians don't like questioning," "White middle-class boys are competitive," or "African American children are kinesthetic learners." If someone on campus has treated you as if you're just another education major, then you have a sense of what it is like to be essentialized. When it comes to referring to rules of thumb for working with different cultural groups, these lists, as well intentioned as they might be, actually create walls that can prevent teachers from recognizing their students' individuality.

If we won't provide you with a rules of thumb list, what can we supply to you to help you negotiate your students' communities? One recommendation is to carefully examine your teaching assumptions and practices from a cultural perspective. Because it is a challenge for us to step outside of ourselves, a video camera can be a valuable tool. Videotape one of your science lessons and then view the lesson, not so much to detect what you are doing but to focus on students. How does their communication style vary as they speak to their classmates as compared to speaking with you? What are the nonverbal aspects of their communication: gesture, eye contact, and intonation? What cues are they offering about their communication that you may not be picking up on when you are in the front of the classroom? See if you can identify some characteristics that weren't as evident because you were concentrating on your teaching at the time.

Another strategy for learning more about your students is to see if you can unobtrusively observe them as they communicate with others in settings outside of your classroom. How do they interact in gym, in the lunchroom, or as they leave school at the end of the day? It is important to develop an understanding of your students while in your classroom and in the wider school environment, because how they participate in science class may be different from the way they interact elsewhere. After all of this work, you will be less likely to essentialize the students, because it will be harder for you to view them as simply members of a group. This preparation will allow you to see them as individual learners.

Genuine knowledge about students drawn from a rich assortment of perspectives allows us to craft instruction that is congruent with their lives. Furthermore, the reasons for understanding our students reach beyond curricular purposes. As Rosebery (2004) explained, teachers need to understand students' ways of "explaining, questioning, arguing, establishing trust, and the like" (p. 6) to identify the features of science within what students are offering in class. What may sound like a students' tangential story may indeed hold a scientific explanation if one knows how to listen. Part of teaching is taking what students offer and shaping it toward a more scientific alternative. To do this well, the teacher needs to recognize what students are offering. This recognition requires knowing your students as both members of groups and distinct individuals.

Point–Counterpoint

The challenge of being effective at teaching science is made even more daunting by the increasingly diverse school populations. Students who are traditionally less successful in science, including those who have immigrated to the United States, present an important responsibility to and require a commitment from teachers. But finding ways to bridge the science of the school and the students' personal and cultural sense-making practices is an endeavor ripe for potential misunderstandings. So in response to the question "How can teachers be effective working with diverse student populations?" we can consult a pair of well-informed notions.

Expanding the Space of Learning in Science

Ann S. Rosebery and Beth Warren
Chèche Konnen Center, TERC (Cambridge, Massachusetts)

We believe that by the time students enter school, they all have acquired sense-making practices in their out-of-school lives that can be an important foundation for learning science. Yet not all students experience success in science. Historically these are students of color, students from low-income households, students whose families speak a language other than English at home, and students whose parents have had limited formal schooling. For the most part schools have been unable to take up the powerful verbal, reasoning, and interpretive practices that students from these nondominant groups learn in their out-of-school lives (e.g., highly attuned listening and observational skills; acute sensitivity to social relationships; skilled forms of language play, storytelling, and argument; and striking and subtle uses of metaphor). Although the academic value of such practices may not be obvious, we have found that they can be powerful tools in learning science.

Researchers at the Chèche Konnen Center are documenting connections between the sense-making practices of students from nondominant groups and those of professional scientists (*Chèche Konnen* means "search for knowledge" in Haitian Creole. It is the name that the original group of teachers gave to this work.) To see these connections, you need to expand your view of science from "the scientific method" to include a wide-ranging repertoire of scientific sense-making practices. Studies of "science in action" have shown that scientists use diverse sense-making practices as they go about the work of developing knowledge, including embodied imagining, argumentation, and metaphor. We have seen students use sense-making practices such as these toward meaningful ends in science. Here's an example:

Third graders in a two-way Spanish–English bilingual program were discussing a student's question, "Do plants grow every day?" They had measured and recorded the growth of their own plants on charts and graphs for several weeks. On this day they debated the pattern of growth and whether they could see their plants grow. Serena, the child of highly educated parents and a "high-achieving" student, explained that perhaps their rulers could not detect the small increments of daily growth in their plants. Elena, the child of immigrant, working class parents who was repeating third grade, approached the question differently. She imagined growth in a plant by imagining her own growth. She responded, "I don't think we could see them grow, but I think they could feel theirselves grow. Sometimes we can feel ourselves grow because my feet grow so fast cuz this little crinkly thing is always bothering my feet. That means it's starting to grow. It's starting to stretch out."

From our point of view, this example illustrates two important scientific practices, one commonly recognized in school and one not. Serena's approach is easily identified as scientific because it conforms to widely held conceptions of scientific reasoning. Using the students' graphs to find and justify an answer to the question, she argues from a perspective outside the plant, viewing growth through the lens of objective measurement. This is an unquestionably important practice in science. However, it represents one tool among many used by professional scientists. Elena's approach is equally scientific and deserving of a place in the classroom, although it is not often recognized as such. In contrast to Serena, Elena thinks about growth from inside her own body, considering its moment-to-moment aspect and how the process of growing feels. Her move to imagine her own growth, and through this the growth of a plant, is akin to forms of imagining used by professional scientists. When trying to puzzle through novel problems, scientists often imagine themselves inside physical events and processes to explore how they might behave.

We regularly see children take on the perspective of organisms (e.g., plants, ants, snails) and physical phenomena (e.g., melting ice cubes, toy cars rolling down ramps, gravity) to explore a scientific question. Some researchers call this "anthropomorphism," suggesting that the students believe that these nonhuman entities possess human qualities. In our experience students know that plants, ants, and ice cubes do not actually possess human attributes. Instead they are temporarily suspending the rules of the real world to imagine what might be possible from a perspective inside the phenomenon itself. These moves are remarkably similar to the ways in which scientists describe their own imagining processes when they are working at the cutting edge of a problem.

We have seen that all students learn more when teachers recognize the connections between their students' diverse sense-making practices and those of science. By way of closing, we return briefly to our example. Elena's imagining led otherwise usually quiet classmates to further explore how growth is conceptualized and how they might "see" it. They explored the thickness of stems and branches, the amount of space their plants occupied, the number of seeds and seedpods, and the number of leaves as additional indicators of growth. This multidimensional conceptualization of growth is closer to a biological view than is the one-dimensional perspective highlighted by Serena and typically found in school science. The children's broad consideration of plant growth additionally led them to wonder about the role of the sun. Following Elena's lead, Serena took the perspective of a leaf, and asked, "How does the sunlight get into the leaves?" showing how such imagining gives rise to challenging scientific questions. Thus in contrast to reform efforts that emphasize the instructional value of enabling Elena to learn from Serena, here we see both Elena and Serena having opportunities to learn from each other. In these ways the space of learning in science expands to include a wider range of sense-making practices and with it wider participation and deeper learning on the part of all students.

Articulating Science Disciplines With Students' Linguistic and Cultural Experiences

Okhee Lee
Science Education Researcher, University of Miami, Florida

When a person enters a foreign country, she has to develop an understanding of the norms and practices common in the new country. Some things are unexpectedly familiar, while other things are completely foreign. Some of the most difficult adaptations to make often relate to the norms that are taken for granted and implicitly understood by native residents. Frequently the foreigner encounters tensions between the norms and practices of her home country and those of the new country. She needs to learn to cross borders between the two sets of expectations. Border crossing is a difficult process, since it requires not only the skills to be able to do so but also the willingness to construct new identities in relation to conflicting norms.

Science has been described as a subculture with a distinct set of socialized norms and practices that members of the scientific community generally agree to uphold and to abide by. Science has also been described as a *Discourse*. Whereas "little d" discourse refers to language in interaction, "big D" Discourse refers to construction of one's identity as well as language (e.g., ways of thinking, valuing, acting, and interacting). Thus learning to enact a science Discourse involves using language according to prescribed norms of evidence and logic and also learning to think, act, interact, and use tools. This science Discourse is foreign to many students, both mainstream and nonmainstream, but the challenges of science learning may be greater for students whose broad cultural traditions and past lived experiences are discontinuous with the Discourses and "ways of knowing" characteristic of Western modern science and normative school science. For example my own research, as well as the larger literature on worldviews, indicates the acceptance of a shared and public Discourse of supernatural, spiritual, animistic, or volitional accounts of nature among many students of nonmainstream backgrounds in the United States and in developing countries around the world.

In a similar way, although learning to conduct scientific inquiry involving testable questions is a challenge for most students, it can present additional challenges for students from societies in which cultural norms prioritize respect for teachers and other adults as authoritative sources of knowledge. Children who are taught to respect the wisdom and authority of their elders may not be encouraged to question received knowledge in ways that are compatible with a Western scientific worldview and Discourse.

The challenge for cultural and linguistic nonmainstream students in learning science is to master a Western scientific way of knowing, while at the same time respecting and accessing the ideas, beliefs, and values of homes and communities. To succeed academically they must learn to negotiate the boundaries that separate their own cultural environments and Discourses from the cultures and Discourses of Western science and school science. At times students may find themselves caught in conflicts between what is expected of them in science classes and what they experience at home, in their communities, and with their peers. If they appear too eager or willing to enact a school science Discourse, they may find themselves estranged from their families or peers. If they appear reluctant or hesitant to participate in science inquiry, they risk marginalization from school and subsequent loss of access to learning opportunities. Although some students successfully bridge this divide between home and school and selectively enact multiple Discourses in context-dependent ways, other students become alienated and resist either the school-based or the home-based conceptions of science and the natural world.

The role of the teacher is critical in helping diverse students to construct these bridges. The teacher needs to articulate scientific disciplines with students' linguistic and cultural experiences and devise ways to link the two (i.e., instructional congruence). The first step generally involves recognition of the linguistic and cultural experiences that nonmainstream individuals and groups bring to the science classroom in relation to the normative school science Discourse. Some aspects of students' lived experience may be discontinuous with traditionally defined Western science. However, the willing teacher may be surprised to identify numerous experiences that can serve as intellectual resources for new learning in science classrooms. Although these experiences may not be easily recognized, my current research is looking at ways in which focused professional development may help teachers learn to better identify and build upon such experiences.

Then the teacher can help students to cross borders between their home practices and the culture and Discourse of Western science. The teacher needs to make the norms and practices of Western science, school science, and home and community explicit, highlighting both similarities and differences. The teacher should initially provide an explicit structure for engaging in scientific inquiry within the context of authentic and meaningful tasks and activities. As students learn to engage in scientific practices, the teacher gradually reduces the degree of structure provided, while encouraging students to take the initiative, explore on their own, and assume responsibility for their own learning. The teacher should consciously maintain a balance between teacher guidance and student initiative, making decisions about when and how to foster students' responsibility for their science learning.

Over time students who successfully participate in normative school science while also valuing the norms and practices of their home languages and cultures will learn to selectively enact the "right Discourses" in the "right" places and at the "right" times. They will also come to better understand the culture of science and their home culture and to behave competently across social contexts. In the end such students will achieve academically in science classrooms, while also maintaining their cultural and linguistic identity.

Helping Negotiate Between Communities

Although you should use what you've come to understand about your students in planning instruction, in terms of both what you will teach and how you will teach it, we suggest for you to consider going beyond this. Find out who within your students' communities have jobs related to science. As you help your students appreciate that science is not all lab coats and test tubes but also logical thinking and problem solving, they begin to see many trades as scientific. When we conceive of scientific literacy as involving the identification of a problem, choosing potentially relevant sources of data, and then drawing conclusions based on that information, then many community members can be appropriately viewed as using science: auto repair, landscaping, food preparation, and construction, for example. Invite people with those jobs into your classroom, preparing them to speak about the science involved in their work: measuring, predicting, and so on. More than being models of possible career options, they can enlighten students about the relevance of science to daily life. For instance a mechanic can explain combustion, a doctor can explain inoculations, a physical therapist can explain torn ligaments, and an electrician can reinforce science lessons about conductors and insulators. Help students appreciate that science is already an aspect of their communities and that the knowledge of science resides within their communities. This represents another way to make science teaching more equitable. This will happen because you are relying on your efforts to negotiate science and the community and then drawing on those communities to reinforce these connections.

> The students' cultural diversity and the families' "lived experiences" need to become part of the school. … They must become part of the classroom learning environment and the development of curriculum. (McCaleb, 1994, pp. 192–193)

For many teachers who first begin to work with students from lower-income families, there is a tendency to see education as a one-way street. In this mind-set the school is perceived as being rich in knowledge and resources whereas "the home" is regarded as not having much in the way of educational utility. However, to think and act in such a manner ignores the fact that working-class and immigrant families often want to help with their child's education and they have the capacity to do so. This idea of families serving as reservoirs for helping students learn has been termed *funds of knowledge,* indicating a shifting perspective about who or what constitutes a source of useful information (González, Amanti, & Moll, 2005).

Funds of knowledge serve as a foundation on which learning can be built, as tools for connecting school knowledge to daily life, and as a mechanism for inviting diverse cultures into the classroom. This should not suggest that the goal of relevance implies a simplification of learning. Showing how science lessons have a bearing on everyday life does not require teachers to compromise their expectations of students. If anything the funds of knowledge concept is an antidote to the assumption that homes are devoid of much in the way of educational resources (McIntyre, Rosebery, & González, 2001). When school and curriculum materials push a skills-based approach and emphasize the need to provide foundational and basic knowledge before moving to more sophisticated (and interesting) topics, the professionalism of teachers and the value of home life are sold short. There is no magic formula for implementing funds of knowledge into elementary or middle school science teaching. But a shift in perspectives is more than sufficient for our immediate purposes: recognizing that the families and communities of our students can provide intellectual resources to reinforce what we are trying to teach is a concept that not enough teachers have come to accept.

For Reflection and Discussion

Suppose that your science methods instructor was new to the United States and had little understanding of you and your background aside from what he or she could glean from your transcripts. What are some strategies she or he might use to uncover your funds of knowledge in a way that would make his or her teaching more relevant to you but wouldn't also make you uncomfortable about revealing information about yourself?

The Classroom as a Community for Negotiation

Recognize that your classroom is one of your students' communities and that it is worth considering how they operate in this community. It is important to ask your students what they are interested in learning, how they are interested in learning it, and what their own goals for science learning and schooling are. Although the families and communities can tell us a great deal about our students' expectations, patterns of communications, and cultural norms, we need to also understand our students as individuals within these broader communities and cultures. The most effective way to do this is to talk with your students, in class and outside of class.

As we have mentioned elsewhere, your relying solely on whole group discussion can provide a distorted portrait of students' knowledge, goals, and desires, as students are selective in what they want to portray in front of their classmates. Share lunch with groups of your students on a rotating basis (to avoid charges of favoritism and to learn more about each of your students), go to after-school activities such as athletic events or clubs, or ask for their help in organizing the science materials or preparing activities. Be sure to take these personal steps with those students who are most unfamiliar to you, and do not become comfortable seeking interaction with only the more friendly and familiar faces. As we have suggested, it is important for teachers to consider the distinctions of various groups of learners in their classrooms, and it is important for teachers to closely examine patterns of behavior that fail to hold for individuals in those groups. As teachers we can use knowledge of the groups to craft instruction, but knowledge of individuals within those groups is essential for honing that instruction. In short get to know what is important to your students on an individual basis, and analyze the ways they communicate in your classroom. This will allow you to take a major step toward instructional congruence.

Gradually our novice teacher deepened her knowledge about the students. By dedicating occasional planning periods for visits to other classrooms, she began to identify patterns of instruction that were familiar, comfortable, and productive for her students. Talks with other teachers helped her to pinpoint techniques that were alien to her (such as writing out directions on the overhead for activities, giving "appearance points" to notebooks, and devoting entire class sessions to note taking), and she saw ways she could improve. Incorporating other teachers' techniques was strengthening her repertoire of practices, because she was weaving approaches recognizable to her students into her science lessons. This didn't mean that she was sacrificing science. Instead she was coming to appreciate that she needed to adjust her methods so they were more closely aligned with her students' experiences. For example she began to identify the parallels between the science her students were engaged in and the science as performed by professionals in the community. In this regard she was able to draw on her own work in labs and field studies. Along the way she discovered that many of her students' family members were employed in jobs that involved science: quality assurance, environmental monitoring, nursing, and agriculture.

Our teacher made adjustments to her teaching practices. She came to realize her students' resistance to the open-ended inquiry activities was an understandable reaction to an approach that was completely unfamiliar to them. Her initial teaching was difficult, because she was using a method that was new to the students while unknowingly devaluing the classroom practices with which they had become familiar. Although she was confident her science methods instructor would cringe if he found out, she began a weekly routine of four days of note-taking and question-and-answer sessions, culminating with one day of structured inquiry. As the weeks progressed, she gradually reduced the amount of time spent lecturing, shifting to more discussions. She explained to her students that she was going to ask some questions where there was not a single correct answer. In addition she provided a rationale for using Wait Time One and showed how she would use a hand signal on those occasions where everyone was to pause and think before answering. She was very judicious in how she used this strategy, because she had noticed the students tended to chime in quite rapidly. But she held to the belief that there were times when a quick answer was not as valuable as a thoughtfully considered response.

A certain comfort level developed, especially as the teacher found ways to chat with her students outside of class. This rapport provided her with insights into their lives, aspirations, and concerns. One community issue of which she had not been aware was the high incidence of AIDS in the area. Rather than using AIDS as the core of a thematic unit, she sought opportunities to weave this topic into their studies of key scientific ideas: DNA, natural selection, germ theory, and so on. This decision seemed to be a watershed decision, as students recognized that what was being addressed in class was salient to their lives. Management problems, although they did not cease, became much less frequent. Students began to understand what was expected of them and the use of the knowledge they were learning. And the teacher made deliberate efforts to continue interacting with her students outside of class. She attended sporting events and school performances and began to do some shopping in the stores in the neighborhood. By year's end, the teaching in this class was not exactly what our novice had hoped for, but she began to understand the need to blend her classroom instruction with knowledge, patterns, and skills drawn from her students' lives.

Negotiating Your Own Communities

Many teacher educators who have been working toward equity argue that to truly understand our students' culture, we must first understand the influences of our own cultures on us (Cochran-Smith, 1995; Helmer & Eddy, 2003; Rosebery, 2004). These authors contend that a teacher's self-knowledge is a prerequisite for understanding her or his students' cultures, and we have come to recognize the wisdom in this perspective. We have reserved discussing this need for self-knowledge until now, because it may be one of the most counterintuitive community negotiations we will address in this chapter.

We will begin with Marilyn Cochran-Smith, who has written extensively about educating teachers for diverse classrooms:

> In order to learn to teach in a society that is increasingly culturally and linguistically diverse, prospective teachers need opportunities to examine much of what is usually unexamined in the tightly braided relationships of language, culture, and power in schools and schooling. This kind of examination inevitably begins with our own histories as human beings and as educators—our own cultural, racial, and linguistic backgrounds and our own experiences as raced, classed, and gendered children, parents, and teachers in the world. It also includes a close look at the tacit assumptions we make about the motivations and behaviors of other children, other parents, and other teachers and about the pedagogies we deem most appropriate for learners who are like us and who are not like us. (Cochran-Smith, 1995, p. 500)

What strikes some people as odd is the notion of needing to study ourselves rather than to study our students or our teaching. Although she's not saying we should ignore our students' backgrounds, Cochran-Smith is making the case that we need to be standing on a clear foundation of our identity before we can fully appreciate the relevance of our students' identities. Once we recognize how our preconceptions influence our interpretations, we can become more accepting of the challenges students sometimes face when they are asked to think, behave, or learn in ways that are unfamiliar to them.

For many of us it is hard to detect the influence of our own culture. In our opening vignette, the novice teacher seemed to cherish questioning and saw the practice of continual critique as a sure step toward students' constructing knowledge. She understood a classroom to be a place where both the teacher and the learners had a voice in what was presented. What was apparently unclear to her was that her views were direct by-products of her background. Her mistake was twofold: not recognizing how her communities had led her to think as she did and failing to appreciate that hers was not the best approach to teach science to any and all students.

We prefer to not question this novice teacher's sincerity. It is clear her motivations were based on a desire to help her students learn science. But her singular view of teaching and learning, borne of her personal and narrow experience, led her down a path that proved to be frustrating to her and her students. It was not until she began to observe other, more established teachers that she detected the clues about where she was falling short of her laudable goals. These teachers taught her that these students valued clear structure, sought the directness of taking notes, and developed a sense of achievement by creating well-designed science notebooks.

To her credit our novice teacher did not dismiss these traditions nor did she simply conform to them. Typically when there are cultural incongruities between subject matter and students, the response is often that the teacher's culture is the one taken as given and the students are expected to adapt, or face the consequence of failing grades. Rather our teacher came to realize that her challenge was to negotiate between her views of science teaching and the teaching and learning practices established in this school. She fought against the temptation to fall in line with the school's very regimented practices because she was tightly and appropriately holding onto the culture of science. She was determined to guide her students to appreciate science as a powerful way of viewing the world, but she knew she couldn't accomplish this if she denied the culture of the students and the local community. Because our novice teacher was so culturally different from her students, the rest of the school, and the wider community and because there were teachers who were experiencing some success with the students, she saw the value in modifying her instructional approaches. Along the way she began to reconsider the influences her upbringing had played in her decision making.

The practice of instructionally congruent science teaching depends on our having knowledge about the cultures of the students and also making teaching decisions so classroom practices are aligned with the learner's culture. But the first requirement is a willingness to understand the ways in which your culture has come to influence you (Bennett, 1993). We must move beyond a blindness to own culture and overcome the assumption that our cultural expectations are the standard against which all others can be appropriately judged. An **ethnocentric** view "refers to the tendency to view one's own cultural group as superior to others" (Reagan, 2000, p. 5). When ethnocentric teachers encounter students from another culture, they unconsciously judge those students by their own cultural frames of reference. That is the problem of difference blindness: invariably in an attempt to treat all students the same, teachers use the cultural guideposts of their own cultures, accepting and supporting what is familiar to them and rejecting or marginalizing that which is unfamiliar.

For Reflection and Discussion

In what ways can an ethnocentric perspective be an understandable feature of a person's thinking? How might the persistence of an ethnocentric view compromise a teacher's effectiveness in working with diverse student populations?

Ethnocentric teachers fail to recognize how their expectations and beliefs are culturally laden, and such teachers cannot begin to understand how and why students may think and behave differently from the ways the teacher expects. Ethnocentric teachers fail to see the influence of culture, so anything that deviates from the norm is odd or wrong. Thus the actions and behaviors of students from families, backgrounds, or countries different from that of the teachers can be seen only as wrong. In our own teaching we have had experiences with students behaving in ways that we felt at the time was inappropriate, such as the following:

- students refusing to maintain eye contact during our attempts to discipline them;
- students feeling comfortable loudly offering jokes and criticizing classmates in classrooms;
- students balking at answering questions in class discussions in those same classrooms with those same students;
- students refusing to turn in homework; and
- students pleading to be allowed to copy notes from the chalkboard or overhead projector rather than participating in a whole class discussion.

In the moment, within the midst of a tiring day, week, or month of teaching, such behaviors seem downright contrary to most us, seeming to indicate the students' failure to participate in class and in their own education. Without further thought, these students, like those we described in the vignette at the outset of this chapter, can be thought of as unteachable. It is not until we as teachers begin to understand that students' behaviors are not wrong but instead part of the students' cultures and ways of understanding and interacting with the world, that positive movement becomes possible.

NSES Teaching Standard B: Recognize and respond to student diversity and encourage all students to participate fully in science learning.

How can a teacher rise above an ethnocentric vantage point? How might you move toward an understanding of the role of culture in schooling, become capable of appreciating difference, and ultimately use this knowledge to craft instruction responsive to all of the students in your science class? Many teacher educators suggest that moving past ethnocentrism starts when a teacher carefully evaluates his or her cultural assumptions (Bennett, 1993; Cochran-Smith, 1995; Rosebery, 2004). Robert Kohls (1984) proposed a collection of core values typically shared by Americans (see Table 14.1). The list shows values typically shared by White, middle-class Americans juxtaposed with values common to many other cultures. Helmer and Eddy (2003) suggested treating these as extremes along continua and then identifying where along the continua our values lie. Then we should locate the values of our students on these same continua: where on each of these are the students situated? Seeing these comparisons may help teachers begin to identify ways in which they can adjust their instructional practices.

Misconceptions With Negotiating Communities

There are a few cautions to offer as we conclude our examination of the communities of practice that must necessarily be negotiated for equitable science instruction to occur. Just as there are common ways that cause learners to stumble in their attempts to explain phenomena scientifically, there are some common cultural ideas that can make even teachers with the best intentions fall short of the ideals of instructional congruence.

The notion of fairness is a strong sentiment and a value central to many of us. However, as teachers working toward equitable science instruction, we need to move past the idea that equity means treating everyone the same. We must recognize that sameness is typically defined by the cultural lens of the dominant group. In supposedly "fair" science classrooms, everyone is treated

Table 14.1. Contrasting Values for Different Cultures

Value Systems	Values of Mainstream Middle-Class Americans	Values Common Within Many Other Cultures
Control of the world	Within one's personal power	Fate, destiny, natural
Change	Due to personal efforts	Involves entire community
Value of time	Control of time important	Human interaction valued
Fairness	Everyone is equal	Hierarchy, rank, status
Individualism	Privacy and independence	Group interdependence
Helping oneself	Personal initiative	Birthright, inheritance
Achieving personal best	Competitive achievements	Cooperative effort
Control of self	Future orientation	Past orientation
Orientation toward work	Action orientation	"Being" orientation
Speech and attire style	Informal	Formal
Openness and opinions	Assertiveness	Indirectness, ritual, "face"
Philosophical view	Practicality, efficiency	Idealism
Materialism	Possessions are valued	Spiritualism, detachment

Note: Adapted from Kohls (1984).

like a White, middle-class American student. Although that may seem acceptable, the approach is much more likely to undercut rather than support the desire of science for all. Instead we should strive toward the idea of equitable science instruction, holding the same goals for all our students while recognizing that the paths to those goals vary from student to student.

Another potential stumbling block on the path to equitable instruction is that of essentialism. Although on the surface it seems sensible to want to describe cultural differences to ease our work as teachers, such descriptions typically obscure more than they inform. Generalized descriptions of social groups fail to recognize the variations among people within a single community. Thus although a rules of thumb list titled "ten ways to teach _____" (fill in the ethnic group) may be attractive for its apparent simplicity, the simplification is much more likely to perpetuate inappropriate stereotypes. Instead, as teachers we should generate such guidelines ourselves by closely examining our students, their families, and their wider communities.

The last major stumbling block to providing instructionally relevant science experiences is a deficit mentality, an idea that we introduced in the first chapter. In teachers' attempts to understand the influence of culture on students, they occasionally describe their students' backgrounds as voids to be filled, with teachers being responsible for filling in the gaps. There is a certain goodness in teachers who use this as a justification for taking students to the zoo and natural science museums or buying individual subscriptions to *Ranger Rick* magazine. However, some might perceive such actions as a form of charity by which the teacher wants to compensate for supposed deficiencies. The good-heartedness might actually be concealing the teacher's perceived shortcomings of the students' families.

The teacher may be subconsciously regarding his or her own culture as worth more and other cultures as worth less. If a teacher is genuinely dedicated to helping a student, then a negotiation between different cultures should be undertaken—not a one-way transmission of favors. The latter denotes a **deficit mentality,** a belief that something needs to be provided for students that they don't already have and that their experiences are limited because they don't resemble ours. It is a perspective that erases existing student culture and replaces it with a hole, a hole to be filled with the cultural practices familiar to the teacher. Such a mentality burdens students and their families to assimilate toward the dominant culture's expectations, while shifting the burden of responsibility for learning away from the teacher. A deficit mentality prevents us from recognizing the science already present in our students' lives.

Realistic But Ambitious Purposes

We realize that we have set incredibly high expectations of the individual science teacher. He or she must be relatively conversant in the culture of science to be able to make science applicable to students' lives. Furthermore, he or she must also be familiar with his or her own cultural biases, assumptions, and values—even though up until now culture may have been seen as something "others" have. Related to this is the need to uncover and understand the cultural norms of other communities: the schools, the families, and the neighborhood. How can we expect a novice teacher to achieve all of this?

First, be aware and receptive. Then be reflective, analyzing yourself in relationship to the content and the learners. Also have a host of investigative tools to access the necessary information, tapping into the funds of knowledge embedded within the local community, the students' families, the effective veteran teachers, and others who can provide insights into the communities' ways of knowing. Find ways to learn firsthand through casual conversations with students and informal observations in nonacademic settings, and tap into their personal interests and ambitions. It is considerable work for teachers to learn enough to be successful at providing instructionally congruent science teaching. Simply not rejecting this goal and beginning to consider ways to make it a reality for your own science teaching is a very important starting point.

Chapter Summary

- Learning science has a clearly cognitive component, but it is also composed of so much more. When we take into consideration the value of teaching science to a wide range of students, we realize components of science in particular and learning in general that must be incorporated into the educational process. In focusing too tightly on mastering teaching methods, teachers may not be sufficiently appreciative of the roles that the students' backgrounds and worldviews can play in learning science.
- Developing instructional congruence between the students' backgrounds and aligning those with the purposes and goals of science education is a challenge and opportunity for those teachers who work with diverse populations.
- Teaching science in an equitable fashion is far more involved than treating all students in the same way. The degree to which the students' backgrounds depart from those of their teacher suggests that it is actually unfair to treat all students the same. To disregard cultural, ethnic, language, and social class differences clearly places those students who have less in common with their teacher at a disadvantage in the classroom.
- A new consideration for teachers who are committed to providing quality science experiences to all students is that of a community negotiator. Teachers and students navigate through a variety of communities: their neighborhoods, their friends, their families, and the classroom. The incongruities between the borders of these communities can serve as barriers. Consequently, the teacher must become familiar with the norms of the communities and then use this knowledge to guide his or her students to negotiate these differences.

- To recognize the restrictions our own backgrounds place on our views of teaching is not an easy task. However, to begin to consider that each of us is a product of our respective cultures and that none of us are independent of our social histories is one of the keys to good science teaching.

Key Terms

Color-blind: a perspective about human diversity that describes that differences in language, culture, ethnicity, social class, and so on are inconsequential.

Deficit mentality: the inappropriate belief that a group or individual has differences that represent flaws, gaps, or limitations because of a nonmainstream cultural background.

Equitable science teaching: an approach to science instruction in which each child is given access to the knowledge, resources, and experiences that will contribute to his or her ability to understand the culture of science.

Essentializing: viewing each person in a social group is essentially the same as other members of that social group. By using this pattern of reasoning, one ignores or minimizes differences between members of social groups.

Ethnocentrism: tendency to view the cultural group of which you are a member as superior to other cultural groups.

Funds of knowledge: the concept that families serve as reservoirs of knowledge and skills that are useful in helping students learn. This concept represents a serious shift from the perspective that only schools or libraries represent the source of useful information knowledge and skills.

Instructional congruence: the degree of alignment between the concepts, patterns of communication, and required habits of mind employed in school settings and the students' own language, cultural experiences, and thought processes.

Meritocracy: a social system in which people achieve economic or social success in proportion to their effort, talent, and ability, as opposed to one in which social class, wealth, or ethnicity is the controlling factor.

A Favorite Science Lesson

The Education Development Center unit for grades four and five titled "Bones and Skeletons" makes effective use of one of the most unusual objects in science teaching: the owl pellet. Although it sounds gross, elementary and middle school students enjoy dissecting an owl pellet, which contains the regurgitated and unbroken bones of an owl's lunch. Instead of the common approach (which is very deductive) where the teacher explains to the students what an owl pellet is and then allows the students to take one apart, within "The Mysterious Object" activity, the identity of the owl pellet is left undisclosed. After taking the pellet apart, students are led through a series of activities in which they compare the bones from the object to information about the human skeleton. Gradually the students are able to make inferences about the bones: their origin, their use, and sometimes even the species. Although the object under study begins with the contents of an owl pellet, students develop understandings of the interactions of bones and muscles within their bodies while also becoming aware of the diversity of skeletons within the animal kingdom.

Suggested Readings

Farenga, S. J., Joyce, B. A., & Ness, D. (2003). Balancing the equity equation: The importance of experience and culture in science learning. *Science Scope, 26*(5), 12, 14–15.

> Although these three authors, all college professors, provide too much in the way of demographic data, their article does provide a quick introduction to some issues related to student diversity and science education. Despite the very general approach to the topics raised in this chapter, the authors should be commended for alerting the science teaching audience about the significance of student diversity.

Watson, S. (2004). Opening the science doorway: Strategies and suggestions for incorporating English language learners in the science classroom. *Science Teacher, 71*(2), 32–35.

> This article provides a number of practical strategies for teaching science to English language learners (ELLs). The strategies were developed by educators participating in science–ELL workshops and through the author's own experience as a science teacher of students with limited English proficiency. One aspect that is consistent with the learning cycle is giving learners multiple experiences with concepts and not simply relying on definitions.

References

Alsop, S. (2005). *Beyond Cartesian dualism: Encountering affect in the teaching and learning of science.* New York: Springer.

Au, K. H. (1980). Participation structures in a reading lesson with Hawaiian children: Analysis of a culturally appropriate instructional event. *Anthropology and Education Quarterly, 11*(2), 91–115.

Banks, J. A., & Banks, C. A. M. (Eds.). (1993). *Multicultural education: Issues and perspectives* (2nd ed.). Boston: Allyn and Bacon.

Bennett, M. J. (1993). Towards ethnorelativism: A developmental model of intercultural sensitivity. In R. M. Paige (Ed.), *Education for the intercultural experience* (pp. 21–71). Yarmouth, ME: Intercultural Press.

Cochran-Smith, M. (1995). Color-blindness and basket making are not the answers: Confronting the dilemmas of race, culture, and language diversity in teacher education. *American Education Research Journal, 32,* 493–522.

Demastes-Southerland, S., Good, R., & Peebles, P. (1995). Students' conceptual ecologies and the process of conceptual change in evolution. *Science Education, 79,* 637–666.

Gonzalez, N., Amanti, C., & Moll, L. (2005). About culture: Using students' lived experiences to build curriculum. In A. Rosebery & B. Warren (Eds.), *Teaching science to English language learners.* Washington, DC: National Science Foundation.

Gutiérrez, K., & Rogoff, B. (2003). Cultural ways of learning: Individual traits or repertoires of practice. *Educational Researcher, 32*(5), 19–25.

Heath, S. B. (1983). *Ways with words: Language, life, and work in communities and classrooms.* New York: Cambridge University Press.

Helmer, S., & Eddy, C. (2003). *Look at me when I talk to you: ESL learners in non-ESL classrooms.* Toronto, Canada: Pippin Publishing Corporation.

Howard, G. R. (1999). *We can't teach what we don't know.* New York: Teachers College Press.

Kohls, R. (1984). *The values Americans live by.* Washington, DC: Meridan House International.

Lee, O. (2003). Equity for culturally and linguistically diverse students in science education: A research agenda. *Teachers College Record, 105,* 465–489.

Lee, O., & Fradd, S. H. (1998). Science for all, including students from non-English language backgrounds. *Educational Researcher, 27*(4), 12–21.

Lynch, S. J. (2000). *Equity and science education reform.* Mahwah, NJ: Lawrence Erlbaum.

McCaleb, S. P. (1994). *Building communities of learners: A collaboration among teachers, students, families, and community.* New York: St. Martin's.

McIntyre, E., Rosebery, A., & González, N. (2001). *Classroom diversity: Connecting curriculum to students' lives.* Portsmouth, NH: Heinemann.

Moje, E., Collazo, T., Carrillo, R., & Marx, R. (2001). "Maestro, what is 'quality'?": Language, literacy, and discourse in project-based science. *Journal of Research in Science Teaching, 38,* 469–498.

Peercy, M. (2004). *Continuities and disruptions in the discursive formation of two English as a second language teachers.* Unpublished doctoral dissertation, University of Utah.

Reagan, T. (2000). *Non-Western educational traditions: Alternative approaches to educational thought and practice.* Mahwah, NJ: Lawrence Erlbaum.

Rodriguez, R. (2004). *Hunger of memory: The education of Richard Rodriguez.* New York: Bantam Doubleday.

Rose, M. (1990). *Lives on the boundary: A moving account of the struggles and achievement of America's educational underclass.* New York: Penguin Books.

Rosebery, A. (2004, May). *Some thoughts about culture and the preparation of science teachers for urban classrooms.* Paper presented at the Wingspread conference on Urban Science Teacher Preparation, Racine, WI.

Southerland, S. A., Kittleson, J., Settlage, J., & Lanier, K. (2005). The intersection of personal and group knowledge construction: Red fog, cold cans, and seeping vapor. *Journal of Research in Science Teaching, 42,* 1032–1061.

Strike, K. A., & Posner, G. J. (1992). A revisionist theory of conceptual change. In R. A. Duschl & R. J. Hamilton, (Eds.), *Philosophy of science, cognitive psychology, and educational theory and practice* (pp. 147–176). New York: SUNY Press.

Tedick, D. J., & Walker, C. L. (1994). Second language teacher education: The problems that plague us. *Modern Language Journal, 78,* 300–312.

Tharp, R. G. & Gallimore, R. (1988). *Rousing minds to life.* Cambridge, UK: Cambridge University Press.

Appendix A
How to Calculate Scores on the MCI (My Class Inventory)

For each statement a student receives a score of 1, 2, or 3. For most items when the "Yes" is circled, this counts as a 3 and a circled "No" response is worth 1. Statements that are left blank or are otherwise invalid (such as when both choices are circled) receive a score of 2. Some statements have their number underlined, and include an R in the teacher column. This indicates the wording of the statement is reversed and the scoring is reversed. For only those items a "Yes" answer is worth 1 and a "No" answer is worth 3. Using this procedure you can establish a score for each statement. The next step is to find the score for each subscale.

At the bottom of the MCI are five abbreviations corresponding to the subscales (S = **S**atisfaction, F = **F**riction, Cm = **Com**petitiveness, D = **D**ifficulty, and Ch = **Coh**esiveness). To determine the Satisfaction subscale score, you simply add the scores for the first statement in each block (i.e., Statements 1, 6, 11, 16, and 21). The total for the second subscale, Friction, is calculated by adding the scores for the second statement in each block (i.e., Statements 2, 7, 12, 17, and 22). You use this same process for determining scores on all five subscales.

At this point, you have the scores for each student. If you wish to create a class profile, then you need to calculate the average score for each subscale. The final level of sophistication is to administer the MCI twice: once with students indicating how the classroom actually is, and then filling in a second sheet indicating how they prefer the classroom to be. The subscale where the gap between the actual and the preferred is the area that is in most need of teacher attention.

Fisher, D.L. and Fraser, B.J. (1981). Validity and use of My Class Inventory. *Science Education, 65*, 14–156.

Name _____

My Class Inventory

<u>Directions:</u> This is not a test. This is to find out about your class. Draw a circle around

Yes   if you AGREE with the sentence

No   if you DON'T AGREE with the sentence.

If you change your mind about a response, cross it out and circle the new response.

Respond to the statements as your classroom actually is OR as you prefer your classroom to be. (Your teacher will tell you which to use.)

This Is How I Think About My Classroom	Circle Your Answer	Teacher Use Only
1. Students enjoy their schoolwork in my class.	Yes No	_____
2. Students are always fighting with each other.	Yes No	_____
3. Students often race to see who can finish first.	Yes No	_____
4. In our class the work is hard to do.	Yes No	_____
5. In my class everyone is my friend.	Yes No	_____
6. Some students are not happy in class.	Yes No	R_____
7. Some of the students in our class are mean.	Yes No	_____
8. Most students want their work to be better than their friends' work.	Yes No	_____
9. Most students can do their schoolwork without help.	Yes No	R_____
10. Some people in my class are not my friends.	Yes No	R_____
11. Students seem to like the class.	Yes No	_____
12. Many students in our class like to fight.	Yes No	_____
13. Some students feel bad when they don't do as well as the others.	Yes No	_____
14. Only the smarter students can do their work.	Yes No	_____
15. All students in my class are close friends.	Yes No	_____
16. Some of the students do not like the class.	Yes No	R_____
17. Certain students always want to have their way.	Yes No	_____
18. Some students always try to do their work better than the others.	Yes No	_____
19. Schoolwork is hard to do.	Yes No	_____
20. All of the students in my class like each other.	Yes No	_____
21. This class is fun.	Yes No	_____
22. Students in our class fight a lot.	Yes No	_____
23. A few students in my class want to be first all the time.	Yes No	_____
24. Most of the students in my class know how to do their work.	Yes No	R_____
25. Students in our class like each other as friends.	Yes No	_____

S _____ F _____ Cm _____ D _____ Ch _____

Appendix B
Skills Required for Success in Inquiry

The rubric on the following page is entitled Skills Required for Success in Inquiry (SRSI), and it was designed by Sharon Maroney and her colleagues during their work on The Science in the Mainstream: Retooling the Scientific Inquiry Process Project in Western Illinois.

Because we realize that students success in scientific inquiry is determined in large part by the inquiry skills they bring into the classroom, it is important to consider both what the student is capable of and what skills the activity requires. The SRSI is designed to structure and stream-line that consideration. In the planning stages of an activity, the teacher can use the SRSI to closely examine the kinds of inquiry skills the activity requires. Then the teacher can consider the skill level of the entire class, as well as any students with learning disabilities. Through this comparison the teacher can determine if the activity is within the skill level of her students, or if particular accommodations need to be made in advance. Maroney and her colleagues explain that the use of this rubric facilitates the inquiry process for everyone and eliminates many of the interruptions that commonly occur in mainstream classrooms. Certainly, this structured examination of the activity in comparison to student skill level will allow for a more careful selection of activities and a preparation for student success.

Too, the SRSI is useful to analyze the development of student inquiry skills. We all realize that as students participate in inquiries, they are honing their inquiry skills. Thus, we should expect students' skills to develop over a school year. The SRSI is a way to document this development.

Reference:

Maroney, S.A., Finson, K.D., Beaver, J.B., & Jensen, M.M. (2003). Preparing for successful inquiry in inclusive science classrooms. *Teaching Exceptional Children,* Sept./Oct, 18-25.

SRSI: Skills Required for Success in Inquiry

Inquiry Activity:

Rating of Importance of Skill:
3 = High 2 = Middle 1 = Low NA = Not Applicable

	Importance of Skill in This Activity	Evaluation of Student Skill Level					
		Classwide Skill Level	S1	S2	S3	S4	S5
Classroom Behavior Skills							
Listens quietly to directions and instruction							
Follows classroom rules							
Follows directions accurately							
Is prepared with needed materials							
Begins work promptly							
Works quietly							
Asks for help when needed							
Completes assignments on time							
Completes work at acceptable level							
Accepts criticism and corrections							
Social Skills							
Interacts appropriately with others							
Has acceptable conversation skills							
Thinks before acting							
Shows a friendly attitude							
Uses language appropriately							
Group Coping Skills							
Works cooperatively in a group							
Contributes to group work							
Expresses opinions							
Disagrees politely							
Listens to others							
Negotiates and compromises							
Accepts criticism							

Rating of Importance of Skill:

3 = High   2 = Middle   1 = Low   NA = Not Applicable

	Importance of Skill in This Activity	Evaluation of Student Skill Level					
		Classwide Skill Level	S1	S2	S3	S4	S5
Basic Academic Skills							
Can read and comprehend required materials							
Has necessary writing skills							
Can understand information presented							
Has required math and measurement skills							
Knows basic science concepts to be used							
Understands vocabulary to be used							
Can use equipment and materials							
Has skills needed to succeed in this activity							
Science Procress Skills							
Gathers information through observation							
Communicates observations and findings							
Makes an educated guess or hypothesis							
Uses experimentation to solve a problem							
Uses measurements to record results							
Uses graphs and diagrams effectively							
Uses classification skills							
Forms generalizations							
Makes reasonable predictions based on data							
Inquiry Skills							
Understands the problem							
Generates simple questions							
Generates complex questions							
Uses previously learned information to solve problem							
Is motivated by inquiry							
Can accept more than one answer							
Displays confidence in own ideas							

Index